TRAVEL CAREER DEVELOPMENT

9th Edition

Patricia J. Gagnon, CTC

Marty Sarbey de Souto, CTC

Brief Contents

Table of Contents

Dear Future Travel Professional:

Congratulations on your decision to enter the travel and tourism industry. We, at The Travel Institute, applaud your decision and wish you a fulfilling and prosperous career.

As you can imagine, travel and tourism evolve as quickly as the world changes. Politics, economics, geography, weather, cultural events, and a host of other factors continually affect travel and tourism businesses. Accordingly, the paramount role of The Travel Institute is to encourage and facilitate professional development and continuous learning for individuals at all career stages.

The Travel Institute's professional designation and certification programs address core and advanced knowledge requirements needed by all travel professionals.

The Travel Institute maintains a unique position in the world of travel and tourism. We are the only professional, not-for-profit industry organization that is politically neutral and open to all. We strive to provide a forum for healthy debate of industry issues.

Visit www.thetravelinstitute.com to learn about membership and all of the benefits available to each and every member of our Institute family.

Sincerely,

Jack E. Mannix
Chairman of the Board of Trustees
The Travel Institute

945 Concord St., Framingham, MA 01701 • tel: 781.237.0280 • 800.542.4282 • fax: 781.237.3860 • www.thetravelinstitute.com

Preface

Hundreds of thousands of students have used *Travel Career Development* as a key to unlocking a career in the travel industry. Since its introduction, *Travel Career Development* has been widely used as a core text in survey courses, as an office reference for new employees, and as the centerpiece for various programs on specific aspects of the travel industry. The ninth edition continues to provide a systematic, comprehensive overview of the travel and tourism industry. Its content is organized into four parts:

■ Part 1: Exploring the World of Travel sets the foundation for the rest of the book, introducing students to basic concepts and topics.
■ Part 2: The Travel Product examines the key sectors of the travel industry one by one.
■ Part 3: Marketing Travel provides both an overview of basic principles and a discussion of effective practices for selling travel products.
■ Part 4: The Travel Workplace gives a practical introduction to key aspects of working in the travel and tourism industry. It discusses the essential tasks of communicating and managing money in travel offices and the operation of home-based travel businesses. It also offers guidelines for finding employment and building a successful career.

Travel professionals have experienced major changes since the eighth edition of *Travel Career Development* was published, and this edition has been thoroughly updated to reflect the current realities and many opportunities facing the industry.

Special Emphases

To address the needs and interests of future travel professionals, *Travel Career Development* offers a real-world focus, bridging the gap between the classroom and the workplace. Several features of the textbook address this goal.

■ Each chapter includes On the Spot features, which present scenarios of situations faced by travel professionals; these should help students sharpen their critical thinking and problem-solving skills. Each chapter also offers a Close-Up box that gives a personal account of day-to-day work on the job in the travel industry; these invite students, in effect, to step out of the classroom and learn about the challenges and rewards experienced by travel professionals.
■ Marketing, selling, and customer service receive attention throughout *Travel*

Career Development. Chapter 1 introduces these topics, and they are the subject of Chapters 9–11. In addition, Chapters 2–8 include Close-Up boxes that focus on selling and customer service, and sections of Chapters 4–8 discuss how the travel products addressed in those chapters can be sold successfully.

■ Careers in all segments of the travel industry are explored. Close-Up boxes throughout the book describe specific positions in the industry. In addition, Chapters 15 and 16 are devoted to the subjects of finding employment and building a career. These chapters include such key topics as how to prepare for and apply for that first travel job, career advancement, professionalism, ethics, skill-building, and continuing education.

Learning Aids

Any comprehensive introduction to the travel industry must consider a broad range of subjects as well as many technical details. To help students master this content more easily, *Travel Career Development* includes several special elements:

■ *Chapter outline and questions.* Each chapter opens with a general outline of the chapter, including the key question(s) addressed by each major section of the chapter.

■ *Objectives.* Numbered objectives appear at the beginning of each chapter, giving students a framework and a set of goals to use as they begin their reading.

■ *Check-Up.* Each major section of the chapter ends with a brief review, encouraging students to check that they have mastered key points in the section before they move on.

■ *Chapter Wrap-Up.* Each chapter ends with a section that provides (1) a summary of the chapter's key points organized by the numbered Objectives listed at the beginning of the chapter; (2) a list of the chapter's key terms; and (3) questions for review and discussion.

In addition, numerous lists, tables, and figures throughout the book highlight key points, provide supplementary information, and use graphs or illustrations to help illuminate points in the text.

Special Features

To enhance interest and emphasize key themes and skills, the text also includes these special features:

■ *Close-Up: On the Job.* This feature provides personal accounts of what particular travel jobs are like day to day. Included are such varied positions as an intern in a travel agency and a tour escort.

■ *Close-Up: Careers.* This feature, which appears in Chapters 1–8, supplements the discussion of careers in Chapters 1, 15, and 16. Each Close-Up: Careers focuses on one segment of the travel industry and gives typical job descriptions and the requirements for selected positions. These Close-Ups were prepared by Karen Rubin, author of *Inside Secrets to Finding a Career in Travel.*

■ *Close-Up: Selling.* Appearing in Chapters 2–8, this feature focuses on the selling and customer service skills needed when dealing with particular travel products and provides supplementary information and tips.

■ *On the Spot.* Realistic cases put students in the position of travel professionals, inviting them to apply the discussion in the text to situations and problems encountered by industry professionals in their daily work. Each On the Spot includes recommendations for dealing with the scenario presented.

Key Changes in the Ninth Edition

Every chapter in the ninth edition has been updated and revised. Updates address some of these important changes in the travel and tourism industry:

- The expectations of today's travel client above and beyond just reservations and how the travel counselor must adapt to meet those expectations.
- The importance of enhanced research capabilities on the part of travel counselors as the Internet continues to grow in importance.
- The continued growth of home-based travel counselors/independent contractors versus traditional brick-and-mortar travel agencies.
- The dramatic trend toward specialization, offering careers in fields such as cruising, family travel, adventure travel, honeymoon/wedding planning, meetings/event planning, women-only travel, luxury travel, and many others.
- The trend of more and more travel agencies charging service or booking fees.
- The recognition of inbound (receptive) travel as an important contribution to a country's economic health and a new awareness of careers in this sector.
- The growing importance of the role of tour operators as travel packagers of group tours and independent packages.
- The growing recognition of the importance of marketing in all facets of travel and tourism and how all employees, whatever their positions, must participate in ongoing marketing within their job descriptions.
- The trend toward employee compensation via base salary plus performance pay, rather than straight salary.
- Continued changes brought about by safety concerns and their costs since 9/11 and today's political realities.
- The growth of social media and how the travel/tourism industry is incorporating it in their marketing plans and budgets.

Organization and Content

To provide an engaging and comprehensive introduction to the travel industry, *Travel Career Development* includes sixteen chapters, divided into four parts.

In Part 1, Chapters 1–3 introduce the key topics covered in the book. Chapter 1 presents an overview of the travel industry, the travel market, and travel careers. Basic geographic terms and concepts as well as issues unique to international travel are introduced in Chapter 2. Chapter 3 gives the background that students will need in order to understand later discussions of how the Internet and other technologies are used throughout the industry.

In Part 2, Chapters 4–8 present the building blocks of travel, from air travel and hotels to cruises, tours, and ground travel. Each chapter in Part 2 discusses a different sector of the travel industry, examining how businesses in that sector are organized; the products and services they offer; how to sell them; and how suppliers, sellers, and travelers interact.

In Part 3, Chapters 9–11 examine key concepts and skills needed to market travel. The basic elements of marketing, steps in selling, how to close a sale, the role of outside agents, and the importance of customer service and specialized travel markets are considered. Corporate travel, meeting and incentive travel, and selling to groups and to travelers with special needs receive particular attention.

In Part 4, Chapters 12–16 discuss issues pertaining to the travel workplace. Chapter 12 discusses how to communicate effectively. Chapter 13 focuses on the financial aspects of operating a travel agency. Home-based work and basic issues in setting up a business at home are examined in Chapter 14. Chapters 15 and 16 discuss how to find employment in the travel industry and how to develop satisfying careers. Sample résumés, advice regarding interviews and career advancement, and a description of opportunities for continuing education are all included. Also discussed are important issues related to professionalism and ethics in the travel industry.

The Glossary includes definitions of the terms that appear in bold italic in the chapters.

The Student Workbook

The *Student Workbook* is an important learning resource specifically designed for use with *Travel Career Development*. Its worksheets, objective tests, and practical exercises emphasize hands-on learning and will help students
■ Understand key terms.
■ Find information on the Internet.
■ Analyze tour brochures.
■ Increase their knowledge of geography.
■ Compare travel products.
■ Develop critical analysis and problem-solving skills.
■ Become familiar with resources and practice finding up-to-date information.
■ Go beyond the text to apply concepts to current and anticipated future conditions in the travel industry.

The Instructor's Resource Manual

Instructors can use *Travel Career Development*'s resource manual to plan lectures and to reinforce their teaching strategy. Among the tools included are
■ Answers to the Review Questions in the text.
■ Answers to *Student Workbook* exercises.
■ Suggestions for classroom activities.
■ A list of Web sites related to select chapter topics.
■ Test banks and answer keys.
■ Additional information about The Travel Institute's testing and certification programs.

The Travel Institute's Testing Programs

Travel Career Development is the primary resource text for the national TAP Test developed by The Travel Institute and the American Society of Travel Agents (ASTA). This entry-level competency test consists of 100 multiple-choice questions that measure knowledge of all segments of the travel industry.

The Travel Institute also offers a test exclusively to students who complete a course of study using *Travel Career Development*. Students who pass the Travel Career Development Test receive The Travel Institute's Travel Career Development Test Certificate. This basic test is a 100-question multiple-choice examination that is administered by instructors and scored by The Travel Institute.

Instructors who would like more detailed information about the Travel Career Development Test and the TAP Test are encouraged to visit www. thetravelinstitute.com or contact The Travel Institute's testing department at 1-800-542-4282.

Acknowledgments

The Travel Institute wants to acknowledge the generosity and dedication of the following educators who provided evaluations and suggestions that were of invaluable help in the development of this new edition:

- Martha Nell Beatty of Frosch International Travel
- S. Scott Feinerman, director of the Travel/Tourism Program at West Los Angeles College
- Amy Fink, owner of retail home-based agency Blue Ribbon Travel
- Sharon Hack, director for many years of the travel program at Foothill College
- Paula Tucker of Mountain Travel
- Debbie Wilson, director of the travel industry online program through Los Medanos College
- Lance Hendry, independent cruise specialist with Landmark Travel
- Jim Prchlik of Rail Europe
- Terry Regan, president of Berkeley's Northside Travel
- Anne Wood of adventure company, Mountain Travel
- Sybil Norwood, copyeditor and interior book designer

The Travel Institute
945 Concord St.
Framingham, MA 01701

Welcome

You're cordially invited to join us in one of the most exciting industries in the world. Why is it exciting? For many, many reasons. Those of us who work in this field do so for some of the following reasons:

- We love that it's a global industry and that we meet people from all over the world.
- It's a "people" job—talking and dealing with the public—rarely locked away in our own little box.
- It's an upbeat job as most clients are looking forward to a trip. And when they are traveling for unhappy reasons, it can be gratifying to help them in a difficult situation.
- It's a satisfying job as we often feel we help people realize a dream or a personal goal.
- It's an education—we are constantly learning something new, building our storehouse of knowledge and our career.
- And lastly, we enjoy our own opportunities for personal travel, visiting parts of the world we might never visit if we were in another career.

If those are reasons that appeal to you, then please join us on this career journey.

Prepare Yourself

In many years past, one might walk into a travel agency, an airline office, a hotel or other tourism company and find employment easily without previous training. Today travel-related companies are more diversified, and reading this book is a good start towards preparing yourself to qualify for the positions the industry offers.

Who Are You?

You may be the re-entry mom who left the workforce to raise her family and now wants to return to work in a new field. You may be a recent college graduate with a good education who has traveled a bit and wants to find an interesting and challenging career path. Perhaps you're a recent retiree with years of business experience and some personal travel and looking for a second career. Maybe you've just completed high school and find the excitement of travel beckoning. Or perhaps you're an international student away from home and planning to return to your country to practice your career. Wherever you are in life, there's probably a place for you in this fascinating and rewarding industry.

We're an industry of all ages, all nationalities, all walks of life. This study program will help you prepare yourself and analyze your own strengths and weaknesses to see where you may be a "good fit" and where you may need to sharpen personal skills.

Employment Requirements

While each industry position may require knowledge of specific subject matter (which you'll be studying here), most segments of the industry look for candidates who possess the following attributes:

- A pleasant, gracious telephone demeanor—with clients, colleagues and suppliers.
- The ability to meet the public, speak with clients in a positive, upbeat and friendly manner, and a willingness to be patient if they are indecisive.
- Knowledge of basic office skills and protocol.
- The ability to read, write, spell, and speak English correctly.
- An understanding of world geography and a bit about the various nations.
- Basic math competency.
- An attention to detail.
- The ability to research—on the Internet and elsewhere.
- The ability to get along with co-workers and often work as a team.
- The ability to work alone and solve problems thinking on your feet.
- Dependability.
- Time management skills and knowing how to prioritize.
- A willingness to "go the extra mile."
- The ability to multi-task.
- The ability to see the big picture—pull lots of facts and pieces together into a whole.

Certain areas of the industry may find other attributes helpful. For example, a tour operator that specializes in Latin America might find you more valuable if you speak some Spanish and have traveled in Spanish-speaking countries. An adventure company offering challenging trips that include hiking and whitewater rafting would be more likely to hire an outdoor person who knows how to pitch a tent rather than one who prefers gambling at a luxury hotel in Las Vegas. With so many specialty travel agencies, applicants can focus their employment search on companies that match their particular lifestyle, interests, and personal qualifications.

Ready, Set, Go

So we invite you to prepare for a wonderful journey . . . the journey through life in an incomparable field.

—Marty Sarbey de Souto, CTC

Part 1:
Exploring the World of Travel

Chapter 1
Overview of the Travel and Tourism Industry

Chapter 2
Geography and International Travel

Chapter 3
Using Technology

Overview of the Travel and Tourism Industry

CHAPTER 1

OBJECTIVES

After completing this chapter, you should be able to

1. Appreciate the evolution of the industry—its past and where it is going.

2. Explain the difference between travel and tourism.

3. Explain inbound versus outbound travel.

4. Describe the major segments of the industry and how they are related.

5. Explain Stanley Plog's psychographic analysis of American travelers.

6. Describe the skills needed for most positions in the travel industry.

If you love the travel/tourism business and work hard at it, success can be yours in the largest industry on the planet. The industry includes businesses as diverse as airlines and theme parks, huge international hotel chains and small neighborhood retail travel agencies, cruise lines and campground operators, outdoor adventure operators, and online booking sites. What are the major segments of this industry, how do they interrelate, and which segment may be the best match for you? What should you know about the travel/tourism market to succeed? What are the career opportunities; what skills are required? In this chapter, a brief industry overview addresses these basic questions.

Our Industry: Past and Present

■ WHAT ARE THE MAJOR PARTS OF THE TRAVEL/TOURISM INDUSTRY?

From Moses' journey to the Promised Land, to Marco Polo's trip to the Far East, to the migrations to the Americas, travelers have shaped history. The first "business travelers" may have been people who went to another

FIGURE 1.1

Milestones in the History of the U.S. Travel Industry

1829 First U.S. luxury hotel, the Tremont House in Boston, opens.

1869 Railroad across the United States is completed, cutting travel time to six days.

1903 Wright brothers take the first flight, at Kitty Hawk, North Carolina.

1926 First motel opens, in California.

1927 Pan Am is the first U.S. carrier to operate scheduled international service.

1938 U.S. government establishes agencies to promote safe air travel.

1939 First commercial flight crosses the Atlantic.

1946 Avis opens a rental car counter at an airport.

1958 First U.S. jet is put in service for civilian travel. More travelers fly across the Atlantic than sail by ship.

1970 First wide-bodied jets are put in service.

1971 Amtrak begins service.

1976 First airline computer reservation systems are established.

1978 Airline Deregulation Act introduces a new era of competition among airlines and travel agencies.

1988 Royal Caribbean and Carnival cruise lines christen the first megaships.

1994 Airlines introduce electronic ticketing.

1995 Major airlines put first caps on travel agency commissions.

2000 The Internet emerges as a vital force.

2001 September 11 terrorist attack on New York City and Washington, D.C., damages all parts of the travel industry.

2002 Major U.S. airlines eliminate base commissions to travel agencies.

2004 Cunard's *Queen Mary 2*—the longest, tallest, widest, and most expensive passenger vehicle at that time—replaces the *QE2* for luxury transatlantic crossings.

2010 Some airlines eliminate meal service and free baggage.

2011–2012 The earthquake/tsunami in Japan and the *Concordia* accident off the coast of Italy deal blows to tourism.

encampment to sell their produce. Other people traveled just to find out what was on the other side of the hill. For business or pleasure, people have sought out every corner of the globe. Only in modern times, however, have masses of ordinary people been able to travel for pleasure. And today, whether travelers from our country visiting abroad or those from other countries coming to visit us, travel is a two-way street, outbound and inbound.

The Difference between Travel and Tourism

Throughout this text, the terms "travel" and "tourism" will be frequent. What do they really mean, and is there a difference between the two? *Merriam-Webster's Dictionary* refers to travel as "to go from place to place, to journey, to move in a given direction or path, to traverse…." On the other hand, tourism is defined as "the practice of traveling for recreation, the guidance or management of tourists, the promotion or encouragement of touring."

In the industry, tourism is usually perceived as the larger of the two terms, implying both inbound (receptive) and outbound visitors. In terms of statistics, tourism brings business into a city, town, hotel, or given business and is seen favorably in a country's balance of payments. On the other hand, travel involves participants purchasing services for going away, such as airline tickets or hotels in another city or country.

In many countries, travel agencies may operate both inbound and outbound services. First-floor windows of a travel agency in London may advertise sun destination trips to Greece or Madeira or Miami—designed to catch the eye of a British client walking by. On the other hand, upstairs in this same agency, the company may be operating a receptive office to handle groups and individuals coming into London. In the United States, most travel offices handle only outbound travel—that is, travel to other spots in the United States as well as to overseas destinations. Inbound (often called receptive) services are usually handled by separate companies called Destination Management Companies.

Evolution of the World's Largest Industry

While we don't know exactly who built the first roads or inn, we *do* know that people were traveling on religious journeys, to trade their goods, and to pay their taxes in biblical times. In medieval Europe, wealthy landowners and prosperous merchants made religious pilgrimages. In the fifteenth and sixteenth centuries, young English aristocrats spent one to five years on a trip through Europe known as the *Grand Tour*.

By the nineteenth century, thousands of Europeans and Americans were traveling for pleasure or for self-improvement. The coming of railroads allowed them to expand their horizons. Because rail travelers needed lodging, the railroads also spurred the growth of hotels along the route (see Figure 1.1). Porters at the hotels helped travelers arrange for train trips and future lodgings and thus became the forerunners of the modern travel counselor.

The golden age for train travel extended from the late 1800s through the early 1900s. By the middle of the twentieth century, both automobiles and airplanes were competing with the railroads, and the railroads fell into a long decline in the United States. After the end of World War II, pent-up spending burgeoned and Americans began to buy cars again after such purchases had been prohibited because of wartime restrictions. In the 1950s, as auto travel became extremely popular in the United States, motels (motor hotels) sprang up across the country to meet the needs of the driving public. Then, in the 1960s and 1970s, jets and wide-bodied aircraft reduced the time and cost of air travel, putting it within reach of millions of Americans eager to travel. Europe and Asia, now well recovered from the damages of World War II, also became a market for business and vacation travel.

The growth of air travel challenged the shipping lines that had carried passengers across the Atlantic between Europe and North America. To survive, some lines adapted by converting oceangoing vessels into cruise ships.

The new cruise industry illustrated a simple law of business life: to sell its product or service, a business must provide customers with some *value*. Once airlines could transport people across the seas faster than ships, transportation by ship could survive only if the ships provided some value in addition to transportation, and that is what cruises do. Rather than simply transporting people from point to point, cruises offer complete vacations. Cruise ships have become floating resorts, with everything from atriums to wave pools, and their new product was "Vacations at Sea." Many cruise lines also started offering intellectual enrichment on board with a lineup of speakers, classes, and activities available to satisfy passengers' interests.

Even the most impressive cruise ships would not have succeeded without other changes that encouraged the growth of travel in the 1990s. The number of people with the time and money to travel soared. Global corporations emerged and sent employees on business trips around the world. And travel businesses became more skillful at creating alluring services for travelers.

Technology played a major role in this story. In the nineteenth and twentieth centuries the introduction of new technologies for transportation—railroads, large steamships, automobiles, and airplanes—created the foundation for the modern travel industry. In the 1970s and 1980s, computerization allowed airlines to keep track of the ever-growing numbers of planes and flights and passengers. In the 1990s, personal computers and the Internet sparked more change. These tools allowed increasing numbers of travel professionals to work out of their homes. They gave all travel professionals easier ways to obtain information and communicate with one another and with clients.

The Internet also made it easier for consumers to obtain information and book travel arrangements on their own without going to a travel agency. And many of them continue to book their own trips directly on their home computers. However, a number are gradually returning to travel agencies to handle their arrangements once they learn how detailed and time-consuming it can be to do it yourself. The difference is that nowadays, these Internet-savvy travelers expect travel professionals to not only book their travel arrangements to save them time, but also to be able to enhance their travel experience with additional knowledge and services. Their heightened expectations have provided new career opportunities for professionals who can adapt and acquire additional skills to act as true travel counselors rather than just as booking reservation agents.

As the twenty-first century began, political and economic conditions slowed the travel industry. Terrorism, wars, and economic downturns discouraged travelers. Still, travel and tourism today, with all its many subindustries, constitute what is recognized by many as the largest industry in the world.

Myths and Realities

Myth You can't get a job in travel without experience.

Reality Most employers would like to hire experienced people. (Wouldn't you?) But where were these "experienced" people a year ago? Everyone in the industry started without experience.

Today's Travel/Tourism Industry and Its Segments

Millions of people now have the time, money, motivation, and means to travel, whether for pleasure or business. A complex industry has evolved to promote travel and to serve the needs of travelers. There are many segments of the industry; however, the main segments fall into three major categories: suppliers, distributors, and supporting organizations (see Figure 1.2).

- *Suppliers* own the goods and services that travelers use, including transportation, food, shelter, entertainment, and attractions. Airline and railroad companies, car rental companies, hotels, and cruise lines—all are major suppliers. Restaurants, nightclubs, museums, theaters, and others also may be considered suppliers, though on a smaller scale.

- *Distributors* act as intermediaries between suppliers and travelers, helping travelers obtain the goods and services owned by suppliers and helping suppliers promote their products in the marketplace where travelers can find them. Examples of distributors include tour operators/packagers and travel agencies.

- *Supporting businesses and organizations* either provide travel-related services, such as maps and travel insurance, or aid or regulate the travel industry. For example, the *American Society of Travel Agents (ASTA)* is a trade association that lobbies governments, presents educational programs, and speaks to the public on behalf of its members. The *Travel Industry Association of America (TIA)* represents more than 2,100 U.S.

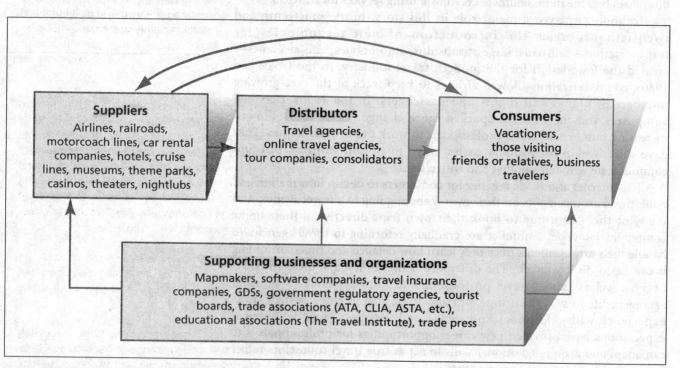

FIGURE 1.2 The Modern Travel/Tourism Industry

This diagram lists just some of the key groups involved in the modern travel/tourism industry. It puts them in categories based on their key relationships to one another and to travelers, but the boundaries between groups are blurred: suppliers, for example, can also be distributors, thus selling directly to the public and bypassing the retail travel agency.

travel-related organizations and works to promote travel within the United States. It is also known as the U.S. Travel Association. *National tourist offices (NTOs)* are government agencies that promote travel to their countries; for example, the German National Tourist Office with offices in New York and Los Angeles promotes travel *to* Germany *from* the United States.

These three segments of the travel industry are closely linked, and the divisions between them are not sharp. For example, airlines supply the seats

---

CLOSE-UP: ON THE JOB WITH LISA SYNOWIECZ, TRAVEL COUNSELOR

Lisa Synowiecz is a travel counselor at Vacations Unlimited, an agency with four full-time and two part-time employees. Lisa has been with the agency for almost five years.

"What's an average day like for me? Well, that's easy to answer because there is no average day. The following are my notes from one day.

"This morning I attend a breakfast seminar given by a cruise line. Coffee and rolls come from 7:15 to 7:45 A.M.; then a breakfast plate arrives and the program begins. A video on their newest ships, a few sales techniques, a look at the new brochures, questions and answers, and they are done at 8:30 A.M. Though I don't like getting up at 6:00 A.M. to make this meeting, I'm glad I came. I'm learning more about cruises and trying to decide if it's an area I want to specialize in. I meet a nice agent from another agency and we exchange cards. I'll give a report on the seminar at our Friday morning 'quick meeting.'

"I get to the agency a little after 9:00. I work on some basic airline reservations for two travelers from our small commercial accounts. One of them goes all over the face of the earth—well, the United States anyway. He gives seminars in college towns, and that makes for odd connections. If he finishes a talk in Poughkeepsie and has his next one in Peoria, it's Poughkeepsie to LaGuardia to O'Hare to Peoria. He never does the same trip twice. I hadn't even heard of half these places the first time he called.

"At 11:00 I have an appointment with a lady who is planning a cruise for her husband and herself for their anniversary. Often, Muriel handles our cruise clients. She's cruised many times and has gone to Miami for seminars and cruise ship inspections in port. But I've handled this client before and we seem to hit it off. Besides, if I'm going to specialize in cruises, I need to jump in and learn, and I can always get help from Muriel. We pick out an itinerary, a ship, a date, a cabin—the whole works, subject to the OK from her husband (but we both know it's her decision).

"This morning was productive, but the afternoon is not going so well. The Poughkeepsie guy (that isn't where he is going this time) e-mails me asking if I can get him an earlier connection. Back to the drawing board—well, the computer, actually. The phones start ringing, and I am the only one who's not talking to a client already, so I start answering all the calls.

"An hour later and I haven't gotten much done except two messages for Muriel (who is on the phone), one for the manager, and two shoppers who didn't seem impressed with my best selling techniques. I've got to get Mr. P. a hotel and car in each of his destinations.

"It's almost 3:00 P.M. and I haven't looked at my e-mails, except the ones I know are from regular clients. I also need to send messages requesting commissions that a hotel and a car rental company never sent. My uncle calls and wants to go to Las Vegas again. Maybe I'll take some brochures home, see what's on the Internet for Vegas, and work on his trip tonight.

"Chris, our receptionist, brings a client back to me who just walked in. She wants to send her son a ticket to fly from San Diego back to our town but wants to make sure that he can't cash it in because then he won't come. 'Not to worry,' I tell her. After she pays by credit card, she starts telling me her life story, explaining that she can't send a ticket to the correct address or her ex-husband might find it first. Finally, the phone rings, and I extend a 'thank you, come again' to my current client, who leaves.

"It's getting late, but I'm determined to finish all of Mr. P.'s bookings today, answer or file my e-mail messages, and complete at least one of the things that have been sitting on my desk for a few days.

"Well, that's one day. Tomorrow is likely to be completely different. I might be booking Europe or researching China. And this is the slow season. As we start to specialize—one of us will do most of the domestic leisure travel, another will take care of international travel, another one (or two) will sell cruises—things should be easier. In the meantime, I'm coping—and I wouldn't give it up for the world."

and service for air travel, but they also distribute their products, marketing and selling directly to consumers as they have done for many years. More and more suppliers distribute their products directly to consumers on the Internet. Furthermore, a few large corporations may own companies in each segment of the industry; for example, one corporation may own hotels, rental car companies, travel agencies, and companies that make software for the travel industry. Let's take a quick look at some major participants in the industry and how they intersect. (Later in Chapters 4–8, we will examine each of these segments in detail.)

Travel Agencies. A *travel agency* sells travel products and services directly to the public. We like to think of them as retail stores with a wide selection of products on the shelves, just like a supermarket. We may sometimes refer to them as full-service agencies. These agencies usually sell products produced by other sectors of the industry, rarely producing their own products. Agencies sell two major types of travel: leisure travel (also referred to as vacation travel) and business travel (also referred to as corporate travel). Some agencies sell both; others may specialize in one or the other. There are also many sub-types. For example, some vacation travel agencies may specialize in adventure travel only. There are some corporate travel agencies that may concentrate on meeting/convention handling. We'll learn more about specialization in Chapter 11.

The people who do the selling in travel agencies go by several names, including *travel agent, travel manager, sales representative, travel consultant,* and *travel counselor.* We prefer the title **travel counselor** because those who sell travel to the public should be able to offer professional advice to the client, above and beyond just booking the needed travel arrangements. Many travel agency counselors work in the physical agency itself (termed a bricks-and-mortar agency). However, a growing number of agents are now working from their home while linked to the agency—whether the agency is in the same town or hundreds of miles away. (See Chapter 14 about home-based agents.)

Travel agencies have complicated relationships with the public and with the rest of the travel industry. They act on behalf of travelers, but they also represent suppliers to the public. To a great extent, the suppliers control who may sell their products and how they are sold. For example, some travel products are sold through a **conference system,** which is an arrangement where an organization of suppliers appoints travel agencies to sell their products. The Airlines Reporting Corporation (ARC) is an example of a conference. Travel agencies must meet certain standards (discussed in later chapters) in order to receive an appointment from conferences and thus be authorized to sell their products.

Travel agencies receive their income from both the traveling public and suppliers. The vast majority of travel agencies charge clients directly for their services through fees, service charges, or markups. They also earn income when suppliers pay them a **commission**—a fee or percentage of the sale—for selling their products to the public. Some years ago airlines generally paid retail agencies an automatic commission for selling their product. That is no longer true today. Many travel agencies must negotiate the right to receive a commission from an airline or must belong to a consortium of agencies that negotiates commissions on behalf of the member agencies. In fact, many agencies no longer issue air tickets; they buy them on behalf of their clients directly from the airline or through an airline consolidator (more about this later in Chapter 4).

In addition, travel agencies earn income from suppliers by establishing *preferred supplier relationships,* which are commitments from the travel agency to certain suppliers to maximize their use of those suppliers and to steer clients to them. For example, an agency might steer clients to one tour operator for all British tours. In turn, the suppliers may offer the agencies higher commissions and/or *overrides,* which means an extra payment for a large volume of sales, as well as other benefits, such as training programs and even familiarization trips (fam trips) for the agency's sales staff. The vast majority of travel agencies have lists of preferred suppliers that they want their counselors to use with clients, whenever possible, if the travel product is suitable for the particular client. In this way, the agency maximizes its profit and builds its relationship with the particular supplier, often benefiting the client through special services and attention.

What do travel agencies offer in return for these payments by travelers and suppliers? Airlines and railroads provide transportation; hotels provide lodging. What is the value provided by travel agencies? What do they add to the travel product that makes it worthwhile for the supplier or the traveler to pay them?

Basically, travel agencies save time for travelers or suppliers, and they provide expert knowledge about travel products. They can also offer clients the pleasures of a personal relationship. Travel counselors who add value to the travel product are those who know what to book, when to do so, and what other possibilities exist. They use expert knowledge to find and recommend appropriate products to help clients satisfy their expectations.

They know, for example, the best discounts available on car rentals; they can advise a couple so they can choose the ideal hotel for their honeymoon; they can excite a group of travelers about their area of specialization, such as the ruins in Peru or cooking tours in Italy. They also keep up to date on new routes, a company's latest product offering, and the most recent visa regulations or airline baggage rules. Those who have been counselors for some time know which products are most appropriate for certain ages, budgets, and lifestyles, as well as a supplier company's reputation and standing in the industry.

Online Travel Agencies.

Most travel agencies have their own Web sites, but the term *online travel agency* refers to a travel agency that exists *only* online, for example, Travelocity and Expedia. A site that operates much like an online agency is Orbitz, which is owned by major U.S. airlines.

Airlines.

The world's major airlines and hundreds of regional carriers, as well as airports, air traffic controllers, and federal aviation agencies, are all part of the complicated air travel industry. Nearly every facet of the travel industry interacts with air travel. Car rental sales rely on travelers who fly to destinations and then need a private car. Most cruise passengers fly to their embarkation ports. Air passengers spend tens of billions of dollars at hotels when they arrive at their destination. Everyone in the travel industry should be knowledgeable about air travel whether or not they actually book air reservations for clients.

Until recently, airline tickets accounted for most of the income earned by U.S. travel agencies. The airlines paid travel agencies commissions for the airline tickets the agencies sold. In the late 1990s travel agencies handled more than 80 percent of the tickets for domestic air travel and 85 percent of those for international air travel. But to increase their profitability, the airlines intensified their efforts to sell seats directly to consumers, bypassing travel agencies, and in 1995 began cutting the commissions paid to agencies. Most airlines no longer automatically pay commissions to agencies for selling tickets on domestic flights within the United States. Selling air tickets in other countries may vary considerably as many governments underwrite their national air carriers financially, whereas airlines must stand on their own in the United States.

Rail Travel. As air and automobile travel soared after World War II, U.S. rail travel declined. In fact, passenger train service in the United States was saved from extinction in 1970 when the government set up and subsidized Amtrak as a corporation to operate passenger rail service between U.S. cities. In many other countries, however, railroads have remained a key means of travel, including the government-financed high-speed rail systems *TGV* in France and Japan's *Bullet Train*.

For their international travelers, U.S. travel agencies sell tickets and passes for European rail travel as well as group tours and independent packages using rail travel. But for years, selling Amtrak tickets to the U.S. domestic market was a money-losing proposition for travel agencies, and many refused to do so. Today, many agencies sell Amtrak tickets for travel along the Boston–New York–Washington corridor, which is important to business travelers, as well as for Amtrak tours and packages. Many agencies are also reconsidering whether to handle other Amtrak trips. They must determine whether the commission or goodwill earned is worth the time and effort involved. If that is not the case (and it usually isn't), they may charge a fee for helping a client to plan a schedule, book the reservations, and handle the tickets.

On the other hand, special train journeys are having a comeback. Entrepreneurs are refitting and designing elegant railroad cars and attaching them to various rail lines to provide upscale rail journeys that can be sold as part of a trip or as a trip unto itself. Grandparents are proudly taking their grandchildren on train rides, remembering the great days of U.S. trains with names like the *California Zephyr* or the *City of New Orleans*. American travelers are now intrigued with trips on famous trains, such as the *Orient Express*, *Blue Train*, and *Glacier Express*. And some innovative companies are coupling rail travel with a cruise, advertising "No Air Travel Necessary" to a public wary of flying and tired of standing in long airport security lines.

Other Ground Transportation. The vast majority of trips in the United States are by car, and more than a million rented cars, vans, and other vehicles are on the road each day, a large percentage booked by travel agencies. Most car rentals occur at airports.

Travel agencies also handle car rentals for travel overseas, both on vacation and on business, as well as arrangements for limousine service, motorcoaches, and private cars with a driver/guide. Overall, only a small percentage of U.S. motorcoach tickets are sold through travel agencies, whereas motorcoaches are a key component of many group tours.

Accommodations. Every year Americans spend $100 billion on hotel stays. The industry that supplies this service is known as the **hospitality industry** and sometimes referred to as the lodging industry. It is a worldwide industry and is the most people-intensive part of the travel/tourism industry, said to employ more than a million people in the United States alone. Many of these people have mastered such specialized fields as managing room inventories, food service, meeting/convention handling, event handling, and security.

Hotel rooms vary greatly, and the choice of lodging is often critical to the success of a trip. Thus, the expertise of a travel counselor may be very valuable in selecting accommodations. Nevertheless, travelers make more than half of the bookings for these rooms directly on their own. This accommodations segment also includes other sleeping arrangements, such as villas in Tuscany, ski lodges in the Rockies or Alps, and even campgrounds in national parks.

Cruise Lines. From Antarctica to Alaska, Maine to Tahiti, and just about everywhere in between, travelers can find a cruise. The cruise business probably ranked as the most successful part of the travel industry in the last years of the twentieth century and into the 21st. Cruise lines built the market for their product as they launched new and bigger ships. Today, large cruise ships are like small cities, and other cruising options include smaller, intimate cruise ships for river and coastal cruising.

Some cruise lines have set up their own Web sites and their own travel agencies, or so-called cruise stores, to fill their ships. Still, the vast majority of cruises, particularly the more upscale ones, are distributed through travel agencies. And there are many agencies that only handle cruises or have departments devoted to selling cruises with cruise counselor specialists who have personally traveled on many of the great cruise lines of the world and can bring their personal experience to the sale.

Tours/Packages. Tour companies are in the business of packaging various aspects of a trip, such as transportation, accommodations, and attractions. The packages they create come in all lengths and types. On some, participants travel together as a group and are escorted by an expert tour leader. On others, travelers are on their own and never see anyone connected with the tour operator. Some tours include air and ground transportation, lodging, food, and attractions, such as theme parks or museums; others include only air transportation, a hotel, and a rental car. There are tours arranged around special events such as the Olympics and tours devoted to special interests, such as golf, bird watching, classical music, or archaeology. However, one thing all tours and packages have in common is that they are sold as a unit and prepaid at a set package price. The traveler does not pay each hotel or each service, credit card in hand, as the trip progresses. Many "tours" do not actually tour; they go to one place and stay there, taking local side trips from their headquarters hotel.

Because there are so many tours and packages from which to choose and so many tour companies, people often need help deciding which tour or package is best for their particular interest, needs, and budget. A large percentage of tours and packages are sold through retail travel agencies. Some tour companies, however, sell directly to the public, and many retail travel agencies create their own tours, even selling them through other travel agencies—in effect, becoming tour operators themselves.

Destination Marketing. As travel has grown, governments, as well as businesses, have seen the benefits to be gained by encouraging tourism. Countries, regions, states, cities, and groups within cities have created organizations to bring tourists to their area. National tourist offices, local tourist bureaus, and city convention centers, for example, publish promotional materials, host Web sites, participate in industry trade shows, and help groups organize events at the destination. For example, international travel into the United States from abroad is now one of the country's leading exports and helps in trying to build the country's balance of payments. It is linked heavily to the exchange rate between the U.S. dollar and the currency used by the country in question at the time.

The modern travel industry includes
✔ Suppliers, which develop, own, and sell their travel products.
✔ Distributors, which act as intermediaries between the traveling public and suppliers.
✔ Businesses and other organizations that provide travel-related services, support businesses in the travel industry, or regulate that industry.

Retail travel agencies earn their income from
✔ Commissions and overrides paid by suppliers.
✔ Fees, service charges, or markups paid by travelers.

Major suppliers include
✔ Tour operators (packagers).
✔ Airlines.
✔ Rail lines.
✔ Car rental companies.
✔ Hotels and other accommodations.
✔ Cruise lines.

The Travel Market: Basic Concepts

■ HOW DO TRAVEL BUSINESSES ATTRACT TRAVELERS?

■ WHAT ARE SOME KEY DIVISIONS WITHIN THE TRAVEL/TOURISM MARKET?

If you wait for customers to come to you, a competitor is likely to find them first. A successful travel business works to bring people to the business and to ensure that those people buy the product, come back as repeat customers, and refer their friends. Meeting these goals requires skill in marketing, selling, and customer service, as well as expert knowledge of the buyers and products.

Marketing Fundamentals

Marketing is a series of decisions and actions taken by a seller to create a match between consumers' preferences and a product or service. The match is not likely to happen by chance; businesses research and analyze the marketplace in order to develop a marketing plan.

One key element of a marketing plan is the definition of the *target market*—the consumers that the business will try to reach. Some companies try to serve the needs of the greatest possible number of clients; others try to appeal to particular *market segments*, or clusters of individuals who have similar needs. *Market segmentation* is the process of identifying clusters of individuals who can form a target market.

There are many ways of segmenting the market; here are a few of them:
■ *Demographic segmentation* categorizes people according to characteristics such as age, sex, or marital status. For example, senior citizens might form one market segment and singles another.
■ *Price segmentation* divides a population into segments based on how much people are able and willing to pay for a product.
■ *Psychographic segmentation* groups people with similar attitudes, interests, and beliefs into distinct target markets. White-water rafters and art lovers, for example, might each form a market segment.

- *Usage segmentation* divides people according to the purpose to which they would put a product. For example, some travelers are taking a trip for business; some for a vacation, others, for education.

Besides defining a target market, a marketing plan describes basic decisions about how a business will be handled. What will be sold and where? How will it be promoted and distributed? What price will be charged?

Chapter 9 discusses the elements of marketing plans. Suppose you are offering a new travel product. Should you promote it on the basis of price or convenience or service? Products are not equally suitable to each of these approaches. To the extent that people view a product as a *commodity*—an item that varies little—they are likely to buy it wherever it is most convenient or least expensive, unless they are very loyal to a particular seller. Airline seats, for example, are usually considered a commodity; cruises are not.

Essentials of Selling

Marketing skills bring people to your doorstep or Web site. *Selling* is the aspect of marketing that ensures that they purchase your product and service. Making a sale requires the ability to meet three goals:

- *Identify the customer's needs.* For example, suppose John Doe wants to travel from Charleston to Chicago. Is he looking for the quickest way to get to a business meeting or the most scenic route to a tourist attraction? Is luxury or economy important to him? How long will he stay?
- *Identify the products or services that will meet those needs.* What types of transportation, accommodations, or other services are most likely to meet the needs you have identified? You need to know the marketplace, the various companies within it, and the products each offers.
- *Translate the features of products and services into benefits for the customer.* A *feature* is an inherent characteristic of a product or a service; a *benefit* is the positive result that a feature brings to a particular client. For example, being located just outside an industrial park may be a feature of one motel. For travelers interested in a city's nightlife, this feature might bring no benefit at all, but for many business travelers, this location brings the benefit of convenience. To sell the motel to a business traveler, you would describe the convenience it offers.

Making a sale is more art than science, but people can and do learn how to sell. When selling is conducted through person-to-person contact—a process called *personal selling*—it helps to think of the sale in terms of eight steps, which are detailed in Chapters 10 and 11.

Understanding Travelers and the Travel Product

To sell a product, you must identify clients' needs. To do that, the most basic question to answer is why they are traveling. Is it because they choose to travel or because their work requires traveling? In other words, is the trip *nondiscretionary* or *discretionary*? Those are the two very broad types of travel.

Business (Nondiscretionary) Travel. Nondiscretionary travel is usually *business travel*, which is also called *corporate travel*. This category includes all trips that are purchased by businesses and other organizations and made for the purposes of the organization. In selling business travel, you must meet the needs of the business paying for the travel, the person who is doing the traveling, and the person arranging the trip (often an administrative assistant).

Business travel includes two special types of trips: meeting travel and incentive travel. *Meeting travel* consists of trips to organized gatherings such as conventions. *Incentive travel* is travel that is offered by an organization as a reward, often for meeting goals such as sales quotas.

Both meeting and incentive travel involve a host of special needs. Arranging a meeting, for example, requires selecting a site and planning transportation to and from and around the site, as well as activities at the site, schedules, food, procedures for registering participants, and numerous other details. Incentive travel involves not only the details of the trip itself but also the goals of the incentive program and the rules for determining and announcing the winners. These types of travel are discussed in Chapter 11.

Discretionary Travel. More than three-fourths of the trips taken by Americans are discretionary. These trips fall into two broad categories:
- *VFR travel,* which is travel to visit friends or relatives.
- *Leisure travel,* which is travel for pleasure or vacation travel. Some leisure travel can be classified as *special-interest travel,* which consists of trips devoted to a particular activity or interest, such as shopping, golf, or art.

Analyzing Leisure Travelers. Unlike business travelers and those on VFR trips, leisure travelers choose where they travel. Can you predict whether a person would enjoy Tonga more than Miami Beach for a vacation? Stanley Plog, a travel researcher, developed one influential way of analyzing why people choose particular destinations (see Figure 1.3).

Plog suggests that psychological differences predict whether people will prefer to visit exotic places or familiar ones. According to Plog, all travelers

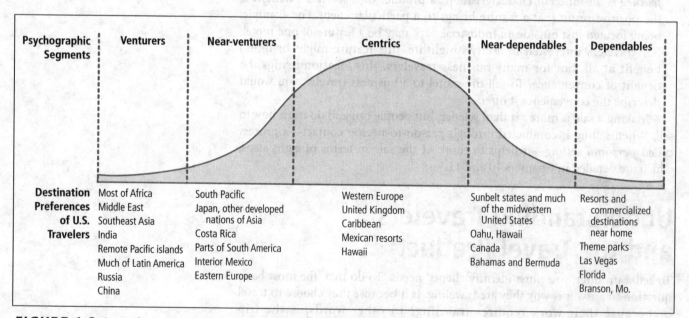

Psychographic Segments	Venturers	Near-venturers	Centrics	Near-dependables	Dependables
Destination Preferences of U.S. Travelers	Most of Africa Middle East Southeast Asia India Remote Pacific islands Much of Latin America Russia China	South Pacific Japan, other developed nations of Asia Costa Rica Parts of South America Interior Mexico Eastern Europe	Western Europe United Kingdom Caribbean Mexican resorts Hawaii	Sunbelt states and much of the midwestern United States Oahu, Hawaii Canada Bahamas and Bermuda	Resorts and commercialized destinations near home Theme parks Las Vegas Florida Branson, Mo.

FIGURE 1.3 American Travelers: A Psychographic Analysis

Stanley Plog proposes that psychological characteristics predict the types of destinations that leisure travelers are likely to prefer. He places travelers on the spectrum of psychological types shown here. Examples of some destinations people of each type are likely to prefer are listed.

Source: Adapted with permission of NFO Plog Research, Inc., New Brunswick, N.J.

can be placed somewhere on a spectrum, with venturers at one end and dependables at the other. *Venturers* center their lives on varied interests. They are outgoing, confident, curious, and eager to be among the first to discover a new vacation spot. In contrast, *dependables* focus on everyday problems and value familiarity and comfort. They are unadventurous and prefer places that offer reassuring signs of home.

Plog's analysis suggests that most international travelers are likely to be venturers and near-venturers. Dependables take almost no international trips.

Of course, both the popularity of a destination and the needs of travelers change throughout the year. For the tourist industry, there are three basic seasons: *high season*, when rates and traffic peak; *low season*, when rates and traffic are at their lowest; and *shoulder season*, a period between high and low seasons. When it is high season in one destination, it is low season elsewhere. For Europe, for example, the high season is generally summer, which is low season in Israel.

✔ CHECK-UP

Market segmentation
✔ Identifies clusters of individuals who can form target markets.
✔ May be based on characteristics such as demographics, price, psychographics, or usage.

Success in selling requires the ability to
✔ Identify the customer's needs.

✔ Identify the products or services that will meet those needs.
✔ Translate the features of products or services into benefits.

The main types of travel are
✔ Business or corporate travel, which includes meeting/convention travel and incentive travel.
✔ VFR travel.
✔ Leisure travel, which includes special-interest travel.

Travel/Tourism Careers: Paths to Success

■ WHAT SKILLS ARE NEEDED FOR WORKING IN TODAY'S TRAVEL/TOURISM INDUSTRY?

■ WHAT IS YOUR REALITY?

Most jobs in this industry are challenging, exciting, and satisfying. They also tend to be exhausting, stressful, and intense. Travel careers are for people who savor dealing with others, have a passion for travel, and for helping others to travel as well. And they are for people who enjoy hard work. Just ask the flight attendant who wakes up at 4:30 A.M., drives to the airport, "crews" six takeoffs and landings in turbulent weather, serves hundreds of drinks and snacks by 6:00 P.M., and still has a smile for departing passengers on her last flight.

A travel worker may be the CEO of a major company or may be the baggage handler at the airport; he or she may be self-employed or work for a worldwide corporation. Careers in computer programming, Web site design, accounting, law, marketing, and other fields may also be pursued in travel-related companies. Table 1.1 lists some of the many employment opportunities that make up this huge industry.

Starting Out

It is not too soon to begin thinking about your own career path. On the one hand, you may have a fixed idea as to what segment of the industry you'd like to work in. On the other hand, you may not have any idea as to where you'd fit in best. Throughout this course, you will learn about new possibilities and may change your mind several times. We suggest you look at Table 1.1 for the broad view of some of the diverse career possibilities throughout the many industry sectors.

You may wish to think through some basic life decisions around these possibilities. Do you live in an area where all these possibilities exist? Or are

TABLE 1.1 Careers in Travel: A Sampling

Industry	Positions	Positions	Industry	Positions	Positions
Travel agencies	Accounting assistant	Leisure travel counselor, domestic	Car rental companies (continued)	Fleet manager	Service agent
	Accounting supervisor			Human resources specialist	Station manager
	Agency manager	Leisure travel counselor, international			
	Corporate account manager		Rail and bus companies	Conductor	Onboard attendant
	Corporate travel counselor	Marketing assistant		Customer service agent	Reservationist
	Cruise sales manager	Marketing director		Marketing manager	Station manager
	Cruise salesperson	Meeting planner		Motorcoach driver	
	Customer service agent	Outside sales agent			
	Database administrator	Quality control agent	Hotels	Assistant manager	Front office manager
	Group agent	Receptionist		Catering manager	General manager
	Group sales manager	Ticket control clerk		Concierge	Group services manager
	Human resources director	Webmaster		Convention sales director	Guest services representative
Airlines	Accountant	Pilot		Executive housekeeper	Human resources specialist
	Account executive	Rate desk agent		Food and beverage manager	Reservationist
	Administrative manager	Regional sales manager			Sales manager
	Crew scheduler	Reservationist, domestic		Front desk clerk	Sales representative
	Customer services representative	Reservationist, international		Front desk supervisor	Security specialist
		Sales representative			
	Dispatcher	Sales support agent	Cruise lines	Accountant	Public relations director
	District sales manager	Station manager		Account executive	Purser
	Flight attendant	Ticket agent		Analyst of revenue management	Regional sales manager
	Group sales support agent	Tour and convention sales manager			Reservationist
	Human resources specialist			Cabin steward	Reservations manager
	Marketing automation software developer	Tour desk reservationist		Group and charter manager	Sailing coordinator
		Traffic manager		Host/hostess	Sales representative
	Marketing manager	Yield management analyst		Human resources specialist	Schedule director
	Personnel representative			Marketing manager	Secretary
				Passenger services representative	Social director
Travel trade and tourism organizations	Cartographer	Public information officer			Youth counselor
	Climatologist	Research director			
	Convention and visitors' bureau representative	Sales representative	Tour companies	Costing coordinator	Quality assurance manager
		Secretary		Director of tour guides	Reservationist
	Convention sales manager	Travel photographer		District sales manager	Sales representative
	Convention services manager	Travel video producer		Group supervisor	Step-on guide
	Group travel coordinator	Travel writer		Product coordinator	Tour guide or director
	Marketing director	Webmaster		Product development manager	Tour planner and operator
	Market research analyst				Webmaster
Car rental companies	City manager	Rental agent			
	District operations manager	Reservationist			
	District sales manager	Sales manager			

you willing to relocate? For example, the majority of employment opportunities with cruise lines are in Florida where most cruise companies have their headquarters, although a few lines have offices elsewhere. If you can't relocate to Florida, you might consider becoming a cruise specialist within a retail travel agency in your town. Can you work full-time or only part-time? If so, you might prefer to become a tour guide and work as an independent contractor only at certain times. Can you be away from home to take advantage of some of the many familiarization trip possibilities that will be there to help you enhance your learning? Or would it be difficult to leave home and family for a five-day fam trip to Paris?

In addition, you may want to analyze your strengths and weaknesses. Do you have the following attributes, or can you work on developing them in preparation for your new career?

- *Interpersonal relationships.* Successful travel professionals must be empathetic. In other words, you must be able to understand your clients' needs and to communicate that understanding. In addition, enthusiasm, patience, and a positive outlook on life will smooth your way through many tough situations.
- *Language.* The ability to speak and write clearly with correct spelling, grammar, and pronunciation is very important. Knowledge of a second language may be a requirement for a few positions (particularly in receptive tourism or companies that deal in the ethnic market) but is not mandatory for most others.
- *Math.* Computers handle much of the basic math requirements today. Nevertheless, many positions still require enough fluency with basic math to understand and, in some cases, to calculate fares, rates, and commissions; to convert currencies and measurement units; and to handle money. In addition, it's important to understand financial terms, including net, gross, and markup.
- *Technology.* Most businesses use technology throughout; many promote, sell, and work with clients through the Internet and e-mail, and many have their own Web sites.
- *Ability to learn.* In any position in any company, there will be routines and procedures to learn, as well as changing facts and changing skills to master. Flexibility will be expected of employees as the industry continues to change daily. The ability to research will prove important.

All of these are considerations. You may find that once you begin your career, you will move from one sector of the industry to another as your life changes. Many have and have grown in the process. But at the outset, your primary concern is to find entry level employment in the industry and to know what skills you need to bring to the job.

You might also ask yourself if you are you willing to intern or spend the first year of your new career in an entry-level position, such as receptionist or clerk. Many travel counselors begin their career by answering phones, greeting clients, ordering and filing brochures, delivering travel documents, logging refunds, and doing research for others in the office, for example. Tour operators need beginners to produce hotel rooming lists, help prepare the tour leader for departure, or handle computer records. Remember, beginners in all professions need experience; even top graduates of the best medical schools serve as interns. The fact that you may already have traveled to 79 countries and are an expert on the wines of France may eventually be a boon to your employer but what management needs first may be something much more mundane, such as greeting the public graciously or filing materials in the right country folder.

Building a Career

If you begin your career in an entry-level position, how do you advance to a position with more responsibility? To win trust and advance in your career, professionalism is essential. *Professionals* are people who train themselves to become experts in a field, use that expertise to benefit clients, and do so in an ethical manner.

Courses like this one are a first step toward becoming a professional, providing the basics for developing expertise. By itself, however, a basic education will not allow you to meet professional standards. Personal travel will help, but no one can go everywhere. Moreover, the travel/tourism industry changes quickly, with new destinations, new technology, new tastes and trends, new competition, and new selling techniques. One year, knowledge about ancient sites in Mexico may be in demand; the next year, you may need expertise in finding accommodations for the Olympics. Even after years on the job, travel professionals are likely to encounter questions

CLOSE-UP: CAREERS WITH TRAVEL AGENCIES

Each travel agency is a business with sales and marketing functions and administrative tasks to be performed. In small agencies, one person may perform all of these tasks, acting as owner/manager as well as travel counselor. The larger the agency is, the greater the specialization.

Most employees of travel agencies receive most of their income through salary, but many receive a salary plus a bonus that depends on their sales, and others receive only commissions. Discounts on travel are an extra benefit. Opportunities and jobs vary tremendously. Generally, the smallest agencies and the largest corporations offer the best opportunities for those just starting their careers. Many people work for travel agencies as independent contractors; Chapter 14 is devoted to home-based agents.

■ **Position** Travel associate

Description This position provides support for a team of travel counselors and is an excellent way to learn the business. Responsibilities are likely to include processing travel documents and invoices; coordinating mailings; maintaining office supplies, brochures, and videos; conducting research; sorting e-mail messages; and answering phones.

Qualifications This entry-level position requires a travel school diploma, knowledge of a global distribution system (GDS) and the Internet, strong organizational skills, and the ability to manage details.

■ **Position** Leisure travel counselor

Description The "face" of the travel industry, this job entails an amazing array of activities: in the span of an hour, the leisure travel counselor may plan an African safari, book an airline ticket to Cleveland, and answer an

e-mail from a client wondering about the weather in spring in Heidelberg. The leisure travel counselor has a dual responsibility: to serve the customer's needs and to sell travel arrangements. The counselor helps clients select travel arrangements, after researching destinations and travel products; helps clients obtain the best possible value for their travel dollar; and makes bookings.

Qualifications A travel counselor must be able to operate a specific GDS, use the Internet, have good selling skills, and know about destinations and travel products. The job also requires patience, very close attention to detail, and an ability to listen and to enjoy dealing with people. Some people move into the job from positions as outside sales agents or reservationists.

■ **Position** Corporate travel counselor

Description This type of counselor books travel services for business travelers. Usually, the corporate travel counselor does not have face-to-face contact with the traveler and often communicates through the traveler's secretary. The counselor provides information about fares and availability via the computer, makes and changes reservations, and handles many bookings, at a fast pace, throughout the day. Service, rather than advice, is key. The counselor may work at an agency or work for the agency on-site at the client company. Working for a corporation's travel department is another option.

Qualifications This very fast-paced job requires a lot of stamina, skill at communicating on the telephone, the ability to handle details and enter data with speed and accuracy, and professionalism. A beginner with good computer skills may be able to become a productive corporate travel counselor in a short time.

(continued on next page)

they cannot answer or problems they do not know how to solve at first. Is it safe, for example, for a client to travel to Belize? Is transportation available from the airport in Belize City to the archaeological site of Caracol?

Of course, travel professionals cannot know everything, but they can and should know where to look for the answers. Chapter 16 discusses opportunities for continuing education and the additional skills that are important for travel professionals. The Travel Institute (publishers of this book) offers continuing education and the well-recognized CTA, CTC, and CTIE certifications.

The many changes in the travel industry during the 1990s and the first part of the 21st century highlighted the importance of continuing education and the ability to adapt. Less than two decades ago, for example,

CLOSE-UP: CAREERS WITH TRAVEL AGENCIES (cont.)

■ **Position** Corporate account manager

Description The person in this position serves as the liaison between the agency and the client, which in this case is a business. The account manager oversees daily operations in order to maximize profitability, provide quality control, and maintain high levels of service. The manager also implements programs aimed at the professional development of on-site corporate agents. Additional responsibilities include implementing the client's travel programs and ensuring compliance with the client's travel policies.

Qualifications This position requires excellent communication skills, professionalism, and a strong background in client services. Employers will also look for a record of skill in time management, financial analysis, presentations, selling, and negotiating. Experience with a GDS, additional computer skills, and the ability to travel may also be necessary.

■ **Position** Outside sales agent

Description The job of an outside sales agent is to bring new clients to the agency. The person may work inside or outside the agency but goes into the community to promote and sell travel services, perhaps giving presentations to clubs, hosting cruise nights, and offering travel seminars. Some outside agents handle all aspects of the transactions for their clients; others just make the sale while the agency handles details such as ticketing. Most outside agents work on a commission basis; many are independent contractors, not employees.

Qualifications Excellent communication and interpersonal skills, including the ability to conduct public presentations, as well as creativity and resourcefulness are required for this job. The person must be able to devise leads and promotions and follow through on projects. An ability to manage a database is desirable.

■ **Position** Customer service agent

Description This position provides support in order to enhance quality control and ensure the satisfaction of customers. Tasks include analyzing procedures and implementing programs to improve customer satisfaction and efficiency; serving as the liaison among clients, the agency, and vendors; ensuring the accuracy of customer profiles; and handling written responses to clients' queries.

Qualifications Proficiency with personal computers and GDSs is required for this position. It also demands excellent communication skills, extensive background in travel operations, and superior skills in analyzing, planning, organizing, and providing customer service.

■ **Position** Webmaster

Description This professional is responsible for building and maintaining a company's Web site. The job involves not only the creation of Web pages but also endless efforts to improve the site and streamline the process of entering and exchanging data. The webmaster may also provide software support and handle minor hardware updates, reports to management on the use of the site, and e-mail connectivity programs.

Qualifications This position requires a solid background in software and software languages as well as search engines and Web design and management. The webmaster must have a feel for what users will want from the Web site and be able to work with macros, databases, spreadsheets, and data migration. An understanding of local area networks (LANs) and relevant hardware is an asset.

■ **Other positions** Cruise (or destination) specialist; database administrator; group sales agent; meeting planner; sales administrator/coordinator; systems administrator; technical leader/trainer; vendor negotiator.

Source: All Close-Ups on careers are based on information from Karen Rubin, president of Travel Executive Search (a recruitement company in Great Neck, New York, that specializes in the global travel industry) and author of *Inside Secrets to Finding a Career in Travel* (Indianapolis, Inc.: Jist Publishing, 2001).

almost no one except scientists and academics used the Internet. Successful travel professionals met the challenge of building a new travel world in which Web sites and e-mail are everyday tools, and they are now looking to the social media, new computer applications, and other ground-breaking possibilities that come along almost daily.

Once you are on the job, you will be expected to continue the learning curve and there are many opportunities to help you do so. Most suppliers offer annual seminars as they launch each year's new products. Membership in industry professional organizations often mean access to special training and insider knowledge. Networking opportunities abound where you can exchange ideas with your peers. Webinar invitations come in almost daily— some excellent, some not so. In short, the industry is usually making continuing education opportunities available; it's only up to you to find the time, energy, and dedication to become involved.

In short, to be successful in the travel industry, you need to learn all that you can about your business as soon as you can, learn while on the job, and then prepare to learn more as the industry and the world change.

CHAPTER WRAP-UP

CHAPTER HIGHLIGHTS

Those who work in the travel/tourism industry are helping people meet a very important need. In this chapter we have given an overview of this industry and the role of the true professionals in this field. Here is a review of the objectives with which we began the chapter.

1. **Describe the major segments of the travel industry and how they are related.** The industry can be divided into suppliers, distributors, and supporting organizations. The major suppliers are the airlines, rail companies, cruise lines, car rental companies, and lodging companies. Major distributors are travel agencies and tour companies. Supporting organizations include trade associations such as the American Society of Travel Agents (ASTA) as well as national tourist offices (NTOs) and businesses and organizations that sell travel-related products or regulate the industry.

   All parts of the industry are interdependent, and the line between suppliers and distributors is often blurred. Many suppliers, for example, also distribute their products to the public. As distributors, most travel agencies earn their income from both travelers and suppliers. Most agencies charge travelers through fees, service charges, or markups. They earn commissions from some suppliers, and many agencies establish preferred supplier relationships and earn overrides as a result.

2. **Outline basic techniques for marketing and selling travel.** As the travel industry has become more competitive, marketing, selling, and service have become ever more important to success. Like other businesses, travel businesses develop marketing plans for their products. These plans define a target market, often through market segmentation. Ways of segmenting the market include demographic segmentation, price segmentation, psychographic segmentation, and usage segmentation.

   To ensure that interested consumers become actual buyers, travel professionals need skill in selling techniques, such as qualifying clients, translating features into benefits, and closing the sale. And they need knowledge of their products and customers in order to give high-quality service.

3. **Describe key characteristics that shape a traveler's needs.** Psychographics and

demographics are important, but usage provides the key division in the travel market. That is, some travel is nondiscretionary and is for the purpose of business; other travel is discretionary. Different needs are associated with each type of travel. Business or corporate travel includes meeting travel and incentive travel. Discretionary travel includes VFR travel and leisure travel. Psychological characteristics—such as whether people can be characterized as venturers or dependables—shape whether leisure travelers prefer exotic or popular destinations.

4. **Describe the skills needed for most positions in the travel industry.** People in almost all entry-level positions need skills in interpersonal relationships and in language. In addition, they must be able to handle basic math and to use standard office technology. Finally, they require skill in learning itself so that they can master the routines of specific positions and adapt to changes. To win greater responsibility and advance in a travel career, professionalism is required. One component of professionalism is a commitment to continuing education.

KEY TERMS

A list of key terms introduced in this chapter follows. If you do not recall the meaning of these terms, see the Glossary, which begins on page 393.

American Society of Travel Agents (ASTA)
benefit
business travel
commission
commodity
conference system
corporate travel
demographic segmentation
dependables
distributor
feature
high season
hospitality industry
incentive travel
leisure travel
low season
marketing
market segmentation
meeting travel
national tourist office (NTO)
online travel agency

override
personal selling
preferred supplier relationship
price segmentation
professional
psychographic segmentation
selling
shoulder season
special-interest travel
supplier
supporting businesses and organizations
target market
travel agency
travel counselor
Travel Industry Association of America (TIA)
Usage segmentation
VFR travel
venturers

REVIEW QUESTIONS

1. Name at least 10 major developments in the history of the U.S. travel/tourism industry.

2. How would you describe the role of technology in the past and in the future of the travel/tourism industry?

3. What value can a travel counselor add to a travel product?

4. Applying usage segmentation, identify several target markets for travel, and suggest what travel products might be appropriate for them.

5. Would you describe yourself as a venturer or a dependable? Why? How would these psychological characteristics affect your needs as a traveler?

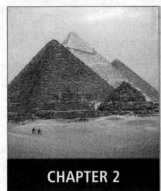

Geography and International Travel

CHAPTER 2

OBJECTIVES

After completing this chapter, you should be able to

1. Identify the characteristics that shape the appeal of destinations, ensuring that people want to visit.

2. Explain how to locate a destination and how to calculate time differences.

3. Outline the major factors that shape the climate of a destination.

4. Describe at least five key sources of information about destinations.

5. Outline the requirements that governments place on international travelers visiting their countries.

6. Identify reliable sources of information about possible dangers abroad and common problems encountered by international travelers.

7. Suggest four methods of handling currency exchange for an international trip.

If a client wants to find a place where she can go horseback riding during the day and attend a top-notch opera at night, where would you send her? If a colleague says that a trip from the pyramids of Giza to the pyramids of Teotihuacán is just an easy day's journey, does he know what he's talking about? Are you likely to get a chance to practice your Spanish in São Paulo? Can someone who likes gambling at casinos find a destination that also provides opportunities for time at the beach and water sports?

These questions touch on aspects of *destination geography,* the study of those characteristics of locations that influence travel. This knowledge is essential to help organize various categories of sites that would appeal to different travelers. It also helps to understand and to narrow down choices for clients as they describe the type of art tour, extreme adventure experience, or city environment that they may want. In this chapter, we consider some basic terms and concepts necessary for learning destination geography. We also consider other information that travel professionals should master, such as passport and visa requirements, customs regulations, and health and safety issues to help travelers going abroad.

OUTLINE

LOCATIONS AND DESTINATIONS
- What makes a location a popular destination?

LOCATIONAL AND PHYSICAL GEOGRAPHY
- How do you describe the location of a destination and calculate time differences?
- What determines a destination's climate?

LEARNING ABOUT DESTINATIONS
- What are good sources of information about destinations?

CROSSING BORDERS
- What rules and regulations govern international travelers?

HEALTH AND SAFETY ABROAD
- What are reliable sources of information about dangers when traveling abroad, and what health precautions should travelers take?

DEALING WITH MONEY AND OTHER DIFFERENCES
- How are currencies and measurements used in other countries converted, and what other everyday differences should travelers be ready to handle?

Locations and Destinations

■ WHAT MAKES A LOCATION A POPULAR DESTINATION?

Not every place on earth is a destination. A ***destination*** is a location that a traveler chooses to visit. In 2011, for example, more than 63 million people from other countries were projected to make the United States their destination. Worldwide, the countries that were projected to send the largest number of international travelers to the United States were Canada, Mexico,

CLOSE-UP: CAREERS IN DESTINATION MARKETING AND PROMOTION

Businesses and governments alike aggressively develop destinations and promote tourism. The task has many facets—from researching potential sites for a new resort to publishing promotional materials to finding volunteers who will make conventioneers feel welcome and coordinating travel arrangements for incoming travelers and groups.

Among the many destination marketing organizations are local tourist bureaus, city convention and visitors' bureaus, state travel offices, regional travel organizations, and associations created by businesses such as ski resorts. A new specialty is sports commissions, charged with bringing major sporting events to a destination. These marketing organizations are frequently divided into departments devoted to convention sales, tourism sales, and membership services; often there is a division between domestic and international markets. In places that are just beginning to focus on tourism, even those with little experience may find excellent opportunities to begin work at a relatively high level. The best place to start is your hometown, but often the way to advance is by moving from city to city and from state to state.

■ **Position** Senior staff assistant

Description The person in this position provides administrative support while learning the fundamentals of the sales, tourism, or communications department. The job includes work on special projects such as helping to coordinate familiarization trips.

Qualifications This is an entry-level position. It requires good communication skills, common sense, and attention to detail.

■ **Position** Agent (for a national tourist office)

Description To promote travel to their countries, many other nations have tourist offices in major U.S. cities. Agents who staff these offices help to raise awareness of the country, promote a positive image of it, and assist

potential travelers. They answer questions, send out information, greet visitors, and conduct seminars for travel professionals.

Qualifications Enthusiasm for the NTO's country, knowledge about the country, and interpersonal and communication skills are needed for this position. Knowledge of the nation's language is also usually required. Many of these employees are natives of the country concerned.

■ **Position** Special events coordinator

Description This specialist develops, prepares, and manages events and related programs designed to increase tourism to a destination. Attendance at functions, which sometimes occur on a weekend or in the evening, might be required.

Qualifications Though the coordinator is often an entry-level position, prior experience in putting together events—perhaps at a hotel or a meeting planning company—is desirable. A similar position focused on organizing sporting events is becoming more prevalent.

■ **Position** Convention sales manager

Description Opening new markets for meetings, conventions, and trade shows is the responsibility of this position. The convention sales manager makes sales calls, attends trade shows, and implements sales blitzes in order to develop leads and help to close sales on behalf of a local convention center or convention bureau and the local hospitality industry. This person also has responsibility for the marketing budget.

Qualifications Typically, these positions are filled by people coming from hotel sales. The position requires the ability to make presentations to high-level decision makers, to provide top levels of service, and to be creative in finding leads. The job also involves considerable travel, possibly even internationally.

(continued on next page)

United Kingdom, Japan, and France. However, projections and actualization can be two different things. As an example, both Japan and Mexico have been popular destinations in the past for U.S. citizens. But today's drug and crime problem in Mexico and _the earthquake_ and _tsunami_ that _hit Japan_ are proving to be stumbling blocks for continued high-volume tourism from U.S. citizens, many of whom may view those countries as less desirable destinations at present.

Key Characteristics of Destinations

What turns a location into a popular destination? Attractions alone do not guarantee success. The UNESCO World Heritage site of Great Zimbabwe is "one of the shining mysteries of Africa . . . the continent's largest structure south of the Pyramids" (_The New York Times_, January 18, 1997, page 4). Here, as early as 350 A.D., Shona-speaking farmers first settled an area, leading to the formation of the Great Zimbabwe state, and eventually to the building of a great city of towers and

---

CLOSE-UP: CAREERS IN DESTINATION MARKETING AND PROMOTION (CONT.)

■ **Position** Convention services manager

Description The person in this position works with the organizers of conventions and meetings, finds out what they need, and then notifies convention bureau members (such as hotels, restaurants, ground transportation companies) so that they can bid for the business. The manager is responsible for keeping costs to a minimum; for recommending amenities, venues, speakers, and themes; and for being sure that contracts with the convention bureau are fulfilled. Responsibilities may also include handling housing and assigning registration personnel. Attendance at functions on weekends and evenings might be required. Over time, the convention services manager develops relationships with local businesspeople.

Qualifications Interpersonal and communication skills as well as knowledge of the destination are needed.

■ **Position** Group tour specialist/group travel coordinator

Description This specialist locates groups or organizations that are potential visitors as well as those that generate group travel (such as travel agents, tour operators, civic organizations, special-interest groups). Once the group is sold on the destination, the specialist hands the booking over to members of the hospitality industry. In order to stimulate tourism, this specialist may also create packages and itineraries that travel agencies or tour operators can sell.

Qualifications Experience in sales, hotels, or other areas of the travel industry is usually required. This position demands creativity, tenacity, excellent communication skills, the ability to relate to people, and excellent follow-through and attention to detail. Previous experience in tour packaging is helpful.

■ **Position** Public information officer

Description This professional develops programs designed to increase the number of visitors and to enhance the destination's image. Other responsibilities include planning; writing and disseminating information through various media, including the Internet; and designing and producing official publications distributed to residents, tourists, businesses, and media representatives. The public information officer may also organize media events and familiarization trips.

Qualifications Prior experience in public relations or marketing is usually required; budgeting and the ability to analyze cost-effectiveness may also be necessary.

■ **Position** Global sales agent (for a corporate travel management company or a destination marketing organization)

Description The person in this senior sales position is responsible for securing international companies or internationally based divisions or subsidiaries of U.S.-based multinational companies as clients. The sales agent must travel a great deal, sometimes 80 percent of the time, building relationships abroad and following through on the sale to be sure all aspects of the contract are understood.

Qualifications Knowledge of the regulations and customs for doing business in other countries and the ability to understand a client's needs are essential, along with follow-up abilities, professionalism, excellent communication skills, and the ability to travel frequently. A second language is a strong asset.

■ **Other positions** Cartographer; market research analyst; travel photographer; travel writer; webmaster.

stone walls thirty-five feet tall and fifteen feet thick built without mortar. Yet only about 20,000 people visit the ruins annually. Why? Perhaps it's because this fascinating site has little promotion and is far away and expensive to visit. Perhaps it's because the country has had an unstable government and other safety issues. And although there has been a nearby small airport and town as well as a choice of hotels in recent years, other interesting competitive sites are easier and less expensive to access.

In contrast, in 1963 a U.S corporation took an area of citrus groves and cattle ranches in Florida and turned it into a tourist mecca that now attracts millions of visitors each year—Walt Disney World. Similarly, in the late 1960s Fonatur, a Mexican government agency, searched for an ideal site to create a beach resort and succeeded spectacularly with Cancún.

What makes a successful destination? Destinations are distinguished from each other primarily by climate, attractions (both natural and human-made), costs, standard of living, accessibility, culture, and competition:

- *Climate.* The *climate* is the average weather over a long time, and it greatly affects the appeal of a destination.
- *Attractions.* What is there to see or do at a destination? Does it have natural attractions such as magnificent scenery or created attractions such as an unusual amusement park?
- *Costs and standard of living.* What kinds of food and lodging are available and at what cost? Can visitors obtain the day-to-day services to which they are accustomed, such as a good cup of coffee or dry cleaning? Will they be able to go on the Internet or watch television? Is quality health care available in an emergency? The more exotic a destination, the more prepared the traveler must be to forgo some services that are commonplace at home or to pay an exorbitant price for them.
- *Accessibility.* How far away is the destination, and how do travelers get there? Can they fly directly to the location on a reliable, well-known air carrier? Both the physical features of a location and the transportation available locally influence its accessibility. For example, you can travel the 4,000 miles from London to Nairobi, Kenya, in less time than it takes to go the 200 or so miles from Nairobi to the gorilla preserve in Bwindi, Uganda. Not everyone believes that "getting there is half the fun."
- *Culture.* Are there customs or laws that would make a visit difficult? Are there cultural differences that the traveler will enjoy? Does the destination offer art or dance or music or architecture with special appeal? Does the destination have particular historical significance?
- *Competition.* Are there other destinations that may be just as interesting, but are less difficult and expensive to visit and have better publicity?

Some characteristics of destinations can change suddenly. Political conflict may make a destination temporarily inaccessible; fluctuations in the exchange rates for currency may alter the affordability of a destination; a hurricane may destroy a key attraction. Changes like these may drastically alter an area's popularity.

The appeal of a destination may also shift with little apparent cause. Sometimes, destinations grow in popularity like a fad. Adventurous travelers find a place off the beaten track, and word of its attractions spreads, luring the less adventurous. Thus, some destinations may begin as exotic places for the few and eventually become familiar to almost everyone. Jamaica, for example, was once an exclusive retreat; now it is a popular destination for tours, cruises, resorts, and all-inclusives.

Like clothing, destinations go in and out of fashion. Some destinations, like denim jeans, manage to retain their popularity. Others, like hemlines, rise and fall cyclically. Still others, like starched collars, disappear, seemingly forever. Ultimately, popularity depends on people and their changing tastes. Whether the culture or climate or other characteristic of a destination draws visitors depends on how travelers view these features and what travelers are looking for, and what competitive sites may offer.

Destination Management

Persuading people that a particular destination is worth visiting is one of the tasks of people who work in the field of *destination management and promotion.* People in this field communicate knowledge about destinations, develop and promote destinations, and help tourists when they come to those destinations. *National tourist offices (NTOs),* for example, are organizations established by governments to promote travel to their countries. Most NTOs do not sell travel arrangements but work to attract travelers and to present the country in the best light to potential travelers from around the world.

Similarly, smaller political units—states, provinces, cities, and so on— fund offices that try to attract visitors to the area and to serve travelers once they arrive. There are *tourist bureaus, visitors' information centers,* and *convention and visitors' bureaus,* which aim to bring meetings, conventions, trade shows, and tourists to an area and promote its convention centers. Often, businesses are members of these organizations and help fund them. Private groups such as the chamber of commerce, tour operators, and a city's hotels also set up their own marketing organizations.

CLOSE-UP: ON THE JOB WITH MANDY HALLET, CONVENTION AND VISITORS' BUREAU REPRESENTATIVE

Mandy Hallet has worked for the convention and visitors' bureau of a major city on the West Coast for almost two years. She is currently assistant manager of its downtown public facility. During the summer she supervises a staff of six to eight, most of whom are seasonal employees or interns in tourism and public relations.

"I work in a tourist office on the ground level of a downtown building. After going in and meeting the marketing director of our convention and tourism bureau, I left my résumé and a letter explaining how much I loved our city and what it offered, even though the bureau had no positions at that time. I kept in touch afterward, too, and when there was an opening, I got an interview. The pay wasn't great to start, but I was in a supervisory role very quickly. At slow times I do some research and planning for the busier season.

"We all love to talk to people who come in because they are genuinely seeking information about our city. They want to be sold on it. I especially enjoy talking to international visitors. I never thought about it before, but it's amazing that we have the whole world visiting us. Still, the majority of our walk-ins are other Americans from out of town. We ask them where they are from and usually have them sign a register to help keep track.

"Individual tourists are fine, but bringing in conventions and people by the hundreds or even thousands is where the expansion is. More and more hotels are being built, and more and more conventions are choosing our area. It's the convention and tourism bureau's job to enhance the possibility of that happening as often as possible.

"Our office talks to convention managers and meeting planners and sells them on our city for dates years into the future. We coordinate this with the other groups that are coming in, and especially with the hotels and convention center or other meeting places. Once we think they are on a course to come here, we step aside and let the groups and hotels negotiate with each other to set up the details. But we are always ready to give backup support.

"This seemed like just fun at first, but now I can see an entire career in it. I enrolled in evening business and communication courses and should have a chance to move into the marketing part of the office in the future."

Characteristics that distinguish one destination from another include
✔ Climate.
✔ Attractions.

✔ Costs and standard of living.
✔ Accessibility.
✔ Culture.
✔ Competition.

Locational and Physical Geography

- HOW DO YOU DESCRIBE THE LOCATION OF A DESTINATION AND CALCULATE TIME DIFFERENCES?

- WHAT DETERMINES A DESTINATION'S CLIMATE?

People who develop and promote particular destinations obviously need expertise about those destinations, but all travel professionals need knowledge of their products, and for the travel industry, destinations *are* products. Knowledge about them comes from *geography*—the science that studies the earth, its features, its life, and how these interact.

In particular, travel professionals need some understanding of the three types of geography: *locational geography*, which covers the location of places; *physical geography*, which examines natural features such as terrain and climate; and *cultural geography*, which studies how people and their environments interact. As a first step, travel professionals should know how to find the answers to three of the most often asked questions about destinations: Where is it? How long does it take to get there? And what will the weather be like?

Where Is It?

Every place on earth has a unique "address" based on a *grid*, or network of lines, created by geographers. The two basic lines of this grid are the equator and the prime meridian:

- The *equator* is an imaginary line that circles the globe halfway between the North and South Poles. The distance measured in degrees north or south of the equator is the *latitude* of a location.
- The *prime meridian* is an imaginary line running through Greenwich, England, that connects the North and South Poles. The distance measured in degrees east or west of the prime meridian is the *longitude* of a location.

New York City, for example, is located at 40°45′ north latitude, 74° west longitude (or 40°45′N, 74°W); no other place on earth has this particular address. However, if you were trying to explain New York City's location to someone, you would most likely never quote the latitude and longitude to them.

In fact, few people know the latitudes and longitudes of different locations. For the traveler and travel professional alike, this precise address or *absolute location* is less important than relative location. Where, for example, is Cancún? Its latitude and longitude are 21°N, 87°W. But for most people a more meaningful answer would describe the location of Cancún by giving its *context—a beachside resort on the tip of the Yucatan Peninsula of Mexico.* Where is it in relation to larger natural features? Answering this question requires the use of a few basic geographic concepts and terms, such as the terms for large areas of land and water.

Describing the Earth. Most of the earth is occupied by a huge body of salt water with four major divisions known as *oceans:* the Arctic, the Atlantic, the Indian, and the Pacific. At the borders of these oceans are *seas,* which are smaller bodies of salt water surrounded by land (such as the Mediterranean and the Caribbean Seas), and *gulfs,* which are bodies of salt water bordered by a curved shoreline (such as the Gulf of Mexico). The oceans embrace seven large landmasses called *continents:* Africa, Antarctica, Asia, Australia, Europe, North America, and South America. (Some people consider Europe and Asia as one continent, Eurasia.)

The continents are used by some geographers to define even larger areas of the globe: the Eastern and Western Hemispheres. North and South America constitute the *Western Hemisphere;* the other continents make up the *Eastern Hemisphere.* Geographers use the equator to divide the earth into a *Northern* and a *Southern Hemisphere.* Thus we can locate Cancún by saying that it is in the Northern and Western Hemispheres on the North American continent, bordering the Caribbean Sea.

More specific descriptions of the location of a destination distinguish smaller bodies of land and water. Cancún, as mentioned before, is on the Yucatán peninsula. A *peninsula* is a body of land with water on three sides. In contrast, an *island* is a body of land completely surrounded by water, and an *isthmus* is a narrow body of land connecting two larger bodies of land. A *strait* is a narrow channel of water connecting two larger bodies of water, whereas a *sound* is a long, wide body of water connecting two larger bodies of water. A *river* is a natural-moving channel of fresh water that flows over the land and empties into a body of water, such as an ocean or lake. The end point is referred to as the *mouth.*

Reading a Map. A map is the key tool for locating places, an invaluable source of information about destinations. Remember, though, that every map is a simplified picture of reality. No map can show everything; every map reflects choices about what to include and what to omit. Furthermore, maps must distort reality because a map is flat and two-dimensional; the earth is spherical and three-dimensional. It is impossible to represent a spherical object on a flat surface without distortion.

Many maps include the grid that shows latitude and longitude. The east-west lines that measure latitude are called *parallels.* The north-south lines that mark off longitude are called *meridians.* (Recall that *latitudes* are distances north and south of the equator; *longitudes* are distances east and west of the prime meridian.)

Most maps offer several aids to help readers understand them:
- An *index* lists in alphabetical order the places and features that are noted on the map.
- A *legend* (or *key*) explains the symbols that are used on the map, such as a star for the capital of a country.
- *Compass points* show where north, south, east, and west are in relation to the map. Usually, north is at the top of the map.

FIGURE 2.1

24-Hour Clock

On the 24-hour clock each day begins at 0000 (midnight) and progresses through each hour of the day from 0100 (1:00 A.M.) to 2300 (11:00 P.M.). The last two digits give the minutes. To convert 24-hour time to A.M./P.M. time, subtract 1200 from hours greater than noon. To convert A.M./P.M. time to the 24-hour clock, add 1200 to hours after noon.

A.M./P.M. Time	24-Hour Time
Midnight (12 A.M.)	0000
1 A.M.	0100
2 A.M.	0200
3 A.M.	0300
4 A.M.	0400
5 A.M.	0500
6 A.M.	0600
7 A.M.	0700
8 A.M.	0800
9 A.M.	0900
10 A.M.	1000
11 A.M.	1100
Noon (12 P.M.)	1200
1 P.M.	1300
2 P.M.	1400
3 P.M.	1500
4 P.M.	1600
5 P.M.	1700
6 P.M.	1800
7 P.M.	1900
8 P.M.	2000
9 P.M.	2100
10 P.M.	2200
11 P.M.	2300

- A *scale* indicates how the size of the map is related to real-world distances. For example, one inch on a map might represent 700 actual miles (or 1,126 kilometers).
- A *relief key* shows how **altitude,** or elevation above sea level, is represented on the map. Often, changes in altitude are indicated by changes in color or shading.

When Will I Get There?

Knowing where a place is does not answer one of the most frequently asked questions: When will I get there? Sometimes, determining the answer requires use of both the 24-hour clock and a map of the world's time zones.

Figure 2.1 shows the **24-hour clock.** It eliminates the A.M./P.M. distinction, providing a different numeral for each hour of the day. It is used often by airlines and the military. Many people in the travel industry prefer to use it as it avoids errors, although computers in the United States are programmed to show A.M. and P.M. because so many Americans are not accustomed to using the 24-hour clock in their daily lives. For example, many flights that leave around midnight are scheduled to leave at 23:59 (one minute before midnight) or at 00:01 (one minute after midnight)—note, only two minutes apart but actually two different dates!

Figure 2.2 shows how the world is divided into twenty-four time zones, starting from the prime meridian at Greenwich, England. There is a 1-hour time difference between most adjacent time zones. The time at Greenwich is called **Greenwich mean time (GMT)** or **universal time coordinated (UTC),** and the time elsewhere in the world is expressed as plus or minus GMT or UTC. New York, for example, is −5 GMT—in other words, 5 hours earlier than GMT.

About twelve time zones from Greenwich, on the opposite side of the world in the Pacific Ocean, is the **international date line.** It is an imaginary line roughly corresponding to 180° longitude that, by international agreement, separates one calendar day from another. When it is noon in Greenwich, England, on the prime meridian, it is midnight on the international date line. West of the international date line, toward Asia, it is one calendar day later than east of the line.

Figure 2.2 also describes how to use a map of time zones to calculate both time differences and the duration of a trip. Note, though, that these calculations get more complicated at certain places and times. A few countries do not follow the international time zones in setting their clocks. China, for example, uses only one time zone throughout the entire country; the time is the same no matter where you are in China. Furthermore, most countries adjust their clocks during the summer to create *daylight saving time,* and places have varying rules about when they move their clocks forward and backward. The computers used in travel agencies called GDSs (Global Distribution Systems) and many Web sites are set to calculate time differences and travel times for you.

Airline schedules indicate the local time in a particular place on a particular date. In some cases, you may arrive at your destination before you left home! For example, in flying eastward from Asia to the United States, you might leave Singapore and arrive in the United States earlier on the same date you left Singapore. Another factor affecting flight schedules is wind. For example, flights from New York to San Francisco take longer than flights from San Francisco to New York, due to prevailing tail winds flying eastward and headwinds flying westward.

What Is the Climate Like?

No one can tell a traveler what the weather is going to be at a destination on a certain day, but travel professionals should be able to describe the weather that prevails, the average weather over a long time—in other words, the climate. For example, areas with what is called a **Mediterranean climate** have warm, dry summers and mild, wet winters. A Mediterranean climate occurs not only in countries along the Mediterranean but also in southern California, central Chile, and parts of the southern coasts of Africa and Australia.

To calculate the time difference

1. For each location, find the local time and its relationship to GMT on an international time chart.
2. If both locations are either ahead of GMT (GMT+) or behind GMT (GMT–), subtract the smaller from the larger figure.

    For example, Toronto is GMT –5 and San Francisco is GMT –8. Subtracting 5 from 8 gives 3, so there is a 3-hour time difference between the two locations.
3. If the local time is ahead of GMT (GMT+) at one location and behind GMT (GMT–) at the other location, add the figures.

    For example, New York is GMT –5 and Rome is GMT +1. Adding 5 plus 1 gives 6, so there is a 6-hour time difference between the two locations.

To calculate the elapsed travel time

1. Convert departure and arrival times to 24-hour clock time.
2. Subtract the departure time from the arrival time.
3. When traveling east, subtract 1 hour for every time zone crossed. When traveling west, add 1 hour for every time zone crossed. The result is the actual travel time.

    For example, suppose the departure time from Paris is 12:15 P.M. and the arrival time in New York is 1:25 P.M. Converted to 24-hour time, the departure time is 1215 and the arrival time is 1325. The difference is 1 hour and 10 minutes. Because 6 time zones are crossed going west from Paris to New York, add 6 hours to the result. Thus the elapsed travel time in this case is 7 hours and 10 minutes.

FIGURE 2.2 Time Zones

There is a 1-hour difference between most adjacent time zones. But the twelfth time zone is two half zones, as the map shows. The international date line crosses this zone at about 180° from Greenwich. East of the date line, it is a day earlier than it is west of the line.

Temperature, precipitation, atmospheric pressure, winds, humidity, altitude, and the percentage of cloudiness and sunshine together define the weather and climate. Temperature is often the salient feature, but it can be overshadowed by other characteristics. Humidity, for example, has a major effect on whether a particular temperature is comfortable. A very hot, dry area is much more tolerable than a hot, humid one.

In many places, patterns of precipitation dominate life. Arid deserts are one example. Major deserts include the Sahara in northern Africa, the Gobi in Mongolia and China, the Kalahari in southwestern Africa, and the Atacama in northern Chile.

Precipitation patterns are also a dominant fact of life in regions that experience monsoons. A *monsoon* is a wind system that reverses direction seasonally, but the word is often used to refer to the heavy rains that come with the wind. In northern Australia and parts of southern Asia, for example, the wind comes from the south or southwest for about six months, blowing in moisture from the Indian and Pacific Oceans and bringing torrential rains. For the next six months, the winds reverse direction, and little rain falls.

What creates differences in climate? Many factors interact, but the key ones include a location's latitude, altitude, proximity to bodies of water, and winds.

Latitude. All year, because of the way the earth tilts on its axis, the equator receives the most direct rays of the sun; the North and South Poles get the least amount of direct sun. Thus the closer a place is to the equator, the warmer it tends to be. Also, the closer a place is to the equator, the less difference there is likely to be between seasons. North of the equator, winter occurs during December, January, and February and summer during June, July, and August. The seasons are reversed south of the equator.

Latitude is the basis for one ancient and very simple classification of the world's climates. This classification describes five zones that circle the globe. In the far north, at the Arctic Circle, is a *frigid polar zone,* where summers are cool despite up to 24 hours of sunlight and winters are cold with 24 hours of darkness. South of the polar zone is a *temperate zone.* Next, straddling the equator, lies the *tropical zone,* where the average temperature every month is about 80°F. South of the tropical zone is another temperate zone and then another polar zone.

This very broad picture of the world's climates can be useful, but dramatic differences occur within climate zones. Places at about the same latitude (such as Seattle, Washington, and Fargo, North Dakota) often have very different climates because latitude is not the only key to climate.

It also should be noted that sunrise and sunset times vary greatly during the seasons at the extreme north and extreme south zones. However, close to the equator there is little difference between the time the sun sets in the winter and in the summer. This can affect tourism greatly, as long periods of light in the evening can make for additional opportunities for sightseeing activities, driving times, and social events.

Altitude. One factor that may overshadow the influence of latitude is the altitude. The higher the altitude, the cooler the climate is likely to be. The temperature along a beach at sea level may be 85°F, while just a few miles away, on top of a high mountain, the temperature may be only 40°F. If you are at the equator but in the mountains 9,000 feet high (as in Ecuador, for example), it may be very cool. Many travel industry novices make the mistake of assuming that it's always hot if you are near the equator—not so! Among the most famous peaks on earth are Mount Everest (at 29,028 ft) in the

Himalayas on the border of Tibet and Nepal, Mount McKinley (at 20,320 ft) in Alaska, Mount Kilimanjaro (at 19,340 ft) in Tanzania, and Mount Fuji (at 12,388 ft) in Japan.

It is important that travel counselors become aware of high altitude destinations as many travelers have health issues at altitudes of 9000 feet and above. And adventure travelers need to be reminded that if climbing Mt. Kilimanjaro they will start their climb wearing light summer clothing and continually add clothing as they approach the summit.

Proximity to Bodies of Water. Water usually moderates temperature. In summer, the closer you are to a body of water, the cooler it will be. In winter, the closer you are to the water, the warmer the temperature.

Winds. Paris and London do not experience many days below freezing, even though they are at the same latitude and altitude as places in central Canada where the temperature may be –40°F during the winter. Why? Prevailing winds bring warm Atlantic air to western Europe for many miles inland from its coast. The air is warm because it passed over the *Gulf Stream,* which is a warm ocean current that flows north from the Caribbean through the Atlantic. In contrast, winds that blow across ocean currents coming from the polar regions can bring cooler temperatures.

Mountain ranges often create interesting variations in climate by blocking the prevailing winds. As air passes over mountains, it rises and is cooled; it also loses moisture. Thus the climate on the **windward** side of the mountains, which is the side exposed to the wind, will differ from the climate on the **leeward** side, the side sheltered from the wind. For example, if a mountain range blocks a warm ocean wind, then its leeward side will have a cooler and drier climate than its windward side.

Conclusions. Understanding the geographic characteristics we have discussed can lead to educated guesses about where to look for a certain type of climate, as well as the wisdom not to jump to conclusions. Some areas have weather that rarely changes; in other places the weather varies considerably. In some places one climate prevails over hundreds of miles; elsewhere the climate changes within just a few miles. San Francisco may be foggy and cool in the summer, for example, while a few miles inland skies may be clear and the temperature can be hot. How to find good information about the climate and other characteristics of a specific destination is the topic of the next section.

✔ CHECK-UP

The largest features of the earth are its
✔ Four oceans: Atlantic, Arctic, Indian, and Pacific.
✔ Seven continents: Africa, Antarctica, Asia, Australia, Europe, North America, and South America.

The earth's time zones
✔ Are measured from the prime meridian, which is at Greenwich, England.
✔ Are one hour apart.

The weather is defined by
✔ Temperature.
✔ Precipitation.
✔ Atmospheric pressure.
✔ Winds.
✔ Humidity.
✔ Percentage of cloudiness and sunshine.
✔ Altitude.

Learning about Destinations

■ WHAT ARE GOOD SOURCES OF INFORMATION ABOUT DESTINATIONS?

No one can be an expert on all destinations, but every travel professional should be acquainted with the most popular destinations and should know how to find other information when it is needed. Personal travel, general education, and formal courses on travel provide the foundation for this knowledge.

Travel and Education

There is no substitute for a personal visit as a way of learning about a destination. Governments as well as suppliers, such as cruise lines and tour operators, sponsor *familiarization trips (fam trips).* These are trips offered to bona fide travel professionals at a reduced rate so that they can inspect hotels and restaurants, sample attractions, and experience the local culture as well as learn about the services of the sponsoring companies. They are usually short, concentrated learning trips in a business format.

A brief visit, however, cannot provide a comprehensive picture of a

---

CLOSE-UP: SELLING THROUGH KNOWLEDGE

The idea that travel professionals need to know where to find answers, rather than the answers themselves, can be taken too far. To make a good first impression and to gain the confidence of a new customer, travel professionals should be able to talk to the customer about a destination, at least briefly. And to plan a trip, travel counselors will need to answer the following basic questions:

■ *Where is the destination located?* Suppose a couple wants to go to Kaanapali. Do you know where it is?

■ *How does a traveler get there?* How easy or difficult is the trip? Are there nonstop flights to Kaanapali, Maui? Direct flights? How many connections will the traveler need to make? How long will the entire trip take, including the transfer from the airport to the destination?

■ *What is the climate at the destination?* Does it vary much throughout the year? Are there particularly unpleasant times, or are there weeks best suited for particular activities?

■ *When are the best times to go?* The answer depends on more than the climate. For example, crowds and prices might vary greatly—and might be worst when the climate is best. Of course, the clients' interests may shape what type of weather is "best."

■ *What are the health conditions, safety concerns, culture, and people like at the destination?* Is the novice traveler likely to be comfortable there, or is this a place better suited to experienced and sophisticated travelers?

■ *What are the major reasons people go to the destination?* What activities are available there? What are the major sights?

■ *How does a traveler get around at the destination?* What local transportation is available?

■ *Where would the traveler stay and eat?* Are there a lot of choices? Can travelers find the brand names they are accustomed to? Can they find unusual types of lodging and food?

■ *What is the price range of a trip?* Can travelers on every budget find transportation and accommodations, or is the destination too expensive for most? Are there accommodations that would suit travelers looking for a luxurious destination?

To help yourself prepare to sell a trip to a destination, plan a trip for yourself and a loved one as if you were going to make the journey. If you feel as if you are actually making the trip, you will remember the information for a very long time.

---

destination, and places may change rapidly. Travel professionals must go beyond their limited personal experience and learn from others.

Almost anything that contributes to your general education can also build your knowledge about destinations. Conversations with other people, books, magazines, newspapers, Web sites, travel videos, documentaries, even movies and novels—all of these sources help travel professionals to enrich their understanding of the world and to keep in touch with the latest trends and events. Many travel professionals continue their learning after they are employed by speaking with their clients when they return from a trip, by talking with colleagues, and by attending industry seminars and participating in familiarization trips. More discussion of these opportunities may be found in Chapter 16.

Making sense of this flood of information can be difficult. The backbone of a travel professional's knowledge about destinations comes from reference works such as maps, guidebooks, textbooks, and personal research. Mastering all the information they offer becomes far easier with the help of the systematic, formal study offered by colleges, travel schools, professional associations, and suppliers. For example, *The Travel Institute,* the educational organization for travel professionals and the publisher of this book, offers Destination Specialist courses that examine specific areas of the world in depth.

Chapter 16 describes such opportunities for further education. Our focus here is slightly different: If you need an answer to a specific question about a location to solve a problem, where do you turn? You might find help from the following sources:

- Colleagues. Your colleagues can be helpful especially if they are experts on the destination and have seen the specific spot you are asking about.
- Tour operators. These companies usually have employees who are very familiar with the destinations they offer and are often willing to share their knowledge with their travel industry colleagues.
- Government tourist offices. Their staffs include people with an intimate knowledge of the destinations they represent, and many can provide leads to other knowledgeable people as well as promotional aids such as annual guides to the destination.
- Other government sources. As we discuss later in this chapter, government agencies such as the U.S. State Department and Centers for Disease Control and Prevention are the best source for some types of information on destinations, particularly information about safety and health issues.

Often, however, finding answers requires the use of references—in print or online—such as atlases, guidebooks, newspapers, magazines, brochures. and Web sites. These sources are worth a closer look.

Some Key References

Maps and Atlases. You can answer many kinds of questions by finding the right map. Besides maps that focus on physical features, there are also maps that give historical and cultural information. A compilation of maps is called an *atlas.* A good atlas should be visited frequently, like an old friend.

Guidebooks. Hundreds of guidebooks are published every year. Leading series of guidebooks include the following:
- *Eyewitness.* These highly visual guidebooks are very attractive, and they include mini-essays on all aspects of a destination's culture.

- *Fodor.* This is a comprehensive series of guides. Most books in the series cover sightseeing, walking tours, attractions, nightlife, and shopping and provide hotel and restaurant reviews. Fodor also offers travel kits, which contain guidebooks, language cassettes, and phrasebooks/dictionaries.
- *Frommer.* This series includes country and regional guides that provide pricing, walking maps, and sightseeing information, as well as the authors' insights, recommendations, and advice. Frommer's "Dollar-a-Day" and city guides emphasize accommodations, restaurants, and sightseeing. Most Frommer guides contain "Ten Best" lists, which make them a good quick-reference tool.
- *Insight.* These books offer superb photography and essays that provide excellent background on a country or area.
- *Let's Go.* This series emphasizes budget travel. It is geared toward student travelers, and much of it is written by students but is used by many others.
- *Lonely Planet* and *Moon Publications.* Designed for the budget traveler, these series give in-depth commentary on the local scene.
- *Michelin.* Michelin's *Red Guides* list hotels, restaurants, and garages (for tires); the *Green Guides* provide detailed historical and sightseeing information, as well as maps.
- *Rick Steves' Europe.* These city and regional guidebooks also include tips on preparing for a trip.
- *Rough Guide.* This is a practical, analytical, and down-to-earth series.

Keep in mind that no book is infallible and that much of the information in guidebooks is not updated frequently.

Newspapers and Magazines. Newspapers and magazines are often excellent sources; many have both online and print editions. Four categories of publications are most useful: (1) consumer magazines devoted exclusively to travel, (2) general consumer publications not devoted exclusively to travel but with occasional helpful travel columns, (3) specialty consumer publications, and (4) travel industry trade publications. Below are some samples of these publications for readers in the United States. Similar publications are available in many other countries as well.

Consumer magazines devoted exclusively to travel include *National Geographic Traveler, Travel and Leisure, Condé Nast Traveler,* and *Budget Traveler. Luxury Travel Advisor* is an online publication.

General consumer magazines with occasional travel articles or columns include *Harper's, New Yorker, Atlantic Monthly, Elle,* and *Sunset.* The Sunday travel sections of some key U.S. newspapers are also a good source. Particularly notable are *The New York Times,* the *Los Angeles Times, The Boston Globe,* the *Chicago Tribune.* The *Wall Street Journal* is also noted for its business travel coverage and, in particular, its reports on the airline industry.

Specialty consumer magazines with travel features include *Outside* for adventure travelers or *Bon Appetit* for food enthusiasts interested in excellent restaurants while they travel or international cooking schools.

Travel industry trade publications are newspapers, periodicals, and online newsletters aimed specifically at those who work in the industry, not at the consumer traveler. Associations of travel professionals, such as the American Society of Travel Agents (ASTA) and the Pacific Asia Travel Association (PATA), publish magazines and annual guides. The trade newspapers *Travel Weekly, Jax Fax, Travel Agent, TravelAge West,* and *Travel Trade* publish articles and supplements. And other trade magazines exist for those in the hospitality or restaurant segment of tourism. Most have both print and online versions.

Brochures. Brochures are far from objective; tour operators and suppliers create them to present destinations in the best possible light. Still, brochures often present useful information about local customs, health precautions, visa requirements, currency, shopping, and sightseeing activities in the area. Sometimes the quickest way to get an overview of the attractions of a destination is to read the itinerary of an escorted tour in a tour operator's brochure or catalogue.

Web Sites. Much of the time and money that companies once devoted to creating brochures now go to designing and maintaining Web sites. In fact, you can find just about everything about destinations online. Most of the publications mentioned in the previous sections have Web sites. And almost every national tourist office has a site, as do many tourist offices representing regions, cities, states, provinces, and other entities. A major advantage of a Web site over print media is that it can be updated frequently with current information, as it becomes available. However, print media may offer more in-depth coverage.

Beyond these standard references, the Internet offers innumerable other sources of information about destinations. The sites of many suppliers and online travel agencies include destination guides. Often you can find useful sites by searching under a topic—castles or skiing, for example. We cannot underestimate how searching for information has changed since being able to "Google" just about any question one has.

How do you sift through and use all this information? Here are two suggestions:

1. *Remember to be skeptical.* Identify the source and its date, and judge the information accordingly. Is the source likely to be biased? Does the information come from someone with first-hand, recent experience of the location? Many Web sites have names and addresses that make them sound as if they were created by tourist offices when, in fact, they are maintained by private companies selling their services or by individuals describing places they love. Many are not up to date.

2. *Develop a list of favorite Web sites and other sources that you know to be reliable and easy to access.* Travel professionals who know how to search efficiently for reliable information can save valuable time and money for their companies and their clients. Periodically review broad topics in a search engine as new, reliable, informative Web sites continue to be created and can expand your list of sources.

✔ CHECK-UP

You can develop a foundation of knowledge about destinations through
- ✔ Travel, including personal travel and fam trips.
- ✔ General education.
- ✔ Systematic courses of study offered by colleges, travel schools, and professional associations.
- ✔ Seminars usually sponsored by suppliers such as government tourist office, tour operators, and cruise lines, among others.
- ✔ Webinars—online seminars, also usually sponsored by suppliers.

Key references for finding specific information about a destination include
- ✔ Maps and atlases.
- ✔ Guidebooks.
- ✔ Newspaper and magazine articles.
- ✔ Brochures.
- ✔ Web sites.

Crossing Borders

McDonald's may well be on the street corners of Tokyo, Paris, and Moscow, but international travel is still unlike domestic travel in whatever country you live. If you travel through Papua New Guinea, for example, you could come across 862 local languages. Visitors in the Gobi Desert might be invited to spend the night in white tent-like homes called *gers*. Travel abroad can bring both exotic experiences and perplexing challenges. Government regulations and differences in currencies, customs, and languages of the many nations making up our world can be frustrating for the unprepared traveler.

The flow of citizens between countries reflects the relationship between these nations. Each country decides whether to welcome or not welcome visitors from other nations and establishes laws accordingly. Many times such laws are based on reciprocity between two countries. Economic, social, political, medical, and natural events can all influence the number of people willing and able to visit other lands.

Every country has rules that restrict the passage of people and goods across its borders, through its airports, and into its ports. Is a Ukrainian citizen who is a resident of the United States allowed to enter Guatemala without a visa? Can U.S. travelers buy ivory in Africa and bring it home? The travelers themselves are responsible for determining and following the rules, but the travel professionals who counsel them should be able to help them with answers to such questions. And the answers often require research.

Disasters such as the March 2011 earthquake and subsequent tsunami in northeast Japan, the 9/11 attacks, Hurricane Katrina in New Orleans, the worldwide financial downturn with massive loss of employment, and the fear associated with outbreaks of certain diseases all take their toll on world tourism and complicate issues of travel documentation. Nevertheless, the tremendous growth of international travel in past years (both for vacation/leisure and business) requires that those employed in the travel/tourism industry understand the documentation requirements of travelers in today's world and know where to go for answers to often-complicated situations.

Today many people may be *residents* of a country but not necessarily be *citizens* of that same country. For example, a citizen of Australia may be living and working in the United States, and planning to visit Brazil on vacation. While living in the United States, that person must have a *residency card* (often called a *green card*). It's important that the travel counselor verify that client's citizenship/nationality so as to provide accurate information regarding entry requirements for Brazil as well as re-entry requirements for the United States. The counselor should never assume the traveler's citizenship. Let's look at some of the documentation terminology and requirements.

Entry Documents

Passports. A *passport* is a document issued by a government that establishes an individual's identity and nationality of that particular country and requests protection for the citizen while abroad. For example, a U.S. passport is issued to U.S. citizens by the State Department's Bureau of Consular Affairs and is valid for ten years from date of issue (except for those younger than 16 when they apply; their passports are valid for only five years). In the past U.S. citizens did not need a passport for some international travel, such as to the Caribbean, Mexico or Canada. Today U.S. citizens need a passport any time they are leaving the United States. Note that some countries require that passports are still valid for six months after entering the country; some have increased that to nine months, and a few only require three months.

When leaving the United States by air, passengers must prove to airline personnel at check-in that they have proper documentation to enter the destination country when their plane arrives. The airline is subject to a fine and must provide return transportation to any passenger not allowed to enter the destination. Therefore, airline personnel check travelers' documents carefully and do not allow people with incomplete documentation to board.

Where and How to Obtain a Passport.
The following information pertains to U.S. citizens only. Citizens of other countries should follow the instructions of their individual country.

For U.S. citizens, up-to-date information is available from the U.S State Department's Bureau of Consular Affairs. Their Web site (www.travel.state. gov) includes full information on passport books versus the new passport cards, where to apply, items needed for applying, fees, special rules for minors, first-time passports versus renewals, among other information. Below are a few basic points from the Web site, but please note that information can change, sometimes with little or no notice.

An adult (age 16 or older) can obtain application forms at many U.S. Post Offices, court houses, and other stipulated sites. The completed application form must be accompanied by: (1) a birth certificate that is certified with the registrar's signature and has a raised, impressed, embossed, or multicolored seal (or if born abroad, a certificate of naturalization); (2) evidence of U.S. citizenship such as previous passport, certified birth certificate, or naturalization certificate (not a drivers' license, draft certificate, Social Security card or a voting card); (3) one photo in color 2x2 inches in size, full-face view on white background, taken within the last six months; (4) payments of $110 application fee, $25 execution fee and additional fees for expedited services, if any.

Rates for minors vary, and effective April 1, 2011, birth certificates for a minor applicant must have the names of both parents. Young people under age 18—traveling alone or with someone—are under special scrutiny when traveling internationally. Some countries, notably Mexico, require written, notarized approval by one or both of the nontraveling parent or legal guardian for minors to enter another country. Travel professionals should be sure to notify clients accordingly.

Travelers should apply for a passport three months in advance, if possible, although the State Department's Web site indicates that passports usually arrive within four to six weeks for routine service or two to three weeks for expedited service. However, the backlog can reach three months at busy times. The site suggests that it is best to apply between September and December.

It's good practice for travel counselors to ask the client to send a copy of the inside data page of the passport. Because the name of the passenger listed on the air ticket must match exactly the name spelled on the passport, this doublecheck avoids check-in problems at the airport. This also gives the travel counselor an opportunity to verify the expiration date and other important details. It is suggested that travelers make several photocopies of the inside data page of the passport—one to keep at home and one to carry on the trip. One photocopy should be kept with them or in a safety deposit box in their hotel. Having a copy and an extra set of passport photos helps facilitate replacement if the passport is lost or stolen. If necessary, the nearest overseas U.S. embassy or consulate can provide a temporary replacement for urgent travel, but it has limited validity. (*Embassies* are the offices of the ambassadors who represent a nation in another country; *consulates* are regional offices of embassies.)

Visas. Whereas a passport is required to travel abroad and is issued by the country of one's citizenship, a *visa* is issued by a country and allows the individual to *enter* that country. Visas are generally stamped on a page of the passport, although in certain cases they may be issued on a separate paper. Not all countries require visas, however.

For example, a U.S. citizen visiting Brazil would require two things: a U.S. passport *and* a Brazilian visa required by the Brazilian government for U.S. citizens to enter the country (Figure 2.3). In the case of an Australian citizen living in the United States, the travel counselor must verify that the traveler has a green card (U.S. residency) to be able to return to the United States after traveling to Brazil. And the travel counselor must check with the Brazilian consulate as to whether an Australian citizen needs a visa to enter Brazil.

Different types of visas allow visitors to enter a country for varied purposes and periods of time. Each has different governing rules, length of permitted stay, and cost. For example, visitors who travel to study in another country and stay for an academic year may need a *student visa*; business people entering to conduct business may need a *business visa*. Some countries require all visitors, even those who are just passing through, to obtain a *transit visa*. Many countries do not require a visa if a traveler is staying for less than 24 hours or is making a flight connection and does not leave the airport. For most tourists, the appropriate visa is a *tourist* or *visitor visa*. Visitor visas are usually valid for a specific period but can often be renewed without leaving the country. Some tourist visas permit multiple entries. Most tourist visas do not permit the traveler to work in the country concerned.

Requirements for obtaining a visa vary. Some countries charge a fee. Other requirements for a typical visitor visa include

- A passport signed and valid for a minimum of six months after arrival in the country concerned.
- A completed visa application form signed by the applicant.
- A passport-size photograph taken within the past six months.
- A printout of the traveler's flight reservations.

Requirements for obtaining a typical business visa might include everything required for a visitor visa plus letters from the host company being visited and from the employer. The employer's letter states the purpose of the trip, the company's guarantee of financial and moral responsibility while the employee is in the country, and the name and address of a reference.

Although some countries, Egypt and Turkey, for example, offer tourist visas upon arrival, many experienced travel counselors believe that travelers should obtain their visas before leaving home. If the traveler is taking a prearranged tour, the tour operator might take care of the process. Travelers who are obtaining their own visas should apply to the consulates or embassies of the countries they plan to visit. Application forms from many countries can now be obtained on the Internet.

Travelers must submit their passport with each visa application one at a time, so obtaining visas for several countries might take months. An alternative is to use a visa service company, which can obtain several visas in a

19 - Purpose of trip (check one item that is the most applicable to the circumstances of your trip)

☐ In-country provision of services of temporary or permanent nature, including in-field services under contract and/or intra-company activities such as project management, technical support, training, auditing/accounting.

☐ Headquarters-based business development activities, including negotiating contracts, executive meetings, marketing assessment, specifying orders in contracts, customer relations related activities, performance assessment, establishing framework for doing business in Brazil.

ЯΞ   REPÚBLICA FEDERATIVA DO BRASIL
MINISTÉRIO DAS RELAÇÕES EXTERIORES

| **Pedido de Visto** |
| **VISA APPLICATION FORM** |

| Protocolo | Visto |

PLEASE TYPE OR PRINT. ANSWER ITEMS 1 THROUGH 26 (FIRST AND SECOND PAGE) AND SIGN. INCOMPLETE FORMS WILL BE RETURNED.

A - DADOS PESSOAIS (PERSONAL INFORMATION)

01 - First/Middle/Family Name)

02 - Place of Birth (city/state/country)

03 - Date of birth
Day   Month   Year

Attach
2" x 2"
photo
here

04 - Nationality   05 - Sex   06 - Marital Status

07 - Passport #   08 - Issuing Country   09 - Expiration Date (D/M/Y)

10 - Parent's Name and Nationality
Father's:
Mother's:

11 - Home Address   12 - Telephone #
(   )   13 - Profession

14 - Business Address   15 - Telephone #
(   )   16 - Employer

17 - Job Position or Title   18 - E-mail

PARA USO OFICIAL (FOR OFFICIAL USE ONLY)

A - Consulta à SERE	B - Autorização da SERE	C - Tipo do Visto
OF TEL No. _____	DESP DESPTEL No. _____	
D - Concessão Denegação Renovação	E - Entradas Uma Múltiplas	F - Prazo de Entrada _____ anos/dias	G- Data ____/____/____
H - Observaçõs		I - Assinaturas
		Funcionário Chefia

Brazilian Embassy in Washington – VISAPPFRM-01/2000

FIGURE 2.3 A Visa Application

This visa application for Brazil can be completed online and printed; then the application is mailed or brought to Brazil's embassy in Washington, D.C., or to one of its consulates in the United States.

relatively short time. They are usually well worth the fees they charge, particularly when time is short or when several different visas are required for a complicated trip. Their service fee is *in addition to* the consulate's fee, if any, and any additional fees for expediting the process.

To summarize, up-to-date information on the requirements for U.S. citizens to enter each country is available from the State Department's Bureau of Consular Affairs. Rules vary from nation to nation and often change, sometimes with little or no notice. Depending on the country visited, travelers may need to provide proof of citizenship, a passport, a visa, or a tourist card.

Tourist Cards. Some countries, such as Mexico, require a **tourist card** for entry instead of a visa. Often these are "landing cards"—cards given to travelers when they check in for the flight, part of which they must turn in on arrival at their destination airport, and the other part that they must surrender when they leave their destination. They are often used by the country as a way of keeping visitor arrival statistics.

Conclusions. The need to check for changes in the requirements for entering and leaving a country cannot be overstated. Since 2001 the United States has been revising and tightening rules and procedures to closely track all kinds of people; as of 2012 changes are still under way. For example, particular controversy has surrounded proposals about encoding information on electronic chips on U.S. passports and about making it more difficult for people to obtain visas to enter the United States. As the United States tightens the rules on international visitors, other nations sometimes threaten to retaliate, making it more difficult for U.S. citizens to enter other countries.

Customs Regulations

Every country in the world restricts the items that can be brought across its borders and assesses a charge, called a **duty**, on items whose value exceeds a certain allowance. Travel counselors should alert clients to the regulations published by the U.S. Customs Service. All returning residents of the United States, citizens or not, must observe these rules.

Articles Free of U.S. Duty. Anything taken from home can be brought back into the United States duty-free. However, the traveler may have to prove to a U.S. Customs officer that some items were bought in the United States. For example, a Japanese-made camera bought in the United States is liable for duty if the traveler cannot provide proof of purchase. Owners of internationally made articles should take the bill of sale with them or register the item with a U.S. Customs office well before departure. Similarly, travelers should bring a bill of sale or appraisal for valuable items such as furs or jewelry.

In the past, some products from certain countries were exempt from any duty to stimulate the economies of developing countries. However, this policy, the Generalized System of Preferences (GSP) expired Dec. 31, 2010, and has not been reinstated by Congress at this writing. Travelers should check with the U.S. Customs Service for detailed information at www.customs.gov.

Travelers who are overseas can mail home to themselves personal clothing or articles that they do not need without paying duty if the items were not bought abroad. Also, travelers may mail home items that do not exceed a market value of $200. Gifts purchased abroad and mailed back to friends or relatives are not subject to duty if their fair retail value in the country where they were purchased does not exceed $100. No recipient can receive more than $100 worth of items in one day. Such packages should be marked "Unsolicited Gift" and the value noted on the outer wrapper. You may not send such gifts to yourself.

The Personal Exemption. Each U.S. traveler may bring back into the United States as accompanied baggage valued up to $800 in duty-free purchases if one has been out of the country at least 48 hours and has not had a similar exemption within the past 30 days. This duty-free exemption is called the (personal exemption.)If travelers bring back goods worth more than the personal exemption, they must pay duty of a flat 3 percent on the next $1,000. Items to be sent later may not be considered accompanied baggage and may not be included in the $800. The value of each item is based on its fair market value in the country where it was purchased. Antiques that are at least 100 years old and fine art may enter the United States duty free, but folk art and handicrafts are generally not exempt. Certain differences apply when returning from U.S. insular possessions (the U.S. Virgin Islands, American Samoa,or Guam) as well as some Caribbean countries. Check the "Know Before You Go" section of the Web site carefully.

U.S. federal regulations allow the personal exemption to include up to 100 cigars (non-Cuban) and 200 cigarettes. Also, it may include up to one liter of alcohol if the passenger is at least 21 years of age. However, some states prohibit the importation of alcohol or tobacco products regardless of federal regulations. Information on these state regulations is available from U.S. Customs and from local alcoholic beverage control commissions.

On the flight or cruise back to the United States, passengers complete a customs declaration form that U.S. Customs inspectors examine upon arrival. All items acquired abroad beyond the personal exemption must be listed, and receipts are requested for substantial purchases. Receipts should be presented with the declaration form.

Forbidden and Restricted Items. Some items cannot be brought into the United States at all. These include narcotics and dangerous drugs, fireworks, switchblade knives, dangerous toys, automobiles that do not conform to standards set by the Environmental Protection Agency, endangered species, and most threatened species. The United States also forbids the importation of any articles made from whale teeth, African ivory, tortoise shell, alligator skin, and many kinds of furs, except for certain limited purposes with advance permission. These articles are regarded as contraband, and they will be seized *without reimbursement* by U.S. Customs officers. Importing them is a felony and may result in a heavy fine.

Severe restrictions exist on other items, including firearms and ammunition; fruits, vegetables, and plants; meat, livestock, and poultry; money; and pets. Detailed information is available from the U.S. Department of Agriculture's Animal and Plant Health Inspection Service (APHIS).

If travelers must carry prescribed medicines, they should:
- Be sure that cough medicines, diuretics, heart drugs, tranquilizers, sleeping pills, antidepressants, and similar medicines are in their original containers and are clearly labeled.
- Carry only the amount needed for the trip.
- Have a copy of the prescription with a doctor's statement that the medicine is necessary.

Duty-Free Ports. In an effort to attract tourist dollars, many countries have *duty-free ports.* These are ports in which no duty or tax is charged on goods either entering or leaving the country. For example, in St. Thomas in the U.S. Virgin Islands, Swiss watches are imported without any duty; they can then be sold to visitors, who can take them out of St. Thomas without duty or tax.

Duty-free ports can theoretically offer goods at lower prices than they cost elsewhere. In reality, this does not always happen. The traveler contemplating a spending spree in other countries would be wise to comparison-shop at home first.

Remember that an item bought in a duty-free port is only duty-free at the place of purchase. When it is brought back to the United States, the normal regulations regarding duties apply. Duty-free ports are not to be confused with duty-free airport shops.

Duty-Free Airport Shops. When leaving the United States, travelers may wish to make some purchases before boarding their outbound aircraft. Liquors, perfumes, cameras, and other luxury items on which there is normally a high U.S. tax are particularly good buys. If purchasing something that will be used completely while abroad, there's no need to be concerned about paying import taxes on it when returning to the states. However, if a partially used or never-used item is brought back into the United States, it counts as part of the duty-free allowance or it is taxed by U.S. Customs officials on re-entry.

✔ CHECK-UP

Depending on the country visited, a U.S. traveler may need to supply
- ✔ A passport, which is issued by the U.S. government to its citizens.
- ✔ A visa, which is issued by an international government to those wishing to enter its country.
- ✔ A tourist card.

For U.S. residents returning to the United States, duty-free articles include
- ✔ Items taken from home and brought back.
- ✔ Items mailed home to one's self by the traveler that do not exceed a market value of $200.
- ✔ Gifts mailed home to friends or relatives that do not exceed $100 in value.
- ✔ Goods produced by certain countries, as may be specified by government agreements.
- ✔ Items purchased abroad up to the personal exemption.

Health and Safety Abroad

■ WHAT ARE RELIABLE SOURCES OF INFORMATION ABOUT DANGERS WHEN TRAVELING ABROAD, AND WHAT HEALTH PRECAUTIONS SHOULD TRAVELERS TAKE?

No one can guarantee that a traveler will have a safe and healthy trip, but there are many ways that travel professionals can help travelers avoid unnecessary problems and be prepared for unavoidable difficulties. Just by knowing where to go for expert advice and by understanding some commonsense precautions, the travel professional can provide invaluable help.

Finding Out What Is Safe

Travel counselors have a responsibility to tell clients about potential hazards of certain destinations, methods of travel, and activities. For information, the U.S. government is often the best source. In particular, the *Centers for Disease Control and Prevention (CDC)* provides advice for travelers and information about specific diseases abroad, such as malaria, about recommended or required immunizations, and about current health risks by region.

The U.S. Department of State also has information about serious disease outbreaks, natural disasters, and political conditions. It distributes (in print and online) three types of information for international travelers:

- *Travel warnings.* The U.S. State Department issues a travel warning when it decides to recommend that Americans avoid travel to a specific country.
- *Public announcements.* Whenever the U.S. State Department perceives a short-term threat to the security of American travelers, it issues a public announcement. Past announcements have included bomb threats to airlines and the anniversaries of terrorist attacks.
- *Consular information sheets.* For every country in the world, the U.S. State Department posts consular information sheets online. These usually do not give advice, but they do give important information, such as the health conditions, minor political disturbances, crime, and areas of instability.

Once U.S. travelers are abroad, U.S. embassies and consular offices overseas can provide invaluable help in emergencies. These officials replace passports; help travelers find medical assistance; relay emergency messages to and from home; and help travelers who have lost money to contact family, friends, or employers. However, they do not loan monies to travelers who may be in financial difficulty. They also visit U.S. travelers who have been arrested and work to protect their rights and interests, and they notify families in case of death. U.S. citizens traveling independently overseas should register with the nearest U.S. embassy or consular office. Travelers of other nationalities similarly would turn to the embassy or consular office of their own country.

International organizations are another important source of information about health and safety abroad. The World Health Organization (WHO) has information about every country in the world, detailing health risks, health-related certificates required to enter the country, its recommended vaccinations and medications, and other health precautions.

Vaccinations

Usually, vaccinations are not required for direct travel from the United States to most countries, and the United States currently does not require any vaccinations for incoming or returning travelers. But some nations do require visitors to present documentation stating that they have received a specific vaccination or that they are free of HIV, the AIDS virus.

The Bureau of Consular Affairs at the U.S. State Department can provide the current requirements of various countries. In addition, information about immunizations is available from the CDC, and most cities with major airports have a division of the federal Department of Health and Human Services that provides up-to-date information on vaccinations.

Note that the fact that a vaccination is not required in order to enter a country does *not* indicate that travelers will be safe from contracting the disease within the country. Governments require vaccinations in order to protect their own citizens against incoming travelers. In contrast, the World

Health Organization (WHO) and governments recommend vaccinations as a way to protect travelers. Thus the difference between a recommendation and a requirement does *not* indicate a difference in the degree of risk to travelers.

Yellow fever, cholera, meningococcal meningitis, typhoid, tetanus, and hepatitis A are among the diseases against which immunizations may be recommended. All vaccinations have an incubation period before they become effective, and some require a series of shots spaced several days apart. Thus, travelers should plan to receive shots well before departure. Because many doctors do not have the necessary vaccines in their offices, travelers must often go to major hospitals for them, to the Department of Health, or to travel clinics that specialize in pertinent diseases. Because some hospitals and clinics may offer certain inoculations only on certain days, it's important to plan ahead and schedule accordingly. For each immunization, the doctor issues a certificate standardized by WHO.

Seeking Medical Advice and Aid

If travelers have high blood pressure, should they climb the steps at Machu Picchu? Is there a risk of malaria in Nepal? Technical medical questions such as these should be addressed to doctors in the field of travel medicine. They keep current with health conditions worldwide and can provide predeparture counseling, inoculations, preventive medications, and treatment for maladies that result from international travel. They are often affiliated with medical centers or universities. Other doctors, health departments, the CDC, and the International Society of Travel Medicine can provide referrals.

To prepare for an emergency, travelers can obtain updated lists of English-speaking doctors around the world from several organizations. One of the best known is the International Association for Medical Assistance to Travelers (IAMAT), a Canadian organization that lists English-speaking doctors in many countries with a pre-determined fee schedule.

Neither Medicare nor most private health insurance will cover the cost of medical care for travelers abroad. Before departure, travelers should check with their insurance carriers to determine whether their policies cover travel-related medical expenses and should then decide whether they need to purchase additional coverage. The Health Insurance Association of America offers information about travel insurance, as do most travel agencies.

Other Health Precautions and Problems

Here are a few simple steps for travelers to take before going overseas to avoid or minimize medical problems during a trip. Travelers should:

- Have dental work done.
- See their doctors if they have a health condition or take medications to be sure they're in good health and have enough supply of their prescriptions to cover the time they're away.
- Obtain recommended and required vaccinations.
- Carry a small first-aid kit containing adhesive bandages, aspirin, antiseptic, and any over-the-counter drugs they normally require. Those traveling independently or to undeveloped areas should take more extensive medical supplies than those who are part of a tour group or cruise.

- Carry prescription drugs in original, clearly marked containers to avoid any suspicion that they might be illegal.
- Carry extra eyeglasses or contact lenses or a copy of the prescription.
- Carry a copy of their medical coverage and their doctor's phone number.

To minimize the dangers of serious illness and the discomfort of minor disorders, it helps to know something about the most common health problems encountered by travelers abroad. Here is an overview.

Malaria. A serious and sometimes fatal disease, malaria cannot be prevented by vaccination. It can linger in the bloodstream for many months before it flares up. Pills can prevent it, and drugs can treat symptoms.

Contaminated Food and Drink. Where hygiene and sanitation are poor, travelers should avoid unpasteurized milk and milk products such as cheese. Cooked food is preferable to raw vegetables and fresh fruit, which should always be peeled by the traveler. However delicious they look, salads may contain invisible contaminants.

It is usually safe to drink the water in major cities where it is treated with chlorine. Wherever chlorinated water is not available, travelers should substitute carbonated drinks, bottled water, beer, wine, or beverages made with boiling water. If the water is questionable, ice should be avoided.

Contaminated food or water is usually the cause of diarrhea. The disorder is rarely serious or incapacitating, but severe cases may require medical attention and children are at particular risk. Fruit juices, hot tea, or carbonated drinks can be helpful to the sufferer. Over-the-counter drugs treat some symptoms at the risk of aggravating others.

Motion and Altitude Sickness. Travelers with a history of motion sickness can choose from a number of over-the-counter remedies that can be taken before departure. Most induce drowsiness and react with alcohol. *Sea-Bands* are wristbands that exert subtle pressure on a point inside the wrist, quelling the disconcerting sensation of motion sickness. There are also patches worn behind the ear.

At altitudes of more than 9,000 feet, even healthy people may suffer from *altitude sickness*. Its symptoms include severe headaches, chest pain, shortness of breath, and intense fatigue. Doctors can prescribe drugs to overcome the symptoms, but elderly people and those with heart or respiratory problems should consult their doctors before traveling to high altitudes. All travelers should rest and take it easy the first day when visiting high-altitude destinations, and itineraries should be planned accordingly.

Side Effects of Flying. Flying itself contributes to fatigue. The combination of a high ozone content, low humidity, and constant pressurization in the cabin has a draining effect. Drinking alcohol or overeating worsens the effect; drinking plenty of nonalcoholic fluids can help.

Long flights bring special hazards. First, sitting in one position for a long time may increase the risk of thrombosis (blood clots). To decrease the risk, passengers on long flights should try to exercise in their seats or walk around the plane cabin; they should avoid sleeping through the entire flight. They also may wish to consider compression socks.

Second, long flights may lead to *jet lag* (or *dyschronism*). Its symptoms include the disruption of normal sleeping and eating patterns and mental and physical exhaustion. These may be caused by the fact that a person flying east to west finds a normal day extended; the passenger flying west to east loses hours of sleeping time in the middle of the night. Usually, the worst effects of jet lag are felt on the second or even third day of a trip. Generally, each hour of time differential requires one day of recovery time.

The following steps can minimize the effects of jet lag:

- If possible, schedule arrivals close to the travelers' normal bedtime.
- Schedule time after arrival so that travelers who arrive short of sleep do not immediately rush into hectic schedules. Even a short nap may help.
- Before departure, travelers should adjust their eating and sleeping schedules to the time zone of the country to be visited.
- Most important, travelers should not rush around on the day of departure and should arrive at the airport in plenty of time. Many experienced travelers arrange to stay at an airport hotel the night before their departure flight, and some hotels have packages that include keeping passengers' cars while they are traveling. And some travelers, planning a somewhat strenuous trip, may prefer to arrive at the tour's starting point several days ahead of time to adjust to the new time zones.
- If possible, travelers should avoid travel sickness medicines and other drugs that aggravate jet lag.

Doctors may prescribe sleeping medications to ease the insomnia that accompanies jet lag. Some people claim that melatonin, which is available at health food stores, prevents the insomnia, but the scientific verdict on its effectiveness is still to come. Meanwhile, production of melatonin is not regulated by the Food and Drug Administration (FDA), so the quality and strength of the product vary.

✔ CHECK-UP

The U.S. State Department provides three forms of information about countries around the world:
✔ An online consular information sheet for each country.
✔ A travel warning when the U.S. State Department is recommending that Americans avoid travel to a particular country.
✔ Public announcements about specific threats.

To increase their chances of a healthy trip, travelers should
✔ Verify their medical, dental, and health insurance coverage before departure.
✔ Obtain recommended as well as required vaccinations.
✔ Bring along a basic first-aid kit, a list of doctors abroad, and whatever medications or health aids normally used.
✔ Avoid food or water that might be contaminated.
✔ Arrange their schedule to minimize the discrepancy between their eating and sleeping schedules at home and at their destination.

Dealing with Money and Other Differences

■ HOW ARE CURRENCIES AND MEASUREMENTS USED IN OTHER COUNTRIES CONVERTED, AND WHAT OTHER EVERYDAY DIFFERENCES SHOULD TRAVELERS BE READY TO HANDLE?

If 50 liters of gasoline costs 200 pesos in Cancún, is gas expensive there? Travelers abroad often come up against a question like this. To answer it, at least three issues must be considered.

First, how much is a liter? Many Americans don't know because it is a unit of the **metric system,** a measurement system used by most countries but ignored by many Americans. Table 2.1 summarizes key metric measurements.

Second, what is a peso worth? How many dollars does it take to buy 200 pesos? The answer depends on the current **exchange rate,** the rate at which the currency of one nation can be exchanged for the currency of another.

Third, to evaluate the cost of a product or service, you need to gauge it against other prices in the country. A dollar may fetch 10 pesos in Mexico, but the cost in dollars for a particular product or service may be higher in Mexico. Purchasing power is what counts.

Travel professionals should understand how differences like these in measurements, exchange rates, and prices can affect travelers. They should be able to alert travelers to the kinds of things they need to know and to help them evaluate the cost of a trip.

Currencies and Exchange Rates

One thing travelers should know is that governments have rules about their currencies. For example, anyone entering or leaving the United States with more than $10,000 in cash or negotiable securities must report that fact on a U.S. Customs form. Information about the currency regulations of other nations can be obtained from the national tourist office, consulate, or embassy of the country in question.

Most countries accept only their own currencies, not necessarily U.S. dollars or euros. Table 2.2 on the next page lists a few of the world's major currencies and the exchange rates that applied one day in March 2012. For example, on this particular day $100 could be exchanged for 10,841 Japanese yen because the exchange rate was $1 for 83.39 yen and 1 yen equaled $0.01. Two simple rules describe how to convert currencies:

- To convert dollars into a local currency, multiply the current value of the local currency unit per dollar times the number of dollars.
- To convert a local currency into dollars, divide the amount of the local currency by this exchange rate.

Most large-city newspapers and GDSs publish the exchange rates for major currencies, which also can be obtained from the international exchange

TABLE 2.1 Metric Units

Unit	Description	Formula
Liter (l)	A liter is a little more than a quart. For example, 4 liters is about 1 gallon and 5 ounces. Most liquids that tourists buy (such as gasoline, wine, or water) are sold by the liter.	1 l = 0.264 gallon
Meter (m)	A meter is somewhat more than a yard; 100 meters is somewhat longer than a football field. Someone might tell a visitor, "It's about 200 meters past that next street."	1 m = 3.28 feet
Kilometer (km)	A kilometer is 1,000 meters or a bit more than six-tenths of a mile. Highway distances are given in kilometers. If the next city is 100 kilometers away, then it is 62 miles farther.	1 km = 0.62 mile
Gram (g)	There are approximately 28 grams in 1 ounce.	1 g = 0.035 ounce
Kilogram (kg)	A kilogram is 1,000 grams and equals about 2.2 pounds. Thus a 20-kilo baggage allowance would permit 44 pounds. Most market items such as produce and meats are measured in kilos. A quarter-kilo (250 grams) of sausage is a bit more than half a pound.	1 kg = 2.21 pounds
Celsius (C)	The freezing point of water is 0° Celsius (C), or 32° Fahrenheit (F). For example, 100°C (212°F) is the usual boiling point for water at sea level. Normal body temperature is about 37°C (98.6°F).	°C = (°F − 32) ÷ 1.8

department of your bank. Many Web sites provide currency converters with instant quotes. Fortunately, international travelers today deal with fewer differences in currency than they did just a few years ago thanks to the number of countries that have adopted the euro, the currency of the European Union.

Normally, the changes in exchange rates from day to day are not dramatic, but they can be large during the time between booking and departure or during a lengthy trip. Also, when a country is experiencing very high inflation or a crisis, even day-to-day changes can be significant.

Getting Money Abroad

To pay for purchases abroad, travelers have four basic options—cash in the local currency of a country, travelers' checks, ATM cards, and credit cards. It's recommended that travelers not depend on only one of these options but plan to use several, depending on circumstances.

- Obtain some destination currency before leaving home. In the United States, only large banks or special banks at gateway airports stock other currencies. Many national banks will accommodate currency exchanges if the order is placed in advance and up to two weeks are allowed for delivery of the currency. Currencies or drafts in international currencies also can be ordered online through a limited number of sources. However, it is unwise to carry a lot of cash in any currency; travelers should have enough for the first few days and then have other methods of paying as the trip progresses. Travelers with local currency left at the end of the trip should spend the money to avoid having to exchange the money at higher rates upon returning home.

- Buy traveler's checks before leaving home. These checks can be obtained in U.S. dollars or in other currencies and may be purchased in small denominations so they can be cashed as you go along. They can be bought from American Express, Thomas Cook, Visa, and international banks such as Barclay. Purchasing them often involves a fee each time; nevertheless the advantage is that they are quickly replaceable in case they are lost or stolen. However, some merchants refuse to accept travelers' checks in some areas, due to recent thefts, money laundering, and general crime.

Travelers abroad can find many places to exchange travelers' checks for cash. By and large, banks offer the best rates and the most reliable service but may have odd hours and be closed on local holidays. Alternatives

TABLE 2.2 Exchange Rates, March, 2012

Country	Currency Unit (Code)	Value of Each Unit in US$	Value of US$1
Australia	Australian dollar (AUD)	US$1.06	00.94 Australian dollars
Canada	Canadian dollar (CAD)	US$1.01	00.99 Canadian dollars
European Union members*	euro (EUR)	US$1.32	00.76 euros
United Kingdom	pound (GBP)	US$1.58	00.63 pound
India	rupee (INR)	US$0.01	50.23 rupees
Japan	yen (JPY)	US$0.01	83.39 yen
Mexico	peso (MXN)	US$0.07	12.63 pesos

*As of March, 2012, twenty countries and territories use the euro as their national currency.
Note: The values listed are rounded off slightly from those in effect in March, 2012. Rates are based on the Universal Currency Converter found at www.xe.com.

include stores, restaurants, and hotels; they usually accept the checks to settle bills and give small amounts of change in local currency. Some hotels also cash travelers' checks as a service to their guests but may extract a service charge and use a conservative exchange rate. Exchange bureaus at airports, train and ferry stations, and large tourist or shopping areas usually do not offer very good exchange rates.

- Use an ATM card. Many banks make it possible to obtain money with an ATM card. The traveler should check with his/her own bank before considering this option and be sure to memorize a four-digit PIN number (numbers not letters). A client may want to ask the bank to increase the amount that may be withdrawn daily before leaving. Withdrawals made while traveling will be in the local currency and at an exchange rate stipulated by that bank.

- Use credit cards as they are accepted at many locations, are easy to use for major purchases, and provide a record of expenses. It's suggested that travelers check with the credit card companies before leaving home to see which card has the lowest international exchange charge, which can range from three to five percent. It's also a good idea to inform the card's sponsor of travel plans so that an unusual spending pattern will not trigger an alert and a halt to honoring purchases. Credit cards also may be used for cash.

   A modified version of a credit card, called a prepaid or preloaded card, is also worth considering. It can be loaded with a limited amount of money, which cannot be exceeded if the card is lost or stolen. Special fees apply with these cards.

Everyday Culture

Music, painting, sculpture, architecture, and crafts all form part of the culture that may draw tourists to a country. Everyday life is also filled with the products of a people's culture—rules of etiquette, language, forms of dress, law courts, and technology. These aspects of culture may confront travelers whether they are looking for them or not.

Social Behavior and Laws. Mongolians consider it rude to show surprise or enthusiasm at a guest's arrival. In contrast, travelers arriving on the Marquesas Islands might be crowded by local people greeting them with flowers, songs, and dances. In Saudi Arabia, restaurants, stores, and other public places close for about half an hour when the call for prayer is heard, which happens five times a day.

   Variations like these in customs and etiquette are virtually endless. Some differences can be more problematic, however. For example,

- Some countries restrict what can be photographed or what antiques can be bought.

- Alcoholic beverages and other drugs that are legal in the United States are illegal in some countries, and the penalties for using them may be severe.

- In Saudi Arabia and some other Islamic nations, adult males and females are not free to congregate together in public places, and it is considered inappropriate to touch women. Even intense eye contact that we may use in sales situations in western countries, for example, may be misunderstood.

   Religion, history, and the political system provide the soil and seeds for many of these cultural products. On a very practical level, however, differences in electricity, electronic communications, taxes, and language may be most important to the traveler.

Electricity. Electric current in the United States is 110–120 volts. In Europe, Africa, and many countries elsewhere, it is generally 220–240 volts. As a result, travelers who want to use small electrical appliances (including chargers for cell phones and laptop computers) that were designed for use in the United States will need a transformer that converts voltages unless the appliance works on dual voltage. They will also need an adapter for the appliance so that the plug will fit in the wall outlet; the shape of plugs varies around the world.

Although many major hotels throughout the world have adapter plugs available on request, they rarely offer a transformer to convert voltage. Failure to convert the voltage will ruin an appliance. Before leaving, travelers can purchase converter kits that include a transformer and a variety of adapter plugs at U.S. electronics stores. Some of the more modern hotels may have the 110-120 volts in the bathroom for shavers but not necessarily throughout the rest of the hotel room. Cruise lines generally offer both 110 and 220 voltage.

Computers and Internet Connections. Travelers who want to use their laptop computers or handheld devices to connect to the Internet while abroad should be aware of the following:

- The power adapter on most laptop/notebook computers, unlike many other electronic devices, is able to convert the voltage. People will need to check the information on their current power adapter. Be sure to have a plug adapter only, not a plug adapter/transformer combination.
- In many parts of the world, it's often easier to find dial-up Internet service than a WiFi Hotspot. It's a good idea to check in advance with the hotel to see what options they provide to connect to the Internet.

Alternatives for going online while abroad include Internet cafés, which charge a fee based on the time spent online on their computers. Also, an increasing number of airports and hotels offer hotspots, areas in which computers with wireless access can connect to the Internet. And if travelers have the right equipment and mobile phone service plan, they can plug their mobile phones into their laptops to go online.

Phones. Making international phone calls from a hotel room may be very expensive. Travelers can purchase an international calling card before leaving the United States, but they should verify that the card will work in the country they are visiting. Many popular tourist locations have phones specially equipped for international calls. The traveler purchases a phone card from a nearby store and inserts the card into the phone.

A mobile phone service may be the best option for making international telephone calls. In a number of countries, however, many U.S. cellular phone plans will not work. The Global System for Mobile telephone (GSM) is a standard that is used in 200 countries. Travelers may want to rent a GSM or a satellite phone that provides service in the country they are visiting. World Cell is a company that pays travel agencies a commission for providing clients with global mobile phone rentals.

Taxes. Many nations use a form of tax unfamiliar to most Americans, the value-added tax. It is based on the fact that each stage of manufacture or distribution adds to the market value of a product or service. A *value-added tax (VAT)* levies a tax on this added value at each stage of manufacture or distribution and adds the total to the ultimate cost of the product. For the consumer a VAT is similar to a sales tax, but the amount of the tax is included in the price charged. The VAT rates in European countries can be as high as 25 percent of the total purchase price.

Some European countries encourage tourists to shop by offering a refund of VATs. The procedures vary from country to country. Travelers should always ask about the procedures and the minimum-purchase requirements for obtaining a refund at the stores where they make purchases. Unless making fairly large purchases or all in one store, it's often not worth the time and paperwork needed to obtain the refund. It often requires packing those items in a special area in your suitcase and taking it to the refund counter at the airport before check-in.

Languages. These days, some knowledge of English is widespread in major metropolitan areas around the world. Unless travelers go off the beaten path, their ignorance of local languages may create few difficulties. But in a medical emergency or business negotiation or whenever something important and precise must be conveyed, even those who enjoy dealing with other languages should consider contacting someone to interpret.

Travelers who want to be courteous and prepared should learn at least a few words in the local language. Most useful to know are numbers, names of common things they might need (train station, water, and so on), and basic phrases such as "Hello," "Do you speak English?" "Please," "Thank you," "Where is . . . ?" "Pardon me," and "Good-bye."

CHAPTER WRAP-UP

CHAPTER HIGHLIGHTS

To give advice to their clients, plan trips, or construct itineraries, travel professionals need a working knowledge of world geography and an understanding of differences among destinations. They need to be aware of the political, economic, and physical factors and events that influence travel to destinations around the world. In addition, travel professionals should be well versed in the procedures and requirements that international travelers face when entering and leaving countries and the health, safety, and cultural issues related to international travel. The discussions in this chapter represent the first steps in acquiring this knowledge. Here is a review of the objectives with which we began the chapter.

1. **Identify six characteristics that shape the appeal of destinations, ensuring that people want to visit.** Among the key characteristics of a destination are its climate, natural and human-made attractions, accessibility, costs, culture, and competition.

2. **Explain how to locate a destination and how to calculate time differences and travel times.** A destination can be located precisely by giving its distance from the equator and the prime meridian—in other words, by citing its latitude and longitude. Usually, though, places are located by describing their location relative to natural features such as continents, islands, oceans, and rivers.

   The world is divided into twenty-four time zones, starting at the prime meridian, which is at Greenwich, England. The time at Greenwich is known as Greenwich mean time (GMT) or universal time coordinated (UTC). The time changes by 1 hour at most time zones. To the west, 1 hour is subtracted at each zone crossed; to the east, 1 hour is added at each zone. Halfway around the world from Greenwich in the Pacific is the international date line, where, by international agreement, the calendar day changes. It is one day later west of the line than it is to the east.

3. **Outline the major factors that shape the climate of a destination.** Wind, pressure, temperature, humidity, clouds, and precipitation are atmospheric conditions that define the weather and hence the climate. Among the key geographic factors that interact to create the climate are latitude, altitude, proximity to bodies of water, and prevailing winds. As a result, particular types of climate recur at varying places around the globe. For example, northern Australia and southern Asia experience monsoons, and a Mediterranean climate is characteristic of parts of California and Spain and many popular resort spots. Variations in climate may occur over short distances—for example, between the windward and leeward sides of mountains.

4. **Describe at least five key sources of information about destinations.** Firsthand experience, whether through personal travel or fam trips, general education, and formal courses represent sources of both information and the background necessary to understand and evaluate information about destinations. For specific questions, sources include colleagues, tour operators, tourist offices and other government offices, travel Web sites, and references—in print or online—such as atlases, guidebooks, newspapers, magazines, and brochures.

5. **Outline the requirements that governments place on international travelers visiting their countries.** Governments restrict the movement of both people and goods across their borders. The requirements on travelers vary with the country and the citizenship of the traveler, and they may change with little notice. To enter another country, travelers may be required to produce proof of citizenship, a passport, a visa, or a tourist card. In addition, vaccination certificates may be needed. Travelers also must obey local laws and customs regulations, and they may owe a duty on goods purchased abroad. Many governments encourage tourism by setting up duty-free ports. International travelers may seek help from their own government through its embassies and consulates.

6. **Identify reliable sources of information about dangers abroad and common problems encountered by international travelers.** Government agencies and international organizations (such as the CDC, State Department, and WHO) are usually the best source of information on health and safety issues abroad. Among the most common health problems encountered by international travelers are diarrhea, motion sickness, altitude sickness, and jet lag. Travelers can often alleviate or avoid these by taking commonsense precautions. Travelers to regions where serious illnesses such as malaria, cholera, and yellow fever are a danger should protect themselves with the appropriate medications or vaccinations.

7. **Explain how to convert one currency into another, and outline other differences that international travelers should be prepared to handle.** To convert a currency, check a GDS, a Web site, a major newspaper, or the international department of your bank to determine the current exchange rate. Next, to convert dollars into the local currency, multiply the exchange rate of the local currency per dollar by the number of dollars. To convert the local currency into dollars, divide the amount in the local currency by the exchange rate.

   Besides planning how to pay for items abroad, international travelers should be prepared to deal with differences in measurement systems, with possible difficulties in phone and electronic communications, with language differences, and with local customs and laws.

KEY TERMS

A list of key terms introduced in this chapter follows. If you do not recall the meaning of these terms, see the Glossary, which begins on page 393.

24-hour clock
altitude
atlas
climate
consulate
continent
destination
destination geography
destination management and promotion
duty
duty-free port
embassy
equator
exchange rate
familiarization trip (fam trip)
geography
Greenwich mean time (GMT)
gulf
international date line
island
isthmus

latitude
leeward
longitude
Mediterranean climate
metric system
monsoon
NTO
ocean
passport
peninsula
prime meridian
river
sea
sound
strait
tourist card
The Travel Institute
universal time coordinated (UTC)
value-added tax (VAT)
visa
windward

REVIEW QUESTIONS

1. What is the difference between latitude and longitude?

2. When it is 1:00 P.M. in San Francisco, what time is it in London?

3. What sources would you consult in order to determine the attractions of a visit to Tonga?

4. What are the three main types of identifying documents that travelers need, and how would they obtain each of them?

5. What is a duty-free port?

6. What two Web sites would you go to first for advice about the health and safety conditions in another country?

Using Technology

CHAPTER 3

OBJECTIVES

After completing this chapter, you should be able to

1. Describe how personal computers and GDSs are used in the travel industry.

2. Outline four major ways that travel professionals use the Internet.

3. Discuss at least three of the many new technological devices that have come into marketplace and how they might be used in the industry by travel professionals.

4. List at least four reasons why travelers would seek out a travel professional despite the existence of online travel services.

Twenty-five years ago, many travel agencies did not have fax machines. Now the Internet, e-mail, smartphones, and personal digital assistants have changed how business is done; most travel professionals could not work without those and other technologies. For many travelers, too, travel and technology go hand in hand; many use their own computers to plan or buy their trips.

The Close-Up describes a few of the many jobs in the travel industry created by new technologies. We focus in this chapter on three technologies: personal computers, GDSs, and the Internet. We also mention a few new devices that can enhance the travel professional's working experience.

Personal Computers and GDSs

■ WHAT ROLE DO PERSONAL COMPUTERS AND GDSs PLAY IN THE TRAVEL INDUSTRY?

Computers are at the heart of the technologies that have transformed the travel industry. It was the marketing of the personal computer in the 1980s that sparked a revolution in American life. A *personal computer* is a computer that has its own *central processing unit (CPU)*, which is a collection of electronic circuitry that allows a single computer to run a great variety of software. Depending on the software used, a personal computer can perform a vast array of specialized tasks such as creating graphs or keeping financial records.

Software for the Office

Personal computers use two basic types of software: an operating system and applications software. An *operating system* is the software that manages the computer system; Microsoft's Windows, Macintosh's OS, and Linux are examples. The earliest operating systems had a **command interface,** which means

---

CLOSE-UP: CAREERS IN E-TRAVEL

More money is spent on travel than on any other category of goods and services sold on the Internet. Every supplier and retailer has been affected by this revolution in the industry. Most now have their own Web sites or link with others who do. The result is a myriad of new professional positions, generally requiring a technical and analytical background, but with a travel bent.

■ **Position** E-business infrastructure technical analyst

Description The person in this position works with other departments to determine the requirements and develop a plan for installation of Web-based applications.

Qualifications This job requires analytical, problem-solving, and communication skills, as well as the ability to handle multiple tasks and to work in a constantly changing environment. It also requires a strong technical background. A college degree in information technology or computer science is preferred.

■ **Position** Manager of database marketing, planning, and analysis

Description This position is responsible for ensuring that information about past and potential customers can be retained and analyzed and for devising direct marketing campaigns (by mail or online) in a cost-effective way. Formulating strategies and executing direct marketing campaigns are also the job of this manager.

Qualifications This position requires proven success with direct marketing, database management, response analysis, and management. A B.A. in marketing is required, in addition to five years' experience in direct marketing.

■ **Position** Programmer analyst

Description This position is responsible for evaluating and implementing new technologies and products. The programmer analyst is often involved in developing specifications, doing design documentation, and overseeing the project and must be able to communicate the status of projects.

Qualifications A B.S. degree coupled with two to three years' hands-on experience with appropriate hardware and software is required. The person in this position needs solid problem-solving and analytical skills, the ability to organize and meet deadlines, strong attention to detail, and the ability both to work independently and to contribute to team efforts.

■ **Position** Technology planning specialist—interactive marketing

Description This professional serves as a member of the team responsible for the operation, infrastructure, and security of the company's Web site. Responsibilities include working with a development team to gather infrastructure requirements, managing external vendors, and analyzing technical recommendations. This professional uses expertise in technology along with project management skills to manage infrastructure projects.

Qualifications The technology planning specialist must be able to work in a fast-paced, changing environment; to set priorities; and to manage multiple projects. The person in this position must have excellent communication skills, project management experience, and a strong technical background.

■ **Position** Manager of Internet marketing

Description This position is responsible for using the Internet as a marketing vehicle, for overseeing strategies for maximizing revenues through the use of Web sites, and for developing new Web sites.

Qualifications Requirements for this position are likely to include a B.S. degree, strong experience in interactive marketing, and a record of successfully evaluating, creating, and executing marketing programs. The person in this position needs an ability to succeed in a fast-paced, changing environment as well as financial acumen and strong communication, leadership, and management skills.

■ **Other positions** Database administrator; online community manager; project manager; software design engineer; webmaster.

---

that users communicated with the computer by typing commands—such as "del c:\travel\clients.wp" to delete a file named "client.wp." Users memorized strings of keystrokes to tell the operating system what to do. Computers became much easier for novices to use when operating systems were created that had a *graphical interface,* which means that users control the computer by using a pointing device such as a mouse to click on commands that are displayed on the computer screen.

Applications software is software that allows the computer to perform specific types of tasks, such as writing letters, creating brochures, managing budgets, or drawing graphs. Some programs are available through software stored on a remote server, a technique known as cloud computing and allowing access from any computer. The basic types that follow are stored on individual personal computers used in offices and include:

- *Word processing software* makes it easy to draft, revise, print, and store letters, memos, and other documents. Microsoft's Word is a well-known example.
- *Desktop publishing software* goes beyond word processing to allow users to integrate text and graphics in sophisticated formats for publications such as brochures and books. Adobe's PageMaker and InDesign software and QuarkXPress are examples.
- *Presentation graphics software* creates high-quality displays of numerical information. With PowerPoint and SlideRocket, for example, you can put sound, charts, and other graphics together for presentations to groups.
- *Database management software* stores and sorts collections of data, which are called *databases.* Examples include Access and FileMaker Pro. With programs like these, you can create profiles of clients and then retrieve the names of clients with particular characteristics, such as a love of cruising.
- *Cash and office management software* provides up-to-the-minute reports of a business's cash flow and financial well-being. Quicken and Sage Peachtree are examples.
- *Internet applications* allow users to send and receive e-mail, to connect to the Internet and to design Web sites.

All of these programs are used by businesses of all types, and they can be bought off the shelf. There are also many programs specifically designed to meet the needs of travel professionals. Very large travel agencies may design their own software or have it custom-made, but even small agencies can buy travel-specific software. Software of particular interest to travel businesses includes the following:

- Database programs such as ClientBase from TRAMS not only organize lists with the usual information (names, addresses, phone numbers, e-mail addresses, and so on) but also make it easy to store and retrieve information about clients' travel history and their likes and dislikes (see Figure 3.1 on the next page).
- Back-office systems handle functions related to accounting and marketing, such as tracking sales by agents, monitoring payments of commissions, and tracking clients' billings and payments. TRAMS® Back Office connects reservation systems with back-office functions such as accounting.
- Integrated software links programs that handle back-office functions with client databases. ClientBase Plus from TRAMS® and WinCruise are examples. Thanks to the integration of systems, when a travel counselor enters a client's name and makes a booking, the computer can automatically bring up on the screen information about the client from the agency's database and immediately transfer information about the booking to the accounting system and the database.

- Specialized Internet applications make it easy for travel agencies to book online. One example of these *booking engines* is VAX VacationAccess, which travel agencies use to book tours and cruises online. Some booking engines now allow *dynamic packaging,* which makes it easy for travel sellers to create and book travel packages themselves. From one online site, they can research and book several travel components (such as a hotel as well as air travel and a rental car) and offer them to the client as a package for a single price.

These and other software packages designed for the travel industry are providing a supplement and even an alternative to what has been the key electronic tool for travel counselors—global distribution systems, which we discuss in the next section.

Global Distribution Systems (GDSs)

Years before computers were on desks in travel/tourism offices, travel professionals were using computer technology every day and communicating with distant computers. The airlines were the driving force behind this

FIGURE 3.1 Creating a Customer Profile

With a program like ClientBase, a keystroke can bring up a profile with information such as where a client likes to sit on a plane and whether a client likes to go to a different Caribbean island every winter or to the same island every year.

Source: Reprinted by permission of TRAMS, Inc.

automation. In the 1950s they began to use computers to keep track of reservations and the seats available on their own flights. In the 1970s United Airlines and then American and TWA began to install computerized systems in travel agencies. These systems allowed travel agencies to obtain information and make reservations for several airlines, and they were the first airline computer reservation systems. A *computer reservation system,* or *CRS,* is a computerized system that links distributors and suppliers to a centralized storehouse of information for the primary purpose of making reservations. It is designed to create and maintain a database concerning reservations. CRSs originally handled only airline reservations.

From CRSs to GDSs. By the late 1970s airlines were installing CRSs in travel agencies throughout North America. For almost two decades, almost 80 percent of the CRSs in travel agencies came from two CRS companies—Sabre (owned by American Airlines) and *Apollo* (United Airlines). Reservations on hundreds of major airlines throughout the world could be made on any of the systems. Travel agencies leased the CRS, including the hardware, from the airline. The system looked much like a personal computer does today, but it was different in an important way. It was a *dumb terminal*; that is, it could exchange information with the airline's central computer, but it could not do any processing of its own.

The 1990s brought many changes to CRSs, partly because of the spreading use of personal computers and the Internet. The systems themselves are now usually called *global distribution systems,* or *GDSs,* and most systems are owned and run by companies independent of the airlines. Other changes in GDSs are more obvious to users. Dumb terminals are a thing of the past; on today's GDSs, users can run a host of programs to perform tasks such as word processing, accounting, and database management. Both command interfaces and graphical interfaces are available. And GDSs offer a wealth of information on all travel products, not just air travel.

With today's GDSs travel counselors can, for example,

- Check the availability of flights on any of the world's major carriers nearly a year in advance.
- Display the schedules of hundreds of airlines and connecting service between cities.
- Quote fares.
- Book the flight reservation and price most itineraries.
- Check the availability of hotel rooms and confirm hotel reservations.
- Confirm car rental reservations.
- Reserve and ticket Amtrak.
- Find information on international rail service.
- Obtain information on tours, packages, and cruises and book them.
- Find information about a destination, such as its weather conditions, theater offerings, and convention facilities.
- Order theater tickets and arrange limousine service.
- Keep files on frequent travelers and their preferences.
- Put the system on their laptops and be travel counselors anywhere.
- Use the Internet to send confirmation to clients and access reservations that were made in the GDS.

The companies that run GDSs are sometimes called *hosts* or *vendors.* They obtain revenue from suppliers that pay to have their services included in the system as well as from travel agencies that subscribe to the system.

Whether the GDS continues to be the travel counselor's best friend or not remains to be seen; some suppliers are rebelling at the fees they must pay the vendor and are looking to circumvent the GDS.

Suppliers, Travel Agencies, and GDSs. Many suppliers have their own computerized reservation systems but still participate in a GDS. They have the choice of various levels of participation at various costs. For example, an airline might have its schedule displayed on the GDS, but not information about the availability of seats on its flights; this is the least expensive level of participation. At more expensive levels, the GDS also indicates the availability of the supplier's product (such as available seats) and allows reservations to be made through the GDS. At the most expensive level of participation, there is a *direct link* between the supplier's own computer system and the GDS.

When a direct link exists, GDS users receive up-to-the-minute information about the supplier's product. When there is no direct link, the information displayed on the GDS may be out-of-date. The difference is critical if you are interested in whether a seat is available on a particular flight or whether a room is still available at a particular price. Travel counselors must determine by experience, on a case-by-case basis, when the information about a particular supplier on the GDS is likely to be reliable.

CLOSE-UP: ON THE JOB WITH DEE DEE DANKAUSKAS, GDS TECHNICIAN

Following her natural interest, Dee Dee Dankauskas began taking advanced classes in computers even before she completed her travel training. She wound up uniquely qualified for emerging jobs because few techie job seekers know anything about how the travel industry works.

"One day in early 2001, dozens of potential travelers went on the Internet and looked up the airfare between two major cities and found that the fare was a dollar. Surely they all knew that the fare was a mistake, but the more enterprising booked the fare and the ticket. The airline was advised by its lawyers that it should honor the fare and so it did. This just shows the importance of the hundreds of people who are putting information into computers every day. Garbage in, garbage out, as they used to say. In this case, garbage in and an almost free ticket out—out of the airline's pocket, that is.

"My first travel job was as an agent at a discount ticket seller/consolidator in Chicago. We dealt directly with clients and with travel agencies. I don't like to be idle for a second, and I found that what I could do best was figure out prices, churn out tickets, and make my computer hum. At least I enjoyed those things better than counseling clients who weren't sure what they wanted or where they wanted to go. I'm not the patient type.

"When I heard from a friend about a position at Galileo, I asked for an interview and got the job and a hike in salary. The work was just as interesting, and I was on the cutting edge of what was happening with computers in travel.

"I started out inputting fares. We all had our own airline that we were responsible for, and we'd send changes to the Galileo mainframe system three times a day. We could change fares three times a day on the same route for that airline, though of course that didn't always happen. But when there was a fare war, our supervisor would just say, 'Plan on working late.'

"In recent years, surcharges, airport taxes, landing fees, customs and immigration fees, and other amounts also changed frequently. They all had to be changed and monitored. Airline ticket agents and travel agents in New Delhi, Cape Town, or Buenos Aires would be charging those fees seconds after I entered them. And if I made a mistake, they'd be charging that wrong amount until it was corrected.

"As a matter of fact, for a while I worked on auditing fares, too. If another airline claimed a mistake had been made in a ticket three months ago, I had to trace the history of what that fare was at the exact moment it was issued. Then if an error was found, we had to determine if it was Galileo's error. Somebody had to pay for it.

"Now I'm at the Help Desk at the Data Center. I help suppliers who are on our system. If any glitch occurs in the computer linkup between Galileo and Hertz, shall we say, a code yellow flashes on my screen and I monitor it. Usually the connection comes right back on and everything is fine. But if other codes are flashed, they are more serious. On a code red, I call the supplier immediately because some problem has broken the connection and agents will not be able to book them.

"Of course there are quality control people monitoring everything I do. Advancement to this area is always a possibility, but so is the possibility of computer jobs with other companies."

To gain access to a GDS, travel agencies generally sign multiyear contracts with GDS companies. There may also be a monthly payment with a small fee for each transaction. The agency may choose to

- Lease the system, including the hardware, with a direct link to the GDS.
- Use its own computer hardware and contract with the GDS for the system's database and reservation capability, with a direct link to the GDS.
- Use its own computer hardware, contract with the GDS for the system's database and reservation capability, and reach it through the Internet.

As their contracts with GDSs run out, travel agencies are looking at other options. They might contract with a third party or host agency that provides access to multiple GDSs, or they might bypass the GDSs by making reservations on suppliers' own Web sites. They might use systems such as VAX VacationAccess, which is free to travel agencies, to book online. Relations between GDS companies and travel agencies are in a state of flux.

GDSs Today. When the airlines owned the forerunners of today's GDSs, people worried that an airline could use its control of a reservation system to gain an unfair advantage in selling tickets. The U.S. Department of Transportation therefore issued and enforced rules to prevent both bias in how information was displayed on reservation systems and unfair practices in contracts with suppliers. In 2004, however, the government ended its regulation of GDSs.

Today, the four major GDSs are *Sabre, Galileo, Amadeus,* and *Worldspan* (see Table 3.1). When people go on the Internet to visit sites hosted by airlines and by online travel agencies, they use the resources of the GDSs. The companies that own the major GDSs are a huge force throughout the travel industry. For example, Sabre Holdings owns Travelocity, among other assets.

TABLE 3.1 Global Distribution Systems

Global Distribution System	Originators of System	Current Ownership
Amadeus	Four European airlines	Amadeus IT Holdings
Galileo (known as Apollo in the United States and Japan)	United Airlines (in partnership with international airlines)	Travelport IT Holding
Sabre	American Airlines	Sabre Holdings
Worldspan	Delta, Northwest, and TWA	Travelport IT Holding

✔ CHECK-UP

Important uses for applications software in travel offices include
✔ Word processing.
✔ Database management.
✔ Cash management.
✔ Presentation graphics.
✔ Internet applications.

The major GDSs are
✔ Sabre.
✔ Galileo.

✔ Amadeus.
✔ Worldspan.

Major uses of GDSs include
✔ Checking the schedules, availability, and fares for flights around the world.
✔ Booking flights.
✔ Finding information about and booking hotel rooms, car rentals, and rail tickets.
✔ Finding information about the weather and attractions at a destination.

The Internet

Years ago, the connection from a travel agency's CRS to an airline's computer hundreds of miles away seemed a rare and wonderful thing. Today, millions of people connect to distant computers as easily as they turn on their TV set by going on the Internet. The *Internet* is a worldwide network of thousands of computer networks; it allows any computer on one of the networks to communicate with any other computer on any of the networks. Computers called *servers* store and distribute the messages at nodes in the networks.

The Internet began in 1969 as a U.S. Defense Department project, but the ideas that turned it into a tool that could be used by the general public only date to 1989. It was then that researchers at a European physics laboratory (CERN) began to circulate the proposals that led to the creation of the *World Wide Web,* a system that makes it easy to present and to retrieve information on the Internet. Most households in the United States are now connected to the Internet, and millions of people not only communicate but also buy and sell online.

Going Online

Going on the Internet requires only

1. A computer with a modem and a phone line. A traditional *modem* is a device that converts the signals from computers and from telephone lines so that messages can be sent from one computer to another over phone lines. Modems are built into most personal computers.
2. Communications software and an account with an *Internet service provider (ISP),* a company that provides the connection to the Internet, like a gatekeeper opening an electronic path to the Internet. The necessary communications software is often installed on computers or provided by the ISP. Well-known commercial ISPs include America Online (AOL), Yahoo!, and Microsoft Network (MSN). Most ISPs charge a monthly fee.

Phone lines and traditional modems, however, are fast being replaced by other ways of going online. Alternatives include connections via digital subscriber line (DSL), cable, and satellite. Speed is the attraction of these alternatives: they offer high-speed Internet access, also called *broadband* connections. They require special equipment, such as cable modems or satellite dishes. But once established, the broadband connection is always "on"; users do not have to dial up to log on to the Internet. More important, with a broadband connection you can *download* (transmit from the Internet) files with large amounts of data, such as videos, much more easily than is possible with the older, traditional "dial-up" access.

Yet another option for a high-speed Internet connection is wireless access, which is especially attractive to people on the move. Wireless access comes in several varieties, including cellular networks, which allow people to reach the Internet by using cell phones and personal digital assistants (PDAs), and *WiFi* (short for "wireless fidelity"), which is a wireless network that broadcasts over a different part of the electromagnetic spectrum than cellular networks do.

The range of a WiFi network is very limited; a *hotspot* is a specific location with access to a WiFi network. An increasing number of airports and hotels offer WiFi hotspots so that their patrons can use their laptops to go online. Meanwhile, many businesses, restaurants, cafés, libraries, and even cities around the globe have set up free WiFi networks.

Using the Internet

Electronic mail, or *e-mail,* is the most often used function of the Internet. Travel agencies, for example, use e-mail in order to communicate quickly with suppliers, clients, or other agencies. (Chapter 12, on communications, discusses tips on when and how to use e-mail.) You need special software to send and receive e-mail, but that software is provided free by many sources. ISPs usually offer access to an e-mail system as part of their service.

Here are some other important uses of the Internet:

- Software or data can be downloaded from other computers by a procedure called *file transfer protocol (FTP).*
- *Usenets* or *listservs* enable subscribers to discuss particular topics via e-mail. When a user posts a message to the list server, either a moderator or a computer sends the message to everyone on the list.
- *Instant messaging* allows e-mail to be received instantly, without any lag time.
- *Bulletin board services (BBSs)* are discussion groups without subscription. People post messages for anyone to read at their leisure, just as they might post a message on a bulletin board at the local supermarket.
- *Telnet* allows a computer to connect directly to a host computer on a network, effectively making that computer part of the other network.
- People can "talk" to others in *chat rooms* by typing their messages at their computers. Chat rooms are usually devoted to particular topics. People make professional contacts in these groups much as they would by joining a club.
- Companies can set up *intranets,* which are communications systems within an organization that are accessible only by people within that organization.
- Companies and other organizations can also set up *extranets,* which are intranets that are partially accessible to authorized outsiders. Extranets allow business partners to exchange information and perform interactions online.
- People can research and publish as well as advertise, buy, and sell products and services to other people around the world on the Internet.

Exploring the Internet

Today almost all that people need to do is point and click with a mouse in order to find the text or images or sounds that they are looking for. The information is organized in a series of interconnected pages, called *Web sites.* The first page of a Web site is known as its *home page.*

Several innovations made this possible:

- *Hypertext,* a process that embeds connections between documents. It creates an electronic link between related pieces of information stored in different documents. Thanks to hypertext, users can click on a highlighted word or image in a document and be taken to a related Web site. For example, on the Web sites of many travel agencies, users can click on a link that takes them to the Web site of a supplier, such as a hotel.
- *Hypertext transfer protocol,* or *HTTP,* which defines rules for sending and receiving information, something like a secret handshake that lets a document in the door.

- *Hypertext markup language,* or *HTML,* the code that makes documents readable by computers that use different operating systems and other software.
- *Web browsers,* software that translates HTML documents and displays them in readable form on a computer. Microsoft's Internet Explorer, Mozilla's Firefox, and Apple's Safari are popular browsers, but, as with everything in the world of technology, new tools can arrive on the scene.
- *Uniform resource locators,* or *URLs,* a standardized system for identifying documents. In other words, URLs give addresses to Web sites.

These tools together make information from the Internet easily accessible.

URLs. To get to a Web site, the user simply types its address, its URL. For example, the URL for the home page of The Travel Institute is http://www.thetravelinstitute.com. This address illustrates the two main parts of a URL:

1. The *protocol:* http://. This tells the browser that the information is located on a server that uses the HTTP protocol.
2. The *domain name:* www.thetravelinstitute.com. The host of a site pays to register a domain name; a nonprofit organization (ICANN) regulates the companies that sell the names. The huge majority of sites today use the suffix ".com" in their domain names; it was originally used to indicate that a Web site was a commercial site. Other common suffixes are ".org" (for a nonprofit organization) and ".gov" (for a government-run site).

After the domain name, URLs may also include a *path* and *filename,* which point to a particular part of the Web site. For example, typing http://www.tia.org/Travel/tvt.asp would take you to the file with the name "tvt.asp" in the Travel section (the path) of the site for the Travel Industry Association of America (TIA), which has the domain name www.tia.org.

Search Engines. If you do not know the address for a Web site, you can go for help to a search engine. *Search engines* are Web sites that provide indexes of Web sites. If you go to a search engine and type the topic you are looking for, the search engine lists Web sites related to that topic (see Figure 3.2). You then point to one of the listed sites and click; that site will appear on your screen.

Not all search engines are created equal—far from it. Search engines have (1) different databases, (2) different ways of retrieving information from Web pages, (3) different indexes, or ways of organizing Web documents, and (4) different ways of ranking their results. If you conduct the same search on different search engines, you will obtain different results. Here are the three most popular search engines in 2012: www.Google.com, www.Bing.com, www.Yahoo.com, and www.Ask.com.

As use of the Internet soared, variations of standard search engines were created, such as meta-crawlers and travel search engines. *Meta-crawlers,* also called *meta-search sites,* allow a single query to be sent to several search engines simultaneously. One query produces a search of numerous search engines, compiling the results on a single page. Examples of the many meta-crawlers are www.dogpile.com and www.mamma.com.

Travel search engines, also called *travel aggregators,* specialize in searching travel sites. Travel search engines such as Travelocity, Kayak, Expedia, and Cheapflights search the sites of travel suppliers and send users to a supplier's Web site to make a purchase.

With the help of search engines, people with little if any expertise or even experience can use the Internet to reach out to people almost anywhere in the world. Today virtually all travel agencies provide Internet access for all staff members at their own workstations. Travel agencies go online for research, for advertising and marketing, and for booking.

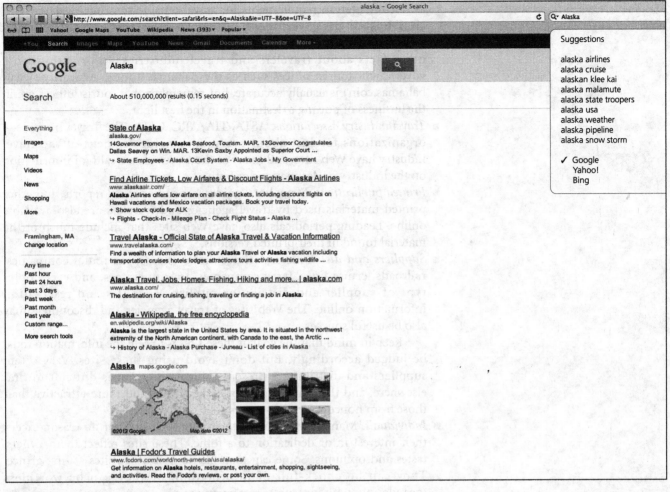

FIGURE 3.2 Searching for Alaska

When "Alaska" was entered as the topic to be searched by Google, this search engine listed more than 510,000,000 Web sites. Usually search engines list the most relevant sites first, but listings can also depend on payments to the search engine by Web site hosts. Notice that Google lists suggestions on the right side of the screen for refining the search. Learning to conduct effective searches will put relevant information at your fingertips quickly.

Researching Online

The Internet is an incomparable research aid; it puts the equivalent of many libraries on your desktop. What kinds of sites are most useful to travel professionals, and what skills are necessary to use them effectively for research?

Sources on Travel. Suppose you are a travel counselor and Jane Doe decides to book the flights you recommended, but she has questions about the trip. She asks about the weather, sightseeing, hotels, car rentals, restaurants, documentation requirements, driving distances, currency conversions, theaters, and parks. You can find answers to her questions online through the following ways:

■ *Government entities.* National tourist offices, countries, states, provinces, counties, cities, and many other government units have Web sites. Often these are the most authoritative, reliable sources available. Information from the U.S. State Department, for example, can be relied on, and its Web site (www.travel.state.gov) is the place to go for information on topics such as documentation requirements for travel outside the United States. Web sites hosted by government offices such as the Federal Aviation Administration offer a seemingly endless supply of reliable statistics and other facts about travelers and travel industries. Information from government tourist offices such as the Bahamas Tourist Authority (www.bahamas.com) is usually accurate, but remember that tourist offices are in the business of putting a destination in the best light.

- *Travel industry associations.* ASTA, TIA, ARC, CLIA, The Travel Institute—organizations for just about every imaginable segment of the travel industry have Web sites, and many of these provide a wealth of information on the industry or destinations or both.

- *Printed publications.* Many hotel guides, consumer travel reports, and other printed materials used by travel agencies and travelers are also available online. Leading periodicals also have Web sites that include much of the material found in their printed versions.

- *Suppliers and distributors.* Airlines, hotel chains, car rental companies, railroads, cruise lines, ferry companies, tour operators, and every other type of supplier and distributor publish schedules and reservation information online. The Web sites of travel agencies and discounters may also be useful sources.

  Keep in mind that the goal of these sites is to sell; the information must be judged accordingly. But don't avoid using these sites. Very often, suppliers and distributors present information that is difficult to find elsewhere, and their sites are often easier to use and more attractive than those from noncommercial sources.

- *Individuals.* Many people put up their own Web sites for no reason except their interest in or dedication to a topic. These sites reflect their owners' tastes and opinions. Some can look like tourist office sites at first glance. They can be chock-full of information, or they can be worthless meanderings with inaccurate statements.

Many Web sites restrict access to certain parts of the site. Some sections may be open only to people who have registered with the site or to people who are members of a certain organization or who have other credentials. Many suppliers, for example, restrict access to part of their site to travel counselors, which strengthens the bond between suppliers and travel agencies, and allows for discussion of some confidential information, such as commissions and other matters to which the client traveler does not have access.

At the same time, most travel Web sites are linked to other sites. For example, many have links to sites that will produce maps of just about anyplace on earth or give conversions for currencies from around the world. The number of possible sources as well as the amount of information on each site can be overwhelming and numbing.

Keys to Effective Research. To use the Internet effectively as a research tool, you need to be able, first, to conduct effective searches. That requires learning how to make the most of search engines. Although their features vary, the basic steps in conducting a search are similar in all search engines. Each has a Help section that provides tips on how to conduct searches.

The key step in conducting an effective search is to use the right combination of keywords and commands in your queries. Figure 3.2 demonstrates a search that is too broad. The searcher typed "Alaska" and received 14 million relevant sites! The Help section on search engines indicates commands that you can use to refine your searches. Learn to use the advanced search features of your favorite search engines so that the engines will give you a short list of the most relevant Web sites. Learn to be more specific, such as "Alaska Inside Passage," for example.

In addition, to use the Internet effectively for research, you need to exercise the same thinking skills that should be applied to any information. Web sites must be examined at least as critically as printed material. In particular,

- *See who is sponsoring the site.* If you go to www.cia.com, for example, you might think you have reached the CIA; in fact, you have reached a critical spoof of the organization. The CIA is at www.cia.gov. Does the host of the site have an interest in pushing a certain point of view? Is it likely to be an unbiased source of information? Note that the vast number of online travel sites can give both consumers and travel professionals the impression that there is much more competition for their business than actually exists. In fact, many online companies have close ties; one may even own the other.
- *Check when the information was last updated.* Finding this information may require a few clicks and scrolling to small type at the bottom of a page.
- *Go directly to the "official" source.* If you find information at a secondary source, validate the information with a primary source. For example, if you read on one site that the U.S. government has a new regulation about airport security, you can check that information on the site of the government agency in charge of airport security (the Transportation Security Administration, or TSA). Perhaps the best feature of the Internet is that it gives you access to official resources; you no longer have to rely on out-of-date information from third parties.

Advertising and Marketing Online

Anyone who has gone online and seen the streamers of ads that appear, unbidden, on the computer screen knows that it is an advertising medium. (In fact, if companies were not willing to pay to advertise online, it could not offer so much information for free.) Some travel agencies advertise online, but a growing number of agencies are more likely to market themselves by hosting their own Web site.

Even grade school children can create a Web site, particularly with the templates available today. But the host of a successful site must accomplish three more difficult tasks:

- The site itself must be designed so that it is simple enough for people to use easily, yet complex enough to meet its objectives.
- The site must be promoted so that people visit it. In order to attract people to their sites, businesses need to advertise (on other Web sites or the old-fashioned way, by handing out business cards, running print ads, and so on) or to pay search engines to feature their sites when people ask for certain types of information. They can also become so expert in one specific area that search engines list them as top choices when someone searches for sites related to that area.
- The site must be maintained continuously.

The difficulty and expense of these tasks depend greatly on the goals set for the site. A travel agency, for example, might consider, Should the site do anything beyond giving information about the agency and its counselors?

How much information should it give about the products that the agency sells? Should it accept bookings online? Chapter 9 discusses these and other questions about marketing online.

Booking Online

The Internet also offers travel professionals additional ways to book online. They might go online and then book by using specialized software or accessing a GDS or going directly to suppliers' sites. To encourage travel agencies to use their sites, many suppliers have agency-only sections through which agencies can book, and some suppliers hook up their most productive travel agencies directly to their own booking software.

The Internet and GDSs. Does the Internet make direct access to a GDS unnecessary? Although travel counselors have increasingly booked directly online, GDSs remain the electronic tool of choice for booking. Using a GDS is still the most efficient way, for example, to switch quickly from one airline's schedule to another, to switch connecting cities, to find the lowest airfares available on alternate dates, and to book itineraries with multiple stops or gaps between flights. In addition, using a GDS is likely to be easier than using the Internet in two situations:

- If you want to book several types of travel products for a trip, such as a rental car, a hotel, and a flight.
- If you need information about a certain category of travel from different companies. A GDS, for example, will instantly list each major hotel that has rooms available this weekend in Philadelphia—whether it is a Marriott, Westin, Holiday Inn, or Wyndham.

These advantages of GDSs may be short-lived, however, as new products and approaches make it easier to book online. The owners of GDSs themselves are in the forefront of offering Web-based tools for assembling travel packages.

Travelers Online. Of course, travelers can also book online themselves. They might book online with a *bricks-and-clicks agency*—a travel agency that has not only a Web site but also a traditional walk-in "bricks-and-mortar" office—but they can also bypass traditional travel agencies when they book online directly. Travelers might go to one of the online travel agencies such as Expedia and Travelocity (see Figure 3.3). Or they might go to an online discounter or directly to suppliers' Web sites. Some suppliers encourage online booking; airlines, for example, offer discounts or extra frequent-flyer miles for booking online. Other suppliers encourage people who visit their Web sites to contact a travel agency.

Auction houses give travelers yet another way to book travel online for themselves. Priceline.com is the best-known example. If travelers choose the "Name Your Own Price" option at Priceline, they name a price for an airline ticket, hotel room, or other purchase. If Priceline finds that a supplier is offering the product for that price (or a lower price), the bid is accepted. But bidders do not know the precise product on which they are bidding. For example, if you place a bid for a hotel room, you do not know exactly which hotel might accept that bid. To compete with Priceline, online travel agencies began offering *opaque pricing,* which reveals the price of products but keeps other details unknown to buyers until they have agreed to purchase the travel arrangements.

Consumers can obtain excellent deals with some auction companies.

Their rules vary. At some auction sites, suppliers offer counterbids. Others auction products to the highest bidder. And others offer "reverse auctions": they post prices, which decline until someone accepts the price. Consumers usually must give their credit card numbers, and sales are generally final.

Recent trends seem to indicate that more and more U.S. travelers have been booking their own travel plans via the Internet, particularly simple air and hotel reservations. However, it also appears that a number of those who have been researching and booking their own trips are turning to travel counselors (or returning to them) because of the investment of time, energy, and knowledge required. That seems to hold especially true for more complicated vacations, such as cruises, escorted group tours, and custom-designed vacations that require more expertise.

✔ CHECK-UP

Common ways of going online today include
- ✔ Traditional dial-up access via phone lines.
- ✔ Broadband connections via DSL, cable, or satellite.
- ✔ Broadband wireless access via cellular networks or WiFi.

Key uses of the Internet include
- ✔ E-mail.
- ✔ Intranets.
- ✔ Communicating with clients, suppliers, and colleagues.
- ✔ Researching information.
- ✔ Advertising and marketing.
- ✔ Booking.

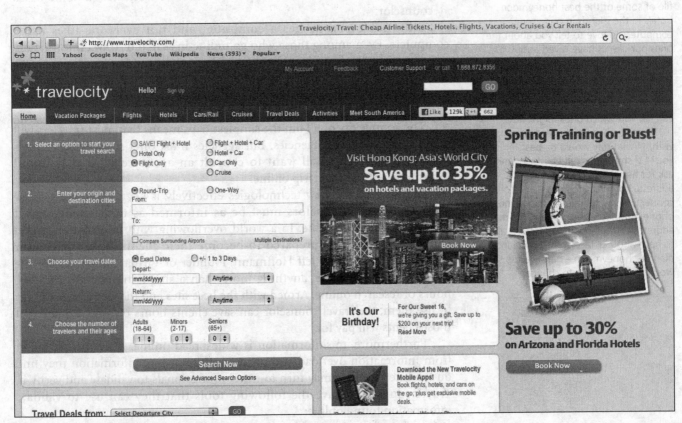

FIGURE 3.3 An Online Travel Agency: Travelocity

The home page for Travelocity illustrates the wide range of offerings available from online travel agencies.

Source: Reprinted by permission of Travelocity.

Meeting the Technological Challenge

■ HOW SHOULD TRAVEL PROFESSIONALS RESPOND
TO THE EXISTENCE OF ONLINE TRAVEL SERVICES?

The Internet has certainly revolutionized the travel industry. Travel ranks first among all types of products and services bought online.

Most travel professionals today use the Internet, but it is not only a tool: it is also a challenge and the home of competitors. Even the airlines, which led the way in the use of computers to promote and sell their products, have found that the public's use of the Internet can bring challenges. The increasing ability of consumers to go online to comparison-shop for airfares is one source of the airlines' financial woes.

The use of online travel sites has posed a special challenge to travel agencies. Thanks to the Internet, travelers with computers now have four choices for booking travel:

1. They can book online with a supplier, a discounter, an auction house, or an online travel agency.
2. They can call a supplier directly.
3. They can book online with a bricks-and-clicks travel agency.
4. They can call or visit a travel agency's office or work with a home-based counselor.

Still, not everyone has a computer, and not everyone likes using computers. Even among those who go online in search of travel information, many are just "lookers," not "bookers." They might not book online because they prefer to talk to a live person or because they are worried about privacy or about the security of credit card transactions or because they want advice or other help.

The complexity of all but the simplest trips means that most travelers will continue to use travel agencies. But agencies must offer services that clients need so that clients will want to consult an agency even if they found information about their trip online.

Learning to use new technologies effectively is key to providing those services. Travel counselors must be as informed as their clients about resources available online. In a world overflowing with information, travel counselors should be prepared to become their clients' "cyberspace tour guide," in the words of Jeff Hoffmann, founder of Virtual Shopping. For the vast majority of people, anything more than a simple transaction can take hours of research online. Armed with the best sites and the knowledge of how to use them, the travel counselor can save clients hours of time, a value that those clients will pay for.

Furthermore, misinformation is widespread online. Many people suffer from information overload and uncertainty regarding information they find on the Internet; they may turn to travel professionals to validate and verify it. Travel counselors have the following tools that they can use to validate information found online:

■ *Knowledge, experience, and expertise.* Travel professionals view the information found online through trained eyes. Extensive knowledge of the industry, suppliers, products, and destinations should enable you to help clients sort through the massive amounts of information available online and to identify relevant, accurate, and useful information for your clients.

- *Travel industry resources.* Travel professionals have access to many industry resources that the public does not. For example, travel counselors can access the "travel-agent-only" section of the CLIA (Cruise Lines International Association) Web site if their agency is a member. Or to learn about a tour operator, they can contact the National Tour Association or the United States Tour Operators Association.
- *Relationships with suppliers.* Clients may benefit from the relationships that travel counselors and travel agencies have built with travel suppliers. These relationships may enable a travel counselor to validate information from

CLOSE-UP: SELLING WITH TECHNOLOGY

The technologies that have revolutionized the travel industry can be used in many ways to sell travel services and serve clients more effectively. Here is one example.

Suppose you are a travel counselor and one of your clients is going to London, where he hopes to indulge a love of East Asian food, theater, and Dickens. If you know how to search online efficiently, you could create a brochure custom-made to match the client's needs and interests. You might include

- The client's itinerary.
- A diagram of the airport to show how to get to the tube (subway).
- The tube schedule and prices.
- A map of the neighborhood near the tube stop where the client's hotel is located.
- Information from the hotel's Web site.
- A list of East Asian restaurants and the menu from one of those restaurants.
- A list of theaters and their phone numbers, a map showing the theater for which the client has tickets, and a list of pubs near the theater that will be open when the play ends.
- Maps of locations mentioned in Charles Dickens's books, a short biography of Dickens, and a menu from one of Dickens's favorite pubs.

The brochure might also include practical information to make the trip easier, such as information on currency and time differences, comments about reaching the Internet and using small appliances, and the local phone number of the airline.

The point is to meet the client's needs and help make the trip as enjoyable as possible. Technology makes it easier to provide the service that delivers real value to clients and earns their loyalty.

Another application of technology is to use travel DVDs as a selling tool. Travel agencies sometimes give them as gifts to clients, sell or rent them in order to produce additional revenue, use them to enhance sales presentations to groups, or loan or show them to clients to help close a sale. Videos can be particularly effective in persuading clients to select a more expensive option or an additional destination and in finalizing the sale of lesser-known destinations.

Many travel videos from tour operators and suppliers contain practical information, showing places to stay, attractions to see, and souvenirs to buy. Other videos emphasize the "flavor" of the destination; these are often produced by tourist bureaus or independent production houses.

The abundance of travel videos can be intimidating if you are trying to select one for a client. Keep these tips in mind:

- A good video should be professional in production, presentation, editing, and sound.
- It should be relatively short and feature practical information such as maps. Undecided clients should usually be given videos no more than fifteen minutes long.
- Music and narration should reflect the culture of the destination but should not obscure the message of the film.
- The video should sell the destination, not the sponsors' products.
- It should look attractive on a shelf, and its content should not date quickly.

As helpful as videos are, they are only tools that can help to make a sale; they cannot replace your own presentation. Also, they should not be given until you have considered the client's needs and desires and know what point the video should make with that client.

In summary, to use videos effectively,

- Preview all videos to make sure they are interesting, accurate, and relevant.
- Offer a video when it will prove certain sales points, show features or benefits you have presented to the client, or enhance a client's enthusiasm about a destination that you believe will meet his or her needs.
- Follow up on the video, elaborating on points it made.

the Internet as well as to provide clients with quality products and services that they may be unable to obtain on their own.

Prospective travel professionals should begin creating their own dossiers of information by keeping lists of favorite Web sites for different categories of information—such as industry news, destinations, airlines, hotels, car rentals, and travel tips.

Travel professionals today also need to know how to use technological tools besides the Internet. Important examples include the computer software discussed earlier and DVDs.

For those dealing with international contacts a great deal, the telephone service *Skype* may be of help, allowing you to talk with your contact face to face. An enhanced cell phone with a built-in camera can be helpful when traveling, allowing you to photograph your recent journeys and then post the photos on your Web site or show to clients. Blackberries, iPads and other tablets, and laptops are a boon to home-based and travel professionals needing to have a virtual office with them at all times. And for group leaders, being able to store travel guidebooks on a light-weight *electronic reading device* such as Amazon's Kindle or Barnes and Noble's Nook will free lots of luggage space.

Knowing when to use a particular technology is also a key to effective selling and service. The information on DVDs, for example, is often also available on the Internet. But a DVD can be easier to access, offer richer content, and have fewer distractions. And as Chapter 12 discusses, sometimes a phone call is a better way to communicate with a client than a fax or an e-mail; sometimes, a letter is better. Will you find an answer faster by looking in a book or by talking to someone or by going online? The answer varies, and experience will teach you which source to turn to first.

Travel counselors have always been information sifters, problem solvers, advisers, and sales clinchers. Clients look to them for ideas, creative itineraries, and reassurance. Technology can never replace people who are able and willing to understand a client's needs and to help solve problems with a smile. And even if you are not a techno-wiz, you can become knowledgeable enough to use technology as a tool for selling travel effectively. Companies need people who can learn to use a technology, continue to learn, change as it changes, and even think up new ways of using that technology. The new uses do not have to be earth-shattering sparks of genius; simple new applications of technology in the right market are enabling small companies in out-of-the-way places to sell to the world.

CHAPTER WRAP-UP

CHAPTER HIGHLIGHTS

Technology has dramatically altered the way travel professionals conduct research, communicate with clients, and market their services. This chapter has described some of the fundamental concepts needed to prepare professionals to meet the resulting challenges. Here is a review of the objectives with which we began the chapter.

1. **Describe how personal computers and GDSs are used in the travel industry.** Like other American businesses, travel professionals use personal computers for word processing, database management, presentation graphics, cash management, and Internet applications. They also use software created specifically for the travel industry, such as databases designed to handle client

profiles, software packages that integrate back-office systems with reservation systems and client databases, and Internet booking engines. The most-used electronic tools, however, are the GDSs. These are the descendants of the reservation systems known as CRSs, which were created in the 1970s. The major GDSs are Sabre, Galileo, Amadeus, and Worldspan. Travel counselors today can gain access to a GDS in several ways, and they use GDSs not only to make airline reservations but also to find information about and to book other types of travel arrangements.

2. **Outline four major ways that travel professionals use the Internet.** E-mail is probably the most popular application of the Internet; travel professionals use it in order to communicate more efficiently with both clients and colleagues. But the World Wide Web opened the way to other uses of the Internet. Just by knowing a Web site's URL or by using a search engine, travel professionals can find information about destinations and suppliers around the world, making the Internet an incomparable tool for research. Travel professionals also advertise and market themselves on the Internet; many travel companies allow travelers to book travel on their Web sites. In addition, travel counselors use the Internet to make bookings for their clients.

3. **Mention three technology devices that have come into the marketplace and how they might be used in the industry by travel professionals.** A number of technology devices have become available that may be helpful to travel counselors and others in the industry. Among those could be the Skype telephone service and enhanced cell phones, partifcularly with cameras for photographing personal travels so as to show them to potential clients. Outside travel counselors and sales representatives will appreciate Blackberries, iPads, and tablets, which allow them to carry a virtual office with them. And tour leaders will appreciate being able to download travel guidebooks into a light-weight electronic reading device to carry with them on tour.

4. **List at least four reasons why travelers would seek out a travel professional despite the existence of online travel services.** Travel professionals should see online travel sources as tools that they should master and a possible source of new opportunities. For travel counselors in particular, however, online travel services can be a major competitor. But travelers will continue to seek contact with a travel counselor if they dislike using computers, worry about the privacy or security of online transactions, want a personal interaction, want advice, or believe that using a travel counselor can save them time or money. Travel counselors can verify information that the public finds on the Internet by using their expertise and experience, their knowledge of travel industry resources, and their relationships with suppliers.

KEY TERMS

A list of key terms introduced in this chapter follows. If you do not recall the meaning of these terms, see the Glossary, which begins on page 393.

Amadeus	graphical interface
Apollo	hotspot
bricks-and-clicks agency	Internet
browser	Internet service provider (ISP)
command interface	Sabre
computer reservation system (CRS)	search engine
database	Skype
direct link	uniform resource locator (URL)
electronic reading device	WiFi
e-mail	Worldspan
Galileo	World Wide Web
global distribution system (GDS)	

REVIEW QUESTIONS

1. The forerunners of today's GDSs were built to sell air travel. For what other arrangements are GDSs useful today?

2. How does the integration of travel software allow travel counselors to be more efficient?

3. How does the ability of clients to book airline tickets from their own computers affect travel agencies?

4. Some believe that the use of computers makes business less personal; others say it frees people from mechanical tasks and gives them the time to be more personal. What do you think? Explain your opinion.

Part 2:
The Travel Product

Chapter 4
Air Travel

Chapter 5
Ground Travel

Chapter 6
Accommodations

Chapter 7
Cruises

Chapter 8
Tours and Packages

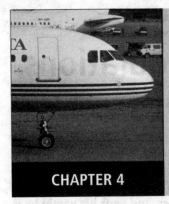

Air Travel

CHAPTER 4

OBJECTIVES

After completing this chapter, you should be able to

1. Outline how the airline industry is regulated and coordinated by the government and suppliers.

2. Describe how airlines differ, and know the codes for some major airlines and airports both in the United States and abroad.

3. Explain three types of flights, five types of journeys, and three classes of service.

4. Describe at least five factors that are likely to affect the cost of a passenger's flight.

5. Outline the procedures involved in taking a flight and common questions and problems that come up in air travel.

6. Show why a good travel counselor needs to know about airline ticketing and how airline tickets are an income source.

Flying, said American astronomer Simon Newcomb in 1903, "is one of that class of problems with which man will never be able to cope." But before the year was out, Orville and Wilbur Wright *had* coped with it. Over the windswept dunes of Kitty Hawk, North Carolina, they completed the first manned, powered flight on December 17, 1903. The twelve-second flight of the 625-pound craft, with Orville Wright manning the controls, managed to stay airborne for 120 feet.

The air transportation industry has progressed tremendously since then; it is now the key long-distance mover of people. During an average daytime hour, more than 100,000 people are airborne over the United States. This chapter examines both international air travel and *domestic air travel,* which includes flights between and within the continental United States and parts of Alaska, Hawaii, Puerto Rico, the Virgin Islands, and Canada. We look first at how the air travel industry is coordinated and regulated. Next we examine the suppliers of air travel—the airlines—and airports and variations in the airlines' products and prices. Finally, we discuss some of the procedures, policies, and problems that most concern the sellers of air travel.

Order in the Skies: Rules and Regulations

■ WHAT IS THE ROLE OF GOVERNMENT IN THE AIRLINE INDUSTRY, AND HOW DO SUPPLIERS REGULATE THE TRAVEL MARKET?

Air travel is amazingly easy. You can buy a ticket for a flight from, say, San Francisco to Chicago on one airline, from Chicago to Miami on another, to San Juan on a third, and then back to San Francisco. You might board a different type of aircraft for each leg of this journey, and your life would be in the hands of different mechanics, flight attendants, and pilots. But at each step on your trip, you could feel confident that your flight would be honored and that the equipment, procedures, and people had all met certain standards and were worthy of your trust.

In just one stop, you will have ordered and paid for services from hundreds of people; the Close-Up on careers describes some of the jobs they perform. In this section we look at how the efforts of all these people are coordinated and regulated.

CLOSE-UP: CAREERS IN AIR TRAVEL

People who are interested in a career in air travel tend to focus on the biggest airlines, but there are also opportunities with regional airlines, private airlines, and international carriers—as well as jobs in airport management, air traffic control, and the Federal Aviation Administration (FAA). Many in-flight and technical positions require licensing by the FAA, but there are plenty of other career opportunities related to sales, marketing, administration, operations, information technology, e-commerce, and security. Many airline employees begin their careers as reservationists or flight attendants.

■ **Position** Reservations agent

Description Reservations agents may work at large airline reservations centers, in city ticket offices, or at airports. At reservations centers they handle telephone requests for tickets as well as questions about fares, seating, schedules, availability, special requests, escorts for juveniles, and ticket policies. Reservationists also reserve and confirm seats on domestic and international flights, issue tickets, and research and resolve passenger problems.

Qualifications This position demands skill in communicating and problem solving. A pleasant voice, a ready smile, the ability to be clear and concise, tact, and good humor are important assets. Training involves mastering the airline's computer system, rules, and policies.

■ **Position** Customer service representative/passenger services agent

Description Providing customer service is the pivotal responsibility of this position. The job is typically fast-paced and physically demanding, with long and inconvenient hours. Duties include answering questions about schedules and fares, initiating and completing flight transactions, maintaining security by checking passengers' ID, helping customers in the check-in and boarding process, and aiding those who have baggage-related questions or who require special help (such as those dealing with missed connections). At some airports, duties also include baggage handling, aircraft cleaning, and other ramp services. Much of the work involves computers.

Qualifications On-the-job training is usually provided for this position. Experience as a reservations agent or ticket agent is helpful. Good "people skills," an unflappable personality, and patience are needed. The flexibility to work weekends and holidays is required.

■ **Position** Flight attendant

Description Flight attendants' primary responsibility is the safety of passengers, but most of their time is spent providing for the comfort of travelers—offering food and beverage service, assisting passengers with baggage, helping sick passengers or those with disabilities, and answering questions. Behind the scenes, they attend preflight briefings, check the cabin for supplies, give first aid, take special care of unaccompanied children, and write postflight reports. Flight attendants may have little choice of home base or routes until they have gained seniority.

(continued on next page)

The U.S. Government and the Airlines: A Brief History

From the start, the airline industry and the U.S. government have had a complicated relationship. Its history divides into three eras: from the birth of the industry until 1978, from 1978 to 2001, and the present.

The Era of Regulation. At first, the only way for airlines to make money was to obtain a contract from the government to fly the U.S. mail. By 1938 American, Eastern, TWA, and United had emerged as major airlines, and the government had set up the Civil Aeronautics Authority (CAA) to regulate the new industry. The CAA was soon reorganized and renamed the *Civil Aeronautics Board*, or *CAB*.

The CAB had two goals: to promote the new airline industry and to protect the interests of passengers. It decided whether an airline was fit to fly, which routes it flew, and how much the airline could charge. Airlines received subsidies from the government to serve remote areas.

As the airline industry grew and changed, so did the government's regulatory structure. The government allowed the airlines to work together through the *Air Traffic Conference (ATC)* to establish a standard sales contract,

---

CLOSE-UP: CAREERS IN AIR TRAVEL (cont.)

Qualifications Prior customer service experience is desired. Airlines look for poise, personality, a well-groomed appearance, good sense, physical stamina, rapport with people, grace under pressure, and the ability to work as part of a team. In addition, flight attendants must be at least 19 years old and meet requirements regarding vision, size, and fitness. Candidates must complete a 4- to 6-week training course. For international services, speaking other languages is a must; the ability to travel in and out of the country is essential.

■ **Position** Airline sales representative

Description This position provides a liaison with travel counselors, tour operators, and corporate accounts. Responsibilities include selling new accounts, building sales from existing accounts, and servicing special requests (such as upgrading VIP passengers). Sales representatives are in the field much of the time calling on agencies, making presentations, and participating in civic functions, seminars, and trade shows. They may become involved in promoting the airline's image and the destinations it serves.

Qualifications Selling and presentation skills are required for this position, along with knowledge of "your" airline—its strength, policies, and destinations.

■ **Position** Account executive, corporate sales

Description Responsibilities of this position include marketing airline services to companies within an area and negotiating volume-based agreements; helping corporations to prepare Requests for Proposals from travel agencies; and working with meeting sales and group sales. Frequently, account executives also coordinate arrangements with those car and hotel vendors that are the airline's partners.

Qualifications Typically, the person in this position is promoted from a job as a reservations or passenger services agent or from a business-to-business sales position in another airline or related travel company.

■ **Position** Marketing automation software developer

Description This professional is responsible for special projects and new technologies, including Internet-related marketing activities. The position involves a variety of tasks related to system and software engineering, from analysis to design, coding, testing, and maintenance of software.

Qualifications This position requires a B.S. in computer science or equivalent experience as well as at least two years' experience in software development and support. An understanding of database design and implementation, organizational and communication skills, and the ability to handle multiple tasks simultaneously are needed. The job may require working evenings or weekends.

■ **Other positions** Advertising and sales promotion for foreign flag carrier; aircraft mechanic; customer relations for frequent-flyer programs; gate agent; station manager; strategic market planning analyst; yield management analyst.

appoint travel agencies to sell air travel, and set up ways to transfer baggage and handle reservations. In 1958 the government established the *Federal Aviation Administration,* or *FAA,* to license pilots, certify aircraft as safe, and enforce rules regarding passenger safety. In 1967 the *National Transportation Safety Board (NTSB)* was created to investigate accidents, and the FAA became part of the Department of Transportation (DOT).

Market Control. In 1978 the *Airline Deregulation Act* ended the government's economic control of U.S. airlines. Airlines were given the power to determine their own routes, fares, and commissions. The CAB and ATC were phased out of existence.

The effects of deregulation came quickly. New airlines were established, competing with old carriers. Some airlines expanded; some merged; some went bankrupt. Of fifty new jet airlines that started up after deregulation, thirty-five had gone out of business fifteen years later.

For travel counselors and travelers alike, deregulation brought uncertainty and confusion. Before deregulation, there might have been three possible fares for one route; now there might be hundreds. Schedules changed frequently; fares changed daily, sometimes hourly.

There were other dislocations. Some small towns and cities lost air service. Travelers who could not adjust their schedules faced high fares. Service before and during flights deteriorated. And beginning in 1995 the airlines began cutting the commissions paid to travel agencies for selling air tickets. Airlines and travel agencies, once seen as partners, became competitors.

But deregulation also delivered important benefits. Entrepreneurs tried out new ideas. Travelers with flexible schedules could find bargain fares. U.S. airlines made impressive innovations, such as using electronic ticketing and selling tickets over the Internet. By 2000 record numbers of Americans were flying; that year the airlines carried more than 730 million people.

In 2000 most of the complaints about air travel seemed to reflect the industry's success. As more and more Americans took to the air, flight delays and cancellations soared. The airlines fought off calls for new government regulation by promising to improve service.

Then the hijackings of September 11, 2001, by terrorists pushed concerns about service into the background and threw the airline industry into turmoil. Demand plummeted. The industry needed the federal government to bail it out financially and to reassure the public that it was safe to fly.

Economic deregulation obviously had not abolished the need for rules and agreements to keep order in the skies. Today, both the federal government and the airlines themselves play important roles in keeping this complicated industry in shape.

The U.S. Government's Role Today. Even after economic deregulation, the federal government retained the authority to protect airline passengers and to police unfair practices by airlines. The key issue still regulated by the government was safety, but until September 11, 2001, implementing many safety procedures—including screening passengers and their baggage—was the responsibility of the airlines. This arrangement seemed to work. In every year of the last two decades of the twentieth century, fatalities at U.S. railroad crossings far outnumbered fatalities in the air. But when terrorists hijacked four U.S. planes on September 11, 2001, and used them to attack New York and Washington, D.C., weaknesses in the system were tragically exposed.

Concerns focused on security at airports. After a wave of hijackings in the 1970s and early 1980s, U.S. airports had hired security guards and installed metal detectors. The FAA provided guidance about security procedures to airlines and airports, and in the largest airports federal security managers oversaw procedures for protecting passengers. Generally, though, airlines and airports were responsible for planning and carrying out security measures, subject to FAA approval. That changed after September 11, 2001.

Two months after the attacks, federal legislation established the *Transportation Security Administration (TSA)*. For the first time, airport security became a direct federal responsibility. Congress provided additional funds for new personnel, including baggage screeners to ensure that all passengers and carry-on bags are thoroughly inspected. In 2002 the Department of Homeland Security (DHS) was established, and the TSA became part of this department, along with other government agencies that are responsible for protecting the nation's transportation systems and supervising the entry of people and goods into the United States.

Table 4.1 summarizes the federal agencies that play important roles in air travel today. In particular,

- The FAA licenses commercial pilots, oversees maintenance programs and procedures for all aircraft, and certifies the airworthiness of planes.
- The NTSB investigates all accidents involving aircraft.
- The FAA also runs the air traffic control system.
- The TSA is responsible for developing policies to ensure the safety of U.S. transportation, including airport security and the prevention of hijacking.
- The federal government also enforces rules regarding issues such as liability for lost and damaged baggage, treatment of travelers with disabilities, and compensation when boarding is denied.

Interline Agreements and ARC

Many aspects of air travel are governed by agreements among the airlines themselves—*interline agreements.* Airline ticketing is one important example. After deregulation, the airlines worked together through the *Air Transport Association (ATA)*, the trade association of major U.S. airlines, to adopt a system remarkably similar to the one that existed during the era of government regulation. This system has two key features.

TABLE 4.1 The Key Regulators of U.S. Domestic Airlines

Government Body	Description
Department of Transportation (DOT)	The cabinet-level department of the federal government that is responsible for mass transportation. It oversees the formulation of national transportation policy. Other responsibilities range from negotiating international transportation agreements to enforcing airline consumer protection regulations.
Federal Aviation Administration (FAA)	An agency of DOT. The FAA has primary responsibility for airline safety regulations. It develops, maintains, and operates the air traffic control system; reviews the design, manufacture, and maintenance of aircraft equipment; sets minimum standards for crew training; and establishes operational requirements for airlines.
Transportation Security Administration (TSA)	Part of the Department of Homeland Security. The TSA is responsible for developing policies to ensure the safety of U.S. transportation, including airport security and the prevention of hijacking.
National Transportation Safety Board (NTSB)	An independent federal agency. The NTSB investigates all aviation accidents (as well as significant accidents in other modes of transportation) and recommends enhancements for safety. It also tracks aviation fatalities, publishes annual safety statistics, and conducts special studies of transportation safety issues.
U.S. Department of Justice	Has become involved in issues of consumer protection.

Sources: Air Transport Association, (www.air-transport.org), FAA, (www.faa.gov); TSA (www.tsa.gov).

First, the ATA created a *standard ticket,* which let passengers fly on many airlines with just one ticket. As we discuss later in this chapter, purchase of an airline ticket brings into force a contract between the airline and the passenger. The exact terms of the contract vary from one airline to another, but the standard ticket identifies the important areas, such as airline liability in cases of delays, injury, or death.

Second, the ATA created **ARC,** the **Airlines Reporting Corporation,** to regulate the distribution of airline tickets. ARC, which is owned by major U.S. airlines, accredits travel agencies. Any nonairline company that issues airline tickets must have ARC accreditation, and every individual involved in the sale of airline tickets must work for or contract with an ARC-accredited company. ARC also supplies documents used in selling airline tickets, rail transportation, and related services, and it provides a centralized system for processing these sales.

The ARC sets the requirements that allow a travel agency to sell airline tickets. Among other things, the agency must:

- Be located in and authorized to do business in the United States, U.S. Virgin Islands, or Puerto Rico. (It may be located in a private residence, as long as it meets the local jurisdiction requirements).
- Provide a bond, a letter of credit, or a cash deposit of at least $20,000.
- Meet the personnel standards of Section IV-B of the Agent Reporting Agreement. Those include having
  - One person who is a full-time employee of the agency, at the place of business, who exercises daily supervision of, and responsibility for, the operations at that agency location and has the authority to make management decisions.
  - The person who has completed and passed the ARC Specialist exam and will represent the agency as the ARC Specialist Qualifier. (Note: the management qualifier and the ARC Specialist Qualifier may be the same person.)
- Meet ticketing security standards of Attachment 8 of the Agent Reporting Agreement.

There is an application fee, as well as an annual fee.

International Rules of the Skies

Each nation owns the right to the sky above it, and it has the right to protect that airspace and to say whether airplanes can fly into its skies. The ability of travelers to zip across the heavens from nation to nation depends on the fact that countries have agreed on rules that balance two goals: preserving the sovereignty of nations over their skies and enhancing the freedom of people to travel.

One milestone occurred in 1944, when fifty-two nations signed the Chicago Convention. Among other things, this agreement set out principles called *freedoms of the air* that describe what a carrier of one nation may do in another nation; other freedoms were agreed to later. These freedoms have provided the basis for negotiations among nations about how their airlines will operate.

Over the years, much of the negotiating about international air traffic has occurred through **IATA,** the **International Air Transport Association.** Founded in 1919 and reorganized after World War II, IATA is an association of 230 international airlines that aims to create order and stability in international aviation.

Ultimately, however, governments must approve the decisions of IATA. In fact, the U.S. government has periodically challenged the authority of IATA and turned to *bilateral agreements* (agreements between two countries) to supersede IATA. Thus international fares reflect agreements between governments, which also negotiate agreements regulating the carriers, routes, frequency, and number of seats on international flights.

In recent years many governments have backed away from regulating air travel. During the 1990s the U.S. government led the way in urging an *open-skies policy* under which carriers can fly where they choose, charge what they wish, and make deals with each other. It reached open-skies agreements with several European nations. It also granted immunity from antitrust laws to several U.S. airlines so they could form alliances with airlines of other nations. Continued deregulation seems likely, but ultimately, political decisions will determine the power corporations will have over the international skies.

IATAN

Like sales for domestic flights, selling seats on international flights also requires coordination and regulation. Since 1945, IATA has a screening program to approve travel agencies that can serve international airlines. It still operates this network outside the United States. But in May 1985 *IATAN,* the *International Airlines Travel Agent Network,* replaced IATA as the organization that appoints U.S. travel agencies to sell tickets for international airlines serving the United States.

IATAN operates as a subsidiary of IATA and links its members with U.S. travel agencies. IATAN serves three primary functions:

- It endorses travel agencies that meet specific standards of financial stability, security, professional integrity, and experience.
- It acts on behalf of its subscriber airlines and other suppliers to appoint agents to sell their products according to the suppliers' standards.
- It promotes professional practices within the international travel industry.

IATAN also sponsors the *IATAN ID Card,* which identifies those carrying the card as industry professionals (see Table 4.2).

TABLE 4.2

Qualifications for the IATAN Identity Card

To qualify for the ID card, applicants must

- Be an owner, employee, or independent contractor of an IATAN-accredited location.
- Be registered with IATAN.
- Devote at least 20 hours per week to the business of selling travel.
- Have earned at least $5,000 in salary and/or commission in the previous 12 months.
- Be at least 18 years of age.

The card is valid for one year and costs $25 online or $30 by mail.

✔ CHECK-UP

After the Airline Deregulation Act of 1978,
- ✔ U.S. airlines were free to set their own fares and routes.
- ✔ The federal government continued to enforce rules to regulate safety and to ensure fair treatment of passengers.
- ✔ The airlines themselves established rules and policies to govern the ticketing of air travel.

Key roles in the system that coordinates and regulates domestic air travel are played by
- ✔ The airlines.
- ✔ ATA, the trade association of major airlines, and ARC, which is owned by the major airlines.
- ✔ The Department of Transportation, which has primary responsibility for enforcing airline consumer protection regulations.

- ✔ The FAA, an agency of the Department of Transportation that has primary responsibility for safety regulations.
- ✔ The NTSB, an independent agency that investigates all accidents.
- ✔ The TSA, an agency in the Department of Homeland Security that has primary responsibility for security.
- ✔ The U.S. Department of Justice, which gets involved in consumer issues.

Key roles in the system that regulates international air travel are played by
- ✔ IATA, which is an association of international airlines.
- ✔ Airlines.
- ✔ Governments.
- ✔ IATAN, which appoints travel agencies to sell tickets for international airlines serving the United States.

Airlines and Airports

■ WHAT ARE THE MAJOR AIRLINES AND AIRPORTS?

The world of aviation includes military aviation and *general aviation* (that is, crop dusters, corporate jets, and other planes not used by commercial airlines) as well as **civil aviation,** which includes all air service that is offered to the public for hire, whether for passengers or for cargo. Passenger service includes both **charters,** which are specially scheduled flights reserved by a private group or tour operator, and **scheduled service,** which consists of flights for designated routes offered to the public according to a published timetable.

The first years of the twenty-first century were not kind to the airlines and airports that provide scheduled service. First, fears of terrorism and an economic slowdown dampened demand for air travel; then war and rising fuel and security costs and taxes put new financial pressures on the industry. (Chapter 9 says more about the strategies that some airlines have used to survive in this environment.) Who are the major players in the airline industry?

U.S. Airlines

The United States is home to the largest civil aviation system in the world. Table 4.3 lists some of the best-known U.S. airlines offering scheduled service. As the table shows, every airline is assigned a two-letter code, which is used on GDSs (global distribution systems), schedules, and tickets.

The hundreds of U.S. airlines offering scheduled service do not fit neatly into simple categories. The average traveler probably divides them into (1) major airlines such as United, (2) commuter lines, and (3) budget lines such as Southwest. The government takes a different approach. It categorizes airlines with scheduled service into three types based on the amount of revenue generated.

■ *Major airlines* generate annual operating revenues of more than $1 billion. They provide service nationwide (and sometimes worldwide).
■ *National airlines* generate annual operating revenues of $100 million to $1 billion. Many of these airlines serve specific regions of the country, but some offer long-haul or even international service.
■ *Regional airlines* generate annual operating revenues of less than $100 million. Most regionals offer service only to one region of the country. The government further classifies regional airlines into large, medium, and small regionals based on their revenue. *Small regionals* are also called **commuter airlines.**

Most regional lines today either are owned by major airlines or have **code-sharing agreements** with them. Major airline alliances, such as Skyteen, The Star Alliance, One Family, also use code sharing. These agreements allow an airline to use the code of a larger, better-known airline. Many code-sharing agreements also call for the companies to coordinate their schedules and marketing efforts. When there is code sharing, travel sellers are required to tell clients in writing which airline they are actually flying. Whatever the type of airline, the FAA applies the same safety standards to all scheduled service with aircraft that have 10 seats or more.

TABLE 4.3

A Sampling of Some Major U.S. Airlines and Their Codes

Airline	Code
Alaska Airlines	AS
American Airlines	AA
Delta Airlines	DL
Frontier Airlines	F9
Hawaiian Airlines	HA
JetBlue Airways	B6
Southwest Airlines	WN
United Airlines (including Continental)	UA
U.S. Airways	US

The Hub-and-Spoke System

Since economic deregulation allowed the airlines to determine their own routes, they have increasingly used a hub-and-spoke system. In a *hub-and-spoke system,* an airline uses certain cities as connecting centers, or hubs, for as many flights to and from outlying cities as possible. Passengers from outlying cities must fly first to the hub and from there catch connecting flights to their different destinations.

Figure 4.1 shows an example. In this case, by using two hubs—Dallas and Chicago—along with eleven shorter "feeder routes," the airline can come up with forty-two different route combinations. The airline could not profitably operate daily flights from, for example, Jackson, Mississippi, to Omaha, Nebraska, because the *passenger load factor*—the percentage of available seats on a flight that is actually sold—would be extremely small. Instead, it flies travelers who want to travel between Jackson and Omaha through the Dallas and Chicago hubs. By using hubs, the airline maximizes passenger loads from small cities; it also saves fuel by minimizing departures from small cities.

For the airlines, the hub-and-spoke system offers a strategy for serving as many passengers as possible while maximizing efficiency. For travelers, though, the hub-and-spoke system means fewer direct flights, more connections, and an increased risk of delays. By decreasing competition, the hub-and-spoke system may also lead to high fares. At some hubs, one airline is so dominant that there is little competitive pressure on fares.

The hub-and-spoke system also creates winners and losers among airports. Airports chosen as hubs often host administrative and maintenance centers for the airlines, generating jobs and revenues. But for airports that are mere "spokes" in the system or that lose air service, the popularity of the system can be disastrous.

U.S. Airports

Table 4.4 on the next page lists some of the busiest North American airports. Every city and airport served by an airline is known by a three-letter code. If a city has only one airport, the same code is often used for both the city and the airport. Cities served by more than one airport have

FIGURE 4.1

A Hub-and-Spoke System

This sample hub-and-spoke system creates forty-two possible route combinations.

one code for the city and others for the airports. The codes are easily found in reference books, online, and GDSs, but many employers check to see if prospective counselors know their codes.

Today, many employees new to the travel industry do not know their airport codes because they depend on the GDS for them. However, experienced counselors will tell you how important knowing the codes is to assure accuracy and avoid making fateful errors.

TABLE 4.4 A Selection of Major North American Airports

Airport	Code	Airport	Code	Airport	Code
United States		Lihue, Kauai, HI	LIH	San Francisco, CA	SFO
Albuquerque, NM	ABQ	Little Rock, AR	LIT	San Jose, CA	SJC
Anchorage, AK	ANC	Long Beach, CA	LGB	Seattle/Tacoma, WA	SEA
Atlanta, GA	ATL	Los Angeles, CA/ Burbank	BUR	Sioux Falls, SD	FSD
Baltimore, MD	BWI			St. Louis, MO	STL
Bismarck, ND	BIS	Los Angeles, CA/ International	LAX	Tampa, FL	TPA
Boston, MA	BOS			Tulsa, OK	TUL
Buffalo, NY	BUF	Los Angeles, CA/ Ontario	ONT	Washington, DC/ Dulles	IAD
Charleston, SC	CHS	Louisville, KY	SDF		
Charlotte, NC	CLT	Memphis, TN	MEM	Washington, DC/ Reagan-National	DCA
Chicago, IL/Midway	MDW	Miami, FL	MIA		
Chicago, IL/O'Hare	ORD	Milwaukee, WI	MKE	West Palm Beach, FL	PBI
Cincinnati, OH	CVG	Minneapolis/St. Paul, MN	MSP	Wichita, KS	ICT
Cleveland, OH	CLE	Nashville, TN	BNA	**Canada**	
Columbus, OH	CMH	New Orleans, LA	MSY	Calgary, Alb	YYC
Dallas/Fort Worth, TX	DFW	New York, NY/ Kennedy	JFK	Montreal, Que/Dorval	YUL
Daytona Beach, FL	DAB			Montreal, Que/Mirabel	YMX
Denver, CO	DEN	New York, NY/ LaGuardia	LGA	Ottawa, Ont	YOW
Des Moines, IA	DSM			Toronto, Ont/Pearson	YYZ
Detroit, MI/ Wayne County	DTW	New York/Newark, NJ	EWR	Vancouver, BC	YVR
		Oakland, CA	OAK	**Mexico and the Caribbean**	
El Paso, TX	ELP	Omaha, NE	OMA	Acapulco, Mexico	ACA
Fairbanks, AK	FAI	Orlando, FL	MCO	Bermuda	BDA
Fort Lauderdale, FL	FLL	Philadelphia, PA	PHL	Cancún, Mexico	CUN
Hartford, CT	BDL	Phoenix, AZ	PHX	Guadalajara, Mexico	GDL
Hilo, Hawaii, HI	ITO	Pittsburgh, PA	PIT	Mexico City, Mexico	MEX
Honolulu, Oahu, HI	HNL	Portland, ME	PWM	Montego Bay, Jamaica	MBJ
Houston, TX/ Bush-Intercontinental	IAH	Portland, OR	PDX	Nassau, Bahamas	NAS
		Providence, RI	PVD	Puerto Vallarta, Mexico	PVR
Houston, TX/Hobby	HOU	Raleigh/Durham, NC	RDU	San Juan, Puerto Rico	SJU
Indianapolis, IN	IND	Rapid City, SD	RAP	St. Croix, USVI	STX
Jacksonville, FL	JAX	Richmond, VA	RIC	St. Maarten, Netherlands Antilles	SXM
Kahului, Maui, HI	OGG	Sacramento, CA	SMF		
Kansas City, MO	MKC	Salt Lake City, UT	SLC	St. Thomas, USVI	STT
Kona, Hawaii, HI	KOA	San Antonio, TX	SAT		
Las Vegas, NV	LAS	San Diego, CA	SAN		

For example, Portland, Oregon (PDX) is a long way from Portland, Maine (PWM) and San Jose, California (SJC) should definitely not be confused with San Jose, Costa Rica (SJO). Many cities have more than one airport, such as New York City (NYC) with Kennedy (JFK), La Guardia (LGA) and nearby Newark, New Jersey (EWR). It would be essential for a passengeer flying from California through New York and on to Europe that the passenger make connections in and out of the same New York airport.

Even worse can be misunderstandings over international airports. One letter different, and you're in a different country. For example, landing at Iguassú Falls on the Brazilian side (IGU) would be an error if the traveler's destination were the Sheraton International Hotel on the Argentine (IGR) side.

Major U.S. airports are owned by public authorities (city, county, or state). The airlines rent space from the airport and pay landing fees for each flight. The airports get their revenues from these payments and from concessions such as restaurants, rental car counters, newsstands, and other shops.

Amenities and Design. Some large airports offer far more than the traditional newsstands and gift shops. They also feature health clubs, business service centers, WiFi hotspots, mini-hotels, nail salons, and more.

For greater comfort, travelers willing to pay about $250 to $450 a year, plus an enrollment fee or frequent-flyer miles, can join an airline-sponsored club that operates members-only lounges at many large airports. The lounges provide comfortable easy chairs and sofas, a relaxed atmosphere, newspapers, magazines, television, and a place to store coats and baggage while passengers shop or go to restaurants. There are also bars, fax machines, facilities for making telephone calls and cashing checks, computer ports or WiFi for Internet access, and meeting rooms. Members can receive boarding passes at the lounge and enjoy complimentary soft drinks, coffee, or light snacks. Cocktails and other drinks are also available at many international clubs.

To many travelers, none of these comforts is as important as easy access. How quickly can they get to the gate for a flight, especially a connecting flight? Where do they pick up transportation? You can find diagrams depicting the layouts of airports on the Web sites of most airports.

Many airports use a *satellite design,* which means that central buildings are attached to boarding areas by passageways. This design minimizes the distances that travelers must cross to reach their planes. Some newer airports, like those in Orlando, Tampa, and Denver, are connected by light rail systems; most have moving sidewalks.

Security. After the attacks of 9/11, many new rules went into effect to tighten airport security. Here are some of the rules that directly affect passengers.

- Air travelers may take onboard only one carry-on bag and one personal item (such as a purse or a briefcase).
- Travelers must show a government-issued, picture ID when they check in. They may be asked to produce this ID at several points before boarding, and the name on their air ticket must match exactly the name on their IDs.
- Only ticketed passengers are allowed beyond screening checkpoints except for those with specific medical or parental needs.
- Parking and curbside check-in are subject to new controls, which vary among airports and airlines.
- Knives of any length, cutting instruments, metal scissors, metal nail files, and corkscrews are among the items that cannot be carried onboard. (Tweezers, safety razors, and nail clippers are permitted.)

■ All visitors (noncitizens) must be finger-scanned and digitally photographed upon entering the United States. (*Finger scanning* is digitized, inkless fingerprinting.)

Note that security procedures may change with little or no notice. The government has increased the searching and "pat-downs" of passengers as they go through security. And it has been revising systems for obtaining information on passengers and using that information for its "no-fly" lists—lists of people who are stopped from boarding planes. Current information regarding airport security is available from the Tranportation Security Administration.

International Airports and Airlines

In many airports abroad, security procedures have long been tighter than those in the United States. Passengers may be interviewed extensively and searched before boarding. Even before the terrorist attacks of 2001, check-in times were usually one and a half to two hours before flight time; they may be as long as three hours. The U.S. government requires international airlines and airports to meet certain standards of security in order for flights to serve U.S. airports.

Airports at major international *gateways* (cities that serve as arrival or departure points for international travel) are listed in Table 4.5, along with their codes. Almost all of the listed airports are served by major U.S. carriers as well as international carriers.

Any aircraft that flies the international skies must be registered in and accountable to a particular nation. The flag of that nation is painted somewhere on the plane, and it is known as a *flag carrier*. Table 4.6 on page 92 lists many of the major international flag carriers.

Outside the United States, many countries owned major airlines. In recent years, however, many governments have gotten out of the airline business. Some experts predict that in the future airlines of different countries will merge to form multinational carriers that will dominate international skies.

In the meantime, airlines based in different nations have been forming code-sharing and marketing alliances. To the prospective traveler it may look as if one airline offers service to a far-flung city when, in fact, the trip to that city might require several connections and flights on different airlines.

Alliances among international airlines now number in the hundreds. As part of their agreements, allied airlines often market and sell each other's flights, link their frequent-flyer programs, and pool revenues and divide profits for the routes involved. In a small percentage of alliances, one airline actually acquires stock in the other.

The airlines argue that these alliances give travelers more choices, easier booking, and smoother service between destinations. Critics respond that travelers will ultimately have fewer choices and face higher fares. Lack of interline agreements between rival airline alliance groups often limits interline ticketing and baggage acceptance.

ON THE SPOT

Ms. Girard, one of your business clients, has called you on her cell phone from the airport just before 5:00 P.M. Her flight has been delayed at least an hour, and the airline still does not have a departure time listed. She would like you to rebook her so that she can get to her destination for an important conference the next morning. What would you do?

Some travel counselors might say to themselves, "She's right there at the airport. Why is she calling me for help?" But that comment shows little knowledge of the situation at airports today. While many delayed passengers are waiting to be rebooked in lines that may take more than an hour, others may be doing it a smarter way—using laptops to access the Internet or calling the airline reservations desk directly. Your client is depending on you to navigate these possibilities and find the quickest way. This is your agency's chance to show Ms. Girard and her company the value of working with you. She is giving you an opportunity, not a problem; use it and help her.

✔ CHECK-UP

The large regional airlines
✔ Typically fly shorter routes than the major carriers.
✔ Are governed by the same safety standards as the major and national carriers.
✔ Are often owned by major airlines or have code-sharing agreements with them.

Trends that have greatly influenced U.S. airports in recent years include
✔ The popularity of the hub-and-spoke system.
✔ The use of a satellite design.
✔ Increased security measures.

Service in the Air: Variations in Air Travel

■ WHAT ARE THE MOST SIGNIFICANT VARIATIONS IN THE FLIGHTS AND SERVICES AVAILABLE TO AIRLINE PASSENGERS?

When Western Air Express flew from Los Angeles to Salt Lake City for the first time in April 1926, passengers rode on folding seats in the mail compartment. By 1928 Western's passengers on a flight from Los Angeles to San Francisco were served meals prepared by a first-class Los Angeles restaurant. But airlines could not make money on passenger service until American Airlines introduced the DC-3 in 1936. It could carry twenty-one passengers, could travel coast to coast in sixteen hours, and had seats set in rubber to decrease vibrations.

Today's travelers have easier, faster trips and more choices than those early fliers did. In this section we look at variations in the trips travelers might take, the planes they fly on, and the amenities they are offered.

TABLE 4.5 A Selection of Major Airports outside North America

Airport	Code	Airport	Code
Amsterdam, Netherlands	AMS	Madrid, Spain	MAD
Athens, Greece	ATH	Manchester, U.K.	MAN
Auckland, New Zealand	AKL	Milan (Malpensa), Italy	MXP
Bangkok, Thailand	BKK	Moscow (Vnukovo), Russia	VKO
Barcelona, Spain	BCN	Munich, Germany	MUC
Beijing, China	PEK	Nairobi (Jomo Kenyatta), Kenya	NBO
Berlin (Tegel), Germany	TXL	Oslo (Gardermoen), Norway	GEN
Bogotá, Colombia	BOG	Paris (De Gaulle), France	CDG
Brussels, Belgium	BRU	Paris (Orly), France	ORY
Buenos Aires (Ezeiza), Argentina	EZE	Prague, Czech Republic	PRG
Cairo, Egypt	CAI	Quito, Ecuador	UIO
Caracas, Venezuela	CCS	Rio de Janeiro (Jobim International), Brazil	GIG
Copenhagen (Roskilde), Denmark	RKE	Rome (Da Vinci), Italy	FCO
Delhi, India	DEL	San José, Costa Rica	SJO
Dublin, Ireland	DUB	Seoul, South Korea	SEL
Frankfurt (International), Germany	FRA	Shannon, Ireland	SNN
Geneva, Switzerland	GVA	Singapore	SIN
Helsinki, Finland	HEL	Stockholm (Arlanda), Sweden	ARN
Hong Kong, China	HKG	Sydney (Kingsford Smith), Australia	SYD
Istanbul, Turkey	IST	Tel Aviv (Yafo), Israel	TLV
Johannesburg (Jan Smuts), South Africa	JNB	Tokyo (Narita), Japan	NRT
Lima, Peru	LIM	Vienna, Austria	VIE
Lisbon, Portugal	LIS	Warsaw, Poland	WAW
London (Gatwick), U.K.	LGW	Zürich, Switzerland	ZRH
London (Heathrow), U.K.	LHR		

Note: Some cities have more than one airport, each with a separate code.

TABLE 4.6 Some Major International Airlines

Name of Airline	Code	Country
Aer Lingus	EI	Republic of Ireland
Aeroflot	SU	Russia
Aeromexico	AM	Mexico
Air Canada	AC	Canada
Air France	AF	France
Air India	AI	India
Air Jamaica	JM	Jamaica
Air New Zealand	NZ	New Zealand
Alitalia	AZ	Italy
Asiana	OZ	Korea
Austrian	OS	Austria
Avianca	AV	Colombia
Bahamasair	UP	Bahamas
British Airways	BA	United Kingdom
Cathay Pacific	CX	Hong Kong, China
China Airlines	CI	Taiwan
Egypt Air	MS	Egypt
El Al	LY	Israel
Emirates	EK	Dubai
Eva	BR	Taiwan
Finnair	AY	Finland
Iberia	IB	Spain
Icelandair	FI	Iceland
Japan (JAL)	JL	Japan
KLM	KL	The Netherlands
Korean Air	KE	Korea
Lan	LA	Chile
Lot Polish	LO	Poland
Lufthansa	LH	Germany
Olympic	OA	Greece
Philippine Airlines	PR	Philippines
Qantas	QF	Australia
Royal Air Maroc	AT	Morocco
Royal Jordanian	RJ	Jordan
Scandinavian Airlines System (SAS)	SK	Denmark, Norway, Sweden
Singapore	SQ	Singapore
South African Airways	SA	South Africa
Swiss	LX	Switzerland
Taca	TA	Various
TAP-Air Portugal	TP	Portugal
Virgin Atlantic	VS	United Kingdom

Types of Flights

For most people traveling by air, about the only things that matter is that their flight is safe, on time, and as fast and simple as possible. Its simplicity depends on the stops.

A *stop* occurs whenever a plane lands, and there are different types. A *connection* is a stop that occurs when the passenger gets off a plane with the sole purpose of boarding another plane. A *stopover* is a planned break in a journey. Stops count as stopovers whenever the traveler stays at a domestic location for more than 4 hours—or, for international flights, 24 hours—unless no flight to the destination is available on that airline. If such a flight is available, the passenger must take the next available flight to avoid paying for a stopover.

Depending on the stops involved, travelers might take three different types of one-way flights, as Figure 4.2 illustrates.

- A *nonstop flight* has no intermediate stops.
- A *connecting flight* has a stop that requires the passenger to change planes.
- A *direct,* or *through, flight* has one or more stops at which the passenger does not have to change planes. In fact, some so-called direct flights change aircraft at the stop, requiring passengers to switch planes, even though these flights are listed not as connecting flights but as a "change of equipment." The government requires that clients be notified in writing when a flight with a change in aircraft is listed as direct. This is usually indicated on the client's itinerary.

Airlines will often list a direct flight that requires a change of equipment; that means it really is a connecting flight. In other words, a direct flight can be a nonstop flight or a flight that makes stops en route to a destination. It is always important to advise a customer if a direct flight is not a non-stop. Often a connection can be faster than a direct flight that makes three or more stops en route to the destination.

FIGURE 4.2 Types of Flights

The difference between nonstop and direct flights can be very important to travelers, who often confuse the two.

FIGURE 4.3

Types of Journeys

Types of Journeys

Whatever the type of flight, travelers take four basic types of journeys, as Figure 4.3 shows.

- A *one-way trip* is a journey from an *originating city* to a *destination city*, with no return to the origin. The journey may be made on one or more flights and may or may not require the passenger to change planes.
- A *round-trip* is a journey that returns to the city where it began, without additional stopovers. Thus the ultimate destination is the originating city, with the same route used going and coming.
- A *circle trip* is like a round-trip except that the route on the return trip differs from the route on the outgoing trip. The journey involves two or more stopovers and returns to the originating city.
- An *open-jaw trip* is like a round-trip except that the passenger either (1) returns to a city different from the point of origin or (2) departs for the return trip from a city other than the original destination. For example, a passenger might go from Seattle to Boston by plane, then to New York by car, and then return to Seattle by plane from New York. Thus, the traveler uses some form of transportation in addition to air.
- A *double open-jaw trip*. Often for fare purposes, airlines will allow a double open-jaw, often found in itineraries where there is more than one airport in a city. One example is Oakland to La Guardia, returning Newark to San Francisco. Some international airlines allow an APEX fare with a double open-jaw, such as San Francisco to Frankfurt, returning from Munich to Los Angeles.

Types of Aircraft

Most modern aircraft have two to four jet engines for propulsion. Basically, there are three types of jet engines: *turbojets; turbofans,* an improved version of turbojets; and *turboprops (propjets),* which use the jet engine to turn a propeller. Turboprops fly more slowly and at lower altitudes than other jet aircraft. On all jets that fly at high altitudes, the air pressure inside the plane is artificially increased to approximate the air pressure at ground level.

Jet aircraft come in two broad types: *wide-bodied planes,* with two aisles and a middle section of seats, and *narrow-bodied,* with seats on either side of a single aisle. For each aircraft, several models or series are likely to exist, as the manufacturer makes improvements on the original plane. For example, there are fifteen models of the Boeing 747.

The largest commercial airline is the Airbus A380. The initial version is designed to carry up to 555 passengers, but it could eventually hold up to 800.

It is important to know the kind of aircraft. Most GDS systems have a way to decode the aircraft listed for a flight. Clients need to be advised if they are flying on a turbojet. There are big differences between traveling on a 30-seat plane with limited space for seating and carry-on luggage and a 300-passenger jet aircraft.

Classes of Service

Some budget airlines offer only one class of service. But on most aircraft, movable partitions called *bulkheads* divide the plane into compartments, and the airline offers different classes of service in the different compartments.

Most airlines offer two *classes of service* on most flights: first class and coach. For long flights (particularly international flights), many airlines offer a third option, business class, and now some have four classes.

Most passengers (including those flying on discount fares) travel *coach* class. On international flights, coach class is more often known as *economy class.* Large jets have several compartments for coach seating. Coach passengers may receive free soft drinks and sometimes free meals or snacks, but they usually must pay for alcoholic beverages. If movies are shown, coach passengers often pay for the use of headsets. The seating in coach has become steadily less comfortable as more and more U.S. flights feature fewer amenities and crowd more and more coach seats into the cabin.

The *first-class* section is located at the front of the plane and features more legroom and seats that are wider and, usually, more heavily padded than those in the coach compartment. First-class passengers receive personalized service, such as separate check-in desks and more flight attendants per passenger, as well as free alcoholic beverages and free headsets on flights with movies. Meals are elaborate, and passengers are offered more choices, often served on china with cloth napkins, rather than plastic and paper.

Business or *executive class* falls between first class and coach in the amenities. Drinks may be free and the seating is in a quieter area than the coach section; sometimes the seats are more comfortable and the meals better. Some airlines offer business class in addition to first class and coach; others substitute it for first class.

International flights often provide amenities beyond those we have described. For example, they may have onboard ATMs (so that passengers can exchange currencies), personal TVs, and even full-length beds (if passengers are willing to pay for them). Some airlines still offer smoking sections on international flights.

Aircraft Seating

The layout of the cabin has much to do with passenger comfort. Airline policies, not the manufacturer, determine seat space. Even when airlines use the same type of aircraft, seat space varies from flight to flight. It is determined by a combination of three factors: seat pitch, seat width, and configuration of the aircraft.

Pitch (often referred to as leg room) is the term for the front-to-rear spacing of seat rows. On U.S. domestic routes seat pitch in coach averages between 31 and 35 inches. The average pitch in first class is 40 inches, although in wide-bodied aircraft it may be as much as 57 to 60 inches. Seats are mounted on tracks in the floor, which the airline uses to adjust the spacing.

Seat width is the total side-to-side space at seat cushion or chest level. Like seat pitch, it is determined by airline policy, but it cannot be adjusted as easily as pitch.

The *configuration,* or layout, of seats in each row also influences comfort and the feeling of roominess. At any given width, seats installed in pairs provide the most comfortable arrangement; this configuration puts every passenger beside either an aisle or a window. If seats are installed in groups of three or more and the plane is full, then at least one passenger in each row is in a middle seat between two other passengers. Most jet aircraft have a seating configuration of three across; some may have two across. Wide-bodied planes may seat four or five across in the middle section.

In the first-class compartment, all seats should be equally comfortable. In

You are a meeting manager and must arrange air reservations for Mr. Kaplan, who is presenting his company's new products at a meeting in St. Thomas. Mr. Kaplan is arriving the day before his presentation on a close connection through San Juan. The travel counselor assures you that even if Mr. Kaplan misses his connection, he can always find more flights from San Juan to St. Thomas. What should you be concerned about?

Trying to persuade Mr. Kaplan to take an earlier flight is probably a good idea. That way, if his flight is very late or canceled, he still has a chance of salvaging his trip. You should also try to find a flight from San Juan with a longer connecting time. Then if he arrives on time to make an earlier connection, fine; if not, he still has a guaranteed seat.

Perhaps more important, even if Mr. Kaplan makes the connection, his baggage might not. The luggage from large jets is often delayed when connecting to small commuter flights. He should ship whatever he is using for his presentation to the hotel ahead of time. In this case, delayed luggage could be as bad as lost luggage.

coach, where people sit can make a difference, especially on flights of long duration such as Los Angeles to Sydney, Australia.

- Seats over the wings generally provide a smoother ride, but the view is obscured, and the area may be noisy because of the engines.
- Seats in emergency exit rows often have extra legroom because the pitch must provide access to the exit. For the same reason, seats in front of the exit row do not usually recline. (To sit in emergency exit rows, passengers must be physically capable and willing to perform emergency actions such as opening the exit door.)
- Aisle seats provide easy access to the bathrooms and a chance to stretch cramped legs.
- Bulkhead seats offer extra legroom, but they have no space below the seat to stow carry-on luggage. Often, bulkhead seats are reserved for families with babies and bassinets or for anyone with an onboard seeing eye dog.

Checked Baggage

Regulations on the baggage that can be taken without charge vary somewhat from airline to airline and even from flight to flight. In the past, it generally was assumed that passengers could check through two standard-size suitcases per person, but that is no longer the case. Many airlines now permit only one bag free of charge plus additional bags at a per-bag fee. Some airlines are even charging a fee for the first checked bag. Outside the United States, the standard limit is 20 kilos (44 pounds) and 60 pounds for first class.

There are also limits on the size and weight of baggage. Usually, no piece of luggage may weigh more than 50 pounds, and the largest piece should not measure more than 62 inches in total dimensions. To determine a case's total dimensions, add its length, height, and width. For example, if a suitcase's longest side measures 28 inches and it is 20 inches high and 5 inches deep, then the case's total dimensions are 53 inches.

All checked baggage must bear an identification tag on the outside giving the owner's name and address. It is advisable to put another tag inside the luggage in case the outside tag comes off. Checked bags can be opened and inspected by TSA security.

Domestic airlines now charge for checked bags. There are exceptions and the fees vary with different airlines. Check the airline's Web site in advance to be able to advise passengers about luggage fees and limitations. Airlines have found baggage fees an important revenue source, like selling meals and beverages on the aircraft. Moreover, airlines will assign an aisle or window seat for an extra fee—again, a new revenue source.

If passengers have unusual baggage, the airline should be alerted beforehand. If a person has more baggage than permitted, an extra fee is charged. The *excess baggage charge* varies from airline to airline but has been about $50 per extra bag. The amount of excess baggage permitted is limited, but a passenger is unlikely to reach that limit. Most airlines accept sporting equipment—such as bicycles, surfboards, skis, and golf clubs—for the same excess baggage charge, but always check the Web site of the airline concerned.

Other Services on Domestic Flights

Travelers who save money by flying on a budget airline may find that they must do without conveniences standard on most airlines. Their luggage may not be transferred automatically to other carriers; they may not be able to obtain a seat assignment; and they may fly into small airports with very limited connecting flights. But some budget airlines actually offer *more* service and better amenities than the major airlines, as Chapter 9 (on marketing) discusses.

Seat Assignments. Most airlines allow passengers to choose a seat when making a reservation, but there are important limitations. Sometimes passengers booked at discount fares cannot make advance seat selections, and some airlines do not allow seat assignments to be made more than 30 days in advance of the flight. If passengers have not selected a seat in advance, they may make a choice when they check in at the airport, but their desired seating may not be available at this late date.

No matter when a seat is selected, passengers may be disappointed with the results. Airlines reserve many seats for their frequent flyers and hold some seats to be assigned at the airport, so passengers might not be able to reserve a particular seat on a particular flight.

Assistance for People with Disabilities. Under the 1986 Air Carrier Access Act and the 1990 Americans with Disabilities Act, travelers with disabilities are guaranteed the same service and access as other travelers on domestic flights. Airport terminals, for example, must have telephones equipped with telecommunication devices for the deaf (TDDs) for those with hearing or speech impairments.

Wheelchairs are available for those who need them and must be requested in advance at the time of booking, along with passengers who want to take their own wheelchairs or who have other special needs. Also, they should ask for a wheelchair to meet their arriving flight.

Special Meals. Few meals are now offered on domestic U.S. flights. Passengers can bring their own food, and increasingly airlines are selling meals onboard. Depending on the airline, when meals are offered with a flight, travelers may be able to order children's meals, seafood platters, low-calorie meals, pasta dishes, or vegetarian and lacto-vegetarian (no dairy or egg products) meals. There are also meals to meet the medical restrictions for diabetics and the religious requirements for Hindus, Muslims, and Jews. Special meals must be ordered at least 12 to 24 hours in advance; extremely unusual meals should be ordered at least a week in advance. Many airport restaurants prepare boxed meals that travelers can buy to carry onboard.

Pets. Advance reservations are needed for pets. Some airlines will transport animals either in the passenger cabin or in the pressurized cargo hold. However, other airlines will not take pets or will limit pets in cargo to certain seasons. There is an extra charge for pets transported as cargo. Check with the specific airline about their pet policy.

Seeing Eye dogs are exempt from the rules forbidding large pets in the cabin. Passengers with Seeing Eye dogs should have bulkhead seats so that the animal has room to lie down.

Electronic Gadgets. Passengers who want to stay "wired" into their earthbound lives may use their own computers, cellular phones, or other electronic devices when a plane is at its cruising altitude. But electronic devices must be turned off while the plane is on a runway, while it is climbing, and while it is descending below 10,000 feet.

More and more planes are equipped with Wi-Fi, another source of revenue for the airlines Cell phones may be used only when the plane is on the ground before take-off and after landing.

Some airlines offer special electronic devices for entertainment. Again, check with the specific airline concerned as to what entertainment features are available on specific flights and whether they are complimentary or cost.

Airfares

■ WHAT ARE THE MOST IMPORTANT FACTORS DETERMINING THE COST OF AN AIRLINE TICKET?

To those new to air travel, nothing may be more bewildering than the fares. Two persons sitting next to each other in coach on a flight from Los Angeles to New York may be holding round-trip tickets, one at $399 and the other at $2,200. A 500-mile trip at noon tomorrow may cost $400; a 1,000-mile trip may cost $99.

Once upon a time, before deregulation, fares could be looked up in published lists called *tariffs*. Now the fares may change at any moment. A fare is guaranteed only when the ticket is purchased. Still, we can make some useful generalizations about airfares.

Domestic Fares

Some variations in domestic airfares are straightforward. The airlines set different fares for (1) different routes and (2) different classes of service. In addition, though, the airlines offer an ever-changing array of discounted fares. In fact, on average more than 80 percent of passengers fly on some sort of discount.

Routes and Classes of Service. The fare for a flight depends first of all on the route. In theory, the airlines charge the same fare for connecting as for direct flights—for example, for a one-way nonstop flight from New York to

Los Angeles and for a one-way flight from New York to Los Angeles with a connection in Chicago. In practice, however, discount fares on the nonstop flight would sell out first. Knowing this, the airline may set a lower fare on the flight with a connection.

The fare through a connecting point is called a *through fare* when it involves a connection between flights of the same airline. When the connection involves different airlines that have agreed on one published fare, that fare is called a *joint fare.*

If a passenger makes a stopover anywhere along the route, the situation changes. Fares from one stopover point to another are called *point-to-point fares,* and they are usually more expensive than through or joint fares. Thus, flying from Boston to Washington with a required connection at New York, the fare charged will be a through fare from Boston to Washington. But if the client wants to fly from Boston to New York with an overnight stay in New York and then fly on to Washington, the trip will involve point-to-point fares from Boston to New York and from New York to Washington.

Airfares also depend on the class of service selected. Coach fares are sometimes called *straight coach, normal,* or *straight Y fares* (because the code used for coach when booking a flight is *Y*). A client who arrives at the airport without a reservation and wishes to travel at the last moment will usually pay the straight coach fare. First-class fares (for which the primary code is *F*) may be only 10 to 20 percent higher than straight coach fares. Business-class fares (coded as *C*) may be 5 to 10 percent higher than straight coach fares.

Discounts for Selected Demographic Groups.
Variations in fares begin to get complicated once discounts are considered. Airlines may offer special fares to specific age groups or to people in specific situations. Each airline has its own rules and fare levels, but special discounts may be available to

- Seniors (with varying definitions; minimum age may be 62 or 65).
- Active members of the armed forces.
- The bereaved—that is, those attending funerals or traveling to be with close relatives who are seriously ill.
- Children.
  The fares and rules for children vary with the age of the child. They also vary from airline to airline.
- Children under the age of 2 are considered infants, and one infant per adult travels free on domestic flights. The infant is not guaranteed a seat, but airlines often try to assign an empty seat next to the parent, if available. To reserve a seat for an infant, parents pay the cost of a child's fare; some airlines have infant seats.
- Children 2 through 11 years old who fly with an adult may qualify for a fare discount.
  Unaccompanied children, however, are charged the adult fare plus a fee. If an unaccompanied child is taking a flight with a connection, a higher fee is charged because of the need for an escort between the flights. Children must be above a certain age (often, age 5) to be allowed to fly unaccompanied. When booking an unaccompanied chiuld, always check with the airline in question as to their procedures.

Promotional Fares.
Other discounts are even less predictable than those for specified groups. An airline may offer a lower fare known as a *promotional fare* or *discount fare* when it opens a new route; when it wants to promote travel between particular destinations during the off-season, if at

certain times of the day, or on certain days of the week; or when a competitor has offered a discount. For example, airlines usually offer promotional fares between the Northeast and Florida during the summer. A promotional fare may be only half the cost of a straight coach fare, or even less.

Promotional fares come with a variety of restrictions. For example, to obtain the promotional fare, passengers may be required to purchase the ticket several weeks in advance, and often they cannot take advantage of other discounts (such as children's fares). Table 4.7 describes some common types of restrictions on promotional fares; the details vary from airline to airline and change frequently.

Many of the restrictions on promotional fares exist simply to ensure that

CLOSE-UP: ON THE JOB WITH NADIA JONES, AIRPORT TICKET AGENT

For two years Nadia Jones has worked as an airport ticket agent at a large regional airline. Here is how she describes her job.

"Although many of my days have become routine, I never lose the excitement of coming to the airport every day. Hearing the planes overhead as I am driving in and just being there dealing with person after person flying to places far off—it gives me a thrill every day.

"I work the ticket counter, so I'm the first person from the airline that most travelers deal with face-to-face. The pilots, reservationists, accountants, baggage handlers, mechanics—the many, many behind-the-scenes employees all depend on us to present a good image to the public and give good customer service.

"Most of my job consists of checking in and tagging luggage, checking tickets, issuing tickets to those who don't have them, writing down the gate number for the traveler, checking that the customer's ID matches the ticket before going to airport security, and answering questions.

"I learned that good customer service is more than just the technical functions of the job. We need to smile at each traveler, use their names when we can, make eye contact, and be ready to be extra helpful if they have special needs. Sometimes we can notice or anticipate customers' needs before they even ask.

"So it sounds pretty routine—until flight delays occur. Then the entire job changes. You can feel the mood in the crowd change. Actually, 99 percent of the travelers are understanding, but there is usually at least one who gets somewhat nasty when things aren't going right. And there isn't a darn thing we can do.

"Once we had to cancel the last flight out because a fog rolled in and practically closed the airport. There wasn't much we could do except send everyone home or suggest hotel space. 'Well, I'm sorry that you just have to be there early tomorrow morning, but you should have left yourself more leeway in planning' is what I'm thinking of telling a traveler who just stands there not believing that he can't go. But I just calmly explain the situation again and try to be as helpful as possible without being too apologetic.

"Of course, other times it's a mechanical delay, which theoretically is our fault—though it happens to all airlines. We try to keep travelers aware of exactly what is happening with the flights. We had a special seminar on 'giving people the bad news' as soon as possible and keeping them informed of changes. People hate 'no news' more than 'bad news.'

"What is really tough, though, is then trying to reroute them on other flights when one flight is canceled. Of course, the next flight out is already almost full. And we have to put them on a standby list, with no guarantee they'll get on that next flight—it's that uncertainty again that people don't like. I'm almost surprised how well most people take it.

"I got this job starting with a group interview. There were about twenty people there. I knew from my travel classes that they look for assertive, friendly, and communicative people, so I spoke up as soon as I could.

"They called me back for a personal interview, and I was conditionally hired to start training. Training was fun but intensive. They gave us a list of city codes to have memorized before we started training. The test was on the second morning. My roommate said she only missed one code. She was sent home; she was history as far as the airline was concerned.

"I was a little scared when I faced my first travelers at the counter, but I was assisting another agent and eased into it. On the first day I was taking care of many of the passengers on my own already. And now I get that thrill of heading out to the airport every day."

discount-fare passengers travel when the airline would otherwise have empty seats. For example, promotional fares on shuttle flights between New York and Boston, which primarily serve business travelers, may be available on weekends but not on weekdays, when the flights are likely to be full without the lure of discounts. In effect, passengers who travel at the full fare are paying for the freedom of flying without such restrictions.

Airlines usually introduce promotional fares with no warning to travel agencies and implement them as speedily as possible. Sometimes, travelers hear about a new fare before travel counselors or even the airline's own reservations agents are aware of it.

Some promotional fares are available only if passengers book tickets on the Internet. These online purchases save the airlines money because they bypass the airlines' phone reservationists, travel agencies, and GDS fees. Airlines periodically offer reduced fares on the Internet in order to encourage clients to buy online.

The Whys of Airfares

Is there some logic to the bewildering array of fares and discounts? Sometimes, airlines offer discount fares to attract new clients for future travel or to generate a quick increase in sales in order to meet cash commitments.

TABLE 4.7 Restrictions on Promotional Fares

Minimum/maximum stay. Many promotional fares are round-trip fares and require the traveler to stay a minimum amount of time at the destination, such as a Saturday night; some set a maximum stay, such as 30 days. Thus a traveler might depart on a Sunday and return the following Sunday or depart on a Saturday and return the next day. One-way discounts are not governed by this rule. (Most round-trip fares can be used on open-jaw itineraries or circle trips; the fare is then calculated by taking half of each of the round-trip fares.)

Advanced booking. The reservation must be made in advance, such as 7 or 14 days before departure.

Advanced ticketing. The ticket must be paid for in advance. Often, it must be paid within 24 hours of making the reservation, but the restriction may specify a certain number of days before the flight. Some fares required instant ticketing and are capacity-controlled.

Cancellation and change fees. Promotional fares are nonrefundable, and a fee is charged for changes. The fee may be anywhere from 100 percent of the fare to cancel a reservation to $50 to change it. If the ticket is changed, there will be an additional charge if the fare has been increased or if the old fare no longer exists. (Nondiscounted fares are usually fully refundable for a year or longer.)

Effective dates of fare sale. Fare sales are often advertised suddenly and are then good only for a short time, such as 2 weeks. Tickets must be purchased within that time, but sometimes the time limit is extended at the last minute. Generally, other restrictions apply to the date of travel (see next item).

Effective dates of travel. A fare may be good only for travel within certain calendar dates. Usually, travel must start and end within these time limits. For example, tickets bought in a fare sale that is in effect only between September 1 and September 14 may require that travel occur between September 15 and December 15.

Blackout dates. Many discounts do not apply during busy travel periods such as holidays. Thus many promotional fares will be "blacked out" certain days of the week on the day preceding and the Sunday after Thanksgiving, around Christmas, or even around school holidays such as Presidents' Day. Careful planning may find holes in blackout times; for example, December 25 is often not blacked out.

Capacity control (Inventory control). Only a certain percentage of seats (a percentage known to the airline) is offered at the discount fare. Even though a fare is not blacked out, it may be sold out because of high demand or because only a small number of discounted seats were available in the first place. (Some controversy exists as to how many seats a carrier must make available when advertising such a discount fare.)

No interlining. On many discount fares the itinerary must use only one carrier or partner carrier.

Discount levels. Fares may be slightly higher or lower on different days of the week (for domestic flights, cheaper days generally are Tuesday, Wednesday, and Saturday) or even at different times of the day. These restrictions can vary greatly.

Routing. Some promotional fares require stopovers; others require that travelers fly direct.

More generally, airline fares reflect the same simple goal that drives prices in similar businesses. They aim to sell the most they can at the highest possible price, which may be limited by competition or concerns about the effects of the price on consumer behavior. For the airlines, this strategy translates in its simplest terms to "Let's try to fill the planes up as much as possible at the highest possible fares."

At a more sophisticated level, the airlines' fare structure, including promotional fares, can be explained as a strategy of *yield management*. *Yield* is the average amount of revenue earned per passenger mile; it is computed by dividing total passenger revenue by the total number of passenger miles flown. The airlines' fare structure is an effort to manage the yield in a way that produces the most revenue. To achieve this aim, the airline may need to offer promotional fares in order to increase the passenger load (the percentage of available seats on a flight that is actually sold).

Thus the promotional fare is the airlines' version of a sale. But unlike many businesses, airlines cannot wait to put their product on sale after it fails to sell at a high price. If they wait, it will be too late, because each seat on each flight is *perishable;* that is, if a seat remains empty for a particular flight, that revenue is lost forever. The opportunity to sell a seat on that flight occurs only once.

Successful promotional fares rely heavily on the airlines' ability to predict which flights would have a large number of unsold seats at the regular fare. Airlines can adjust the frequency of flights and the size of aircraft to match broad seasonal changes, but they cannot make these changes from day to day. They cannot fly a large plane one day and a small one the next. The restrictions on promotional fares represent an attempt to direct discount-fare-buying passengers to flights that might otherwise remain unsold and thus to avoid diluting revenue from full-fare passengers. The rules may be bizarre and complicated, but they reflect an effort to achieve the rather simple goal of increasing revenue.

Frequent-Flyer Programs

Bonus programs that reward consistent patronage are another technique for increasing revenue over the long haul. Although each airline has a different name for its bonus program, these programs are known generally as *frequent-flyer plans.* For example, after traveling 40,000 miles on an airline, a client might be rewarded with a free unrestricted domestic ticket; 10,000 miles might earn a free upgrade from coach to first class.

All frequent-flyer plans generally work the same way. The traveler signs up with an airline and then makes sure that the mileage for each flight is credited to his or her account. Depending on the plan, this means that the traveler might be required to put a sticker on each flight coupon, submit a certificate at the gate, show a membership card, or (most commonly) provide a number when making a reservation or checking in. The airline records the mileage on the participant's account and sends the participant periodic summaries of accumulated credits.

Frequent-flyer programs have become so popular that businesses of all kinds have established tie-ins with the programs. Airlines have formed partnerships with hotel chains, car rental companies, credit card companies, online shopping companies, and telephone companies. These partnerships allow frequent-flyer members to earn so-called air miles by buying these services or to cash in their air miles for these services. For example, members of one frequent-flyer program can cash in 10,000 to 12,000 air miles for a three-day car rental with any of several car rental companies, and they can earn air miles by taking a cruise, obtaining a mortgage, or buying a specialty cake with one of the airline's mileage partners.

Some people use a bank credit card that has a tie-in with an airline—for example, the Chase Bank credit card with United. They then try to put as many of their monthly expenditures as possible on that specific card, from groceries to college tuition, in an effort to build their mileage points even though they haven't actually flown anywhere that month.

To some extent, frequent-flyer programs have become victims of their own success. They are costly to operate, and they no longer give a competitive edge because every major airline has one. Most frequent-flyer members today belong to several frequent-flyer plans, and they collect miles on whatever airline they can.

Flights are capacity controlled as to the number of travelers on board who are flying on frequent flyer miles that day. Therefore, many travelers are often disillusioned when they wish to use their earned miles and find that it may take many, many months for them to be able to get the desired seat to fly to the destinations of their choice.

Domestic Taxes and Surcharges

Often, an airline's advertisement might say, for instance, "The fare is $398 plus tax," instead of noting that the fare is $438.73 including all taxes and service charges. Airline fares are subject to a number of taxes and surcharges. Although a computer can calculate the total cost, sales agents should understand the basic taxes. Current taxes on domestic flights include (1) a federal transportation tax, (2) a segment tax, (3) an airport passenger facility charge at some airports, and (4) a security fee.

The federal transportation tax is known as the *U.S. ticket tax*. It is charged on tickets purchased within the United States when air travel meets one of the following conditions: it is (1) within the continental United States or (2) within the states of Alaska and Hawaii or (3) between the continental United States and a 225-mile *buffer zone* that extends from the U.S. border into Canada and Mexico or (4) within this buffer zone, which is shown in Figure 4.4 on the next page.

For flights from the continental United States to Alaska or Hawaii, travelers pay only a portion of the U.S. ticket tax based on the percentage of the flight that occurs across the continental United States and Alaska or Hawaii. (Travelers to Alaska and Hawaii are also assessed the U.S. international travel facilities tax.)

The *segment tax* is charged for each takeoff and landing. This tax has been increasing yearly since its inception in 1997.

A *passenger facility charge (PFC)* is levied at almost all U.S. airports. The FAA allows airports to collect this surcharge for airport improvements. Up to two PFCs may be charged on each portion of an itinerary. Thus, on a one-way flight, up to two PFCs may be charged, but on a nonstop flight, only one PFC would be charged. Up to four PFCs may be charged for round-trip itineraries.

The *security fee* was established in 2001 to pay for increased security measures.

Airlines also add fuel surcharges at times when the price of oil increases, but those are considered part of the fare.

International Airfares

Like U.S. domestic fares, international airfares vary with the class of service, the time, the day of the week, and the season. As in the case of domestic travel, some discounts are available on international fares for travelers who can meet certain restrictions.

In other important ways, international airfares are very different from domestic fares. They are based on agreements between governments and, broadly speaking, are set by one of two systems:

- A *routing system,* in which the fare depends on the specific route flown.

FIGURE 4.4 Buffer Zone

Notice that the only large Canadian city outside the buffer zone is Edmonton, Alberta. The only large Mexican city within the buffer zone is Monterrey. Thus international taxes apply to airline tickets from the United States to Edmonton and domestic taxes apply to airline tickets from the United States to Monterrey.

- A *mileage system,* in which the fare generally depends on (1) the origin, (2) the farthest point on the trip, and (3) the number of miles flown.

Fares based on the routing system are much simpler than those based on mileage, and we begin with them.

Fares Based on Routing. When an international fare is based on the route, the traveler must go to specific connecting or stopover cities. For example, a fare may be cited for a flight from New York to Nice, France, with a connection in Paris.

Most international discount fares use the routing system and feature many of the same restrictions as domestic discount fares. The lowest fares to Europe generally allow no stopovers, but discount fares to Asian and South Pacific destinations may allow stopovers. The most frequently used discount fare for international travel is called the *APEX fare* (for advance purchase excursion).

Fares Based on Mileage. Most economy, first-class, and business-class fares apply the mileage system, which ties the fare to the number of miles flown. Basically, when the mileage system is used, the fare depends first on the through fare for a flight from the origin to the farthest point of the trip, which is called the *destination city.* Stopovers are usually allowed. The through fare between the origin and the destination city is charged unless either of two qualifications applies.

1. If passengers wish to make stops that bring the trip over a certain allotted number of miles, called the *maximum permitted miles (MPM),* they pay the through fare plus a surcharge. For every pair of cities around the world for which international fares are published, IATA has established an MPM, which is greater than the nonstop mileage between the cities. As long as passengers stay within this allotment, stopovers do not usually add to the fare.

2. If a fare between two cities on an itinerary is higher than the through fare between the origin and the destination city, passengers pay the higher fare. A nearer but more expensive city on the itinerary is called a *higher intermediate point (HIP).* In other words, the passenger must be charged the highest fare between any two cities on the itinerary.

These two qualifications are just the most basic of the detailed, complicated rules called *construction principles* that are used in calculating mileage-based fares. In practice, travel counselors and reservationists make only limited use of these principles. For simple round-trips without stopovers, GDSs identify the best fare. Knowledge of the construction principles is mainly needed for itineraries that include a series of stops in different countries. But even for these, help is available from GDSs and from *rate desks,* a part of an airline or travel agency staffed by specialists in international airfares.

Airline Rate Desks. An airline rate desk will calculate the fare for any itinerary if the passenger begins the trip with its airline or takes the first substantial international flight with it—provided the passenger has made a reservation. Rate desks have another limitation: they may take 24 hours or more to quote the fare for a complex itinerary. Thus if a client asks for an approximate fare before deciding on a trip, the travel counselor must be able to give at least a fairly accurate quotation. Rate desk quotes are often prevalent for group tour operators. Rate desk quotes may not be available in the GDS—only by fax, phone, or e-mail.

Each fare calculation provided by a rate agent bears an identifying number, which the travel counselor or airline ticketing agent should enter on the ticket. This number helps to guarantee the fare if it is ever challenged. For this reason, any complex fare should be checked with the airline rate desk and a rate number obtained. Agents at airport ticket counters have been known to require additional payments from passengers whose tickets lacked a rate number.

Neutral Units of Construction (NUCs).

If a traveler is flying from Chicago to Frankfurt to Athens, what currency would be used to calculate the fare? Under the system established by IATA, international airfares are cited in two ways: (1) in the currency used by the country where the trip begins and (2) in special counting units called *neutral units of construction*, or *NUCs*.

IATA set the value of one NUC as being equal in value to one U.S. dollar. Four times a year, IATA publishes a *rate of exchange (ROE)* for other currencies around the world. Multiplying the fare in NUCs by the ROE for a currency gives the fare in that currency. For example, if a fare is cited as 976 NUCs and the current ROE for the euro is 0.9, then the fare amounts to 878.4 euros. As currencies change in value in relation to one another, this system keeps fares in balance so that people do not buy tickets with weak currencies in those countries.

Taxes and Surcharges.

Taxes and fees add to the cost of international flights and can be considerable. For flights to or from the United States, possible taxes and fees include the following:

- The U.S. international *departure tax* on individuals flying out of the United States or any of its possessions.
- The U.S. international *arrival tax* on individuals flying into the United States or any of its possessions.
- The passenger facility charge levied by certain U.S. airports.
- The U.S. security fee.
- International departure taxes levied by many other governments. They usually collect the tax at the airport before the departing flight, and often it must be paid in the local currency. Occasionally, the ticket includes this tax.

Consolidators and Other Sources of Discounts

For international travelers looking for low fares, consolidators may be the answer to their prayers. *Consolidators* are distribution companies that negotiate with airlines to buy seats on international flights at bargain rates and then sell the tickets to consumers, either directly or through travel agencies. They are called *bucket shops* in Britain. Their agreements with airlines allow consolidators to offer international tickets for substantially less than normal discount fares. Their fares often appear in tiny newspaper ads that show a list of cities with fares but no airline names.

Evaluating Consolidators.

For the airlines, consolidators offer the guaranteed sale of large blocks of seats or a way of selling at the last minute seats that would otherwise go unsold—without officially lowering their fares. The airline sets aside a portion of its inventory of seats to be available only to the consolidator. It makes a specific agreement with the consolidator to sell the seats at a reduced price but does not lower its fares across the board. The airline may also allow the consolidator to bypass some restrictions on discounted fares, such as requirements for advance booking.

For the traveler, consolidators offer low fares, sometimes on short notice. But even when travelers buy tickets from consolidators through travel agencies, using a consolidator has drawbacks. In particular, when a ticket is sold through a consolidator,

- Severe penalties may apply for any changes in travel plans.
- Routings may be unusual and time-consuming, requiring several connections.
- Travelers may be required to use an airline with which they are not familiar.
- Frequent-flyer plans may not be offered or may not apply.
- Seat assignments may not be possible until the day of the flight.
- Funds paid for flights may be tied up or lost altogether if the consolidator goes out of business.
- Travel insurance offered by the traveler's credit card company may not apply.
- A fee may be charged for using a credit card.
- The ticket may be totally non-refundable and non-changeable.

Rules change and vary among consolidators; check the conditions of purchase each time with a consolidator, and travel insurance is important.

For travel agencies, consolidators represent an opportunity. By using consolidators, travel agencies can serve clients who might otherwise find international travel too expensive, and the results can be profitable. Some consolidators pay commissions to travel agencies; in some cases the consolidator quotes the agency a net rate with no commission, and the agency sets its own markup on the ticket instead of receiving a commission. Also, travel agencies can negotiate with an airline to become consolidators themselves.

Obviously, consolidators should not be used blindly; nor should they be rejected out-of-hand. Travel counselors should be sure that

- The consolidator is reputable and reliable.
- The consolidator's ticket meets the client's needs.
- The client understands the advantages and disadvantages of purchasing a ticket through a consolidator.

Charters. Whereas consolidators purchase seats on scheduled flights, *charter* companies own or lease entire planes and then sell seats to the public or to tour operators. Consolidators have reduced the market for charters, but hosted tours (discussed in Chapter 8) often use charters. Some tour operators charter and fill entire planes weekly to popular destinations such as the Caribbean, Hawaii, and Mexico, packaging the cost of the charter flight into the total tour package rate for opaque pricing.

Charters offer reasonable prices and direct flights to destinations that require connecting flights on regular scheduled service. But charters also bring many of the same disadvantages as consolidators, plus the following:

- Because charters are sold with the goal of filling every seat, some may be more crowded or provide less service than other flights. (Others provide superior service.)
- Charters generally provide little flexibility in schedule. They may offer only weekly flights; travelers cannot extend their stay for a day or two.
- Because charter tickets are not accepted by scheduled airlines, a passenger who must change plans during the trip usually has no options.
- Any delays may be prolonged because replacement aircraft may not be available and because scheduled flights are usually cleared to take off first after delays caused by weather.

ON THE SPOT

Jose and Maria Ortiz and their ten-year-old son want to fly to Spain this summer. Jose, a contractor who often books business trips with your agency, has seen a bargain airfare to Spain advertised in the newspaper. After some research, you have found that you can get this fare through a very reliable consolidator that your agency has used for years. The consolidator will guarantee the arrival and departure dates but cannot specify the airline and schedule yet. You have also found that you can reserve a nonstop flight to Spain directly from the airline; it will cost $175 more per adult and $75 more for the child than the tickets from the consolidator. When the Ortiz family comes in this afternoon, what will you say to them?

First, check all the details that surround the consolidator's tickets. For example, what connections are required? Will frequent-flyer mileage be awarded? Are advance seat assignments possible?

Be prepared to compare the two trips for the Ortiz family, contrasting not only the monetary costs but also any costs in convenience and peace of mind. Be sure Mr. and Mrs. Ortiz understand what the consolidator does, and explain any benefits of the more expensive nonstop flight. For example, they will know the carrier, can check the frequent-flyer programs it is associated with, and can be sure that the family will sit together on the flight. Also, if they must change their plans, the consolidator's tickets might be difficult or more costly to change. Is it worth paying extra for peace of mind and a guarantee of the most convenient flights?

Let the Ortiz family make the decision, but lead in the direction you think is best.

Fare Sales. Bargain hunters have yet another option for low international fares: Internet sales by the airlines. Some airlines post special low international fares on the Internet just as they do for domestic tickets. Generally, these extra-low fares are available for only a limited number of tickets, to specific destinations, on short notice, and for brief stays.

✔ CHECK-UP

A passenger's fare is affected by
✔ The route taken.
✔ The class of service selected.
✔ Whether the passenger qualifies for a discount based on his or her age or special situation.
✔ Whether the passenger can accept restrictions that permit a promotional fare.

Among the major restrictions on promotional fares are
✔ Minimum stay.
✔ Advance booking and ticketing.
✔ Lack of refundability.
✔ Effective dates.
✔ Limited availability in the booking inventory.
✔ Routing.

Federal taxes on domestic air travel include
✔ The U.S. ticket tax.
✔ The segment tax.

✔ The airport passenger facility charge (PFC).
✔ The U.S. security fee.

Taxes that apply only to international flights include
✔ The U.S. international departure tax for individuals flying out of the United States.
✔ The U.S. international arrival tax for individuals flying into the United States.
✔ The U.S. Customs fee, immigration (INS) fee, and animal and plant health inspection service fee.
✔ International departure taxes levied by the governments of other countries.

Sources for low fares for international flights include
✔ Traditional discount fares from the airlines, such as APEX, which usually are based on the routing system.
✔ Consolidators.
✔ Charters.
✔ Internet-only fares offered by airlines.

Selling Air Travel: Policies and Challenges

■ WHAT ARE THE KEY POLICIES AND CHALLENGES RELATED TO AIR TRAVEL?

For decades, some writers have been predicting that automation would make people redundant in the selling of air travel. As we discussed in Chapter 3, travelers can now find detailed information about the availability of flights online by themselves and buy those flights without talking to anyone. But flights are still sold with the help of travel counselors or reservations agents. Salespeople are far from obsolete.

What do these people do? Their job is to
■ Listen carefully to the customer.
■ Gather all relevant information concerning travelers and their needs. (The Close-Up on selling looks at this step in more detail.)
■ Determine the best schedules and fares for the client.
■ Close the sale, booking the flight and determining whether any additional services are needed.
■ Provide the client with the documents and information needed to make the journey as smooth as possible.

In this section we introduce some of the procedures and policies that travel professionals must understand in order to carry out these tasks.

Finding a Flight

Finding the schedule and fare that match a client's needs best is the most important service provided by the sales agent. A study by the Public Interest Research Group dramatized the difference that good travel sellers can make. When travel counselors in the Boston area were asked to find the lowest fare available for twenty-three trips all over the country, no two counselors came up with the same fares. The highest fares quoted were often more than twice the cost of the lowest ones.

Using a GDS, sales agents can search out airfares by giving the GDS the command to show all fares for all airlines or fares for a particular airline; they might even use software that automatically searches multiple GDSs and the Internet for the lowest possible and lowest available fares. They can also use the Internet, just as the general public can, to check for low fares offered only online by the airlines, discounters, or auction houses. But sales agents must still interpret the results and explain the advantages and disadvantages of each fare to their clients.

Making a Reservation

In order to make a reservation, the sales agent needs to know
- The full, legal names and titles of all travelers, matching the names on their travel IDs.
- The ages of any children or senior citizens.
- The address and work or home phone number of at least one traveler.
- The departure and return dates and the origin and destination cities.
- The class of service desired.
- The form of payment for the tickets.

To make the reservation, the sales agent enters into the computer a *PNR,* or *passenger name record,* which is the complete record of a reservation stored by the airline's reservation system. (Multiple passengers may be on the same PNR if their itineraries are exactly the same.) The *mandatory fields,* or required parts, of a PNR are the following:
- **Phone number** of the passenger(s), including the area code.
- **Record** of the person requesting the reservation.
- **Itinerary,** with complete information on the travel segments booked. (The travel segment may be not only a flight but also a car rental, hotel, tour, and so on.)
- **Name** of the passenger(s) exactly as it appears on the ID.
- **Ticketing** arrangements, such as the date by which the passenger must pay for the ticket. (Discount fares may require almost immediate payment, but for some fares clients may wait to buy the ticket up to an hour before flight time.)

You might remember these fields by the first letter in each name, which spells *PRINT.* But the computer arranges the fields in the order *NIPTR.*

The itinerary field of the PNR in the computer includes the following information in the following order:
- Airline name.
- Flight number.
- Class of service.

- Date of departure.
- Departure city/airport.
- Destination city/airport.
- Number of seats.

For each PNR, the computer assigns a *record locator number,* a combination of six numbers or letters that is used to retrieve the PNR. But if a traveler forgets his or her record locator number, the PNR can also be retrieved by using the traveler's name and flight number or date of flight.

CLOSE-UP: SELLING BY IDENTIFYING NEEDS

One key to success in selling is the ability to size up a client's needs by asking the right questions. If you are selling air travel, what are those questions?

In order to search for a schedule to meet a client's needs, you need to know
- The number of persons traveling.
- The destination.
- The preferred dates of departure and return.
- The desired class of service. A client who is leaning toward an unrestricted coach fare is a good candidate for being upgraded to business or first class because the difference in prices for these classes of service is usually relatively small.

To find the lowest fare for the client, you also need to know the ages of any children who are traveling, and you might ask questions such as the following:
- Do you have any flexibility in your departure or arrival date in case fares are lower on those dates?
- Can you return on Sunday instead of Saturday? Or can you leave on Saturday instead of Sunday?
- Do you need a nonstop, or would you be willing to take a connection if one is available at a lower fare?
- Can you leave earlier in the day? Later? On a different airline?

Knowing when, how, and to whom to ask these questions takes some experience and judgment. Asking these questions of many business travelers might be a waste of your time and theirs. Asking these questions of a student trying to get home for the holidays may be absolutely necessary.

With repeat clients, you might also ask whether they have access to e-mail and the Internet. If so, you might tell them about how to receive postings of special fares.

In addition, you should ask
- Whether the client has a seating preference. Although this information is optional, asking for it is a standard service. Ask whether the client prefers an aisle or a window seat (no one prefers a middle seat). If two

clients are flying, give one the preferred seat and the other the middle seat. If three are flying, assign them three seats across if possible.
- Whether the client will need a car rental, hotel room, and other auxiliary services.

Other services that you might suggest in appropriate situations include
- Assistance for those with disabilities
- Special meals.
- Reservations for pets.
- Airport transfers.
- A tour package.
- Travel insurance.

For international travel, travel sellers must consider additional needs, as discussed in Chapter 2. Here is a checklist of basic questions regarding each overseas destination.
- Is a visa required? How much is the fee? How long is the visa valid and for how many entries?
- Are financial data required in order to enter the country? Must the traveler have an onward or return ticket?
- Are immunizations or a certificate that the traveler is free of HIV required?
- What are the currency regulations?
- What are the restrictions on imports and exports?
- Is there a departure tax? (The traveler should be sure to have enough cash in the local currency to pay it.)
- Is the airline or airport known for any particular problems?
- Is the reservation confirmed in writing?

In addition, the International Society of Travel Medicine recommends that travel counselors should
- Inform travelers of immunizations required for entry into a country and advise them to seek expert advice regarding recommended immunizations.
- Warn clients if there is a risk of malaria at a destination.
- Advise clients to consult a health care provider or an expert in travel medicine. They may need information about food and beverage precautions and protection against insect bites, for example.
- Be able to discuss the availability of travelers' health insurance policies.

Flights are said to be **confirmed** when they are reserved. In fact, the airline must respond in order to confirm the flight, but this usually occurs instantaneously. When the airline's computer does not respond instantaneously, the flight is said to be *on request*.

If space is not available on a particular flight, clients may choose to be **waitlisted**, which means that they are on a list of people seeking a sold-out service. As other people cancel, waitlisted clients are confirmed in the order in which their reservations were received. Waitlisted clients usually reserve another flight in case the first flight is never confirmed. Waitlisting is seldom allowed on discount fares.

A person without a confirmed reservation is referred to as "waitlisted" only until the day of the flight; once at the airport, a person who was waitlisted is called a **standby** or is said to be flying *space available*. That person may get on the flight because of **no-shows**—people who do not cancel or change their reservation but who, nevertheless, do not appear for the flight.

Tickets and Boarding Passes

After reservations are made and paid for, sales agents issue the ticket as an electronic ticket. An **electronic ticket** (or e-ticket) exists only as a computer record; the information is stored in the computer but not printed on a conventional ticket. The "ticketless travel" provided by electronic tickets saves money for the airlines and saves passengers from worrying about lost, forgotten, or stolen tickets. A passenger with an electronic ticket is given a record locator number and a printed itinerary or confirmation, as well as a receipt if the ticket is purchased at a travel agency.

Most travelers now use electronic tickets, and many airlines charge fees as high as $50 for paper tickets. But a few passengers still prefer to have a conventional **paper ticket** in hand, particularly for international travel and to less-developed areas. Having the conventional ticket does save time if passengers must change airlines at the airport. As this is written, if passengers with e-tickets need to change airlines, they usually must first go to the original airline's counter in order to obtain a paper ticket or voucher to present to the new airline.

The airline ticket provides

- Authorization to travel.
- Evidence of payment.
- An accounting link between the distributor and the airline (discussed in Chapter 13).
- Acceptance of the contract between the airline and the passenger. When people purchase air tickets, they enter into a contract and accept the airline's terms and conditions for transporting them and their baggage.

But a ticket does not allow a passenger on a flight; a **boarding pass** does. Travelers obtain a boarding pass at the airport ticket counter, at curbside check-in from skycaps, or at e-ticket counters, which are self-check-in kiosks. An increasing number of airlines are also allowing online check-in: travelers can check in for their flights online 60 minutes to 36 hours prior to departure and print their boarding passes from their own computers or store the boarding pass on their phone. For international flights, which require passport verification, the boarding pass is at the airline check-in desk.

A boarding pass is usually required to pass through security, although the TSA is considering a revision to this policy. Agents at the gate can change seat assignments and reissue boarding passes as needed.

Passengers' Rights and Responsibilities

In the ideal situation, clients have their tickets and seat assignments before reaching the airport. If they have only carry-on luggage, they arrive at the airport, check a monitor for the gate assignment of the flight, obtain their boarding pass, go through security, and board the plane. Passengers with luggage check it at the airline's ticket counter or with the skycap outside, if permitted. Clients who do not have a ticket or who wish to change anything about their tickets must wait in line at the ticket counter.

Reality, of course, is often more complicated. What is the liability of the airline when things go wrong? When does it owe the traveler some type of compensation? The answers depend in part on the contract that the traveler has with the airline.

The Ticket as Contract. Each airline has its own contract. The airline ticket does not include an actual copy of the terms of the contract but is available online. The standard ticket printout only identifies the important issues covered in the contract.

Issues covered in the contract include the airline's liability for personal injury and death; restrictions and procedures for filing claims; the right of the airline to change the terms of the contract without advance notice; the airline's rights and liabilities for delays, schedule changes, reroutings, or failure to operate; the limitation of liability for lost or damaged baggage; and the availability of excess valuation insurance. Here we discuss a few of the issues that frequently affect travelers.

Airline Default. Serious problems may arise even before a flight if an airline files for bankruptcy and ceases operations, leaving travelers with useless tickets and travel agencies with unhappy customers. Travelers may seek recompense in the bankruptcy courts. If they paid for the tickets by credit card, many credit card companies will protect them, ensuring that they do not pay for services not received. Also, some travel insurance policies cover defaults; these policies are discussed in Chapter 11.

Check-In Times. Passengers sometimes cause problems themselves by ignoring check-in times. After September 2001 passengers on domestic flights were told to be at the airport 2 hours before their flights, but check-in times may be changed at any time. In practice, the airlines hold clients' seats until 15 to 20 minutes before flight time; then they may release seats to standby passengers, and late passengers lose their rights to their reserved seats. The airlines will try to get full-fare passengers aboard confirmed flights. But if they cannot seat late arrivals, those travelers are put on the next available flight of that same airline.

Check-in times are longer for international flights. Even before the 2001 terrorist attacks, international passengers were usually told to check in 1 1/2 to 2 hours before flight time, but check-in times now are usually 3 hours, particularly because of lengthy security check-in times.

Overbooking and Bumping. Having a ticket is no guarantee that it will be honored. Airlines often *overbook* their flights; in other words, they sell more tickets than there are seats in order to compensate for no-shows. (Ticket contracts announce that they do so.)

Generally, the number of no-shows equals or exceeds the number of overbooked passengers, and everyone gets on the plane. But occasionally the number of confirmed passengers who show up for a flight exceeds the number of seats. At that point, the flight is said to be *oversold*. The gate agents then ask for volunteers who will give up their seats on the flight in return for both (1) passage on the next flight and (2) either a free ticket in the future or a voucher for varying amounts of money to be applied against the cost of a future ticket.

Occasionally, even the offer of free tickets does not produce enough volunteers to make up for overbooking. As a result, some confirmed passengers cannot get on the flight; they are said to be *bumped*. For every 10,000 passengers on U.S. airlines, one is likely to be bumped.

If the airline cannot get a bumped passenger to his or her destination within 1 hour of the originally scheduled time, the person is entitled to *denied boarding compensation*. The amount of compensation depends on how much the ticket cost and on how quickly the airline can deliver the passenger to the destination. The amount also depends on the airline and on whether the flight is domestic or international.

Each airline has its own policy, but generally, for U.S. domestic flights,

- If the scheduled arrival is more than 1 hour but less than 2 hours later than the original arrival time, the bumped passenger must be paid the face value of the ticket, up to a maximum of $200.
- If the scheduled arrival is more than 2 hours later, the compensation doubles, to a maximum of $400.

For international flights, different rules specify how much compensation is due for involuntary bumping, and they vary from country to country. Each airline's policy regarding denied boarding compensation can be found in the "Contract of Carriage" section of its Web site.

Cancellations and Delays. Note that flight cancellations due to weather or mechanical difficulties do not constitute bumping. Airlines are not required to compensate customers for cancellations and delays. They do try to rebook passengers from canceled flights as soon as possible. Sometimes airlines pay for a passenger's hotel room when a flight delay strands a passenger overnight, but they are not required to do so.

Unfortunately, flight cancellations and delays are far from rare. Flights are counted as being "on time" if they operate less than 15 minutes after their scheduled time. Most GDSs show how often a particular flight has been delayed during the most recent reported month; the Web site of the U.S. Department of Transportation's Aviation Consumer Department also offers information about on-time performance.

Liability for Baggage. Lost or damaged baggage continues to be a problem. Passengers should report baggage problems immediately to the office in the airport's baggage claim area. The airline will not assume liability for damage to bags that the passenger carried onboard or for damage to checked luggage caused by the passenger (for example, by overstuffing bags or packing fragile items improperly).

If luggage seems to be lost, the traveler fills out a form, presents the ticket and baggage claim check, and describes the luggage and its contents. At the discretion of the airline's airport station manager, a small cash advance may be offered to allow the passenger to buy emergency articles until the baggage is found. Any cash advance is deducted from the final liability settlement.

In fact, the vast majority of bags reported lost are only delayed and are delivered the same day or the next day. If the luggage is located, it is delivered to the passenger's home or destination as soon as possible. Most major airlines allow 3 to 5 days to trace lost baggage; then the luggage is officially declared to be lost. At that time the passenger submits a claim, which is forwarded to the carrier's central office. Most claims are settled within 6 weeks to 3 months.

The airline makes its own assessment of the depreciated value of lost or damaged luggage. For domestic flights, the airline can invoke a ceiling of $3,300 per fare-paying passenger on the amount it will pay for lost or damaged luggage. If the value of luggage and its contents exceeds this limit, the passenger may want to declare a higher valuation when checking the baggage and pay an additional charge. But the airline may refuse to sell excess valuation on especially valuable or breakable items such as cash, jewelry, bank notes, antiques, and negotiable securities. Passengers may still be covered for the loss by their homeowner's or renter's insurance, by their credit card company, or by baggage insurance, as discussed in Chapter 11.

The Role of Travel Counselors

Even though travelers can make their reservations and purchase tickets themselves on their own computers, many still look for advice from travel counselors before they complete their transactions. Good salespeople can convert these people into long-term clients by providing good service and a personal touch.

Travelers may need help with any number of questions and possible snafus. Travel counselors should be prepared, for example, to

- Serve as a guide to useful Web sites.
- Answer questions about the rationale for a fare. Although they need not understand the subtleties behind specific fares, travel counselors should be able to discuss the general strategy behind airfares.
- Explain the layouts of the most commonly used airports, and use their knowledge of these layouts to evaluate connections and to give clients tips on parking, restaurants, and other services.
- Point out connections and layover times to be sure the client is comfortable with them.
- Recognize a code share in the computer, and let clients know that they will be connecting to or from a different line and what type of aircraft is being operated.
- Sign up to receive information about Internet-only fare sales and other offers so that they can offer clients the best available fares as often as possible.

Countless other items could be added to this list.

Although travel agencies no longer receive automatic base commissions from airlines for selling domestic air tickets, they can still earn revenue from air travel. They do receive commissions from preferred airline relationships, and they may receive service fees from their clients for processing domestic airline reservations as most travel agencies now have a schedule of fees in place for most transactions, including air tickets. (In Chapter 13 we discuss the economics of selling domestic air tickets.) Furthermore, most airlines do pay commissions for reservations for international air travel, and international travel becomes a more important source of revenue for most travel agencies every year. Offering service to the customer is essential if travel agencies are to hold on to this market.

One key service is providing information about the special requirements of international travel. These requirements (discussed in Chapter 2) can seem like a maze to novice travelers. Travel counselors should make sure that travelers who are planning to leave the United States will be permitted to enter the countries they wish to visit, that they will be allowed back into the country, and that they do not unknowingly break any laws regarding the import or export of goods. Travel counselors also have the responsibility to warn travelers when they are planning trips to areas with known medical risks. The Close-Up on selling (page 110) includes a checklist of basic questions that should be considered for each overseas destination.

CHAPTER WRAP-UP

CHAPTER HIGHLIGHTS

The first years of the twenty-first century brought many challenges to the airline industry and to those who sell their products, but the growth of the global marketplace has reinforced the importance of air travel to the travel industry as a whole. Here is a review of the objectives with which we began the chapter.

1. **Outline how the airline industry is regulated and coordinated by the government and suppliers.** Since the Airline Deregulation Act of 1978, U.S. airlines have been free to set their own fares, routes, and commissions. But the federal government continues to set rules to ensure airline safety and to prevent unfair practices, particularly through the work of the TSA, FAA, NTSB, DOT, and DOJ. Many other aspects of airline travel are governed by policies set by the airlines themselves through interline agreements and groups such as ATA, which created a standard ticket, and ARC, which determines who can sell domestic airline tickets.

   International air travel is regulated through international agreements and IATA. In the United States IATAN, a subsidiary of IATA, appoints travel agencies to sell international airline tickets.

2. **Describe how airlines differ, and know the codes for major airlines and airports.** Passenger airlines may offer scheduled service or charters. Airlines with scheduled service include major, national, and regional airlines. (Small regional airlines are often called commuter airlines.) Regional airlines often join with larger carriers in code-sharing agreements.

3. **Explain three types of flights, four types of journeys, and three classes of service.** The type of flight depends basically on whether the stops include connections or stopovers; flights may be nonstop, connecting, or direct (also called through). Journeys may involve one-way trips, round-trips, circle trips, open-jaw trips, or double open-jaw trips. Classes of service include first class, coach, and business or executive class. Bulkheads typically divide compartments set aside for each class. One key advantage of first-class over coach service is its greater seat space, which depends on pitch, seat width, and configuration. Some flights substitute business class for first class or offer only first class and coach; budget airlines may offer only one class of service. On international flights coach class is often known as economy class. International flights often provide amenities beyond those available on domestic flights.

4. **Describe at least five factors that are likely to affect the cost of a passenger's flight.** A passenger's fare is affected first of all by the route flown and whether there are stopovers. The resulting fare may be a through fare, joint fare, or point-to-point fare. Other factors are class of service and whether the passenger is applying a bonus from a frequent-flyer plan, fits into a category

eligible for a discount (such as children), or can accept the restrictions placed on a promotional fare (also known as a discount fare). Taxes—including the U.S. ticket tax, departure and arrival taxes (for international flights), PFCs, and the segment tax—and surcharges and fees (such as security, immigration, and customs) also influence the cost of a flight.

For U.S. domestic flights, the fare structure is set by the airlines and reflects sophisticated yield management strategies. For international flights, governments play a role in setting the fares.

5. **Outline the procedures involved in taking a flight and common questions and problems that come up in air travel.** When a passenger's planned flight is confirmed, the reservation record in the computer is known as a PNR. A client who cannot obtain a reservation may wish to be waitlisted and may even go to the airport as a standby in the hope that no-shows may make a seat available. Clients may receive either a paper ticket or an electronic ticket. The ticket entitles the client to a boarding pass, which is needed in order to board the plane. Passengers who do not arrive within the specified check-in time lose their right to a seat. They may also lose their seats if the airline's overbooking leads to an oversold flight. But if passengers are bumped, the airline must either get them to their destination within an hour of the originally scheduled arrival or pay denied boarding compensation. The airline is also liable for lost or damaged luggage that has been checked. Rules regarding liability and compensation for lost luggage and other problems vary for domestic and international flights.

KEY TERMS

A list of key terms introduced in this chapter follows. If you do not recall the meaning of these terms, see the Glossary, which begins on page 393.

Airline Deregulation Act
Airlines Reporting Corporation (ARC)
Air Transport Association (ATA)
APEX fare
arrival tax
boarding pass
buffer zone
bulkhead
bumped
business class
charter
circle trip
civil aviation
classes of service
coach
code-sharing agreements
commuter airlines
configuration
confirmed
connecting flight
connection
consolidator
construction principle
denied boarding compensation
departure tax
direct flight
discount fare
domestic air travel
double open-jaw trip
economy class

electronic ticket
excess baggage charge
executive class
Federal Aviation Administration (FAA)
first class
frequent-flyer plan
gateway
higher intermediate point (HIP)
hub-and-spoke system
interline agreement
International Air Transport Association (IATA)
International Airlines Travel Agent Network (IATAN)
joint fare
maximum permitted miles (MPM)
mileage system
National Transportation Safety Board (NTSB)
neutral units of construction (NUCs)
nonstop flight
no-show
one-way trip
open-jaw trip
open-skies policy
overbook
oversold
paper ticket

passenger facility charge (PFC)
passenger load factor
passenger name record (PNR)
pitch
point-to-point fare
promotional fare
rate desk
record locator number
round-trip
routing system
scheduled service
seat width
security fee

segment tax
standard ticket
standby
stop
stopover
through fare
through flight
Transportation Security
  Administration (TSA)
U.S. ticket tax
waitlisted
yield
yield management

REVIEW QUESTIONS

1. Name three important airlines in your area. List their codes.

2. From an airline's point of view, what are the advantages of the hub-and-spoke system?

3. Why would a travel agency avoid using a consolidator to obtain air tickets for a particular client?

4. Airline Web sites, discount travel sites, and other Internet sources sell air tickets directly to the public. How can travel counselors use these as tools to serve their clients?

5. How would you summarize the most important differences between domestic and international air travel?

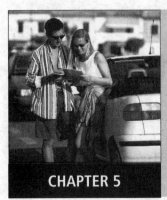

Ground Travel

CHAPTER 5

OBJECTIVES

After completing this chapter, you should be able to

1. Describe rail service in the United States and Europe.

2. Outline the services provided by car rental companies and the requirements that renters should expect to meet.

3. Identify the functions played by motorcoaches.

4. Explain the comparative advantages of traveling by rail, car, or motorcoach.

5. Discuss the roles of transfers and other ground services that travel counselors might offer.

OUTLINE

RAIL TRANSPORTATION
- What is the state of rail travel today?

RENTAL CARS
- What services do car rental companies provide, and what requirements should car renters expect to meet?

MOTORCOACHES
- What are the various uses of motorcoaches?

SELLING GROUND TRANSPORTATION
- What are the advantages of each form of ground transportation?
- What other ground services can counselors offer?

The second most popular attraction in the Washington, D.C., region (after the Air and Space Museum) is Potomac Mills, a mega-mall in Virginia. It attracts more than 4 million visitors each year, including more than 3,000 groups and chartered tours. In fact, around the country, millions of tourists flock to shopping malls. They go by bus and they go by car; they can't go by plane. If you never took a train or bus or car, your travels would be limited indeed.

More than 90 percent of the trips Americans take involve some form of ground transportation. Most of these trips do not require professional travel planning, but ground transport is vital to the travel industry. Without the motorcoach, for example, tours would find it difficult to operate, and without rental cars most traveling business people would be at a loss.

For travelers, ground transportation can provide a pleasant, relaxing, and often inexpensive alternative to air transportation, as well as access to places not served by airlines. For businesses like Potomac Mills, as well as countless motels, restaurants, and attractions, an efficient ground transportation industry is a key ingredient to success. And for hundreds of thousands of Americans, the ground transportation industry is a source of employment. (The Close-Up on careers describes a few of the positions in the industry.) In this chapter we look at three major elements of ground transportation: intercity and international train service, car rentals, and motorcoaches.

Rail Transportation

"Empire Builder now departing for Fargo, Devils Lake, Rugby, Wolf Point, Cut Bank, Glacier, Spokane, and points west on Track Four," drones the stationmaster. "Aaaall aboard!" To some who hear that sound, the romance of the rails still lives, and travel by train is their first choice.

Trains offer many potential advantages. Compared with air travel, they provide a more leisurely trip. Travelers can sit back, enjoy the scenery, and meet other passengers. Train travel is also an alternative for those who fear flying, and often it is cheaper than flying. Sometimes it is more convenient, partly because many train stations sit in the heart of a city, whereas airports lie on the fringes. Procedures for traveling by train are often simpler and faster than those required for air travel. And, of course, some places served by train do not have regular air service.

In much of the world, trains are popular or essential or both. Japan has one of the fastest, safest, and most punctual rail systems in the world. Its high-speed passenger trains, known as **bullet trains** (*Shinkansen*), reach speeds of more than 170 miles per hour. But Asia's largest railway system belongs to India; its railroads blanket the country. Our focus in this chapter, though, is primarily on rail transportation in North America and western Europe, plus some unusual train trips famous around the world.

Amtrak

Freight trains and commuter trains as well as passenger trains make up the U.S. railroad industry, but only intercity passenger service represents a key part of the travel industry. That service is just a shadow of what it once was.

A Brief History. The first steam locomotives made their appearance in 1825 in England and 1830 in America. Rail travel developed rapidly, thanks in part to land given up by the government in order to promote the railroad industry. Between the 1860s and the 1930s, the railroads were the dominant means of transportation and one of the mightiest industries in the United States. Fortunes were made from the railroads; thousands of towns and world-famous hotels grew near the tracks. Rail was king.

Beginning in the 1920s, Americans' love for driving their own cars helped push passenger trains toward the fringes of the transportation market. Train travel dropped further after World War II, as air travel became more affordable. By the late 1950s a trip from Chicago to Los Angeles took 40 hours by train and just 4 hours by jet. By 1960 passenger miles by air surpassed those by rail. While government-owned-and-subsidized trains in Europe were constantly modernizing, the privately owned passenger trains in the United States became ever less competitive with other forms of transportation. By 1970, while freight business remained strong, railroad companies were eliminating passenger trains. It began to look as if passenger rail travel might disappear from the United States.

To keep passenger trains running, the federal government in 1970 established the National Railroad Passenger Corporation, known as Amtrak.

Today, *Amtrak* is a private corporation that operates intercity passenger rail service with the help of funding from the federal government. Its board of directors is appointed by the president of the United States, and the U.S. Department of Transportation holds the majority of its stock.

When Amtrak began operating in 1971, it immediately cut routes and services but also began to modernize. It improved tracks, cars, and onboard amenities, and it introduced a national reservation system. In 2000 it finally launched a train—the *Acela Express*—similar to the high-speed trains that

CLOSE-UP: CAREERS IN GROUND TRANSPORTATION

The ground transportation industry is not as glamorous as the airline industry, but it offers more career opportunities. There are thousands of car rental and motorcoach companies. Like other parts of the travel industry, these companies have jobs in marketing and sales, international sales, e-commerce, and franchising. There are also fascinating positions related to logistics and the acquisition of fleets. Openings at Amtrak are few because turnover is low among its unionized employees, but opportunities exist for employment with specialty trains.

■ **Position** Car rental agent

Description Most car rental agents work at airport locations and deal directly with customers. They greet renters, complete the paperwork, and check credentials before handing over the car keys. Sales of insurance or upgrades may also be part of the job. The starting salary may be little over the minimum wage, but the position is often a stepping-stone to other positions.

Qualifications This entry-level position requires a professional manner, excellent interpersonal and communication skills, and a customer-service orientation.

■ **Position** Car rental customer service representative

Description Customer service representatives are responsible for resolving rental complaints, answering inquiries from customers, and solving problems concerning rates.

Qualifications This entry-level position requires articulate, personable individuals with the ability to communicate well. Common sense, patience, and tact are also needed.

■ **Position** Onboard attendant, Amtrak

Description Like airline flight attendants, train attendants serve the needs of their onboard clients and watch out for their safety. Seniority governs choice of routes.

Qualifications This position is ideal for individuals with a background in food or transportation service.

■ **Position** Revenue manager

Description Many ground transportation companies need a professional to implement pricing tactics to spur sales without cutting into profitability. The revenue manager works with marketing, sales, and reservations departments to identify market opportunities and to design and implement products. The revenue manager must also keep abreast of what competitors are doing.

Qualifications A B.A. or B.S. in economics, finance, marketing, or statistics or equivalent experience is necessary; an M.B.A. is a strong plus. This position also requires two or more years' experience with pricing tactics, excellent analytical skills, strong communication and organizational skills, and the ability to work independently.

■ **Position** Marketing coordinator

Description Responsibilities of this position include managing the frequent-renter club, direct-mail or online marketing to members, and promotions of discounts, vacation packages, and the like. The marketing coordinator verifies that criteria are met for those being enrolled in the frequent-renter club, provides customer support for members, works with programmers to create and enhance the customer database, and helps book reservations for members.

Qualifications This is a step up from a sales representative and requires knowledge of both marketing methods and list acquisition and management as well as the ability to analyze results.

■ **Position** Customer service manager (also called station manager)

Description The person in this position hires, trains, schedules, supervises, and evaluates staff—including service agents, rental sales agents, and shuttle bus drivers—and ensures efficient daily operation of the station. Responsibilities also include servicing customers, overseeing fleet control, monitoring daily computer reports, and undertaking local marketing programs.

Qualifications This position requires attention to detail and excellent organizational and managerial skills, along with analytical ability.

■ **Other positions** Account executive; account manager; fleet manager; motorcoach driver.

have long operated in Europe and Japan. In 2003 it announced a five-year plan to upgrade and improve equipment and services. But for decades Amtrak has struggled to deal with changes in the marketplace and declining federal subsidies.

Rail has been the stepchild as U.S. government subsidy to the rail industry is dwarfed by that granted to air and road traffic. Nevertheless, ridership has been increasing, particularly since the 9/11 terrorist attacks when many U.S. travelers avoided air travel in favor of ground travel, and some innovative tour operators developed packages combining rail travel with cruises, motorcoach travel, and other industry sectors.

Routes and Equipment. Figure 5.1 shows Amtrak's major routes. The longest route, the *Sunset Limited* between Orlando and Los Angeles, covers 2,768 miles. The long-distance routes, such as Chicago to Los Angeles and New York to Miami, are used mainly by leisure travelers; the short-distance, or *corridor,* routes serve a high percentage of business travelers. Many states are working with Amtrak to develop plans for regional high-speed service; whether these plans will be carried out depends on the potential for riders and on support from Congress and the states.

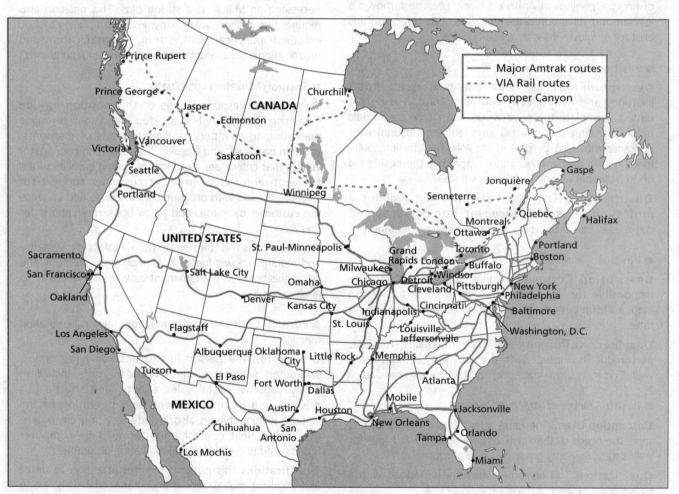

FIGURE 5.1 Major Passenger Rail Routes of North America

This map shows major routes offered by Amtrak and by VIA Rail of Canada, plus the route of Mexico's most famous train, through the Copper Canyon. On Amtrak the busiest routes include the Northeast corridor from Washington to Boston and the California coastal route from San Francisco to San Diego.

Amtrak's fleet includes single-level and bi-level trains, coach cars and sleeping cars, food service cars, and lounges (see Table 5.1). The trains that are used vary with the route. Among Amtrak's modern trains are

- The *Acela Express*, which offers high-speed service between Boston, New York, and Washington, D.C. The 150-mile-per-hour Acela can make the trip between New York and Boston in 3 hours and 18 minutes and between New York and Washington in 2 hours and 43 minutes.
- The *Pacific Surfliner*, a double-decker train that travels the San Diego–Los Angeles–San Luis Obispo route.
- The *Auto Train*, which carries cars and their passengers from a Virginia suburb of Washington, D.C., to Florida.
- The *Cascades*, fast Talgo-manufactured trains (with many amenities) operating in the Pacific Northwest.

Onboard Services. Amtrak offers several classes of service: first class, business class, coach class, and sleeping accommodations, as well as club class—an extra level of service for coach passengers. *Coach* class features two reclining seats on each side of an aisle. Usually seats have fold-down trays, leg rests, and individual reading lights. There are restrooms at the ends of the cars. Power outlets for laptop computers are also available on some trains. Club service brings amenities such as a complimentary beverage and newspaper.

Travelers willing to pay more than coach fare may be interested in *business class*, which offers a private car, complimentary nonalcoholic beverage, and newspaper on the *Acela* only. *First class* provides deluxe reserved seats, meals and beverages served at the seat by an attendant, hot towels, and complimentary daily newspapers. *Sleeping accommodations* represent first class on long-distance trains. The traveler receives a private room in a sleeping car, personal service, complimentary meals, and other amenities. Table 5.1 describes the variety of sleeping accommodations available.

TABLE 5.1 Selected Trains on Amtrak

SLEEPING CARS

Viewliner. Single-level cars, with standard and deluxe bedrooms.

- The standard bedroom has two reclining seats that convert to a bed plus an upper berth that pulls down from the ceiling. A sink and toilet are in the room; a shower is nearby.
- The deluxe bedroom features an armchair and a sofa that converts to a bed. An upper berth folds down from the wall. Shower, sink, vanity, and toilet are all in the room. Two deluxe bedrooms can be combined to create a suite for four people.

Superliner. Bi-level cars with standard, deluxe, and family bedrooms.

- The standard bedroom features two reclining seats that convert to a bed; an upper berth pulls down from the wall. Restrooms and a shower are nearby.
- Deluxe bedrooms are on the upper level and feature an armchair and a sofa that converts to a bed; an upper berth folds down from the wall. Sink, vanity, shower, and toilet are all in the room. Some deluxe bedrooms can be combined to form a suite.
- The family bedroom features windows on two sides. A sofa and two seats convert to two lower berths, and upper berths fold

down from the wall, to provide total sleeping room for two adults and two children. Restrooms and a shower are nearby.

Note: Both *Viewliners* and *Superliners* also have bedrooms designed to be accessible to those with special mobility requirements, including space for a wheelchair.

SELECTED DAY TRAINS

Acela Express. A single-level high-speed train.

This train's features include plush seats, movable armrests and headrest, laptop computer outlets, conference tables, deluxe restrooms, and a café car.

Talgo. A single-level train.

Known for its European style, this train offers plush seating, laptop computer outlets, onboard movies, bicycle and surfboard racks, luggage cars, a bistro car, and a dining car.

Surfliner. A spacious bi-level train.

Features on this train include panoramic windows, spacious seating, outlets for laptop computers, bicycle and surfboard racks, and a café car.

Not all classes are available on all trains. What you get on Amtrak depends on where you are going and when. Generally, long-distance trains provide more amenities than trains on corridor routes. The services available on specific trains are indicated on Amtrak schedules, as you can see in Figure 5.2.

Most Amtrak trains offer some type of food service. On some there are dining cars that serve complete sit-down meals. Other trains offer only lounge and café cars—where travelers can buy sandwiches, snacks, and beverages—or dinette and club cars, which offer tray meals. These cars also provide places for socializing and playing games. On some trains the lounge cars offer movies or domed windows for sightseeing.

11			‹ Train Number ›			14
Daily		Ⓐ	‹ Normal Days of Operation ›			Daily
Ⓡ 🛏 ✕ ☕			‹ On Board Service ›		Ⓑ	Ⓡ 🛏 ✕ ☕
Read Down	Mile	▽		Symbol	△	Read Up
		🚆 Amtrak Thruway Connection—Vancouver, BC/Seattle, WA				
5 30A	0	Dp	Vancouver, BC (PT) —Pacific Central Station	●🛏	Ar	12 20A
R5 50A	12		Richmond, BC —Sandman Signature Hotel	○ ○		D11 50P
R6 20A	29		Surrey, BC–Pacific Inn	○		D11 20P
9 00A	144	Ar	Seattle, WA–Amtrak Station 🚆(PT)	●ⓠ	Dp	9 15P
9 45A	0	Dp	Seattle, WA (Victoria, BC 🚢) (PT)	●🛏&ⓠ	Ar	8 45P
10 31A	39		Tacoma, WA	●🛏&ⓠ		7 11P
11 21A	75		Olympia-Lacey, WA	○&ⓠ		6 22P
🛏11 45A	94		Centralia, WA	●🛏&ⓠ		5 57P
12 29P	137		Kelso-Longview, WA	○&ⓠ		5 14P
1 08P	177		Vancouver, WA	●🛏&ⓠ		4 36P
1 50P	187	Ar	Portland, OR	●🛏&ⓠ	Dp	4 20P
2 25P		Dp	🚆 Pendleton, Boise—see back			3 40P
3 37P	239		Salem, OR	●🛏&ⓠ	Ⓔ	2 03P
4 10P	267		Albany, OR 🚆 Corvallis, Newport—see back	●🛏&ⓠ		1 30P
5 10P	310		Eugene-Springfield, OR 🚆 Ontario, Coos Bay—see back	●🛏&ⓠ		12 44P
8 08P	432		Chemult, OR 🚆 Bend, Sunriver —see back	○🛏		9 40A
10 00P	505		Klamath Falls, OR (Crater Lake) 🚆 Brookings—see back	●🛏&ⓠ		8 25A
12 35A	610		Dunsmuir, CA (Mt. Shasta) Ⓓ	○&		5 04A
2 21A	665		Redding, CA	○&		3 14A
3 50A	739		Chico, CA	○🛏		1 55A
6 35A	824		Sacramento, CA	●🛏&ⓠ		11 59P
6 50A	837		Davis, CA	●🛏&ⓠ		11 33P
7 34A	881		Martinez, CA	●🛏&ⓠ		10 54P
8 04A	901		Richmond, CA	○🛏&ⓠ		10 20P
8 15A	908	Ar	Emeryville, CA	●🛏&ⓠ	Dp	10 07P
8 25A		Dp	🚌 San Francisco—see back		Ar	9 57P
8 40A	913	Ar	Oakland, CA–Jack London Square	●🛏&ⓠ	Dp	9 42P
8 50A		Dp	🚌 San Francisco—see back		Ar	9 32P
9 55A	954	Ar	San Jose, CA (Caltrain)	●🛏&ⓠ	Dp	8 39P
10 07A		Dp		⊠	Ar	8 27P
11 48A	1021		Salinas, CA 🚌 Monterey, Carmel —see back	●🛏&		6 36P
1 38P	1119		Paso Robles, CA	○&		4 45P
3 20P	1157		San Luis Obispo, CA (Morro Bay)	●🛏&ⓠ		3 43P
6 17P	1274		Santa Barbara, CA	●🛏&ⓠ		12 48P
D7 05P	1310		Oxnard, CA	●🛏&ⓠ		11 55A
D7 38P	1341	Ar	Simi Valley, CA	○🛏&ⓠ		R11 23A
D8 05P	1358	Ar	Van Nuys, CA–Amtrak Station	●🛏&ⓠ		R10 52A
D8 15P	1363	Ar	Burbank-Bob Hope Airport, CA ✦	○&		R10 42A
9 00P	1377	Ar	Los Angeles, CA ✦ (PT)	●🛏&ⓠ	Dp	10 20A
796			Connecting Train Number			763
Daily			Days of Operation			Daily
10 10P	1377	Dp	Los Angeles, CA ✦ (PT)	●🛏&ⓠ	Ar	8 50A
10 40P	1403	Ar	Fullerton, CA	●🛏&ⓠ		8 15A
10 49P	1409		Anaheim, CA (Disneyland®)	●🛏&ⓠ		8 06A
10 58P	1413		Santa Ana, CA	●🛏&ⓠ		7 57A
11 09P	1423		Irvine, CA	●&ⓠ		7 46A
11 23P	1435		San Juan Capistrano, CA	●&ⓠ		7 31A
11 55P	1464		Oceanside, CA	●&ⓠ		7 01A
12 11A	1480		Solana Beach, CA	●&ⓠ		6 45A
12 50A	1505	Ar	San Diego, CA (PT)	●🛏&ⓠ	Dp	6 10A

How to read the timetable

By reading across the table, you can determine which trains arrive and depart from a station at which times. Check the bold vertical arrow to determine whether to read up or down the page.

Ⓐ During holiday periods, days of operation may vary.

Ⓑ Services available on each train are indicated by the symbols: the R in the square: coach reservations are required; a bed: sleeping accommodations; the knife and fork: a dining car with sit-down meals; a cup: casual dining with sandwiches, snacks and beverages.

Ⓒ The gray shading indicates a connecting train, van, or bus.

Ⓓ Nearby cities and points of interest are listed in parentheses. The large star indicates that an Amtrak travel vacation is available at the destination.

Ⓔ The symbol of a wheelchair with no box indicates that all facilities are fully accessible to persons using wheelchairs. The wheelchair within a box indicates that although there is barrier-free access between the street and station and train, not all station facilities are fully accessible to those in wheelchairs. A suitcase indicates that luggage can be checked.

Ⓕ An open circle designates an unstaffed station; a solid circle shows a staffed ticket office although the office may not be open for all train departures. *QT* is a Quik-Trak self-serve ticketing kiosk.

FIGURE 5.2 Amtrak Schedules and Services

This example of an Amtrak timetable shows some of the symbols that indicate the services available.

Source: Adapted by permission of Amtrak.

Checked baggage service is available at most Amtrak stations. Passengers may check up to three bags at no additional cost, and they are allowed to bring no more than two pieces of carry-on luggage.

Other Services. Amtrak's Guest Rewards program lets riders earn points every time they travel on Amtrak. As points accumulate, they may select from a variety of rewards: free travel on Amtrak, hotel and car rental awards, airline miles, and gift certificates from nationally known retailers. Frequent travelers on the *Acela Express* and on New York's Empire trains (running from Buffalo to Albany to New York City) may register for the complimentary Executive Privileges program, which offers special incentives and discounts.

First-class passengers with a same-day ticket may use Amtrak's Metropolitan lounges and ClubAcela facilities. The Metropolitan lounges, in Chicago, Miami, New Orleans, Portland (Oregon), Raleigh, and St. Paul/ Minneapolis, provide comfortable seating, complimentary soft drinks and coffee, and ticketing assistance. ClubAcela facilities also have free use of photocopy and fax machines and conference rooms. Both may have Internet access. ClubAcelas are in Boston, New York, Philadelphia, and Washington, D.C.

For some cities not served by Amtrak, the railroad offers Amtrak Thruway Bus Service, which guarantees connections to bus service from the Amtrak station. The cost of the bus trip is included in the rail fare.

Customized vacation packages are also available from Amtrak; they are listed in Amtrak's *Travel Planner* and on its Web site. With one type of package, Amtrak reserves and books rental cars and hotel rooms along with the train ticket. Another type of package includes a motorcoach tour with a professional tour director, as well as hotel accommodations and meals. With the Amtrak Air-Rail travel plan, travelers can depart for their vacations by train and return by United Airlines or United Express, or vice versa.

Fares/Products. Amtrak has two major types of fares/products to choose:

- Basic *Point-to-Point tickets* vary in price based on a number of factors, such as advance purchase, time of day, number of changes, and type of equipment on the route. The price includes either seat or sleeper accommodations.
- *USA Rail Pass* comes in a variety of options: up to eight segments within 15 days, up to 12 segments within 30 days, and up to 18 segments within 45 days. Purchase of the rail pass does not constitute a reservation; space in this category is limited each day. Reservations for specific dates must be booked well in advance to assure confirmation of the dates desired for each segment. Reservations must be booked within 180 days of the pass purchase date. Note: A segment means one trip without stopping over; if a stopover is made in the middle of a segment, it counts as two segments.

Like the airlines, Amtrak also offers promotional discounts on certain routes at certain times of the year in an effort to fill seats that would otherwise go empty. Amtrak also offers year-round discounts for children ages 2 to 15, for those age 62 and over, for people with disabilities, for those in the military, and for high school and college students who enroll in Amtrak's Student Advantage program.

For sleeping accommodations, travelers pay the rail fare plus an accommodations charge. Discounts apply only to the rail fare. Although the rail fare is charged per person traveling, the accommodations charge is calculated per accommodation. Thus if three people share a bedroom, the total cost includes three rail fares plus one accommodations charge.

Even with the accommodations charge, the cost of traveling overnight by train can be very reasonable because it covers transportation, accommodations, and meals. Budget-minded travelers can buy a coach fare, purchase reasonably priced food onboard, and—at no extra cost—sleep in seats that recline to an almost-horizontal position.

Ticketing, Reservations, and Commissions. Reservations are necessary for sleeping accommodations, first class, business class, and long-distance trains. For coach seats on certain trains, reservations are not required. But seats at discount fares are limited, and reservations may be sold out months ahead during the summer.

Travel counselors may book Amtrak service in one of three ways:
1. By calling Amtrak directly
2. By using the travel agency's GDS (requires an ARC or CLIA appointment)
3. By booking through the Rail Europe Web site (is only available to qualified travel agencies or counselors))

In the past, many travel agencies have been hesitant to offer Amtrak services to their clientele because of the time involved for little or no commission earnings. Commission is paid for long-distance overnight trains through either the GDS or RailEurope's site. No commission is paid on day corridor service on Amtrak. A service fee is available only through RailEurope. However, because RailEurope has now been appointed as portal for Amtrak, booking through the RailEurope Web site allows the counselor to add a service fee of up to 15 percent of the entire booking package.

Also note that while there are no commissions on the day or corridor trips, such as the *Acela* or the *Capital Corridor*, the long-distance Amtrak trains *do* pay eight percent commission on the entire package, including accommodations and meals. The commission for these Amtrak sales is sent to the agency by check at the end of each month as part of its payment for any RailEurope products the agency may have sold during that time.

After booking, a written confirmation with itinerary will be e-mailed to the agency for the client. However, for an actual boarding pass or paper ticket, the client must check in at the boarding rail station or kiosk for one. If the client is boarding at a stop without a kiosk or an agent, see the Web site for instructions on how to obtain a boarding pass as the traveler will not be allowed to board with only an e-mail confirmation.

Train Travel in Canada and Mexico

Both Amtrak and *VIA Rail*, Canada's passenger train network, operate routes that cross the border between the two nations. (Look again at Figure 5.1.) Travelers can go from the United States to Canada and return, without changing trains, on at least four routes: (1) between Vancouver and Seattle and points south on the West Coast, (2) between Toronto and New York, (3) between Toronto and Chicago, and (4) between Montreal and New York.

VIA Rail links more than 450 Canadian communities from the Atlantic to the Pacific, offering intercity as well as transcontinental journeys. Of particular interest are

■ The *Canadian,* Canada's best-known train, which takes a 2,800-mile, three-day journey from Toronto to Vancouver, passing through northern lakelands, prairies, and the Rocky Mountains—one of the world's great train trips. The train has been restored to its 1950s style and features observation cars, dining car, bar, and lounge. Luxury class offers private sleeping compartments and intimate dining.

- The *Hudson Bay*, which travels north from Winnipeg to Churchill, the "polar bear capital of the world," on Hudson Bay and the edge of Canada's Arctic.
- The *Chaleur*, which takes travelers from Montreal northeast through quaint towns and villages to the Gaspé Peninsula, and the *Ocean*, which goes from Montreal through rural communities to Nova Scotia.

Dining service and sleeping accommodations are available on some VIA Rail routes, and there are connections to bus and ferry service at selected points. With 24 hours' notice, those planning an adventure in Canada's wilderness areas can arrange to be dropped off or picked up at points where there is no scheduled stop. (But checked baggage service is not available on all trains.)

VIA Rail offers discount programs for seniors, children, meetings, and groups, as well as a frequent-traveler program. Because VIA Rail is a member of ARC, U.S. travel agencies can make reservations and issue tickets conveniently through a GDS. Reservations can also be made by calling VIA Rail or by visiting its Web site.

In Mexico the highlight of train travel is the ride on the Chihuahua al Pacífico Railway through the Copper Canyon. The train travels between the desert city of Chihuahua to Los Mochis for about thirteen hours, through spectacular mountain scenery over the Sierra Madre and through coastal plains. The journey includes eighty-six tunnels, thirty-nine bridges, and many hairpin turns from elevations ranging from 8,000 feet to sea level. It has been described as the most dramatic train ride in the Western Hemisphere, and some tour operators have developed interesting rail/motorcoach tours that include stays at lodges along the way and visits to the Tarahumara Indians.

Otherwise, travel by train in Mexico appeals mostly to dedicated train fans or those with plenty of time on their hands. It is generally slow and often irregular; most local people take the bus. Tourists who want to take the train anyway should be advised to travel first or luxury class. Local travel agencies in Mexico as well as a few U.S. tour operators offer information and reservations.

European Rail

From its origins in the first half of the nineteenth century, rail travel in Europe grew rapidly to become the dominant mode of transportation. Even through the twentieth century, trains remained popular—thanks in part to political and economic factors that slowed the purchase of private automobiles, to the short distances between major European cities, and to the high cost of air travel for short European flights. Furthermore, European governments continually subsidized and improved their rail systems, modernizing tracks and trains. Thus European train travel escaped the decline that occurred in the United States.

Today, travelers in continental Europe can use the train to take a quiet, swift, businesslike journey from one city center to another or to enjoy an intimate experience of the land, its people, and its customs. *InterCity (IC) trains* are domestic trains running within a country's borders; major international trains are called *EuroCity (EC) trains*. The trains are fast and dependable. When travel to and from airports is taken into account, it may be faster to get from the heart of one city to another by train than by plane (see Figure 5.3 on the next page). France's **TGV** (*train à grande vitesse*) and Germany's **ICE** (InterCity Expresses) travel close to 200 miles per hour. Other high-speed trains include *Frecciarosa* in Italy, *AVE* in Spain, *X2000* in Sweden, and Thalys Paris to Amsterdam and Cologne.

Since 1994 travelers can even take a train from England to continental Europe. *Eurostar* operates through the ***Chunnel***, the tunnel beneath the English Channel that links England and France. Eurostar makes the trip from St. Pancras Station in London to Gare du Nord in Paris in 2 hours and 15 minutes; the trip from London to Brussels Midistation is 1 hour, 51 minutes. About 20 minutes are spent in the Chunnel itself.

Onboard Services. Some European trains still offer traditional compartments (small rooms) that have six seats arranged in two rows of three seats facing each other; the compartments open to a corridor that runs along one side of the car. Virtually all new and high-speed trains have *bank seating* like that on most American trains and buses, with seats on each side of a central aisle. First-class configuration is two seats, an aisle and then one seat. Second-class is two seats, an aisle, and then two more seats. Restrooms are located at the ends of most train cars.

Most European trains have first-class and second-class seating and compartments. Seats in second class are usually perfectly comfortable, but first-class compartments are roomier and the seats have more cushioning. The cost of the extra comfort that first-class provides means that fares tend to be 40 to 60 percent more than those for second-class.

Sleeping accommodations require the payment of a supplement in addition to the basic fare. On most overnight trains, there are sleeping cars that offer private compartments with single or double berths. The cost may be the same as for a moderate hotel room, depending on the country. Sleeping cars usually have a washbasin, towels, and linens; toilet facilities are at the ends of each car.

Another form of sleeping accommodation is the ***couchette***, which is a compartment with six bunk beds (three on each side); it has little headroom and not much luggage space. Couchettes are not private, and beds are assigned without regard to gender. (Some trains have four berths and may be

FIGURE 5.3

Europe by Train and by Plane, 2011

The actual flight time between many major European cities is often little more than an hour, but total travel time—including the trip to and from the airport's check-in time and clearing security—is usually more than three hours. Most Europeans prefer to take the train for these trips. Second-class rail fares average about one-third less than the first-class fares shown here.

Source: Rail fares and times from Rail Europe, as posted at www.raileurope.com.

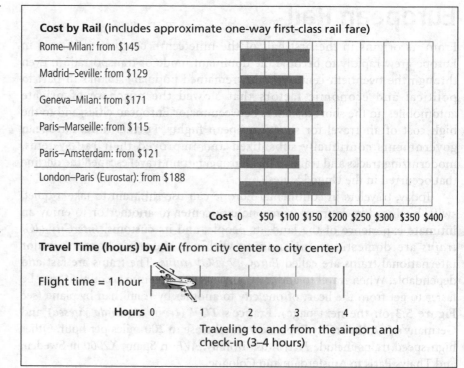

Cost by Rail (includes approximate one-way first-class rail fare)

Rome–Milan: from $145
Madrid–Seville: from $129
Geneva–Milan: from $171
Paris–Marseille: from $115
Paris–Amsterdam: from $121
London–Paris (Eurostar): from $188

Cost 0 $50 $100 $150 $200 $250 $300 $350 $400

Travel Time (hours) by Air (from city center to city center)

Flight time = 1 hour

Hours 0   1   2   3   4

Traveling to and from the airport and check-in (3–4 hours)

reserved for families or members of the same gender.) Linen for the berth and a pillow are provided. Couchettes are inexpensive but should be described carefully to travelers.

For food, travelers may just pack a lunch and bring something to share with their compartment neighbors. But many long-distance, international day trains have dining cars, which are sometimes quite elegant and serve good and not-too-expensive meals. Most high-speed trains and many overnight trains do not have dining cars. Those that don't often have café cars with drinks and light food options. Many trains have trolley service where vendors pass through the train selling drinks and snacks.

Drinking water must be purchased separately from vendors or brought along by the traveler. Tap water from sinks is not for drinking.

It is important to travel light on European trains. On most of them, luggage must be stowed either in overhead storage racks or in luggage areas at each end of the car, and most European rail stations do not have porters. Traveling with a suitcase on wheels is highly recommended.

Stations and Procedures.
Travelers on European railways need to check not only that they get on the right train at the correct platform but also that the car is going to their destination. Cars that start out on the same train may end up at different destinations. Casually changing seats and cars during the ride could bring the traveler to an unexpected destination or separate the traveler from his or her luggage. It is also wise to keep all tickets and passports handy, as they are often inspected during the trip and sometimes collected upon arrival.

Many members of the European Union now allow border crossings with no document checks, but travelers should be prepared to produce any required travel documents. Officials board the train to check these documents while the train is en route, even on simple one-day excursions.

Travelers also need to check the specified station for their departure or arrival location. Many large cities, and even some small ones, have multiple train stations.

Larger stations are mini-malls. They feature the usual ticket counters, information desks, waiting rooms, and newsstands. But there are also currency exchange booths, post offices, and shops. Many have baths and showers, a hotel-finding service, cafés, restaurants, supermarkets, hair salons, and hotels attached to the station. Rome's Termini has a chapel and even a morgue.

Ticketing and Reservations.
Reservations are necessary for all sleeping accommodations as well as for all high-speed trains and certain other trains. On most local trains, reservations are not required. But travelers who are taking a long trip, who are traveling at peak times, or who want to be assured of a seat should make a reservation if it is possible; not all trains take reservations. There is always an extra charge for a reservation.

The Thomas Cook European Timetable gives rail schedules for trains in Europe (and Britain). Information is also available from **Rail Europe,** a company owned by Swiss and French railroads that acts as a U.S. booking agent for virtually all trains in Europe.

Tickets can be ordered through Rail Europe's toll-free number (1-800-848-7245), by fax, or at its agent's Web site (agent.raileurope.com). Tickets for Eurostar may be booked through either Rail Europe or BritRail. Often, however, instead of purchasing a point-to-point ticket, the best course for a traveler will be to purchase a rail pass.

Rail Passes

For train travelers seeking the freedom to change their itineraries on a whim and add extra trips, a rail pass may be ideal. *Rail passes* allow train travel for a specified time and region with unlimited stops and unlimited mileage. They can provide savings as well as convenience. A pass does not guarantee a seat, however, unless a reservation has been made. Even with a pass, all high-speed trains tightly control reservations.

To determine whether a rail pass will bring savings, add up the point-to-point rail fares on an itinerary and then compare that figure to the cost of the pass. Usually, the pass will not turn out to be cheaper if the traveler is taking just one long trip. To get the best use of an unlimited mileage pass, plot an itinerary that follows a continuous loop. Or take a hub-and-spoke approach, setting up several base cities and fanning out from each city on a series of one-day trips.

Rail passes are available in many nations. Each rail pass has its own advantages and restrictions. Some are available to anyone; some only to youths. Some are valid only in one country; others in several. Some must be bought outside the country in which they are used. BritRail passes are an example; they may be purchased only outside the United Kingdom. The granddaddy of rail passes is the European pass, known as the Eurailpass for years, and now called the Eurail Global Pass.

Eurail Global Pass. Introduced in 1959, *Eurail Global Pass* allows unlimited first-class travel through 23 European countries for a specified time—15 days, 21 days, 1 month, 2 months, or 3 months. The 23 countries are Austria, Belgium, Bulgaria, Croatia, Czech Republic, Denmark, Finland, France, Germany, Greece, Hungary, Italy, Luxembourg, the Netherlands, Norway, Portugal, the Republic of Ireland, Romania, Slovakia, Slovenia, Spain, Sweden, and Switzerland (see Figure 5.4).

Variations of Eurailpass include

- *Eurail Flexipass,* which allows first-class travel in the 23 countries for any 10 or 15 days within a 2-month period.
- *Eurail Selectpass,* which allows first-class travel in any three to five bordering countries out of the 22 that are connected by train or ferry. (Slovakia is not included in the Selectpass.)

Most passes have a *Youthpass* equivalent (for those under the age of 26), which costs less and provides second-class travel; a *Drive* counterpart, which combines train travel and a rental car; and a *Saverpass* equivalent, which requires two or three people to travel together.

Eurailpasses are also good for free or reduced-rate passage on many steamers and scenic bus trips. The passes are often used for trips on ferries connecting Ireland and France, Greece and Italy, or Sweden and Finland as well as for steamers on the Rhine, the Danube, and Lake Lucerne. Certain passes also provide a discount for fares on Eurostar.

For decades Eurailpasses could be purchased only outside Europe. Today, the passes can be purchased in Europe at special Eurail offices, but the charge is 10 percent higher, and few travelers will want to wait until arrival to plan their itineraries. In effect, Eurailpasses remain an excellent and almost exclusive marketing tool for North American travel sellers. They can be purchased through Rail Europe in the same way as Eurail tickets.

Before boarding, passengers must have their passes validated and passport numbers inscribed; this can be done at a ticket or information window at any railway station. Eurailpasses are nontransferable, and passengers may be required to show their passports along with the pass. Passes do not include seat-reservation fees, meals, sleeping accommodations, or port taxes. Very important: Even with a rail pass, all high-speed trains require a seat reservation, and increasingly the number of seats for rail pass holders are limited because of capacity controls. Although it diminishes the historical legacy of flexibility, it is essential for travelers to make reservations as far in advance as possible. Currently, most trains can be reserved up to 90 days in advance.

For travelers visiting only one European country, the rail pass offered by that country may be a better bargain than a Eurailpass. Many European countries offer their own passes, good for travel within their country.

BritRail Pass. A *BritRail pass* allows travel throughout England, Scotland, and Wales. The pass can be purchased for periods ranging from 4 days to 1 month; either first-class or second-class service is available. Other variations include the following:

■ Children and those 60 years or older are eligible for discounts through the BritRail Family Pass and Senior Pass.

FIGURE 5.4 Participants in the Eurailpass and the BritRail Pass

Twenty-three countries are part of the Eurailpass system. Ireland, Greece, and the three countries of Scandinavia are reached by ferry, which is included in passes at no extra cost.

- The BritRail Flexipass allows travel on a specific number of nonconsecutive days within a 1-month period.

Other passes are available for people who plan to visit only certain parts of Britain or to travel in Ireland along with Great Britain. There is also a package that combines a trip on Eurostar with a special Flexipass that allows travel around Britain on any 4 or 8 days out of a 3-month period.

BritRail passes must be purchased outside Britain. They are distributed by BritRail Travel International.

Canrailpass. VIA Rail offers **Canrailpass,** which provides 12 days of unlimited travel during a 30-day period anywhere in Canada. Anyone can purchase a Canrailpass, regardless of residence. Sleeping accommodations must be purchased separately, but the cost is reasonable.

In addition, a *North America Rail Pass* is available to anyone. It is good for unlimited travel aboard VIA Rail and most Amtrak trains for 30 days.

Specialty Rail

Travelers take *specialty trains* mainly for the experience, not the transportation. Getting there isn't half the fun; it's almost all the fun.

In the United States a modest growth industry exists in small railroads that offer local sightseeing tours. One of the best known is the *Durango and Silverton Railroad* in southwestern Colorado. This narrow-gauge, coal-burning train has been operating since 1882 and travels through superb scenic mountains and valleys on a three-hour journey between two historic mining towns. The *Napa Valley Wine Train* is a privately owned excursion train between Napa and St. Helena, California.

Other specialty trains can be found all over the United States. Some are dinner trains to the beach or mountains; some can be leased; and on some, private cars can be chartered.

Abroad, many international specialty trains use restored equipment to evoke nostalgia for a past era and feature elegant meals and deluxe service. Fares should be compared to the cost of a deluxe tour or a cruise. Some famous specialty trains of Europe include

- The deluxe *Orient Express,* named after one of the most famous trains of the past, which journeys between Venice and London.
- The *Royal Scotsman,* which features vintage carriages, ornately decorated Pullman sleeping cars, and an observation car with an open veranda on which to sit and watch the Highlands pass by.

Among the trains in Asia and Africa that offer chances for unique journeys are the following:

- India's *Palace on Wheels* travels for 8 days, with modern facilities and luxurious service, past marble palaces, temples, and colorful markets.
- Japan's luxurious trains include the *Twilight Express,* which makes a 21-hour journey from Osaka to Sapporo, and *Cassiopeia,* which travels from Tokyo to Sapporo in 17 hours.
- South Africa boasts two deluxe trains: the *Blue Train*—which travels between Cape Town and Johannesburg (Pretoria), a distance of 994 miles, in 26 hours—and *Rovos Rail,* which covers various itineraries.

The world's longest overland train trip is far from deluxe: it is Russia's *Trans-Siberian Railroad* from Moscow to Vladivostok. It covers 5,778 miles and 11 time zones in 7 days. This fascinating journey ranks anywhere from an adventure to an ordeal. An alternate route goes through Mongolia to Beijing, China.

Passenger rail service in the United States
✔ Is provided by Amtrak.
✔ Includes busy corridor routes that serve many business travelers as well as long-distance routes used mainly by leisure travelers.
✔ Features amenities and service options that vary from route to route.

Unlike Amtrak trains, on European trains
✔ Much of the seating is in compartments, rooms of six passengers.

✔ Most trains have first- and second-class compartments.
✔ Cars are often switched from one train to another during the trip, and many cities have more than one train station.

Rail passes
✔ Do not by themselves guarantee a seat.
✔ Usually will be cheaper than point-to-point fares only if the traveler is taking more than one long trip.
✔ Can be most efficiently used by plotting an itinerary that follows a continuous loop or that takes a hub-and-spoke approach.

Rental Cars

■ WHAT SERVICES DO CAR RENTAL COMPANIES PROVIDE, AND WHAT REQUIREMENTS SHOULD CAR RENTERS EXPECT TO MEET?

A car is an expensive nuisance in cities that have excellent public transportation or extreme congestion. On long trips, taking a car is exhausting for the driver, and it may be uncomfortable for the passengers. Often, though, these disadvantages pale beside the advantages of renting a car. Car rentals offer

■ Freedom to change an itinerary. Business travelers can pursue a new lead or rearrange appointments. Vacationers can follow their whims and take the road less traveled.

■ Flexibility to combine different modes of transportation, such as flying and then renting a car rather than driving many hours.

■ Access to destinations unreachable by other means. Car rentals permit vacationers to stay at country inns, farmhouses, or less expensive hotels hidden in the countryside. In a great many places, such as Florida and California, getting around without a car is extremely difficult.

■ Room for baggage. A car is like a huge extra suitcase, enabling travelers to carry loose items such as books, food, or sports gear without difficulty.

■ Economy. The larger the group traveling together and dividing the cost of the vehicle, the more economical the rental becomes.

Americans certainly appreciate these benefits: In the past, they have put more than 1.7 million rental vehicles on the road annually.

U.S. Car Rental Companies

The history of car rental companies goes back to 1916, but it was the expansion of air travel that transformed car rental into the major enterprise it is today (see Table 5.2 on the next page). Overall, about 65 percent of U.S. car rentals occur at airport locations, and a majority of the jobs are there, too.

Some companies, though, do most of their business, not with people at airports, but with people who rent cars in their hometowns because their own cars broke down or were stolen. Enterprise, for example, rents most of its cars to this *replacement market;* 94 percent of its transactions occurred at nonairport locations in 2003. About 50 percent of U.S. car rentals are made through travel agencies.

For a car rental company, the ups and downs of economic life are tied to the state of the auto industry. When auto manufacturers are hungry for sales, car rental companies can obtain their cars on favorable terms. Boom times for the auto industry translate into tough terms for the car rental companies and declining profits.

Competition among car rental firms is stiff, but there is little difference in the cars they offer. To distinguish themselves in the marketplace, some companies emphasize full service (Hertz, Avis, and National) and others emphasize savings (Thrifty and Dollar). The categories are far from absolute, however. "Full-service" companies may try to compete on the basis of price and sometimes cost less than those that emphasize savings, and "economical" companies often give good service. Also, companies may change strategies. Budget, for example, has been categorized as a company that targets customers looking for savings, but in the late 1990s it emphasized its service in order to attract business travelers. Generally speaking, business travelers expect high levels of service from a car rental company, whereas many leisure travelers are willing to sacrifice service to save on the rate.

Fleets and Services

Companies use slightly different terms to describe their fleets, but generally the cars fall into six classes:
- *Economy* or *subcompact,* which are small cars that are suitable for one or two persons and have few options.
- *Compact,* which are slightly larger than subcompacts and may have a few more options.

TABLE 5.2 Leading U.S. Car Rental Companies

Five car rental companies dominate the industry, although dozens of small and local companies also compete successfully.

Company	U.S. Cars in Service (avg.) 2010	# U.S. Locations	2010 U.S. Revenue Estimated (in millions)
Enterprise Holdings (includes Alamo Rent A Car, Enterprise Rent-A-Car, National Car Rental)	850,689	6,187	$9,800
Hertz (includes Advantage Rent-A-Car)	290,000	2,300	$4,158
Avis Budget Group	270,000	2,100	$3,850
Dollar Thrifty Automotive Group	108,000	464	$1,540
All others	110,872	6,072	$1,203

Source: Data from *Auto Rental News,* as posted at www.fleet-central.com, July 2011.

- *Intermediate* or *midsize,* which are suitable for three or four persons for short distances and may include amenities.
- *Standard* or *full size,* which can seat four persons comfortably.
- *Luxury* or *premium,* which are expensive deluxe models.
- *Sport utility vehicles (SUVs) and vans,* which seat seven or have extra cargo area.

Car renters can reserve a particular class but usually not a specific make or model. If the customer has a reservation and the confirmed class is not available at the time of rental, the customer is usually given the next higher class at the rate of the confirmed class.

Large companies usually have convertibles, SUVs, and minivans in their fleet. They may or may not be able to meet requests for sports cars, jeeps, and other specialty cars. Some companies specialize in motor home rentals.

If travelers want child safety seats, four-wheel drive, bike racks, ski racks, or tire chains, they must request these and pay extra. Daytime running lights and hand controls are other options. Cellular phones and computerized navigational systems are available as optional features in most cities, although they may be available only in luxury models. Some companies offer CD players; some are experimenting with in-car shopping catalogs and "concierge service" for travelers who need urgent help.

Full-service companies might aim to provide
- Speedy handling of phone reservations.
- Speedy check-in, pickup, and drop-off procedures.
- More convenient locations.
- Drop-off freedom (renting the car in one city and returning it in another).
- New cars with few miles.
- Cars with more amenities.
- Clean cars.
- More locations to switch cars (in case something is wrong with the first one rented).

To promote customer loyalty, car rental firms have three types of programs:
- *Service clubs,* which give members preferential treatment. For example, National offers the Emerald Club Aisle Service. Members can reserve a car an hour in advance, and they can bypass the rental counter and personally select their own cars.
- *Frequent-renter plans,* which reward renters with free upgrades or rentals after a certain number of paid rentals. For example, Alamo's True Blue program gives renters points for each rental; they can use their points for rentals and priority service.
- *Tie-ins* with frequent-traveler programs offered by airlines and hotels. For example, for each rental day with Alamo, members of Alaska Airlines' Mileage Plan earn 50 air miles. Most major rental companies have partnerships with numerous frequent-flyer programs.

Requirements and Procedures

A hotel room does not move away from its rental location, and an airline chooses its own extremely qualified "drivers." In contrast, the car rental firm loses control over its expensive investment the moment that the unknown client drives it away. This difference is reflected in the conditions that car renters must meet before they are approved.

The renter must
- Have a valid driver's license.

- Be at least 25 years of age, ordinarily. Those who are 18 to 24 years old may qualify with certain companies under certain conditions, such as if they hold a credit card or if an employer or parent fills out certain forms.
- Be creditworthy. Holding a major credit card usually satisfies this requirement. If the traveler does not have an acceptable credit card, a travel counselor may issue a prepaid voucher. A person who has neither a credit card nor a prepaid voucher may still be able to rent a car, but it may take several days to make the arrangements. The company may need to verify the renter's address, telephone number, employment, bank account, and even references.

In addition, in some states the potential car renter's driving record will be checked—but not until the person appears at the counter. Drivers with serious violations such as driving while using alcohol or leaving the scene of an accident will be denied the rental.

Other terms and conditions may apply at different times and places; for example, there may be restrictions regarding what state lines may be crossed, and violators may face substantial fees. Satellite positioning systems allow rental companies to track their cars.

CLOSE-UP: ON THE JOB WITH FRANK SCIATA, CAR RENTAL AGENT

Frank Sciata works for one of the largest car rental companies in the country. It emphasizes economy first and serves a higher percentage of leisure customers than other big car rental companies. Most of Frank's day is spent behind the rental counter dealing with people who have just flown into the city.

"I started out 'hiking cars,' or that's what I called it—it was transferring cars from one location to another, usually from downtown to the airport, part-time. If there was nothing to be driven, I'd help out cleaning the cars. Then I started driving the van from the airport to the agency and back. This was fun because I've always liked to drive.

"After a while, though, I realized there wasn't much advancement unless I got to work in the office, and there weren't many openings. When there was one and they hired an outsider, I figured maybe they'll just always think of me as a driver, so I applied somewhere else and got hired right away at a larger company. They sent me for sales and computer training and then put me right to work as a rental agent.

"My past experience was an advantage. I knew little things about the cars, how they were serviced, and the inventory, and I could discuss the aspects of each car with clients. I have to check each person's driver's license and credit card. Most people have a reservation when they come in. If their license and credit card check out, they get the car. If they don't have a credit card, they may not get the car unless they've made prior arrangements for us to check out their job and credit. But there's a lot more to it than that.

"I have to make sure the client understands the rental agreement and charges. Better they understand it now than after they are finished using the car. It happens quite a few times that people come in after the rental and argue about the bill. They didn't bother to take a good look at it when they got it. And some people bring the car in early and then wonder why their bill isn't less. Sometimes it is, but if they got a special discount for a weekend or week, it may even cost more if it's returned early. A deal is a deal. Bring the car in early and it's a different deal and a different rate. They can't believe it; I wonder what business they are in.

"A lot of people make a reservation for the best price they hear but might not actually want that car when they arrive. A lot of times it's for the least expensive car, which is not as strong and safe and not as large as the car they're used to driving. It's my job to see if a better car would suit their needs.

"Usually business travelers have reserved the car they want and stick with it. But the vacationers are all over the lot on this. They think they're going to fit seven kids into a compact car. So I always explain the next size or two larger to them and how much it will cost. Often we have a special if they upgrade their car then and there. It may not cost them that much more.

"I'm fairly good about selling larger cars, waivers, and fuel options. I always reach my monthly quota. The business has been growing every year, and I'm looking for advancement to shift manager and maybe station manager in the long run, if I stick with it. I'm also going to school taking business classes."

Rental Rates

Cars are rented on a 24-hour basis. If you pick up the car at 3:45 P.M. on one day and drop it off by that time the next day, a 1-day rental will be charged. There is usually a 59-minute "grace" period, after which additional charges apply.

The cost of renting a car varies widely among cities; it may even change with the pickup point within a city. Generally, companies offer different rates for different classes of cars and for daily, weekly, and weekend rentals. Weekly rates are usually substantially lower than seven times the daily rate. Weekend rates are usually less than weekday rates.

In addition to the charge for the time rented, there may be a mileage charge. The different ways of handling mileage yield three types of rental rates:

- *Time plus mileage.* The car renter is charged a fee for a certain amount of time plus a fee per mile driven; for example, the rate might be $19 a day and 3 cents per mile.
- *Time with mileage cap.* The car renter is charged per day, with a certain number of miles allowed; for additional mileage, there is a charge. For example, the rate might be $29 a day with 100 included miles and 29 cents per mile above 100 miles. If the car is rented for 1 day and driven 120 miles, the charge would be $34.80.
- *Time with unlimited mileage.* The car renter can drive any number of miles for the same price. If the rate is $29 per day and the car is driven 500 miles, the charge is still $29.

Car renters may obtain discounts on the standard rates if they belong to frequent-renter plans, certain organizations such as the American Association of Retired Persons (AARP), or motor clubs. The best-known motor club is the **American Automobile Association (AAA),** which offers members a variety of travel and motoring services. Also, renters may receive discounts if their companies participate in a corporate discount program.

Rental rates generally cover oil, minor repairs, public liability insurance, and property damage insurance. But because of additional charges, the car renter's final fee may be more than double the quoted rental price. Additional charges might include

- Drop-off charges. Dropping the car at a location different from the pickup point usually brings an extra charge, if it is permitted at all.
- Special equipment. Bike racks and ski racks are examples.
- Fuel. If the gas tank is not full when the renter returns the vehicle, a charge of close to double the regular cost of fuel may be applied. To avoid this fee, some companies offer clients the option of buying a full tank in advance at current prices; the renter gets no credit for gas left in the tank upon return.
- Additional drivers. Nonregistered drivers may void the car rental contract and make the renter liable for any damages or injuries.
- Taxes. Up to three local taxes, including an airport surcharge, are added to the car rental in some cities.

One other important possible cost covers insurance. Rates and rules are complex and vary from state to state and from company to company. We take a closer look at this troublesome topic in the next section.

Insurance and Waivers

Car rental agreements include—at no extra charge—liability for damage to persons, to other cars, or to property. But who pays for damage to or theft of the rented car itself? Rental agreements state how much the company will pay.

In many cases, the agreement leaves the renter liable for thousands of dollars or for the entire cost of the car.

For an additional charge, car rental companies in many states offer

- A *collision damage waiver (CDW),* which waives the rental company's right to charge the renter for damages if the rental car is involved in an accident.
- A *loss damage waiver (LDW),* which waives the company's right to recover damages resulting from theft or vandalism as well as from collisions.
- *Personal accident insurance (PAI),* which covers bodily injury to the car renter. PAI is sometimes included with a CDW or LDW or is offered at a low rate.
- *Additional liability insurance (ALI)* or *extended liability insurance (ELI),* which adds insurance for injuries to persons or property up to $1 million above what is covered by the renter's own car insurance and what the rental company is mandated by state law to cover.

State laws differ regarding the amount of insurance that car rental companies must themselves provide. In some states, laws prohibit the sale of some of these forms of insurance. The cost of CDWs and LDWs has traditionally been very high.

In fact, many travelers do not need any of this coverage, or they can get it more cheaply elsewhere. Often, the renter's own car insurance or the credit card used for the rental will cover any damage to the rented car. However, this coverage may not be in effect for special situations (such as antique automobiles, certain vans, motorcycles, or recreational vehicles) or if the car is rented for more than 2 weeks.

In any event, a travel insurer may offer the same coverage for less than half the cost of a CDW or LDW from the car rental company. For example, car renters can purchase CDW-equivalent coverage over the phone or on the Internet through Travel Guard International. Similarly, the car renter's own health and life insurance is likely to provide the coverage offered by PAIs.

Whether car renters need additional insurance coverage should be determined ahead of time. Renters are very likely to find it difficult to read and understand all of the fine print of the car rental agreement while standing at the rental counter, and it may be impossible at that point for them to determine whether their personal insurance is adequate. It is the client's responsibility to determine whether the coverage provided by a CDW, LDW, PAI, or ALI/ELI is needed. But travel counselors should explain the matter as clearly as possible so that the client will know what information is needed.

International Car Rentals

Cars can be rented practically anywhere in the world. In fact, in much of the world you can find offices of the major U.S. car rental companies. Auto Europe, Europe by Car, and Kemwel are other well-known companies that arrange rentals with various car companies in Europe. These companies offer a number of helpful services. For example, Auto Europe offers maps with estimated drive times between cities, rather than just listing mileage.

Driving Abroad. Travelers who want to drive while abroad should check whether their U.S. driver's licenses allow them to drive at their destinations. Major European countries accept U.S. driver's licenses. Some countries elsewhere require an *International Driver's Permit (IDP),* which is essentially a translation of the bearer's driver's license into an internationally recognized format. The IDP is available from the American Automobile Association

(AAA) at a fee of $15 for members or $25 for non-members plus the cost of photos. To obtain an IDP, travelers must present a valid license, pay a fee, and submit two passport-size photos. Some countries, however, require local driver's permits, and a few allow only chauffeur-driven service. The car rental company should be able to provide information about these regulations.

Driving in certain countries is more of a challenge than in others. For example, cities observing the typical Mediterranean work schedule have four major rush hours; drivers are bound to get caught in one rush hour or another. The German autobahn has no speed limits. Driving is on the left side of the road in Japan, Thailand, Britain, and most members of the British Commonwealth. Those who plan to drive while abroad should familiarize themselves with international signs before their departure (see Figure 5.5).

Traffic abroad often moves faster and more aggressively than in the United States, and in some countries the injury and death rates for auto collisions are far higher than in the United States. Drunk-driving regulations in most countries are stricter than those in the United States, ranging from prison to death. Note that American insurance is not valid in Mexico whether driving a rental car or one's own car.

Rentals Abroad. Perhaps the most important point to keep in mind about international car rentals is that they should be reserved in advance. In most cases, car rentals are substantially less expensive if they are booked or paid for before the traveler leaves the United States or Canada.

Procedures for renting a car abroad are quite similar to those in the United States. Only the type of car, not the model, can be guaranteed. Rental fleets vary from country to country. Cars familiar to Americans may be given different names abroad. To help renters, most firms renting European cars publish pictures of their fleets in their brochures and on their Web sites.

There are some other differences between renting a car in the United States and abroad.

- Luggage space will generally be somewhat smaller than in cars in the United States. If a roof rack is needed, it must be ordered in advance.
- Automatic transmission must be specifically requested in advance; the cost varies greatly.
- Air conditioning must be specifically requested. It may not be available in

FIGURE 5.5 International Signs

The American Automobile Association and any good road atlas have a complete list of international signs.

many countries or on mini, compact, economy, and intermediate cars; it probably will be available only on the largest and most expensive cars.

- Fuel prices may be significantly different. In some popular destinations they can be two to four times those in the United States.
- Value-added taxes (VATs) may not be included in the general rates and can range from 10 to 25 percent of the total rental charge. (Travel counselors should quote the rate and add the tax for the client.)
- Cars rented in one country may not be taken across a border into another country. Or special documents may be needed to do so.
- U.S. auto insurance policies usually do not cover rentals abroad.
- Some rental companies in a few countries may have a maximum age limit as well as the usual minimum age requirements.

Alternatives to Car Rentals. Renting may not be the best solution for everyone who wants access to a car when abroad. Clients who need a car for a month or more might instead consider *leasing*, which is essentially a prearranged purchase/repurchase plan. Leased cars come new from the factory and usually cost less than long rentals. Furthermore, a leased car is not subject to the high taxes levied on rentals in European countries. Insurance is usually completely covered in the lease rate.

International car purchase may offer advantages for those on a lengthy overseas trip, depending on the currency exchange rate. The car must meet visa regulations, however. Also, U.S. regulations often change regarding

---

CLOSE-UP: SELLING AND QUALIFYING

Because cars are so familiar, it may seem as if renting one would not require much thought. But clients who reserve a car that is too small or who do not understand drop-off restrictions or fuel charges could end up with an uncomfortable or unnecessarily expensive trip. Not informing clients about insurance regulations could have worse consequences.

A first and most obvious question is whether a client needs a rental car at all. Business travelers may not need one if they are handling business at a hotel that offers an airport shuttle or if they are doing most of their work at a central location in a city with good public transportation or limo service—such as New York, Chicago, Paris, London, and Tokyo. In cities like these, taking a taxi or public transportation will cost less in money and energy than a car rental. Similarly, leisure travelers staying in the centers of many cities are likely to find walking, taking buses and subways, or taking taxis much more pleasant than driving. In most other cases, unless they are being escorted on a tour, both business and leisure clients will find a car essential.

Once you have determined that a traveler needs a car rental, what else do you need to know in order to serve the customer? Here are the key questions.

- Does the client meet the requirements for renting a car?

- When and where will the client pick up the car and drop it off?
- What kind of car does the client want to rent? (A good way to match car and driver is to ask what type of car the client owns and then ask if he or she wants a similar one.)
- Is the client a member of a frequent-traveler plan? (The possibility of earning points or air miles, or of using the rewards from one of these programs to rent the car, might determine the choice of rental company. Also, if the client is a member of a frequent-traveler plan, the membership number should be added to the reservation.)
- Is the client eligible for discounts? (If the client has a discount coupon or saw an advertised sale, get the accompanying code number.)
- For how long does the client want the car?
- What is the approximate itinerary or number of miles that will be driven?
- What will the charges be?
- What extra charges might be added on?
- Does the client understand the insurance included and the insurance offered by the rental company? Does the client understand how to determine whether the additional insurance offered is needed?
- Is the client also traveling by air on the trip? (If so, note the arrival time and flight number.)

whether the car is considered used when shipped to the United States—an important point for tax purposes. It is wise to use a company that specializes in factory-delivered cars in order to obtain the latest choice of purchase plans and the latest shipping and import information.

✔ CHECK-UP

U.S. car rental companies may be roughly classified according to whether they emphasize
✔ Rentals to air travelers or to those who rent from their hometowns.
✔ Competing through full service or through price.

Rental fleets generally include six types of cars:
✔ Economy or subcompact.
✔ Compact.
✔ Intermediate or midsize.
✔ Standard or full size.
✔ Luxury or premium.
✔ Sport utility vehicles (SUVs) and vans.

Motorcoaches

■ WHAT ARE THE VARIOUS USES OF MOTORCOACHES?

For many Americans, bus transportation is the last resort. They expect buses to be slow and uncomfortable. Today, however, some buses are equipped with plush seats, restrooms, bars, DVD players with multiscreens throughout the coach, and WiFi. Specially designed coaches intended for a small number of passengers may have lounge chairs, sofas, and tables. This upgrading is reflected in the fact that buses are now called *motorcoaches;* the term *bus* usually connotes a vehicle with few amenities that is used only for short trips, such as the buses used for public transportation within cities.

In thousands of American communities, buses are the only alternative to cars; no other public mode of transportation serves these communities. For those who do have a choice among bus, rail, and plane, intercity bus service traditionally offered the advantage of being the cheapest way to travel. But bus companies have had difficulty maintaining this competitive advantage. Although about a hundred privately owned companies still provide regularly scheduled bus service between U.S. cities, Greyhound Bus Lines is now the only nationwide bus carrier.

Intercity travel represents only one of the uses of motorcoaches. Others include
■ *Transfers*—that is, transportation between hotels and airports, docks, or railroad stations. Motorcoaches are often the most efficient transportation for transfers and for trips from a hotel to a restaurant or to a special activity such as skiing.
■ Sightseeing within a city and its surrounding area.
■ Motorcoach tours run by bus companies themselves or by travel agencies or tour operators. (Chapter 8 covers tours in detail.)
■ Charters by private groups such as church organizations and clubs. Trips to dinner theaters, casinos, historic sites, and shopping malls are especially popular.

More than 4,000 independent motorcoach companies offer charters and local sightseeing. Many local sightseeing lines have connections with two of the largest sightseeing companies, Gray Line and Sightseeing.com (formerly American Sightseeing International, a worldwide association of sightseeing tours and charter companies).

Selling Ground Transportation

- WHAT ARE THE ADVANTAGES OF EACH FORM OF GROUND TRANSPORTATION?
- WHAT OTHER GROUND SERVICES CAN COUNSELORS OFFER?

Each form of ground transportation has an important place in travel. Rail offers opportunities for meeting other passengers and for relaxing—viewing the scenery, walking about, eating and drinking comfortably. Auto travel provides flexibility—the opportunity to drive to and from almost all lodgings, restaurants, or places of interest—and the ability to carry much more luggage. For transfers, though, a motorcoach is often the best means of transportation.

Although the sale of domestic ground transportation is not known for its glamour, these forms of transportation are certainly significant to travelers. For example, more than one-fifth of all business trips involve use of a rental car. Ground transportation represents a market opportunity that travel professionals cannot afford to overlook.

For travel counselors, selling ground transportation offers chances both for earning revenue directly from the sale and for giving the kind of service that earns the loyalty of clients. With little extra effort, for example, travel counselors can increase sales by suggesting rental cars to their air travelers. Providing good service, however, might be more important in the long run. Arranging for transfers and preparing travelers for their arrivals represent two important services provided by travel counselors.

Transfers

Because of their small cost and brief duration, transfers are easy to overlook when planning a trip. Unfortunately, the result can be memorable. Arriving in a strange city half asleep from jet lag, loaded down with luggage, and confused about what to do next is no way to begin a journey.

Sometimes it might be appropriate to have clients met and helped by interpreters or to sell clients vouchers for transfers. In some cases, arranging for limousine service may be the best option for clients. Book-A-Limo is one of the fastest-growing limousine services in the United States; it also offers service at many international destinations. Carey International is a well-known limousine service available in 550 cities in 60 countries.

Just giving information may be a significant service. For example, a travel counselor might want to tell travelers ahead of time that after arriving on Capri they will transfer by *funicular* (a cable railway), with porters wheeling their bags in carts. This bit of information can both enhance the travelers' trip and heighten their esteem for the travel counselor.

Taking the extra step to find out if their hotel provides shuttle service (vans) to and from the airport will contribute to clients' feeling that they are well taken care of by their travel counselor. When hotels don't provide shuttle service, they often have information regarding local, independent shuttle services that make regular stops at their property. Many of these local companies allow advance reservations.

If taxi service is the best choice for a transfer, a travel counselor can provide clients with approximate taxi rates in advance. Armed with this information, travelers will know how much money to have ready and will be confident that they are paying a reasonable fare.

Additional Services

Technology offers ways of improving service. Travel counselors can use the Internet to obtain for their clients a local map, a description of ground transportation from the airport, and schedules for public transportation or (for clients who are driving) exact directions from one destination to another. Travel counselors can reserve a seat on a train in Australia as easily as one on Amtrak. They can meet travelers' needs before the travelers are even aware of those needs. Check the many passes offered on Rail Europe's Web site (http://agent.raileurope.com), for example, and imagine a new traveler trying to decide among them. Travel counselors can help clients choose the right pass—and, along the way, can sell other products as well.

Other services counselors can provide to their clients could include a car and driver, an airport meet and greet, a translator, and other offerings from a variety of specialty companies.

Except for car rental companies and Amtrak, most ground transportation companies are not included on GDSs but might be found online. Look for the section of the Web site that is reserved for travel agencies; it will offer inside information and indicate if and how services are commissionable. If the site does not have such a section, call or e-mail the company to establish a relationship.

CHAPTER WRAP-UP

CHAPTER HIGHLIGHTS

Smooth transportation by rail, car, or motorcoach can be critical to the success of any traveler's journey; knowing about ground transportation and how to sell it can be key to a travel professional's success. Here is a review of the objectives with which we began the chapter.

1. **Describe rail service in the United States and Europe.** Amtrak provides almost all of the passenger train service available in the United States. Amtrak offers coach, business, and first class, as well as sleeping accommodations, but not all classes of service are available on all trains. Reservations are always required for all classes of service except coach. Food service is available on most routes, and meals are included with sleeping accommodations. Types of fares include basic Point-to-Point tickets, the USA Rail Pass, and numerous discounts and promotional fares. Amtrak also offers many vacation packages.

The railroads of continental Europe are known for their high-quality service and high-speed trains (such as France's TGV and Eurostar). Accommodations include compartments and *couchettes* as well as private sleeping accommodations.

For many tourists, rail passes are a convenient, economical way to travel. Amtrak offers a rail pass known as USA Rail. Unlike the Canrailpass from VIA Rail of Canada, which can be bought in Canada, the USA Rail pass can be purchased only outside the United States. The Eurailpass is good for unlimited first-class train travel in 23 European countries for specified periods. There are also many variations of the Eurailpass, such as Saverpass, Youthpass, and Selectpass. Other passes exist for individual countries or combinations of countries; the BritRail pass is one of the most widely used. Rail Europe provides a convenient portal through which U.S. agencies can book both European and Amtrak rail travel.

2. **Outline the services provided by car rental companies and the requirements that renters should expect to meet.** There is little difference in the cars offered by different car rental companies, and renters usually can reserve only a particular class of car, not a specific make or model. Some companies emphasize the service they provide—such as cars with the latest gadgets, speedy check-in, or drop-off freedom. The car renter must have a valid driver's license. Possession of a major credit card is important and often necessary; renting a car without one requires either a prepaid voucher or a thorough credit check. Those under 25 years of age must also make special arrangements to qualify for a car rental. Rental companies may refuse cars to those with poor driving records. The renter might pay daily, weekend, or weekly rates. Most companies offer unlimited mileage, but some add a charge for each mile driven over a certain number or for all miles driven. Renters may incur extra charges for drop-off fees, special equipment, fuel, additional drivers, or various taxes. Car rental companies also sell collision damage waivers (CDWs), loss damage waivers (LDWs), personal accident insurance (PAI), and additional liability insurance (ALI) or extended liability insurance (ELI), but many renters are adequately covered without these.

Overseas, car fleets may be different, and familiar cars may appear under different names. Cars are likely to offer less luggage space. Automatic transmission and air conditioning must be requested and paid for, and fuel is likely to be significantly more expensive than in the United States. In some countries travelers will need an International Driver's Permit (IDP), which can be obtained from AAA. In most cases, booking the overseas rental before leaving the United States is much less expensive than booking it when abroad.

3. **Identify the functions played by motorcoaches.** In many American communities, motorcoaches are the only form of public transportation available. Motorcoaches are used not only for intercity travel but also for transfers, sightseeing, tours, and chartered trips by groups such as church organizations.

4. **Explain the comparative advantages of traveling by rail, car, or motorcoach.** Rail provides the opportunity to meet other passengers, to walk around, and to relax. Auto travel provides flexibility and the ability to carry much more luggage, and if several people are traveling together and sharing car expenses, it can be very viable financially. For transfers, though, a motorcoach is often the best means of transportation.

5. **Discuss the roles of transfers and technology in the selling of ground travel.** Arranging transfers provides an opportunity not only to gain revenue but also to provide an important service that can help gain a client's loyalty. In different circumstances, motorcoaches, limousines, shuttles, or taxis might be the best choice for a transfer; some destinations offer unusual options such as a funicular. Learning to find information about these options online is just one way that travel counselors can use the Internet to improve the service they offer clients.

KEY TERMS

A list of key terms introduced in this chapter follows. If you do not recall the meaning of these terms, see the Glossary, which begins on page 393.

Acela Express
additional liability insurance (ALI)
American Automobile Association (AAA)
Amtrak
BritRail pass
bullet train
Canrailpass
Chunnel
collision damage waiver (CDW)
couchette
Eurailpass (Eurail Global Pass)
Eurostar
extended liability insurance (ELI)

International Driver's Permit (IDP)
loss damage waiver (LDW)
motorcoach
personal accident insurance (PAI)
Point-to-Point tickets
Rail Europe
rail pass
specialty train
TGV
transfers
USA Rail pass
VIA Rail

REVIEW QUESTIONS

1. What kinds of clients might prefer to travel by Amtrak rather than by car or plane?

2. What types of clients might benefit from a Eurailpass?

3. In which situations or places might a car rental be necessary?

4. An economy car rental is advertised at $99 per week with unlimited mileage. For what kinds of clients might this car be inappropriate? What extra charges might be applied to this rental?

5. Why might a client refuse to buy a collision damage waiver or personal accident insurance?

6. Explain how you can use the Internet and e-mail to obtain information on additional ground services for independent travelers.

CHAPTER 6

Accommodations

OBJECTIVES

After completing this chapter, you should be able to

1. Identify at least 10 of the 20 types of properties listed that exist worldwide.

2. Discuss the major trends in how accommodations are owned and operated, and describe some key market segments.

3. Outline the roles of hotels and travel counselors in selling accommodations.

4. List the characteristics that may affect the price of a room.

5. Make a checklist of the information that is needed when making a hotel reservation for a client.

What does this word *accommodations* mean? In the travel/tourism industry it generally is recognized as somewhere to sleep. Other terms are **lodging**, the **hospitality industry**, or the *hotel* industry. Or as one author put it succinctly, "It's a home away from home."

Within the overall tourism industry, this sector is the largest employer, with the largest number of opportunities, and often provides young people with their first jobs. Best of all, the sector is found worldwide with many different types of **properties** making up this multi-billion dollar industry. And employees interact with many other parts of the travel/tourism industry, such as travel agencies, tour operators, restaurants, meeting and event planners, and the entertainment industry.

Accommodations may be found in big cities and in the countryside, in the mountains and at the seashore, in campsites and in private homes, in dormitories and in apartments. But regardless of the many different kinds of properties, all must meet basic requirements. They must be:

- clean
- quiet
- secure
- comfortable
- attractive

This chapter first explores the characteristic of the hotel industry, then looks at accommodations themselves and how to sell them.

FIGURE 6.1

Milestones in the History of U.S. Hotels

U.S. hotels have kept pace with the country's rising living standards, progressing from rooms with telephones to rooms with computers.

1829 Tremont Hotel in Boston is the first U.S. hotel to offer indoor toilets and private bedrooms with locks on the doors.

1907 E.M. Statler opens his first hotel in Buffalo, New York. It has individual rooms with private baths and caters to business travelers.

1907 The Plaza Hotel in New York City installs telephones in each room.

1919 Conrad Hilton opens his first hotel, the Mobley, in Texas.

1925 The first motel, Mo-Tel Inn, opens in San Luis Obispo, California.

1927 Radio reception is made available to guests at the Boston Statler.

1929 The first U.S. airport hotel is built at the Oakland Municipal Airport.

1934 The Detroit Statler is the first hotel to air-condition every room.

1945 Sheraton becomes the first hotel company to be listed on the New York Stock Exchange, and Travelodge becomes the first economy hotel corporation.

1946 The first casino hotel, the Flamingo, opens in Las Vegas.

1947 New York City's Roosevelt Hotel installs television sets in every room.

1949 Hilton becomes the first international hotel chain.

1952 Kemmons Wilson opens the first Holiday Inn in Memphis, Tennessee.

1958 Sheraton installs a centralized reservation system.

1964 Holiday Inn establishes a computerized reservation system.

1968 The first all-inclusive resort, Club Med, begins marketing to Americans.

1981 In-room movies are available in 500,000 U.S. guestrooms.

1995 Radisson and Holiday Inn go online, allowing Internet bookings.

1999 Choice International becomes the first chain to test making in-room PCs a standard amenity.

2004 Ninety-eight percent of hotel rooms offer cable or satellite television.

2011 Many U.S. hotels offer guests Internet access.

The Business of Accommodations

■ WHAT ARE THE DOMINANT TRENDS IN HOW ACCOMMODATIONS ARE OWNED, MANAGED, AND MARKETED?

The U.S. hotel industry has more than 4 million guestrooms and directly employs close to 2 million workers. It pays $186 billion in travel-related wages and salaries. (The Close-Up on careers describes some of the job opportunities.) How did this economic giant develop, and what keeps it running?

A Brief History

The history of accommodations goes back at least to the times described in the Bible, which includes many references to lodgings. Travelers from ancient Rome were required to carry official documents that granted them permission to travel and stay in private *mansionis*. In medieval Europe, inns for travelers in dangerous regions were often run by monks. More than four hundred years ago, the Incas of South America kept inns (called *tambos*) along a road thousands of miles long. But it was only in the late 1700s that large, comfortable lodgings like today's hotels appeared. Figure 6.1 describes some milestones in the history of hotels in the United States.

Over the years, transportation and accommodations have evolved together. In the United States, cities in the Northeast became transportation centers, for example, they also became home to the first luxurious hotels. As trains opened up the West to travelers in the late 1800s, railroad companies built some of Canada's grandest hotels. And in the early twentieth century, the growing popularity of automobiles paved the way for the rise of motels (short for *motor hotels*).

It was in 1925 that the word *motel* was coined. Arthur Heineman gave the name Mo-Tel Inn to his long one-story establishment on Route 101 in San Luis Obispo, California. Motels introduced many Americans to steam heat, tile bathrooms, sliding glass doors, and radio—features that were promoted on hundreds of motel signs along the highways. Motels caught on because they allowed motorists to be close to their vehicles and belongings, to park easily, and to avoid dealing with hotel lobbies after a tiring, dusty drive. Also, motels usually cost less than hotels because motels were built on less expensive land on the outskirts of town and did without large lobbies.

The 1930s Depression devastated the hotel business; after World War II the U.S. industry was rebuilt as Americans took to the road and to the air. The railroads were deteriorating, air travel was expanding, and in 1956 the federal government began building the interstate highway system. City hotels suffered from both the loss of railroad travelers and their inability to provide enough parking for the increasing number of motorists. Travelers on the new highways looked for lodging more convenient than the downtown hotels. Motels sprang up everywhere. Many were built by chains and offered swimming pools, televisions, and convenient reservation systems. The small mom-and-pop cabins, called **tourist courts**, built in the 1920s could not compete.

Economic changes during the 1970s and 1980s produced other innovations in accommodations. As air travel boomed, new hotels were built near airports. As major American cities were revitalized, large hotels came back to the downtown areas. In fact, by the late 1980s there were too many

Mobility is excellent in the accommodations industry, the segment of the travel industry that employs the most people. Pay levels tend to be low for entry-level positions, but you can rise rapidly to better positions. Opportunities are greatest at the largest chains and smallest hotels. The best way to get in the door is by working part-time, on weekends, or on the night shift. But be prepared to give service. The accommodations industry puts great demands on your time and personal life. To climb the career ladder, you may have to relocate frequently.

■ **Position** Front desk clerk

Description The front desk clerk checks guests in and out, makes reservations, and handles requests from guests. At some hotels, the clerk may also perform office duties such as posting payments and maintaining records.

Qualifications Typically, this is an entry-level position that is part of the hotel's management training program. Companies look for a person with some background in customer service, a polished appearance, and a personable manner. The ability to speak other languages may be an asset at some properties.

■ **Position** Sales manager

Description Soliciting and booking business is the heart of this job. Depending on the hotel, it might involve dealing with corporate accounts, convention organizers, tour operators, travel counselors, international clients, and so on. The sales manager participates in trade shows, makes sales calls, and delivers presentations. The sales manager usually has latitude to spot and pursue untapped markets and to help fashion packages or pricing programs.

Qualifications Employers look for prior sales experience. A sales assistant might move up to this job.

■ **Position** Food and beverage manager

Description Directing the production and service of food and beverages is the essence of this position. It involves training dining room and kitchen staff, ensuring quality control, planning menus, budgeting and purchasing ingredients, and selecting wine and liquor.

Qualifications Usually, this position requires experience in management and training from a hospitality or culinary arts program. It also demands a keen interest in food and wine, knowledge of food trends and guests' tastes, and a willingness to work long hours under pressure and ability to supervise and work collaboratively with food and beverage personnel.

■ **Position** Catering manager

Description This manager sells food and beverages and related services for banquets. The job involves working directly with the staff and the clients—such as convention organizers and local groups—as well as supervising the banquet service.

Qualifications Sales experience, interpersonal skills, a talent for details, and a flair for entertaining are needed.

■ **Position** Executive housekeeper

Description This key position brings responsibility for training, scheduling, and supervising all housekeeping personnel and for purchasing supplies.

Qualifications Housekeepers may be promoted to this position, but in some hotels it requires management experience. Leadership ability and knowledge of inventory control, scheduling, hiring, and training are needed.

■ **Position** Concierge

Description The concierge recommends and makes reservations for restaurants, activities, and attractions and answers guests' questions about how to get around, what is open and when, and where to find just about anything. The concierge also arranges limousines and babysitting services, books accommodations in other cities, and provides information on an incredible variety of subjects. In short, the concierge aims to satisfy a guest's every wish.

Qualifications Prior experience is not essential, but the concierge must possess a wealth of knowledge and great resourcefulness, as well as a polished, professional demeanor and can-do attitude. Other prerequisites include personal knowledge of the destination, excellent interpersonal skills, understanding of the hotel industry, and proficiency in two or more languages.

■ **Position** Programmer analyst (for a hotel company)

Description This professional is responsible for the day-to-day operation and support of the forecast management system as well as programming enhancements.

Qualifications Employers look for two to three years of programming experience, experience in developing Web-based applications, and a thorough understanding of relevant technical subjects such as relational database design.

■ **Other positions** Convention sales director; engineering and facility maintenance specialist; resident manager; sales representative; security specialist.

rooms and too few guests. When the economy weakened, the hotel industry lost money for six straight years.

In the 1990s the lodging industry responded to economic challenges by expanding overseas and competing with many of the world's most famous hotels (see Figure 6.2) by developing new forms of ownership and management, and by marketing itself aggressively. As the U.S. economy boomed, the 1990s became the most profitable era ever for the hotel industry. It took advantage of new technology to improve management, marketing, and services. For example, most hotels of any size set up their own Web sites. They put computers, fax machines, and photocopiers in "office centers" for guests and installed dataports in rooms. And increasingly, hotels used computers to track the preferences of frequent guests and to gear services such as in-room snacks and kinds of pillows to those guests.

Today, the U.S. landscape features motor hotels around small cities and towns, large downtown city hotels, airport lodgings of all kinds, and resorts for every budget. Two trends that helped spark the industry's growth in the

FIGURE 6.2 A Sampling of Some of the World's Great Hotels

City	Hotel	Comments
Athens	Grand Bretagne	Built in 1842, originally a private mansion. Fabulous views of the Acropolis and Parthenon.
Bangkok	Oriental	Opened 1899. List of celebrities who have stayed here reads like Who's Who. On the banks of the Chao Phraya River.
Cairo	Mena House	Built in 1869. Lies at foot of Pyramid of Cheops. Former royal hunting lodge turned luxury resort.
Hawaii	Halekulani	Much-loved Waikiki Beach hotel, know as "House Befitting Heaven" in the Hawaiian language.
Hong Kong	Peninsula	Opened 1928. Flagship property of Peninsula Hotels. Rooftop heliport for guests, famed for afternoon tea in the lobby.
London	Savoy	Opened 1899. Built with profits from Gilbert & Sullivan operas. Famous for its dance bands and Art Deco jazz era.
New York	Plaza	Founded in 1907. Landmark property, setting of Eloise children's books and many films. Afternoon tea a must.
Paris	Ritz	Opened 1898. Fashion designer Coco Chanel and author Ernest Hemingway lived here for years. Diana, Princess of Wales, dined here before her 1997 death in a car crash.
Quebec	Château Frontenac	Opened 1893. Overlooks St. Lawrence River. Built by Canadian Pacific Railway, managed by Fairmont.
Rio de Janeiro	Copacabana Palace	Opened 1923. Home of rich and famous, including Elton John, the Rolling Stones, and Madonna. Faces Copacabana Beach.
Singapore	Raffles	Opened 1899. Singapore Sling cocktail originated here. Hangout for authors Ernest Hemingway and Somerset Maugham.
Tokyo	Imperial	Opened 1890. Landmark hotel, withstood 7.9 earthquake because of Frank Lloyd Wright's design.
Vienna	Danieli	Formerly 14th-century home of noble Venetian family. Handmade Murano glass chandeliers, carved marble columns.

1990s continue today: (1) consolidation of ownership and management and (2) specialization in the product offered, as a result of aggressive marketing.

Ownership and Organization

Some of the world's finest hotels still operate independently, and travelers can still find *properties* (lodging establishments) with a unique character. But much as the local coffee shop has given way to Starbucks and the family diner to McDonald's, large companies dominate the lodgings market. Chains of one sort or another have spread around the globe.

Hotel Affiliations. A *chain* consists of a group of affiliated properties that bear the same name, follow the same operating procedures and standards, and share a reservation system. Holiday Inn, Sheraton, Hilton, Marriott, Ramada, and Days Inn are familiar examples. Chains of every size and kind are available.

The success of chains is easy to understand. A chain is like a *brand* name: people expect consistency from one example of the brand to the next. Travelers who go to a motel with the same name at an airport in Topeka and at the seaside in Galveston expect to get the same level of service and the same amenities, in a similar atmosphere, at similar prices relative to other motels in the area. To the travel counselor, the chain represents an easily accessible inventory of rooms with predictable standards. Reservations can be easily confirmed. Tour operators love the consistency of rooms for groups so that all tour participants receive equal rooms. Thus a chain provides a sense of security: the seller knows what is being sold, and the client knows what is being purchased.

More difficult to understand than the popularity of chains is the variety of ways they are organized. Some chains are owned by other chains or by a conglomerate (see Table 6.1 on the next page). For example, Marriott Hotels, Courtyard by Marriott, and Ritz-Carlton are all owned by Marriott, catering to different market segments. Many fast-growing chains are actually franchise operators. The *franchise company* provides the use of the name, a central reservation system, advertising, and training. The *franchisee* owns the hotel but pays a fee to the parent company and must meet its standards.

Management contracts represent another approach to ownership and management. Hotel companies manage hotels under contract with the owners. The management contract gives the operator the right to manage the property without the owner's interference; the owner is responsible for operating and financing costs.

Best Western International is an example of yet another arrangement: a *membership organization*. The "members" are individually owned and operated hotels that share a reservation system as well as marketing, purchasing, and other services. Member properties retain their independence and individuality, but they benefit from their identification with the image of Best Western, which is marketed to the public.

Hotel Representative Firms. Whatever its type of ownership and management, a hotel might turn to a hotel representative firm for help in staying competitive. *Hotel representative firms*, or *repping firms*, accept reservations and provide marketing and sales help. Rep firms in the United States include Leading Hotels of the World, Preferred Hotels, and Utell.

For hotels, repping firms provide

- Reservation systems that use toll-free numbers.
- A staff that works extended hours.
- Tie-ins with the major GDSs (global distribution systems, discussed in Chapter 3).
- Pooled marketing, including direct mail, sales calls to agencies, advertising, and participation at trade shows.
- The enhanced image that comes from being represented by a well-known firm.

Thus a hotel repping firm acts like a large sales force. These firms can be especially helpful to individually owned or remote hotels that cannot afford their own sales force.

For travel agencies, repping firms may provide

- Up-to-date information on "what's new" at a given hotel.
- Information about what rooms are available in a city.
- An easy way of making reservations for overseas hotels.
- Confirmation of reservations immediately, or within 24 hours for remote properties.
- Substantial discounts in many cases.
- A personal, perhaps local, "face" to a property.
- Speedy commission payments.

Some repping firms are, in effect, consolidators for hotels in a number of big cities. **Hotel consolidators** buy up blocks of rooms from hotels at favorable prices and then resell them at discounted rates; Hotel Reservations Network is an example. Consolidators may be able to provide rooms when a hotel is sold out or offer rooms at prices lower than those offered by the hotel itself.

TABLE 6.1 A Sampling of Largest Hotel Companies and Their Brands, 2011

Organization/Web Site	Properties	Major Brand Names
Accor www.accor.com	4,229 in 90 countries	Motel 6, Ibis, Novotel, Pullman, Studio 6, Mercure, Sofitel, Adagio, and others
Best Western www.bestwestern.com	4,000 in 90 countries	All hotels independently owned but carry Best Western name
Choice Hotels www.choice hotels.com	5,800 in United States and 30 other countries	Clarion, Comfort Inn, Econo Lodge, Mainstary, Quality Inns, Rodeway, Sleep Inns, Suburban Extended Stay, and others
Hilton Worldwide www.hiltonworldwide.com	3,750 in 84 countries	Conrad Hotels & Resorts, Doubletree, Embassy Suites, Hampton Inns, Hilton Garden Inn, Hilton Hotels & Resorts, Homewood Suites, Waldorf Astoria Hotels, and others
Intercontinental Hotels Group www.ichotelsgroup.com	4,500 in more than 100 countries	Candlewood Suites, Crowne Plaza, Holiday Inn, Holiday Inn Express, Hotel Indigo, Intercontinental Hotels and Resorts, Staybridge
Marriott International www.marriott.com	3,150 in United States and other countries	Courtyard by Marriott, Marriott Hotels, Resorts and Inns, Renaissance Inns, Ritz-Carlton, Springhill Suites, Townplace Suites
Starwood Hotels www.starwoodhotels.com	929	Aloft, Element by Westin, Four Points by Sheraton, Sheraton, St. Regis, The Luxury Collection, Westin, W. Hotels

Source: Individual Web sites for each firm listed.

Marketing Segments

Aggressive marketing has been another response of the lodging industry to increased competition. The industry has created an ever-wider variety of specialized types of accommodations, targeting more specific *market segments*. What are these segments?

The accommodations market can be segmented in numerous ways, including the following:

- *By location.* A company might aim to attract travelers needing accommodations at airports, downtown, or at the beach, for example.
- *By purpose of the usage.* Figure 6.3 applies this type of market segmentation, analyzing whether guests at U.S. hotels are traveling for business, pleasure, or other purposes.
- *By current needs.* Honeymooners, families with children, and people attending a religious convention, for example, are likely to look for different things in a hotel.
- *By attitudes and interests*—in other words, *psychographics.* People who enjoy scuba diving and those who want to spend their time shopping are likely to be attracted by different features.
- *By price,* probably the most often used basis of segmentation. Analyzed by price, the lodging market can be divided into six segments: strict budget, economy, budget luxury, mid-priced, first class, and luxury. Table 6.2 describes accommodations that target each of these segments.

Many large hotel companies target specific market segments by developing or buying up brands for different market segments. The Marriott chain is one example. It operates Fairfield Inn for the economy segment; Courtyard for the mid-priced segment; Marriott Hotels, Resorts, and Suites for first-class lodging; and Ritz-Carlton for luxury.

FIGURE 6.3

U.S. Lodging Customers, 2010: Segmentation by Usage

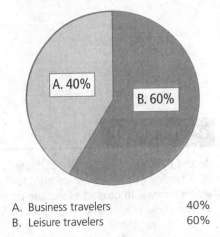

| A. Business travelers | 40% |
| B. Leisure travelers | 60% |

This chart shows the main purposes for the trips being taken by guests at U.S. hotels.

Source: Data from *AH&LA 2010 Lodging Profile.*

TABLE 6.2 Segmentation of Hotels by Price

Segment	Description	Examples
Strict budget	Basically, these are no-frills hotels that offer the lowest rates. They have only a small lobby or no lobby, no restaurant, and few amenities in the rooms. There may be just a rack to hang clothes and limited drawer space and furniture.	Motel 6, Microtel
Economy	Compared with strict-budget properties, these offer slightly expanded amenities—such as slightly upgraded decor, an extra chair, larger double-bed rooms, and sometimes a continental breakfast. Many have a restaurant and an outdoor pool.	Super 8, Red Roof Inn, Fairfield Inn, Travelodge
Budget luxury	These may have only small lobbies and few facilities. However, the rooms may have more furniture and be slightly larger than those in economy lodgings. They are more likely to have outdoor swimming pools and room amenities such as shampoo and lotion, and they may have more offerings for continental breakfast.	Comfort Inn, Hampton Inn
Mid-priced	Compared with budget-luxury lodgings, these provide more room amenities and facilities, a 24-hour desk attendant, restaurants, lounges, and room service. Often, mid-priced hotels are located near convention facilities.	Holiday Inn, Quality Inn, Ramada Inn, Courtyard Inn
First class	These offer tastefully furnished, very comfortable, and well-designed public areas and rooms; a choice of restaurants and bars; 24-hour room service; and health clubs. Some have an indoor swimming pool and concierge service.	Sheraton, Hilton, Marriott, Embassy Suites
Luxury	These may be extravagantly lavish or exceptionally tasteful and elegant. They have impeccable service, lobbies of marble and brass, health clubs, spas, in-room minibars, haute cuisine restaurants, concierge service, and many suites.	Ritz-Carlton, Westin, Four Seasons, Hyatt, Wyndham

Successful companies adapt to changes in market segments, as the history of Club Med illustrates. Established shortly after World War II as a tent village on the Mediterranean island of Majorca (Mallorca) for a French clientele, Club Med introduced vacations featuring fun, sun, and *joie de vivre* for one fee covering transportation, lodging, three meals a day, and a multitude of sports and leisure activities. It first catered to young singles and couples. As its clientele aged and had children, Club Med adapted. At many locations, it set up activity centers for children of different ages (including Baby Clubs, Petit Clubs, and Mini Clubs). Parents can drop their children off at the centers for the day. Today, Club Med has 75 resort properties in 25 world destinations.

✔ CHECK-UP

Recent trends in the structure of the lodging industry include
✔ A decline in the number of individually owned properties.
✔ An increase in properties that are part of chains.
✔ The expansion of chains into countries around the globe.

For customers and sellers, the advantages of lodgings that are part of a chain include
✔ Predictable standards.

✔ Readily confirmed reservations.

Two important ways of segmenting the accommodations market are segmentation
✔ By the purpose of the guest's trip.
✔ By price, which yields six segments: strict budget, economy, budget luxury, mid-priced, first class, and luxury.

Evaluating Accommodations

■ WHAT ARE THE MAIN TYPES AND KEY CHARACTERISTICS OF ACCOMMODATIONS?

While the world may be getting smaller, what a lodging should provide differs in many countries. Many Europeans, for example, might not expect a private bath but would be shocked to find no bidet (a fixture useful for bathing the genitals and posterior parts of the body). On the other hand, many Americans might be surprised to find no elevator or baggage service in some of the less expensive European lodgings. Likewise, Americans who rent a car in Europe are often frustrated to find their lodging has no garage or parking lot. So travel counselors well informed about the different types of worldwide accommodations are better equipped to match their clients' needs with an appropriate property.

But giving good advice can be challenging, largely because (1) accommodations vary tremendously and (2) judgments about accommodations are unusually subjective. Travelers often develop expectations that can be hard to define and even harder to match. A good first step in learning to evaluate accommodations is to become familiar with some of the major types of lodgings that are available.

Kinds of Accommodations

1. **Commercial hotels** are generally located in a city. They are most used by business travelers, particularly during the week and then by leisure travelers more often on weekends, both individually and as part of package tours.

2. *Convention hotels* cater to business travelers, groups that do not need to leave the property to conduct their business. Convention hotels are usually first class and up. Sometimes they are directly attached to or connected to a city's convention center or sometimes they may have trade/exposition space available within the hotel itself.

3. *Airport hotels* are convenient for travelers departing on early-morning flights and for those not needing to go downtown. They are increasingly offering "Parking Packages" for travelers who may like to leave their car at the hotel for a week or two while they are traveling. Most airport hotels have complimentary shuttle service between the property and the nearby airport. Many airport hotels are members of major chains.

4. *All-Suites* offer rooms that have separate sleeping and living areas. The typical all-suite unit provides a living room, sleeping area, and kitchenette. Some all-suites are termed *extended-stay hotels*. These cater to people intending to stay for weeks or even months and also offer such services as weekly housekeeping and coin Laundromats but may eliminate amenities such as plastic wrapping on glasses and daily maid service. They are popular with business people planning to be in a sales area or territory for some time or for families that are relocating to a different city but have not yet found permanent housing. An example would be Courtyard by Marriott. In Europe on the Mediterranean coast, all-suites are sometimes called self-catering apartments.

5. *Bed and Breakfasts* (B&Bs) should appeal to travelers looking for lodging with a unique character and a taste of the local life. The concept began in Britain, where the B&Bs are best suited for budget travelers. In the United States a beautiful old home that offers a full breakfast in the morning is usually thought of as a B&B. In practice, the building can be almost anything; but to be called a B&B, it should be a small establishment that emphasizes personal attention and offers individually decorated rooms with some special character. Usually they are individually owned and operated, often by retired couples.

   B&Bs have the advantage of being homey and friendly, but they may allow less privacy than other accommodations. Guests often have to share bathroom facilities and follow the rules of the house, such as when to play the television (if there is one). Sometimes the hosts will offer complimentary afternoon tea or perhaps a glass of sherry in the evening. Also some B&Bs have evening lock-out hours.

6. *Inns* are generally somewhat larger than B&Bs, offer a dining room and function more like hotels. Still, a true inn provides a great deal of local character and personal service. In practice, however, the term is used very loosely.

7. *Hostels* are usually dorm-like accommodations and used to be called youth hotels, with rather rigid rules, hours, and the like. Today, they are usually open to those of all ages in most of the world

8. *Motels* (short for motor hotels) cater to motorists. The classic motel is a building with just one or two stories, ample parking (usually at the guestroom door) and very limited food service, if any. Today's motels are often more elaborate than the classic model. When they consist of several stories and offer food service and recreational facilities, they are sometimes classified as *motor inns*. Other classifications distinguish motor hotels and motor lodges, but the differences among all these are rather slight and the various names are often used interchangeably.

9. *Resorts* provide a vacation in themselves. These are not places just to spend the night. They are meant to attract guests for a lengthy stay. In fact, many

resorts, especially in the Caribbean will not accept guests for less than three nights, and many resort packages are sold in one-week segments only. Most resorts are in the first-class or deluxe category. They may have wide-ranging facilities for daytime entertainment, nightlife, dining, shopping, and special activities such as golf, tennis, skiing, water sports, or gambling. Group and convention business is a staple for many resorts; new ones are built with special facilities for meetings.

10. **All-inclusives** are resorts that charge one basic rate for just about everything. Meals, entertainment, sports, educational classes, and the room are usually included in the price. The pioneer of all-inclusives is Club Med. Other popular all-inclusives are Super Clubs and Sandals to mention just a few of a wide-selection of properties. Some cater to special markets such as families, newlyweds, adults only, etc. One specialty all-inclusive is the **dude ranch** found in many U.S. western states. Such facilities include extensive horseback riding excursions and classes, hayrides, square dancing, and other ranch-style activities.

11. **Spas** are a special type of resort that emphasizes health, diet, and fitness. They have a long history in Europe; often they were built near mineral

CLOSE-UP: ON THE JOB WITH TAMMY JOHNS, FRONT DESK CLERK

Tammy Johns's hotel is a first-class establishment, but one without luxuries such as a huge lobby. Tammy handles the check-in process, but employees are trained to take responsibility for anything a guest might need. Most of her time is spent behind the check-in desk.

"My basic job is to rent rooms. But my real job is to be as pleasant as possible so people will enjoy their stay from the moment they enter. Even if people don't look too friendly when they walk in, I've got to remember they may be tired from working all day, or even from traveling and sightseeing.

"I greet them and ask for their name. I ask them how their day or trip was while looking up their reservation. I assign them a room, have them sign a charge slip, and give them their key or coded door card. I give directions to the room and ask if there's anything else they need.

"If they don't have a reservation, I ask how many persons are with them, how many beds they need, and so on, and then quote them a rate. This is usually fairly routine, but not always. At certain times, we have a lot of empty rooms and I'm graded on how many walk-ins I can convert and at what price. I'm given a sample rate, which is already lower than our regular rate. I can then go down from there if I think the client will walk out. A lot depends on the time of day the client comes in and how he or she looks.

"Sometimes you can tell just by how people walk in that they are staying at this hotel no matter what. Others, you are not too sure of, especially if they ask about the rate as their first question. When you lower your rate, you give

some reason—maybe they get a corporate rate or belong to a motor club. Then again, maybe they're not and you say, 'I can give you that motor club rate anyway tonight because of such and such.' Or, 'Oh, I see I have a room on the lower floor toward the back for only X dollars; it's the last one left there. It's a good value if you don't mind being at the end of the corridor.'

"The important thing is that you don't want them to walk out. On the other hand, there is a limit to what we can do with the rate, and we can't go below a certain level. Our manager keeps records of how many walk-ins we sell and what the average rate is and compares us to each other.

"We help out on phones when the reservationist is out to lunch, update computer records, and try to answer clients' questions. I like clients who ask questions about where they are because then I can play concierge. Our hotel is fairly large, but it's nowhere near the point where it would have a concierge. We visited with one on a trip to Phoenix. I decided that that is something I would really like to do.

"Anyway, just ask me about places to eat in my town, and I'll be ready with an answer and make a reservation for you. And I'm ready with information on the city or the airport. We have information in racks, but I'm ready with schedules and updates at the desk. I've compiled many of them myself, and I leave it for the others at the front desk. There's usually a front desk cashier who handles checkout. But when she's busy, I can do that also.

"I was hired directly after graduating from a hotel program at a two-year college. I plan to make this my career."

springs. (The name comes from the first letters of the Latin phrase *salus per aqua*, which means "health through water"). European spas typically have a medical focus; visits may be prescribed as treatment for illnesses and may be paid for by health insurance. Throughout history many royal families and bon vivants took to the spa to compensate for a social season of over-eating and names like Bath, Baden-Baden, Marienbad, and Saratoga Springs came to be known in literature. In the United States, the popularity of spas has soared. Many resorts feature spa treatments and day-spas have come of age as well.

12. *Pensions* (pronounced *pahn-see-ohn*) are usually small family-run lodgings in Europe that may be operated much like a hotel or B&B. In German-speaking countries, a pension might be called a *gasthaus*, in Italy a *pensione*. Other countries have different names. They usually serve three meals a day included in the price (full pension or board) while some operate on the basis of breakfast and dinner (demi-pension or half-board). Similar lodgings in Japan are called *minshukus* and follow Japanese traditions.

13. *Châteaux*, *castles*, and *villas* might be described as very upscale inns. Visitors might stay in one room of a medieval castle or rent an entire villa. Villa rentals, with chef and private swimming pool, have become very popular in Italy, Mexico, and other areas and are an attractive offering for small groups of friends or extended families.

14. The *parador* in Spain and the *pousada* in Portugal are specialized inns that may be housed in a castle, palace, or fortress. These are government-owned and-run and carry ratings from mid-priced to luxury. Puerto Rico also uses the *parador* designation for a limited number of its local inns, often simpler than those in Spain.

15. *Ryokan* are found in Japan and are local upscale inns that retain many Japanese traditions, such as sleeping on futons on the floor on atami mats, wearing *yukatas* (cotton sleeping kimonos), and featuring Japanese cuisine. Beautiful gardens or natural scenery often surround the ryokan. Usually only Japanese is spoken. Traditional baths, geisha entertainment, and massage are often available.

16. *Tented camps* and *tree lodges* are for travelers on safari. They consist of structures built on stilts, usually above an animal watering hole, and can be found in eastern Africa. Some can be simple and rustic; others are extremely deluxe complete with oriental carpets on the floor. In southern Africa, circular lodgings known as *rondavels* may provide inexpensive accommodations. Some offer neither bedding nor bath; others are comfortable, air-conditioned cottages with fully equipped kitchens.

17. *Boatels* are motels for those who may arrive by private boat, rather than by car, obviously located on rivers, inland waterways, etc. The lodging itself may be on boats as well.

18. *Casinos* are often operated in conjunction with hotels or major resorts, such as in Las Vegas, Atlantic City and other areas where gambling may be legalized.

19. *Retreat-Style Accommodations* are often a full complex designed for organizations or companies that wish to have a retreat for meetings, educational activities, and the like. Often they are somewhat rustic in nature, perhaps with cabins surrounding a central meeting house and dining facility. An example would be Asilomar Conference Grounds overlooking the ocean at Pacific Grove on the Monterey Peninsula in Northern California.

20. *Lodges* may often be found in U.S. National Parks, usually historic and rustic in appearance, but not necessarily inexpensive. Examples are the

Ahwahnee Hotel in Yosemite, Grand Canyon Lodge on the north rim of the Grand Canyon, or Old Faithful Inn in Yellowstone Park. These lodgings are heavily booked during the summer months, often a year in advance.

21. **Self-catering rental apartments** are furnished flats or apartments, available in some major cities such as London, Paris, Sydney, Istanbul and in some beach communities such as Spain's Costa del Sol. They provide a good option for families and business people seeking a more home-like atmosphere when on a business trip.

Rating Systems

In some countries the government runs a formal rating system for accommodations. For example, both Spain and Italy rate their hotels from one star (strictly budget) to five stars (deluxe). The United States has no official rating system, but many references and guidebooks publish their own. Among the best known are

■ The ten-category classification system designed by the *Official Hotel Guide* (*OHG*) and used by the *Hotel & Travel Index* (see Table 6.3).

TABLE 6.3 OHG Classification System

1. **Superior Deluxe** An exclusive and expensive luxury hotel, often palatial, offering the highest standards of service, accommodations, and facilities; elegant and luxurious public rooms; and a prestigious address. Establishments in this category are among the world's top hotels.

2. **Deluxe** An outstanding property offering many of the same features as Superior Deluxe. May be less grand and offer more reasonable rates than the Superior Deluxe properties, yet in many instances may be just as satisfactory. Safe to recommend to most discriminating clients.

3. **Moderate Deluxe** Basically a Deluxe hotel, but with qualifications. In some cases, some accommodations or public areas may offer a less pronounced degree of luxury than that found in fully Deluxe properties. In other cases, the hotel may be a well-established famous name, depending heavily on past reputation. The more contemporary hotels may be heavily marketed to business clients, with fine accommodations and public rooms offering Deluxe standards in comfort, but with less emphasis on atmosphere and/or personal service.

4. **Superior First Class** An above-average hotel. May be an exceptionally well-maintained older hotel, but more often a superior modern hotel specifically designed for the First-Class market, with some outstanding features. Accommodations and public areas are expected to be tastefully furnished and very comfortable. May be a good value, especially if it is a commercial hotel. May be recommended to average clients and in most cases will satisfy the discriminating ones.

5. **First Class** A dependable, comfortable hotel with standardized rooms, amenities, and public areas. May have a superior executive level or wing. May be safely recommended to average clients not expecting Deluxe facilities or special services. Should also be satisfactory for better groups.

6. **Limited-Service First Class** A property offering full First-Class quality accommodations but limited public areas, food service, and facilities. Usually moderate in size, the hotel often utilizes a residential scale and architecture, and many offer complimentary breakfast and evening cocktails in the lobby or in a small, informal restaurant. Geared to the individual business/pleasure traveler.

7. **Moderate First Class** Essentially a First-Class establishment with comfortable but somewhat simpler accommodations and public areas. May be lacking in some features (e.g., restaurant). Some of the rooms or public areas, while adequate, may tend to be basic and functional. Usually suitable for cost-conscious clients.

8. **Superior Tourist Class** Primarily a budget property with mostly well-kept, functional accommodations, some up to First-Class standards. Public rooms may be limited or nonexistent. Often just a place to sleep but may have some charming or intimate features. May be good value. Should satisfy individuals (sometimes even discriminating ones) or groups on a budget.

9. **Tourist Class** Strictly a budget operation with some facilities or features of Superior Tourist Class, but usually no (or very few) First-Class accommodations. Should not be recommended to fussy or discriminating clients.

10. **Moderate Tourist Class** A low-budget operation, often quite old and may not be well maintained. Should only be used in a pinch if no others are available. Clients should always be cautioned what to expect.

Source: Official Hotel Guide (OHG).

- The five-star rating system in the *Forbes Travel Guide* (formerly the *Mobil Guides*), which is available at most bookstores. One star indicates that the lodging is good; five stars indicate that it is one of the best in the country.
- A similar five-diamond rating system in the *AAA Guidebooks*, which are available to any member of AAA.

What Affects the Price of a Room?

The variations in accommodations are at least matched by the variety in their prices. The **rack rate** is the "regular" posted or "off-the-street" price of a room. It is generally the highest rate charged for that room except during special events such as the Olympics. However, a standard twin-bedded room of the same chain may run $450 per night in London or $109 in a suburb of Akron, Ohio. Although the two rooms are not exactly identical, why the huge difference? The difference in rate is striking! But even more striking; at any given hotel, people will be paying many different rates within the same hotel for identical rooms the same night.

Like the airlines, hotels practice *yield management* (discussed in Chapter 4): They aim to maximize rates and occupancy to produce the highest daily average revenue for all rooms on any given day. Computer reservation systems permit them to adjust prices on a day-to-day, often moment-to-moment basis. As demand weakens, the hotel offers lower prices or discounts requiring advance bookings. As demand builds, consumers must pay more for the same product.

In fact, accommodation rates can vary almost as much as airline rates. Airlines will at least have particular rules in effect at a given moment. Accommodation rates sometimes depend on a decision by the person taking the reservation. Still, there are some constant factors that affect the price of a room. In this section we look first at the factors that influence the room price and then at different types of rates. Note that the prices quoted by hotels may or may not include taxes, various fees, and service charges, which can be significant and should be queried.

Location of the Lodging. Location within a particular city or area is the single most important factor influencing the cost of a room. Commercial hotels located in the heart of a city close to convention facilities will be more expensive than those on the fringes of the city. Resort hotels on a beautiful beach can command top prices; an identical room one block from the beach would cost much less. If a hotel is the only lodging in sight in a popular area, it can charge high prices. In some countries the government controls the number and variety of hotels in resort areas to ensure that overdevelopment does not produce either a low **occupancy rate** (the percentage of rooms occupied) or damage to the environment.

Location of the Room. Another factor affecting price is the location of a room within a hotel, which may influence the guest's convenience, view, and exposure to noise. Often, the most expensive rooms are those with the best views. An ocean view on a high floor may command top price; rooms with parking-lot views and rooms on lower floors may be the least expensive. Sometimes proximity to sources of noise influences the price. Rooms on upper floors—far from public areas such as the lobby and pool—tend to be quieter. Rooms close to elevators are noisier, because of the opening and closing of doors and the sounds of guests in the halls.

Linda Chadwick is taking her laptop computer on a business trip for the first time. She calls and asks whether she will be able to plug it in at her hotel room and go on the Internet and what amenities she can expect in the room. What kind of information can you give her, and how would you find it?

The easiest way to find an answer might be to visit the Web site hosted by the chain or by the specific hotel. For example, suppose Ms. Chadwick is going to stay at the Four Seasons in London. According to its Web site, the rooms have high-speed e-mail and Internet access; help connecting the computer as well as a fax machine can be requested. Rooms also have DVD players, speaker phones, exercise equipment, and much more. Remind Ms. Chadwick that electric current, electrical sockets, and phone jacks are often different abroad.

Room Size and Furnishings. Old hotels tend to have rooms of many different sizes, and luxurious hotels usually have suites that are much like small apartments. In these hotels the price reflects the size of the room. But in new hotels almost all rooms are the same size; for these rooms, types of fixtures or decor, rather than size, shape the price.

Most Americans take for granted that a hotel room will contain a comfortable bed, chairs, a dresser, a desk, good lighting, a closet with hangers, a television set, a telephone, a private bathroom with sink, a toilet, a bathtub with shower, and, of course, heat and air conditioning. Beyond these items, amenities such as balconies, two-line phones or two phone lines, WiFi, and ergonomic chairs may add to the price of a room.

Occupancy. Different rates may be cited depending on the number of beds as well as the number of occupants. A room with one double bed, one queen- or king-size bed, or two twin beds usually has two rates: *single* (one person) and *double* (two persons). A room with two double or two queen- or king-size beds may have four rates: single, double, *triple* (three persons), and *quad* (four persons). Or the hotel may simply have an add-on rate for each extra person in a room. Triple may often be a twin room for two with a rollaway brought in for the third person. Rates for more than four persons in a room are usually not offered.

Most hotel rooms are designed for two people. When a room is rented as a single, a hotel loses revenue, not only on the room, but also on possible purchases of food, drink, and activities. Thus hotels may charge as much for a single room as for a double room—which means that the person with a single room is paying twice as much on a per-person basis as those in a double room. Some hotels, particularly older hotels, may actually have single rooms, but such rooms should not be sold as being "better." Often they are the maid's room made over or similar inferior rooms.

Friends or family members may ask for **adjoining rooms,** which are rooms located next to each other that have separate entrances and no means of going directly from one room to the other, or they may ask for **connecting rooms,** which are linked by a common door inside the rooms. There is no extra cost for adjoining or connecting rooms, but travel counselors must be careful to be sure the client understands the different terminology.

For little or no extra cost, most hotels provide cribs or rollaway beds for small children sharing a room with their parents. Many chains have a "kids free" policy: there is no extra charge for children occupying the same room as long as no additional beds are needed.

Meals. Room rates in the United States usually do not include meals unless specifically stated. Outside the United States, hotels usually offer the following choice of meal plans:

- *European plan (EP).* No meals are included.
- *Continental plan (CP).* A light, or continental, breakfast is included.
- *Bermuda plan (BP).* A fully cooked breakfast is included.
- *Modified American plan (MAP).* Breakfast and one other main meal, usually dinner, are included. This plan is called *demi-pension* in Europe. Some hotels provide a *dine-around plan;* it gives MAP guests a credit toward dinner at other hotels or restaurants within the same resort property or around town.
- *American plan (AP).* Usually three meals are included. This is also called *full board* or *full pension*.

Table 6.4 describes these plans in more detail. EP and BP are desirable when various affordable restaurants are nearby; AP and MAP may be attractive if a hotel is isolated or if nearby restaurants are expensive. MAP makes it easier to predict the total cost of a vacation, and the plan saves guests the cost and inconvenience of transportation to and from restaurants. Also, it is usually less expensive to eat dinner as an MAP guest than to select items from the menu.

Other variations in meal service include whether the hotel offers *table d'hôte* (a set menu at a fixed price) or serves *à la carte* (with a choice of individually priced items from a menu). *À la carte* dining, where one may order whatever one wants from the menu, is offered only on very deluxe tours.

Special Facilities and Service. Hotels follow the lead of their guests in determining what is a frill and what is a necessity. For example, even strict budget properties in most climates usually have free swimming pools. But kiddie pools, tennis courts, beach clubs, saunas, game rooms, nightclubs, golf courses, racquet clubs, health clubs, room service, and having both indoor and outdoor pools are all special features that are reflected in room rates. One new trend is to charge a daily resort fee, even if guests do not use the amenities.

Hotel companies are vying with one another to provide useful technology for business travelers. An increasing number provide high-speed Internet access in the rooms. Many hotels have an office center on their ground floor with computers, printers, copy and fax machines, and various business supplies. Most of these features are complimentary, but others such as teleconferencing and clerical service are arranged and paid for as needed.

Quality of service also makes a difference. If a hotel offers round-the-clock room service or a *concierge*—a staff member who provides information and other help to guests—then the extra attention is likely to show up in the price of the room.

Price Level and Currency Value. The general price level in an area also influences room rates. Many things besides hotel rooms are more expensive in New York and Tokyo, for example, than in Durham, North Carolina, or Milwaukee, Wisconsin.

For lodgings overseas, the room rate also varies with fluctuations in the currency exchange rate. For clients who pay a hotel bill in U.S. dollars or U.S.

ON THE SPOT

As a hotel concierge, you have been trying for two weeks to find tickets for a guest for a very popular opera. You have called the box office and local ticket brokers almost daily, hoping for cancellations, with no luck. Your guest is arriving in a week, and you feel as if you might as well tell him the bad news. What should you do?

Does your hotel have other job openings? You are going to have to develop some new resources and contacts if you want to survive as a concierge! Have you talked to your manager or to other concierges? Have you gone to the theater manager in person? Does your hotel manager have contacts? You can get this done.

TABLE 6.4 Meal Plans

EP: European plan No meals are included. This is typical in the United States and many big cities around the world. Many U.S. hotels, however, now offer coffee in the room or in the lobby, and there is a trend toward offering continental buffet breakfasts.

CP: Continental plan A light breakfast is provided, but the quantity and contents vary with local customs. For example, in the United States, France, Italy, and Spain, it is likely to include croissants or bread, jams, and coffee or tea. In Germany and Scandinavia, other items would be added, such as a buffet of meats, cheeses, cereals, fruits, and even boiled eggs.

BP: Bermuda plan A fully cooked breakfast is provided but no other meals. Generally speaking, hotels that offer BP are resorts.

MAP: Modified American plan (or demi-pension) Breakfast and one other main meal, usually dinner, are included. In many countries dinner is the midday meal. MAP is popular in the resorts of the Bahamas, Bermuda, the Caribbean, and Mexico. Some hotels limit choices from the menu for MAP guests; diners who want a specialty such as lobster pay a surcharge. Some U.S. hotels give MAP clients a coupon valid for a meal in a specific dining room up to a specified dollar amount; guests pay for anything beyond that limit.

AP: American plan (or full board or full pension) All three meals are included. Ranches, spas, and resorts that are isolated or at which clients spend almost all their time usually offer AP. Cruise ships and all-inclusive resorts offer AP, although they may not use the term.

traveler's checks, the exchange rate used will be the rate in effect on the *day of payment,* not the day of booking. If a hotel advertises a rate in U.S. dollars, this amount reflects the exchange rate on the day the brochure or advertisement was printed and is not guaranteed. Travel counselors should quote rates in the local currency, if possible, and explain them to travelers. For those who pay an international hotel by credit card, it's the day the transaction clears the bank that is pertinent.

Length of Stay. Some hotels offer discounts for long stays such as a week or more. If a client is staying for a week, a lower rate should at least be requested. *Day rates,* which are available for those not staying overnight, are sometimes used for meetings, by people in the middle of long international trips, or by those who need to stay long after the check-out time.

Day and Season. If the demand for rooms fluctuates greatly with the date, the price of a room is likely to change as well. Many of the most popular vacation destinations have great seasonal fluctuations in demand and therefore in room rates. Sometimes the fluctuation depends on the weather at the destination, and sometimes on the weather that clients are trying to escape (such as northern winters).

Often the busy and expensive seasons for hotels are the same as the peak seasons for airfares. In particular,

- For almost the entire Caribbean and the beach destinations of Mexico, peak demand runs from approximately December 15 to April 15. Prices during this time may be double the rates during the rest of the year. Demand is usually lowest during late spring and autumn (hurricane season).
- European beach resorts are most popular in the summer (especially August, when entire countries, it seems, go on holiday). Lower prices prevail during the rest of the year, but the weather is just barely warm in many areas and it may be rainy.
- During the summer, when business travel slows, major European cities may be less crowded, but small tourist towns or resorts will be packed.

Peak seasons should be checked, not guessed at. For example, Bermuda's seasons are more similar to European than to Caribbean seasons. In Cambodia, southwestern China, and many other countries, the best seasons for travel depend greatly on the timing of the monsoons.

Demand and prices may also vary with the day of the week. Rooms at resorts are likely to be in demand on the weekends, so rates are higher then; the resort may offer special packages for midweek stays. In contrast, hotels that cater primarily to business travelers offer very low weekend rates or special packages that may include meals, drinks, or other extras at a large discount.

Special Rates. Besides promotional rates, hotels have special rates for guests who come as a group or who are members of certain groups.

- The **corporate rate** is sometimes offered to all business travelers, sometimes only to listed corporations, and sometimes to anyone who asks.
- The **negotiated corporate rate** is a rate that has been negotiated with a company or its affiliate or association. The hotel hopes to become that company's automatic choice for lodging; the company generally guarantees that it will rent a minimum number of room nights per year.
- A **group rate** represents a discount offered to a group that uses a certain number of rooms on the same night. As many as twenty rooms or as few as five might be required to qualify for a group rate, depending on the season and projected occupancy rate.

- The **Run-of-the-House (ROH)** rate is a flat rate that the hotel may offer to a travel agency for its clients. It would apply to any of its available rooms, whatever their location, at time of check-in with the understanding that the client will receive a stated minimum type of room or better if the upgrade is not available. Although the ROH rate is often offered for groups, it is not a wise policy to accept unless all members of the group can be upgraded. Group tour members are not happy clients if some receive better rooms than others when all are paying the same group price.
- The **convention rate** may reflect the largest discount. This reflects the fact that competition for meetings and conventions is keen because they typically use so many services at the hotel, giving the hotel many opportunities to increase revenue (particularly from the bar and catering services).

In addition, many hotel chains offer **frequent-guest programs,** which reward repeat guests with bonuses such as a free room night, services, merchandise, and discounts. Hotels have innumerable tie-ins with airlines' frequent-flyer plans and with car rental companies.

CLOSE-UP: SELLING TO THE BUDGET-MINDED

One night, a call was made to the toll-free number for a hotel chain that owns a downtown hotel in one of the nation's largest cities. The following conversation occurred:

Customer: "What would the rate be for a single room for January 27 and 28?"
Hotel chain reservationist: "Let's see. I can get you the rate of $115, um, oops, no. We can offer a rate of $95 for those nights. Would you like to place a reservation?"
C: "Do you have any weekend rates or packages?"
HCR: "Yes, we have a promotional weekend rate of $89. Can I book that for you?"
C: "No, not at the moment. I was just checking rates right now and will call back."
HCR: "OK, one second. Oh, you know, on that Saturday night I can offer you the supersaver rate of $69 and then make a separate reservation for the promotional rate of $89 for the other night. How's that? Would you like to hold that? And I can transfer you to our travel club. Once you're a member, you get a 5 percent rebate on all hotel reservations with us as well as $20 in free gas coupons."

When so many rates might be charged for a room, how can you be sure your rate is not too high? Here are some techniques for helping a client get the best rate:

- If you are dealing with a corporate client, be sure you find out ahead of time about any specially negotiated corporate rates.
- Determine in advance if your client is a member of AAA (American Automobile Association), AARP (American Association of Retired Persons), or any other organization that may make the client eligible for a discount. Many hotels have a special rate or immediately discount the rate 5 to 10 percent for members. Many give a special senior rate even to guests who are not members of AARP.
- Ask for the rate first to establish a starting point. You might say something like, "What is the least expensive rate for the nights of _____?" or "Could you please quote the lowest rate available?"
- Ask for specials, corporate rates, packages, or discounts for weekends, off-season times, or lengthy stays. Often the hotel reservationist will not offer discounted rates unless asked about them.
- Compare each discount. A weekend package rate may be lower than a corporate or AAA discount.
- Insist on the least expensive type of room if that is what your client desires. Some upscale chains pitch their more expensive rooms very aggressively. If you ask for the best rate on a standard room, you might still be given the rate for a deluxe room. But if you reject that rate, you will quickly be given the lower one.

Preferred supplier agreements (discussed in Chapters 1, 13, and 16) can also yield better rates. Agencies too small to establish these relationships on their own may get similar benefits by joining a consortium (a group of companies that pool their resources).

Sometimes better prices can be found by talking, not to the hotel, but to hotel consolidators or to hotel representative firms or by checking bargain sites online. You will discover with experience which sites really offer bargains and which are simply marketing devices.

Be sure that searching for a deal is worth the time to your agency. The room, after all, may not be commissionable, and clients looking for a bargain may not be willing to pay a service charge to the agency.

Accommodations designed to provide a unique atmosphere include
- ✔ Bed-and-breakfasts.
- ✔ Inns.
- ✔ Overseas: paradores, pousadas, ryokans, pensions, and minshukus.

Types of rates charged by lodgings include
- ✔ The rack rate.
- ✔ Special rates for groups: the corporate rate, negotiated corporate rate, group rate, run-of-the-house (ROH) rate, and convention rate.

- ✔ Promotional rates that respond to changes in anticipated demand.

Other important factors influencing the price of a room include
- ✔ The location of the property.
- ✔ Room characteristics, such as its location in the lodging, size and furnishings, and number of beds and occupants.
- ✔ Special facilities and the quality of service.
- ✔ Competition in the immediate area.

Selling Accommodations

- ■ HOW DO HOTELS SELL THEIR ROOMS?
- ■ WHAT DO TRAVEL COUNSELORS NEED TO KNOW WHEN THEY MAKE A HOTEL RESERVATION?

The selling of accommodations has become a very sophisticated business. As we discuss in Chapter 9 (on marketing), hotels have found new ways to fine-tune their services to meet the changing needs and expectations of their guests. Thanks to powerful software and the Internet, hotels have also been able to target and communicate with potential guests in new and more effective ways, and many travelers now book their own hotel reservations directly on the Internet without the help of travel counselors.

Despite the Internet, travel counselors remain an important source of sales for the hotel industry for two reasons. First, travel counselors are effective promoters of hotels.

Second, travel agencies are a relatively inexpensive way for the hotel industry to promote and distribute its product. Hotels do not pay a commission to an agency until the guest completes a stay; commissions average 8 to 10 percent. Many strict-budget properties do not give commissions on sales, and some corporate sales are also noncommissionable.

For travel agencies, the relationship with hotels is sometimes testy, often because of lost commissions. If a client changes his or her arrival date, the hotel creates a new booking, information about the agency is deleted, and no commission is received. Similarly, if a client receives a lower rate when checking in than the originally quoted rate, then the hotel creates a new booking, and again the agency receives no commission. In addition, some commissions are lost simply as a result of mistakes in keeping track of millions of hotel rooms.

The relationship between hotels and travel agencies might be easier if it were not so loosely defined. No uniform procedures guide the relationship. However, some hotels and agencies now participate in third-party clearinghouses (such as Pegasus Commission Processing), which ensure that commissions are paid to travel agencies in a timely and thorough manner. Also, some large hotel companies have centralized systems for paying commissions.

For travel agencies, the accommodations market represents a potential source of growth. If you are a travel counselor, how do you go about tapping this market? In this section we look at some basic tasks involved in selling accommodations, as well as some problems frequently encountered by customers.

Recommending the Right Hotel

At the Broadmoor in Colorado Springs, Colorado, at the foot of the Rockies, guests can enjoy priceless art treasures from Europe and Asia in its halls and grand rooms. The resort was founded in 1918 by a couple who made a fortune in gold and copper mines. The Grand Hotel Suites of Raffles in Singapore contains rare prints, fine Persian carpets, and fourteen-foot ceilings. Opened in 1887, Raffles is noted not only for its Old World opulence but also for a history of famous and adventuresome guests.

These are just two of the world's legendary hotels. You might want to visit them, but if you were a travel counselor, would you recommend them to your clients? Matching the accommodation to the client is one of the most challenging aspects of travel counseling. The task requires knowledge of both hotels and clients.

Learning about Lodgings. The sheer number of lodgings complicates the task of finding the right hotel. A first step is to know the major companies, their brands, and the characteristics of those brands. (Look again at Tables 6.1 and 6.2.)

Second, to decide whether to recommend a particular hotel, travel counselors should know

- *The type.* For example, is it a bed-and-breakfast? A motor hotel?
- *Location.* For example, is it on the beach or a mile away? Downtown or in a suburb?
- *Food service.* Is there a restaurant on the site? Room service?
- *Amenities.* Are there recreational opportunities? Entertainment? A courtesy van? A concierge?
- *Price.* What is its price segment? Are the features comparable to those at other lodgings for this segment? What discounts and packages are available?
- *Special advantages.* Do the rooms themselves offer anything extra? Is there a special attempt to meet the needs of business travelers or families or seniors?

Where would you go to find this information? For years, three references were the "bibles" for the lodging industry: *STAR Service,* with subjective critiques of more than 10,000 hotels by travel writers and correspondents; the multivolume *Official Hotel Guide (OHG),* with as many objective facts as possible about approximately 30,000 hotels; and the *Hotel & Travel Index,* with the barest facts about 45,000 hotels, plus copious advertising.

All three of these references are now owned by the same company (NorthStar Travel Media), and new editions of STAR Service are available only online (see Figure 6.3 on the next page). OHG now shares a Web site with *Hotel & Travel Index,* with more than 70,000 properties listed. New domestic editions of OHG are not being printed, but print versions of the *Official Hotel Guide Worldwide (OHGW)* have been available for sale to travel agents abroad.

Even these three "hotel bibles" could not adequately cover all of the world's lodgings. Guidebooks and tourist offices have filled the information gap for years; today, GDSs and the Internet offer other options. For example, BedandBreakfast.com provides more than 27,000 listings of bed and breakfasts, country and urban inns, guesthouses, lodges, cabins, historic

The St Regis Houston

1919 Briar Oaks Lane
Houston, TX

Rates: $395-$685 (USD)

Phone: 1 713-840-7600
Fax: 1 713-840-8036
Toll Free: 877-787-3447
E-mail: res247.st.regishouston@stregis.com
Web: http://www.stregis.com

Year Renovated: 2002
Check in Time: 3:00 PM
Check out Time: 12:00 PM
Number of Floors: 12
Total Number of Rooms: 232
General Manager: Ron Lamers

STAR Rating: ★ ★ ★ ★ ★   Amenity Rating: ✓ ✓ ✓ ✓ ✓

This 13-story property with a sleek concrete facade, cascading garden terraces and large fountains at the entrance exudes taste and refinement. At less than half of the size of its competitor, Four Seasons Houston, this place feels a bit like a charming inn.

Yet, this place manages to put together similarly stunning dining and recreational options, a sap, stunning pool and enviable meeting space. Both properties boast world-class service, but the decor both share in common—crisp, contemporary style with soothing residential overtones—has a heavier hand here. This place imparts the kind of lavish black-lacquer-and-Chesterfield-leather look that distracted Daddy Warbucks.

With that said, recent updates have tempered some of the common areas with a more urban sensibility, and the hotel's briefcase-palette is slowly being phased out in lieu of brighter, happier hues. While it remains predominately a business hotel it has become a wee bit more cheerful over the last few years. Like its competitors, with the exception of the Four Seasons, it is situated in a lovely residential neighborhood comfortably close to the Galleria.

Once a Ritz-Carlton (R-C is constructing a 53-story hotel-condo tower up the road), it continues to be governed by a meticulous staff. Arrivals are greeted in a reception area of elegantly understated marble and light oak enriched with antiques, very formal floral arrangements and original art. Fine leather seating areas and classical music welcome guests in the lobby. A few well-chosen Asian antiques lend an Oriental-Occidental air, most notable in the lounge.

A New American menu with regional flair is prepared for all meals, including the popular Sunday brunch, in Remington, an elegant garden restaurant with airy conservatory styling, antique murals, potted greenery and a stylish private alcove. Garret Fujieda is head chef. The tasting menu is a hit and a bargain.

The adjoining lounge with rich mahogany paneling brightened with contemporary art also offers a light menu. Live entertainment, featuring light jazz and dance music, is offered on the weekend. Guests enjoy tea in the fancy English lounge as a harpist plucks away.

The fitness center is well-equipped, and the highly touted spa offers treatments including Ayurvedic rituals, Shirodhara and marine therapies. Lovely segregated locker rooms sport relaxation areas and steam rooms. Guests also enjoy privileges at an area health club. The lavishly appointed outdoor pool is large and surrounded by a tiled deck and backed by fountains and a formal landscape.

Function space runs the gamut from finely appointed boardrooms for as few as 12 to a lavish ballroom for 400. The renovated meeting space on the mezzanine level speaks of this hotel's devotion to the commercial set. There is also a research library and a

FIGURE 6.3 Hotels on the Web: An Example

Suppliers' Web sites, such as the one shown above, are just one source of information online about hotels. The excerpt shown here comes from Northstar Travel Media, which provides candid information about hotels and cruise ships worldwide. The service requires a subscription.

hotels, small resorts, guest ranches, and farmhouse accommodations. You can search the site by various categories such as location, amenities, or special needs. GotRooms.com is an online reservation site endorsed by the **American Hotel & Lodging Association (AH&LA),** which is the trade association that represents the lodging industry in the United States.

There are Web sites that are huge databases with listings of all sorts of lodgings around the world as well as sites that specialize in a particular type of lodging such as spas or hostels. You can also find relevant Web sites through links on other sites. For example, suppose a traveler wants to stay at an out-of-the-way inn in a tiny town in the Cotswolds in England. If you go to the Web site of VisitBritain, it offers an index of accommodations as well as links to regional tourist boards—such as the one for the "West Country," which includes the Cotswolds, where you can find lists of particular types of lodgings, including out-of-the-way inns.

Learning about Clients. Along with knowledge about lodgings, travel counselors need an understanding of their clients. What matters to them? WiFi in a room may be more important than the soap. Vacation travelers complain most about service; business travelers about hotels that book more guests than they have rooms.

With information like this, though, you are still left with the question of whether a particular accommodation will suit a specific client. An individual client cannot be understood simply through data about market segments. In fact, from one trip to another, the client's motivation, needs, and expectations may well change. A client may want a budget hotel for an overnight stay on one trip and then, a few months later, something luxurious for a vacation.

Regarding any potential lodger, travel counselors should of course know who is traveling and when and where lodgings are needed. But they should also understand

- *The purpose for the trip.* Is it for business? Pleasure? To visit family?
- *The clients' needs and requirements.* For example, do they need smoking or nonsmoking rooms? Do they need cribs or babysitting services? Would they appreciate the brighter lighting and large-button telephones that some hotels offer in rooms for senior travelers? As we discuss in Chapter 11, some hotels now offer special services for elderly guests as well as for business travelers, children, people with disabilities, singles, and women.
- *The clients' preferences.* For example, do they expect to eat at the hotel, to play there, or to be entertained there? Or do they prefer to get away from the hotel? The more adventurous may wish to stay at a monastery in Tibet or in rooms above a pub in Ireland, whereas others may feel comfortable only in a familiar Holiday Inn. Asking clients what hotel they enjoyed in the past can shed a lot of light on what lodging is likely to suit them next time.

Contacting a Hotel

Once a hotel is selected, it can be contacted directly (by GDS, the Internet, letter, phone, fax, or e-mail) or indirectly (through a repping firm, consolidator, or tourist bureau). The best method depends on circumstances.

Travel agencies still make most of their hotel bookings through GDSs, and many hotel chains have a direct link to GDSs so that counselors see exactly what the hotel's own reservationists are seeing. Of course, some lodgings (such as some budget hotels and unusual properties) are not listed in GDSs.

Increasingly, travel agencies are booking hotel reservations directly on the supplier's Web site. Many hotel companies (Marriott and Hilton are two examples) now provide a "best-rate guarantee" for those who book on their sites. Travel agencies protect their commissions by making the reservations through the travel-agency section of the hotel's site.

The old-fashioned way of communicating in writing is sometimes best. Letters or e-mails are useful when booking very small hotels months ahead if the staff does not speak English well enough to handle a phone conversation comfortably.

The more upscale the hotel is, the greater the likelihood that a telephone call will be worthwhile because reservations tend to be more complicated for deluxe hotels. Toll-free numbers may connect either to the hotel chain or to the hotel itself.

Making a regular long-distance call to contact a hotel is sometimes appropriate despite the cost. For example, sometimes you can obtain a room by calling the hotel directly even though both the GDS and a call to the hotel's toll-free number indicated that the hotel was sold out, because the hotel was holding a few rooms in reserve. Most international hotels have English-speaking personnel available, especially during regular business hours. (Keep time differences in mind.)

Contacting the hotel by e-mail or fax offers advantages, particularly for complex reservations and especially for groups. An e-mail or fax allows counselors to make sure details are correct; something as simple as the client's name, for example, can be misconstrued over the phone. Also, sending e-mail or a fax avoids language and time zone problems. The receiver will have time to get translations, if necessary, and the message can be sent anytime and received anytime.

Sometimes, instead of using any of these methods to contact the hotel or hotel chain directly, it makes sense to contact a hotel representative firm, consolidator, or tourist bureau. Hotel representative firms handle many of the hotels that are not members of chains and do not have toll-free numbers. Consolidators sometimes offer lower prices or have rooms available when the hotel says it is sold out; many are on the Internet. (Most travel agencies deal only with consolidators that are on their "preferred" list or that they know are reliable.) Also, some tourism offices and convention bureaus have reservation systems to simplify accommodation bookings in their area. They operate much like hotel representatives, but payments are made directly to hotels.

Making a Reservation

When making a reservation, travel counselors should be prepared to give the following information:

- Client's full name as it appears on ID (or passport, if an international booking).
- Number of people in the party.
- Ages of children or listing as senior citizens (if eligible for rate reductions).
- Type of room desired (such as location, view, or amenities).
- Number and type of beds.
- Club memberships, such as membership in the hotel's frequent-guest program, a motor club, or AARP, which may entitle the guest to a discount or special service.
- Special requests, such as wheelchair-accessible rooms, cribs, or rollaway beds.

- Dates of arrival and departure.
- Time of arrival. (As we discuss later, this information is crucial.)
- Type of payment, and names and numbers of credit cards.

One client's name is sufficient when booking one room and usually sufficient for more than one room. But booking separate rooms under separate names has advantages. Clients can then receive their own confirmation numbers and can give their own names if they arrive separately. Counselors will have separate reservations for tracking commissions. But each separate booking also creates extra work. If one member of a family or small group is booking for everyone, one reservation and name may be enough. If the other people are known and might prefer the reservation in their own names, book them separately.

All reservations carry a confirmation or reservation number; it should be carefully noted, along with the reservationist's name and the date if the room was booked by phone. The rate, tax and service charges, and commissions due to the agency should also be noted. Be aware that commissions are paid on the hotel rate only, not on taxes and service fees.

Group Reservations

The mechanics of making a reservation for a group are in many ways the same as for an individual, but there are some differences. For example,

- Even the largest group may be booked in one name, but individual names (the rooming list) must be supplied to the hotel by a specified date before arrival.
- The hotel will require a deposit and signed contracts. Watch carefully for a nonrefundable deposit and dates.
- The group rate quoted may include the agency's commission, or it may be a *net rate,* which means it does not include a commission. If the rate is net, the agency adds its own markup.

Usually, hotels have a separate department or specialist to handle reservations for groups. Travel counselors should become thoroughly comfortable making individual reservations before handling groups.

Many group reservations are made as part of a tour. The rates will be net, and the discount will depend on the size of the group, the hotel's occupancy, and the buyer's negotiating skills. Ask about a free room for the group leader and the number of sold rooms required for granting a complimentary one.

Other group reservations are made for conventions, meetings, and seminars. Large groups with many special needs are generally handled by specialists—*meeting planners*—who deal directly with the hotel, negotiating rates and conducting on-site inspections. Hotels are often booked years in advance for conventions and other meetings. This is a growing market, and we discuss it further in Chapter 11.

Dealing with Policies and Problems

How long is a reservation held? If travelers have reservations, are they certain to get rooms? And can they cancel without penalty? Most hotels follow the same general policies regarding these issues.

Guarantees and Late Arrivals. Most hotels have a *hold time,* the deadline for holding the room without payment. The traveler must arrive by the hold time to secure the reservation. After that time, the reservation is canceled and the room may be given to the first person who arrives. If the traveler arrives later and a room is still available, no doubt the hotel will be glad to provide it; but if the hotel is full, it is under no obligation to do so.

The hold time is generally 4:00 P.M. or 6:00 P.M., but it can vary and should always be checked. All times refer to the hotel's clock.

If the traveler is planning to arrive or might arrive after the hold time, the reservation can be held by paying a deposit for the room; the reservation is then *guaranteed for late arrival.* The deposit is usually made by credit card, but a check may be sent if time permits. If the room is guaranteed by a deposit, the traveler may arrive at any time; the room will be held because it has been paid for. Be sure that clients understand that if they fail to appear they will be charged for one night.

Some hotels ask for a credit card just to hold a reservation. In effect, these hotels are making all reservations "guaranteed."

If travelers have guaranteed reservations and wish to cancel, they can usually do so without penalty by calling before the hold time. But policies regarding cancellation time vary and should always be checked. Some resorts, for example, require that the cancellation be made days or even weeks in advance to avoid a penalty. Cancellations, like confirmations and reservations, are assigned a number, which should be carefully noted.

Overbooking. Hotels know that a certain number of guests with reservations will not arrive. Deposits or guarantees do not solve the problem because clients sometimes dispute these charges, and hotels then have a difficult time collecting them from credit card companies. To be assured of a full house each night, hotels overbook their rooms, much as airlines overbook their seats. They calculate how many rooms to overbook for specific days of the week and seasons. Sometimes, though, they miscalculate and end up with more confirmed guests than rooms.

The same result may occur, not because of overbooking, but because of *overstaying.* Guests do not always check out when they say they will. Most local laws state that innkeepers have the right to request a guest's departure if the room is needed for an incoming guest, but most hotels are reluctant to evict paying guests.

What happens to the unlucky confirmed guest when the hotel has no rooms available? The policy varies, but typically the hotel tries to substitute nearby accommodations of equal or better quality. This is called *walking the guest.* Some hotels pay the entire price for the substituted room; usually, though, the hotel pays the difference if the new room costs more. It also provides free transportation to the substitute hotel. The hotel urges guests to transfer back as soon as space is available, and it again pays for transportation. It's wise to advise the clients to arrive earlier in the afternoon, if possible, or to call the hotel during the day if it looks as though they may be late.

CHAPTER WRAP-UP

CHAPTER HIGHLIGHTS

Like many other industries, the accommodations industry has been marked by the expansion of chains at home and abroad. At the same time, market segmentation has produced wide choices for travelers. In fact, the variety of lodgings and rates creates a constant challenge for travel professionals trying to help travelers make wise choices. This chapter provided the background necessary to meet that challenge. Here is a review of the objectives with which we began the chapter.

1. **Identify the major trends in how accommodations are owned and operated, and describe some key market segments.** Lodgings may be owned and operated as independent properties or as one of a number of properties that are affiliated through chains, franchises, management contracts, or membership organizations. The dominant trend is away from independent properties and toward consolidation. Around the globe, many lodgings are part of chains, which in turn are part of large hotel companies. In order to capture a large market, some hotel companies establish many brand names, each of which is designed to appeal to a particular market segment. Markets can be segmented by the purpose for traveling, by current needs, and by location, as well as by price. Based on price, market segments include strict budget, economy, budget luxury, mid-priced, first class, and luxury accommodations.

2. **Describe key types of lodgings and characteristics that affect the price of a room.** U.S. lodgings can be classified into the following key types: motels, commercial hotels, convention hotels, airport hotels, all-suites, resorts, spas, all-inclusives, bed-and-breakfasts (B&Bs), inns, lodges, casinos, and hostels. Abroad, minshukus, paradores, pensions, pousadas, and ryokan are significant types in certain countries.

   Many characteristics distinguish one accommodation from another and can affect the price. Location is most important, but other key factors are special facilities and services (a concierge, for instance) and characteristics of the room—its location within the lodging, its size and furnishings, the number of beds and occupants. Sometimes, the length of stay and meal plan have an effect. The season, the day of the week, and the demand of the moment are also important. Applying yield management, hotels project an occupancy rate and may vary their prices accordingly on a day-day basis.

   The price to a particular guest will also vary depending on whether the guest pays the rack rate or is eligible for a corporate rate, negotiated corporate rate, group rate, convention rate, run-of-the-house (ROH) rate, or special promotional rate. Hotels often quote net rates for a group; the agency then adds its own markup to the quote.

3. **Outline the roles of hotels and travel counselors in selling accommodations.** Hotels have fine-tuned their services in order to increase sales, and increasingly they sell rooms to the public on the Internet either directly or through consolidators. But travel agencies remain an important source of sales for the lodging industry. To be successful in tapping this market, travel counselors must know how to match the client with the right accommodation. They need to know how to find information about specific hotels, understand their clients' needs, and learn which methods to use to contact hotels.

4. **Identify the information needed when making a hotel reservation.** Whether the reservation is made with the hotel, hotel chain, or hotel representative firm (rep firm), the travel counselor should be able to provide the name, number of people in the party, number and type of beds necessary, date and time of arrival, date of departure, age of the client, membership in any program or club that might qualify the client for rate reductions, any special requests, and the manner of guaranteeing the reservation, if necessary.

   The travel counselor should also be sure to check the cancellation policy and hold time and determine whether the reservation should be guaranteed for late arrival. The confirmation number should be carefully noted. But despite the travel counselor's best efforts, a hotel might walk the guest as a result of overbooking by the hotel or overstaying by other guests. Last, but not least, counselors should always verify whether the hotel will pay commission on the booking, and, if not, they may need to add a service fee to compensate.

KEY TERMS

A list of key terms introduced in this chapter follows. If you do not recall the meaning of these terms, see the Glossary, which begins on page 393.

adjoining rooms
airport hotel
all-inclusive
all-suite
American Hotel and Lodging
  Association (AH&LA)
American plan (AP)
bed and breakfast (B&B)
Bermuda plan (BP)
boatel
brand
casino
chain
château, castle, and villa
commercial hotel
concierge
connecting rooms
Continental plan (CP)
convention hotel
convention rate
corporate rate
demi-pension
dine-around plan
dude ranch
European plan (EP)
extended-stay hotel
franchise company
frequent-guest program
full board
group rate
guaranteed for late arrival
hold time
hospitality industry

hostel
hotel consolidator
hotel representative firm
inn
lodge
lodging
management contract
market segment
membership organization
minshuku
Modified American plan (MAP)
motel
motor inn
negotiated corporate rate
net rate
occupancy rate
parador
pension
pousada
properties
rack rate
rep firm
resort
retreat-style accommodation
rondavel
run-of-the-house (ROH) rate
ryokan
self-catering rental apartment
spa
tented camp
tourist court
tree lodge
walking the guest

REVIEW QUESTIONS

1. Why would one hotel company operate under many names?

2. Why is the choice of accommodations sometimes more complicated than the choice of transportation?

3. What features is a business traveler likely to look for in a hotel? What features are likely to appeal to a vacationer touring by car?

4. Which factors most affect the cost of a hotel room?

5. Name several of the different meal plans that hotels may offer and how they may vary in different countries.

6. When and why would you go first to the Internet to find information about a hotel where your client wants a room?

CHAPTER 7

Cruises

OBJECTIVES

After completing this chapter, you should be able to

1. Describe the key types of cruise lines and other ships available to tourists.

2. Identify the five most popular cruising areas.

3. Outline the key attractions of life onboard a cruise.

4. Explain major benefits and possible disadvantages of the typical cruise.

5. Name the factors that determine the cost of a cruise.

"Follow the sun," the ad might say. "Awake each morning to see new vistas. From sumptuous food to Broadway shows and a spa, you'll find everything you want on our incomparable ship."

Taking a cruise like this is the dream vacation for millions of Americans. *Cruise ships* are all-inclusive floating resorts that move from port to port. For travelers, they offer constant pampering, a chance to sample the life at different ports, and opportunities for both relaxation and excitement. Cruises are also convenient. The price of the cruise takes care of transportation, accommodations, meals, most entertainment, and more, and passengers can visit different places without constantly packing and unpacking. In this chapter we look first at the industry that provides these services, then at the cruising experience and at how cruises are sold.

The Modern Cruise Industry

■ HOW DID THE CRUISE INDUSTRY HELP TO CREATE A GROWING MARKET FOR TRAVEL BY SHIP?

About 13.5 million North Americans took cruises in 2009, generating more than $3 billion for the U.S. economy and creating nearly 314,000 U.S. jobs.

Since the 1970s cruising has been one of the fastest-growing segments of the travel industry, and career opportunities in this field should continue to expand, particularly because only 20 percent of U.S. residents have ever sailed, leaving a huge, untapped market. (The Close-Up on careers describes some of these jobs.)

CLOSE-UP: CAREERS WITH CRUISE LINES

Positions in the cruise industry are more plentiful onshore than aboard ships, but opportunities abound. Onboard, all employees are referred to as crew, and most of the positions are like those at resorts. Typically, they are contracted for six months. Hours are long, accommodations are tight, and privacy is almost nonexistent. But because crew members do not have to pay for room and board while on the ship, they can pocket a tidy sum. Shoreside positions are like those for hotel companies or tour operators, with interesting positions in marketing, sales, reservations, operations, and finance. Most shoreside opportunities are at the cruise line's headquarters office, most of which are in Florida.

ONBOARD POSITIONS

■ **Position** Youth counselor

Description Watching passengers' children and conducting youth activities are the responsibility of the youth counselor. The hours are long—from 8:00 A.M. to late into the evening. The position generally requires working for three to six months at a time, followed by four to six weeks off.

Qualifications Cruise lines look for people with experience as camp counselors or with a background in education or child care. Having taken some college courses in physical education or childhood development helps. Certification in CPR and first aid is usually required.

■ **Position** Cruise staff

Description A person in this position does everything to entertain passengers, from being a costumed character to playing bingo or giving lectures.

Qualifications Gregarious people, perhaps with a background in entertainment, are suited for this position. It does not require prior cruise experience.

■ **Position** Future cruise reservations manager

Description The primary responsibility of this manager is to sell future cruises to the passengers. (If a travel agency booked the passenger on the current cruise, the agency will receive the commission for the future booking made onboard.)

Qualifications Extensive knowledge of the cruise line's products is required. Previous travel industry or sales experience is preferred.

ONSHORE POSITIONS

■ **Position** Sailing coordinator

Description This shoreside position brings responsibility for making all travel accommodations for air and sea passengers (airline, rail, hotel, transfers) and for maintaining and updating passenger records.

Qualifications This position requires at least one year of experience as an airline reservationist or as a travel counselor with GDS experience. Strong organizational skills, a good command of the English language (both written and oral), and the ability to work in a fast-paced environment are also needed.

■ **Position** Reservations manager

Description Supervising the reservations staff is the heart of this job. The reservations manager is responsible for developing procedures, implementing training, and motivating people, as well as for gauging demand in order to schedule staff efficiently. The manager must also keep other departments informed about booking volume.

Qualifications Prior background as a reservationist and some management experience in a call center are necessary for this position.

■ **Position** Agency marketing manager/sales representative/account executive

Description The agency marketing manager promotes a cruise line's products to travel agencies in a specified territory. He or she is responsible for increasing sales by promoting awareness, generating product loyalty, and identifying and developing key accounts. The manager participates in trade shows and often helps travel agencies sell cruises to groups. This position requires travel within the territory and a willingness to work evenings.

Qualifications A sales or marketing background, preferably in the travel industry, is needed for this position. A gregarious personality and cruise experience are assets; presentation skills are essential.

■ **Other positions** Airfare coordinator; analyst, revenue management; barber; cabin steward; documentation agent; entertainer; fitness trainers; hairdresser; host/hostess; hotel manager; nurse; photographer; pricing analyst; purser; reservations agent.

The growth in cruising did not just happen by chance. The cruise lines themselves have been key in creating a profitable market for cruising.

The Cruise Lines

When the first nonstop passenger flights crossed the Atlantic from New York to Europe, the death knell sounded for the luxury ocean liner. The growth of jet travel forced shipping lines to retire the ships that had carried millions from continent to continent. Some lines began to focus on shipping cargo; some went out of business; others created the modern cruise industry.

The industry began to take shape in the early 1960s, when some shipping lines converted their ocean liners into cruise ships. Later in the 1960s new companies developed year-round cruises to the Caribbean and introduced ships specifically designed for cruising. In the 1970s Carnival Cruise Lines became the first line to market cruising as a vacation experience rather than as a way to get from one place to another. The new era in cruising was marked by the founding of the *Cruise Lines International Association (CLIA)* in 1975. It promotes cruising through public relations and advertising as well as by training travel counselors. In 2006 it merged with the International Council of Cruise Lines (ICCL), a sister entity created in 1990, dedicated to participating in regulatory and policy development for the cruise industry.

Since the 1980s cruise lines expanded their market by offering travelers new itineraries and new activities, as well as discounts. They repackaged cruises into vacations that could appeal to a wide range of the public. They also invested in a huge building boom, putting colossal new ships to sea. Meanwhile, cruise lines themselves were being bought, sold, and consolidated. *Parent cruise companies* often own several cruise lines. In fact, by 2000 the three largest parent cruise companies—Carnival, Royal Caribbean, and Princess—controlled about two-thirds of the berths on North American cruise ships.

The parent cruise companies have created brands of cruise lines (Table 7.1 on the next page), much like the hotel brands discussed in Chapter 6. By selecting destinations, activities, ship designs, and themes, they create an identity for a cruise line that will appeal to particular segments of the market. For example, Carnival owns not only Carnival Cruise Lines—which offers popularly priced, resort-style cruises—but also six other brands, including the somewhat sedate Holland America; the deluxe, elegant Cunard line; and Seabourn, a cruise line known for its smaller ships and luxurious amenities.

CLIA categorizes the lines into the following major types:

- *Contemporary, resort-style brands.* These offer midsize to huge ships, rich with activities, in a generally casual style at a moderate price. For example, Carnival's *Dream* strives for a beach-party atmosphere on seven-day cruises to the Caribbean. It has a capacity of 3,646 passengers.
- *Premium brands.* These lines feature midsize to large ships with the extensive diversions offered by resort-style brands plus some upscale features such as art collections and gourmet-style cuisine. One example is Celebrity's *Eclipse,* with five specialty restaurants and onboard classes, among other amenities.
- *Luxury brands.* Unparalleled personalized service, a spacious environment, and luxury on small to midsize ships are offered by the luxury brands, such as Silversea Voyages, along with exotic ports.
- *Specialty/expedition brands* (also called *niche brands*). These lines offer cruises with a distinct focus; most emphasize discovery of the cultures of their destinations. Prices range from moderate to deluxe.

- *Value brands* (also called *traditional brands*). These lines offer the standard features of a cruise at a more economical price than other brands, typically on small to midsize ships. Hurtigruten Cruises, famous for its Norwegian fjords cruises, is an example.

The ships themselves are key to establishing a cruise line's identity.

The Ships

The old language of the sea is still used to describe cruise ships (see Figure 7.1 on page 178). Thus the front of the ship is the **bow** and the back is the **stern;** anything toward the front is **fore** and anything toward the rear is **aft.** Speed is measured in knots (1 **knot** is equivalent to about 1.15 land miles per hour). Round windows are *portholes*, kitchens are *galleys*, and ramps by which passengers get on and off ship are *gangways*. The vessels are always referred to as *ships*, never as boats.

Comfort, Health, and Safety. Seasickness is one tradition of the sea that modern cruisers can usually avoid. All cruise ships have **stabilizers,** which are devices that extend from both sides of the ship and minimize roll. **Roll** is the

TABLE 7.1 The 26 Cruise Lines Belonging to CLIA

Cruise Line	Web Site	Ships	Comments
AMA Waterways	www.amawaterways.com	10	Rivers of Europe, Russia, southeast Asia
American Cruise Lines	www.americancruiselines.com	5	Various U.S. rivers
Avalon Waterways	www.avalonwaterways.com	14	Europe, China, Egypt, Galápagos. Part of Globus family of brands
Azamara Club Cruises	www.azamaracruises.com	2	Europe, Asia, Panama Canal, Atlantic Crossings, less-traveled Caribbean
Carnival Cruise Lines	www.carnival.com	25	Alaska, Canada, New England, Caribbean, Mexican Riviera, Panama Canal
Celebrity Cruises	www.celebritycruises.com	11	Alaska, Bermuda, Pacific Northwest, Canada, New England, Caribbean, Europe, South America
Costa Cruises	www.costacruises.com	17	European style, Europe, Russia, Baltic, South Amemrica, Dubai, Asia, Seychelles, Madagascar
Crystal Cruises	www.crystalcruises.com	2	Virtually everywhere; 25 percent international guests. Voted best large ship line by *Condé Nast Traveler* and *Travel and Leisure* magazines
Cunard Line	www.cunard.com	3	Worldwide itineraries, British tradition since 1840, unique lecture series, trans-Atlantic crossings again
Disney Cruise Line	www.disneycruise.com	4	Caribbean, Mediterranean, Baltic; emphasis on families and children
Holland America Line	www.hollandamerica.com	15	All seven continents, marked 137 years of service in 2010
Hurtigruten	www.hurtigruten.us	13	Smaller ships, Norwegian fjords, Iceland, Greenland, Antarctica and Arctic, Chilean fjords; mature clientele; scenery; wildlife
Louis Cruises	www.louiscruises.com	9	Cyprus-based; France, Italy, Greece and its islands; international clientele
MSC Cruises	www.msccruisesusa.com	11	Italian style and service; world destinations including unique stops; Malta, Balearics, Ukraine, Portugal, South Africa

(continued on next page)

ship's side-to-side movement; it is the primary cause of seasickness. (The ship's movement up and down is called *pitch*.) Because of the efficiency of modern stabilizers, most passengers will be perfectly comfortable a fair distance each side of midship.

To minimize other potential hazards at sea, travelers rely on governments to make and enforce regulations. However, cruise ships are not subject to U.S. laws when they are at sea. Each cruise ship has a ***country of registry;*** the ship operates under the maritime laws of that country. U.S. laws require that ships registered under the U.S. flag be built in the United States and operated by American crews, which is an expensive proposition. Operators save huge sums by registering ships under the flags of other nations. When a company registers its ships under another country's flag to avoid the regulations or taxes of its home country, it is said to "fly a ***flag of convenience***."

Whatever its country of registry, ships that serve U.S. ports must meet certain health and safety requirements. For example, they must follow the ***Safety of Life at Sea (SOLAS) regulations***. These are rules established by the International Maritime Organization, which is part of the United Nations. The rules cover the configuration of ships and equipment and are designed to prevent and control hazards such as fires.

In addition, the U.S. Public Health Service regularly checks and grades the cleanliness of ships sailing from U.S. ports in order to minimize the risk of disease on the ships. Under the *Vessel Sanitation Program (VSP)*, any ship that has an international itinerary, carries 13 or more passengers, and calls on a U.S. port is subject to unannounced twice-yearly inspections. The Summary

TABLE 7.1 The 26 Cruise Lines Belonging to CLIA (cont.)

Cruise Line	Web Site	Ships	Comments
Norwegian Cruise Line	www.ncl.com	11	World destinations, originator of "freestyle cruising," array of cruising options
Oceania Cruises	www.oceaniacruises.com	4	Country club elegance; Down Under, India, Africa, Southeast Asia, Black Sea, and more
Paul Gauguin Cruises	www.pgcruises.com	1	Year round in Tahiti, French Polynesia, South Pacific; onboard water sports marina
Pearl Sea Cruises	www.pearlseacruises.com	2	Canadian Maritimes, Great Lakes, New England, Caribbean, Central America
Princess Cruises	www.princess.com	17	Sailings to all seven continents, home of the original "Loveboat," which was used in the 1970s television series of the same name
Regent Seven Seas Cruises	www.rssc.com	3	All-suite ships, 300 worldwide destinations, upscale educated clientele over age 45
Royal Caribbean International	www.royalcaribbean.com	22	Major destinations, itinerares from three to 14 days, home of megaships *Allure* and *Oasis of the Seas*
Seabourn Cruise Lines	www.seabourn.com	6	Top-rate, small-ship cruise company voted #1 by *Travel and Leisure* readers in 2011
SeaDream Yacht Club	www.seadream.com	2	Ultra-luxury mega yachts, seven-day sailings to Greek Islands, Mediterranean, Caribbean, Croation coast
Silversea Cruises	www.silversea.com	6	Wordwide destinations, small ultra-luxury vessels able to put in at smaller ports
Uniworld River Cruises	www.uniworld.com	11	500 departures on 30 itineraries on 11 rivers in 20 countries including Europe, Egypt, China
Windstar Cruises	www.windstarcruises.com	3	Operates 4- and 5-masted sailing ships, carries 145–312 guests, couples oriented

FIGURE 7.1 Shiptalk

Here are some of the basic terms used to describe locations on a ship.

of Sanitation Inspections, commonly called the **green sheet,** is posted on the Web site of the Centers for Disease Control (www.cdc.gov). Ships with unacceptable scores, however, are not stopped from sailing.

Finally, the *International Council of Cruise Lines (ICCL),* which represents the seventeen largest cruise lines serving the North American market, sets guidelines regarding medical care onboard cruise ships. For example, the guidelines state that cruise ships should provide reasonable emergency medical care, adequate infirmary care, and a medical staff competent in life-support techniques and cardiac care. The medical staff should be able to administer emergency first aid and to diagnose, stabilize, and facilitate the evacuation of seriously ill or injured persons to the nearest onshore hospital.

Note that these guidelines are limited. There might be no surgeon onboard, and medical equipment might not be up-to-date. Furthermore, there is no agency to enforce the guidelines or to certify that a cruise line follows them.

Comparing Ships: Size and Age. Nothing can quite compare with the sight of a huge cruise ship slipping gracefully away to sea. Each ship has its own personality, but age and size represent key differences among ships.

Although modern ships offer the latest in technology, comfort, and amenities, some travelers prefer older ships. Their rooms are more varied in size, their histories can be fascinating, and their characters are distinctive.

The size of a cruise ship may be cited in terms of the number of possible passengers, the number of berths, or its **gross registered tonnage (GRT),** which is the amount of enclosed revenue-producing space. *Megaships* measure at least 70,000 GRT and hold more than 1,600 passengers. One example is Royal Caribbean's *Allure of the Seas,* currently the world's largest cruise ship. Its GRT is 225,282, and it carries up to 6,360 passengers and 2,384 crew members.

Is bigger better? On large ships, motion is reduced to a minimum. Large ships also bring economies of scale, so they offer amenities that smaller ships cannot match. Also, the extra space on megaships permits attractions and activities unthinkable a few years ago. For example,

- Norwegian Cruise Line's *Norwegian Epic*. Built in 2010 as a 155,873 GRT vessel, its 19 decks hold as many as 5,183 passengers. There are 20 different dining options on board, a sports complex with climbing wall and full-sized basketball court, and a spa offering a wide range of treatments including teeth whitening and botox.

- MSC Cruises *Fantasia*. The 137,936-GRT ship debuted in 2009 and carries a maximum of 3,900 passengers. Italian owned and styled, it attracts many Europeans as well as Americans, particularly couples and families. The casino offers free gaming lessons.

- Cunard's *Queen Mary 2*. Launched into service in 2004, this 151,000-GRT beauty has a maximum guest capacity of 2,620. In addition to its cruise schedule, it offers transatlantic service between Southampton and New York. Unique on-board lectures, a book club, workshops, performances, and other intellectual/cultural offerings are provided by representatives of London's Royal Academy of Dramatic Art, the Royal Astronomical Society, and the Juilliard School of Music.

Despite the excitement offered by megaships, some travelers prefer the more intimate, quiet atmosphere of smaller ships. Small ships have the additional advantage of being able to visit destinations that are inaccessible to large vessels because of the depth of the harbor or the dockage space. Also, a small ship may have more room per person and therefore feel more spacious. One measure of spaciousness is the **space ratio,** which is the ship size in GRT divided by the number of passengers. A space ratio of 50 is luxuriously spacious; a space ratio of 20 might feel crowded. For example, one crew member to every three passengers would not provide the personal service that one crew member to every 1.5 passengers would.

The cruise lines continue to expand their fleets with ships large and small. Ships not distinguished by their large size are likely to feature unusual destinations, innovative programs designed for special market segments, or an unusual degree of luxury. New trends include Internet access for passengers and the concept of dine-around in several onboard restaurants.

The Cruise Market

Once upon a time, only the rich took cruises. Cruise lines exploit this old association, presenting cruising as an opportunity to experience unusual luxury. But they have also made cruises affordable to a broad range of travelers. Because cruise prices include transportation, accommodations, and food, the cost compares well with that for land-based vacations.

Who are the people taking cruises? Of all cruise passengers in the world, more than 75 percent are North American. Recent cruisers from the United States include a balanced mix of people, as Figure 7.2 shows on the next page. People of all ages and incomes can be found on cruises.

This variety among cruisers is matched by the variety among cruises. Look again at the description of the types of cruise lines on page 176. As we noted earlier, the parent cruise companies have aimed to create cruise lines for different market segments. As a result, today, there is a cruise for almost every budget and for almost every age. For example, many cruises offer services that appeal to young clients. Some promote a partylike atmosphere and offer special singles get-togethers. Ships that cater to families offer children's fares, babysitting services for a fee, and special events and programs for children.

There are also cruises for all interests. Specialty or *niche cruises* include jazz, blues, country-and-western, and oldies' rock cruises; sports and celebrity cruises; and adventure, heritage, gourmet, mystery, and chocoholics cruises.

Cruise companies also aim to accommodate different lifestyles. Most cruises still have one or two nights when women wear formal dresses and gentlemen wear tuxedos or dark suits, and the typical cruise seeks to preserve the tradition of elegance set by luxury ocean liners. But new ships have become increasingly informal. Casual dress is normal during the day; for most dinners, passengers dress as they would in a good restaurant back home. On large ships passengers can choose from multiple restaurants and dining rooms to find the atmosphere and dressing standards they prefer. There are sailing cruises that require little more than a bathing suit all day and a cover-up for the evening.

Cruises of different lengths tend to differ in price, clientele, and atmosphere. More than half of all cruises last from six to eight days. The longer the cruise, the more expensive it is and, generally speaking, the older the clients. Long cruises are also more likely than short ones to have a formal atmosphere and to emphasize service, ports, and gourmet cuisine. Short cruises of three or four days tend to attract those looking for pure escape; they exude an informal, often partylike, atmosphere and serve to attract the client who then may book longer, more expensive trips in the future.

Other Ship Travel

Besides traditional cruises, other forms of travel by ship are also popular. The main options are yachts, large sailing ships, freighters, and ferries.

FIGURE 7.2 Who Is Cruising?

Among those who have taken cruises during the last five years, the typical cruiser is a married fifty-year-old who has a college education and above-average income and is still working. But as the data shown here illustrate, cruisers include a broad range of people. And the popularity of the family cruise, including children, teenagers, and grandparents, often alter the statistics.

Source: *CLIA 2011 Market Profile Study.*

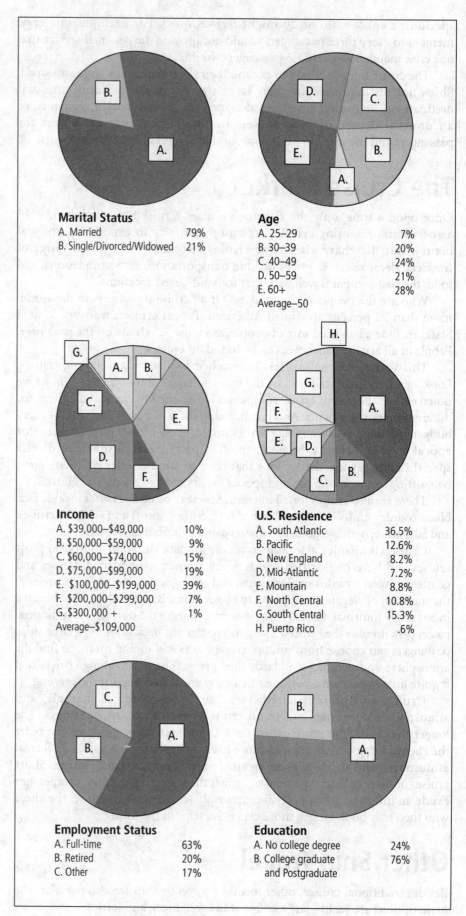

Marital Status
A. Married	79%
B. Single/Divorced/Widowed	21%

Age
A. 25–29	7%
B. 30–39	20%
C. 40–49	24%
D. 50–59	21%
E. 60+	28%
Average—50	

Income
A. $39,000–$49,000	10%
B. $50,000–$59,000	9%
C. $60,000–$74,000	15%
D. $75,000–$99,000	19%
E. $100,000–$199,000	39%
F. $200,000–$299,000	7%
G. $300,000 +	1%
Average—$109,000	

U.S. Residence
A. South Atlantic	36.5%
B. Pacific	12.6%
C. New England	8.2%
D. Mid-Atlantic	7.2%
E. Mountain	8.8%
F. North Central	10.8%
G. South Central	15.3%
H. Puerto Rico	.6%

Employment Status
A. Full-time	63%
B. Retired	20%
C. Other	17%

Education
A. No college degree	24%
B. College graduate and Postgraduate	76%

Yacht Charters. *Yachts* are boats used for private pleasure excursions. On a typical yacht charter, groups of four to ten people hire the boat for a certain number of days. They choose the itinerary, subject to the advice of the operator and the crew. A professional crew sails the boat and cooks the meals.

Experienced sailors may charter yachts that they sail themselves, without a professional crew; this is known as a **bareboat charter.** The boat operator requires evidence of sailing experience and expertise; some operators give a written exam or conduct a trial at sea. If the prospective skipper and crew pass the tests, they receive their boat complete with charts, safety equipment, and everything necessary to sail.

Many large yachts migrate seasonally. The Caribbean season begins around Thanksgiving and runs through April; peak time is Christmas week. The Mediterranean season begins in mid-May, peaks in July and August, and ends in October. New England charters are at their height in July and August; the season runs from June through Labor Day. The Moorings offers both bareboat and crewed yacht charters in a variety of world destinations.

Sailing Ships. Large sailing ships with multiple sails are called **windjammers.** For example, Star Clipper's 227-passenger *Royal Clipper* has five masts and 42 sails. Windjammers are large for sailing vessels but much smaller than cruise ships and usually less luxurious.

Informality is the hallmark of windjammer cruises. Passengers may help sail the ships and often pick up a smattering of nautical knowledge. But note that windjammer cruises are not charters. Berths are sold to the public on a per-person basis, and the operator determines the itinerary.

Some large sailing ships are computerized and use both sails and motors; they are classified officially as **schooners.** They take advantage of modern technology without sacrificing the beautiful lines of a sailing vessel. Windstar Sail Cruises and Club Med have been offering cruises on schooners much like traditional cruises. Passengers can enjoy swimming pools, casinos, and other amenities in a very informal atmosphere.

Freighters. Ships that have the principal purpose of carrying cargo are called *freighters,* but the typical freighter may also carry passengers. Most are modern vessels with stabilizers, climate control, and some amenities.

Most freighters take up to twelve passengers. The cabins are comfortable, the food is varied, and the table conversation may be entertaining. But onboard activity is limited. Passengers should take plenty of good books, plan their own shore excursions, and pack hand-washable clothing. Freighters are best suited for people with time to spare, few fixed commitments, and the ability to stay friendly with eight to ten other people in fairly close quarters for many weeks. Ports on the itinerary are those desirable for cargo purposes, not necessarily ones that tourists may prefer.

Ferries. Around the world, *ferries* carry passengers, vehicles, livestock, and supplies across bodies of water on regular schedules. The trips take from a few minutes to several days, although most take less than a day. Ferries can be as small as a rowboat or as large as a small cruise ship. But unlike cruise ships, ferries act simply as a means of transportation; the price does not include food, accommodations, or other activities. Service is what you might expect on any public transport.

Sometimes ferries are the only practical way to get to a destination. But travelers also take ferries by choice rather than necessity. Some construct entire vacations around ferry travel along the Alaska coast, the Norwegian coast, or the Greek islands. Hong Kong has some of the most famous ferry trips in the world, notably the *Star Ferry* that travels between Hong Kong Island and Kowloon.

✔ CHECK-UP

Megaships
- ✔ Measure at least 70,000 GRT and hold at least 1,600 passengers.
- ✔ Offer economies of scale, amenities, and activities that smaller ships cannot match.

The cruise market
- ✔ Includes a balanced mix of people of varying ages, incomes, and interests.

- ✔ Has been stimulated by the success of cruise companies in creating brands to appeal to varied market segments.

Compared with cruise ships, freighters
- ✔ Carry few passengers.
- ✔ Are designed to carry cargo efficiently.
- ✔ Offer few onboard activities.

Destinations: Cruising Itineraries

■ WHAT ARE THE MOST POPULAR DESTINATIONS FOR CRUISES?

Most cruises last three to fourteen days, but travelers can cruise for several months if they choose. However, most cruisers seem to be selecting cruises that last from six to eight days.

Today's cruise ships average about 16 knots; thus they have a maximum daily range of about 450 to 550 miles, which is about the distance from Boston to Washington, D.C., or from San Francisco to San Diego. They visit ports in every corner of the world. When a harbor is too shallow or too crowded for a ship to dock, passengers go from ship to shore and back on small boats called *tenders.* The cruise might allow several days or just a few hours onshore.

To fill the growing number of ships, cruise lines have added service from new originating, or *embarkation, points.* They have also expanded the destinations they visit, or *ports of call.* Each year cruise lines offer new itineraries.

Traditional Cruising Areas

According to CLIA, the most popular destinations for cruise ships have been the Caribbean, the Mediterranean, Europe, Alaska, and Mexico. Other popular cruising areas include Panama Canal crossings, Bermuda, and South America. Newly popular areas include the Baltic, Russia, China, and the Adriatic Coast from Venice, Italy, to Dubrovnik, Croatia.

The Caribbean and Bahamas. When people talk about the Caribbean, they often mean not only the islands in the Caribbean but also the Bahamas, which are islands in the Atlantic (see Figure 7.3). The largest percent of the cruising public visits the area.

Cruise-goers prefer one-week trips in the Caribbean to cruises of any other length. But two- to four-day cruises are also very popular. Many islands are close enough to one another for ships to visit one island all day and sail on to another at night. Many itineraries are offered, but here are three popular types:

- One-week cruises of the *eastern Caribbean,* including San Juan, Puerto Rico; St. Thomas (one of the U.S. Virgin Islands); St. Croix; and the Dominican Republic. The familiar American ports of San Juan and St. Thomas are especially popular with first-time passengers. San Juan provides Las Vegas–style entertainment, and St. Thomas has duty-free shopping and beautiful beaches.

- One-week cruises to the *western Caribbean,* including Jamaica, the Cayman Islands, Key West, and Mexican sites, such as Cozumel and Tulúm, near Cancún. A fun atmosphere and the cultures of Jamaica and Mexico are highlights of these cruises.

- One-week cruises to selected islands of the *southern Caribbean,* such as St.

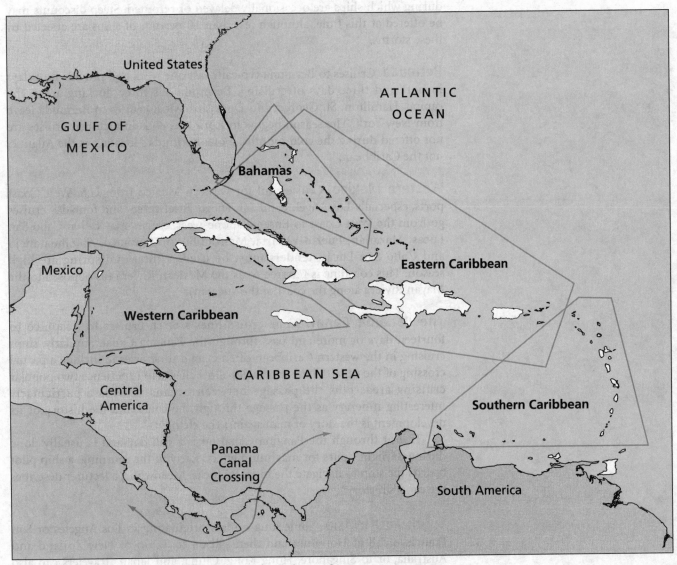

FIGURE 7.3 Cruising the Caribbean and the Bahamas

Cruise lines carve dozens of itineraries out of the four regions of the Caribbean: western Caribbean, eastern Caribbean, southern Caribbean, and Bahamas. (To find the specific islands the text mentions, see a map of Middle America and the Caribbean in an atlas.)

Maarten, Antigua, Martinique, St. Lucia, Barbados, Grenada, Curaçao, and others. Different southern Caribbean itineraries offer varied attractions—from opportunities for shopping and nightlife to islands with an unhurried atmosphere and a hint of the exotic. This itinerary makes an excellent second or third Caribbean cruise.

Cruises to the eastern and western Caribbean and to the Bahamas typically depart from Florida; those to the southern Caribbean, from San Juan, Puerto Rico.

Several cruise lines offer Caribbean itineraries lasting ten to twelve days. Typically, the extra days are used to push farther eastward in the Caribbean or to travel farther south to the Panama Canal or to the coast of South America. Caribbean cruises rarely exceed two weeks.

Peak season for Caribbean cruising runs from mid-December to mid-April. Many ships offer extended gala cruises during the Christmas and New Year period at slightly higher prices. The official low season in the Caribbean is summer and fall. This is the season for tropical storms and hurricanes, during which ships are occasionally delayed or rerouted. Steep discounts may be offered at this time, although less than 10 percent of ships are affected by these storms.

Bermuda. Cruises to Bermuda typically last one week and provide four days in port and three days of cruising. Bermuda has three docking areas: the capital, Hamilton; St. George; and Dockyard. Most cruises to Bermuda leave from New York. The season begins in April and ends in October; cruises are not offered during the cold months. Note: Bermuda's location is the Atlantic, not the Caribbean.

Western Mexico. Cruises sail for western Mexico from U.S. West Coast ports, especially Los Angeles and San Diego. Brief three- and four-day cruises go from the West Coast to Ensenada; one-week cruises may call at Cabo San Lucas, Mazatlán, Puerto Vallarta, Manzanillo, or Acapulco. At Zihuatanejo and Cabo San Lucas, tenders must be used. Winter and spring are high season. This coastline is referred to as the Mexican Riviera (as opposed to the Mayan Riviera along the coast of the Yucatán).

The Panama Canal. Some cruise lines stretch cruises to Acapulco to fourteen days or more and pass through the Panama Canal. Similarly, ships cruising in the western Caribbean often extend itineraries to include a partial crossing of the canal. These itineraries allow clients to experience two popular cruising areas plus the passage between oceans. This is a particularly interesting itinerary as the passage through the canal and the history of its development is the story of man against the elements.

Transit through the Panama Canal takes a full day and is usually done during daylight hours for maximum effect. Early in the morning, a ship pilot boards the ship to navigate the intricate locks. Meanwhile, a lecturer describes the canal's history.

South Pacific/Asia. Some long cruises originating in Los Angeles or San Francisco call at Honolulu and then sail on to Tahiti or New Zealand and Australia, or to Singapore, Hong Kong, China, and Japan. Travelers can also take cruises to China or the South Pacific from ports such as Osaka, Hong Kong, Singapore, or Sydney. Usually cruises in the South Pacific take at least two weeks; often these are segments of a world cruise. Only occasional departures are offered.

Alaska. On cruises to Alaska, passengers can be pampered on the most deluxe of ships, or they can select a no-frills tour that emphasizes learning about the people, history, and geography of the area. *Inside Passage* cruises travel along the coast of Canada's British Columbia to ports of southeastern Alaska. The ship is never out of sight of snowcapped mountainous land. Highlights include the spectacular scenery of Glacier Bay; the once-rowdy frontier town of Skagway; the capital city, Juneau; Sitka, with its Russian history; and the modern Canadian cities of Vancouver and Victoria. The Inside Passage season runs from mid-May to late September.

Canada and the U.S. East Coast. During the summer, ships sail from New York and call at Canadian ports in Nova Scotia, Prince Edward Island, and Quebec, as well as at New England ports, such as Bar Harbor, Boston, and Newport. The crossing between New England and Nova Scotia can be rough. Smaller ships may also call at places along the New England coast, such as Gloucester, Nantucket, Martha's Vineyard, Portland, and New Bedford. In the autumn, several lines add special cruises for viewing the colorful fall foliage. Other cruises visit southern ports, such as Savannah, Charleston, Hilton Head, St. Augustine, and small cities along the Chesapeake Bay.

The Mediterranean. Popular cruise stops for the western Mediterranean include Cannes or Nice on the French Riviera; Barcelona, Spain; the islands of Malta and Sicily; and Naples and Livorno, Italy (see Figure 7.4 on the next page). A one-week cruise might depart from Venice and call at Corfu in the Adriatic Sea, Palermo in Sicily, Valletta in Malta, Costa Smeralda in Sardinia, Portofino in Italy, and Nice in France. Genoa, Italy, is an ideal port of embarkation for a circle cruise of eastern and western Mediterranean ports.

The eastern Mediterranean offers some of the world's finest ports. Cruising lasts from April to October. One arm of the Mediterranean, the Aegean Sea, is "Europe's Caribbean." It offers an abundance of small islands within easy sailing distance of one another. The islands are the sites of legendary civilizations; they also provide beautiful beaches and a relaxed lifestyle. There are regular departures from Piraeus, the port of Athens.

Cruises that touch the coast of Turkey usually spend a day at Istanbul and include a stop to visit the ancient ruins of Ephesus from the ports of Izmir or Kusadasi. Because St. Paul is said to have preached here, many religious groups market these itineraries as "In the Steps of Paul" cruises. Stops at other ports can be brief and are affected by tidal conditions.

Cruises are also available during the summer from Southampton, England, into the Mediterranean or down the coast of Portugal to North Africa and the Canary Islands. These cruises range in length from one to three weeks.

Northern Europe. Popular cruises in northern Europe cover the North Cape or the Baltic. These cruises are generally fourteen days long.

The North Cape of Europe is the geographic and scenic equivalent of Alaska. From a port such as Copenhagen or Hamburg, the cruise heads up the Norwegian coast as far as Tromsø and Hammerfest in Lapland. Here cruisers see Norway's mighty fjords; in late June and early July they enjoy the "midnight sun," which never dips below the horizon. Cruising season runs from June to late August.

Other cruises head into the protected waters of the Baltic Sea and call at major port cities, such as St. Petersburg, Helsinki, and Stockholm. Each Baltic stop offers a multitude of sightseeing and shopping possibilities, in contrast to the simple quiet of North Cape towns.

South America. South America offers a variety of cruise experiences. A trip along the east coast can combine calls on Forteleza, Recife, and Salvador de Bahia with stops at the notorious Devil's Island and at Rio de Janeiro for Carnival. A trip around the tip of South America that includes Tierra del Fuego, Beagle Channel, and Cape Horn attracts naturalists and adventurers alike. An interior exploration of the Amazon as far as Manaus, Brazil, has been popular for several seasons. And occasionally cruise lines have given up their annual winter around-the-world itineraries for interesting itineraries

FIGURE 7.4 Major European Ports and Cruising Areas

This map shows only key destinations mentioned in the text.

around the South American continent with stops in Chile, Peru, and Ecuador. Adventure cruises to Antarctica sail during South America's summer to the white continent of Antarctica, primarily from Ushuaia in southern Argentina.

Nontraditional Cruises

Wherever there is a body of water, somebody is likely to be sailing across it. Experienced cruisers in particular may be interested in some of the many options beyond the traditional cruising areas.

The Grand Tour (The World Cruise). Some upscale ships offer a return to the golden era of the Grand Tour. One cruise from January through April takes passengers through the Atlantic, Indian, and Pacific Oceans, crossing the equator twice and stopping at thirty-eight ports, from Zanzibar and Ushuaia to Acapulco and Hong Kong.

Clients who cannot afford the time or money for a complete world cruise might purchase segments of an itinerary. For example, one ninety-six-day cruise goes from Fort Lauderdale to Los Angeles by way of South America, Africa, and Asia—but clients can book just parts of the cruise, such as a twenty-eight-day segment from Fort Lauderdale to Buenos Aires, or a ninety-day trip from Fort Lauderdale to Honolulu, or even shorter segments. The World Cruise usually is a winter cruise.

Theme Cruises. For years, cruise lines experienced slow periods during late September through November, post-Christmas into January, and again from late April through early May. To attract passengers during these times, cruise lines began offering cruises with special themes—such as preholiday shopping sprees, Improv at Sea Comedy, fall foliage tours, celebrity guest sailings, Murder Mystery at Sea, ethnic festivals, and beauty and fitness programs. Bookings are now sometimes difficult to obtain during these once-slow seasons.

Repositioning Cruises. Cruises in Europe, Alaska, and Bermuda are not offered during cold months. As the cruising season draws to a close in one area, ships can be seen sailing away. For example, in the fall, ships sail from Mediterranean and European ports to the Caribbean and South America. And although cruises operate year-round in the Caribbean and western Mexico, many ships relocate from there during the summer. Rather than sail empty with a skeleton crew, cruise lines market these seasonal migrations as *repositioning cruises.* These trips combine ports of call that are not part of a ship's usual itinerary. The same phenomenon takes place along the U.S. West Coast. In fall, ships relocate from Alaska down the coast through the Panama Canal. In the spring, the ships return from their winter season in the Caribbean, through the canal and back up the coast to Alaskan or Western Canadian waters.

Repositioning cruises offer an ideal opportunity for veteran cruisers to try an unusual itinerary with their favorite ship. The trips frequently feature special themes and entertainment. Often cruise lines also give substantial discounts on repositioning cruises, especially on luxury ships.

Transatlantic Crossings. A number of lines offer crossings between Europe and the United States. Many of these trips are actually repositioning cruises. Travelers can choose a crossing as short as six days, taking a Cunard cruise from New York to Southampton, England, or perhaps as long as twenty-three days, taking a cruise from Fort Lauderdale to Lisbon.

River Cruises. A phenomenon that has developed in recent years is the popularity of river cruising. As megaships have become larger and larger, many cruise passengers have become enamored of the opposite trend—small ships plying the world's great rivers in style. Four particularly popular river cruise companies—AMA Waterways, Avalon Waterways (part of the Globus Family of Brands), Uniworld River Cruises, and Viking River Cruises—have created a new type of cruise experience somewhat akin to a floating tour.

Passengers buy a total package of airfare to and from the ship, cruise accommodations, meals, onboard lectures, light entertainment, and sightseeing/shore excursions. Unlike traditional cruises, the basic shore excursions are not an additional cost. Passengers are close to the shore, and stops are frequent. For those wishing to see a great deal of Europe, these offer an alternative to motorcoach tours.

Most of these cruises began on the rivers of Europe—the Danube and the Rhine, which is famous for the vineyards and castles lining its banks, the Rhone through the heart of Provence, and the Mosel, which connects with the Rhine in western Germany. The completion of the Rhine-Main-Danube canal in 1992 joined the Rhine/Main and the Danube to create a single waterway from the North Sea all the way to the Black Sea, opening European river cruising to a great many new itineraries.

In addition to Europe, river cruise companies have now expanded their offerings to include Egypt (the Nile), China (the Yangtze), Russia (the Volga and inland canals), Vietnam (the Mekong), and others. In addition to river cruise ships, even smaller vessels such as *cabin cruisers* (power boats with living accommodations) sail the Thames in England and slow-moving *barges* (flat bottomed boats) cruise the inland waterways of France.

Special-Interest Cruises. Every cruising area offers a culture that appeals to particular tastes and interests, but some lines go further and design cruises to appeal to people with specific interests. The subjects can be varied: a jazz or big-band dancing cruise or renown guest lecturers speaking on topics ranging from the habits of polar bears to the causes of the 1929 crash. It also could be a cruise to a specific spot in the middle of the ocean to watch an eclipse or to anchor in Rio's Guanabara Bay for Carnaval.

Sometimes such cruises are referred to as **adventure cruises** or even **expeditions** when they are venturing to new areas or are highly specialized in scientific inquiry. They usually appeal to passengers with time, money, and deep intellectual curiosity. The ships are often small, accommodating between 90 and 250 people, and feature world-famous experts and lecturers in a given subject. Companies such as Lindblad Expeditions, partnering with National Geographic, and a British company, Swan Hellenic, are examples of companies providing specialized cruises.

✔ CHECK-UP

Peak seasons for cruising are
- ✔ In the Caribbean, from mid-December to mid-April.
- ✔ Along the Inside Passage of Alaska, from mid-May to late September.
- ✔ In the Mediterranean, from April to October.
- ✔ In Scandinavia, from June to late August.

Nontraditional cruises include
- ✔ Theme cruises.
- ✔ Repositioning cruises.
- ✔ Transatlantic crossings.
- ✔ River cruises.
- ✔ Special-interest and adventure cruises.

Life on a Cruise

For many experienced cruise passengers, the ship is their true destination. Ports of call are a secondary consideration; they take a cruise for the way of life onboard.

Accommodations

Deck plans of a ship show the locations of cabins and public rooms; Figure 7.5 on the next page gives an example. A cabin amidships is the ideal location for passengers prone to seasickness. An outside cabin may have a porthole that looks out over the ocean; inside cabins have no access to natural light. Note, though, that portholes cannot be opened to allow fresh sea breezes into cabins. In fact, on older ships, caps are sometimes secured over the portholes on the lowest decks to make them safe for rough seas.

Cabins, which are sometimes called *staterooms* or simply *rooms,* are smaller than comparable hotel rooms, but cabin size varies from ship to ship. Large cabins have both a sleeping area and a separate living space. Many ships have cabins with large bathrooms and extra-large doorways to accommodate wheelchairs. (For a discussion of the accessibility of cruise ships for those with wheelchairs or other special needs, see page 281 in Chapter 11.) Many cabins, especially on new and upscale ships, have private balconies or verandas.

The typical cabin has two lower twin *berth*s; new ships and some refurbished ones offer double, queen-size, and even king-size beds. In some cabins, beds convert to sofas during the day or recess into the wall. Families or young people traveling as a group may prefer the cabins with upper berths recessed into the walls above twin beds; the berths can be pulled out to provide sleeping accommodations for two additional persons.

Passengers with a typical cabin can expect small closets, a dresser with mirror, a toilet, a washbasin, and a shower. Usually, only expensive cabins have tubs. Luxury ships offer amenities such as hair dryers, minibars, refrigerators, in-room safes, and terry bathrobes depending on the stateroom category or resort refurbishing. Most ships offer radio or limited-channel television in the cabins. Nevertheless, cruise cabins are never as spacious as hotel rooms.

Food Service

Cruise ships are famous for the quantity and quality of their food. The reputation for cuisine varies from ship to ship, but all offer an abundance of opportunities to eat.

A traditional dining room onboard has tables for six or eight, but many ships accommodate requests for private tables for two or four. Usually, passengers receive their table assignments after they board, but some cruise lines preassign tables. Large ships often schedule two sittings in the dining room; passengers indicate their preference for first or second sitting. Early-to-bed and early-to-rise passengers as well as families with young children will probably prefer the first sitting. Those who plan to dance or gamble the night away will probably prefer the second sitting. Ships with only one sitting are considered more gracious as service is less rushed.

Norwegian Cruise Lines (NCL) pioneered changes in how cruisers dine. Its Freestyle Cruising program does away with assigned seats and designated times for dining. Its ships have up to ten restaurants each, and passengers choose where and when to eat. As a result, they may have to wait in line to dine, but many of the restaurants take advance reservations.

Some cruises now have 24-hour restaurants. Most will arrange private parties; deliver continental breakfasts, sandwiches, and cocktails to cabins by request around the clock; and accommodate most special diets (salt-free, fat-free, and so on) if notice is given well in advance.

The variety of food is impressive. On many ships, menus include "lite" fare and heart-healthy choices. Many feature an array of casual eateries, such as pizza and burger joints, small supper clubs, and ethnic restaurants. Some of the larger ships may have as many as 20 different onboard dining options.

FIGURE 7.5 Deck Plans: A Sample

Deck plans are shown for illustrative purposes for *Seabourn* ships.

Other Services

On most cruises passengers can find an array of services:

- *Infirmary.* The ship's doctor provides treatment for routine medical problems and is on call for emergencies. Hours and fees are posted in the daily news. Cabin calls are a costly extra.
- *Duty-free shops.* Open daily while the ship is at sea, shops sell gifts, clothing, souvenirs, tobacco, candy, and necessities.
- *Beauty salon and barber shop.* These facilities are usually open whether the ship is at sea or in port. Facials and manicures are usually available.
- *Laundry.* Laundry and dry cleaning can be left with the cabin steward for a fee; this service normally takes two days. Some ships have free self-service laundries.
- *Religious services.* Some ships offer Jewish, Catholic, and interdenominational services; others offer only interdenominational services. Services for particular religions or sects are offered on holy days such as Easter. Special services may be arranged on some cruises for couples interested in renewing their marriage vows.
- *Communications.* Each ship publishes a daily newspaper that summarizes news, sports, financial information, and shipboard activities. Nowadays major ships have onboard Internet services available with a range of prices. Purchasing or renting a cell phone with international capabilities is also an option. Onboard technologies that use satellite equipment may be subject to temporary outages of any satellite-connected shore-side service. Passengers should check with the particular cruise line in question for full details as to specific communication services each ship has.
- *Library.* Most ships offer a small library that may include DVDs for rent.

On most cruise lines, it is the **hotel manager** who ensures the smooth running of all services. The manager's office is chiefly responsible for passenger accommodations and (like the front desk of a hotel) offers banking services, safety deposit boxes, postal communication, and customs and immigration information. The **purser,** who reports to the hotel manager, handles financial matters and operates the information desk.

Activities and Entertainment

For many passengers, eating, sleeping, and relaxing are the most popular activities on cruises. For anyone who chooses a more active life, most cruise ships offer an amazing array of activities.

Onboard Fun. When the ship is at sea, shops and casinos are open, as is the library, the card room, intimate bars, and lounges featuring soft music. Most ships also have a cinema and discotheque. Passengers can also jog around the deck, try skeetshooting off the stern, or drive golf balls into the ocean. They might play Ping-Pong, bridge, bingo, chess, Scrabble, backgammon, or shuffleboard. Many ships offer a sauna and a gymnasium. There is usually no charge to use exercise equipment or attend aerobics classes. Many upscale cruise lines feature full-service spas with a complete menu of services, such as aromatherapy, hydrotherapy, and herbal wraps for a fee. The spas are usually run by outside companies. For example, the *Queen Mary 2* features Canyon Ranch, with facilities in Tucson, Arizona, Lenox, Massachusetts, and Miami Beach, Florida. A deep-cleaning, 50-minute facial is priced at $149, plus tip. It is suggested that clients book spa/beauty services ahead or immediately upon boarding.

A captain's welcome-onboard cocktail party, gala farewell dinner, and theme night (a masquerade, talent show, and so on) are traditional events on cruise ships. Most ships have a large ballroom or lounge for dancing and for shows featuring professional entertainers. Larger ships offer theaters with revolving stages, retractable domes over swimming pools, eighteen-hole miniature golf courses, and nightclubs fifteen decks above the sea. Entertainment rivals Las Vegas revues. An entire deck may be devoted to the casino or shops.

The cruise director and staff arrange a nonstop flow of activities from dawn to dusk and beyond if the ship is at sea for all or part of the day. While the ship is in port, limited activities are featured for those who do not wish to go ashore. Classes may be offered on topics as varied as dancing, flower arranging, tennis, and photography. Figure 7.6 shows an example of the schedule for a day aboard one ship. Passengers are free to choose as many or as few activities as they please.

Usually, a talk each day familiarizes passengers with the attractions of the next destination. Topics include history, major sights, shopping hints, optional shore excursions, and local customs. Long cruises or those with an emphasis on a certain theme or destination often have experts as guest lecturers.

Excursions. Shore excursions run the gamut from two-hour city tours to extravagant overnight adventures exploring the depths of the Amazon. They are conducted by local tour operators under contract with the cruise line. On some cruises passengers may purchase all shore excursions as a package. The cost of the package is considerably less than the sum of the components purchased separately. However, shore excursions purchased onboard cruise ships vary greatly in quality and value.

Some travel counselors excel at pre-booking private shore excursions or activities for their clients. A number of river cruise companies and adventure cruise companies include most shore excursions in the cruise package. For some excursions individuals can make their own arrangements. But if several cruise ships are in port, they may find that tour operators have booked all available transportation onshore, as well as all tickets to local attractions.

Onboard Expenses

Although the price paid for a cruise covers accommodations, meals, entertainment, and many activities, passengers do incur other expenses. Tipping is one important addition to the cost.

Usually, shipboard tips come to at least $12 a day per person. Ship's officers are never tipped. Bar personnel, wine stewards, and cocktail waiters are tipped the normal 15 percent whenever a tab is paid. Tips to the dining-room steward, the busboy, and the cabin steward are normally given at the last dinner or the evening before leaving the cabin. On long cruises, however, tips are given every week or every two weeks, not just at the end of the cruise. Some cruise lines advertise a no-tipping-required policy, but passengers may want to recognize outstanding service. Most cruise lines provide passengers with tipping guidelines. In fact, many cruise lines, depending on their nationality, automatically put tips on your shipboard bill to simplify matters. Check with individual cruise lines as to their policy.

Other expenses not covered by cruise prices that may be incurred onboard include

- *Personal expenditures.* Passengers pay extra for purchases in shops, certain medical expenses, and casino gambling, as well as for the use of special facilities (such as the beauty salon and spa) or certain sports equipment or activities.

- *Liquor and soft drinks.* On most lines passengers pay for wine at dinner, other alcoholic beverages, specialty drinks, soft drinks, and even bottled water to take onshore.

Refreshing Morning

6:00 A.M. – Noon
The Wake Show!
Wake up with Kelvin & Matt – Channel 21, Crew's Choice

6:00 A.M. – Onwards
Daily Brainteasers & Sudoku
Available in the Library, Deck 5 Midship

6:00 A.M. – 10 A.M. approx.
Scenic Cruising in Tracy Arm (Weather Permitting)
During our time in Tracy Arm, there will be a commentary on deck, Horizon Court & Channel 35 of your stateroom television with Naturalist Julius Talarica

7:00 A.M. – 10:00 A.M.
Up Close & Personal
Watch out for our Photographers on the open deck this morning as we sail through beautiful Tracy Arm

7:00 A.M. – 11:00 A.M.
Tracy Arm Outpost
Binoculars, cold weather gear, books, souvenirs, sundries and much more. Lido, Deck 14 Midship

9:00 A.M. – Arrival
Fine Jewelry Silent Auction – Day 2!
Learn how to bid on our private collection of Fine Jewelry. (and sailing until midnight) Facets, Deck 7 Midship

10:00 A.M.
Body Sculpt Boot Camp
Aerobics Studio, Deck 15 Fwd

10:00 A.M. – Noon
Bridge Play & Lecture with Donald Hennigan
Vivaldi Dining Room, Deck 5 Midship

10:15 A.M.
Free Seminar: "Arthritis & Back Pain Relief"
With Sarah Licensed Acupuncturist. Hearts and Minds, Deck 7 Fwd

10:15 A.M. Zumba Time!
Another chance to Zumba. Wear your workout clothes. Club Fusion, Deck 7 Aft Crew's Choice

10:30 A.M. Ice Carving Demonstration
Neptune's Reef & Pool, Deck 14 Midship

11:00 A.M.
Knitting & Crochet Get-Together
Crooners Bar, Deck 7 Midship

11:00 A.M. $60 Texas Hold'em Tournament
Followed by a $1/$2 No Limit Cash Game. Register with the Casino Cashier from 10:30am. Grand Casino, Deck 6 Fwd

11:00 A.M. Free Seminar: "Non-Surgical Facial Rejuvenation"
With Dr. Jariel. Hearts & Minds, Deck 7 Fwd

11:00 A.M. How to Get Around & What to see in Juneau & Skagway
Last minute VIP cards, coupons, and maps for Juneau and Skagway. Atrium, Deck 5 Midship

11:00 A.M. – 2:00 P.M. Reindeer Chili Cook-Off
Calypso Pool, Deck 14 Midship

11:15 A.M. $1300 Snowball Jackpot Bingo Crew's Choice
Could go in 53 numbers, plus 3 other cash prizes. Cards available until 11:15 A.M. Club Fusion, Deck 7 Aft

11:15 A.M. Morning Trivia with the Cruise Director's Staff
Explorers Lounge, Deck 7 Midship

11:30 A.M. Free Seminar: "Secrets to a Flatter Stomach"
Aerobics Studio, Deck 15 Fwd

FIGURE 7.6 Sample Morning Schedule from the *Sapphire Princess'* Daily Activity Newsletter

This schedule of the activities available illustrates a typical first-day schedule for cruisers.

■ *Shore excursions.* Unless specifically stated to the contrary, shore excursions are an option that passengers may purchase before or during their cruise.

Policies for paying for onboard services and purchases are usually stated clearly in brochures and on the cruise line's Web site. Most ships establish a credit account for passengers as soon as they board the ship; then passengers sign for these services onboard. Passengers who do not have credit cards may be required to deposit cash with the purser at the start of the voyage to cover onboard purchases. Accounts are settled at the purser's office at the end of the cruise. Cash, credit cards, or traveler's checks are usually accepted.

✔ CHECK-UP

Typically, onboard expenses not covered by a cruise fare include
✔ Tips.
✔ Personal expenditures.
✔ Liquor.
✔ Shore excursions.

Usually, passengers must pay extra for certain services, including
✔ Cabin calls from the ship's doctors.
✔ Dry cleaning.
✔ Videos.
✔ Herbal wraps.

Selling Cruises

■ WHAT ARE THE POTENTIAL BENEFITS AND DRAWBACKS OF CRUISING?

■ WHAT IS THE CORRECT BOOKING PROCEDURE?

Statistics point to the potential for future growth in cruise sales. Past CLIA studies have found that 90 percent of first-time cruisers were extremely or very satisfied with their trips and that nearly 51 million Americans intended to take a cruise in the next three years. According to CLIA's study *The Overview: 2011,* the typical cruiser last took a cruise for about 7.2 days and expects to cruise again within the next two years.

These numbers suggest the importance of the cruise market for travel agencies. More than 90 percent of cruises are sold through travel agencies, and cruise sales represent more than 50 percent of many agencies' vacation sales volume. For the agencies, cruises represent a very profitable market. Booking a cruise often requires only one phone call or GDS entry. Furthermore, the price on which the commission is figured for a cruise, unlike a typical land vacation, includes meals and entertainment.

Acquiring Expertise

Although cruises are sold on the Internet, the vast percentage of sales comes through travel agencies that have special cruise departments or counselors (either onsite or often home-based) specializing in cruises. There are even "cruise-only" agencies. Selling cruises requires expertise. Often, the seller must overcome clients' misconceptions, and the sheer number of ships and itineraries can be overwhelming to clients and counselors alike.

Fortunately, opportunities for learning about cruises abound.

- Both CLIA and ASTA (American Society of Travel Agents) offer training programs for selling cruises; they are described in Chapter 16.
- Some cruise lines offer training videos, seminars, courses, and webinars on how to sell their products. A cruise line may reward travel counselors who complete its courses by designating them as certified sales experts and listing them on its Web site.
- Travel counselors can also learn about specific ships by taking part in familiarization trips, ship inspections, trade shows, and "cruise nights" offered by cruise lines.

CLOSE-UP: ON THE JOB WITH HILLARY PENNELL, AGENCY MARKETING MANAGER FOR A CRUISE LINE

Hilary Pennell works as an agency marketing manager—often called a sales representative—for a deluxe cruise line that has five ships. Her territory consists of three states, and much of her job is on the road.

"I started out as an intern at a travel agency while still going to travel school. After graduating I took a job in reservations with a tour wholesaler. A year later I moved into marketing and sales with that company. I was basically the inside sales representative. We sold exclusively through travel agencies, so I dealt mainly with them; at the same time I was learning about advertising and marketing. Since then I have been a sales representative for an airline and now a cruise line. In between I worked briefly for a company that represented an entire group of small suppliers.

"This isn't an entry-level job, but you can move into it fast if you prove yourself. My main job is to help my distributors sell my product. That means getting travel counselors to fill our ships. I feel my main duty is to differentiate my product from the others. I explain to travel counselors—in a way that they can explain to their clients—what makes my cruise line different, what experiences travelers are going to get that they won't get on another cruise line. Of course, I have some tough competitors. In competing with the one or two that are very similar, my job is to establish a relationship with my agents that will be so strong they will tend to sell our ships first.

"One key way I do this is to give ideas to the counselors on how to sell our ships. Of course, what I learn from one agency is strictly confidential. But I can share general ideas on how to promote, advertise, and sell, hoping they take the ball and run with it. I meet with the rest of our sales reps from all over the country, and we share ideas about things people are doing in other places. The idea is to help agents sell. Of course, I give the most help to those who most help themselves.

"I work out of my home and have a territory that I cover.

Counselors can e-mail me at any time. I check my messages constantly, whether I'm at my home office, in an agent's office, in the airport, or (believe it or not) on the beach in Barbados, where our ships visit. The 'inside rep' at the national office can help them with things if they don't need me. I give my local phone number and e-mail to the counselors that I work closely with, so they can get me more directly on occasion.

"I may spend one day a week working in 'the office' (home). The rest of the time is usually spent visiting agencies or meeting with home-based counselors. I try to make more and more of my calls have a specific purpose. I try to make an appointment to see the manager or speak to the counselors in a group, maybe an early-morning staff meeting.

"I start out by telling them anything new that is happening on our side—new ships debuting, new policies—and reviewing past innovations that they might have forgotten. Then I ask them what is new with them. The more they talk, the more I listen—and see if I can glean something that will help. Otherwise, we take a few minutes just to socialize and make that bond stronger.

"A certain number of evenings during the year I spend at trade shows, conducting our own cruise seminars, and attending cruise shows or cruise nights that agencies or their cruise specialists put on and that feature our cruise line in particular. I escort a couple of familiarization cruises a year also. On these, we'll choose some of our top agencies and those that we think have potential and invite them for a cruise. If other functions are going on in the agency community, I'll try to attend those, such as industry association meetings where one can network well.

"Our side of the business is going to have a lot of growth and opportunity. I plan to be a big part of it. I want to show agencies and their associated home-based cruise counselors how they can be a big part of it also."

Even if you take advantage of these educational opportunities, it is next to impossible to know every cruise ship afloat. The names, itineraries, sizes, schedules, and services of ships and cruise lines change constantly. One strategy for dealing with this problem is to choose a preferred supplier for each category of cruise line and learn its ships intimately.

For answering specific questions on departure dates, ports of call, and cruising areas, the *CLIA Cruise Manual* and the *Official Steamship Guide International* are dependable guides. The latter lists more than 70 cruise lines, many of which may not be members of CLIA, such as Hapag Lloyd, Fred Olsen, and others. Travel counselors should also be familiar with the Web sites of the major cruise lines; these offer a wealth of information. But don't expect the Web site to have all of the best price information. The cruise lines phone, e-mail, or fax information on discounts and special promotions to cruise specialists. Usually the Web sites of cruise lines steer the general public to consult a travel agency, but many do take reservations directly.

The Web sites for most cruise lines have a special section reserved for travel counselors; access requires an agency's IATA (International Air Transport Association) or CLIA number. This section often includes

- Information on commissions, discounts, and group bookings.
- Information on how to arrange group transfers or special gifts for clients.
- Information on how to set up cruises for meetings or incentive travel.
- Booking or reservation forms.
- The capability of taking reservations online, directly on the cruise line's booking engine.
- Sign-ups for an e-mail newsgroup.
- Details on who's who in the sales department and how to reach them.

For finding information on the thousands of smaller ships, ferries, and boats that ply the seas of the world, the Internet is almost indispensable. Almost every shipping company has a Web site. However, travelers must recheck schedules when they arrive at a destination, and often tickets must be purchased locally.

Understanding the Benefits and Drawbacks of Cruising

A first step in selling cruises is to identify which travelers are likely to enjoy a cruise. What do cruises have to offer them, and what are the drawbacks of cruising?

The most important benefits of cruises include the following:

- *Relaxation and entertainment.* The sea has a romantic allure. The combination of the constant gentle movement of the ship, the brisk sea air, and the unhurried pace makes a cruise relaxing. Passengers are insulated from anything that reminds them of everyday responsibilities. Everything is within easy walking distance, including good restaurants and evening entertainment. Also, passengers unpack and pack only once. They can be as busy or as lazy as they like. Those who travel alone are never at a loss for opportunities to socialize.
- *Prepayment.* Because most expenses are prepaid, clients can accurately predict the cost of their vacation and avoid carrying large sums of money.
- *Service.* Cruise ships pamper passengers with personal service and gracious touches. The crew anticipates as many of the passengers' needs and desires as possible.

- *Variety of destinations.* On a typical cruise, passengers cannot explore destinations in depth. But they can get a taste of different locales while enjoying the convenience of returning to the same lodging each night. In one CLIA study, 50 percent of cruisers said that they expected to return to a destination they visited during their cruise for another type of vacation. The cruise provided a preview of possible destinations for future vacations.
- *Value.* Although cruises may look expensive at first glance, their cost compares favorably with that of many resorts and other prepaid vacations and package tours. The base price for a land-based vacation is likely to be lower than the price of a comparable cruise, but the base price for the land-based vacation often does not include essentials that are covered by the cruise's price, such as meals and entertainment. Furthermore, cruises can offer intangibles unmatched elsewhere, such as the romance of the sea and the atmosphere on the ship. The result, for many clients, is that cruises give them the best value for their money.

Not everyone is a good candidate for a cruise. Poor candidates include the following:

- Although seasickness can usually be avoided, those who fear storms or the sea should try a different kind of vacation.
- Those who dislike waiting in lines or being in crowds are likely to find a large cruise irritating. People who tend to be claustrophobic should avoid extended cruises and small ships; once at sea, there is nowhere else to go.
- Travelers who are eager to study the world and its peoples in depth may be disappointed by a typical cruise. Passengers may have time to do little more than take a standard sightseeing tour, visit a beach, or check out local markets and stores. A typical cruise allows only fleeting impressions of the destinations visited.

Matching Clients and Cruises

Notice that the short time spent at each destination can be either a benefit or a drawback, depending on a person's viewpoint. Even among people who enjoy cruises, attitudes and preferences vary greatly.

Knowing the client is one key to success in selling a cruise. For example, travelers who fear they might feel claustrophobic on a typical cruise might enjoy a short cruise or a megaship. If one member of a couple is ardently pushing for a cruise while the other is reluctant, a short cruise might represent a workable compromise. Another choice might be a cruise that focuses on a special interest that both people share.

Different clients weight various factors differently. Sometimes, the client's own location is important. Caribbean cruises are most popular among clients from the U.S. northeastern, mid-Atlantic, and midwestern states. Cruises of western Mexico are especially popular with people from the U.S. West and Rocky Mountain states.

To other clients, the ship itself is key. Some passengers develop an affection for a particular ship and return to it year after year. Some eagerly await inaugural cruises so that they can be among the first to sail on a new ship. One client may be looking for elegance onboard; another, for excitement.

The right cruise for an individual client is likely to depend on the itinerary and its length and on the ship itself and its size, style, and service. All of these factors also influence the cost of a cruise, and sometimes their importance depends on their effect on cost. It is said that cruises may be classified into four types: (1) those with limited budgets and limited time;

(2) those with ample budgets but limited time; (3) those with ample time but limited budgets; and (4) those with ample budgets and ample time. There are cruises for each type.

The Price of a Cruise

The prices quoted by cruise lines are for one person sharing a cabin with another. Singles pay a charge called a **single supplement** and occupy a cabin that is built for two. However, some lines allow those traveling solo to avoid paying the single supplement if they are willing to share a cabin with another traveler of the same gender. In that case, they pay the **guaranteed share rate;** if no other single traveler books, they still pay this lower rate. Unfortunately, some cruise lines do not offer those traveling alone an attractive single occupancy rate; it may be as high as paying for two.

If a third or fourth person shares a cabin, it costs the cruise line very little extra; therefore the **third/fourth person rate** is very low. Dividing the total cost among all three or four persons in a cabin can reduce the cost for all. Third and fourth passengers occupy "upper" bunks that retract into the wall during the day.

Cruise prices are often compared by the *per diem* (daily) cost per person. In general, the price of a cruise depends on its length, the season, the ship, the cabin, discounts, and the location on the ship.

Length of Cruise. To some extent, the number of days devoted to a cruise determines its price.

The Season. Shoulder and off-seasons are known as the **value seasons.** Value-season prices can be as much as 20 percent less than regular prices.

CLOSE-UP: SELLING CRUISES BY DEALING WITH OBJECTIONS

Selling a cruise begins with knowing the client and the product and using that knowledge to find a good match between the client and a cruise. No matter how much you learn, though, a client's lack of knowledge may create problems. Because many people are unfamiliar with cruises, they will probably have questions, misconceptions, and objections about any recommendation, however good it may be.

The most frequently heard objections from clients include the following:
- I'll get seasick.
- It's too expensive.
- I don't like dressing up.
- I'll feel stuck.

The facts that address each of these concerns are discussed in the chapter. To present them effectively, try these guidelines.
- Remain positive, not defensive. The objection is not about you personally.
- Listen to the objection carefully, without interrupting.

- Before countering the objection, show that you understand it by paraphrasing it. (For example, "A lot of people worry about that. Getting seasick certainly would spoil things.")
- Then give clear, practical solutions to the problem.

Suppose, for example, that your client is concerned that bad weather could spoil a cruise. In fact, the captain uses radar to avoid storms whenever possible, but cruises are vulnerable to bad weather. When rough seas cannot be avoided, they can cause physical discomfort and make movement around the ship difficult. Even prolonged rain or cloudiness can sharply reduce the passengers' enjoyment of a cruise despite the multitude of indoor activities available.

How, then, could you respond to the client's concern about the weather? You might say that—because of the size of ships, their technology, and indoor activities—weather is no more a factor than it is on any trip, and note that cruisers are more satisfied with their vacations than any other type of traveler.

The Ship. A ship that offers more space and more crew members per passenger generally is more expensive. Luxury cruises may have as many as one crew member for every one and a half or two passengers.

The efficiency of a ship's design also influences price. For example, new ships built specifically for short cruises usually have many small cabins, are fuel-efficient, and require fewer crew members than older ones. As a result, their fares may be lower than those for cruises on other ships.

The Cabin. Size, design, and special features of the cabin influence price. For example, bathtubs and balconies may add to the cost. The location of a cabin is also important.

- Usually the higher the deck is, the more expensive its cabins. Higher decks tend to be closer than lower ones to most public areas; lower decks are closer to the engine room and may be noisier.
- The cost of a cabin is also dictated, to some extent, by its proximity to the bow or stern of the ship. Most people prefer a cabin midship, which is usually more convenient to public areas and may offer a smoother trip, so these cabins cost a bit more.
- Outside cabins are more expensive than inside cabins of comparable size and comfort.

Discounts. Agencies that simply sell cruises for the rates listed in brochures are not likely to be competitive. Discounts come in many guises.

- Most cruise lines offer discounts if passengers book soon after the cruise is open for booking, usually from 6 to 12 months in advance. The price might gradually rise toward the brochure rate during the first few months of booking, or the discount might simply end at a certain date.
- Cruise lines may also offer discounts close to the date of departure when there is excess space.
- Typically, cruise lines offer to help travel counselors promote group tours, and they give discounts for groups with ten to fifteen passengers. They also may offer a free berth to the group leader based on volume.
- Agencies obtain group rates from cruise lines that the agencies can offer to the general public on certain dates; sometimes a broad selection of dates is available to the agency and its affiliated counselors.
- Discount brokers also offer attractive rates. They advertise their toll-free numbers and Web sites in newspapers and magazines.

Additional Costs

Beyond the quoted price of a cruise, passengers must pay for the onboard expenses that we discussed earlier—tips, personal expenditures, liquor, and shore excursions. In addition, two other costs should be considered when evaluating the total cost of a cruise: (1) port charges, fuel surcharges, and fees and (2) transportation to and from the embarkation point.

Port Charges. *Port charges* are fees assessed by the cruise line that cover fees charged by governments or port facilities for the use of a port. Cruise lines may also include as port charges various fees for services such as handling baggage and security on the gangway. A seven-day cruise might bring $120 in port charges.

Not all quoted prices include the port charges. Since 1997 most cruise lines serving the U.S. market have agreed to include these charges in their advertised prices, as part of the settlement of lawsuits. But occasionally, port

ON THE SPOT

Herbert and Eva Robertson, both retired, had long dreamed of taking a cruise. After talking with you, looking at brochures, and talking some more, they had almost decided on a cruise to the Caribbean with a quoted price of $1,299. Then Herb called with new doubts. They had just seen an ad for a trip to the Caribbean for $599, he said, and it looked like a better deal. What would you say to them?

A wise sales counselor gets clients thinking value rather than price as soon as possible. A hamburger at a fast-food chain costs much less than prime rib at a good restaurant, but many people choose the prime rib every day; they are putting a value on the cuisine, atmosphere, and service. In this case, not only may the cruise give much greater value, but the price might even turn out to be less.

Since Herbert and Eva have dreamed of taking a cruise, it probably offers greater value to them than sitting in one place on an island. Discuss the price with them so that they understand the two options. For example, what will three meals a day cost them in the Caribbean? And will they be able to order whatever they want at all these meals? What if they want entertainment on several days and evenings? If you add up cover charges, drink minimums, and taxis or other transportation, the sum is substantial. The total costs of the two trips will probably end up somewhat similar.

To make the sale, remind them of why they wanted to take a cruise, and mention additional benefits. Would they like to unpack only once and yet visit four or five destinations? Would they like to have meals and entertainment just steps away from their door? Would they like to travel with a large group of like-minded fun-lovers? If you have determined their wants and needs correctly, they will find the cruise an excellent value.

"After that ordeal, the first two days will be lost!" complained Tanya Hardstone. "We'll be too frazzled to enjoy them." Tanya and her husband, Jeff, had purchased a Caribbean air/sea package from the West Coast. When their documents arrived, they discovered that they are booked for an all-night flight to Miami in order to arrive on the day of embarkation. Is there anything you can do for them now?

Although cruise lines usually cannot tell you a client's exact air schedule ahead of time, they might have been able to give you an idea of sample schedules had you asked. You would have been able to prepare the clients for the schedule or to suggest alternatives, such as flying in a day early or booking the cruise and the flight separately. You still may be able to get them a flight out a day earlier. (A flight on the day of the cruise is risky.) Contact the cruise line's air department and then the airline. Perhaps a bottle of champagne in their room on arrival would be a nice idea.

charges are omitted from advertised prices. Also, cruises that operate in other parts of the world may not follow this policy. It's always wise to query the cruise line on this matter. It's also a good idea to ask if there have been any fuel surcharges or additional costs since the cruise price was published.

Air/Sea Packages. Passengers also need transportation to and from the embarkation point. Most fly to it. They might arrange and pay for their travel to the port on their own and pay a *cruise-only rate* for the cruise itself. But to provide incentives for people to book cruises, cruise lines offer special *fly/cruise* arrangements. These *air/sea* packages come in three varieties.

- The cruise line organizes an air charter between major cities and the port of embarkation.
- The cruise line gives passengers an air credit. Passengers then choose their own air itinerary, class of service, and route. If their chosen flight costs more than the air credit, they pay the difference. Some passengers may elect to use their own frequent-flyer miles.
- The cruise line negotiates a schedule and rate with the airline and pays for round-trip air service to the embarkation point. Passengers have little or no say in the choice of airline or schedule. Any desired changes should be made through the cruise line's air desk as soon as possible. Sometimes passengers are charged for changes.

When passengers buy an air/sea package, the cruise line is responsible for getting them to the ship. If delays or cancellations prevent them from making a departure, the cruise line will fly them to the next port, issue refunds, or do whatever is necessary. In contrast, when passengers make their own arrangements, they are responsible for getting to the ship on time, and no refund is given for missing the ship.

Transfers to and from the airport and pier are included in air-sea packages purchased from cruise lines. Passengers who buy their own air transportation have the option of buying round-trip transfers from the cruise line—an option that is usually more economical than paying taxi fares.

Making the Reservation

To reserve a cruise, travel counselors should have the following information:
- Names of all travelers (with names exactly as listed on passports).
- All travelers' complete birthdates, proofs of citizenship, passport numbers, and dates of expiration.
- Ship, date, and city of departure.
- Preference for type of cabin. Counselors should help clients choose the general type of cabin that they prefer. But it's best if the client does not select a specific cabin or location because it is very likely that the cabin will not be available. Typically, cruise lines assign cabins within a particular category on a first-come, first-served basis, starting midship and working toward the bow and stern.
- Preference for first or second sitting in the main dining room.
- Preference for a smoking or nonsmoking cabin—unless the entire ship is smoke-free.
- Any special occasions the client is celebrating.
- An indication of whether the client is a repeat cruiser on this ship or line.
- Prebooked shore excursions desired, when available.
- Package choices, if any, for before and after the cruise.

Most travel counselors still book cruises by calling the cruise line's toll-free number, but they can make bookings in other ways. They can book most cruise lines on GDSs. Agencies that sell many cruises usually have a direct link with the cruise lines' computers. As a result, the agency's computer shows almost the identical information available to a reservationist for the cruise line, and the agency can book and confirm cabins and prices instantaneously. Travel counselors can also book reservations on the cruise line's Web site once their agency has registered on the site.

Reservations should be made as early as possible to secure the best rates and cabins. The exception occurs when clients want to gamble on obtaining steep discounts during the last few weeks before departure. But if the cruise line foresees a full ship, there will be no discounts, and clients will be left with the highest prices and least desirable cabins, if any. For group bookings, reservations should be made with the cruise line's *group desk* 8 to 20 months in advance. Cruise lines generally give group space as a **spread**—that is a range of cabins in various price categories. It is rare to obtain a **block** of cabins for a group all at the same price.

When a cruise is reserved, the cruise line cites an **option date,** which is the deadline for payment of a deposit. It also states the date for final payment and the total for each payment, including port charges and air taxes.

Travelers sometimes obtain a **guaranteed rate,** which means that the cruise line promises that they will receive either a cabin in their requested price range or an upgrade at no additional cost. In no instance should travel counselors tell clients that an upgrade is guaranteed.

Serving the Customer

Because cruising is associated with pampering and luxury, many travel counselors perform special services for cruise clients. They may purchase a bon voyage gift such as a bouquet, which the cruise line places in the client's cabin, or a bottle of wine, which the waiter presents at dinner. Special requests to a cruise line should be made by telephone or computer, but a follow-up e-mail to the line helps ensure that the request is met.

For many cruisers, information may be a more important service. Counselors should
- Supply all cruise passengers with information about U.S. customs and immigration regulations (discussed in Chapter 2).
- Be sure clients understand that cruise lines reserve the right to change an itinerary, at the captain's discretion, without refunding passengers. Changes are usually dictated by weather or political events.
- Be sure passengers are aware of the limitations of onboard medical care. Those with medical conditions should consult their physicians. (Many travel agencies have their clients sign a disclaimer indicating that this information has been communicated to them.)

Travel counselors might also recommend that clients ask their doctors for advice about medication for seasickness. Dramamine, Marezine, and Bonine are over-the-counter drugs taken orally before sailing to prevent seasickness. Drowsiness is often a side effect of these drugs. Sea-Band is a band worn on the wrist that prevents motion sickness through pressure; no side effects have been reported. Sea-Band is drug-free and is endorsed by CLIA.

Clients are also likely to welcome information on destinations, independent sightseeing, tipping, shopping, and dressing. They frequently ask for advice about what to wear in the evening; because fashions do change, counselors should consult the individual line at the time of booking. Clients can also be given advice about how to arrange special events, how to avoid lines, which onboard activities they might enjoy, and how to avoid certain tourist traps or dangers at destinations.

Travel counselors can also enhance their clients' cruise by booking shore excursions for them in advance—if the cruise line permits—which increases the chances that clients will be able to take the excursions that match their interests. And the travel agency will earn a commission on the excursions (which does not happen if clients book the excursions through the cruise line after they're aboard). Travel counselors can book these excursions through experienced receptive ground operators who specialize in the destination. (Chapter 8 discusses tour operators.)

Many clients check the Internet before calling or stopping at an agency, and travel counselors should be familiar enough with the offerings there to know what their clients are seeing. Clients who spend a lot of time online may appreciate receiving e-mail with attachments of stories from various sites about their destination. Whether or not you search the Internet for appropriate information for your clients or refer to the sites of a handful of cruise lines with which you work frequently, nothing beats your ability to kindle excitement in clients and to find just the right itinerary and ship to meet their needs. Clients will find that calling you with their questions and comments is better than their staring at a computer screen in the long run and builds the rapport between you and the clients.

Where Is the Cruise Industry Headed? As the cruise industry matures, it is becoming ever more popular and diversified. Though currently dominated by the North American market, globalization is increasing as more international passengers enter the market. Expectations are for continued interest in the return of some transatlantic crossings, expedition and exploratory style itineraries, small-ship offerings on the world's rivers and inland waterways, and megaships with their many onboard offerings. More focus also is foreseen for special markets such as families, singles, upscale retireds, actives, and LGBTs (lesbian, gay, bisexual, and transgender). (See Chapter 11 for a discussion of specialized sales).

CHAPTER WRAP-UP

CHAPTER HIGHLIGHTS

Here is a review of the objectives with which we began the chapter.

1. **Describe the key types of cruise lines and other ships available to vacationers.** Cruise ships are all-inclusive floating resorts that move from port to port. The cruise industry helped expand its market in part by creating different brands of cruise lines that could appeal to people of almost every income, age, or lifestyle. As a result, the lines fall into five main types: resort-style, premium, luxury, specialty/expedition, and value brands. The ships themselves help create the brand. Recently built ships include megaships. Because of their size, megaships can provide amenities, attractions, and activities unthinkable a few years ago.

   In addition to traditional cruise ships, vacationers also travel in smaller river cruise ships, windjammers, schooners, yachts, freighters, ferries, and tenders.

2. **Identify the most popular cruising areas.** The Caribbean/Bahamas is the most popular area. Peak season there runs from mid-December to mid-April. Four other popular areas include the Mediterranean (with cruising from April to October), Europe (from June to late August), Alaska (with Inside Passage cruises from mid-May to late September), and Mexico year-round.

3. **Outline the key attractions of life onboard a cruise.** Cabins vary greatly, but cruises generally are famous for their personal service and for the quantity and quality of their food. Many ships now offer alternatives to the traditional dining room, including restaurants as well as casual eating spots. Most cruise ships also provide a nonstop flow of activities, but passengers are free to choose to do as much or as little as they wish. On most ships passengers can also find an array of useful services—such as an infirmary, duty-free shops, beauty salon and barber shop, laundry, religious services, a daily newspaper, and access to other forms of communication.

4. **Explain benefits and possible disadvantages of the typical cruise.** A cruise offers opportunities for both relaxation and entertainment. Prepayment alleviates financial worries and allows vacationers to predict the cost of the trip. Pampered personal service is found on most ships. The ship itself and the ability to visit many ports of call while unpacking only once are added benefits. Possible disadvantages include the fact that calls at port do not allow enough time to get an in-depth feel for the area or its culture. Also, bad weather can make a cruise miserable, and some people find cruises too confining. Seasickness is another potential problem, although cruise ships have stabilizers to minimize the ships' roll.

   Of course, whether a feature of a cruise is a benefit or a drawback depends on the individual traveler's perception, and travelers evaluate the importance of different features differently. The right cruise for an individual client is likely to depend on the itinerary and its length; on the ship's size, style and service; and on the cost.

5. **Name the factors that determine the cost of a cruise.** The length of the cruise, the timing (for example, during a value season or high season), and the ship itself all influence the price. The number of people per cabin also has an effect. Solo passengers can avoid paying a single supplement by taking the guaranteed share rate offered on some cruise lines; families or groups can save by taking advantage of the third/fourth person rate. Characteristics of the cabin—such as its size, design, feature, and location—also influence the price as do current world events and competition from other cruise lines.

   The quoted price covers accommodations, meals, choices of entertainment at night, a full program of daytime activities, and transport to each port on the itinerary, as well as a ship's newspaper, special events, and other amenities. Some important costs, however, are usually not included in the price; these include port charges, tips, personal expenditures, liquor, and shore excursions. Transportation to and from the embarkation point may also add to the cost. Many travelers, however, save money by obtaining fly/cruise packages from the cruise lines, as well as discounts on the fare.

KEY TERMS

A list of key terms introduced in this chapter follows. If you do not recall the meaning of any terms, see the Glossary, which begins on page 393.

adventure cruise	berth
aft	block
air/sea	bow
bareboat charter	cabin

country of registry
Cruise Lines International Association (CLIA)
cruise ship
deck plan
embarkation point
expedition
ferry
flag of convenience
fly/cruise
fore
freighter
green sheet
gross registered tonnage (GRT)
guaranteed rate
guaranteed share rate
hotel manager
knot
megaship
niche cruises
option date

pitch
port charges
port of call
purser
repositioning cruise
roll
Safety of Life at Sea (SOLAS)
  regulations
schooner
single supplement
space ratio
spread
stabilizer
stern
tender
third/fourth person rate
value season
windjammer
yacht

REVIEW QUESTIONS

1. Which cruises attract older clients? Wealthier ones? Those with families? Why?

2. What costs are not included in the price of a cruise?

3. How does river or canal cruising differ from ocean cruising?

4. Why might one purchase shore excursions in advance?

5. Why might clients prefer an inside cabin?

6. Where would one find information on ships to be launched next year?

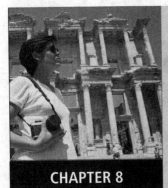

CHAPTER 8

Tours and Packages

OBJECTIVES

After completing this chapter, you should be able to

1. Identify at least five types of tours and packages.

2. Describe the key components of tours and packages.

3. Explain the tour contract and the responsibilities and liabilities of tour operators.

4. Discuss key criteria for selecting a tour operator.

5. Identify benefits that tours offer travelers and travel counselors.

If you are in the market for a home computer, you might select and buy each component separately—monitor, printer, keyboard, drives, and scanner. Or you might avoid a lot of work by buying the entire system as one package.

In much the same way, many travelers turn to tours and packages. Through one retailer, they buy various trip components—transportation, accommodations, meals, sightseeing, and other features. A *tour* offers a package of features for purchase as a single unit and is prepaid by the traveler before departure. The traveler is not given a breakdown of the price of each component and does not pay at each hotel, restaurant, or event.

The traveler might, for example, buy a tour that includes a flight to Miami, Florida, and the use of a rental car for a week—or a tour that includes a flight to London and a motorcoach trip with a guide meandering all over England and Scotland for two weeks with stays at ten hotels. In the typical case, tour operators or tour wholesalers assemble the components of the tour, buying features from suppliers such as airlines, car rental companies, and hotels and then market them as a package. The vast majority are sold to the public by travel agencies and their counselors, although a number are also available online.

The world of tours offers a wealth of opportunities for travelers and travel professionals alike. For travelers, tours offer bargains, convenience, security, and expert guidance. For travel professionals, the tour industry includes a fascinating range of career opportunities; the Close-Up on careers describes a few of them. In this chapter we consider the variety of tours available, how the components are put together, and how they are sold.

A World of Tours

■ WHAT ARE THE MAIN TYPES OF TOURS AND PACKAGES OFFERED TO TODAY'S TRAVELERS?

In the early 1840s an Englishman named Thomas Cook became the first to organize a group of travelers for a tour. For decades he and his son took British travelers all over Europe, Africa, and the Middle East. Even now, any standard tour of a place is called "the Cook's tour."

The process of taking people on tours, however, has become far more sophisticated than in Cook's time. It involves suppliers, such as airlines and hotels, as well as ground operators and destination management companies, which sometimes coordinate the operation of tours at the destination. Key jobs are performed by tour operators, tour wholesalers, and travel agencies, although their roles often overlap.

In fact, the terms *tour wholesaler* and *tour operator* are often used

CLOSE-UP: CAREERS IN TOURS

Careers in tour operations offer some of the best opportunities in the travel industry for fulfilling dreams of traveling to exotic places and doing adventurous things. The amazing variety of tour companies includes companies that specialize in international travel, in escorted travel by groups, in tours for inbound travelers, in adventure and special-interest tours, in travel for specific markets such as museum societies, and more. Companies other than tour operators (such as hotels, tourism bureaus, cruise lines, and motorcoach companies) often have departments devoted to tour operations. Positions in tour operations utilize just about every background and specialty, but the biggest growth is occurring in positions related to quality control, marketing, and e-commerce.

■ **Position** Sales agent/tour consultant/reservationist

Description The person in this position books tours, usually by telephone and most often for travel counselors. Duties include eliciting information in order to make recommendations, suggesting ways to combine the tour with other travel, determining the costs of a tour, and communicating deposit requirements and cancellation policies. Communicating with other departments about bookings and handling complaints from customers are also part of this job.

Qualifications This is sometimes an entry-level position. It requires study at a travel school or two years' experience as a travel agent or experience for one year with a tour wholesaler. It also requires excellent communication skills, a personable manner on the telephone, knowledge of geography, computer literacy, and the ability to follow through on many details.

■ **Position** Quality assurance manager

Description The quality assurance manager is responsible for troubleshooting complaints and problems and then incorporating corrective measures in tour products and procedures. In order to improve customer service and efficiency, the person in this position also works to implement customer evaluation processes, increase awareness of quality concerns within the company, and improve interdepartmental communication.

Qualifications The star performer in reservations or customer service usually assumes this role, but a company may also go outside the industry to hire someone who has completed college and postgraduate programs in quality assurance.

■ **Position** Group sales representative

Description This position specializes in travel by groups and has responsibility for planning, packaging, and selling air and motorcoach tours. Specific duties include helping clients by designing and costing out a suitable itinerary, working with overseas offices and vendors to obtain services, sending written proposals to clients, booking, maintaining communication with clients, assisting in creating promotional materials, working with the operations coordinator on travel documents, preparing profit/loss analyses, and working with the customer service department to resolve complaints.

Qualifications Qualifications include study in travel school or two years in a tour operation or four years in another facet of the travel industry. Excellent communication skills, a pleasant telephone manner, an understanding of geography, and the ability to work as part of a team are also needed.

(continued on next page)

interchangeably, but strictly speaking, we can distinguish between them. Typically, a **tour wholesaler** assembles the components of the tour into a package and pays a commission or offers a net rate to the tour seller; the wholesaler leaves tour operations to others. In contrast, **tour operators** not only assemble the package but may also operate aspects of the tour, own facilities or vehicles used on the tour, and employ personnel such as escorts and drivers. Tour operators may also sell directly to the public, and some own travel agencies. For simplicity, we use the term *tour operator* to refer to either wholesalers or operators.

The lines between tour operators and travel agencies are also blurred. Much as tour operators sometimes act like travel agencies by selling to the public, some travel agencies operate and sell their own tours.

Each year, thousands and thousands of tours and packages are sold. The reasons for this popularity are many because tours themselves come in many shapes and sizes to satisfy the varied needs of travelers.

Types of Tours

There are tours that will take you to Antarctica or the wilds of the Amazon for weeks with expert guides—and other tours that offer only a rental car and vouchers for a weekend at a hotel in Las Vegas. Because they are so varied, tours can be classified in many ways. One significant distinction is whether

---

CLOSE-UP: CAREERS IN TOURS (cont.)

■ **Position** Product development manager

Description This manager creates tour packages. Duties include conducting research on destinations and site inspections, planning logistics, creating the itinerary, negotiating for space and rates with suppliers, costing, keeping track of sales and clients' comments, and analyzing competitors' programs. The job may also entail participation in producing brochures, marketing, and training sales agents.

Qualifications Tour companies look for three or more years' experience with a tour operator and knowledge of the destination as well as personal contacts with hotels, attractions, and ground handlers. The position also requires creativity, the ability to follow through on details, and sensitivity to travelers' preferences. Analytical skills are an asset.

■ **Position** Tour manager/tour escort/tour director

Description This person leads a tour group and is responsible for the well-being of the guests, handling any emergencies, and providing information. Typically, the tour manager conducts a particular series of tours within a specific area for months at a time. This is often a contract position.

Qualifications This position requires specialized knowledge about a destination and its people—the history, economy, politics, geology, geography, flora, and fauna. It

requires leadership skills, common sense and resourcefulness, the ability to remain calm in an emergency, good communication and organizational skills, attention to detail, the stamina to make it through long days, and enthusiasm for doing the same tour over and over for months. Tour companies look for experience in travel-related customer service, such as customer contact in the hospitality industry. They may also expect a specific educational background and language skills.

■ **Position** Director of tour escorts

Description This position is responsible for supervising the staff of tour guides—hiring, training, scheduling, briefing, and managing them in the field (which can be far-flung points throughout the world). Other duties include preparing reservations and instructions for each tour departure, writing tour manuals and routings for tours, and being on call 24 hours a day to deal with emergencies.

Qualifications This position is usually held by a person with managerial ability who has spent years in the field as a tour manager.

Other positions Business analyst; client services specialist; costing coordinator; district sales manager; manager of database marketing, planning, and analysis; product coordinator; step-on guide; tour guide; webmaster.

---

tours are marketed to the general public or to specific groups. Tours marketed to groups include:

- Tours arranged for **affinity groups,** people who share a particular interest, age, or background and belong to a club, team, or other organization.
- *Convention tours,* designed for members of associations or corporations who are attending a convention, trade show, or similar gathering.
- *Incentive tours,* offered as a prize or reward to employees of a company, usually for productivity or sales performance.

Tours can also be divided into *custom-designed tours* and *prepackaged tours.*

Custom-Designed Tours

Until the 1960s many travelers had their arrangements custom-made to fit their individual requirements. Transportation, hotels, and other features of a trip were selected and bought in advance for the traveler, just to fit that person's needs. Today, a custom-designed tour is often called an **FIT.** The initials originally stood for "foreign independent tour"; nowadays, the term is used whether the tour is international or domestic. It is usually applied only to trips taken for pleasure, even though arranging a complicated business trip is often like arranging an FIT.

The market for FITs has been rather small. Because FITs are individualized, their packagers cannot obtain volume discounts from suppliers. As a result, FITs are more expensive than prepackaged tours. Generally, FIT wholesalers require that an FIT consist of at least 3 destinations and accommodations for at least 6 nights plus transfers and sightseeing at each destination.

FITs are usually more expensive than ready-made tours because they are custom-designed to the traveler's dates, needs, interest, and specifications. This would be analogous to having a suit custom-designed and tailored for you versus buying one "off the rack" at a department store. Designing FITs is time and labor intensive and requires an experienced employee to successfully operate such personalized trips.

As booking engines become increasingly powerful and sophisticated, the limitations on custom-designed tours seem to be easing. Some booking engines allow *dynamic packaging,* which is the ability to quickly put together a travel package involving multiple components (such as air, car rental, and hotel) from a variety of sources and offer it at a single price. A dynamic packaging tool gives you a direct connection to suppliers, providing access to the real-time availability and prices of the travel products. It allows you to obtain the components at net prices, add an appropriate markup, and offer the package at a single price, hiding the price of components (*opaque pricing*).

Although the market for custom-designed tours may be growing, when we refer to "tours" in the following pages, we are talking about prepackaged tours. Depending on their structure, prepackaged tours can be classified as independent, hosted, or escorted, as the following sections explain.

The Independent Tour

For some people, the word *tour* evokes images of ruthless early-morning awakenings, regimented sightseeing, and unceasing hustle and bustle. An **independent tour,** however, has no group and no tour leader, and independent tours are very often called **packages** or *vacation packages.* They usually offer the traveler very good value because the operator gets excellent bulk rates from suppliers. If the traveler is willing to fit his/her plans into the operator's offer, such as choice of hotels or airline, the total trip package price is usually considerably less than trying to do it on one's own.

Participants travel independently; they may depart and return any day and can adjust the tour length to suit themselves. They may not even realize that they are on a tour. But it is a tour because participants buy some arrangements in advance as a package: they receive vouchers for the arrangements from the travel agency and give the vouchers to suppliers such as hotels.

These independent packages may include many components of a trip or only a few. Many provide only transportation to a destination, round-trip transfers from the airport to hotel, and accommodations at one hotel for the number of nights the participant chooses. This kind of package is popular in resort areas where vacationers want only to relax and in cities that have public transportation and popular sightseeing tours.

Other packages include car rentals or stays at multiple hotels or both. The advertised car is usually compact or economy size, but participants may pay to upgrade it. When hotels are part of the package, participants often choose from a list of hotels with varying prices. They may arrive any day of the year (although they may pay surcharges during especially popular periods), and they may extend their trip by paying a fixed rate for each night beyond the number specified for the tour. They set their own pace and arrange each day to suit themselves.

A *fly/drive* package includes air transportation, a car rental, and a number of hotels. Often participants can stay at any of a specific chain's properties. Fly/drives are suited for travelers who wish to tour a particular region, stopping at a different place every night or two and enjoy the freedom of driving themselves.

The Hosted Tour

On a *hosted tour* individuals travel independently, but a host is available at each destination to help them arrange activities. The *host* is a representative of the tour or ground operator. Typically, hosted tours include basic sightseeing or entertainment and offer optional arrangements for purchase.

Often, participants in a hosted tour may arrive on the day of their choice, choose from a range of hotels, and adjust the length of their stay. Some hosted tours include more than one destination. In each city, participants normally receive round-trip transfers from airport to hotel, one sightseeing tour to orient themselves, and the services of a host.

Other hosted tours offer less flexibility. On some, participants take a chartered flight and must stick to the dates selected for the flight. But even though they arrive together, the participants spend the tour as independent travelers, not as a group.

What does the host do? On most hosted tours, the host greets the participants when they arrive, gives them a brief orientation, and lets them know when he or she is available for further assistance. Usually the host does not accompany travelers on any sightseeing tours. The typical host can be found at the desk in the lobby of each hotel on the tour. When the host is not at the hotel, tour members can receive help by calling the tour operator's local representative.

The Escorted Tour

On an *escorted tour* participants travel together as a group and are always accompanied by a professional *tour escort,* who is responsible for ensuring that the tour goes smoothly. Participants enjoy a structured program of sightseeing, meals, transportation, and accommodations. Details and difficulties are taken out of their hands.

Movement characterizes escorted tours. Unlike independent and hosted tours, escorted tours usually move from one place to another every one to three days—usually by motorcoach. Participants do not select specific hotels; instead, they choose a grade of tour—such as budget, economy, classic, or deluxe (see Figure 8.1). During the tour they stay as a group at hotels of the grade selected.

Tour escorts (also called *tour managers, tour leaders,* or *tour directors*) are usually gold mines of information, but the term **tour guide** is often reserved for local specialists on particular topics. Guides (sometimes called **step-on guides**) often join escorted tours briefly to conduct sightseeing of a city, museum, or art gallery. In fact, many cities require that locally licensed guides lead all sightseeing tours.

People who do not want to compromise may not enjoy escorted tours. If the motorcoach is leaving, tour members must be ready to leave—even if they would rather sleep or shop an extra hour. A well-run tour tries to meet each individual's needs, but by its nature an escorted tour limits the traveler's options. Traditionally, from the moment an escorted tour departs, participants travel together.

Recently, many tour companies have made their tours more flexible in order to suit independent-minded travelers. Some offer *modules:* instead of a full two-week escorted tour of Australia, for example, the traveler might be able to choose certain segments, such as three days in Sydney, three days in Melbourne, and four days on the Barrier Reef.

CLOSE-UP: ON THE JOB WITH SANDY JOHANSEN, TOUR ESCORT

Sandy Johansen, a teacher, applied in February for a position as a tour escort during the summer. The tour company could not guarantee how much work it could offer her, but it scheduled Sandy for two training sessions in April and a couple of one-day training tours on Saturdays in May. Sandy did well on the training tours.

"I just loved it. Of course, what really helped was working with an experienced tour manager who let me ease into things. I greeted people, learned their names, introduced them to each other when I could, and found out a little about them if there was time. Trying to learn their names was hard for me. I wish they had had name tags, but Happy Seniors Tours didn't use them, at least on this tour.

"I checked off their names on the manifest and kept track of who had not arrived yet. At the same time, I tried to overhear what Jan, the regular escort, was telling our motorcoach driver. I was probably the most nervous when I was getting on the microphone to introduce myself. It was one thing to talk to travelers individually and another to see all thirty-three of them seated and looking in my direction. But Jan made it easier, and once I heard my voice going out there—well, I knew I'd be able to do this. It might just take a little getting used to.

"I studied the itinerary, which was an all-day wine châteaux tour in California. Jan mentioned in earlier training that I wouldn't be expected to know it all—a guide at each of the three vineyards would be the expert, and I could learn along with everyone. Whatever I did know was a bonus.

"Jan gave me a few prepared things that I could point out on the way to the first winery. Our coach also had television monitors at various intervals, and we played a tape about winemaking to get everybody in the mood; I made the announcement before the tape. Jan had a few good jokes related to what happened on the last tour to someone who got a little carried away with the winetasting. The clincher was that we might be picking that person up this time because he never made it back to the bus. I think the real moral of the story was, 'If you're not back, we're leaving!'

"In any case, it worked out well. Teaching will be a breeze when I go back in September—if I go back. I guess I will because the number of tours slows down dramatically in the late fall. But in a few years, who knows?"

In other ways, too, tour operators are blending the categories of tours as they compete for travelers. Some independent tours, for example, now include escorts or hosts for city tours as optional elements.

Special-Interest Tours

Competition for travelers is the basis for another trend in tours: the development of *special-interest tours,* which are tours designed to appeal to people with an interest in a particular topic or activity—such as photography or skiing, scuba diving or Russian, baseball or Buddhism. One family might choose a Working Cattle Drive tour, during which they learn to ride horses, get to sleep in a lodge, and gather around the campfire at night. Another might tour southern China to attend InspirAsians Cooking School, where they can learn culinary secrets from local chefs and taste local delicacies.

Special-interest tours provide exceptional opportunities for both traveler and travel professional. What is it worth to take cooking lessons from a famous French chef or to travel with twenty other people who share your love of butterfly collecting? On a special-interest tour, the expertise required of the tour operator and the tour leader will be more in depth and focused.

FIGURE 8.1 An Escorted Tour

Tours are available to appeal to almost any location and interest.

Source: Reprinted by permission of Collette Vacations.

One type of special-interest tour is the **adventure tour,** which focuses on outdoor physical activity—horse or camel riding, biking, backpacking, canoeing, or sailing. Adventure tours are often classified as hard or soft. **Hard adventures** feature strenuous activity (for example, kayaking or mountaineering), remote locations, or risk. **Soft adventures** involve physical activities that offer little physical challenge or danger, such as walking from inn to inn or river rafting on a mild river. Tours that appeal to an interest in the environment—*ecotours*—are also popular. An ecotour may consist of trips to view natural wonders, such as unusual birds or waterways, or trips in which participants work to repair environmental damage. The International Ecotourism Society (TIES) defines *ecotourism* as "responsible travel to natural areas that conserves the environment and improves the well-being of local people." Many ecotours are also classified as adventure tours.

Other special-interest tours include

- Ski, dive, golf, or tennis tours, which center on hotels that feature all the equipment, staff, and services needed for the particular sport. They also offer special courses or well-known instructors.
- Cultural tours, which may focus on art, architecture, history, anthropology, or similar subjects.
- Tours to special events, such as the Olympics, music and theater festivals, Mardi Gras, Oberammergau—the list grows every year.
- Religious tours, which visit shrines and are often led by a member of the clergy.

Gourmet, winetasting, horticultural, gambling, shopping, and photography tours are among the many other types of special-interest tours offered. Many of these special-interest tours are led by key figures with a following and are referred to as "**Pied Pipers.**"

✔ CHECK-UP

Putting together a tour may involve work by a host of travel professionals, including
- ✔ Suppliers.
- ✔ Tour wholesalers and tour operators.
- ✔ Travel agencies.
- ✔ Ground operators and destination management companies.

Two basic types of tours are
- ✔ Custom-designed tours.
- ✔ Prepackaged tours, which may be independent, hosted, or escorted.

Popular types of special-interest tours include
- ✔ Adventure tours, with hard adventure or soft adventure.
- ✔ Ecotours.

Creating and Evaluating Tours

- ■ WHAT ARE THE MOST IMPORTANT VARIATIONS IN THE COMPONENTS OF TOURS?

- ■ WHAT ISSUES ARE COVERED BY THE TOUR CONTRACT, AND WHAT ARE THE RESPONSIBILITIES AND LIABILITIES OF THE TOUR OPERATOR?

Successful tours require the combined skills and resources of many people. What do they consider in choosing the components of the tour, and how are the pieces put together?

Components of a Tour

If you were developing a tour, what would you include? Obviously, the answer depends on the intended market. Some tours offer a minimum of elements; others are all-inclusive. Table 8.1 outlines many of the variations to be considered.

Transportation. Most tours include transportation as part of the package. We discussed a *fly/drive,* which combines air transportation and a car rental. An *air/sea* or *fly/cruise* combines air and ship transportation; a *rail tour* includes transportation by train; a *motorcoach tour* uses buses to carry tour participants from destination to destination to visit major attractions. Many tours also include transfers to and from airports, hotels, and rail stations.

Itineraries. Years ago, most tours packed in as wide an area with as many stops as possible. Today's tours are more likely to aim for an in-depth exploration of a smaller area.

For escorted tours, going from site to site within countries is a large part of the trip's enjoyment, but the hallmark of a good tour is a relaxed pace. A trip that changes hotels every night takes a lot of energy. Long stays at key destinations distinguish deluxe tours. As a rule, tour operators avoid more than 10 hours of travel or 350 miles in a day, and they average substantially fewer miles per day.

For any intercontinental trip, consider time zones and jet lag when judging an itinerary. The day of departure, the day of arrival, and the departure day on the return often amount to "lost days" for clients. An

TABLE 8.1 Components of Tours

Component	Special Features
Transportation	Air travel: type and class
	Departure point
	Airline
	Ground transportation: type and class
	Transfers
Itinerary	Number of stops
	Time spent at each stop
	Amount of time traveling
	Amount of leisure time
Accommodations	Class of lodging
	Location of lodging
	Choice of room types
	Location of rooms
Meals	Number of meals
	At restaurant or hotel
	Choice of meals and meal plans
Other	Sightseeing: included or optional
	Special events: number and kind
	Side trips
	Luggage handling
	Luggage allowance
	Tips: Included or optional
	Leadership

"eight-day, seven-night" tour to Europe, for example, might consist of only five days of touring.

Tours tend to use one of three types of itineraries:

- A *circle itinerary*, which brings travelers back to their starting point via a different route. Passengers experience varied sights and places throughout, without retracing their steps. This approach suits tours that aim to cover a broad area, such as "Highlights of Central Europe."

- An *open-jaw itinerary*, which begins and ends in different places. For example, a "Highlights of Italy" tour might visit Milan, Venice, Florence, Pisa, and Rome—without returning to Milan. This type of itinerary works well when returning to the starting point means retracing steps or visiting less desirable locations.

- A *hub-and-spoke itinerary*, which is an increasingly popular approach. Travelers set up their base at a hotel in one city for several days and take day trips into the surrounding area, thus avoiding packing, unpacking, and moving baggage. They might also spend one night away from the home base. The hub-and-spoke approach allows travelers to explore a region in depth. For example, on a "Highlights of France" tour, travelers might be based in Paris and take day trips to the numerous sights within striking distance of the City of Light, such as Versailles or Giverny.

Accommodations. Proximity to sightseeing attractions, transfer services, parking for the motorcoach, and accessibility for people with disabilities may all be important in selecting hotels for a tour. Hosted and independent packages usually offer participants a choice among several hotels in different price ranges. On escorted tours, participants stay together at a hotel. Thus hotels selected for escorted tours must be able to register groups efficiently, serve group meals, and (because all tour participants pay the same price) provide similar rooms for everyone in the group.

Meals. Tour operators can cut their costs substantially by requiring tour participants to pay for their own meals or by adjusting the kind of meals offered. A tour operator that includes five dinners and five lunches is offering more than an operator that includes ten breakfasts. A tour operator that permits an unlimited choice from the menu (à la carte) is offering more than an operator that arranges a set menu or limited choice. (Look again at Table 6.4, page 161, for a description of various meal plans.)

Escorted tours typically start after breakfast on the first day and conclude before dinner on the last. When meals are included in the tour but not provided at the hotel, participants are usually served at well-known restaurants. Often the restaurant provides special tour menus (table d'hôte) or limits choices to four or five entrées. Deluxe tours offer à la carte dining.

Sightseeing. Tours usually include some attractions that are standard tourist draws, such as Walt Disney World, Busch Gardens, and Cypress Gardens in Florida. On an independent or a hosted tour, travelers generally receive sightseeing vouchers and admission tickets ahead of time or pick them up at the first stop on their trip.

On an escorted tour, attractions might be added during the tour, depending on the interests of the group. Most attractions are prepaid, and the tour escort will have tickets or vouchers for members of the tour. Sometimes these must be obtained at the attraction itself, in which case the tour escort precedes the group and pays the admission fee.

Tour operators can significantly lower the cost of a tour by reducing the number of attractions included. An escorted itinerary that includes phrases such as "Balance of the day at leisure" or "Today you are free to explore" may reflect such cost cutting. But the result may actually suit many travelers. They may like the idea of having free time and independence and prefer not paying for a constant schedule of activity. If they wish, they can purchase optional sightseeing tours on the spot.

Tour operators can also lower costs by selecting lesser-known attractions. Again, travelers may prefer this cost-cutting option. Going to lesser-known areas rather than traditional tourist hotspots may provide a better chance to experience the local culture and obtain an in-depth look at a destination. Increasingly, vacation packages and tours incorporate nontraditional sightseeing, such as visits to local farms and walking tours.

Other Components. The fare for some tours includes services such as baggage handling or covers tips, service charges, or taxes. Some tours also offer items such as flight bags, free drinks, or other "gifts"—elements that might be of little value to many travelers.

Price. Whatever the components of a tour, travelers are likely to weigh them against its price. A small percentage of tours are quoted per couple (the most obvious are honeymoon packages). But the vast majority of prices are given *per person, double occupancy,* which means that each person pays this price when sharing a room with another. Single occupancy prices are higher, sometimes much higher; the additional price paid by a person traveling alone is called the **single supplement**. A few tours try to find a roommate for a traveler who does not wish to pay the single rate. When the tour operator will not guarantee a roommate, the traveler may have to pay the single supplement, often referred to as a **forced single**.

Developing and Operating Tours

Planning and Negotiating. Whatever a tour's components, its creation begins with planning, as Figure 8.2 indicates. Ideas for a tour come from many sources, including customers, but having exciting ideas does not ensure success. Market research should be a key component of the planning stage. It can help both to generate ideas for tours and to test the viability of ideas. Identifying the needs of the target market and evaluating what a destination has to offer to meet these needs are crucial tasks.

In recent years market research has often encouraged specialization. Tour operators and agencies may specialize by concentrating on tours for certain demographic segments—seniors or the youth market, for instance—or on certain destinations—such as the South Pacific or Costa Rica—or on special interests. Specialization can be the key to success, or even survival.

Negotiations with suppliers are the second step in creating a tour. Hotels and other suppliers typically reduce their prices for tour operators when the operators have generated a predetermined volume of business; tour operators make their money by selling the same tour to many clients. Once prices have been negotiated, an itinerary is created.

Setting the Price. Next comes the process of establishing a selling price for the tour. To set the price, some tour operators first calculate how much each participant in the tour will cost them. To this cost the tour operator adds a markup sufficient to cover all promotional costs, staff salaries, commissions it

FIGURE 8.2

Developing a Tour

The process of creating a tour involves the chain of linked steps outlined here. Any break in the chain can make the tour a failure.

Step 1: Planning
The idea for creating a tour might come from market research, a customer, inspiration, or just about anywhere. The planning process might involve steps such as site inspections and market research. It's wise to allow a lead time of one year.

Step 2: Negotiations
Secure the services of suppliers. Negotiate prices and create an itinerary.

Step 3: Costing
Determine the cost of each component of the tour. Add in all the costs of promotion, sales, and overhead to determine net cost. Mark up the net cost to establish the price.

Step 4: Promotion
Produce a brochure and Web page. Promote the tour through advertisements, direct mail, group presentations, or a Pied Piper.

must pay to travel agencies selling the tour, and other overhead. Finally, the operator adds a markup to allow a profit, setting the price for the tour.

Determining the cost of a tour, however, is an art, and it often requires a great many assumptions and estimates. A motorcoach, for example, costs a tour operator a flat fee no matter how many people take the tour, but its cost per participant depends on how many tours are sold. Tour operators can economize on their costs by adjustments in four main areas: meal costs, hotel quality and location, length of stay in principal cities, and sightseeing.

Promoting the Tour. Promotion is the fourth step in developing a tour. Tour operators produce brochures, catalogues, and Web pages describing the features, terms, and conditions of their tours. These are important sales tools.

Usually the front of a brochure describes the tour operator's credentials and experience along with key characteristics of tours and explanations of terms used in the brochure. The main section of the brochure lists each tour and describes its itinerary, highlights, and costs. (Some operators put the costs at the end or in a special insert.) At the back are the "terms and conditions" of the contract between the tour operator and the traveler.

Web sites for tours generally present the same information as brochures. They must be well designed so that they are easy for people to understand and to navigate when they are looking for specific information. The Web sites of many tour operators allow you to print or e-mail an electronic version of their brochures. Sometimes the operator has created these e-brochures by adding information to a *template*.

Once brochures and Web pages are produced, the tour operator promotes the tour through selected advertising media. The promotional campaign might include some combination of commercials on radio or television, advertisements in newspapers or magazines, ads and links on other Web sites, mailings and flyers, and presence in the social media—all depending on the clientele one is trying to reach.

After the Sale. The job of tour operators does not stop with the sale. They are also responsible for:
- *Documentation.* Incoming reservations must be processed; invoices for passengers' final payments must be issued; tickets, vouchers, baggage tags, and so on must be sent to all confirmed participants.
- *Operation.* The components of the tour must be coordinated by a tour manager, escort, host, or ground representative.
- *Relations with suppliers.* All suppliers must be given correct and final information, such as the names and special needs of participants, their passport data, and rooming arrangements. Payment schedules must be established and followed.

The Tour Contract

In the back of their brochures, operators must disclose the provisions of the contract with travelers. The details of this contract are extremely important to both the traveler and the seller. The following are five key issues.

Items Not Included. How many meals are included on the tour? (Clients need to budget for those not included.) What sightseeing is included? What is "optional" or "suggested"? (Clients need to budget for independent sightseeing or for extra, optional tours.) What tips, if any, are included?

Unless a brochure clearly states that a feature is included, assume that it is not. Many tour operators state explicitly what is not included.

Deposit and Payment Schedule. For prepackaged tours, the payment schedule is usually as follows:

- All tour operators require a deposit to hold a reservation more than a few days. The deposit must be received by the tour operator within a specified time (often 7 to 15 days) after the reservation is made or it will be canceled.
- The balance, or final payment, is due no later than 30 to 60 days before departure, or as specified in the brochure.

After the deadline for final payment has passed, tour operators usually still accept reservations, with full payment due immediately if space is still available.

The procedure is different for FITs. Usually the FIT wholesaler/operator requires a nonrefundable deposit before beginning work and then sends a suggested itinerary and a cost quotation to the travel counselor. Once the client accepts the itinerary and the price, the FIT operator secures confirmations of all arrangements and the deposit submitted earlier is credited against the tour purchase.

Cancellation and Refund Policy. Tour operators reserve the right to cancel a tour before departure. The cause may be political events, social conditions, or weather. Escorted tour operators also cancel tours when there is an insufficient number of participants for a particular date; their cost for hotel accommodations, sightseeing, and the motorcoach is based on a minimum number traveling together.

If clients cancel before departure, they are usually liable for a *cancellation penalty,* particularly if the cancellation is made close to departure. To cover this penalty, travelers can obtain *cancellation insurance* through the tour operator or through an insurance agency; this insurance is discussed in Chapter 11.

If part of the tour is canceled, clients are typically entitled to a refund for the value of the portion missed. Most tour operators reserve the right to substitute tour elements with or without notice. If the substitution lowers the quality of an element, the client receives a refund for the difference between the costs of the original and the substituted element, either on the spot or after returning home or the operator may provide a substitute.

Once the tour is under way, most tour operators reserve the right to expel tour participants for due cause—without compensation.

Limitations on the Operator's Responsibility and Liability. Tour operators point out that they cannot be held responsible for the actions of airlines, hotels, bus companies, or any other supplier or its employees. They also disclaim responsibility for any loss, damage, or delay caused by events outside their control or by tour participants.

Status of Fares and Rates. The tour brochure describes whether costs differ according to seasons or departure dates. Most tour operators set their rates for an entire year.

Some tour operators quote prices for the tour plus airfare from large cities. Almost all operators also have **land rates,** which are rates that exclude transportation costs between the traveler's home and the start or end of the tour. Land rates apply for the effective dates covered by the brochure and typically do not change if the tours are within the United States and are quoted in U.S. dollars.

ON THE SPOT

Mr. and Mrs. Sargent have just returned from a cherry blossom tour of Washington, D.C. They walk into the travel agency with itinerary and sales brochure firmly in hand. With barely a word of greeting, they explain their mission. "Look at this! In black and white, clear as day, the brochure promised that we'd 'see such historical monuments as the Washington, Lincoln, and Jefferson memorials.' But we rode right by them on the bus! The driver wouldn't let us off to see them! We want a refund. At least a partial one! This is outrageous." If you were the travel counselor, what would you say?

First, you should be sure to hear the Sargents out completely without interrupting and to show that you understand their complaint and sympathize with their point of view. Do not argue. But do remind them that you had gone over the itinerary and brochure with them before the trip and that neither mentions stopping at or visiting the monuments. A lot depends on your agency's policies for dealing with dissatisfied clients. But generally speaking, no refund would be made under these circumstances.

That is why it's important that clients understand before purchasing the tour the difference between seeing or viewing a place (as from the outside in passing) versus visiting a place (as going inside with the admission fee paid by the tour operator).

For tours outside the United States, the land rates are also usually quoted in U.S. dollars, and most tour operators reserve the right to adjust prices if currency fluctuations affect them. Once final payment has been received, most do not impose any surcharge to cover currency changes. However, airlines may incur fuel surcharges up to the time air tickets are issued.

✔ CHECK-UP

If a tour operator wants to economize, key possible targets are
- ✔ Meal costs.
- ✔ Hotel quality.
- ✔ Length of stay in principal cities.
- ✔ Number of sightseeing attractions.

Essential information in a tour brochure includes
- ✔ What is included in the tour and covered by the price and what is not included.
- ✔ The deposit and payment schedule.
- ✔ The operator's cancellation and refund policy.
- ✔ Limitations on the operator's responsibility and liability.
- ✔ The status of the fares and rates published in the brochure.

Selling Tours

- ■ HOW WOULD YOU CHOOSE A TOUR OPERATOR?
- ■ WHAT BENEFITS DO TOURS OFFER TRAVELERS AND TRAVEL AGENCIES?

Each tour is a unique product, and brand-name tour companies are few. The public often needs help in making decisions concerning which tours and operators are best. Thus it is not surprising that only a small percentage of travelers book tours online. There are so many tours to choose from and so much is riding on those choices that the travel counselor is likely to remain important in selling tours for years to come. The travel counselor's task is to choose among tour operators and tours in order to satisfy the client's needs.

Choosing Tour Operators

There are more than 2,000 tour operators in the United States. There are tour companies specializing in international travel, domestic escorted travel, inbound travel, and adventure travel as well as travel for specific markets such as the families, teens, students, or museum societies.

Out of all of these possibilities and more, travel counselors must find tour operators that can be trusted to provide all arrangements as advertised and to offer substitute arrangements of the highest possible quality if unforeseen circumstances arise. Obviously, the tour operator selected should be experienced, reputable, and financially stable.

Membership in Professional Organizations. One measure of a tour operator's quality is whether the operator has met the standards set for membership in professional organizations. Two of the best known are the United States Tour Operators Association and the National Tour Association.

The **United States Tour Operators Association (USTOA)** is a professional association for worldwide tour operators that conduct business in the United

ON THE SPOT

Clients Pat and Jane Ward come to your office and ask if you can get them a bargain tour that they saw on the Internet. What can you do for them?

There is a small chance that if the Wards bring a printout or Web site address, you will be able to look into the details of the tour, discover if it is offered by a reputable operator, and take the steps to book the tour. But it is more likely that you will not find the tour they are referring to or that it has been operating for only a short time or that it is run by an operator you know nothing about. Ask yourself: If this was such a "bargain," why didn't they book it on the spot? (You might be tempted to ask them, but don't.) They came to you because of your advice in the past and their trust in you. Find out what attracted them to this tour (besides price), and proceed as you normally would. Sell the preferred operators you know you can rely on.

States. Active members of USTOA must first of all be tour operators. According to USTOA, a tour operator is an entity whose primary purpose is to plan, arrange, and market tours or vacation packages, which are commissionable to travel agents who sell the product to the public. In addition, active members of USTOA must pledge adherence to a code of ethics and (1) have 18 references from reputable travel industry organizations and financial organizations, (2) have had the same ownership or management for at least 3 years, (3) handle a certain volume of bookings, (4) carry a minimum of $1 million of liability insurance with worldwide coverage, and (5) post $1 million in security for participation in *USTOA's consumer protection plan*. Under this plan, consumers are reimbursed for any tour deposits and payments lost as a result of a member's bankruptcy or insolvency. A list of active members is available at www.ustoa.com.

The *National Tour Association (NTA)* includes more than 600 tour operators—most of which are motorcoach tour operators—as well as 2,225 suppliers and 800 destination marketing organizations. Members must post a $1 million professional liability insurance policy and comply with the NTA Code of Ethics. If an NTA operator files for bankruptcy, clients may be reimbursed for payments up to $250,000.

Additional Criteria. Answering several questions can help you narrow the field of tour operators to the most promising candidates.

- *Is the operator known for consistent operation?* Does the tour operator have a history of canceling scheduled departures or raising prices between the date of reservation and departure?
- *Is the operator a specialist?* Operators that specialize in particular markets tend to know their product in depth.
- *How long has the operator been in business?* In the travel business, longevity may be a meaningful measure of quality. The older tour operators have established relationships with their suppliers over the years, and clients traveling on their tours receive preferential treatment. Certain tour operators—because of their contacts, their experience, and the repeat business they provide—can insist on special arrangements and considerations for their clients.
- *Is there a strong relationship between the operator and the travel agency?* Clients benefit from close relationships in the form of better accommodations, superior service, and acceptance of last-minute changes or payments. If the operator is a preferred supplier, travel agencies may also benefit by earning higher commissions.

Identifying the Benefits of a Tour

Selling a tour requires that counselors have a solid grasp of how the features of a tour might translate into benefits for their clients. Some clients may be interested in purchasing a tour just to save money on airfare; others may want a particular destination or a chance to socialize with people of like interests.

Chapter 10 discusses how you can determine which features of a trip a particular client is likely to perceive as benefits. In general, however, tours offer four key benefits:

- *Known costs.* Tours are prepaid, and additional travel costs can be calculated with fair accuracy in advance. As a result, tour participants need to carry less money with them than other travelers and often are protected against unfavorable currency fluctuations or other unexpected expenses.

- *Savings.* Tour operators negotiate discounts from suppliers. As a result, prepackaged tours can be significantly less expensive than the same trips arranged by individuals.
- *Guaranteed entrances.* Tour operators make block purchases of tickets to attractions and events in order to ensure that their clients have access to them. Individual travelers may find it impossible to obtain tickets that are available to tour participants. Tour participants also avoid lines for attractions, such as world-famous museums.
- *Reliable sightseeing features.* Tour operators use their long experience to design tours that provide tried-and-true sightseeing attractions and other activities.

Other benefits depend on the format of the tour. For example, independent tours enable clients to obtain the benefits of volume discounts and prearranged guaranteed rates without sacrificing independence and flexibility. Escorted tours require clients to sacrifice some flexibility, but their disadvantages are matched by other benefits, such as

- *Security.* On escorted tours, hotels, restaurants, and attractions are chosen with security in mind.
- *Peace of mind and relaxation.* Travelers feel safer with escorts along. They know that if problems arise, the escort is there to help. And they do not have to worry about getting from the airport to attractions or waste time each day finding hotels. For many people, escorted motorcoach tours are the most relaxing form of transportation. When the motorcoach starts in the morning, the sightseeing begins; when the motorcoach stops, it is magically in the right place for a visit, a meal, or an overnight stay. Border crossings, airport arrivals and departures, hotel check-ins, and baggage are all handled by someone else.
- *Efficiency.* Escorted tours are carefully planned by people who know the area intimately in order to make the best use of time and know which dates and times certain sites are closed.
- *Expertise.* Clients are assured that the operator knows where to take them and that local advice and assistance are available for special tastes. The escort or tour director often points out customs, traditions, and unusual phenomena that independent travelers miss.
- *Sociability.* People on escorted tours can meet and socialize with fellow travelers interested in the same places. Many tour members make lifelong friends.

In short, escorted tours provide structure and security, which may be especially desirable on trips to exotic locations. Thus it is not surprising that a high percentage of leisure travel in Africa, Asia, and South America involves escorted tours. (Hosted and independent tours are popular at beach destinations in the Bahamas, the Caribbean, and Mexico.) The features of escorted tours are also likely to be seen as benefits by first-time travelers abroad, by dependables, and by older travelers.

Helping Clients Choose a Tour

The selection of tour operator for a client is of utmost importance. While some travelers may feel comfortable enrolling with an unknown operator online, most do not know how to select a reputable operator and, if left to their own devices, may select a fly-by-night company that looks beautiful on a Web site but is lacking in substance.

Matching clients with the right tours is not easy. Operators' brochures and catalogues are indispensable tools both for learning which tour would suit which client and for selling the tour to the client. The Close-Up on selling includes tips on how to use them to select tours. On many of the Web sites for tours you can ask for lists of tours that meet certain criteria—such as tours to a certain destination or tours with a particular theme or tours of a certain type—thus making it easier to narrow your search for a suitable tour.

In theory, travel counselors should know the details of every tour in every brochure in their offices and be able to lead the client deftly through the features of each. In practice, travel counselors must limit their detailed knowledge to the offerings of the tour operators whose products they sell frequently. Developing preferred supplier relationships (as discussed on pages 9 and 326) simplifies this job. However, in some case, these operators may not offer a tour that matches the traveler's needs, and the counselor may offer a tour with some other well-known operator that does not have a preferred supplier arrangement with the travel agency.

Ultimately, it is the client's trip, and the choice of the tour is the client's. But here are a few steps that can help clients make a wise choice.

- Offer clients one or two choices that seem to match their desires. Mark important sections with a highlighter.
- Highlight sections to mark points unique to that trip in order to help clients examine and compare the components of the tour.
- Go through all the details to make certain the clients understand them.
- Take the initiative to summarize the provisions of the tour operator's contract, although clients should be encouraged to read each part of the contract. In particular, review what each tour does and does not include,

CLOSE-UP: SELLING THE RIGHT TOUR THROUGH BROCHURES AND WEB SITES

The USTOA suggests using this ten-item checklist when reading a tour brochure or visiting the operator's Web site in order to find the perfect tour for a client:

1. *Price.* Read the fine print to see exactly what is included in the tour price—and what is not—in order to compare prices of similar tour itineraries. Look specifically to see if airfare, meals, transfers, hotels, and sightseeing are included in the rate.

2. *Itinerary.* Find out the client's must-see sights, and find a tour that matches those interests.

3. *Pace.* Do your clients want to see five countries in ten days or to explore a single region at a leisurely pace or to have a great deal of independence during their stay? Look at the itinerary to determine whether clients see a lot in a short time or have a lot of free time on their own.

4. *Size of group.* Choose the tour or package that offers clients the exact group size they want. Small groups may be more desirable but pricier.

5. *Terminology.* Explain to clients that travel terms used in other countries may not be the same as in the United

States and that brochures may use unfamiliar language. Most brochures classify hotels and clearly state which amenities are standard for each level of classification. The brochures also explain meals as well as what is and is not included.

6. *Single supplement.* If a client is traveling alone, see if the tour operator charges a supplement for singles.

7. *Conditions.* The fine print on the conditions page in the brochure can be tedious, but it is important to the sales process. This is the section that clearly states the tour operator's and the client's rights.

8. *Consumer protection.* Is the operator a member of an organization such as USTOA that provides a consumer protection plan?

9. *Questions.* Is there something in the brochure or anything about the package you don't completely understand? Call the tour operator and ask for more information.

10. *Preferred supplier.* Pages 9 and 326 discuss the reasons for using preferred suppliers and the potential for a conflict of interest.

Source: Adapted with permission from USTOA.

the deposit and payment schedule, the cancellation policy, the limitations on the operator's responsibility and liability, and the status of fares and rates in the brochure.

Once the tour operator and tour have been chosen, the booking requires just a toll-free call to the tour operator or an entry at a computer. Many tour operators can be reached through GDSs, and almost all have Web sites. Electronic booking bypasses the possible nuisance of being put on hold, but it does not allow for the immediate discussion of questions. Most tour bookings are still made by phone though tour companies are encouraging use of the GDS or Internet whenever possible.

Benefits to Travel Agencies

Selling tours offers important advantages to travel agencies. It allows them to provide clients with time-tested products that give good value for the price. Other benefits to travel agencies include

- *Speed and efficiency.* The features of a tour can be purchased from a single source—the tour operator. Dealing with a tour operator may require only one telephone call, one written communication, and one payment. The operator prepares the documentation.
- *Maximum earnings.* Selling tours may increase commissions. The price on which the tour operator pays a commission typically includes the cost of items that clients would otherwise pay for out of their pockets at the destinations, such as meals, special events, tips, and taxes. In addition, agencies can earn higher commissions from tour operators based on the volume of bookings made.
- *Objective advice.* Operators specialize in particular destinations, and they know their territory. They can provide travel counselors with advice about accommodations, sightseeing, climate, culture, and current trends.

Operating their own tours is also an attractive option to some travel agencies. Doing so allows them to add their own markups instead of being dependent on suppliers' commissions. But agencies should be careful before operating their own tours. It is a complicated, time-consuming, and risky business. Usually, the costs for staff and promotion must be incurred before a single sale is made. Also one must often place advance deposits with hotels and airlines in order to hold space, thus requiring cash flow. Agencies should first work with experienced operators, "sell into" existing tours, have tour operators dedicate a tour for a specific group, and then learn the ropes by operating small local tours.

CHAPTER WRAP-UP

CHAPTER HIGHLIGHTS

In this chapter we outlined basic facts and concepts needed to find one's way through the ocean of information about the multitude of tours. Here is a review of the objectives with which we began the chapter.

1. **Identify at least five types of tours.** Tours may be divided into those marketed to the general public and those intended for members of specific groups, such as affinity groups. Tours may also be classified into custom-designed tours, or FITs, and prepackaged tours. Depending on their structure, prepackaged tours are classified as independent, hosted, and escorted tours; independent tours are very

often called packages or vacation packages. On both independent and hosted tours, participants travel independently, not as a group; but on hosted tours, a host is available to help travelers at each destination. On escorted tours, participants travel as a group and are accompanied by tour escorts. Many tours of various types are special-interest tours, designed to appeal to people interested in a particular topic or activity.

2. **Describe the key components of tours.** The major components of tours are transportation, itinerary, lodging, meals, and sightseeing. Typically, the components are packaged by a tour operator or tour wholesaler for sale by a travel agency; however, some travel agencies also package tours, and some tour operators sell their tours to the public themselves. Tour packagers usually obtain the components at reduced prices from suppliers and add a markup to the total cost to establish the selling price. The price is usually given per person for double occupancy. Tour packagers can economize on their costs primarily by adjusting meal costs, hotel quality, the length of stay in principal cities, and sightseeing.

3. **Explain the tour contract and the responsibilities and liabilities of tour operators.** Tour operators publish their contract with tour participants in their brochures, catalogues, and Web sites. They set out what is included in the tour, the payment schedule, the cancellation and refund policy, the status of fares and rates, as well as limitations on the operator's responsibility and liability. Many operators explicitly state in their brochures what is not included in the tour. Tour contracts vary, but generally they require a deposit; final payment is usually due at least 30 to 60 days before departure. Tour operators reserve the right to cancel a tour before departure, and most reserve the right to expel tour participants for due cause without compensation. Prices may vary with the date of the tour, and for tours abroad most operators reserve the right to adjust prices to reflect currency fluctuations. Reliable tour operators accept responsibility for fulfilling the terms and conditions described in their brochures. But they disclaim responsibility or liability for the actions of suppliers and for any loss or delay caused by passengers or by events outside their control.

4. **Discuss key criteria for selecting a tour operator.** The ideal operator is experienced, reputable, and financially stable. The operator's membership in professional organizations such as USTOA or NTA, its relationship with the travel agency, its reputation for consistent operation, its specialization, and its longevity are specific factors worth considering when choosing an operator.

5. **Identify benefits that tours offer clients and travel counselors.** For most clients, benefits include knowing the cost before the trip and receiving a good price, assured entrances to attractions, and reliable features. Tour guides provide additional benefits on hosted and escorted tours. Of course, benefits vary with the traveler and the type of tour. For many travelers, escorted tours provide additional benefits such as security, peace of mind, an efficient use of travel time, and opportunities to socialize. For travel counselors, the advantages of selling tours include the speed and efficiency of booking many elements through one source, the income generated for the time expended, and the advice available from expert operators.

KEY TERMS

A list of key terms introduced in this chapter follows. If you do not recall the meaning of these terms, see the Glossary, which begins on page 393.

adventure tour	FIT
affinity group	fly/drive
cancellation penalty	forced single
ecotour	hard adventure
escorted tour	host

hosted tour
independent tour
land rate
National Tour Association (NTA)
package
Pied Piper
single supplement
soft adventure
special-interest tour

step-on guide
template
tour
tour escort
tour guide
tour operator
tour wholesaler
United States Tour Operators
Association (USTOA)

REVIEW QUESTIONS

1. What are the differences between an independent tour and a hosted tour?

2. What does the price of a tour usually exclude?

3. For some participants on escorted tours, enjoyment of the tour depends on the tour escort. Why?

4. Clients often object to the high cost of traveling as a single. How would you deal with this objection?

5. What can travel counselors do to keep clients booking with them rather than directly on the Internet, and how can travel counselors harness the Internet for tour sales?

Part 3:
Marketing Travel

Chapter 9
Marketing

Chapter 10
Making a Sale

Chapter 11
Specialized Sales

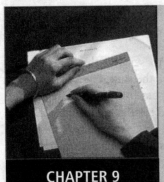

Marketing

OUTLINE

THE MARKETING PROCESS
- What are the basic components of the marketing process and the marketing mix?

WHAT TO SELL: DEFINING THE PRODUCT
- What decisions must travel businesses make when they define their product?

HOW TO SELL: PROMOTING THE PRODUCT
- How do travel businesses promote their products?

WHERE TO SELL: SALES AND DISTRIBUTION CHANNELS
- How do travel businesses get their products to buyers?

HOW MUCH TO CHARGE: SETTING THE PRICE
- What pricing strategies are most often used by travel sellers?

OBJECTIVES

After completing this chapter, you should be able to

1. Outline the marketing process and name the four Ps.

2. Summarize key decisions that a travel business must make about its product.

3. Describe the major forms of promotion.

4. Identify the distribution system and selling sites most often used by travel businesses.

5. Describe pricing strategies frequently used by travel suppliers and travel agencies.

Chapters 4–8 focused on the principle products and services that the travel industry sells to the public. But before travel companies can sell anything they must decide what to sell, whom to sell it to, what price to set for it, and how to sell it. These decisions are part of *marketing*—a series of decisions and actions taken by a seller to create a match between consumers' preferences and a product. Notice that consumers are at the heart of the process.

The changes in travel agencies, starting in the 1990s, illustrate marketing decisions at work. At the start of the decade, travel agencies maintained traditional offices and depended on airline sales for their survival. Agencies rarely charged clients directly; the agencies received almost all of their income from commissions from suppliers. Then the slide in commission rates began, and many travel agencies faced financial disaster. Additional challenges soon followed as the Internet gave travelers a new way to arrange travel directly. Would travel agencies go the way of buggy drivers and shoeshine stands?

In short, travel agencies faced a severe challenge to their marketing methods. Like all businesses, they had to find ways to match what they wanted to sell with what consumers wanted to buy and to do so in a way that produced a profit—or go out of business. Many small neighborhood agencies closed or consolidated into larger agencies. However, a great many of the travel agency industry defied the doomsayers by surviving and survived by changing. The industry began selling more tours and packages, cruises, rental cars, and hotel rooms—decreasing its reliance on airline sales—and emphasizing service. Agencies set up Web sites to promote themselves, and many people in the industry began working from home offices. Charging various kinds of fees became common practice.

Travel agencies no longer limit themselves to serving the surrounding community. Many have developed a clientele across the state, country, and even overseas. With the electronic communication possibilities available today, forward-looking counselors use e-mail, Skype, and similar methods to expand the reach of their agency.

The changes made by travel agencies demonstrate concepts of marketing that affect all travel sellers—from airlines to tour operators, hotels, theme parks, and dozens of other travel-related entities. In this chapter we consider the basic elements of marketing, beginning with an overview of the marketing process.

The Marketing Process

■ WHAT ARE THE BASIC COMPONENTS OF THE MARKETING PROCESS AND THE MARKETING MIX?

Developing a marketing plan is critical to the success of any business. A *marketing plan* selects a target market and describes how to handle four basic characteristics of the business, called the *marketing mix* or the *four Ps: product, promotion, place,* and *price* (see Figure 9.1). In other words, the marketing plan should answer four basic questions:

1. What product will we sell?
2. How will we promote it?
3. Where—at what place—will we sell and distribute it?
4. At what price will we sell it?

Conducting market research is a first step toward answering these questions.

FIGURE 9.1 Components of a Marketing Plan

A marketing plan describes the marketing mix and the target market. Thus it defines the product to be sold, how it will be promoted, its price, and the place of sale.

Market Research

At the center of marketing is the relationship that businesses build and maintain with their customers. Thus the basis of marketing is an understanding of the customer's needs, wants, and demands and an attempt to find ways to satisfy them. As the world changes, customers change. Understanding their needs, wants, and demands requires market research.

As the name indicates, **market research** is the gathering and analyzing of information about consumers and products. Even a small company can do useful market research. For example, travel agencies and tour operators can ask new clients to fill out a form about their preferences and interests. They can ask clients returning from a trip specific questions to discover what was most liked and disliked about the trip.

Sources of Information. The information used in market research includes both primary and secondary data. *Primary data* consist of information that a company collects for the specific purpose of the research, such as the results of questionnaires sent to clients. *Secondary data* consist of preexisting information, such as data in reference books on the Internet and surveys conducted by research firms.

Test marketing—experimenting with an idea by introducing a product or service on a limited scale—is another form of market research. For example, cruise ships might offer special sailings to a limited number of people before the official inaugural sailing of a new ship to test the services provided. The cruise line can then evaluate its marketing strategy based in part on the input from these test passengers.

Uses of Market Research. Information gained from market research is useful at each stage of the marketing process, beginning with market segmentation. Recall that *market segmentation* categorizes people into potential target markets. (Table 9.1 reviews key forms of market segmentation.) Research on market segmentation might tell a local travel agency, for example, that its community includes a large number of middle-aged people and many golfers but very few wealthy people and few students.

The results of research on market segments allow a company to identify which segments might serve as target markets and to develop a marketing plan accordingly. Many companies have discovered that their company may serve several different submarkets, each needing separate travel products and a separate marketing plan. An adventure tour company that begins serving a young, extremely active clientele may find its marketing plan needs to change as its clients grow older, raise a family, and ultimately want less strenuous destinations and itineraries. A company that specializes in honeymoons may

TABLE 9.1 Types of Market Segmentation

Type	Defining Characteristics of Segment
Demographic	Age, sex, race, income, and so on
Psychographic	Attitudes, interests, and beliefs
Location	Distance between client and travel company—in town, out of state, overseas
Usage	Purpose (business, leisure, VFR, meetings, and incentive travel)
Price	Willingness to pay

ON THE SPOT

Bruce is an old veteran of the travel industry, but he has decided that even he can and should learn some new tricks. His small neighborhood travel agency has been successful for years, but Bruce knows that many of his old friends in the business have decided that they can't compete with the large travel agencies anymore. And he's drowning in paper at his office. Bruce has decided that it's time that he enter the computer age, and he has asked Ann, his new assistant, for help. He wants her to set up a database of the agency's clients. What should she do to get started?

Scott Ahlsmith, CTC, of 23 TouchPoints offered this advice in *Travel Professional*: A spreadsheet such as Excel is a quick and simple way to begin. It's like a spreadsheet on training wheels. Most of us already have a spreadsheet on our computer. Once you outgrow a spreadsheet, you can upgrade to a database with more features. Several generic databases can help you store the data that build strong client relationships.

Define the minimum data you need to be effective. This might be as few as three pieces of information: the traveler's name, e-mail address, and where the traveler would next like to travel. Once you start collecting and storing data, you can and will add more information. Once you have the first three pieces of traveler information, obtain additional pieces. Identify a basket, envelope, shoebox, or bowl to temporarily hold new data you plan to enter. Every day enter one piece of data for a new traveler or update information about an existing traveler. Great databases are dynamic and receive additions and deletions every day.

Source: Adapted with permission from Scott Ahlsmith, "Gotta Get Going on That Database!" *Travel Professional*, February/March 2004, pp. 22, 24.

discover it needs to develop new travel products and marketing plans to include anniversary or renew-your-vows trips. Research also helps a company identify trends that might affect its market, such as changes in

- *Demographics.* Changes in birthrate, family size, divorce rate, and the average age of a population are all examples of demographic change. These changes may point to coming trends in the demand for certain types of travel. Recent demographic changes in the United States, for example, include a rise in the average age of the population, an increase in the number of elderly people, and an increase in the number of people with a Hispanic background. The U.S. Census Bureau is a good source for such information.
- *Laws.* For example, specific laws dictate how services and products can be advertised, how contests must be structured, and who can and cannot gamble.
- *Politics.* Unrest in an international country affects both business investments and travel.
- *Economics.* Rates of income growth, inflation, unemployment, and consumer debt, as well as changes in how consumers spend their money, all influence a business's costs, revenues, and ultimate profitability. By definition, discretionary travel is sensitive to changes in the economic climate.
- *Technology.* Advances in transportation may open up new destinations; advances in computers and communications may influence what and how clients buy and how businesses can market their services.

A company cannot control trends, but if it pays attention to market research, it can spot them and adapt to them. Wise travel sellers, for example, see the growing number of people over age forty-five as an opportunity to market cruises and overseas travel to clients in their peak earning years. They are certain not to rely too much on travel to one area, such as the Middle East, in case of political turmoil. They view technological change as an opportunity to change tactics or strategy faster than their competitors.

Research is also key to monitoring and improving a company's performance. Do employees have ideas for improving how they do their jobs? Are customers satisfied? Why or why not?

Customer Relationship Marketing. As business competition has heated up, obtaining feedback and following up on it in order to improve customer service have become essential to survival. For example, surveys of female business travelers led Wyndham Hotels to add library-style pubs for after-work drinks. Hotels and cruise lines often use guest comment cards and surveys online to obtain feedback from their customers; then they can adjust their services based on that feedback. To encourage their customers to participate in surveys, airlines and car rental companies award bonus points to frequent flyers or frequent renters who complete the surveys.

Information from surveys can be easily collected, sorted, resorted, analyzed, and retrieved rapidly thanks to computerized databases. With a sophisticated database of a travel agency's clients, for example, you might select the names of all clients who (1) live in a zip code of mostly affluent people, (2) have recently flown overseas, and (3) are interested in winter sports—and then put these names on a mailing list to receive information about European ski resorts. This is a simple example of *customer relationship marketing.* Using the information gathered and compiled in a database system, businesses contact customers with promotions and services that match their clients' preferences and interests. The focus is on serving their clients' needs while building relationships rather than making individual sales.

Marketing Strategies in a Changing Industry

Decades ago, businesses usually followed a *product-oriented marketing strategy:* they sensed that a product would be profitable, and then they looked for customers to buy it. For example, a tour operator might decide that it could offer motorcoach tours profitably, so it developed the tours and then searched for customers.

Today, a second type of marketing strategy is more common: a *market-oriented strategy,* which is also called *customer-oriented marketing.* Companies first define the needs of a target market and then try to develop a product to meet those needs.

Suppose the manager of a travel agency hopes that expanding into the sale of group tours will help the agency stay competitive and successful. Should the agency begin with a tour and then try to find a buyer or start with a group that wishes to go somewhere? In the first approach, the manager might have a team develop a tour and then try to find a market for the tour. But this product-oriented strategy stacks the odds against the would-be operator. Great amounts of advertising and effort might be necessary to identify and reach a market segment with unserved needs that would be met by the new tour. Travel professionals today are more likely to favor a customer-oriented strategy.

Focusing on the Customer: The Four Cs. The focus on customers can be seen in the changing marketing methods and strategies used by the travel industry. As its customers' needs and expectations have changed, each sector of the industry has adapted. Table 9.2 on the next page summarizes these changes. Many of them have been discussed in earlier chapters; others will be discussed as we explore the elements of the marketing mix in this chapter.

You might have noticed that the four Ps describe the marketing mix from the seller's point of view. Some marketing experts have suggested a way of looking at the marketing mix instead from the customer's point of view. The result is the *four Cs:*

Four Ps	Four Cs
Product	Customer value or solution
Promotion	Communication
Place	Convenience
Price	Cost to the customer

In today's view of marketing, it can be summed up as the delivery of customer satisfaction at a profit.

The emphasis on customers is reflected in the development of **customer relationship management (CRM),** a strategy that combines personalized service and technology to meet the specific needs of customers, enabling businesses to provide excellent service and build lasting relationships with their clients, thus increasing customer loyalty.

For example, Ritz-Carlton employees provide memorable experiences to their guests by treating them as individuals. They record specific guest preferences in the company's database, which holds more than 500,000 individual customer preferences, accessible by all hotels in the worldwide Ritz chain. A request made in Atlanta for feather pillows will also be honored without an additional request being made in the Ritz-Carlton in San Juan months later. Technology helps the company build stronger relationships with its guests.

Coordinating the Elements. Whatever marketing strategy is devised, decisions about product, promotion, place, and price must be coordinated if the strategy is to succeed. Suppose you run a travel agency that sells deluxe tours at an office in a pricey neighborhood. If you promote your tours by putting flyers on car windows and jingles on alternative rock radio stations, you are probably wasting your money. These forms of advertising are not likely to be very effective in reaching your target market.

Like the pieces of a jigsaw puzzle, all parts of the marketing mix must fit together. They must be blended into a coordinated program designed to achieve the marketing objectives. In the rest of this chapter we look at each part of the marketing mix.

✔ CHECK-UP

Elements of the marketing process include
✔ Market research.
✔ Identification of market segments.
✔ Selection of target markets and a marketing strategy.
✔ Development of a marketing plan.
✔ Ongoing market research to monitor trends and performance.

A marketing plan includes decisions about
✔ The target market.
✔ The product.
✔ The product's promotion.
✔ The place to sell the product.
✔ The product's price.

TABLE 9.2 Adapting to Changing Customers

Travel Sector	Recent Marketing Methods and Strategies
Travel agencies	Less dependence on air sales; more attention to tours, cruises, rental cars, and hotel rooms Both "bricks" and "clicks" points of contact with customers Emphasis on service Specialization More home-based agents Charging service fees to customers
Airlines	Cost cutting by major carriers Successful business model by low-cost airlines
Ground transportation	Addition of features to cars in rental fleet Increased number of luxury and SUV vehicles in rental fleet Increased availability of light rail, high-speed trains, and specialty rail
Accommodations	Consolidation of ownership but increased variety of brands for targeted market segments Increased use of guest comment cards and online surveys to identify changing needs More features and services that provide convenience to business travelers at commercial hotels and that cater to the needs of families at resorts Increased use of technology to help personalize services and build a loyal customer base
Cruise lines	New and varied products that appeal to different market segments Promotion through varied media with multiple points of contact
Tour operators	Increased flexibility and variety of products Changes in the length and focus of tours to meet a variety of needs

What to Sell: Defining the Product

■ WHAT DECISIONS MUST TRAVEL BUSINESSES MAKE WHEN THEY DEFINE THEIR PRODUCT?

If you were in the business of selling boxes, you might wonder whether you should sell cheap boxes as well as sturdy packages, plain brown boxes as well as decorative ones. Should you offer only certain standard sizes, or should you also offer to order boxes of any size the customer desires? Should you also sell wrapping papers, tapes, and seals? Would you package the boxes when they are purchased or just hand them over to the customer?

These are the types of questions that a marketing plan should address regarding the first *P*—the product. Airlines, for example, must select the routes they will fly; hotels define the amenities they will offer; cruise lines create itineraries. Similarly, travel agencies must determine the range, mix, and level of products and services they will offer. To remain competitive, businesses of all types must keep developing and refining the products they offer.

The Range and Mix of Products

As travelers change, travel sellers must alter their product mix in order to survive. In recent years, for example, more travelers wanted a chance to experience destinations in depth. Successful tour companies responded by becoming more flexible in the length of their tours and the focus of their activities.

Similarly, car rental companies responded to the changing expectations of their customers by adding features and special equipment to their vehicles. They also increased the number of SUVs, sports cars, and luxury vehicles available.

To determine the range and mix of their products, companies use *segmental analysis,* an evaluation of the profitability of different products and services. Which ones bring in the most income relative to the amount of time spent handling the transactions? By providing an answer, segmental analysis helps companies decide how to allocate their resources efficiently.

The recent history of travel agencies demonstrates the importance of decisions about the range and mix of products. Little more than a decade ago, travel agencies churned out airline tickets as fast as fingers could fly over computer keys. Hotel and car reservations were sometimes an afterthought, and many felt that selling tours and cruises just slowed them down. The number of air tickets sold was the name of the game. When the airlines changed the game by eliminating commissions, travel agencies had to adjust in many ways, including changes in the range and mix of products sold. They put more emphasis on selling products other than air travel, such as cruises and tours, and on selling to specific types of travelers (look again at Table 9.1).

Developing expertise in special types of travel was one frequent response. For example, an agency might specialize in

- Particular destinations, such as Las Vegas or Hawaii, western Europe, or the Caribbean.
- Particular demographic groups, such as seniors or families, upscale or budget travelers.
- Particular interests, such as golf vacations or safaris or scuba diving.
- Particular types of travel, such as corporate travel.

Specialization is not an all-or-nothing proposition. Basically, a travel agency may meet the challenge of determining what it will sell in three ways.

- It may operate as a general agency but concentrate on certain products.
- It may carry the first strategy a bit further and develop *niches,* or specialty markets, such as adventure travel, cruises, upscale travel, or budget travel. The agency sells a wide range of products, but it aggressively markets certain types of travel arrangements, and a high percentage of its sales occurs in these specialty areas.
- It may deal with one type of travel to the exclusion of all others, developing a marketing plan that prepares it to succeed through sales only in this niche. Some agencies that take this approach still provide other services when they deem it worthwhile and when they are appointed to receive commissions from the supplier. Many do not; incentive houses (which arrange only incentive travel) and cruise-only agencies are examples.

Most agencies still sell a complete range of travel arrangements—air, rail, auto, hotel, tour, cruise—plus insurance and perhaps miscellaneous products. But being all things to all people is increasingly difficult. Large agencies tend to create special departments to deal with specific types of travel. When many agencies are close to and competing with each other, the tendency increases for each to specialize.

Agencies do not necessarily sell all suppliers. Ultimately, they sell products they can be proud of and that will provide a reasonable profit.

The Level of Services

Whatever a travel agency's decision about the travel products it will offer for sale, in fact it is only helping travelers to lease these products temporarily. Suppliers provide the air seats, cars, and hotel rooms. Travelers can call suppliers or go online themselves in order to book these products. When they go instead to a travel agency, they are purchasing the agency's time and expertise; the agency is providing services that should give the travel products their highest possible value.

What services are travelers looking for from a travel agency? Surveys show vacation travelers are likely to be especially interested in

- Help in getting the most value for their money.
- Assurance that they will get high-quality accommodations and services on the trip from reputable operators.
- A trouble-free trip.
- A counselor available to help if things go wrong.
- Unbiased opinions from a knowledgeable professional.
- Service that saves them time as many are busy professionals themselves.
- Personal contact with a professional.

In effect, the travel agency sells a counseling service that is only as good as its counselors. The agency's success depends on providing a consistent level of service. Training and quality control are therefore vital.

How much time should an agency's travel counselors devote to looking for bargains or checking the quality of a product? Should the agency promise that someone is available 24 hours a day in case something goes wrong? In short, what level of service should the agency's counselors give clients? If ABC agency plans to sell mainly discount-priced trips, then offering a lot of frills is not likely to be profitable. But if its product mix emphasizes deluxe cruises and tours, then it should offer a lot of personal attention—perhaps including limousine service and premium travel gifts free of charge. The level of service provided should mesh with the agency's overall marketing plan.

✔ CHECK-UP

Specialization by travel agencies
✔ May be carried out to varying degrees.
✔ May focus on particular destinations, demographic groups, interests, or types of travel.
✔ Allows counselors to offer travelers detailed, professional knowledge.

The level of service provided by a travel agency should
✔ Be consistent from one travel counselor to another.
✔ Mesh with the marketing plan.

How to Sell: Promoting the Product

■ HOW DO TRAVEL BUSINESSES PROMOTE THEIR PRODUCTS?

Nothing, it seems, sells itself; it must be promoted. **Promotion,** the second *P*, consists of efforts to communicate information about a product or service to the market. It includes

- Advertising, whether in print, on radio or television, or on the Internet.
- Sales promotions, such as discounts, bonuses, and contests.
- Public relations.
- Person-to-person selling.

All of the elements of promotion should help to create a perception of the company—an *image*—that is consistent with the rest of the marketing plan. If a travel agency emphasizes corporate travel with deluxe arrangements, it should not aim to convey an image of homespun friendliness.

How does a business create an image? Many elements can contribute. Carnival Cruise Lines promotes its "Fun Ships" with advertisements that are festive; Royal Caribbean's advertising emphasizes the "royal" treatment its passengers receive through personal service and pampering. Or consider a California travel agency for upscale leisure travelers. It builds its image through

- Its name. It describes itself as "cruise and tour consultants."
- The design and atmosphere of its office, which features teakwood and classical music.
- Its staff's appearance. Their usual attire is relaxed but chic—yet they have been known to don tuxedos and elegant dresses for cruise nights and safari clothing for consumer seminars on Africa.
- Its advertising. It has one ad in the yellow pages but no newspaper ads. The agency prefers to use highly selective direct mail, word of mouth, and its Web site.
- Its treatment of clients. The agency offers its clients chilled canapés and a

choice of beverages; it has a substantial wine list. Counselors meet with clients privately without interruption.

Besides defining an image, a company must also determine the mix of promotional methods to use. Will it rely mostly on person-to-person selling by representatives, or will it reach people mainly through its advertising? How and where will it advertise? Should it devote significant resources to special promotions (such as contests) or to public relations? Each of the many methods of promotion has benefits and disadvantages, which we look at next.

Direct-Mail Advertising

Many companies use some type of *direct mail*—letters, postcards, flyers, brochures, questionnaires, or newsletters distributed through the mail. The mailing lists are compiled from the company's own records, from local directories, or from mailing-list companies.

As discussed in earlier chapters, brochures represent an important form of promotion for travel suppliers such as tour companies and cruise lines. Often they compile a collection of brochures for all of their products into a single publication or catalog. By making the products more tangible to buyers, the brochures become an essential sales tool for travel agencies that sell the supplier's products. Thus brochures include enticing photos, a list of the products' features, and a translation of those features into possible benefits for the buyers.

For travel agencies, direct mail—more than any other kind of advertising—is likely to use a company's own talents, resources, and records. The initial costs are likely to be high, but direct mail offers several advantages.

- It can contain far more information than any other kind of advertisement.
- It stands alone, unlike newspaper advertisements, which compete with other ads for the consumer's attention.
- It may be kept around for days before being discarded, and the recipient may pass it on to others.
- It reaches identifiable segments of the total market. For example, a travel agency might send a special announcement just to those clients who have taken a cruise or to everyone who has not taken a trip in the past year. The piece can be tailored to the audience and its needs.
- It can be sent whenever the company needs to advertise, with little lead time. The company does not have to sign a contract committing it to a series of ads or commercials.
- Its effectiveness can be measured fairly easily by including a response card or return-reply envelope with the mailing.

Figure 9.2 includes some tips for making direct mail effective. Newsletters can be especially informative. They may include many types of reports to stimulate interest and confidence and to build a company's image. For example, a travel agency's newsletter might include reports from staff members or clients about recently visited destinations and news about staff members who have completed special training courses. It might encourage clients to contact a staff member who has specialized knowledge or recent experience with a particular kind of travel. To be most effective, newsletters should be published regularly. Many companies no longer distribute print newsletters but e-mail them instead if they have clients who are Internet savvy.

The best time for a travel agency to promote through direct mail is during a slow period. Consumers usually take nine to eleven days to respond to first-class mail. First-time mailings to repeat customers should be sent four to six times a year; general-response mailings should be sent twice a year. Mailings that arrive midweek have the best chance of bringing a response.

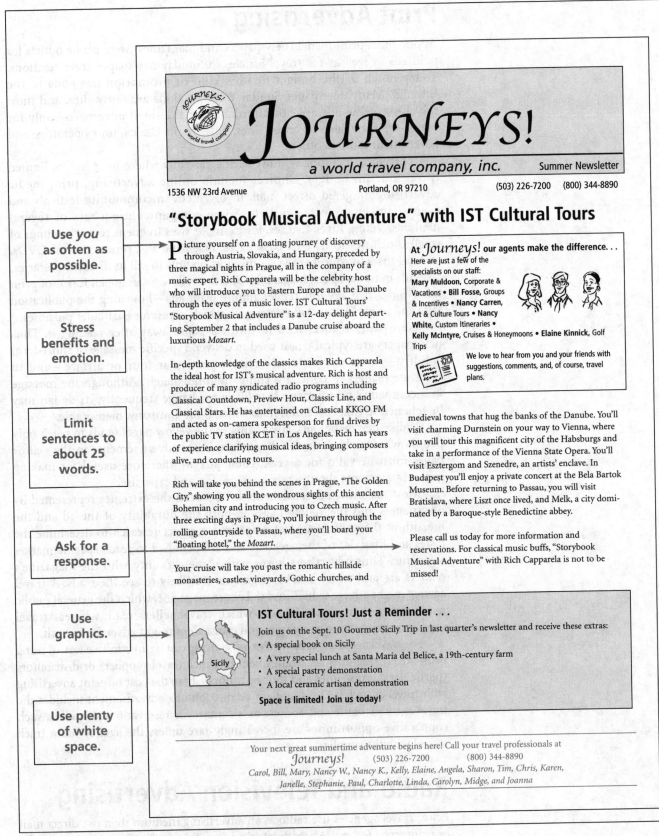

Use *you* as often as possible.

Stress benefits and emotion.

Limit sentences to about 25 words.

Ask for a response.

Use graphics.

Use plenty of white space.

JOURNEYS!
a world travel company, inc.
Summer Newsletter

1536 NW 23rd Avenue   Portland, OR 97210   (503) 226-7200   (800) 344-8890

"Storybook Musical Adventure" with IST Cultural Tours

Picture yourself on a floating journey of discovery through Austria, Slovakia, and Hungary, preceded by three magical nights in Prague, all in the company of a music expert. Rich Capparela will be the celebrity host who will introduce you to Eastern Europe and the Danube through the eyes of a music lover. IST Cultural Tours' "Storybook Musical Adventure" is a 12-day delight departing September 2 that includes a Danube cruise aboard the luxurious *Mozart*.

In-depth knowledge of the classics makes Rich Capparela the ideal host for IST's musical adventure. Rich is host and producer of many syndicated radio programs including Classical Countdown, Preview Hour, Classic Line, and Classical Stars. He has entertained on Classical KKGO FM and acted as on-camera spokesperson for fund drives by the public TV station KCET in Los Angeles. Rich has years of experience clarifying musical ideas, bringing composers alive, and conducting tours.

Rich will take you behind the scenes in Prague, "The Golden City," showing you all the wondrous sights of this ancient Bohemian city and introducing you to Czech music. After three exciting days in Prague, you'll journey through the rolling countryside to Passau, where you'll board your "floating hotel," the *Mozart.*

Your cruise will take you past the romantic hillside monasteries, castles, vineyards, Gothic churches, and

At *Journeys!* our agents make the difference. . .
Here are just a few of the specialists on our staff:
Mary Muldoon, Corporate & Vacations • **Bill Fosse**, Groups & Incentives • **Nancy Carren**, Art & Culture Tours • **Nancy White**, Custom Itineraries • **Kelly McIntyre**, Cruises & Honeymoons • **Elaine Kinnick**, Golf Trips

We love to hear from you and your friends with suggestions, comments, and, of course, travel plans.

medieval towns that hug the banks of the Danube. You'll visit charming Durnstein on your way to Vienna, where you will tour this magnificent city of the Habsburgs and take in a performance of the Vienna State Opera. You'll visit Esztergom and Szenedre, an artists' enclave. In Budapest you'll enjoy a private concert at the Bela Bartok Museum. Before returning to Passau, you will visit Bratislava, where Liszt once lived, and Melk, a city dominated by a Baroque-style Benedictine abbey.

Please call us today for more information and reservations. For classical music buffs, "Storybook Musical Adventure" with Rich Capparela is not to be missed!

IST Cultural Tours! Just a Reminder . . .

Sicily

Join us on the Sept. 10 Gourmet Sicily Trip in last quarter's newsletter and receive these extras:
- A special book on Sicily
- A very special lunch at Santa Maria del Belice, a 19th-century farm
- A special pastry demonstration
- A local ceramic artisan demonstration

Space is limited! Join us today!

Your next great summertime adventure begins here! Call your travel professionals at
Journeys!   (503) 226-7200   (800) 344-8890
Carol, Bill, Mary, Nancy W., Nancy K., Kelly, Elaine, Angela, Sharon, Tim, Chris, Karen, Janelle, Stephanie, Paul, Charlotte, Linda, Carolyn, Midge, and Joanna

FIGURE 9.2 Making Direct Mail Effective

This sample newsletter illustrates a few guidelines useful in all forms of direct mail.

Source: Adapted with permission of Journeys! of Portland, Oregon.

Print Advertising

At one time, print media (newspapers and magazines) were prime outlets for paid ads as well as for travel articles in Sunday newspaper travel sections. Today much of the budget for this kind of promotion has gone to the Internet. Many newspaper Sunday travel sections are fairly slim, and most travel magazine ads are not affordable for the small advertiser—only for major suppliers such as cruise lines, hotel/resort chains, tour operators, and government tourism offices.

Therefore, a company must decide carefully where to spend its limited travel/tourism budget. Choices include online advertising, print media advertising, targeted direct mail, involvement in community festivals and events, and many other outlets. Some companies use a mix of several methods. Viking River Cruises, for example, uses frequent repeat mailings of small brochures to its past passengers, magazine ads, production of DVDs, and webinars to educate travel counselors on how to sell its diverse itineraries.

Ads in newspapers, magazines, and the yellow pages are all forms of *print advertising*. Two key differences among print ads—how long the publication lasts and its audience—help determine which is best for particular purposes.

Newspaper readers tend to throw a paper away after reading it. Thus newspapers are typically best used to deliver a specific message of short-term validity—for example, to advertise a particular tour or airfare—and to motivate readers to contact a company immediately. Although the message in a company's newspaper ads is likely to change frequently, its design may be retained so that repetition makes it, and the company, memorable.

Unlike newspaper ads, advertising in the yellow pages tends to reach only people who are looking for the service. Also, advertisements in the yellow pages must be valid for a year. These ads are therefore useful for making general statements about service, experience, and expertise.

Most magazine advertisements fall between the extremes represented by newspapers and the yellow pages in both the durability of the ad and the breadth of the audience. Most magazines conduct research to determine the tastes and lifestyles of their readers and are designed to reach specific market segments. Thus advertisers know with some certainty who the magazine's readers are and which market segments are likely to see their ads. A travel agency might advertise in *Travel & Leisure* magazine, which the general public reads, but not in *Travel Weekly,* which travel sellers read, whereas travel suppliers such as tour companies and cruise lines might advertise in both.

For travel agencies, **cooperative advertising** can be an effective way of using print advertising; it is an arrangement in which travel suppliers or distributors (particularly cruise lines and tour operators) share the cost of print advertising with travel agencies. The supplier's or distributor's advertisement includes the travel agency's name and address as a contact for reservations. However, such cooperative opportunites are increasingly rare unless the agency has a track record with the supplier.

Radio and Television Advertising

Fewer travel agencies use radio as an advertising medium than use direct mail or print; even fewer use broadcast television. Travel advertisers on these media are more likely to be travel suppliers, especially the large ones. These media have the potential of reaching a large audience, but especially in the case of broadcast television, they have two drawbacks.

- The audience tends to be diverse, including many people outside the target market.
- More problematic is the cost: radio or television advertising tends to be expensive. The cost comes from a combination of the advertising rates charged, the need for repetition, and the production costs.

A typical radio or television advertisement lasts only thirty to sixty seconds and cannot be easily saved and found again. Only repetition ensures that a radio or television advertisement will register on the consumer's consciousness. (Television *infomercials*—commercials that are the length of a program and seek an immediate response from the viewing audience—are an exception to these generalizations.) In small towns, radio may be no more expensive than other forms of advertising despite the need to air the commercials repeatedly. But in large metropolitan areas, the cost of repeating radio advertising exceeds the average travel agency's budget.

One type of effective radio advertising can be when a popular disc jockey acts as a "Pied Piper" and announces that he will lead a group of listeners who share a common interest, such as Big Band music, on a cruise. Broadcast television is usually even more expensive, not only because of the high rates charged to advertisers but also because of production costs. Viewers measure television advertisements by the standards of professional advertising agencies that handle multimillion-dollar accounts. Amateur television advertisements seldom measure up.

Production costs are also high for advertising on cable television, but agencies of all sizes may be able to afford to advertise in small cable markets. Many cable companies offer help in preparing commercials aimed at local subscribers. Advertising on cable can be targeted to particular segments of the market. There are cable television channels directed to sports lovers, culture buffs, news junkies, and other identifiable segments, as well as programs devoted to travel and to particular destinations. Sometimes these travel program hosts want to interview experts for their shows.

Videos or DVDs for home use provide another way to reach potential clients. Tour operators and cruise lines produce videos to send directly to clients or to be distributed by travel agencies.

Advertising on the Internet

The Internet has quickly become the key cog in the marketing machine for many companies. Many people see it as a social tool, a library, or a game room. But it is also a place for distributing products (discussed in the next section) and an advertising medium. It offers the advantage of being available 24 hours a day, every day.

For every traditional method of advertising, the Internet offers an electronic counterpart plus additional options. For example,
- The Internet version of television advertising is streaming videos and downloadable DVDs, complete with high-quality audio and visual components that can be delivered at a fraction of the cost of television ads.
- If radio is your medium of choice, the Internet offers live radio programs that include advertising opportunities in both audio and text formats. Travel Talk Radio (www.traveltalkradio.com) is just one example of an online talk show that focuses on the travel industry. Listeners can catch the show live or listen to the archives at their convenience.
- The Internet's version of direct mail is often called *e-marketing*, in which recipients have agreed to receive e-mail advertisements and promotional

messages direct from travel suppliers or a travel trade news service such as eTurboNews (www.eturbonews.com).

- Because it is a news service, eTurboNews also offers electronic classified ads and press releases, similar to what you find in traditional printed newspapers and magazines.

Electronic brochures, Web sites, banner advertisements, listings in search engines, electronic yellow page listings, and links to other Web sites are a few of the popular forms of advertising on the Internet. We will examine the two most common forms in this section: hosting a Web site and linking to other Web sites. Also check out industry education sources, such as ASTA, The Travel Institute, and CLIA, for a number of publications.

Establishing a Web Presence. Few travel sellers in the future will want to do without a Web site, but the goals of the sites vary. Some travel sellers aim for their Web site to do no more than build awareness of the company and establish it as a reliable, business-like entity to encourage their clients' loyalty. Others expect their site to generate new business. Some sites are designed to increase clients' satisfaction or even to make sales by allowing clients to book on the site itself.

The content and complexity of a Web site obviously depend on its goals, but here are a few general guidelines.

- Web sites should be professionally designed. They should reflect the company's overall image, be pleasant to look at, and be easy to navigate (see Figure 9.3).
- Web sites must be constantly monitored and updated, or they become worse than a waste of time and money. Like a musty out-of-date window display, they can discourage buyers and detract from a company's image.
- Inquiries from clients at the Web site should be answered quickly. What "quickly" means depends on the company's strategy and products, but 24 hours is generally seen as the maximum.
- Other marketing must ensure that people see the site, as discussed in Chapter 3.
- The narrower the market niche and the more specialized the product or service, the greater the chances are that the site will attract interested buyers.

For some specific comments about the steps involved in establishing a Web site, see Chapter 14.

Linking to Other Sites. Most successful airlines, tour operators, and other travel sellers are linked to dozens of Web sites. If you look up travel information on Frommer's site, you will be a click away from hotel providers, tourist bureaus, or travel gear manufacturers, for example. Many wholesalers, tour operators, and tourist offices also give links to lists of travel counselors. These counselors have usually "paid" for the listing by hard work and education rather than advertising dollars.

Many companies find that Web links (both paid and unpaid) are their most effective method of online advertising. Carefully chosen reciprocal links can (1) enhance a company's own Web site by providing more content to its visitors and (2) bring in visitors from other sites that feature a link to it, increasing the company's marketing reach.

There are, of course, innumerable other methods of advertising, from fax blitzes to billboards to skywriting. Each might be effective for some travel seller in some location at some time, if for no other reason than that no one else has tried it for a long time. Effective promotion of a business uses multiple media for advertising, as well as other forms of promotion.

Public Relations

Compared with advertising, public relations is usually a less obvious type of promotion. Any activity conducted to establish recognition and respect within the community is a form of *public relations.* When a newspaper lists a company as the sponsor for a charity event or reports that a company employee has won a community service award, the company's efforts at public relations have succeeded. To gather publicity, companies submit press releases and invite journalists to events.

Hosting special events is a complicated but productive form of public relations. Companies either sponsor or participate in events, such as a golf tournament or a benefit fashion show. Some travel agencies hold regular "travel nights" at which they show films, present speakers, and promote related travel arrangements. Travel sellers also participate in theme events, such as bridal shows with presentations by clothing stores, real estate agents, jewelers, and houseware retailers—as well as by airlines, cruise companies, tour operators, and travel counselors discussing honeymoon destinations.

Like other forms of public relations, hosting a special event should help establish a travel company's image. Often these events provide a means of identifying market segments interested in a particular kind of travel and of better defining the target market. Sometimes they also present opportunities for person-to-person selling.

Suppliers often cooperate with travel agencies to produce special events. A cruise line, for example, might work with a travel agency to organize a

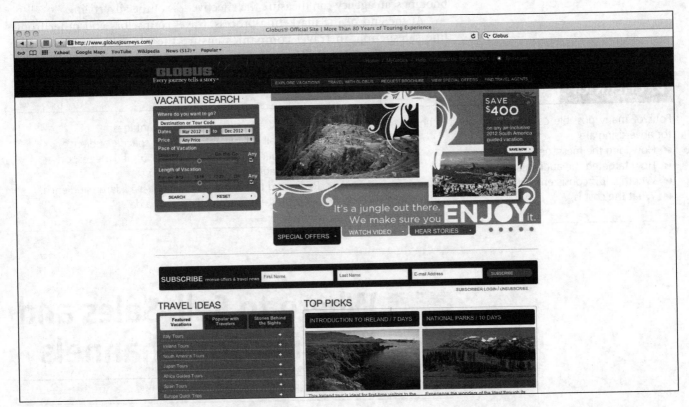

FIGURE 9.3 Advertising on the Internet

Hosting a Web site is one way of using the Internet to advertise a company. The Globus home page is pleasant to look at (especially in color) and easy to navigate.

Source: Reprinted by permission of Globus & Cosmos Tours.

"cruise night" and share the costs of refreshments, decorations, invitations, and door prizes. Representatives from the agency and the cruise line would offer information about cruising itineraries, life onboard, and specific cruises.

Personal Selling

Salespeople are also elements in the promotional mix. As part of the marketing plan, businesses decide how much of their resources they will devote to selling face-to-face and how much to other promotions. Whatever the answer, the salesperson can be an important part of the marketing effort.

Consider the case of travel counselors. Through constant contact with clients, they can gather vital information about tastes, trends, and attitudes. In short, travel counselors conduct informal market research every time a client answers a question. Both counselors and management know what sells, but front-line counselors can detect subtle shifts in why it sells and who is buying it. That knowledge might suggest a new promotional approach.

Travel counselors can also help to ensure that advertising is not wasted by evaluating its effectiveness. They should know what products their agency is advertising. If, for example, an agency has run a cooperative newspaper ad with a cruise line in the Sunday travel section, they can be prepared to deal confidently with clients who respond to the ads. If people do not say that they are responding to an advertisement, counselors should ask if they saw a particular ad. By logging the number of responses and the number of bookings, an agency can measure the effectiveness of the advertising.

At the end of the marketing process, travel counselors and other front-line salespeople in travel companies ensure the ultimate success of the marketing plan. Their selling makes the marketing plan work.

✔ CHECK-UP

Four of many possible considerations in selecting a medium for advertising are
- ✔ How long the message is accessible.
- ✔ How targeted the audience can be.
- ✔ Whether it is consistent with the desired image.
- ✔ What the cost is.

Each form of advertising has its advantages:
- ✔ Direct mail is easily targeted to a specific audience.
- ✔ Newspaper advertising produces immediate responses.
- ✔ Yellow pages ads are long-lasting.
- ✔ Radio and television ads usually have a large audience.
- ✔ Web sites are available 24 hours a day.

Where to Sell: Sales and Distribution Channels

■ HOW DO TRAVEL BUSINESSES GET THEIR PRODUCTS TO BUYERS?

Once you have a product or service, how do you get it to the public? Do you sell it directly or through an intermediary? And where do you locate the points of sale and distribution? Must travelers come to buy your product in person, or can they make the purchase over the phone or online? These questions all address the third *P* of the marketing plan—place (also known as *point of sale*).

Distribution Channels

Many travel suppliers answer the question of place by using a *dual distribution* system: they sell to the public both directly themselves and indirectly, through travel agencies and other intermediaries. Their marketing plans should indicate how much emphasis to give to each of these channels.

One reason for dual distribution by suppliers is the nature of the travel

---

CLOSE-UP: ON THE JOB WITH JOHN ABRUZZI, WEB SITE SPECIALIST

A decade ago, the positions of Web designer and Web programmer would have drawn a blank on the radar screens of most travel employers. Most of these jobs are filled by people who learn computers first and then apply their skills to the travel industry. John Abruzzi is one who kept learning in both fields and became his company's Internet specialist.

"I was just getting into the travel business in the early 1990s. CRSs had been in travel agencies for about fifteen years, and I relished the opportunity to practice what I learned in travel school. Within a few months I was turning out tickets, itineraries, invoices, boarding passes—you name it. Within a year no one could produce them as fast as I could. Little did I know I'd soon be doing computer work that barely existed when I went to school.

"All the travel counselors in our office are very competent in using the GDS, and now they're sharp in using e-mail and the Internet as well. It's up to me, though, to monitor and operate our agency's Web site. It just fell naturally in my lap because I'd been keeping up with the Internet in the mid-1990s and had my own home computer. A number of the other travel counselors were CRS whizzes at work but didn't want to look at a computer when they went home.

"One of the major things I do is make constant changes in the information on our site. We run specials from preferred suppliers, consolidators, and lately even from airline Internet sites. Clients get that great fare even if they don't have a computer or never saw it on the Internet, but they have to pay us a service charge. Still, for a round-trip to London for $800, a small service charge is nothing.

"The specials change constantly, and I have to keep our site fresh so clients will keep coming back to look. We also have our travel counselors' pictures on the site, information on where they've traveled, what their field of expertise is, and even personal information if they wish to share it. As soon as people return from a trip, I add that to their 'résumés' and write a feature for the Web site. Every time I make any significant change on the site, I make sure our counselors are informed and have any relevant information handy.

"I also help other counselors create custom-made brochures with the software we have. It's hard to believe that instead of giving clients the same brochure that a tour company prints in the thousands, we can print one out in color with the client's name on it—and we can print only the particular tour or cruise and the date those clients are considering. And I can do them quickly now. It's called mass customization, a term I learned in a class on using the software.

"We have a receptionist who routes calls; I route Web site inquiries. People who are at our site can e-mail us for a reservation, general information, a brochure, or other requests. I decide who gets the request and check that the client gets an answer within four hours. Often the client gets an answer even faster. I answer a lot of them myself.

"One of our goals is to get clients on the phone as soon as possible because then we can learn much more quickly which clients are qualified buyers. You can hear the tone of their voice, give them an idea of price, and decide if they are serious buyers. We try to hook them right away by emphasizing the special expertise a particular travel counselor has, something they couldn't get anywhere else.

"Our Web site might not look like it provides a lot of direct bookings, but it already produces a lot of repeat and word-of-mouth business. A lot of the time clients will later e-mail or phone, or their friends will. We haven't been tracking this, except informally, but we know quite a bit of this business is there—people who first saw the site and now call or e-mail. Then again, some repeat clients book right on the site. Actually, we have to get back to them; it isn't an instant interactive booking. We take the information and then book it with the supplier.

"If we decide on major changes in the site, such as altering the number of screens or changing how to click from screen to screen, we pay an outside webmaster to do it—someone who's basically a computer whiz but who knows enough about the travel industry to create what we need.

"It seems as though the Internet is such an advanced tool, but I keep reading that its integration into the world of business has only just begun. I'm going to make sure I'm in the forefront of new developments."

inventory. Travel agencies usually do not buy inventory; therefore, the supplier must retain some method of selling whatever agencies do not sell. Moreover, the supplier's inventory is highly perishable; today's airline seat or hotel room cannot be sold tomorrow. The supplier must make the product as available as possible.

During the 1990s, the growing popularity of toll-free numbers and the Internet made it easier for suppliers to sell directly to the public, bypassing travel agencies. As a result, travel agencies now face direct competition from suppliers. In fact, suppliers are tempted to do all of the selling themselves if that would reduce their selling costs. And many retail travel agencies are loathe to sell products from suppliers who are competing with them, in effect, "selling on both sides of the fence."

Consider the airlines. Why did they stop paying commissions to travel agencies for domestic air tickets? The two primary reasons that airlines paid travel agencies a commission to sell their products in the first place were (1) to increase their marketing reach and (2) to use travel agencies as a sales and reservations staff that was far less expensive than hiring employees. But they found a distribution channel that was more economical: the Internet.

Many travel suppliers still prefer to pay commissions to travel agencies rather than employ large sales and reservations staffs of their own. And many still advise consumers, "See your travel agent." Furthermore (as discussed in Chapter 3), consumers still value the unbiased information, convenience, and personal service provided by travel agencies, as indicated by the high percentage of travel sales booked by travel agencies.

Selecting a Site

Like other elements of the marketing mix, the site for an office or retail outlet should be consistent with the rest of the marketing plan. For example, locating a deluxe cruise agency in the poorest area of town is likely to be a mistake. But today, decisions about the place of sale and distribution involve far more than the location of a building. Answering the question of "place" also means deciding the extent to which the company will use an office or retail outlet, telephone, Internet, or other type of location as the site for selling.

The airlines again provide an example. They still sell to the public from airline ticket offices, but the major carriers have closed many ticket offices. Many airline tickets are sold at airports, at ticket machines, over the phone, on the Internet, and—of course—through travel agencies.

Similarly, travel agencies have decreased their reliance on walk-in business at retail outlets. In fact, a great deal of selling occurs outside the travel agency's office. Most corporate sales take place in the office of the client corporation. After this initial sale, primarily to set up the contract and the "ground rules," people from the client company rarely visit the agency; the account is serviced over the phone or on the Internet. Similarly, group travel may be sold at the agent's or decision maker's home or at the headquarters of the group buying the trip. Outside sales agents may do most of their sales at the homes of clients, at their own home offices, or even over coffee at a local café.

The Home-Based Office. Increasingly, the home is an attractive choice for the site of an office. Sales representatives or account representatives for travel suppliers frequently work out of home offices. Often, their company's headquarters is far from their sales territory, and business is conducted at the clients' place of business.

Many sales representatives of cruise lines, tour operators, and airlines have huge territories and rarely manage to visit the agencies spread so far and wide, preferring to keep in contact with agency personnel by phone, e-mail, and educational webinars. The cost of using traditional office and retail space is high, and technology now allows people to perform many tasks at home that once had to be done in a traditional office setting.

Travel professionals working at home fall into three categories:

- Employees doing some or all of their work at home. Using e-mail and the Internet, they can stay in close touch with the home office.
- Part-time or full-time independent contractors, working for themselves.
- Independent entrepreneurs, operating their own businesses.

By using home-based independent contractors, companies save many costs. They save the cost of paying for Social Security taxes; for employee benefits such as health insurance, vacations, sick days, training, and pensions; and for office space and office equipment. They may also save the cost of contributing to their state's funds for workers with disabilities or who are unemployed. But to avoid violating tax laws, the company must be certain that these people are truly independent contractors, not employees in disguise. Chapter 14 discusses the criteria that the U.S. Internal Revenue Service uses to determine whether a person is an independent contractor as well as details involved in establishing home-based offices.

The Internet. The growth in home-based offices owes a lot to the Internet. It can serve not just as an advertising medium but also as a company's "store," or as one of its stores. In other words, the Internet can be a place of sale and distribution in one of two ways: (1) as the sole location for a company's sales or (2) as an alternative point of a sale.

To use the first strategy and succeed without a bricks-and-mortar location, a company must have wide recognition or be able to affiliate itself with other well-known, well-respected companies. The number of travel reservations booked online continues to grow, but the more complex the transaction, the more clients want to talk to or meet a live person. To satisfy clients' needs, travel sellers need to occupy both cyberspace and a piece of real estate—a *bricks-and-clicks strategy*. Even the online travel agencies Expedia and Travelocity list toll-free numbers and have call service centers so that customers can ask questions and talk to someone about reservations.

The more specialized an agency is, the better its chances of gaining the trust of clients to use its Web site and book components other than air, hotel, and car. Travelers planning to take a bicycle trip in Vietnam, for example, will look online either for a supplier of such trips or for a travel counselor who specializes in bicycle trips or in Vietnam. When they find one, they may eventually book a trip—but not until they have called or e-mailed several times with questions and feel confident about the company or the counselor. (Repeat clients may book directly.)

Who is or is not likely to book online? Past statistics have shown that 82 percent of online travel bookers reported booking airline tickets. Candidates for booking online are those clients who are very familiar with air pricing, are certain of the hotel and car they want, may wish a simple package, and need no extra travel management. But frequent business travelers are likely to turn instead to travel counselors to book their arrangements for several reasons: they make frequent changes to their travel plans, their travel arrangements involve numerous details, and their time is very limited. Leisure travelers are most likely to rely on travel counselors if they are seeking advice on a tour or cruise or if they are not familiar with the many possible choices in the marketplace—the companies, their product lines, reputations, and personalities. They also increasingly are turning to travel counselors when they realise the time and knowledge required to find the best choice of product for their particular needs.

This portrait of today's sales and distribution channels suggests two simple conclusions for travel counselors: to attract clients, they should provide multiple types of contact—in person and by phone, fax, e-mail, or online—so that travelers can be served in the way that is most convenient to them, and they should provide clients with additional valuable services, above and beyond simply making a reservation.

✔ CHECK-UP

Key questions about sales and distribution channels include
✔ Whether to use dual distribution, selling both directly and through intermediaries.
✔ Whether to use multiple sites for sales, such as retail offices, the telephone, and the Internet.
✔ How much to emphasize each site if multiple sites are used.

Travel buyers are good candidates for booking online when they
✔ Are very familiar with airfares.
✔ Know what hotel room and car they want.
✔ Do not need other travel management services.
✔ Trust the Web site host.

How Much to Charge: Setting the Price

■ WHAT PRICING STRATEGIES ARE MOST OFTEN USED BY TRAVEL SELLERS?

To customers, the pricing of a product or service is likely to be the most visible marketing decision. Most businesses buy a product at one price, add a markup, and sell it at the resulting higher price. But how high should the markup be? How is the price determined? Prices, the fourth *P*, reflect a basic marketing decision: Will the company compete on the basis of price, or not?

Pricing Strategies

A company can use two basic pricing strategies.

■ It can treat a product as a commodity and sell it at a price that is the same as, or lower than, its competitors' price. Recall that a *commodity* is something that has a specific value. Gold is a commodity because at a given time an ounce of gold has almost exactly the same value anywhere in the world.

■ A company can aim to differentiate its product by offering something that its competitors do not, and then sell the product at the same price as competitors do—or at a higher price. For example, a beautifully crafted gold necklace is not a commodity; its value is determined by how beautiful and worthwhile people deem it to be, and the seller prices it accordingly.

The second strategy is the one more often used by travel suppliers. Chapters 4–8 discussed the prices that suppliers charge for hotel rooms, cruises, and other products. Suppliers generally aim to distinguish their product from others and price it in a way that meets the needs of particular market segments. (Look again at Table 6.2 on page 153.) Deluxe art tours and windjammer cruises, for example, reflect attempts to offer products that differ from other tours and cruises.

Travel Agencies and Pricing. What about travel agencies? For years, their pricing practices presented an exceptional case. They earned their profits, not from markups, but from commissions, mostly from airline tickets, and the airlines set the commission rate and the final price. Most agencies treated their services as commodities. Each travel agency had the same price for the same product. But the elimination of base commissions for domestic flights forced travel agencies into new marketing strategies.

In order to survive, travel agencies had to find sources of income other than commissions. Since 2002 almost 95 percent of travel agencies charge fees for some or all of their services. (For details about these fees, see Chapter 13.) Many agencies had feared that clients would not be willing to pay fees for their services; after all, clients had long thought of travel agencies as working for them for free. But travelers have accepted these fees and demonstrate a high degree of loyalty to their travel counselors even when they move away or change their travel habits and style.

Most travel agencies now aim to differentiate themselves from the competition and price accordingly. This pricing strategy obviously must fit with the rest of the marketing plan. For example, if an agency's target market is an upscale clientele, it might offer limousine service, personally deliver documents for a vacation, set up golf tee times, offer trips with unique luxuries—and set the price accordingly. But if its target market is student travelers on a budget, the travel agency would not provide those extras, but it would know how to offer low-budget trips that give good value and how to provide the service with cheerful efficiency. In both cases, the price and the service can meet the needs of the target market.

Lessons from Airlines. It is easy to oversimplify pricing strategy and its effect on marketing. One might think that low prices require low costs to a company and that low costs mean a low level of service. But the experience of airlines in recent years shows that business is far more complicated.

After 9/11, the airlines faced a general downturn in the economy, a reduction in passenger loads, and rising fuel costs. Many of the major carriers took drastic cost-cutting measures. They reduced schedules in many markets, eliminated meals on most flights, and laid off thousands of employees. New services were introduced that further reduced the cost to the airline. For example, self-check-in kiosks at airports eliminated the need for airline personnel, reducing labor costs for the airline. Still the major carriers lost money.

While the major airlines—referred to as *legacy airlines*—were struggling financially, the low-cost airlines were growing and thriving. Examples of successful low-cost carriers are Southwest, AirTran, JetBlue, Frontier, and Spirit. But low-cost doesn't necessarily translate into less service. In fact, the successful low-cost carriers focus on providing excellent customer service. JetBlue, for example, offers both leather seats and Direct TV on its flights and prides itself on hiring employees who are highly motivated and service-oriented.

The factors that contribute to the success of the new business model of the low-cost airlines include

- Lower prices, making them attractive to consumers.
- Improved cost efficiency due to using a new single type of aircraft, which reduces the costs for airplane maintenance, training, and labor.
- Service efficiency, by empowering employees to provide good customer service.
- Scheduled service to routes that are profitable.

Surviving and Thriving with Competitive Pricing

Price competition among businesses sometimes leads to dubious methods. For example, if you advertise your lowest price and that price is in fact available for only a few restricted items, which you know will sell out very quickly, is that honest? Often only a very thin line separates advertising your lowest price and practicing a *bait-and-switch,* which means advertising something that is not available. Bait-and-switch methods are deceptive, unethical, and usually illegal.

Travel counselors should take action against suppliers that practice a bait-and-switch, but they should also be sure to distinguish it from legitimate pricing practices. For example, counselors should be able to explain to clients the difference between a restricted airfare and a bait-and-switch. In the first, the product is available if you meet the restrictions; in the second, the product is unavailable no matter what you do.

For travel agencies, being successful in an environment of stiff competition requires that the agency and its travel counselors

- Be more resourceful and efficient than the competition in searching out the best price from suppliers. Even those traveling super-deluxe want value for their money. Being able to give clients the best value for their dollar is a service they will pay for.
- Be able either to offer a lower price than competitors or to differentiate the agency's services (by offering more services or more knowledgeable counselors or unique products or a unique style, for example), and then sell the value of the higher-priced product.
- Establish communication and confidence between client and counselor.
- Keep up-to-date with new marketing ideas, new markets, and new technology.
- Offer something that others cannot. In other words, find a niche and specialize. (See Chapter 11 for more ideas on specialization.)

CHAPTER WRAP-UP

CHAPTER HIGHLIGHTS

Professionals in all sectors of the travel industry deal, in varying degrees, with marketing. Understanding marketing and staying focused on the consumer in all business processes is key to success. In this chapter we considered the basic elements of marketing; here is a review of the objectives with which we began the chapter.

1. **Outline the marketing process and name the four Ps.** The marketing process

aims to create a match between consumers' preferences and a company's products. Making that match requires knowledge not only about products but also about consumers' changing needs and expectations. To gain that knowledge, businesses rely on market research. On the basis of that research, they develop a marketing plan, which includes the selection of a target market and decisions about how to reach that market. In other words, it includes decisions about the marketing mix, or four Ps: product (what product is to be sold), promotion (how the product will be promoted), place (where it will be sold), and price. Each of the four Ps must mesh with the others.

2. **Summarize key decisions that a travel business must make about its product.** Travel businesses must determine the range and mix of travel products that they will offer for sale as well as the level of service they will provide. Segmental analysis provides a tool for determining which products and services are most profitable and should be emphasized. Many travel agencies find that to be competitive they must specialize, developing their own niche. Ultimately, however, travel agencies are selling their service to customers.

3. **Describe the major forms of promotion.** Advertising, sales promotions, public relations, and person-to-person selling are the major forms of promotion, and each has a place in the travel industry. Advertising uses many media, including direct mail, newspapers, yellow pages, magazines, radio, broadcast television, cable television, video, and the Internet.

    Each form of advertising has advantages and disadvantages. Direct mail can be tailored to a specific audience, easily changed, and easily tracked, and it can convey much information. Newspapers can deliver a specific message of short-term validity, but they are discarded quickly. The yellow pages attract only interested consumers. Consumers tend to keep magazines longer, and most are more narrowly targeted than newspapers. Radio and television need much repetition to register with consumers and are usually expensive compared with other forms of advertising. Advertising on the Internet is constantly available, but the messages can be easily lost amid the mass of information. The most common ways for travel businesses to advertise on the Internet are by hosting a Web site and by linking to other Web sites. Cooperative advertising with suppliers is a popular way for travel agencies to increase the cost-effectiveness of their advertising efforts.

4. **Identify the distribution system and selling sites most often used by travel businesses.** Many travel suppliers use a dual distribution system, selling directly to the public and through intermediaries. Most travel agencies traditionally used retail outlets as their place of sale, but today many sales occur in clients' offices, over the telephone, in the seller's home, and on the Internet. The Internet may be used as the sole location for sales, but more often it is an alternative point of sale, as part of a bricks-and-clicks strategy. Decisions about how to use a Web site, like other marketing decisions, should be consistent with the rest of the marketing mix and integrated with the overall marketing strategy.

5. **Describe pricing strategies frequently used by travel suppliers and travel agencies.** Travel suppliers usually aim to distinguish their product from others and then sell the product at the same price as competitors or even at a higher price. But the price must be selected so that the particular product at that price meets the needs of particular market segments. A low price does not necessarily mean a low level of service, as the low-cost airlines have demonstrated. Most travel agencies now aim to differentiate themselves from their competition and price their services so that the price and the service meet the needs of their target market.

KEY TERMS

A list of key terms introduced in this chapter follows. If you do not recall the meaning of these terms, see the Glossary, which begins on page 393.

bait-and-switch
cooperative advertising
customer relationship management (CRM)
customer relationship marketing
direct mail
dual distribution
four Ps

legacy airlines
marketing plan
market research
niche
promotion
public relations
segmental analysis

REVIEW QUESTIONS

1. What is the relationship between a travel agency and a supplier?

2. What are the distribution channels for airline tickets? What benefits can travel agencies offer the consumer that other distribution channels cannot?

3. What makes up a company's image?

4. Name three effective methods of advertising travel. How or when would each be most effective? Name one disadvantage of each.

5. Under what conditions are consumers likely to book on the Internet without other contact with the supplier or travel agency?

CHAPTER 10

Making a Sale

OBJECTIVES

After completing this chapter, you should be able to

1. Describe the agency-supplier relationship, which limits the agency's potential liability.

2. Describe the skills that provide a foundation for effective communication by salespeople.

3. Identify eight steps in making a successful sale.

4. State five questions involved in qualifying a client and three ways to close a sale.

5. Discuss the responsibilities of a travel counselor after the sale has been made.

OUTLINE

THE SALES RELATIONSHIP
- What special characteristics mark the relationship between sellers and buyers in the travel industry?

LEARNING TO COMMUNICATE
- What skills do sellers need in order to communicate effectively?

STEPS IN SELLING
- What steps should sellers take in order to make a sale?
- How do sellers qualify clients, and how do they close a sale?

SERVING THE CUSTOMER
- Why doesn't the seller's job end when the sale is made?

Good salespeople are made, not born. Successful selling comes from knowledge about what is sold and from skills such as asking the right questions. Both the knowledge and the skills can be learned by almost anyone who is motivated to become a successful salesperson.

The successful seller depends on certain techniques, but not on a prepackaged presentation, because each client is different. Some clients make quick decisions and focus on the big picture. Others move slowly, considering every option and everything that could possibly go wrong. Furthermore, the sales presentation must vary with the destination, the product, and the client's needs. The business traveler who wants a flight to a meeting in Phoenix, the young family searching for a cheap way home to Atlanta for Thanksgiving, and the retired couple eager to explore museums in eastern Europe—each of these travelers needs something different from the travel seller for their needs to be met effectively.

Variations in selling is the topic of Chapter 11: Specialized Sales. In this chapter, Making a Sale, we examine characteristics that are shared by almost all selling situations, primarily in an office. We look first at the relationship between the seller and the buyer and at the keys to successful communication, an important part of any sales situation. Then we focus on the basic steps in selling and essentials of customer service. These steps may need to be modified when selling a travel product by telephone, e-mail, and other non-traditional office situations.

The Sales Relationship

■ WHAT SPECIAL CHARACTERISTICS MARK THE RELATIONSHIP
BETWEEN SELLERS AND BUYERS IN THE TRAVEL INDUSTRY?

The job of selling travel is shaped by the fact that the "product" is intangible. Unlike a car or stereo or jewelry, travel arrangements cannot be felt, heard, tasted, or tried before buying. You cannot "kick the tires" of a tour. Buyers may spend thousands of dollars on a product they cannot sample. As a result, even more than other salespeople, those who sell travel must try to make the product or service as tangible as possible and to establish their credibility with the buyer.

CLOSE-UP: ON THE JOB WITH TOM MCLAUGHLIN, OUTSIDE SALES AGENT

Tom McLaughlin works for a medium-size travel agency that recently affiliated with a large chain. Tom was the agency's first outside sales agent. It now has a staff of eight full-time travel counselors and six outside sales agents.

"As an outside sales agent I work strictly on commission and am responsible for my own clients. My agency gives me all kinds of support. When I go on vacation, I know my clients will be well taken care of by someone at the agency; I have access to mounds of information; I attend weekly meetings; I feel like an important part of a team. There is no question that this is the way to go, at least for me.

"I'm a full-time agent like any other, but technically I am not an employee of the agency—I'm an independent contractor. They have no control over me. I make my own hours and handle my clients the way I want. As long as my clients are taken care of, the agency is happy. I follow their office procedures, of course.

"When I began, I received 40 percent of the commission, but as I proved myself and built up my volume, I moved to 50 percent. Recently we changed the commission split to 55 percent for me and 45 percent for the agency. Now the agency has a written commission scale for all outside agents.

"I go into the office three days a week and work at home the rest of the time. I have GDS access at home and can queue in a reservation to the agency, and it does the ticketing. I concentrate on tours, cruises, and custom-made trips, along with groups.

"I give clients I know my home phone, so they can call me direct. This can get a little out of hand sometimes, but if I really want some privacy, I can always turn the answering machine on. I got a call from clients one time who arrived in Mexico and the hotel had no record of them and no room. They had paid in full, and I had sent the hotel the payment in full. I was glad I could be there for them at that moment. I was able to talk to the manager and explain that I had used this hotel for clients before and that I had sent the hotel the payment. The manager gave them a room and later found the reservation misfiled—the name was misspelled. My clients probably could have taken care of this themselves with some persistence, but they didn't go on vacation to worry about this.

"I'll do whatever it takes to get clients. I meet with them in their homes. I often meet with them in the agency in the evening after the office is closed. Actually, I prefer this if they have a major vacation to plan. There are no distractions, and everyone can relax; we can talk as long as we need to. I have some coffee, tea, or wine ready. I'll deliver tickets and documents right to their home if they wish. Again, it gives me a chance to build a personal rapport with them.

"I participate in all the travel benefits of any agent. Theoretically, I could take all kinds of discount trips, more than the salaried agents, but I don't have the time. I usually plan my own fam trips as part of my vacation. I once spent the whole day in Cancún walking from hotel to hotel taking notes on them.

"Sometimes I take a total vacation and just sit by a lake. I've seen a lot of the world, but there is a lot left to see in the future. My clients are getting interested in places not even heard of ten years ago. I'll try to get there first."

The Sellers of Travel

Selling occurs in all facets of the travel industry. Airlines and railroads, motorcoach and car rental companies, hotels and cruise lines—these and other suppliers all hire salespeople. Some take calls from consumers and travel counselors; others are sales representatives (like the one described in Chapter 7) who go out to travel agencies and other organizations to familiarize them with their company's products in hopes of future sales.

Travel sellers may work inside an employer's office or in their own home-based offices, or both. They may be salaried employees or *independent contractors*—people who are not employees but are self-employed, working under contract. Independent contractors are not subject to the same rules and control as employees, and many do not receive the same benefits, such as paid vacation time, sick days, health insurance, or pensions. Chapter 14 discusses some of the special challenges and opportunities that come with working out of the home and with being self-employed.

To some suppliers, the travel agency is a buyer, but travel counselors, of course, are also sellers—they sell to the general public. And, as mentioned earlier, many suppliers sell directly to the traveler, bypassing the travel counselor. The Close-Up on careers in Chapter 1 described some of the specific sales positions in travel agencies. There are leisure and corporate travel counselors, account managers, and **outside sales agents**—people whose job is to bring new clients to the agency, attracting customers outside the agency's existing clientele.

Unlike most retail sellers, travel agencies normally maintain no inventory. Sometimes the agency prepurchases blocks of airline seats, hotel rooms, and so forth for resale; but usually agencies place an order only when the client decides to buy. As a result, travel agencies do not risk money acquiring products they may be unable to sell. But the lack of inventory also has a disadvantage: the agency must usually check with a supplier before selling anything. The agency does not control the inventory; suppliers do.

To some extent, travel suppliers also control who may sell their products. As we discussed in Chapter 1, through the conference system, certain groups of suppliers—such as IATAN (International Airlines Travel Agent Network), ARC (Airlines Reporting Corporation), and CLIA (Cruise Lines International Association)—appoint agencies to sell their products.

The Buyers of Travel

Economists talk about travel as being *discretionary* because the demand is *elastic* and *price-sensitive*. In other words, people tend to travel less when budgets are tight and to travel more during periods of prosperity or when prices are slashed or when an obviously good value is offered. For individual travelers, however, trips are often not discretionary but necessary. A person traveling on business, for example, often has no choice in the matter, and people often feel obliged to travel to attend various family gatherings. (Grandchildren may have done more for the travel industry than the Wright brothers.)

Based on differences such as these, we identified three main types of travel in Chapter 1: *vacation and leisure travel; corporate* or *business travel* (any trip purchased by a business and made for the purposes of the organization); and *VFR travel* (travel to visit friends or relatives). For each type of travel, clients are likely to have different needs.

Discovering those needs can be particularly challenging in the case of leisure travelers. The challenge comes in part from the sheer variety of needs and motives. Leisure travelers may be looking mainly for rest or for intellectual stimulation, for a change in routine or for a religious experience. They may be hoping to meet new friends or to learn more about a specific field by joining a tour led by an expert. Table 10.1 describes some of the many specific activities and benefits that people look for when they take a leisure trip.

Beyond conscious purposes like these, travelers may also be influenced by subtler needs. For example,

- A need for *social status* leads some people to travel to a particular

TABLE 10.1 Motives for Leisure Travel

Motivator	Examples of Possible Destinations
Gambling. Because gambling is now legal to some extent in more than thirty states, it is less likely than in the past to be the sole motivation for travel far from home.	Though casinos have proliferated in many states, Las Vegas grows ever stronger as a destination. Atlantic City and Monte Carlo (on the French Riviera) are other famous gambling venues. Many Caribbean islands and cruise ships are selected because of gambling. Riverboat casinos and motorcoach tours to local gambling attractions are other possibilities.
Shopping. All but the most uncommercialized destinations offer shopping, and it ranks among the top activities of domestic and international travelers, here and abroad.	Shopping tours can be organized to almost anywhere, from the local discount mall to Hong Kong. North American malls known as tourist attractions include the West Edmonton Mall in Edmonton, Canada, and the Mall of America in Bloomington, Minnesota.
Religion. For some, religious beliefs require a visit to a particular religious site. For others, it is an opportunity to visit sites of cultural significance.	Jerusalem, the Vatican, and Mecca are key religious destinations. Others include Lourdes, France, and shrines or special places of worship in many locales.
Sun. The urge to get away from cold, gloomy weather or to find someplace warm is reason enough for some people to travel.	The sunny climates of Florida, California, the Caribbean, and the Riviera attract many visitors.
Food and drink. A desire to sample different cuisines or restaurants is often a secondary reason for traveling, but an interest in taking gourmet or winetasting tours may also be the primary reason for a trip.	Cruises are known for the food they offer. Winetasting tours of the Napa and Sonoma Valleys in California and of French vineyards are very popular.
Entertainment. The chance to sample the nightlife of a city sometimes stands on its own as a reason for traveling.	Las Vegas, Hollywood, New York City, New Orleans, Paris, and Rio are a few of the standouts that can satisfy the party crowd.
Arts. People will travel halfway around the world to experience great art and architecture firsthand. Music, opera, dance, and theater all form separate travel niches.	New York and London are especially known for theater tours. Italy attracts opera buffs; Austria, lovers of classical music.
History and culture. Many people travel in order to trace their own roots or to learn about the past by visiting museums or historical sites.	Ellis Island in New York is of particular interest to the American descendants of immigrants who want to trace their past. Those with broader historical interests might be drawn to the archaeological sites and ruins in Greece, Mexico, Peru, Egypt, or Rome; presidential libraries; Colonial Williamsburg in Virginia; the Freedom Trail in Boston; or battlegrounds of the Civil War.
Collecting countries. Some travelers want to see how many countries they can have stamped in their passports (a chore sometimes, because many countries do not bother to stamp passports).	Don't forget to route these travelers through Liechtenstein and Monaco on that European trip. Try San Marino and Andorra as well.

(continued on next page)

destination or to stay at a particular hotel because many of their friends have been there. The same need leads others to travel where none of their friends has been so that they will stand out as leaders.

■ A need for *self-esteem* motivates some travelers to stay at deluxe hotels where they will be treated with deference and motivates others to search for unusual destinations or opportunities for learning.

■ A need for *self-actualization* leads some people to select travel without concern for what others are doing but with the aim of fulfilling themselves, whether that means trekking alone in the Himalayas, going to cooking school in Tuscany, or traveling to Peru to help in a shelter for the poor.

In short, people with differing motives and needs are likely to be satisfied by different destinations, accommodations, and activities. The successful salesperson learns the products of key industry suppliers, such as tours, cruises, and resorts and is able to ascertain which company's product would be a good match for a particular client's needs.

TABLE 10.1 Motives for Leisure Travel (cont.)

Motivator	Examples of Possible Destinations
Meeting people. Travelers may want to meet the people who live at a destination. Others may hope to travel with newfound friends—a motivator that clients do not always mention but that subtle questions may uncover.	Tours for singles are one possibility. For those wanting to meet people at the destination, consider countries such as Ireland that are known for being friendly to travelers. The Bahamas is one of many countries that has a "People-to-People" program: the Ministry of Tourism will arrange for travelers to meet Bahamians with interests similar to their own.
Personal challenge. For some people, a trip alone to another country constitutes a challenge. For others, this motivation may translate into a desire for an adventure such as climbing a mountain or rafting down dangerous rapids.	The possibilities obviously depend on the particular challenge. For white-water rafting, for example, opportunities include going down the Colorado River through the Grand Canyon, the Zambezi River in Zimbabwe, or rivers in West Virginia, Idaho, Costa Rica, and Chile. Dude ranches in Arizona, Colorado, Montana, and Wyoming provide a challenge many travelers enjoy.
Ecotourism. Broadly defined, this motivation includes the desire to see nature's variety and beauty.	Costa Rica, Belize, the Galápagos Islands, African safaris, and national parks all over the world offer opportunities to satisfy this desire.
Sightseeing. Some people derive satisfaction just from knowing that they have seen famous places for themselves. Many tours are purchased on the basis of the number of sights that will be seen.	The Grand Tour offered by European tour companies as well as the Orlando, Florida, and Washington, D.C., areas offer the opportunity to view a large number of sights within a small area.
Special events. There is an endless list of special events and festivals that bring people together, from those famous around the world to local arts and crafts fairs.	Prime candidates include annual Mardi Gras or Carnival celebrations, particularly in New Orleans, Rio de Janeiro, and Trinidad; the sites of the Summer and Winter Olympics; the Passion Play in Oberammergau, Germany; and the tennis matches at Wimbledon, England.
Getting away from it all; relaxation. Someone with a quiet job may consider an action-packed vacation to be the best way to get away from it all; someone with a stressful, exhausting job may want to go somewhere and lie in a hammock for a week.	It is important to note this motivation but then also to determine the type of destination and activity that will meet the client's needs. For those most interested in peace and quiet, a secluded Caribbean island might be the answer.
Active sports. Skiing, golf, tennis, scuba diving, and windsurfing are among the physical activities that many people enjoy. They will travel for the chance to indulge in a particular sport or for the opportunity to experience it in new and unusual settings.	Switzerland as well as Aspen and Vail, Colorado, should satisfy skiers. Ireland and Myrtle Beach, South Carolina, have much to offer golfers. Some places offer travelers the chance to learn a sport; for example, resorts in the Caribbean teach scuba diving.

The Contract between Buyers and Sellers

Ideally, a sale involves a partnership between the buyer and the seller in which the needs of both are met. The buyer obtains something he or she wants; the seller gets the sale. Neither pressure nor manipulation is needed. Reality, of course, often varies from this ideal.

Occasionally, written contracts regulate the relationship between travel buyers and sellers. For example, car rental companies present a contract for signature. But most contracts are implied. The purchase of an airline ticket, implies assent to the airline's contract with passengers, as discussed in Chapter 4. Tour operators and cruise lines state their contracts in their brochures.

Similarly, the contract between a travel counselor and a client is usually considered to be implied. Basically, the counselor is responsible for

- Confirming reservations, sending deposits, checking times and schedules, issuing correct documents, and so forth.
- Protecting the clients' best interests by negotiating on their behalf with suppliers for the best possible arrangements at the best possible price.
- Verifying clients' citizenship if they are traveling to other nations and notifying them about necessary documents such as passports and visas.
- Conveying other needed information—such as cancellation charges and change fees, any negative information about the contracts with suppliers, financial instability among tour operators or suppliers, risks associated with the destination, and the need for travel insurance.

Beyond these responsibilities, however, the contract for services exists between the client and the *supplier*, except when a travel agency is operating its own tour. The travel counselor usually is only an agent of the supplier and is not responsible for the actions of the supplier.

Travel counselors should make sure that clients understand this relationship. By disclosing the agency-supplier relationship, travel counselors may limit potential liability. They can protect themselves further by publishing a *consumer disclosure notice* (see Figure 10.1). The notice should be

---

Palmetto Travel is acting only in the capacity of an agent for the various suppliers of travel services listed on your travel documents and itinerary. This agency is not liable for any personal injury, property damage, or other loss, accident, delay, or inconvenience caused by any supplier or any party not under its control. Your acceptance of travel documents indicates your understanding and agreement to this.

•••••••••••••

I understand that Palmetto Travel is not the source or supplier of the travel services I have requested and acts solely as an agent for the actual suppliers of such services. I have been advised that the suppliers whose names appear in the information supplied to me are those who are actually responsible for providing the travel services I have purchased. I consent to and request the use of those suppliers and agree not to hold my travel agency responsible should any of these suppliers fail to provide the travel services I have purchased.

Client's Signature   Date

FIGURE 10.1 Disclaimer Statements

Here are two sample disclaimers. When clients refuse to take advice, many travel counselors ask them to sign and date a disclaimer like the second one here.

prominently displayed, inserted in client materials, or printed on invoices, ticket jackets, or itineraries. Agencies seeking additional protection ask that clients sign a disclosure or disclaimer.

No disclaimer, however, can protect a counselor who is negligent. A disclaimer of responsibility for the actions of suppliers does not release the travel counselor from responsibility for checking suppliers and arrangements carefully. A counselor who spots inaccuracies in brochures, for example, should draw the client's attention to them. By offering the brochure to the customer, the salesperson is taking responsibility for its truthfulness. By misrepresenting the supplier's product or by being a party to the supplier's misrepresentation, the travel counselor can become legally liable for any problems that the client encounters. We discuss the legal and ethical responsibilities of travel professionals further in Chapter 16.

In the rest of this chapter and the next, we focus on selling by travel counselors. The variety and flexibility of their products relieve them, to a great extent, of the need to pressure customers. The customer wants to travel. The travel counselor has something the customer wants to buy.

✔ CHECK-UP

Sellers of travel include
✔ Sales representatives from suppliers who sell directly to the public.
✔ Sales representatives from suppliers who sell to travel agencies.
✔ Travel counselors who sell to the general public.

Buyers of travel may be planning
✔ Vacation or leisure travel.
✔ Business or corporate travel.
✔ VFR travel.

The relationship between buyer and seller
✔ Ideally results in a sale that meets the needs of both.
✔ Involves a contract, whether written or implied.

Learning to Communicate

■ WHAT SKILLS DO SELLERS NEED IN ORDER TO COMMUNICATE EFFECTIVELY?

Selling is basically just a particular type of communication. If you communicate well, you are at least halfway on the path toward success in selling. Like other types of communication, effective selling requires the ability to (1) create a good relationship, (2) ask questions and listen to the answers, and (3) present ideas or information.

Creating a Relationship

The keys that unlock the door to effective communication are the desire of other people to talk with you and their trust in what you say. Unfortunately, first impressions are indeed lasting impressions, and a bad first impression can permanently block development of this relationship. Here are some tips for creating an impression to encourage rapport with customers.

- Greet customers when they enter your workplace. Make eye contact and smile. Stand to introduce yourself, and extend your hand to welcome them; perhaps direct them to a seat. If you cannot greet clients immediately because you are on the phone or with another customer, acknowledge their presence and let them know you will be with them soon. Provide reading materials such as brochures while they wait. No one likes to feel ignored.
- Look at your workplace from the customer's viewpoint. Is it tasteful and neat? Does it put clients in a relaxed mood? Does the decor whisper of far-off places?
- Place the client's chair next to yours, if possible, not across the barrier of a desk. Offer the customer a cup of coffee.
- Look at your own appearance. Is it professional?
- If your first contact with a customer is by phone or e-mail, rather than in person, you will want to be especially friendly, personal, and helpful in the hope of leading the customer to more discussions or a face-to-face meeting. Many sales today are made without the client and customer ever seeing one another.

Beyond creating a good impression, establishing a link with your customer will be easier if you

- Begin and end each conversation with a smile. Emotions are often infectious.
- Use the customer's name frequently.
- Don't waste time. If you do not know an answer, offer to research the issue and get back to othe customer. Keep frequently used resources close by.
- Use a moderate tone of voice. Adjust it to the speed at which your customer talks.
- Be positive and empathetic. Try to view clients' interests through their eyes. You may never have skied, for example, but if you can imagine the thrill of skiing down the slopes and the taste of hot chocolate in front of the fireplace, you can get excited about the experience.
- Inspire trust by being prepared.

Asking Questions and Hearing the Answers

For the salesperson, questions give structure to the sales process. Before asking any question, you should have in mind where the answer will take the conversation. By asking effective questions but letting the client do the talking, you can lead the conversation toward the desired end.

Three types of questions are useful in different circumstances.

- *Close-ended questions* invite precise answers like "Yes" or "No" or simple facts. They narrow the possibilities and yield specific information.
- *Open-ended questions* invite answers that include whatever facts, opinions, or feelings the client thinks are relevant. Open-ended questions typically begin with *what, how,* or *why;* for example, "What do you have in mind?" "What kind of vacations have you enjoyed before?" "Why do you like the idea of a cruise?" These questions encourage people to "open up," perhaps revealing their attitudes, tastes, preferences, and needs as they discuss the topic.
- *Feedback questions* confirm details that have emerged in the conversation. For example, "So you want a resort with a very sociable feeling, where you can meet people. Is that right?" The other person can simply respond, "Yes," offer minor corrections, or object.

Questioning, of course, should never sound like cross-examination. Effective questioners try to

- Weave their questions into the conversation.
- Combine different types of questions.
- Reflect the client's own language in their questions.
- Phrase questions to elicit a positive answer.
- Limit their own talking. Clients must be allowed to talk freely, even as you guide the conversation into relevant areas.

The purpose of asking questions is to hear the answers, but research suggests that the average listener grasps the significance of only about 25 percent of what was said. Effective listening requires effort. Here are some tips for hearing what another person actually says.

- Shut out distractions. Don't take incoming calls while with a client.
- Don't interrupt, even if the person pauses for a long breath.
- Take notes.
- Keep an open mind. To avoid missing what clients are saying, don't let what they say or how they say it irritate you, and don't jump to conclusions.
- Use verbal and nonverbal signals to indicate you understand and are paying attention. Nodding, eye contact, and phrases such as "I see" all indicate that you are listening.
- Listen for inflections and watch the client's **body language,** which consists of nonverbal signals such as facial expressions, posture, and gestures. These nonverbal signals reveal attitudes and biases; Table 10.2 describes some examples.
- *Recap*—that is, review key points of the conversation.
- Get the client's contact information. Don't let someone leave your office or end a telephone conversation without doing so.

Presenting Ideas and Information

Beyond questioning others to gain information, effective communicators also present their own information persuasively. They know how to make their points both clear and appealing. Here are some techniques that will help you do the same.

TABLE 10.2 Body Language in the United States

Message	Gesture
Defensiveness	Holding arms cross in front of chest Crossing legs tightly Interposing a shoulder or an object such as a handbag or papers
Frustration and aggression	Making clasped fist Holding wrist of fisted hand Holding fist to chin
Thoughtfulness, attempt to reach a decision	Touching chin or cheek Stroking chin Pinching bridge of nose
Readiness to buy	Nodding and smiling Leaning in with a relaxed arm and open hand Leaning back and relaxing

- Adopt the words and style used by your listener. Avoid using jargon the other person might not understand; use everyday language instead. Does your listener really know what round-trip transfers are? He or she will surely understand if you say, "You will be taken from the airport directly to your hotel and back again at the end of your stay in time for your flight."
- Elicit feedback throughout your presentation, mixing questions with your comments. For example, you might ask, "Does that sound good to you?"
- Be prepared with two ideas, but present only one idea at a time.
- Do whatever you can to make the intangible tangible. Use words that create mental pictures; give examples; use visual aids if possible.

In the next section we describe how to apply these techniques to the challenge of selling travel.

✔ CHECK-UP

Successful communicators know how to
✔ Create rapport with listeners.
✔ Ask effective questions.
✔ Listen carefully.
✔ Present ideas and information clearly and persuasively.

Some of the elements needed to develop rapport include
✔ Developing a good impression through your appearance, surroundings, and manner.

✔ Showing interest in the other person.
✔ Demonstrating empathy.
✔ Inspiring trust.

Three types of questions are
✔ Close-ended questions.
✔ Open-ended questions.
✔ Feedback questions.

Steps in Selling

■ WHAT STEPS SHOULD SELLERS TAKE IN ORDER TO MAKE A SALE?

■ HOW DO SELLERS QUALIFY CLIENTS, AND HOW DO THEY CLOSE A SALE?

Every salesperson needs to know what to say, when to say it, and how to say it. So far, we have considered how to say things effectively. In this section we focus on what to say in a sales presentation and when to say it.

In a general way, the steps in selling outlined in Chapter 1 provide the answer; they lay out a framework for progressing toward the sale. Figure 10.2 reviews these steps.

Good salespeople follow a structure similar to the one spelled out in Figure 10.2, but they vary it as necessary to respond to individual situations. Sometimes, for example, clients know exactly what they want and you can go directly from step 3 to step 7, *closing* the sale, which means moving the customer to make a commitment to buy. Often, steps in the cycle must be revisited. For example, you might go from presenting a recommendation (step 5) to dealing with objections (step 6) and then back to presenting a new recommendation (step 5).

Steps 1–3: Acquiring Information

"Hi, do you have any information on Mexico?" Most conversations between a travel counselor and a client start something like this, with a potential customer asking for information. Travel counselors should view these requests as evidence of a desire to travel. If you simply answer the questions without initiating your own presentation, you are doomed to frustrating days with few sales. In this case, for example, you might say something like,

> *Yes, we certainly do. Please have a seat. What got you interested in Mexico? What part have you been thinking about visiting?*

Step 1: Identifying Qualified Clients. Of course, not everybody who contacts you is ready to make a purchase. Counselors need to *qualify* the client; that is, determine how ready and able the client is to make a purchase. Thus a first goal of the sales presentation is to ask five qualifying questions:

1. When would you like to go?
2. Do you know exactly where you would like to go?
3. How many are in your travel party, and who are they?
4. How long do you plan to be away?

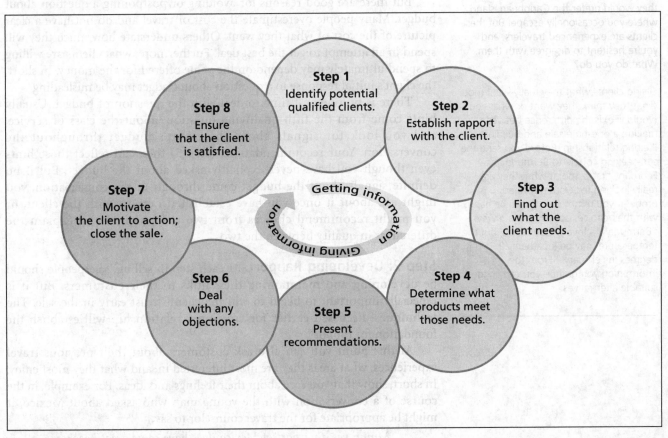

FIGURE 10.2 Steps in Selling

Not every sale requires these eight steps, and sometimes the salesperson must cycle back through some steps. But understanding these steps and keeping them in mind should help you learn to communicate effectively with clients, to meet their needs, and to make the sale. While these eight basic steps work well in a face-to-face selling situation, the counselor will have to modify them if selling by telephone or e-mail.

5. What kind or class of service do you need? You might answer this question by saying, "What kinds of hotels do you usually like to stay in? Should we look for the same type this time?" or "Is this a special occasion?"

Besides indicating whether the person qualifies as a potential customer, these questions should elicit information that will help you narrow the search for the services the customer needs. By starting with these questions, you can avoid getting involved in long inconclusive discussions or confusing the client with too many possibilities.

Occasionally clients immediately announce precisely what they want, or they are eager to book the trip once they have answered the initial questions. In these cases there is no reason to linger on other selling steps; in fact, you may lose the sale if you do not move to the closing. Confirm the information you have received, and be certain that the proposed arrangements meet the customer's needs. If they do, close the sale (step 7).

The Budget Question. Some salespeople like to add a sixth qualifying question, one about the budget, such as "How much do you want to spend?" or "Do you have a total budget in mind?" The answer allows the seller to focus quickly on the appropriate arrangements. Also, asking about the budget helps the salesperson avoid embarrassing or alienating customers by suggesting arrangements that cost far more, or far less, than they intend to spend.

But there are good reasons for avoiding or postponing a question about budget. Many people overestimate the cost of travel and do not have a clear picture of the cost of what they want. Others understate how much they will spend in an attempt to get the best deal. Furthermore, what clients are willing to spend ultimately may depend on the value offered for the money. In short, the client's initial response to a question about budget may be misleading.

There is no one best time to deal with the question of budget. Usually hints come from the fifth qualifying question, about the class of service, and you look for signals about the client's budget throughout the conversation. Your recommendations (step 5) then can reflect those hints even though you have never explicitly asked about the budget. But if no definite signals about the budget come through in the conversation, you might ask about it once you have established rapport with the client, or you might recommend choices from two price ranges and explain the differences in quality between the two.

Step 2: Developing Rapport. At each step in selling, salespeople should be developing and maintaining their links to their customers. But it is especially important to begin to win the client's trust early in the sale. The techniques discussed earlier for creating a relationship will establish the foundation for rapport.

At this point you can also ask customers about their previous travel experiences, what areas they are most interested in, and what they most enjoy. In short, show that you care about their feelings and ideas. For example, in the course of a conversation with the young man who asked about Mexico, it might be appropriate for the travel counselor to say,

> Mmm, yes, that part of Mexico does have some great beaches. It sounds as if you've done some thinking about it.

Try to develop rapport in a way that comes naturally to you, with sincere statements. Select one of the client's statements with which you can identify. Remember that trust is inspired by self-confidence, and self-confidence comes from being up-to-date about what you are selling and from knowing the answers, or where to find the answers.

"Send us to Bermuda," says the middle-aged couple across your desk; they are here to plan their annual February getaway. "We're in the mood for an island in the sun." You know that Bermuda won't be as warm as they would like in February, and you're sure they would prefer the Caribbean island where you occasionally escape. But these clients are experienced travelers, and you're hesitant to disagree with them. What do you do?

Giving clients what they really want (not what they think they want or what you would like) is the difference between making a one-time sale and building a lifelong relationship. Before you send the sun-seeking couple to Bermuda in February, first pinpoint what they are really looking for; you may need to probe. If you're not sure they'll be happy with their choice, politely explain why: "Bermuda is a lovely destination, but the temperature may be less than 70 degrees in February." From the information you gather, you can suggest suitable alternatives.

Step 3: Identifying Wants and Needs. Usually clients' answers to the qualifying questions do not tell you everything you need to know. To pinpoint their needs more precisely, you need to ask additional questions.

Chapters 4–8 identified many of these questions. Recall, for example, the discussions of what travel counselors should ask when selling an airline ticket (in the Close-Up on selling on page 100); when qualifying a client for a car rental (in the Close-Up on page 136); when finding a lodging for a client and making a reservation (page 163); and when making a cruise reservation (page 195). These questions should give you specific facts about your clients' needs.

In addition, in many cases you should elicit more personal information in order to understand the clients' motives, needs, and wants. For example, if your clients do not know where they want to go for a vacation, you should find out why they are taking a vacation and what they would like to do. Most travelers have a mixture of reasons and motives. For clients who just know they want to go somewhere in the Caribbean, for example, you might ask them to rank the importance of the beach, sightseeing, food, nightlife, and shopping in order to narrow the choice of islands.

Depending on the nature of the trip, you might try to develop an even richer understanding of the client. Is he or she motivated by a need for social status or self-esteem or self-actualization? Or where does the client fall on the psychographic spectrum shown in Figure 1.3 (page 14)? Does he or she tend to be a venturer (outgoing, confident, eager to lead the pack) or a dependable (valuing familiarity and comfort)? To understand these characteristics of your clients, you might ask what they did for their last vacation, why they chose it, and whether they enjoyed it. "My friends told me it was just great!" and "I wanted to visit before it was discovered by hordes of people" indicate quite different personalities.

In these early steps, focus on the client and avoid making suggestions until the complete picture emerges. Ask close-ended, open-ended, and feedback questions as we described earlier. Listen carefully and recap the conversation. For example, this step in the sale to the young man who was interested in Mexico might end with the travel counselor saying,

> OK, so let me review this. You're planning to go in late January for eight or nine days, and you want one of the quieter beach locations, one that is pretty new. You don't need a lot of fancy nightlife, but you want at least something to do at night, and you do want a nice place to stay because you need a real mental break. Does that sound about right?

Step 4: Matching a Product to the Client

So far, our hypothetical travel counselor has greeted the client, qualified him, and learned a great deal about what he wants and needs. What next?

Experienced counselors may have just the right recommendations for a trip, but even those who do not know what to recommend should be able to make the sale. They can look for help from several sources, including

- Colleagues. Professionals in all fields regularly consult one another. Also, many agencies keep a file of reports by travel counselors about their familiarization trips.
- Reference materials—in print, online, on DVDs, or on other media.

- Clients. Many agencies solicit and file clients' reactions to their trips. Also, do not be afraid to ask well-traveled clients for their opinions about destinations and suppliers.
- Suppliers. Airlines may help with some questions. Good tour operators try to help travel counselors match clients to their tours and packages, many of which are extremely cost-effective for the client and both time- and labor-saving for the counselor.

As you consider what arrangements will suit a client, remember that not even the wealthy want to be overcharged. Clients seek a price that represents a good *value*. Value, of course, is subjective. To the couple who want to celebrate their twenty-fifth anniversary by returning to their honeymoon hotel in Hawaii, even a very high price may represent an excellent value. Low-cost arrangements that do not meet a client's needs do not represent good value. Sometimes clients may be willing to compromise or eliminate choices because of the price, but they should understand what they are sacrificing.

Many clients say they are looking for a deal. A "deal" does not mean a low price; it means an excellent value for whatever price is paid. A great price for a week in Hawaii that buys a motel-like accommodation in an urban area three blocks from the beach may or may not fit a particular client's needs. Clients get a deal whenever they get excellent value for their money and receive the product that serves their needs and wants.

Usually suppliers prominently advertise their lowest fares or rates. Clients may not note the restrictions that apply. For example, the lowest hotel and car rates are often available only on certain days; the lowest-priced tours, only at the least desirable hotels; and the least expensive cruises, only on certain sailings and for few cabins. Counselors should check and explain the restrictions and suggest alternatives if the client cannot meet them.

Step 5: Presenting Recommendations

Once you are confident that you know what a client wants and that your suggestions will meet those desires, make a recommendation confidently and enthusiastically. In the case of the man who wanted to go to Mexico, the counselor eventually suggested a choice: either Ixtapa or Huatulco, described the features and benefits of each, and had him decide. Clients who are reluctant to choose ("Well, which one do you recommend?") can be gently urged in the direction that you think might be best.

When presenting recommendations, give each possibility its due. Do not eliminate all options. At some point, the real world—in which there are full flights, full hotels, full tours, and full cruises—will intrude. No recommendation should be so exclusive that the client will cancel the trip if one element cannot be booked.

To make your recommendation persuasive, remember to avoid jargon. For example, you might have read a magazine article about Huatulco when it was first being developed as a new resort and say,

> *Huatulco is a new tourism development with new properties. Growth of its infrastructure is just in the inception stage. There are likely to be availabilities for your clients.*

When you give the same information to your client, though, you might say something like the following:

ON THE SPOT

Mr. White, a repeat business client, has asked for help in choosing a hotel. The travel counselor says, "Oh, I'd really recommend the Belvedere rather than the Hartford. It's much more centrally located. The rooms are bigger, and the airport limousine stops right at the door. The Hartford overlooks a smelly paint factory and really doesn't look very nice in this brochure. I don't think you'd want to stay there." What's wrong with this recommendation?

What happens if the Hartford turns out to be the only downtown hotel available when Mr. White wants to stay?

*Huatulco may have that fresh feeling you're looking for. In the
future, the area may get millions of tourists, but right now few
have heard of it. Let's see if there's something available.*

Furthermore, to ensure your effectiveness, incorporate the client's own statements or refer to them. Use your words to paint a picture of your recommendation, as Figure 10.3 describes.

Also use maps, brochures, videos, and the Internet when applicable. In fact, maps are absolutely necessary when planning a wide-ranging itinerary. Remember that brochures paint a rosy picture and that the camera can mislead. Videos can either whet travelers' appetites at an early stage or keep them enthused later. Printouts from Web sites can also keep interest up and may help finalize a sale.

These visual aids are just that—aids. They need to be used at the right time; they are not a substitute for your presentation. Bring out a limited number of brochures (probably two at most), ones that are appropriate and familiar to you and for companies with which your agency has a track record and a preferred supplier relationship. For more specific advice on using brochures and other visual aids, refer to the discussions on pages 73 and 221.

One other guideline is important when presenting a recommendation: link the recommendation to the benefits the client seeks. This is worth some further comment.

Translating Features into Benefits. Clients may be impressed by features, but they will not be motivated to purchase them unless the benefits are clear. As we discussed in Chapter 1, a *feature* is an inherent characteristic of a product or service; a *benefit* is the positive result that a feature brings to a particular client. Effective salespeople translate features into benefits, as Table 10.3 illustrates.

Personalize this translation by restating the client's wants and needs and then relating the specific benefits of features to those wants and needs. For example, a travel counselor might say, "You mentioned that you'd like a relaxing vacation on a beach. This place has its own private beach, giving you the tranquility you're looking for."

Different people may buy the same product because of different features and benefits. For example, one person chooses a particular cruise in order to relax; another, because it stops at interesting ports. Even a single feature can offer varying benefits to different people. Some travelers take a half-day sightseeing tour of Hong Kong because they do not want to try to find places

FIGURE 10.3

Selling a Recommendation

"If your client imagines himself on a trip," writes Marc Mancini, "he's more likely to actually take that trip." You can help clients imagine themselves on a trip by painting mental pictures that put clients at their center. Here are some tips for how to create such pictures.

- **Use visual words to give form to the picture.**

  "When you see this magnificent ship in port, you'll know you're about to begin a very special experience."

- **Stress your enthusiasm.**

  "I was really excited when I found it."

- **Use action words to make the picture move.**

  "You can play volleyball in the sun and enjoy food prepared by a world-famous chef, as you sail up the coast."

- **Comment on the picture, describing exactly the benefits it brings.**

  "I can get you a cabin with its own veranda. That way, you can have your own private view of Alaska's amazing scenery as it passes by."

- **Elicit other senses to make the picture real.**

  "When you get to Glacier Bay, you'll have the incredible experience of hearing huge chunks of ice thundering into the water right in front of you. And there's nothing to compare with that bracing air."

Source: Adapted with permission from Marc Mancini.

TABLE 10.3 Translating Features into Benefits

Features of a Convention Center	Possible Benefits
Small and independent site Unique design and furnishings Intimate atmosphere	Personalized service
Remote location Encourages camaraderie Refreshing tranquility	Few distractions On-site recreation activities for spouses and free time
All meals included	No need to search for restaurants No need to monitor budget for meals
Daytime and nighttime activities	Wide variety of things to do both day and night Can be as active or lazy as you like

on their own; others do so because they want a quick orientation to the city before they begin their own exploration. Emphasize the benefits appropriate to the individual. Knowing which benefits to suggest to each client comes from careful qualifying and listening.

Dangers to Avoid. What you do *not* say to your customers is also important.

Among statements to avoid are

- *Exaggerations, overgeneralizations, and lies.* Avoid saying things like "It's the greatest value in New Orleans"; "It's always lovely at this time of year"; "You don't have to worry about malaria because you'll never catch it in a week." Do not generalize about things you know nothing about: "This hotel is just great. I'm sure you're going to love it."
- *Guarantees of enjoyment by referring to another client's experience:* "I know you'll enjoy this trip because Mr. and Mrs. Jones did." Mr. and Mrs. Jones may have liked it for reasons totally unimportant to the current client.
- *Guarantees of anything beyond your control,* such as the weather, the service, or even the client's reaction. "You'll love it" is a dangerous expression.
- *Apologies for circumstances beyond your control.* Constant apologizing creates the same effect as constant negatives. It also implies that you are responsible to some degree.
- *Overpromises.* If you say you are going to do something, do it.
- *Knocks on the competition.* Clients might mention that another agency did not give good service. The comment should not be answered directly, and your next sentence should focus on the client's needs and perhaps the kind of good service he can expect from your company without denigrating your competitor.
- *Use of the phrase "No problem."* This phrase suggests that no great effort will be taken because none is needed. But also avoid giving the impression that the trip is extraordinarily difficult or likely to be mishandled.
- *The word "cancel."* Instead, suggest that clients can change reservations should the need arise.

Recapping. The recap pulls together details from the conversation and resolves any confusion. It reduces the possibility that a disappointed client may later accuse the seller of not having explained things clearly. An accurate recap also starts the client toward saying "Yes" and can lead easily into an offer to book the trip.

The recap may uncover disagreements or objections; resolving these is the next step, step 6. If the client agrees with the recap, you can proceed to step 7, closing the sale, or first suggest upgrading or adding to the arrangements.

Selling Up and Cross-Selling

If the client agrees with your recommendation, you might increase the scope of the sale with a little effort, through selling up and cross-selling. *Selling up* means upgrading, changing to a more expensive or inclusive version of a product. For example, you might suggest

- An upgraded hotel or an upgraded hotel room. If a client is paying $2,500 for a trip, would an upgraded hotel room with a view of the ocean for $250 more be worthwhile? According to research by ASTA (American Society of Travel Agents), clients splurge most often on lodging. Many clients will be disappointed later if you did not offer this option.

- An outside rather than an inside stateroom on a cruise, or a cabin on a higher deck or with a more central location.
- Larger cars for people who may need the extra space.
- First-class or business-class airfare to those already paying a high nondiscounted fare.

Clients who enjoy their trip may grumble about the cost of things in general but will give you credit for helping them plan a fantastic trip. Suggest an upgrade. Clients will appreciate it.

Cross-selling—selling additional products or services—is another way of increasing a sale while providing more service. Ask simple questions such as, "Do you need a hotel room when you arrive?" and "Do you need a car when you arrive?" Clients may not even be aware that you can arrange tickets for attractions in advance. Or they may forget to ask for services and then make arrangements on their own later, resulting in no commissions for the agency and often higher costs for the clients.

Other opportunities for cross-selling include

- Travel insurance, discussed in Chapter 11. Every client is a candidate for some type of travel insurance.
- Transfer service from an airport to a hotel or ship.
- City and local tours.
- Tickets for theaters or museums, restaurant reservations.
- Stopovers en route to or from the destination. A poor air connection can sometimes be made into a stopover that enhances the entire itinerary.
- Shore excursions for cruise passengers—some private or personalized to meet clients' specific interests.
- Supplementary products and services such as passport pictures, luggage, and travel books. Many travel agencies offer these items in their offices or in conjunction with suppliers.

Step 6: Dealing with Objections

Be prepared for objections to your recommendations. When they arise, take a positive attitude and avoid becoming defensive. Listen carefully, and then evaluate the objection.

Sometimes objections arise from the client's ignorance, prejudice, or misunderstanding of a recommendation. In these cases, try again to explain the recommendation. At other times, objections arise because of real problems with the recommendation. In these cases, suggest alternatives.

Sometimes objections are hidden. For example, if you end a conversation by offering clients exactly what they want and they still seem unwilling to commit, price is almost certainly the principal objection. Suggest ways in which the cost could be reduced without sacrificing too many benefits.

Often clients feel they must consult a spouse or traveling companion before committing to final arrangements. You should fully describe the arrangements and their benefits so that the client can explain the trip positively at home; then set a date to call back.

Sometimes, after objections have been met and resolved, a customer still resists the sale. Several kinds of resistance need to be recognized. One is guilt. Sometimes clients suddenly feel guilty about spending money on themselves. By reviewing how the suggested arrangements meet their needs, you can help them overcome any guilt. And as an antidote to price shock, focus on value by stressing benefits.

Resistance may also be a maneuver by the client. Some clients view the conversation as a kind of negotiation and look for one last concession. They need to feel that they had the last word and struck the best possible deal. As a result, they might raise last-minute objections in the form of requests for impossible guarantees or unusual services. Generally, these objections are not serious; consider them a signal to move forward and offer to book.

Clients may also resist a recommendation because they feel pressured. Most people prefer to delay decisions, especially those that cost money. Some counselors think they are doing their clients a favor by advising them to go home and think it over. Given such advice, most leave. But making a decision is usually followed by a great sense of relief and expectation.

If a client raises unexpected resistance that seems to spring from a desire to postpone a decision, stress that the decision has been reached by mutual agreement. Point out how the arrangements meet the client's needs. Explain that a decision now can avoid disappointment later. In this way, you can help clients overcome the last psychological barrier to a decision.

Step 7: Closing the Sale

Surveys indicate that salespeople fail to ask for the client's business in up to 90 percent of all sales situations. Perhaps they worry about appearing pushy. Yet a missed sale benefits neither buyer nor seller. Closing a sale requires two separate decisions: when to do it and how to do it.

When to Close. Unfortunately, the right moment to close is often unclear. Table 10.2 on body language included several key *buying signals,* signs that the customer is ready to make the purchase. Signals that the client is *not* ready to buy include

- Frowning and avoiding eye contact.
- Leaning back with arms crossed in front.
- Fidgeting.
- Refusing to touch or look at a brochure, flipping idly through it, or reading it very closely (indicating a need for more information).

But far more sales are lost by delaying the closing than by offering to book too soon. Clients are often ready to commit before salespeople attempt to close the sale.

You might offer to book several times and learn much from the attempts. Indeed, counselors may uncover objections or questions only when they try to close the sale.

If a client cannot answer essential questions even after careful questions and recommendations, offer a tentative or conditional reservation (see Table 10.4). Then set a date by which the client must confirm the conditional arrangements, and offer to contact the client on that date. Note, however, that some promotional fares prohibit the use of conditional reservations.

How to Close. There are techniques, procedures, and even specific phrases that can be used to close a sale effectively.

- *Offer to book.* For example, you might say, "Well, what if we see if space is available and hold a reservation while you decide?"
- *Give choices.* You might ask, "What do you think? Do you want to leave on the week of the 12th or the 19th?" or "Well, did you decide on the El Sol or the La Maya hotel?" Do not state the choice as "Would you like to book the cruise or not?"
- *Ask for the preferred method of payment.* "Will that be check or credit card?"

A form of the alternate-choice technique, this approach should be used when you are fairly certain of the booking.

- *Compliment the client.* "I think you've made a very good decision in picking the package to Fiji." If the client has not yet made the decision, he or she will let you know. Otherwise, you may proceed with the booking.
- *Put a clock on the client,* indicating a time limit. "Get it while supplies last" and "Last day of the sale" are popular advertisements in other businesses; equivalent statements in the travel industry are often literally true. If the client does not book now, the space may not be available tomorrow, or the price might be different.
- *Check availability.* Nine times out of ten, what is available now might not be available tomorrow. Thus this approach leads into the technique of putting a clock on the client.

Book while the client is there. If you determine availability via your computer or speak to the supplier on the phone while the client is present, your information gains credibility. If there is any change from the information in an ad or brochure, hearing it firsthand helps. For example, while on the telephone to the cruise line, you might say to the client, "The $799 lead price is currently sold out. They have two cabins left in the $899 category. Shall I put a hold on one for you for a few days to protect you?"

End your sale on a positive note. Thank the clients for their time, assure them that the purchase (if made) is a good one, shake hands, use their names, and be prepared to follow up with a phone call, note, or mailer if needed.

Step 8: Ensuring Customer Satisfaction

Once the sale has been closed, each detail must be processed and monitored. This may be as simple as issuing and filing an airline ticket with an invoice and itinerary or as complicated as carrying out many steps for each part of a long itinerary. In all cases, processing must be done in an exact and timely manner.

Even the most conscientious person will occasionally make a mistake. Mentally walk through the client's itinerary day by day. Check everything twice, particularly documents arriving from suppliers. Some common mistakes include

- Routing clients into one airport in a particular city and out of another without realizing it. Clients may arrive at Orly Airport in Paris with a connection departing from Charles de Gaulle Airport on the other side of the city.

TABLE 10.4 Dealing with Unanswered Qualifying Questions

Qualifying Questions	Response If Question Is Not Answered
Where?	Review needs with the client. Provide more information. Make suggestions. Set up an appointment for the future.
When?	Make transportation reservations (air, cruise, etc.) on the most likely dates, provided there is no cancellation penalty.
How long?	Make definite reservations for outbound transportation, and reserve on the most likely return date, or leave the return temporarily open if that option is allowed.
When and how many?	Make reservations for the greatest number likely to travel. It is always easier to cancel one person from a party than to get a duplicate booking for another traveler later on.
What kind or class of service?	Ask more questions. Provide more information.

- Making a car or hotel reservation for the wrong day. Clients who depart New York in the evening on November 1 will require a car rental or hotel reservation in London on November 2, the day the flight arrives.
- Assuming that clients know that passports are required for overseas travel.
- Failing to mention the need for a visa or proof of citizenship.

Complicated itineraries require a file for correspondence and documents. Even if all communications and reservations were handled via the computer and a complete electronic file exists, most agencies require a hard-copy file to be kept on bookings. Once the trip is over, the file becomes the reference once the current online reservations are wiped out. The records of previous trips constitute the most basic data for the agency's marketing research.

Processing the sale and record keeping are just the most obvious tasks necessary after closing the sale. Successful people in all facets of business know "It isn't over 'til it's over." And in the travel industry, it isn't over even when it is over. Once the sale is made, you must work to keep it made. Also, clients may cancel or change their reservations. And once their trip is completed, follow-up is essential: contact the client; discuss the trip; be sure the client was satisfied. Ask for referrals and even pique their interest in next year's trip. Repeat and referral clients are the lifeblood of a successful agency.

In fact, giving good customer service by following up, keeping in touch, and anticipating a client's needs often separates the successful counselor from the average one. The extra thought shown to a client or the prompt handling of an unexpected problem may earn the client's loyalty for years to come.

✔ CHECK-UP

Techniques for presenting recommendations effectively include the following:
- ✔ Try to paint a mental picture of the recommendation.
- ✔ Translate features into benefits sought by the client.
- ✔ Use visual aids as sales tools.
- ✔ Be prepared for selling up and cross-selling.

After the sale is made, ensure customer satisfaction by
- ✔ Processing and monitoring the sale precisely.
- ✔ Keeping accurate records.
- ✔ Dealing with changes.
- ✔ Checking with the client after the trip.

Serving the Customer

■ WHY DOESN'T THE SELLER'S JOB END WHEN THE SALE IS MADE?

Clients are longing for good service, and most are willing to pay for it. They will be loyal to salespeople who go the extra mile. The possible services that travel counselors might provide leisure travelers, for example, are limited only by their imagination; a few include
- Providing destination information from national tourism offices.
- Saving and offering articles about their destinations, from both print and online sources.
- Sending birthday, anniversary, or welcome-home cards.

It is up to the travel agency or supplier to develop a marketing strategy that defines and supports the services that salespeople are expected to provide, as we discussed in Chapter 9. Not all companies choose to emphasize customer service. Whatever the company's policies, though, customers are likely to expect certain basic benefits from a travel agency; these are our focus in this section.

Following Through and Following Up

In the travel business, a sale may last several weeks or even several months. Clients often pay deposits months ahead of time to ensure space on popular trips; final payment on major trips is usually required 60 days before departure or even earlier.

Keeping in touch with the client throughout this process is a subtle but effective reminder that the agency is keeping an eye on the client's plans. In many cases there may be information from the supplier, visa forms, or receipts to send to the client. If there has been no contact for a month or two, drop a brief note or e-mail or a brochure or newspaper clipping about the destination.

Be sure to tell clients when documents and tickets are expected. If they are not received by that date, check with the supplier to make sure they are on their way and then call to reassure the client. If you wait for the client to call, you may lose some of the client's confidence, especially without a ready answer.

Customers must also be advised of their responsibility to obtain visas and immunizations and to be aware of restrictions that might affect their freedom of movement. Always identify who sets these requirements (a government, an airline), and tell clients how they can easily comply. Some travel agencies provide all clients with an information packet about these requirements (discussed in Chapter 2) and the places to contact with questions or problems. Exceptional agencies go further and provide travel tips and checklists of tasks to complete in preparation for a trip. The tips can include information about the weather, clothing and packing recommendations, suggested readings about the area, and local currency and exchange rates.

Whenever clients visit an agency, whether or not they book, they should walk out with at least three items: (1) your card, (2) either brochures stamped with the agency's information or rates and notes on the agency's letterhead, and (3) a clear understanding of what is going to happen next. Are you going to call? Are you going to send information? Perhaps you and the clients agreed that they will e-mail you with a decision. Maybe you will be calling them to set up a second appointment, by which time you will compile a list of recommendations. Perhaps they are going to send you a deposit. Whatever is agreed to as the next step, follow up on it—whether or not the clients do.

Dealing with Changes

Additional services may be necessary when clients want to change or cancel aspects of their booking. Changes are part of every travel counselor's daily responsibilities. In fact, the ability to make changes quickly and efficiently is one of the basic reasons consumers—especially business travelers—use travel agencies.

Clients may choose to add arrangements, exchange one arrangement for another (such as a change in departure date or class of service), or cancel without rebooking. Before altering arrangements, make sure that the changes are in the client's best interests. In particular,

- Ask the reasons for the changes.
- Restate the benefits of the original choice.
- Quote rates for the new favorite.
- Inform the client that the new choice may not be available.

Never cancel a reservation until the alternative has been confirmed.

Changes may also be involuntary. Insurance can protect the client's investment in the trip in many cases; it is discussed in Chapter 11. A cancellation or change may be necessary because of

- Strikes. Usually, alternatives that provide the same, or virtually the same, arrangements are available. Because an airline strike affects many travelers, speed is vital to secure alternative arrangements for your clients.
- Bankruptcies by suppliers. Travel counselors have the responsibility to choose suppliers carefully in an effort to protect the client. Whenever possible, clients should pay for travel by credit card so that they will not be charged for services they do not receive. However, some agencies now charge a fee for using a credit card.
- Political upheavals, epidemics, and natural catastrophes like earthquakes and hurricanes. Travel counselors should keep up-to-date on political upheavals and threatening weather forecasts. As discussed in Chapter 2, the State Department provides information about current conditions around the world.

Many agencies have specific policies and procedures to help counselors decide how to deal with these situations.

Occasionally an emergency develops while the client is traveling. In most instances, tour operators, airlines, or U.S. foreign service officers take the lead in aiding affected passengers. U.S. embassies and consulates are charged with the responsibility, within reason, of helping citizens who get into trouble while traveling abroad. But in some cases, it is the travel agency's duty to help. The agency may be the only contact that a cruise line, airline, or tour operator has for a client who becomes seriously ill or dies. Travel counselors may need to help relatives make arrangements to transport a sick client or a client's remains back home.

The American embassy or consular office will know local requirements and costs for such arrangements and will send an official to mediate with the host government. The Citizen's Emergency Center in Washington, D.C., can help contact U.S. officials abroad.

Handling Complaints

Travel counselors are likely to have little or no control over the elements of a trip once the client departs. Still—along with flight attendants, customer service representatives, hotel desk clerks, the cruise director's staff, and tour directors—they are part of the front line that receives the full force of customers' complaints.

Clients are likely to complain whenever they find discrepancies between what they thought they had bought and what they received. The source of the problem might lie with the supplier, the travel counselor, or even the client. Whatever the source, the counselor should listen to the complaint.

When faced with a complaint,

- Be courteous. Courtesy often defuses complaints; rudeness provokes them. Remember that clients who honestly report problems are valuable sources of information about suppliers and destinations.
- Listen carefully to the client's full explanation of what occurred. Before

assigning blame, hazarding guesses, or apologizing, obtain all the facts and clarify uncertainties by asking questions about the relevant circumstances.

- Take notes.
- Make the client feel that the complaint is being taken seriously, and try to empathize with the client's disappointment.
- Restate the complaint to show that it has been understood.
- Explain what action can be taken.
- Never admit responsibility for whatever went wrong without first discussing the complaint with the agency manager. Offering a small sum of money could be interpreted as an admission of responsibility.
- Follow through on the promised action.
- Inform the client of the resolution of the problem.

Even if the client is temporarily satisfied, refer any complaint through appropriate channels, preferably put it in writing to the appropriate supplier with full, detailed information. If possible, take steps to see that the problem does not recur.

CHAPTER WRAP-UP

CHAPTER HIGHLIGHTS

Seldom will a salesperson use all the techniques discussed in this chapter for one client; many can be adapted to fit the client and type of sale. In the next chapter we discuss how to vary the selling process to suit particular types of sales. Here is a review of the objectives with which we began the chapter.

1. **Describe the agency-supplier relationship, which limits the agency's liability.** Travel suppliers sell their own goods and services through travel agencies or directly to the public. Travel agencies act as intermediaries, selling the supplier's goods and services to the public. The supplier controls the inventory and in some cases uses a conference system to appoint those who may sell its products. Contracts among the parties in these transactions may be written but usually are only implied. In most cases, travelers are actually contracting for services with the suppliers. The travel agency is not liable for the actions of suppliers, but it is responsible for conveying necessary information to the client.

2. **Describe the skills that provide a foundation for effective communication by salespeople.** To communicate effectively, it is important to be able to make a first impression that encourages the development of rapport and then to establish a link with the client. Successful communication also depends on the ability to ask effective questions and to listen carefully. Questioners should use close-ended, open-ended, or feedback questions as the circumstances require. Listeners should watch the speaker's body language and recap the conversation. Finally, effective communicators must be able to present their information persuasively; it helps to avoid jargon and elicit feedback.

3. **Identify eight steps in making a successful sale.** The first three steps basically help the salesperson acquire information: (1) identify potential qualified clients, (2) develop rapport, and (3) identify the customer's wants and needs. The next steps are to (4) determine what product meets the client's needs, (5) present recommendations to the customer, and (6) deal with any objections to those recommendations. During this process the salesperson looks for opportunities for selling up and for cross-selling. Both the client's body language and his or her comments help the salesperson determine when to attempt to close the sale,

which is step 7. The final step, step 8, is to ensure that the customer is satisfied after the trip.

4. **State five questions involved in qualifying a client and three ways to close a sale.** The basic questions in qualifying a client are When? Where? Who? How long? and What type or class of service? To close a sale, the salesperson might simply offer to book the trip or set a time limit on the decision, or present a choice that assumes that the client is making a purchase. Additional methods include asking for the preferred method of payment or complimenting the client in ways that assume the sale has been made.

5. **Discuss the responsibilities of a travel counselor after the sale has been made.** After a sale, travel counselors must ensure that the sale stays made and that the client is satisfied with the result. Service earns loyalty from the client. Besides processing and monitoring the sale precisely and keeping records, travel counselors might provide extra services by sending additional information about a destination or even surprise gifts. More basically, though, they should follow up on the sale, keeping in touch with clients and informing them of their own responsibilities. Counselors should also be prepared to deal with any changes or emergencies and to handle complaints.

KEY TERMS

A list of key terms introduced in this chapter follows. If you do not recall the meaning of these terms, see the Glossary, which begins on page 393.

body language
close-ended question
cross-selling
feedback question

open-ended question
outside sales agent
selling up

REVIEW QUESTIONS

1. What can you do to develop rapport with a client?

2. What are the advantages gained by asking the five qualifying questions?

3. What would you do if you were not sure what to recommend to a client?

4. How could you find out how much clients want to spend on a trip?

5. What types of objections do clients make, and how should a travel counselor treat them?

6. At which steps in the sales process could you use e-mail to enhance your chances of success?

CHAPTER 11

Specialized Sales

OBJECTIVES

After completing this chapter, you should be able to

1. Describe three key variations in selling situations that travel sellers must adjust to.

2. State four principles to follow when selling a trip to a group.

3. Discuss the distinctive characteristics of business travel.

4. Describe the special challenges involved in arranging meetings and incentive travel.

5. Identify the main types and benefits of travel insurance.

6. Name three specialties prevalent in the travel industry.

All clients have different needs. Some require special meals for religious reasons; some need kennels for their pets. There are clients who are looking only for efficient delivery of an airline ticket at a good price and others who are hoping for inspiration in choosing the trip of a lifetime.

Whoever the client is the salesperson must adapt the sales techniques used to suit the client and the situation. Is selling travel to a seventy-year-old different from selling to a twenty-year-old? How is selling to a group different from selling to individuals? This chapter addresses these and similar questions, examining the special needs of different clients and situations.

OUTLINE

CUSTOMIZING SALES AND SERVICE
- What are the key differences in selling situations that travel sellers should recognize?

SELLING TO GROUPS
- How does selling travel to a group differ from selling travel to individuals?

SELLING BUSINESS TRAVEL
- How does selling business travel differ from selling leisure travel?

MEETINGS AND INCENTIVE TRAVEL
- What special skills and functions are involved in arranging meetings and incentive travel?

SELLING TRAVEL INSURANCE
- How does selling travel insurance benefit both the seller and the buyer of travel, and what are the major types of travel insurance?

Customizing Sales and Service

■ WHAT ARE THE KEY DIFFERENCES IN SELLING SITUATIONS
THAT TRAVEL SELLERS SHOULD RECOGNIZE?

Many travel companies and many travel professionals specialize in selling to clients with particular needs or interests. But even specialists must deal with people who have varying needs and problems. To be successful, travel sellers—whether they are travel counselors or airline reservationists or sales representatives for suppliers—should be prepared to recognize some key variations in the demands of selling situations.

Variations in Purpose

Perhaps the most basic variation in travel is the one introduced in Chapter 1. Recall that travel can be classified into three types based on its purpose: *corporate,* or *business, travel* (any trip purchased by a business and made for the purposes of the organization); *vacation and leisure travel;* and *VFR travel* (travel to visit friends or relatives). For each type of travel, clients are likely to have different needs.

Leisure and Business Travelers. Consider the differences between leisure travelers and business travelers. Years ago, Plog Research asked 12,000 people to rate their reasons for leisure travel; the five most popular reasons were

- To get rid of stress.
- To enrich their perspective on life.
- To bring the family closer together.
- To do what they want, when they want.
- To feel alive and energetic.

In contrast, the key reasons for business travel are

- For sales calls, purchasing, and consultation.
- To handle internal company business.
- To solve problems.
- For training, conventions, or other meetings.

Because they have such different reasons for traveling, selling to business travelers is very different from selling to leisure travelers. The majority of leisure travelers ask for advice on many issues. Business travelers often know exactly what they want; most seek advice only about airlines, hotels, and car rentals. We look at business travel in detail later in this chapter.

VFR Travel. Sometimes, VFR travel is lumped together with leisure travel, but selling VFR travel can be very different. Often, VFR travelers need only transportation. Their plans have neither the complexity of some pleasure trips nor the urgency of many business trips. Usually they are most interested in getting the best fare possible in view of their schedule.

When VFR travel is discretionary, it may be very sensitive to price. If an airfare sale suddenly reduces ticket prices, Aunt Minnie in Missoula may get a visit. If prices are high, Aunt Minnie may have to wait a few months.

Some VFR travel, though, is not seen as discretionary by the traveler. People often consider holiday travel obligatory, for example. Clients who put off their planning for holiday travel may have to pay premium prices in order to travel at peak times, and they may be very willing to do so.

Travel counselors who book VFR travel should be prepared to deal with the special situation of unaccompanied minors traveling by air. Travel counselors must inform the custodians or parents of the procedures that must be followed at the airports.

Travel counselors should also be ready to help families come together when there is a medical emergency or death in a family. Because they typically do not have advance notice in these situations, travelers could end up paying full coach fares. Travel counselors can help them obtain a lower fare by checking for the *bereavement fares* that are offered by most airlines. To qualify for this fare, the traveler needs documentation of the situation that the airline can verify. Travel counselors should compare the airlines' policies and provide the family with advice about the best fares and schedules and the required documents.

Finally, travel sellers who are interested in giving good service to VFR clients might alert them to air sales to cities where they have friends and relatives whom they visit frequently. Travel counselors might also record information about clients' preferences, if any, for car rentals and hotels.

Variations in Interests

Even among leisure travelers, travel sellers must adjust their sales techniques to a tremendous range of interests. Some travelers just want to lie on a quiet beach; others want to dance 'til dawn or challenge a mountain or contemplate medieval masterpieces.

Increasingly, leisure travelers want to get something specific out of their vacations. The number of bookings made by travel agencies for *special-interest trips*—travel planned around a specific theme such as a sport, casinos, hard or soft adventure, and so on—continues to grow. Chapters 8 and 10 outlined some of the many interests that can be the focus of vacations (see Table 10.1, page 254).

Some people believe that only those who share a special interest can arrange a successful special-interest trip. Scuba divers are unlikely to book a trip with someone who does not know what a PADI certificate is; trekkers will expect advice on how to choose between Tibet and Patagonia for their next journey. Certainly it helps to be personally involved in the special interest, or at least to learn a great deal about it. Sellers who know the basics in the field or are active participants will find it easier to empathize with clients and to establish credibility.

Variations in Special Needs

Beyond their purposes and interests, travelers differ in yet another way: demographics. They may be young or old, single or married, for example, and these characteristics often bring with them certain needs.

Single people, for example, may be particularly interested in tours, cruises, or resorts that make a special effort to offer opportunities for singles to meet other singles. Or they may be especially interested in finding accommodations without the single supplement (the higher rate often charged to those occupying a hotel room or cruise cabin by themselves) or in finding suppliers that help singles find roommates to avoid the extra charge.

Honeymooners are another example. Even in difficult economic times, honeymoon travel remains relatively stable. Newlyweds are rarely willing to forgo a honeymoon of some sort. Working on honeymoons is often very time-consuming, but couples who have had memorable wedding trips are excellent sources of repeat business and will speak glowingly of their experience to family and friends, all of whom are potential clients.

Members of some religious groups may also have special needs. They may want to attend services on a particular day or at a particular time each day. They may ask for special diets. They may not be able to travel on certain holy days. If the travel seller senses that a client is interested in any of these topics, it does no harm to ask if there are any other special observances. Clients who request particular foods may have other needs that they do not think of expressing.

There are many other travelers with special needs and products to fulfill their needs. Let's examine a few of the specialties.

Senior Citizens

Senior citizens, those 65 years of age or older, are a large and growing part of the traveling population. What do seniors look for when they are traveling? Some may be eager to return to destinations they loved in the past. Comfort, safety, and pacing are especially important to many. They might prefer rooms close to elevators, for example, and want meals that conform to special diets. Also, compared with people of other ages, a high proportion of senior citizens travel in groups, enjoying the camaraderie as well as the luxury of having someone else worry about many travel details.

But stereotyping is dangerous. People tend to underestimate the stamina and interests of senior citizens. The next senior citizen who calls may be more adventuresome than most thirty-year-olds. Many are sophisticated, energetic travelers who have visited many destinations and are looking for new itineraries. And the current generation of seniors is more active and more widely traveled than their parents and grandparents.

Travel sellers should be prepared to ask seniors the same qualifying questions that they ask other clients, but they should also be ready to determine whether seniors are interested in the special services available to this age group. For example, are they interested in senior discounts? In group travel that caters to seniors? In cruise ships that offer promotional nights for seniors? In the special rooms that some hotel chains provide? For example, some hotels offer rooms for seniors that have bright lighting, large-button telephones, lever-style handles on doors and sinks, and grab bars in showers. Hyatt Hotels and Club Med are two examples.

Family Travel

According to TIA (Travel Industry Association of America), more than 90 million U.S. adults are likely to take a child with them on a trip of a hundred miles or more from home. The importance of family travel as an area of expertise that brings success to travel counselors cannot be overestimated. Many travel suppliers offer services designed to have special appeal to families and to meet the needs of children. For example,

- Car rental companies have car seats (infant, toddler, and youth) available when requested in advance.
- Airlines normally preboard families with young children and can serve children's meals if requested in advance. Baby strollers fit between the aisles in the cabin and can be stowed in the overhead bins, beneath the seat, or in the baggage compartment. Flight attendants can heat milk for babies, but it is unfair to expect them to look after or feed a child or to change diapers.
- Some cruise lines and resorts offer special activity programs for children. The parents are then free to leave them for almost the entire day, if they wish. Most cruise lines offer babysitting services subject to the availability of crew members. Some resort hotels in Hawaii offer children aged 5 through 12 activities such as boogie boarding, ukelele playing, lei making, and hula dancing. Other resort groups have family camps with age-appropriate sports activities.

Many suppliers provide special rates for children accompanying their parents. Cruise lines frequently accept the third and fourth occupants of a cabin at considerably reduced rates or do not charge for them at all. Some hotel chains allow children under age 18 to share a room with their parents at no charge. Airlines frequently offer discounted fares to children flying with a parent. (For more on these discounts, see Chapter 4.) For international travel, however, it is important for travel counselors to advise their clients that children traveling with only one parent or with grandparents need a notarized letter from parent(s) authorizing the guardian to take the child out of the country.

Travelers with Disabilities

Nearly one-fifth of all Americans have some type of disability. By the broadest definition, *travelers with disabilities* are those who have impaired mobility and require special arrangements—such as people who are blind or deaf, confined to wheelchairs or stretchers, mentally challenged, very elderly, extremely obese, or in need of oxygen or a respirator. In the United States— thanks to the 1986 Air Carrier Access Act and the 1990 *Americans with Disabilities Act*—people with disabilities have the right to access the same services as those without disabilities. On non-U.S. airlines, IATA (International Air Transport Association) regulations provide rules regarding accessibility similar to those in the United States.

The *Society for Accessible Travel and Hospitality (SATH)* estimates that about 83 percent of Americans with disabilities are potential travelers. They represent a tremendous opportunity for travel professionals who understand and respond to their needs.

Travel Agencies. Making travel arrangements for people with disabilities may take extra time, but that time is more than compensated for by repeat and referral business from satisfied clients.

Travel sellers should be careful not to stereotype travelers with disabilities. Many persons with disabilities choose adventurous, physically demanding trips. The qualifying questions described in Chapter 10 must still be asked, but travel counselors must also be able to identify unusual requirements. They should ask questions frankly and, if possible, speak directly to the travelers with disabilities—not to companions or assistants.

Travel counselors who make arrangements for travelers with disabilities should check with each supplier as far ahead as possible. If suppliers are given sufficient notice of clients' needs, travelers with disabilities can go almost anywhere. The following sections briefly summarize the services and challenges that such travelers, particularly those in wheelchairs, often encounter when traveling.

Air Travel. Generally speaking, travelers with disabilities prefer as much space as possible. On planes, first-class seats are ideal. In the coach section, aisle and bulkhead seats may be best because they provide the most legroom. Sometimes airlines can leave the middle seat in a row of three empty if a passenger is occupying one of the others. Seating in emergency exit rows is limited to those with the most potential to operate the emergency exit and to help evacuate the aircraft. On most planes, travelers with disabilities find it difficult or impossible to use the small bathrooms, but on the Boeing 767 bathrooms are designed to accommodate Narrowmatic wheelchairs.

The airlines provide many services for passengers with disabilities. They might offer advance boarding, a wheelchair, storage of canes and crutches, an escort, special meals, and fully reclining seats. Service animals such as Seeing Eye dogs may travel in the passenger cabin free of charge on domestic airlines; however, some countries quarantine all arriving animals.

The airlines provide some services automatically, but others must be requested, sometimes up to 48 hours in advance. Computer codes for special service requests (SSR) and for information on other services (OSI) alert the airline to the client's requirements. For clients with wheelchairs, travel sellers should ask whether the wheelchair is self-propelled or battery-operated and note special arrangements needed for battery-operated chairs. Travelers will be switched to an "aisle chair" at the airport unless their chair fits through aircraft aisles. In either case, the wheelchair is then stored.

Rail Travel. Amtrak schedules provide information about the accessibility of rail stations. Amtrak promises that

- Help is available for boarding and detraining.
- On each train at least one coach car has accessible seating and accessible restrooms.
- Trains with sleeping cars have at least one bedroom that is accessible.
- Seeing Eye dogs are welcome onboard at no charge.
- Meals and beverage service will be brought to the passenger's seat.

Reservations and special requests for passengers with disabilities should be relayed as early as possible. Only a limited number of accessible spaces are available on each train. To ensure an accessible space, you must make a reservation for the accessible bedroom accommodation, transfer seat, or wheelchair space (even on an unreserved train). Accommodations can be reserved for passengers with mobility impairments until 14 days prior to departure; then the accessible bedrooms are available on a first-come, first-served basis. Amtrak supplies a Special Services Request Form for noting pertinent details about services being requested, and it has discounts for passengers with disabilities.

On international railroads, accessibility and services vary widely. Travel counselors should consult the U.S. offices of the rail lines for information and should be sure that help will be available for passengers with disabilities at the stations.

Car Rentals. With about 48 hours' advance notice, some major car rental companies can provide cars with hand controls for physically challenged drivers, often at no extra cost. If transfer from the terminal to the car is difficult, the car can be waiting outside the baggage claim area (if airport regulations permit), or a van with wheelchair accessibility may be provided to transfer the passenger to the rental car. Some companies specialize in renting vans designed to carry one or two wheelchair-bound travelers and up to five other passengers. Some small cars, particularly in Europe, do not have room for a wheelchair in the trunk.

Motorcoaches. By law, new U.S. motorcoaches must be accessible to those with disabilities, and motorcoaches must store wheelchairs and help people with impaired mobility to a seat. Old coaches, however, are not required to add special equipment.

Nevertheless, local transportation systems generally have wheelchair lifts, and long-distance companies such as Greyhound have now added services for travelers with disabilities. For example, with 48 hours' notice, you can request a coach equipped with a wheelchair lift. Greyhound provides assistance with boarding and deboarding, with luggage, with transfers, and with the storage and retrieval of mobility devices. Greyhound also extends a 50 percent discount for personal care attendants who are traveling with physically challenged passengers, although there are restrictions.

Tours. U.S. tour operators are required to serve those with disabilities to the best of their ability. An increasing number of operators specialize in tours for travelers with disabilities and use motorcoaches with lifts and enlarged baggage compartments. Tour packages of all kinds—from trips to Disney World to African safaris to around-the-world air tours—are available from operators that have expertise in serving travelers with disabilities. Care must be taken to ensure that the special accommodations provided are appropriate to meet the various and specific needs of each client.

Hotels. The Americans with Disabilities Act requires that new hotels must be accessible to those with disabilities and that existing hotels must do everything that is "readily achievable" to make their rooms and all public facilities accessible.

What makes a hotel or a room accessible? The entrance must be level or provided with a ramp. If no accessible rooms are available on the ground floor, elevators must be large enough to accommodate a wheelchair. In the hotel room, light switches, thermostats, air-conditioning controls, and locks must be low enough to be reached from a sitting position. The bathroom must have a tub with safety bars and be able to accommodate a wheelchair, whether the door is open or closed. The bed should be the same height as the wheelchair to permit easy transfers, and there should be a bedside telephone. For the deaf and hearing-impaired, U.S. hotels are required to provide equipment such as text telephones and flashing lights for alarms and doorbells.

Of course, for travel abroad, conditions in each country must be checked carefully. Some small European hotels have only very small elevators with narrow entrances, many steps, and other situations that are not compliant with the ADA requirements prevalent in the United States.

Cruises. Because cruise lines are technically owned by non-American companies, they traditionally have not been covered by U.S. laws such as the Americans with Disabilities Act. Nevertheless, courts have ruled favorably on lawsuits aimed to force cruise lines to comply with the act. Progress has come slowly, but most cruise lines are improving accessibility, and a growing number offer programs, facilities, and services for those with disabilities.

A statement that a cabin or certain public rooms are "accessible" leaves many unanswered questions. Exactly what public areas are or are not accessible? How are port calls handled? What are bathroom facilities like? What is the staff's attitude toward serving passengers with special needs?

The potential difficulties for people with disabilities on cruises are numerous. Narrow cabin doors and narrow passageways may restrict the ability to maneuver wheelchairs around the ship. Only the latest ships provide some cabins designed to accommodate the needs of wheelchair-bound passengers. At some ports where seas are rough, transporting wheelchair passengers to tenders may be impossible. Many cruise lines require that passengers with disabilities be accompanied by an able-bodied passenger, and many refuse to accept the very elderly or passengers with a history of illness without a doctor's certificate. Most ships will not carry animals, including Seeing Eye dogs, and quarantine regulations apply at international ports.

If the difficulties can be reduced, however, cruises provide distinct advantages for travelers with disabilities. The proximity of restaurants,

ON THE SPOT

A client calls, wanting to fly with her husband to Nassau and stay at a hotel on Paradise Island. She informs you that her husband uses a wheelchair. What will you ask her? What arrangements will you make?

Ask the same questions you would ask of any client. You may find much of what you need to know by asking about the couple's past travels. In addition, ask what kind of help her husband needs. Can she help him from the chair to his seat, or will an airline attendant be needed? What are the dimensions of the chair? Does it fold up? Ask if there are issues you have not addressed that you should know about.

Book the flight accordingly. If you are not certain of the codes needed for requesting wheelchairs, call the airline. If booking a transfer, contact the transfer company directly and describe the needed services. When booking the hotel, don't depend on a simple statement that it has an accessible room; ask for a detailed description. Does it have ledges and sills to get the chair over, or does it have ramps? How wide are the doors? What are the bathroom facilities? Call and reconfirm all details a day or two ahead. Special arrangements often must be double-checked because personnel sometimes changes, people get busy, and the information might be sitting somewhere unread. Recheck everything, and get confirmation of the services in writing and the names of the people you spoke to.

entertainment, planned activities, and open deck space increases their independence. For the travel seller who is able to satisfy the client's needs, a repeat customer is virtually assured because the cruise passenger and the passenger with disabilities are statistically among the most loyal clients.

✔ CHECK-UP

Travel sellers adjust their sales techniques in light of
✔ The purpose for the trip.
✔ The client's interests.
✔ The client's special needs.
✔ The situation.

Unlike leisure travelers,
✔ Most business travelers seek advice only about airlines, hotels, and car rentals.
✔ VFR travelers often require only transportation and sometimes view their trip as obligatory.

Demographic groups that may have special needs include
✔ Singles.
✔ Members of certain religious groups.

✔ Senior citizens.
✔ Families with children.
✔ Travelers with disabilities.

When selling to clients with disabilities, travel counselors should be sure to
✔ Avoid acting on the basis of stereotypes.
✔ Ask the usual qualifying questions.
✔ Ask about other requirements.
✔ Be aware of their clients' rights to accessible facilities as guaranteed by federal law in the United States.
✔ Plan to check with each supplier and to relay reservations and special requests as early as possible.
✔ Plan to spend extra time and effort in handling arrangements for those with disabilities.

Selling to Groups

■ HOW DOES SELLING TRAVEL TO A GROUP DIFFER FROM SELLING TRAVEL TO INDIVIDUALS?

Travelers with disabilities and senior citizens are important potential customers not only as individuals but also as members of groups. Thousands of clubs and organizations—from the local gardening club to the high school French club to a support group for divorced fathers—as well as businesses are potential buyers of group travel.

Making the Sale

If you are selling travel to a group, here are four suggested steps.

First, construct a profile. Selling travel to a group requires careful consideration of the group's makeup. Construct a profile of the average member in terms of age, economic status, background, interests, and whatever other factors may have led the person to join the group.

Second, design a trip for the average member. Use the profile to help determine the approach to take, the choices to offer for destinations, and the special needs to consider.

Third, establish a working relationship with the key decision maker who will act as your contact with the group, communicating the group's desires to you and relaying information back to the members. This person may be a Pied Piper—someone whom others will follow, whose opinions others will respect. Extend VIP treatment to this person. Selling a concept to one person may produce a trip for a group of forty.

Fourth, based on the profile of the average member, prepare one option to sell. You cannot expect a group to reach agreement in an open meeting if they are given a random selection of suggestions. Before the presentation, complete the preliminary work of establishing a destination, travel dates, price, and availability.

Making Travel Arrangements

Ensuring the availability of arrangements and accommodations for a group may require as much as a year's lead time. Arrangements for groups are different from arrangements for individuals in several ways.

- Most suppliers have departments that specialize in handling group business, and reservations for group travel usually go through these specialists.
- Group bookings have special payment procedures and cancellation penalties. Generally, all arrangements for group travel must be completed 30 to 60 days before departure.
- Discounts, upgrades, special amenities, and incentives such as complimentary trips or tickets are often available for groups. For example, a hotel may offer an upgrade to a suite; an airline might offer a special discount or a free seat for each specified number of paying customers.

Anyone arranging group travel should negotiate with suppliers for these special benefits of group travel. The arranger will also need to draw up schedules for reservations, deposits and final payments from participants, payments to suppliers, mailing of rooming lists to hotels, and issuance of tickets.

Travel counselors can take care of all of this, putting the entire travel program together themselves. But this means dealing with hundreds of details. It requires experience, organization, and great energy.

An alternative is to use a tour operator. The operator then takes care of making arrangements for hotels, restaurants, guides, museums, local transportation, and so on. The travel counselor concentrates on selling the trip to the group and on handling details related to communication, documents, payments, pretrip meetings, and instructions for group members.

When travel counselors use tour operators for group travel, they have two choices:

- Book into an existing program. A travel counselor might book a scheduled departure or request a separate departure for the group for an existing tour. If too few people sign up for the trip, it may be possible to switch members to a regular departure of the tour.
- Have a tour operator put together a custom-made trip for the group. This option is often used. The cost is usually higher, but the result may be a trip that most closely meets the group's interests and thus gives high value for the money.

When an existing tour is booked for the group, the agency receives the tour operator's usual or negotiated commission rates. For custom-made group travel, suppliers usually quote *net rates* (without commissions). To set the price for these trips, the travel agency must add to the net rates all of the other costs involved in the trip and its planning: tips, taxes, promotional costs, complimentary trips for the group's recruiters, and any other special items. On top of this, the agency adds a markup as its profit.

How much should the markup be? The answer depends on many factors: complexity of planning, competition, and the expertise of travel counselors, to name a few. One rule of thumb is that when an agency does most of the planning for a fairly complex trip, the markup should be at least 20 percent on the net. When a tour operator does most of the planning, custom-making the trip for a group, the agency's markup might be as low as 15 percent.

✔ **CHECK-UP**

When selling to a group,
✔ Prepare a profile of the average member.
✔ Establish a close relationship with a key decision maker.
✔ Prepare one option to sell.

In arranging travel for a group, travel counselors might
✔ Put the entire trip together themselves.
✔ Book an existing program.
✔ Have a tour operator put together a tailor-made trip.

Selling Business Travel

■ HOW DOES SELLING BUSINESS TRAVEL DIFFER FROM SELLING LEISURE TRAVEL?

More than one-fifth of U.S. adults travel for business each year, taking more than 275 million trips for business purposes. For many travel businesses, this is a very appealing market. Compared with leisure travel, business travel tends to be far steadier in several ways.

■ Business travel (also referred to as corporate travel) varies less than leisure travel during the year.

■ Business travel is less sensitive to changes in the economy. When economic growth slows, many companies tighten their belts and reduce travel, but not as much as leisure travelers do. In fact, some businesses increase travel in difficult times.

■ Business travel is also less sensitive to changes in price. If travel costs rise, most businesses try to pass the cost on by raising their own prices.

Furthermore, corporate travel can generate other business. For example, client companies may turn to their corporate travel agencies to arrange meetings and incentive travel, and business travelers may turn to the travel counselors who arrange their business travel for their VFR and leisure travel.

Businesses handle their travel in varying ways. Some have their own corporate travel departments. Travel managers in these departments work for the corporation, not a travel agency. Some companies go to a general-purpose travel agency or to a *commercial agency,* which is a travel agency that specializes in business travel. And in some companies, a travel agency is hired to establish an outreach office within the company to handle travel arrangements. Success in this attractive market requires the ability to appeal both to the ultimate customer—the company paying for the travel—and to those traveling.

Needs of Business Travelers

In many organizations, travel connotes prestige, and many business travelers enjoy the experience. Often, though, business travelers travel because they must. Their travel is sometimes accompanied by stress, is usually filled with hard work, and often leaves no time to enjoy the place visited. Business travelers take pride in the fact that they are traveling for important reasons, and they focus on the business they must accomplish. They are likely to buy from travel professionals who help them keep this focus.

Among the key needs of the business traveler are

- **Prompt service.** In business travel, "prompt" is likely to mean confirming reservations while the client is on the phone, calling back within an hour, or finalizing arrangements before the day is over. Though ticketless travel is the norm for most air passengers, some business travelers require actual tickets in hand and need them by the end of the business day.

- **Absolutely correct arrangements.** The correct car rental company must be booked, the preferred seating on the plane reserved, the frequent-flyer number recorded, and so on. Excuses for inaccuracies are not acceptable.

- **The ability to change reservations at a moment's notice.** In the business world, plans change frequently.

- **An environment suitable for concentration on business.** For example, business-class sections on airplanes and airport club lounges offer the quiet, comfort, and service that allow businesspeople to work during and between flights. Many hotels offer time-saving breakfast buffets and rooms away from noisy guests.

CLOSE-UP: ON THE JOB WITH AMY MARKELL, CORPORATE TRAVEL COUNSELOR

Amy Markell works for a travel agency whose clients include large corporations. She and another counselor work as a team and are assigned one very large and three very small companies. Most of her day is spent with a headset on; it frees her hands to use the computer while talking with clients on the telephone.

"I don't think I was even very aware of business travel when I was studying to be a travel agent. The people I deal with generally know where they want to go, when, and often how. Sometimes it's cut-and-dried. Other times, they have never been to a city and want you to suggest hotels. Regardless, I always try to add something special. How much a taxi will cost from the airport, if there is a current show or exhibit going on, how to get hockey tickets—things like that, especially if I know something about what my client is interested in.

"And I do know a lot about my clients. Their computer profile contains not only all their credit card information, addresses, phone numbers, airline seat and hotel room preferences, likes and dislikes, and special needs, but also anything else that I can pick up about them. So if I know they particularly liked a Broadway musical one time, I might be able to suggest something in Los Angeles another time. Even if they go to the same city week after week, you try to do something to personalize the transaction, even if it's just a comment on the itinerary like, 'Wow! Podunk again! You must be excited!' You have to use good judgment and know your client. It's the little-mint-on-the-pillow idea:

people don't book the hotel to get that little mint, but it symbolizes the care and personal attention that the hotel is going to give them in a lot of other ways.

"About half the time we don't even talk to the person traveling. We're dealing with the assistant or colleague who makes the reservations. Then not only do we want to add some personal touch for the traveler, but we also want to keep a good relationship with the person making the reservation. We always want to make him or her look good, especially if the person being booked is the boss.

"OK, there's the downside, too: travelers who can't make up their mind or who change their mind. They cancel; they change. It gets a little frustrating. But maybe their work keeps changing. My agency doesn't just look at how much dollar volume I book but also at how many transactions I perform. If I book and cancel a ticket and have to issue a refund, that's two transactions and maybe no money earned (we have to give all the commissions back). If I did my job well, that's not my fault. It's up to the agency to decide if this company's travel is worthwhile. The agency might have to renegotiate the contract or raise the company's service fees.

"We're a fairly large agency and have just joined up with one that operates coast to coast. There's room for advancement. I haven't tried yet, but now I'm ready. We have international specialists, and I think that's what I would like to move to first."

- Special services to enable them to conduct their business. Examples include access to fax machines and the Internet as well as help obtaining translations or preparing presentations.
- Physical and psychological pampering. Business travelers may want exercise facilities or swimming pools to relieve stress. They may look for luxuries to keep their morale high.
- Special amenities for female business travelers. These can include features such as a beauty salon, ironing board and iron in the room, and night-time escort service to and from the car and the parking lot.

The Company's Travel Needs

Even the best service to individual business travelers may not be enough to retain a company's travel business; the company's needs must also be served. Of course, those needs vary, just as do those of individuals. But the cost and efficiency of travel are likely to rank high on a company's list of concerns. Keys to meeting these concerns are negotiations with travel vendors, record keeping and analyses of travel expenses, and development and enforcement of travel policies.

Negotiations with vendors assume importance in part because many special deals are available for corporate travel. Many suppliers are willing to offer favorable rates to win the business of these frequent travelers. A specific company may negotiate with a supplier (with or without the assistance of a travel agency) for a discount available to all of that company's travelers when they use that supplier's services; this is known as a *company-negotiated rate*. In addition, travel agencies negotiate for discounts known as *contract rates*; these are rates available to all business travelers who book the supplier's service through that travel agency.

Record keeping is another tool for controlling travel costs. With the help of computers, it is easy to keep records of travel expenses that categorize those expenses in myriad ways—by traveler, destination, supplier, activity, time period, and so on. Thus the company can see just how its money is being spent and spot inefficiencies.

Analysis of travel costs can help a company design effective travel policies. For example, one company might decide that only employees at a certain level are allowed to fly first class or that frequent-flyer awards are to be turned over to the company, rather than used by the employee.

Travel Agencies and Business Travel

About 81 percent of U.S. travel agencies sell business travel to some degree. Travel agencies have long provided companies with services such as offering a toll-free line available 24 hours a day for assistance. But, today, commercial agencies must also offer more-sophisticated services; they are, in effect, in the business of "travel management." They are selling an array of services to help companies manage their business travel—from reservations and ticketing to vendor negotiations and travel policy development.

Sometimes the desires of the company and the traveler clash. For example, the company might require employees to take the flight with the lowest fare if it gets them to the destination before 9:00 P.M. If the lowest fare requires a connecting flight, the traveler might ask instead for a nonstop flight. The travel agency must follow the company's policy unless it receives approval to meet the employee's request. It is the company, not the traveler, that has hired and is paying the agency. Still, if the company's travelers become dissatisfied with the agency, word is likely to reach the company's decision makers, who may soon choose another agency. Ultimately, the individual traveler's needs must be met, too.

Usually a contract spells out the arrangement between the travel agency and the company. The contract specifies the services that the agency will provide and how quickly those services will be delivered. It usually reflects or incorporates all or part of the company's travel policy, such as when flights with the lowest airfares must be selected. The contract also states what management fees or service charges are to be paid to the agency.

Handling Corporate Accounts. Selling a travel agency's services to a particular company might require only a call from the agency's owner, manager, or corporate sales manager asking for the company's business. Or the sale might require many sales calls over the course of months or even years, with skillful use of all the selling techniques discussed in the previous chapter.

Once a travel agency has a company's business, the corporate counselor must give great service in order to keep the account sold. The advantage of working with business travelers is that they know where and when they want to travel. Often they prefer a particular airline, car rental company, or hotel chain. Furthermore, they may repeat the same trip a number of times. Corporate counselors, therefore, face fewer decisions than leisure counselors, and they seldom need to apply the selling techniques discussed in Chapter 10 in full force.

But speed, accuracy, flexibility, skill at phone communications, and professionalism are especially important when handling corporate accounts. Usually, corporate travel counselors must do a high volume of business for the agency to make a profit. They must also be prepared to make frequent and speedy changes in travel arrangements. And the corporate counselor might handle all the arrangements on the phone, without ever meeting the traveler. The business traveler may never visit the agency. In fact, even on the phone, the commercial counselor often will be dealing with an assistant instead of the traveler. Thus corporate travel counselors must be very good at telephone communications.

Using Technology. The corporate counselor who can provide a high quantity and quality of service is likely to be one who is comfortable with the latest technology. To serve business travelers efficiently, for example, information about their preferences is kept in a profile maintained by a database system, like the one shown in Figure 3.1 (page 60). The client profile might include

- Office, home, and billing addresses and phone numbers.
- Billing preferences and credit card numbers.
- Seating preferences.
- Information on membership in frequent-flyer and other frequent-traveler programs.
- Preferred hotels, types of rooms, and special requests.
- Preferred car rental company and type of car.
- Special airline meal requests.

Much of the information about a client remains the same for every trip. Once it has been entered into the system, one or two keystrokes can move many lines of information into a client's reservation. Each GDS has its own proprietary name for these profiles, such as Star from Sabre.

Commercial agencies also have software that can create reports about almost any aspect of travel that a company wants to track: who traveled; how

---

ON THE SPOT

Suppose you are a commercial travel counselor and one account that you handle is Rollaway Blinds. Travelers at the company hint that they could find lower fares on the Internet than you get them—and Rollaway Blinds wouldn't have to pay the fees to your agency. What can you do to win their confidence and satisfy their complaint?

These travelers may be unaware of the other services that your agency is giving the company, such as expense reports, assistance with setting travel policy, and savings from negotiated rates. They may not know that many Internet fares cannot be changed without penalty. And they probably are not the ones making the decision about where Rollaway Blinds books its travel. But since they are complaining (and most such travelers wouldn't worry about what the company is paying), keep your ears open. Maybe they have a hidden complaint that they aren't sharing. Also, be sure to notify the appropriate person at your agency of the comments that you are hearing; he or she might want to meet with the decision makers at Rollaway. Travel agencies must be prepared to prove their value to the companies and travelers they serve.

many times they traveled; their average hotel rate, airfare, and car rental cost; how many times they used discount fares; and so on. Companies have come to expect this kind of analysis.

In addition, self-service booking systems on the Internet are fast becoming an essential feature offered by corporate travel agencies. These systems allow business travelers to make their own reservations on a site that is customized to reflect the company's travel policy. For instance, preferred airlines may appear more prominently, and only those hotels with which the company has contracts might be presented. These booking systems are set up and managed by travel agencies, and travel counselors are available on the phone to handle questions, problems, and special arrangements. Even small agencies can service corporate accounts that make bookings online through GDS products or online services such as Travelocity, Expedia, and Orbitz; the agency then provides fulfillment and added services for a fee.

✔ CHECK-UP

For the travel counselor, serving business travelers is unlike selling to leisure travelers in that

✔ Their travel is not discretionary.
✔ The traveler's employer as well as the traveler must be satisfied.
✔ The counselor might deal only with an assistant, not with the traveler.
✔ Details regarding the services to be rendered have usually been agreed to, often in a written contract.
✔ The business traveler often has distinctive needs.

Among the services often provided by commercial agencies are

✔ Reservations and ticketing.
✔ Document delivery.
✔ A 24-hour toll-free line for assistance.
✔ Negotiations or assistance in negotiations with travel vendors.
✔ A computerized record of travel expenses.

Meetings and Incentive Travel

■ WHAT SPECIAL SKILLS AND FUNCTIONS ARE INVOLVED IN ARRANGING MEETINGS AND INCENTIVE TRAVEL?

Despite teleconferencing, faxes, and the Internet, businesspeople still feel the need to meet face-to-face. In addition, scientific and educational associations, religious and charitable associations, political and special-interest groups all hold *meetings,* which in this context means association- or corporate-sponsored events that involve an overnight stay. Overall, meetings of one kind or another attract more than 70 million people a year in the United States.

In short, the industry associated with meetings is huge, and it is growing. It arranges conventions, trade shows, exhibitions, and other meetings, as well as incentive travel programs. The 24,000-member *Meeting Professionals International (MPI),* which is represented in sixty countries, promotes the industry, along with other associations such as the *Convention Industry Council (CIC),* the *Center for Exhibition Industry Research (CEIR),* and the *Society of Incentive and Travel Executives (SITE).* These groups provide information, educational programs, and forums for identifying and solving problems.

Meetings and Conventions

Table 11.1 defines the major types of meetings. The suppliers for meetings include companies that provide the physical facilities as well as those that provide the many services used at meetings. The buyers include affinity groups and associations, promotional and marketing companies that are putting on conventions and trade shows, as well as businesses. They may be holding a meeting to train employees or consumers, to introduce or sell products, just to exchange ideas, or for any of a host of other reasons.

Although small meetings can be set up by any agency with an eye for detail, large or frequent meetings are usually handled by specialists called meeting planners. **Meeting planners** act as intermediaries, conveying to suppliers the wishes and requirements of the sponsor of the meeting. These experts may work for meeting planning companies, hotels, exposition centers, or the corporations holding the meetings or conventions. Sometimes they work for divisions of large travel agencies that manage business travel; others are independent contractors. Planners involved in large conventions often work as much as five years in advance, booking convention centers and a city's hotel facilities.

Meeting planning involves much more than the usual travel arrangements. The field is both specialized and broad. The job may involve signing up a former president for a speech, choosing the right wines for attendees, and traveling to analyze locations. Depending on the size and duration of the meeting, as well as the buyer's wishes, the functions of the meeting planner might include the following:

- Clarifying the goals and requirements of the meeting.
- Selecting the site and facilities and negotiating for their use.
- Budgeting for the event.
- Arranging transportation.
- Handling reservations and housing.
- Working with a hotel's group sales department to coordinate the meeting.
- Planning guidebooks, documentation, and registration procedures.
- Planning and managing the setup of function rooms and exhibits.
- Managing food and beverage service.
- Selecting speakers and booking entertainment.
- Scheduling publicity.
- Developing programs for guests and families.

TABLE 11.1 Major Types of Meetings

Type	Description
Clinic	A group session that offers counseling or instruction on a particular topic
Conference	A meeting designed to exchange views or to settle differences
Convention	A large formal meeting of members, representatives, or delegates of an organization, profession, or industry
Exhibition or exposition	The public showing of goods and services as part of a large meeting
Lecture	The exposition of a subject by a speaker before an audience
Panel	A discussion by a group of persons in front of an audience
Symposium	A formal meeting intended for the discussion of a particular issue
Trade fair or trade show	The public showing of goods or services in displays and booths, often open only to members of a profession or industry
Workshop	A meeting or series of meetings for educational purposes in which a small number of participants interact and exchange information

Incentive Travel

Thousands of companies, large and small, use travel as an incentive. They might offer a trip as a reward to employees who have contributed to successful marketing efforts or to dealers and distributors who have achieved a certain level of sales. The trip itself may be strictly for pleasure, or it may combine business and pleasure. More than 100,000 incentive programs are planned each year.

Incentive programs sometimes offer trips to individuals, but most incentive programs offer group trips. In the vast majority of programs, spouses or other guests are allowed to accompany the qualifying employee. Resorts, spas, and cruises are popular choices. To succeed as an incentive, the trip must be a very special experience, with every detail carefully planned.

Making arrangements for activities at the destination requires creativity and close collaboration with suppliers. Theme dinners, parties, special sporting events, and sightseeing might be included. Usually the host company expects some attractions and activities to highlight the company's own goals and activities and to foster corporate loyalty. For example, suppose top salespeople for a company in the fashion industry are on an incentive trip to Ecuador or Bali. An exhibition featuring handmade clothing by local artisans might be created exclusively for them in a country market town when few other tourists are present.

Arranging this type of travel takes expertise and experience. The trip itself is part of a broader motivational program, and its objectives must be clear, realistic, and quantifiable. (Is the main goal, for example, to boost morale and loyalty by encouraging cooperation? Or to boost performance by encouraging competition?) Those arranging incentive travel must shift their focus away from how to sell travel and concentrate on how to use travel as a motivational tool to meet the goals of a specific group. (How high should the standard be, for example, for receiving a reward? Should it be set so that most of those eligible will win or so that only a few will win? How valuable must the reward be in order to work as an effective motivator?) It's important to understand that the trip participants cannot buy their way into the trip. The only way they can qualify to go is to meet the employer's requirements—usually by meeting a predetermined sales quota during a specific period.

Agencies that specialize in this field are called **incentive houses.** About 36 percent of travel agencies that book business travel also plan incentive travel.

Adventure Travel Specialist

One of the most popular specialties in today's travel world is *Adventure Travel*, also sometimes called *active travel*. As more and more travelers look for outdoor activities and have a love of nature, these companies have developed and offer a wide range of choices.

For the very active, companies offer *hard adventure*, which may involve mountain climbing, hiking 30 miles a day, and sleeping under the stars. For those who have slowed down a little in life, there is **soft adventure**, perhaps some daily exercise followed by a bit of village browsing, a glass of wine by the fireplace, dinner and overnight in a cozy inn. And *cultural adventure* is for those who still like to learn, get off the beaten track, and meet interesting people but whose energy and activity level is limited. Strenuous physical participation is not required.

Counselors do not necessarily need to be adventure travelers themselves to sell this specialty but should know which companies work with travel agencies and which don't and be familiar with the various companies and their particular products as well. For example, some companies may offer multi-sport vacations while others have itineraries that focus on one type of sport, such as bicycling trips.

It's also important to know the terminology and safety rules and regulations involved. For example, if selling a dive trip, a counselor must understand that, for health reasons, a client cannot fly within 24 hours of the last dive. And the counselor should know the difference between a shore-based dive vacation and a live-aboard one and be able to screen clients for proper dive certification requirements.

Adventure trips should be sold only with well-known, reputable companies, and such trips are not necessarily inexpensive. Involvement in the adventure travel sector of the industry is a specialty worth considering.

Cruise-Only Specialist

A number of employees and independent contractors in the travel industry specialize in selling cruises. With the huge number of ships at sea, just learning all you need to learn to sell cruise travel well is a challenge unto itself without learning to sell tours, rail travel, air travel, and all the other sectors. In fact, most successful cruise counselors do not represent all cruise lines; they carefully select a handful of the companies that they would like to promote and concentrate on their offerings.

Often the companies and ships they sell will depend on their clientele and their expectations—whether it's a young couple off on their first weekend party cruise all the way to a wealthy, retired couple on an around-the-world winter cruise aboard an upscale cruise line. Of course, many of these successful cruise salespeople take cruises themselves, often as leader of their own small groups on board. They try to learn the "personality" of certain ships and become familiar with the itineraries and practices of the cruise lines

---

CLOSE-UP: ON THE JOB WITH LANCE HENDRY, CRUISE-ONLY COUNSELOR

Lance Hendry is affiliated with a small, upscale northern California agency as its cruise specialist. After a 25-year career in the airlines with Air France, he took retirement and launched his second career. He is now an independent contractor working on commission basis only.

"I love this arrangement. I have a 91-year-old mother whom I care for so I work four days a week out of my home and only go into the office once a week. This gives me the flexibility I need in my life at this stage. I handle nearly all of my business by telephone.

"I deal with perhaps as few as 50-75 clients per year with a heavy repeat factor–some making three cruises a year. I do not advertise; I don't use the social media. I work strictly on referral and about 65% of my clients are nationwide or worldwide. I have ranchers from Arizona, importers from Manhattan, and many other professionals– some elderly who may take 15 grandchildren with them!

"I've been fortunate in taking over 40 cruises in my life,

including 14 Atlantic crossings and six through the Panama Canal, but I also try new ships and new routes, always learning something new. I do not try to sell all cruise lines; I concentrate on several, mostly upscale, lines and I have not sold the new huge megaships carrying 6,000 passengers. My clients prefer ships of a more manageable size and service, service, and more service is the name of the game."

What's important in a job like this? "You need to have passion for what you do, have a good sense of geography and map skills, and the ability to communicate well. Also helpful is the ability to research and to anticipate the client's needs. You must develop their trust, meeting their needs (and sometime demands) but guiding them through it. You also need to know how to qualify them in terms of their education and level of sophistication so as to make suggestions appropriate to their lifestyle and comfort level.

"This is a job that isn't really a 'job.' It's something I love doing and it gives me great personal gratification."

they represent. They also develop pleasant working relationships with the cruise line office personnel so as to be able to service their clientele's special needs and requests.

Some are employees of a full-service retail travel agency, others may be owners of a cruise-only franchise, and still others may simply be independent contractors, perhaps working from their home. Many tend to be mature, retired or semi-retired travel veterans who have built a following of clientele through the years.

Other Popular Specialties

A number of other specialties within the travel industry may be considered. One is termed *ethnic agencies*—travel agencies or tour companies that specialize in travel for persons of a particular ethnic background or language. In some large U.S. cities, such agencies abound for the Spanish-speaking or Chinese-speaking market. Obviously, employees must be bilingual and know the travel products of interest to this market. Many so-called "ethnic travelers" simply buy airfare to and from their native country at key holidays or to visit family. Often the agency has negotiated special airfares with certain airlines serving these destinations. Others specialize in cruises for African-American clientele, perhaps chartering a cruise ship with special foods, entertainment, church services, and jazz performances geared to the taste of their clientele.

Another specialty company is the *inbound travel* company, often referred to as a receptive travel company or destination management company (DMC). These are companies, or subdivisions of other companies, that specialize in individual travelers, or most likely groups, arriving from other parts of the country or from abroad. A second language, a knowledge of one's own city and its attractions, and a sensitivity to the needs and customs of international travelers are a plus for employment in this segment of the industry. Many of these companies are affiliated with their city's convention and visitors' bureau.

There are also specialists in romantic travel, often billing themselves as *honeymoon specialists* but, in reality, handling much more than honeymoons. They usually market themselves with bridal shows and bridal magazines and focus their knowledge on resorts and cruises that are particularly appropriate for the honeymoon couple. Many also offer renew-your-vows trips, anniversary trips, or destination weddings. They must have expertise on the legalities, rules and regulations governing marriages abroad.

Some cities may also have agencies or key employees who are adept at counseling their *LGBT* (lesbian, gay, bisexual, and transgender) clientele. They must know which destinations are gay-friendly and which are not. Agents working in this field are often heavily involved in community events in their own hometown, such as Gay Pride activities.

✔ CHECK-UP

Meeting planners may be employed by
✔ A meeting planning company.
✔ The corporation sponsoring the event.
✔ A hotel or exposition center.
✔ A commercial travel agency.
✔ An incentive house.

Those who arrange incentive travel need to
✔ Be sure the objectives of the program are clear, realistic, and quantifiable.
✔ Concentrate, not on selling travel, but on how to use travel as a motivational tool to meet the goals of the group.

Selling Travel Insurance

■ HOW DOES SELLING TRAVEL INSURANCE BENEFIT BOTH THE SELLER AND THE BUYER OF TRAVEL, AND WHAT ARE THE MAJOR TYPES OF TRAVEL INSURANCE?

For a payment, or *premium,* travelers can obtain insurance against many of the risks associated with traveling. Some travel counselors feel uncomfortable selling travel insurance because discussing the topic tends to emphasize everything that might go wrong on a trip. But there are three reasons for overcoming this hesitancy. First, clients have a right to know that they can protect their investment in a trip, and they may hold a travel agency liable for any losses incurred if insurance is not offered. Second, in many instances, travel insurance protects the travel counselor from liability. Third, insurance sales can improve an agency's profitability.

In Chapter 5, we discussed car rental insurance. Here we describe other types of travel insurance, when they are needed, and how they are sold.

Types of Insurance

Specialized types of travel insurance can be purchased separately, in combination, or as part of a travel package. Besides car rental insurance, there are four basic types: (1) flight, (2) travel accident and health, (3) baggage and personal possessions, and (4) trip cancellation or interruption.

Flight Insurance. Accidents that occur in connection with air travel are covered by *flight insurance.* Coverage begins when the client leaves home and includes the ride to the airport. It ends when flights are completed or after 180 days, whichever comes first. Coverage is extended if scheduling changes by the carrier create delays beyond the client's control.

The benefits paid by flight insurance range up to $1 million for accidental loss of sight, limb, or life that occurs while the insured is on airport premises or is riding as a passenger on a flight or on other forms of transportation used by an airline to transport passengers, such as transfer buses. In the case of death, benefits are paid to the *beneficiary,* a person chosen by the insured.

Travelers may receive flight insurance automatically as a benefit when tickets are charged on certain credit cards. Otherwise clients may buy flight insurance from travel agencies, from tour operators, from cruise companies (on air/sea programs), or from insurance companies that sell it from booths and machines at airports. The premiums for flight insurance seem very low— usually about $4 to $7. But because the premium covers only one trip, the price is very high relative to the average benefit paid.

Travel Accident and Health Insurance. Whereas flight insurance is bought frequently but collected on rarely, the benefits from *travel accident and health insurance* are often needed. It protects the insured in case of accidents (whether travel-related or not) and sickness at all times while away from home. In some cases, travelers' existing health insurance already protects them in these situations. Neither Medicare nor most private health insurance policies, however, cover the cost of medical care abroad.

Most travel accident and health policies do not cover the cost of medical evacuation, and they do not give benefits in cases of illness or death caused by acts of war or by "dangerous activities," which include such sports as mountain climbing, skiing, and hang-gliding. (People who plan activities like these may want to purchase additional special insurance. Also, travelers can purchase additional policies that cover emergency medical transportation, which includes evacuation to the nearest medical facility or home.) Many policies also exclude preexisting medical conditions.

Baggage and Personal Possessions Insurance. For protection in case their baggage or personal possessions are lost, stolen, or damaged while traveling, clients can purchase *baggage and personal possessions insurance.* It picks up where the responsibility of an airline, motorcoach company, or other carrier ends. Normally, only items owned by clients and taken for personal use are covered. Some policies also cover items borrowed just for the trip. Benefits are payable at actual cash value, up to specified limits. The value on clothes is usually based on the value of used clothing, not new replacement value. One premium covers all family members.

There are very specific exceptions and limitations to the coverage provided by this insurance, and clients should read the policies carefully. Most insurance companies limit the amount they will pay for loss of jewelry, furs, currency, or cameras. Clients should be made aware of the procedures required for reporting a loss in order to ensure payment of their claims.

Many homeowner's insurance policies cover loss of or damage to personal possessions even away from home. Unlike most homeowner's policies, however, baggage insurance rarely has a deductible and often covers mysterious disappearances. Some companies offer coverage for emergency purchases that must be made when baggage is delayed or lost.

Trip Cancellation or Interruption Insurance. Many clients already have some form of health, accident, and personal possessions insurance, but travel agencies are among the few sources of *trip cancellation or interruption insurance.* It reimburses clients for (1) nonrefundable prepayments if they must cancel a trip for a reason covered by the policy and (2) any nonrefundable portion of their trip and the cost of transportation home should they have to discontinue a trip. It will also pay for transportation back to a group if clients remain behind temporarily because of an accident or illness covered by the policy.

The reasons for cancellation that qualify for coverage vary with the policy. Most policies provide reimbursement in cases of sudden illness, accident, or death in the family. Some policies also cover cancellations when clients are summoned for jury duty, served with a subpoena, or forced to vacate their home for some reason. Some offer coverage for weather and other natural disasters; this coverage reimburses the client if the natural disaster prevented the airline or other supplier from providing service. A change in plans for personal or financial reasons ordinarily is not covered. Canceling a trip for *fear* of a hurricane, for example, is not covered.

Some insurance companies allow trip insurance to be bought up until the day before departure. Others require that the policy be purchased when the trip is booked or before cancellation penalties take effect.

Trip cancellation or interruption protection should be offered to all clients. The amount that clients should purchase depends on the greatest possible loss that can be anticipated.

Coverage for Bankruptcies and Defaults. The possibility that a travel supplier might declare bankruptcy or become insolvent represents yet another risk. Customers might receive compensation by filing a claim in bankruptcy court—but the refund may be small and slow in coming. For fuller protection, some travel insurance policies offer coverage against defaults. As discussed in earlier chapters, however, protection also comes from

- The consumer protection plan of the United States Tour Operators Association. The USTOA $1 Million Travelers Assistance Program is solely for use in reimbursing consumers for tour payments or deposits lost in the event of a) a USTOA Active member bankruptcy; b) a USTOA Active Member insolvency; c) a USTOA Active Member cessation of business; d) failure of a USTOA Active member to refund consumer deposits or payments within 120 days following its cancellation of a tour(s) or vacation packages(s) or its material failure to complete performance of a tour(s) or vacation package(s).
- The consumer protection plan of the National Tour Association (NTA). It provides refunds to those who book with a company that is a member of NTA if the company officially declares bankruptcy.
- Payment by credit card. Usually, if customers can provide documentation, credit card companies ensure that they do not pay for services not received.

The Role of the Travel Counselor

Travel counselors sell insurance from two types of sources. First, insurance companies appoint travel agencies to sell their policies. The commission from the insurance companies usually runs between 20 and 35 percent. The agency's management usually selects the insurance company the agency will use and all counselors use that one company.

Second, tour companies and cruise lines offer insurance to those booking their tours and cruises, and travel counselors can sell this insurance when they sell the tours or cruises. But selling insurance from these sources has two drawbacks. First, clients are not protected if the tour company or cruise line offering the insurance goes out of business. Second, the commission rate for the insurance sale is the same as for the rest of the package, which is likely to be only 10 percent. However, compared with insurance from insurance companies, insurance from tour or cruise companies may be less expensive for the clients, and processing these insurance sales requires less of the counselor's time. To address this last issue, some insurance companies now allow travel agencies to issue insurance policies online. Many of these relatively inexpensive insurance offers from the tour or cruise company itself are not always true third-party insurance but merely a waiver.

Although it is dangerous to generalize, some form of travel insurance is likely to be very desirable for

- Any tour, cruise, airfare, or other arrangement with high cancellation penalties.
- All charter arrangements.
- All escorted tours when baggage may be left out overnight for early-morning pickup.
- People with conditions or responsibilities that might hinder their departure at the last minute.

Mailing a client a brochure that describes travel insurance may be sufficient to constitute an offer of insurance for legal purposes. Of course, referring to insurance or recommending it during the sales presentation, whether in person or by telephone or mail, is more effective and more clearly an offer in a legal sense. If insurance is offered and refused, that fact should be noted in the client's file, and the client should be asked to initial a spot on the final invoice indicating that the offer was refused.

Whenever insurance seems advisable, travel counselors should

- Advise clients to check their existing health and homeowner's policies and their credit card agreements to see what coverage they already have. (Clients may, for example, want to insure their baggage only for the amount of the deductible on their homeowner's policy.)
- Check all suppliers' cancellation penalties and refund policies.
- Present all the options as clearly as possible and allow clients to determine what is best.
- Be sure the client is aware of what is and what is not covered by the insurance.

CHAPTER WRAP-UP

CHAPTER HIGHLIGHTS

To succeed in selling, travel professionals must respond to the needs of particular individuals and the demands of specific situations. This chapter outlined some of the important variations in these needs and situations. Here is a review of the objectives with which we began the chapter.

1. **Describe three key variations in selling situations that travel sellers must adjust to.** Travel sellers must adjust to differences in the purpose of trips, differences in the interests of travelers, and differences in the special needs of travelers. For example, travelers with disabilities may have special requirements such as rental cars with room for a wheelchair, bathrooms large enough for wheelchairs, hotels with accessible entrances, or accommodations for a Seeing Eye dog. Families may need babysitting services or special activities for children. Members of some religious groups follow special diets and restrict their activities on certain days.

2. **State four principles to follow when selling a trip to a group.** Learn all you can about the makeup of the group. Target the presentation to the average member of the group. Establish a strong relationship with the key decision maker in the group. Select a specific trip to promote.

3. **Discuss the distinctive characteristics of business travel.** Two clients must be satisfied: the company and the traveler. For the company, commercial agencies offer many services that help the company manage travel and reduce costs. Individual business travelers are likely to be especially interested in receiving prompt service with accurate arrangements, being able to change their travel arrangements quickly, and having an environment suitable for working during the trip. They are also likely to be interested in having access to services that enable them to conduct business and to relieve stress during the trip.

4. **Describe the special challenges involved in arranging meetings and incentive travel.** Meetings and incentive programs involve a host of details. Meeting planners act as intermediaries between suppliers and the host of the meeting. Their functions depend on the size and duration of the meeting and the wishes of the buyer, but they might involve just about anything from clarifying the goals of the meeting to selecting wines or speakers. Those involved in arranging incentive travel face the additional challenge of learning to think of a trip as part of a motivational program.

5. **Discuss some of the other specialties within the travel industry that have become popular, such as adventure travel, cruise-only agencies, ethnic**

agencies, inbound travel, romantic/honeymoon specialists and gay/lesbian specialty companies. The market has become splintered into many additional specialties including adventure travel, one of the largest, offering hard adventure, soft adventure, and cultural adventure trips. Another niche is cruise-only agencies, which concentrate on selling the cruise experience only. Some agencies have particular expertise for specific ethnic groups, particularly the Latin-American market and the Chinese market. The reverse face of outbound travel is inbound travel, sometimes called receptive travel, specializing in arrangements for incoming visitors. Honeymoon experts also are a popular niche as are companies that cater to the gay/lesbian market.

6. **Identify the main types and benefits of travel insurance.** Key types of travel insurance are flight insurance, travel accident and health insurance, baggage and personal possessions insurance, and trip cancellation or interruption insurance. Travel insurance protects the client's investment in the trip, protects the travel counselor from many forms of liability, and earns the travel agency a sales commission. Failure to offer insurance could render the agent liable should the client be harmed in some way that insurance would have covered.

KEY TERMS

A list of key terms introduced in this chapter follows. If you do not recall the meaning of these terms, see the Glossary, which begins on page 393.

Americans with Disabilities Act (ADA)
baggage and personal possessions insurance
Center for Exhibition Industry Research (CEIR)
commercial agency
Convention Industry Council (CIC)
ethnic agencies
flight insurance
honeymoon specialist
inbound travel
incentive house
LGBT travel specialty
meeting
meeting planner

Meeting Professionals International (MPI)
Society for Accessible Travel and Hospitality (SATH)
Society of Incentive and Travel Executives (SITE)
soft adventure
travel accident and health insurance
travelers with disabilities
trip cancellation or interruption insurance

REVIEW QUESTIONS

1. How do the needs of the business traveler differ from those of other travelers?

2. Name two things to remember when dealing with the following travelers: (a) travelers with disabilities, (b) seniors, (c) families with children.

3. What forms of transportation appear to be most adaptable to the needs of travelers with disabilities?

4. What would you emphasize about a travel agency in order to inspire confidence in its ability to handle group arrangements?

5. You have booked an escorted tour for clients who want to buy health and cancellation insurance for the trip. You can add the insurance to the reservation with a simple click of the mouse. Should you take this step?

6. Name several specialties mentioned in this chapter, and specify one or two that appeal to you and why.

Part 4:
The Travel Workplace

Chapter 12
Communications

Chapter 13
Money Matters

Chapter 14
Home-based Agents

Chapter 15
Finding Employment

Chapter 16
Building a Career

Communications

CHAPTER 12

OBJECTIVES

After completing this chapter, you should be able to

1. Outline the advantages of the major methods of communication in the travel industry.

2. Describe at least four guidelines for selling travel on the telephone.

3. List five situations in which a travel counselor should communicate by letter.

4. Review at least five guidelines each for effective letter writing and use of e-mail.

5. Describe four methods of interoffice communication.

Like highways to truckers or stocks to Wall Street, communication is key to the travel industry. Clients' needs and dreams; the details of schedules, itineraries, restrictions, and rates; the characteristics and attractions of destinations—these and other facts and ideas must be passed back and forth among innumerable people in the travel industry. Success depends on effective communication.

Chapter 10 (Making a Sale) included tips on how to communicate, but that discussion focused primarily on face-to-face communication in selling situations. Is communication different when you are not face-to-face? Are different skills needed when you are communicating with a colleague rather than a client? This chapter addresses those questions by examining the many types of communication that occur from a distance—through phone conversations, fax messages, e-mail, and letters—as well as interoffice communications.

Methods of Communication

■ WHAT DIFFERENT METHODS OF COMMUNICATION DO TRAVEL PROFESSIONALS USE, AND WHY?

When people communicate face-to-face, much of the message is unspoken; in fact, some claim that words carry only 7 percent of the communication. The tone, volume, speed, and inflection of the voice—all influence how the words are interpreted. *Body language*—facial expressions, posture, and gestures—is often even more important.

When communication is not face-to-face, many or all of these nonverbal cues to meaning are lost. On the telephone, the listener cannot see the smile or the frown on the speaker's face; all of the cues usually offered by body language are lost. In letters, e-mails, and faxed messages, both body language and the voice cues that are available in person and on the telephone are missing. The words themselves must do all the work of communicating. As a result, developing rapport may be more difficult than in face-to-face meetings, and misunderstandings can easily crop up in these other forms of communication. But these communication methods are obviously essential.

How do you select which method of communication to use? Begin by knowing the best way to communicate with specific people. Do they use e-mail? Do they dislike talking on the phone? Do they have trouble understanding your written communications? Whenever possible, use the method with which they feel most comfortable. Don't assume that everyone is as savvy about new electronic methods of communication as you are. Many seniors do not use computers at all or only use them on a limited basis.

When dealing with clients, travel counselors are likely to use several methods of communication—perhaps a face-to-face meeting, phone contact, and e-mail contact. Each method has advantages in particular situations. Whenever give-and-take is needed or one party wants to gauge the other's reactions to suggestions, a phone call is probably best. When accuracy, detail, and permanence are needed, which is usually the case in conducting travel business, communicate in writing. Letters give a personal yet official touch to communications. When a letter would be too slow but something in writing must be sent or the person cannot be reached on the phone, e-mail and faxed messages provide alternatives.

Faxes are written documents that are electronically transmitted over phone lines. Using a fax is rather like photocopying a document and mailing it—but having it received about as fast as a phone call, if the recipient has access to a fax machine. (Fax numbers are noted on stationery, business cards, invoices, tour documents, brochures, and agency reference books.) When speed is important, a fax is likely to be useful for sending material such as

- Lists of client names with exact spellings.
- Itineraries with precise departure and arrival times.
- Invoices with pricing details.
- Visa applications and other document forms.
- Reservation requests with a precise list of client needs.

Today, e-mail is often used to send such material. But faxed messages are not likely to disappear soon. For many people and in many situations, sending material by fax is easier than sending it via computer. This is especially likely to be the case when the document to be sent includes pictures, signatures, other handwriting, formatting, or similar material that must be duplicated precisely in the material received.

Despite the speed of e-mail and faxed messages, delivery by the U.S. postal service or a private company is sometimes the better option. In particular, when the security of the material is a concern, when the material is bulky, or when the sender wishes material to be tracked and signed on delivery, overnight delivery by the U.S. Postal Service's express mail or by a company such as FedEx likely to be the best delivery method. They both offer guaranteed overnight delivery of items of nearly any size, track the material, and provide notification of delivery. These services are especially useful for large packets containing group tickets, clients' bon voyage or honeymoon gifts, and corporate mailings. If mailing passports, send them by a secure method that can be tracked.

Compared with face-to-face communication,
✔ Visual cues from body language are missing in phone conversations.
✔ Visual cues plus auditory cues from the tone of voice are missing in written communications.

Written communications offer the advantages of
✔ Accuracy, detail, permanence, and proof of exactly what was communicated.
✔ Giving senders the flexibility of making the communication at any time.
✔ Giving recipients the flexibility of reviewing the communi–nication carefully and responding at their convenience.

Communicating by Telephone

■ HOW DOES COMMUNICATING AND SELLING ON THE PHONE DIFFER FROM FACE-TO-FACE COMMUNICATION?

The telephone has been so much a part of everyday life for so long that it may seem odd to talk about how to use it, but for travel professionals it is a tool that is worth learning to use effectively. Before looking at some specific situations, we consider general guidelines for communicating clearly and persuasively on the telephone.

Telephone Tips

Communicating on the telephone is different than communicating face-to-face. Telephones tend to decrease the volume of the voice, make it drag, and raise its pitch. To compensate,
■ Speak a little more loudly than usual.
■ Speak very clearly and do not slur words; enunciate.
■ Lower the pitch of your voice if it is normally high.

The absence of in-person interaction and body language presents even more of a challenge to effective communication on the telephone than changes in the voice. You must make your message clear and interesting without the help of eye contact, nods, and other gestures. You need to "read between the lines" to understand the other person's reaction without cues from his or her body language. The following steps should help:
■ Smile. When you smile, the tone and pitch of your voice change, and the caller can hear it. (Try saying "Hello" while keeping a straight or dour face and then say "Hello" while smiling, and you will hear the difference.)
■ Make a special effort to concentrate. Take notes and avoid distractions. Do not try to do anything else, including eating, drinking, smoking, or chewing gum.

On Monday morning you find that Bob Kincaid, a client for years and a nationally known photographer, sent you an urgent e-mail Sunday night. He has been stuck in Iowa for two weeks, and suddenly one of his editors has asked him to leave on a trip to three African countries next Monday to replace someone who came down with malaria. He needs you to make all the arrangements. What would be the best way to communicate with Mr. Kincaid?

Since he sent an e-mail, your first thought might be to e-mail him back. That might not be a bad idea as a backup, but you should realize that you are going to have to use almost every method of communication at your disposal. Call him immediately. You will have to arrange some personal contact because he will most likely have to get pictures and visa applications to you. How will he get the applications? You will have to fax them to him after checking each country's documentation requirements on the Internet, or visa application forms may be available on the Web so you can tell him where to find them. Then overnight delivery to a visa-processing firm in Washington, D.C., will be necessary. What if he doesn't have time to come to your office? A messenger firm might pick up his documents, or you may have to pick them up. You will want to consult with him carefully on the phone (or in person, if possible) about his itinerary. Make sure both of you have hard copies of the itinerary (a fax or a printout from an e-mail) to go over for accuracy. He or his magazine will pay the fees for all these communication services.

- Let the other person know you are listening by at least saying something like "OK," "Uh-huh," or "I see." Remember that he or she cannot see that you are paying attention.
- If you are doing most of the talking, pause every minute or ask a question to be sure the other person has a chance to talk.
- Listen for the other person's tone of voice. It will often tell you when the person is interested or has objections.
- Plan ahead when you make outgoing calls. Know the purpose of the call, the questions you need to ask, and the objections you might encounter.
- Have pen and pad ready to deal with incoming calls. Keep frequently used references nearby.

  To avoid wasting time on "telephone tag," try these guidelines:
- Call busy people early in the morning, midweek, and midmonth.
- Develop secondary contacts who can help you if the person you are trying to reach is unavailable.
- Ask when the best time would be to return the call, and record it for future reference.
- Leave detailed messages so that others can help relay your information.
- Be available when you tell others you will be.
- Remember to take differences in time zones into account.

Also, do not use a speakerphone unless it is absolutely necessary to include others in the conversation and you have asked the caller's permission.

Using Voice Mail

Often the first contact that clients have with a travel business is by telephone, and that first call can create a lasting impression. Today, that first impression is likely to come through *voice mail*, an automated phone-answering system that handles incoming calls. Voice mail irritates some people who do not like talking to machines. But voice mail saves time and reduces errors, offering convenience and efficiency for both callers and businesses. Callers never reach an unanswered phone; they are always able to leave detailed messages.

Here are some tips for using voice mail.
- The greeting should be short and professional. Everyone is sorry they missed everyone else's call; you don't need to state the obvious. If you are making a voice-mail greeting for a personal phone, you might include information about when you can be reached.
- The menu of options should not be overly long.
- Answer your phone yourself when possible.
- Check voice-mail messages frequently, and return all messages.
- When leaving a voice-mail message, state the reason for your call as briefly as possible, but convey the facts necessary for the other person to be ready to answer you. Speak slowly and distinctly. When you leave your phone number, speak even more slowly so that the person can write the number without replaying the message multiple times.
- If you are a home-based counselor, your taped response should sound professional and not have the sounds of children or pets in the background.

Handling Incoming Calls

At some time or other, everyone is likely to serve in effect as a receptionist, fielding calls and transferring them to the person the caller is seeking. Here are some basic rules of telephone courtesy when answering a phone.

- Answer the phone by the third ring. Most people hang up after the fourth or fifth ring. Answering promptly reduces office noise and tension, eliminates distractions, and pleases the caller.
- Use a standard greeting such as "Good morning" or "Thank you for calling." Then identify the company and give your name (and the department, if applicable).
- Ask the caller, "How may I help you?" or "How may I direct your call?"
- Ask the caller's name and use it in the conversation if possible.
- If taking a message, ask the nature of the call and help the caller yourself if possible. The message should include the caller's name, telephone number, and the day and time the call was received. Use a preprinted message pad.
- If you must put the caller on hold, explain why and ask permission ("That line is busy. May I place you on hold?"). Wait for the caller's response before hitting the hold button. Try to get back to the caller within 30 to 45 seconds. If the hold will be lengthy, estimate how long the caller will have to wait and ask whether he or she wants to continue to hold or would rather leave a message. Thank the caller for holding.
- If you must transfer a call, tell the caller you are transferring and say why.
- When the call is complete, thank the caller and let the caller be the first to disconnect.

Selling by Telephone

Even on the phone, sellers should follow the eight steps in the sales cycle discussed in Chapter 10. Many of those selling travel by phone are sales agents for airlines, hotels, car rental companies, tour companies, and cruise lines. They may not give clients the amount of counseling and time that travel counselors typically do, but they do follow the sales cycle.

Reservationists need to establish rapport with a smile in their voice, seek out information from the client, make recommendations, handle objections, and close the sale—and they usually need to do so quickly. Even though others in the company may handle follow-up communications with the buyer, reservationists are often judged by the number of sales made.

In much of the travel industry, those handling phone reservations will be dealing with people they do not know or hardly know. Those working for very large suppliers seldom talk to the same client twice. In contrast, travel counselors try to use the telephone to begin a lasting relationship. They aim to receive a large percentage of their phone calls from repeat clients—people whose needs and preferences they know and who they know will buy.

Clients who phone travel agencies range from *shoppers*—people who merely want information and are not ready to discuss their plans in detail— to *buyers*—those who are already prepared to book. Experience in asking qualifying questions helps counselors distinguish the buyers from the shoppers. Most experienced counselors will not spend time with callers unwilling to give their names, phone numbers, or details about their possible trip. Spending hours with shoppers can be as counterproductive as losing a sure sale from a buyer. But keep in mind that today's buyers were yesterday's shoppers. Many skilled counselors excel at converting shoppers into buyers.

Selling by phone brings some special challenges. Remember that you may have to give extra feedback to clients or ask for more feedback from them to compensate for the absence of cues from body language. Pay special attention to the other person's tone of voice; it may tell you if the person is ready to buy or is too busy or tired to discuss the trip. Because you cannot use brochures, pictures, maps, or other visual aids, stress benefits that clients can visualize and paint verbal pictures. Double-check and then check again to make sure that the picture got across.

Some callers can be difficult to understand because they lack fluency in English, have a heavy accent, mumble, or speak too rapidly. Don't pretend to understand anything that you don't get. Ask them to start over and to speak slowly.

Note that selling via phone can have advantages as well as drawbacks, especially when you do not have all the answers to questions or are not certain what recommendations to make. It is much easier to tell clients you will call them back than it is to ask them to wait in your office or to return the next day. Plus, they won't be able to see the puzzled look on your face.

Videoconferencing or *teleconferencing* or *webcasting* puts the visual element back into the communication process: you can see people and their reactions as well as hear their tone of voice. Using videoconferencing to communicate has become a common way for businesses to communicate. Services such as Webex and GoToMeeting offer free trials and low-cost plans allowing people to work together anytime, anywhere. These services work on any computer or on compatible mobile phones. Skype is a good choice when you need to communicate with people internationally, and it's free.

✔ CHECK-UP

When handling incoming calls,
- ✔ Answer the phone by the third ring and greet the caller.
- ✔ Take accurate and complete messages.
- ✔ Be as considerate as possible if you must put the caller on hold.

Those selling by telephone should
- ✔ Follow the same sales cycle used in face-to-face selling.
- ✔ Take special care to qualify clients.
- ✔ Pay special attention to the client's tone of voice.
- ✔ Remember to compensate for the absence of cues from body language, lack of visual aids, and voice distortion on the phone.

Communicating in Writing

■ WHEN IS IT BEST TO COMMUNICATE IN WRITING?

■ WHAT ARE THE KEYS TO WRITING EFFECTIVE LETTERS AND E-MAILS?

Unlike a phone call, written communications can be sent at any time without disturbing the recipient, and the recipient can take the time to give the message a studied and accurate response whenever convenient. The message can be saved and referred to later. But compared with face-to-face communications, written ones lack not only visual cues to meaning but also auditory cues and the nuances of back-and-forth interaction. Getting one's idea across clearly takes great care. That is why writing well is a skill, sometimes even an art.

Imagine selling a house without writing down all the details that go into the sale; imagine paying for a journey without reviewing the itinerary. Despite its difficulties, there are times when only writing will do.

Business Letters

A letter is the best way to communicate whenever accuracy and some formality are necessary. For instance, a tour operator might phone or e-mail to request a certain number of rooms be reserved for a group; the reply might also come by phone or e-mail. But the reservation will be confirmed by letter or contract. A business letter is generally best to confirm contracts, to introduce a company or personnel, to make or answer a complaint, to ask for payment, and to thank people for their business or services.

For travel counselors, for example, using a letter is usually best in order to

- Request or confirm changes or additions to standard arrangements from suppliers, such as a request to have king-size beds or to join a tour on its second day.
- Explain or confirm complicated or detailed arrangements to the client.
- Advise the client of important information, including deadlines for future payments, visa requirements, and so on.
- Make a record of agreements and details as protection against a client's misunderstanding or future liability.
- Seek refunds on behalf of a client. (If the client cancels arrangements and a refund is in order, the counselor may have to write and enclose documents. If the client returns from a trip with unused prepaid vouchers, these too must be submitted with a written request for a refund.)
- Thank the client for a reservation.
- Promote sales.
- Welcome the client home from a trip.

Sometimes, for people you deal with regularly, e-mails can be used instead of business letters for these purposes. Experience will tell you when that is the case. When in doubt, use a business letter. When precision is important, always use a business letter.

Figures 12.1 and 12.2 show examples of letters. For efficiency, form letters that deal with common situations can be prepared and then modified to suit individual cases.

Whatever its purpose, the fundamental rule of business correspondence is to communicate information as briefly and clearly as possible. Organization is key. In addition, through its appearance as well as its content, a letter should help convey an image of professionalism. Attention to spelling, grammar, and neatness enhances that image and boosts the credibility of the statements in the letter.

In order to meet these goals, try to follow these guidelines.

- Limit letters to one page whenever possible.
- Try to avoid sentences with more than seventeen words.
- Use short paragraphs.
- Use active verbs; for example, "We recommend," not "It is recommended."
- Put important ideas at the beginning of paragraphs.
- Describe rules, requirements, and procedures in your own words. Do not merely quote a source.
- Avoid jargon such as "Unfortunately, your reservation came up no rec."
- Use the first person ("I" or "we") rather than "this office."
- Use simple, straightforward language. Instead of "Please remit your

remuneration," write "Please send payment." Rather than "This agency regrets this inadvertent error," write "We are sorry."

In addition, when sending marketing letters, catch the reader's attention immediately and ask for a response. Most people look at the top and bottom of a letter for a few seconds to decide whether they will bother reading it at all. Make the first sentence strong, use the recipient's name and title, sign your name in color, add a postscript (P.S.), and set a deadline for a response.

E-Mail

Strictly speaking, *e-mail* is simply a method of delivering a written message electronically. It brings many of the advantages of sending a letter—plus

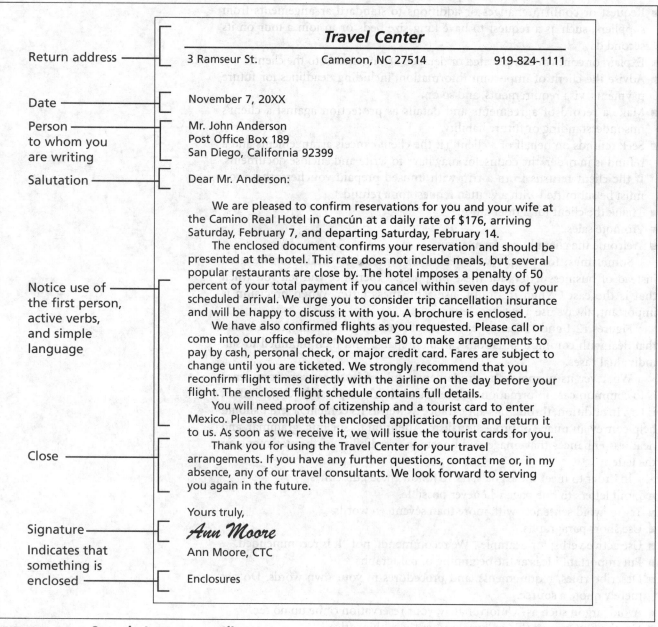

Return address	**Travel Center**
	3 Ramseur St. Cameron, NC 27514 919-824-1111
Date	November 7, 20XX
Person to whom you are writing	Mr. John Anderson Post Office Box 189 San Diego, California 92399
Salutation	Dear Mr. Anderson:
Notice use of the first person, active verbs, and simple language	We are pleased to confirm reservations for you and your wife at the Camino Real Hotel in Cancún at a daily rate of $176, arriving Saturday, February 7, and departing Saturday, February 14. The enclosed document confirms your reservation and should be presented at the hotel. This rate does not include meals, but several popular restaurants are close by. The hotel imposes a penalty of 50 percent of your total payment if you cancel within seven days of your scheduled arrival. We urge you to consider trip cancellation insurance and will be happy to discuss it with you. A brochure is enclosed. We have also confirmed flights as you requested. Please call or come into our office before November 30 to make arrangements to pay by cash, personal check, or major credit card. Fares are subject to change until you are ticketed. We strongly recommend that you reconfirm flight times directly with the airline on the day before your flight. The enclosed flight schedule contains full details. You will need proof of citizenship and a tourist card to enter Mexico. Please complete the enclosed application form and return it to us. As soon as we receive it, we will issue the tourist cards for you.
Close	Thank you for using the Travel Center for your travel arrangements. If you have any further questions, contact me or, in my absence, any of our travel consultants. We look forward to serving you again in the future.
	Yours truly,
Signature	*Ann Moore*
Indicates that something is enclosed	Ann Moore, CTC
	Enclosures

FIGURE 12.1 Sample Letter to a Client

Travel Center

3 Ramseur St.   Cameron, NC 27514   919-824-1111

August 10, 20XX

Ms. Judy Daugherty
Accounting Department
Funway Tours
6259 Griffiths Boulevard
Minneapolis, Minnesota 55469

Dear Ms. Daugherty:

Our clients, Mr. and Mrs. William Murray, were booked on your "Acapulco Plus" one-week tour arriving July 18. Because of overbooking, they could not be given their prepaid accommodations in the Hotel Contessa until July 20. They spent two nights in the Santa Maria Hotel on the understanding that they would receive a refund equal to the difference between the room rates at the two hotels.

By our calculation Mr. and Mrs. Murray are entitled to a refund of $48. Please send your check to my attention. I am enclosing copies of all relevant documents.

Yours truly,

Roberta Fairbairn

Roberta Fairbairn

Enclosures

Travel Center

3 Ramseur St.   Cameron, NC 27514   919-824-1111

December 10, 20XX

Kay Macy, President
Honolulu Tours, Inc.
78324 Kalakaua Avenue
Honolulu, Hawaii 96815

Dear Ms. Macy:

I am writing on behalf of our client, Mr. David Tailby, to express dissatisfaction with your "Four Island Fling," which departed from Honolulu on November 20. Mr. Tailby was a participant in this tour.

Three months before departure we had requested vegetarian meals for Mr. Tailby for the entire two weeks of your tour. Despite such advance warning, Mr. Tailby reports that at each hotel he received the same meal, a cheese omelet. Although this menu fulfills the letter of our request, surely on a deluxe tour like this more variety and imagination could have been shown.

I trust that the unfortunate experience of our valued client will cause you to review your procedure in such cases. I feel Mr. Tailby himself is due an apology and a refund. We look forward to your earliest reply.

Yours truly,

Priscilla Henderson

Priscilla Henderson, CTC

cc: Mr. David Tailby

FIGURE 12.2 Sample Letters to Suppliers

speed close to or equal to that of a phone call. An e-mail message is noninvasive and almost instantaneous, and it allows recipients time to review the message and respond at their convenience. It is less intrusive than a phone call, easier to manage than faxing, and usually less costly than other forms of communication.

E-mails can be received instantaneously or take a few minutes to a few hours to be received. *Instant messaging* is a form of e-mail whereby the sender and the receiver see each other's messages instantly. You respond immediately as in a conversation, and you can immediately clarify or modify what you say. Instant messaging is used mostly for personal communications, but a growing number of businesses use it for interoffice communications or in special circumstances.

Guidelines for E-Mail. Find out whether e-mail is a person's preferred means of communication and whether he or she uses it constantly and checks messages daily. If not, you may wish to call for important decisions.

Even if a face-to-face meeting or a phone call is the preferred option in a situation, it may be desirable to send an e-mail late at night or early in the morning. The e-mail can always request that the client phone you.

If you decide to send e-mail to a stranger or someone with whom you are doing business, follow these guidelines.

- Use meaningful, brief subject lines. Many business e-mails are unopened because the subject line has no message, an inadequate message, or may appear to be spam or a virus threat.
- Be concise and simple. People may receive many messages a day.
- Don't neglect spelling and grammar just because e-mail is quick and easy. E-mail to clients is a form of business correspondence, and it shapes clients' impressions of your competence and reliability. Before pushing the "Send" button, proofread carefully.
- Use the "reply to sender" option only for short answers to specific questions. You can set the Reply button in your e-mail program to exclude the original message in your reply.
- Use words, not capitals, to emphasize your ideas. Capital letters shout at the recipient.
- When writing international e-mails, consider the culture of the recipient. Being overly friendly or informal can be interpreted as a lack of respect or insincerity. Err on the side of caution. Use formal titles and keep a formal tone until you are invited by the recipient to use a less formal title or his or her first name. Keep in mind that the recipient's first language may not be English. Avoid regional idioms, symbols, acronyms, and jargon.
- Learn how to use attachments and links. Lengthy information may be clearer in an attached file than in an e-mail message, which has less formatting. However, many e-mail users will not open unsolicited attachments because they may contain viruses. A link provides quick access to additional information while keeping the e-mail message short and the file size small.
- Send unsolicited information only if you have some basis for thinking the person will appreciate receiving it.
- Always include your contact information (company name and Web address and your name, title, phone and fax numbers, and address). (See Figure 12.3.)
- Carefully read e-mail messages before sending them to be sure they are clear and cannot be misinterpreted. Like other forms of written communication, e-mail is not accompanied by your smiling face or pleasant voice.

- Don't be offended if clients state tersely what they want. Assume a smile on their faces.
- Answer all e-mails within 24 hours, at most. The faster you can answer, the better. If you don't have the answer the person is looking for, e-mail immediately to say when you will have it.

Formats. Systems for e-mail vary, especially in regard to the appearance of messages. What the recipient sees when viewing an e-mail message may look very different from how the message appeared while you were composing it.

The two major types of message formats are
- *Plain text format.* All e-mail programs can display plain text format accurately. Plain text does not support formatted text (colors, varied fonts, and so on), hot links (clickable text that sends the reader to a Web site), or graphics in the body of the text. Photos or formatted documents can be sent as an attachment.
- *HTML (Hypertext Markup Language) format.* This message format supports formatted text, hot links, graphics, photos, backgrounds, and Web pages. The sender might ask if the recipient's e-mail program supports HTML format before sending an e-mail that uses these features. If the recipient's e-mail program does not support HTML format, a message using this format will come through as a meaningless string of symbols.

If the recipient's e-mail system is unknown to you, send the message in plain text format.

Legal and Security Issues. Remember that e-mails leave a permanent record. Clients will likely hold you accountable for what you promise to do "in writing." Furthermore, recipients of your e-mail can print, copy, and forward it. Your e-mail may be seen and read by many people.

Also, your e-mail correspondence can be monitored by your employer. Laws vary regarding ownership of e-mail, but typically your employer owns all e-mail sent and received through the company's computers.

Confidential information should not be sent via e-mail unless security features are set up on your computer system. It is crucial that you know whether the e-mails you are sending are *encrypted* (scrambled into a secret code so that they cannot be read by anyone other than the intended recipient) over a secure connection. When in doubt, do not send confidential information such as credit card numbers via e-mail.

Using Auto-Responders. *Auto-responders* reply to incoming messages automatically, without the need for human intervention. They range from basic to "smart" programs with advanced capabilities. An auto-responder can be set up to respond to all of your e-mail while you are out of the office, telling the sender whom to contact in your absence and when you will return to the office.

Building Business Relationships. With the right clients, e-mail gives travel counselors an ideal way to keep in touch during the weeks or months before a long trip and for follow-up after a trip. They should follow up and keep the connection, even with prospects who did not buy from them. Remember, though, that *spam*—unsolicited e-mail—is unethical; new laws have been proposed to make it illegal. Only send business e-mails to individuals who wish to receive them.

Businesses should give clients the choice and the opportunity to "opt in" and "opt out" of e-mailing lists. They should ask clients and potential clients what type of e-mails they would like to receive. Would they like to receive a monthly newsletter or notification of special promotions and sales? Do they want to receive information regarding their special interests, such as news and special pricing for skiing, sports events, festivals, and so on?

Like other technology, e-mail used properly provides tools that allow you to improve communication. It can help you keep in close communication with clients, provide personalized service, strengthen business relationships, and build customer loyalty.

Regardless of which written communication method you choose, it should be sufficiently formal to appear to be business-like, even if it has a friendly touch. Communication methods such as texting are not acceptable in the business world and are best left to very casual situations.

Occasionally, handwritten notes lend a gracious touch to what otherwise might be cold correspondence. They are appropriate to thank someone for hosting you or referring a client to you, for example.

All written communication, in whatever format, should exhibit proper spelling and grammar. Two excellent reference books on writing should be on your bookshelf: *The Elements of Style* by William Strunk Jr. and B.B. White (MacMillan Publishing Co., Inc.) and *The Associated Press Stylebook*, edited by Norm Goldstein. And, of course, a good dictionary should always be at hand.

Your hotel vouchers have been mailed

File   Edit   View   Insert   Format   Tools   Message   Help

Send   Cut   Copy   Paste   Undo   Check   Spelling   Attach   Priority   Sign   Encrypt   Offline

From:
To: anderson@email.com
Cc:
Bcc:
Subject: Your hotel vouchers have been mailed

Travel Center

3 Ramseur St.   Cameron, NC 27514   919-824-1111

Dear Mr. Anderson,

We are pleased to confirm your hotel reservations for you and your wife for your trip to Cancun arriving February 7 and returning February 14th. I express mailed your hotel vouchers along with a brochure of the Camino Real hotel via U.S. mail today. Your package will be delivered to your home tomorrow.

If you would like to view complete details about the Camino Real Hotel in Cancun, simply click on the following link www.camino-real-cancun.com. This Web site provides detailed information regarding the many amenities that this resort has to offer, room features, and restaurant services.

Mr. Anderson, you and your wife will need to show your valid U.S. passports when checking in for your flight and complete a tourist card to enter Mexico. I have enclosed two tourist card forms in the package I sent, so that you both can fill them out in advance.

Thank you for using the Travel Center for your arrangements. If you have any further questions, contact me or, in my absence, any of our travel consultants. We look forward to serving you again in the future.

Best regards,

Ann Moore

Ann Moore, CTC
Travel Counselor, Travel Center
Web site: www.travelcenter.com
e-mail: ann.moore@travelcenter.com
Phone: 919-824-111, Fax: 919-824-1234

FIGURE 12.3 Sample Business E-Mail

Notice that this sample e-mail contains a descriptive subject line, an e-letter head, a hot link, and a signature.

Two essential elements of an effective business letter are
✔ Organization.
✔ Clear and concise writing.

E-mail has the advantages of
✔ Being almost instantaneous.
✔ Being noninvasive.
✔ Allowing recipients to review the message and respond at their convenience.

Interoffice Communications

■ WHAT ARE THE KEY METHODS OF COMMUNICATION WITHIN TRAVEL OFFICES?

Travel offices are information centers. Information comes in many forms from suppliers, clients, and colleagues. Letters or e-mails that are of interest to everyone in an office can be circulated. Messages via GDS queues, memos, staff meetings, or manuals may be the most efficient way to share other information.

Although most travel employees use e-mail for interoffice communications, GDSs permit users to place messages, reminders, or instructions in storage (on *queue*) for coworkers or others on the system. The queue system is still the official way that rates on complicated itineraries are transmitted, schedule changes are announced, and other changes are communicated between airlines and travel agencies. A permanent record of who accepted the message and what action was taken resides in the PNR (passenger name record; see Chapter 4).

Memos sent via e-mail—*e-memos*—are often the best way of imparting information. They are subject to less distortion than is word of mouth, and they can circulate information almost immediately, before a staff meeting can be arranged. New fares, changes in a political situation, and messages for colleagues who are away from their desks or out of the office require e-memos.

Most businesses in all sectors of the travel industry schedule regular staff meetings. These meetings enable employees and managers to discuss office procedures and propose changes. Upcoming promotions, recent advertisements, and the manager's plans can be discussed. Meetings may also offer opportunities to boost morale or plan responses during crises. Travel agency staff meetings provide an opportunity for counselors who have recently returned from trips to brief their colleagues on destinations. It should be noted that those who are independent counselors, not employees, cannot legally be required to attend staff meetings lest they be considered employees by the U.S. Department of Labor.

Manuals provide another method of interoffice communication. In every office there are certain tasks and problems that everyone should be handling in the same way as well as certain questions that come up over and over again. Describing official policies and procedures in a manual helps ensure consistent service to customers and fairness to employees. It also eases the task of training new employees. In addition, publishing a manual provides legal advantages by proving that certain policies are part of standard operating procedures. The information is stored in a computer, making revisions easy.

Manuals usually include an organizational chart. In addition, they should review

- Policies and procedures relating to customer service.
- Personnel policies regarding dismissal, smoking, performance appraisals, liability, and outside employment.
- Pay issues relating to bonuses, holidays, lunch and break times, overtime, and comp pay.
- Vacation time and benefits, including fam trips in the case of travel agencies.
- Health care, including insurance, pension plans, dental and eye care, and sick days.

Many manuals also describe the company's history, mission statement, and code of ethics.

CHAPTER WRAP-UP

CHAPTER HIGHLIGHTS

This chapter has outlined some basic guidelines for clear communications, the cornerstone of a successful travel business. Here is a review of the objectives with which we began the chapter.

1. **Outline the advantages of the major methods of communication in the travel industry.** Travel professionals are likely to communicate face-to-face, over the phone, with fax messages, by letter, and by e-mail. Which method is best depends on both the situation and the preferences of the people involved. Many nonverbal cues are lost when communication is not face-to-face. Unlike written communications, a phone call allows people to gauge each other's reactions. But written communications offer accuracy, detail, and permanence. Phone, e-mail, and fax have the advantage of speed. Letters give a personal, yet official, touch to communications.

2. **Describe at least four guidelines for selling travel on the telephone.** Follow the steps in selling used in face-to-face interactions, but be prepared to compensate for the lack of visual cues. Smile through the phone, give feedback, and paint word pictures. Listen very carefully, take notes, and review details frequently. Be prepared also for voice distortion. Speak slowly and clearly, and vary your pitch. Remember that both you and the other person may be more easily distracted on the phone than in person; concentrate.

3. **List five situations in which a travel counselor should communicate by letter.** A letter to the supplier is the best way to request special services and to seek refunds. A letter to the client is the best way to state agreements, explain trip details and payment schedules, and say "thank you" for the reservation.

4. **Review at least five guidelines each for effective letter writing and for effective use of e-mail.** The organization of a letter is key to its effectiveness. Place important ideas at the beginning of each paragraph. Keep sentences and paragraphs short and simple. Use short, clear statements and avoid jargon. Use your own words, not quotations of rules and procedures. Limit the letter to one page, if possible. (These principles also apply to e-mail.)

For effective use of e-mail, find out whether the people you communicate with use e-mail and whether they check for messages regularly. Be concise and simple. Do not let the ease and apparent informality of e-mail lead you to neglect good writing techniques. For international e-mails, consider the recipient's culture. Learn how to use attachments and links. Check e-mail messages before sending them. Answer e-mails promptly. If you do not know the recipient's e-mail system, use plain text format. Become knowledgeable about security on your e-mail system. Do not spam people.

5. **Describe four methods of interoffice communication.** GDSs permit people to place messages, reminders, or instructions on queue for coworkers or others on the system. E-memos can circulate quickly in an office and are often the best way to transmit information. Meetings not only allow the staff to discuss office procedures, propose changes, and announce news but also offer an opportunity to boost morale and plan responses during crises. Manuals emphasize more general and long-term issues; they help ensure consistent service to clients and fairness to employees.

KEY TERMS

A list of key terms introduced in this chapter follows. If you do not recall the meaning of these terms, see the Glossary, which begins on page 393.

e-mail	voice mail
fax	webcasting
videoconferencing	

REVIEW QUESTIONS

1. What do you think is the ideal way to answer a phone in an office?

2. The text suggests situations in which a business letter is appropriate. Can you suggest any others?

3. List one situation in a travel business for which each of the following forms of communication would be most desirable: (a) a face-to-face meeting, (b) a phone call, (c) a business letter sent through the mail, (d) a fax, (e) an e-mail.

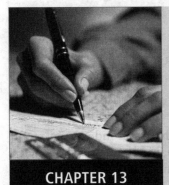

Money Matters

If you are a call-center reservationist, how long should you spend on each call? If you are a hotel manager, should you hire new employees for the busy season or have current ones work overtime? If you are a travel counselor, how much time should you spend with a client planning a deluxe cruise? Should you send a package of brochures by priority mail, use a cheaper, slower method, or suggest the customer look at the supplier's online brochure on its Web site?

Day by day, the impact of the answers to small questions like these adds up, helping to shape a company's reputation for service as well as its expenses, its income, and ultimately its profitability. Collectively, these decisions are just as important as those made by the president of a travel company. Whatever their position, travel professionals should be thinking not only of how their actions fit into the company's marketing plan but also of how they affect its financial status. They should understand where a company earns its money and how it spends it. If they are front-line salespeople such as travel counselors, they must also have a detailed knowledge of how to handle the documents and money that pass between sellers and buyers. This chapter aims to provide the foundation for that knowledge.

The Business of Travel

Consolidation and specialization have marked the travel industry in recent years. Among airlines, hotels, car rental companies, and travel agencies, companies came together to form larger companies, and many parts of the industry targeted increasingly specialized markets.

Since 2001, the new century has brought many changes. The period following the 9/11 terrorist attacks produced nervous travelers and increased security, along with increasing costs associated with new security measures. Other events included the war in Iraq, skyrocketing deficits, rising fuel costs, and a severe economic situation worldwide. The travel industry suffered, too, and is trying to find its way.

How did travel owners, managers, and entrepreneurs make the financial decisions that allowed them to weather the storm of bad news in the first years of the century and to be with us today? At the most basic level, these decisions require a clear picture of a company's financial status and of how payments flow among customers, intermediaries, and suppliers.

CLOSE-UP: ON THE JOB WITH CLAUDIA KEMPTES, AGENCY MANAGER

Claudia Kemptes is the manager of a travel agency in a prosperous suburb of a major city. Its business is split almost equally between business and leisure travel.

"Even though our agency is larger than most, I still wear many hats. Sometimes I'm in personnel doing the hiring and keeping my agents happy. Then I am the advertising and public relations department. I start the training with new agents, but after the first day I delegate that to one of the other agents. Another key area I am in charge of is finances. Everything else depends on this. If we don't make money, eventually we are out of business.

"Our agency has a computerized accounting system. Every transaction that an agent does is entered into the system. This enables me to get a look at how the agency did by the year, quarter, month, week, and even by the day if I ask for it.

"I can keep track of our accounts receivable—that is, who owes us money. I have one agent whose job it is to track this. If she has any doubts about whether this money is going to be paid or the fact that it is taking too long, she notifies me immediately.

"Once we know we have business coming in, my key job is to see how the agents are doing. Each agent has to handle a certain amount of business; that's all there is to it. We have ten agents. If we totaled up all our expenses, our salaries, and our expected profits and divide by ten, then we would know how much commission each agent needs to earn from the business she or he handles. Those who bring in more would get a bonus. We would work with those who bring in less to see if we can get them up to speed.

"Actually, the formula is a bit more complex than this. It isn't divided into ten equal parts. Some agents who have been with us for a while are earning a higher salary and therefore have a higher goal. Others are newer and have a lower goal to meet. We also have two part-time agents who are judged accordingly. And then there's me; I still handle some clients, but not that many. My job is to oversee everything and plan for the future, so my salary goes into the expense category.

"We stress cruises and tours as much as we can. We earn the most commissions from these compared to the amount of time we have to put in. And we stress our preferred suppliers since their overrides will give us more commissions to meet our goals. But mainly we stress what is in the best interest of our clients because we know that is what will make us best off in the long run. I've been in the business almost eleven years and have been the manager for almost three. We're ready to change as the industry changes so that we can be around for a long time."

Income and Expenses

To plan and control their businesses wisely, people need accurate and timely information about where their money is coming from and where it is going—their income and expenses.

Customers may be the ultimate source of most of a company's revenues, but it is important to keep track of the types of purchases that are producing the revenue so that the profitability of different products can be analyzed. For a travel agency, for example, major sources of revenues are likely to include not only commissions from some suppliers but also service fees. These fees partially compensate agencies for products that do not pay commissions, as well as compensate for the expense of the counselors in the agency. For cruise lines, revenue comes not only from the purchase price for a cruise but also from onboard revenues—from shore excursions, casino spending, bar sales, and so on. For many segments of the travel industry, income is seasonal. Tour operators may shut down completely during some seasons. Airlines, hotels, cruise lines, and travel agencies all must plan for slow times of the year.

Expenses are the cost of goods and services used in the process of earning revenue. For anyone trying to control costs, it is important to identify three types of expenses: fixed, variable, and semivariable.

- *Fixed expenses* are costs that remain unchanged during a specific period despite changes in the volume of business. Rent, insurance premiums, GDS computer leases, salaries, subscriptions to reference books, and furniture are all fixed expenses.
- *Variable expenses* are costs that increase and decrease directly and proportionately with changes in business volume. Commissions to outside agents and corporate dividends, for example, should increase when business is good and decline when business is slow.
- *Semivariable* or *mixed expenses* are costs that change in response to a change in business volume, but they change by less than a proportional amount. Some part of the cost is fixed for a certain time, and another part changes with volume. Semivariable expenses include electricity, telephone service, and advertising.

Financial Statements

Usually, recording the daily transactions that create revenue and expenses—checks issued, deposits made, interest payments, and so on—is the job of *bookkeepers*. Analyzing how these transactions add up is the job of *accountants*. Is the company bringing in enough money to update its equipment? Does it have enough cash on hand to weather a slow month? To provide the analysis needed to answer questions like these, accountants produce many types of financial statements that give a financial picture of a company, including the income statement and the balance sheet.

Income Statements. An *income statement* summarizes revenues earned and expenses incurred for a particular period (see Figure 13.1 on next page). It answers the questions

- How much money came in, and where did it come from?
- How much money went out, and where did it go?
- Does the income minus the expenses yield a net loss or a net gain (profit) for that period?

Balance Sheets. The income statement is used to prepare the *balance sheet* (see Figure 13.2); it shows the financial position of a business at a particular time and may compare it to the business's position at the same time of a previous year. The balance sheet indicates

- *Assets,* which are usable resources such as cash in a checking account, money owed to the agency by clients (accounts receivable), office supplies owned by the company, and furniture.
- *Liabilities,* which are claims that other companies or individuals have against the company. For example, it may owe money to a bank, salaries for days that employees have already worked, or payroll taxes.

Palmetto Travel
Income Statement for 20xx

Revenues

Domestic air commissions	$ 33,934
International air commissions	116,134
Consolidator air commissions	45,072
Service fee on every airline and Amtrak ticket Tour and	141,989
package commissions (with overrides and FIT markups)	133,791
Cruise commissions (including overrides)	29,829
Hotel commissions	66,915
Car rental commissions	10,532
Rail commissions	5,733
Travel insurance commissions	11,711
Commission on miscellaneous sales	31,246
Total Revenues	**$626,886**

Expenses

Salaries and bonuses	$343,000
Outside agent commissions	146,387
Rent	35,211
Computers (including GDS fees, hardware, and maintenance)	2,921
Advertising	2,649
Phone	10,742
Utilities	5,680
Furniture and equipment	5,230
ARC, CLIA, and other fees and subscriptions	3,799
Depreciation	3,793
Insurance	26,609
Taxes	5,438
Interest expense	5,000
Office supplies	8,495
Postage	1,926
Miscellaneous expenses	454
Total Expenses	**$607,334**

Net Income (excess of revenue over expenses)	**$ 19,552**

FIGURE 13.1 A Sample Income Statement

Palmetto Travel is an imaginary small corporate agency.

- *Equity*, which is the excess of assets over liabilities. Depending on how the company is owned, the equity may be called *owner's equity* or *stockholders' equity*.

The rule in preparing balance sheets is that a change in the amount of assets necessitates an equal change in the amount of liabilities plus equity. Thus the sum of all assets is constantly equal to the sum of all liabilities and equity. If liabilities exceed assets, the owner must inject more capital soon.

What does the balance sheet tell you? It can allow an accountant to answer questions such as

- Does the company have enough money on hand to pay its bills and meet unexpected needs for cash?

Nirvana Travel Balance Sheet—December 31, 20xx

Assets

Current Assets			
Cash		$50,000	
Accounts receivable		15,000	
Prepaid expenses		500	
Total current assets			$ 65,500
Long-Term Assets			
Tangible assets:			
Furniture and fixtures	$10,000		
Equipment	5,000		
Automobiles	3,000		
Total tangible assets		$ 18,000	
Intangible assets:			
Goodwill	$ 5,000		
Leasehold improvements	3,000		
Total intangible assets		$ 8,000	
Total Assets			$91,500

Liabilities and Capital

Current Liabilities			
Accounts payable—ARC		$35,000	
Accounts payable—other		6,200	
Advance client deposits		5,000	
Total current liabilities			$ 46,200
Long-Term Liabilities			
Note payable		$ 5,000	
Total long-term liabilities			$ 5,000
Capital			
Invested capital		$25,000	
Retained earnings		15,300	
Total capital			$ 40,300
Total Liabilities and Capital			$91,500

FIGURE 13.2 A Sample Balance Sheet

A balance sheet shows a company's assets, liabilities, and equity on a particular date. Unlike this sample balance sheet, some include information about the company's financial position at an earlier date for comparison.

- Is the company using its assets efficiently?
- Is the company generating enough cash to meet long-term liabilities? Will the company be able to stay in business for the foreseeable future?
- How profitable is the company?

An introductory course in accounting describes how to use a balance sheet to compute numbers that answer these and other questions.

Cash Flow. Neither the income statement nor the balance sheet reports directly on another important indicator of a business's status, the *cash flow*—the pattern of income and expenditures that determines the availability of cash. In an ideal world, income would always precede the expenses associated with it. In the real world, companies must pay salaries and other expenses even if their customers have not yet paid money owed. Because of slow periods, even a profitable company may lose money for a particular month or quarter.

Most companies prepare a report called a *statement of cash flows;* it shows how much cash the company generated over a period of time and where it went. The statement shows the company's ability to pay its short-term obligations when due, and the data helps anticipate cash flow needs.

Cash flow is vital to a company. Companies have been forced into bankruptcy, not because they were not doing well or did not have bright futures, but simply because they had no cash to meet current expenses. Furthermore, money on hand is worth more than the same amount promised for some future date because money on hand can be invested in any number of ways to produce income.

✔ CHECK-UP

Expenses are classified as
✔ Fixed.
✔ Variable.
✔ Semivariable (or mixed).

Two basic financial statements are the
✔ Income statement, which summarizes a company's business activities over a period of time—its revenues and expenses.
✔ Balance sheet, which indicates a company's financial position—its assets, liabilities, and equity—for a particular period.

Transactions between Suppliers and Agencies

- HOW ARE FUNDS TRANSFERRED AMONG SUPPLIERS, TRAVEL AGENCIES, AND TRAVELERS?

- WHAT ARE THE BENEFITS OF PREFERRED SUPPLIER RELATIONSHIPS?

The flow of money in the travel industry can get complicated. Suppose a client books a trip with a travel agency that includes flights, rental cars, and hotels. How do the suppliers get their payments, and how does the travel agency get its commissions from the suppliers?

When suppliers work with travel agencies, suppliers may receive payments in four ways:

- Directly from clients.
- From credit card companies.
- In the form of checks from travel agencies.
- Through ARC (Airlines Reporting Corporation).

   Travel agencies receive their commissions from suppliers in three ways:
- Through ARC.
- By deducting commissions before sending payments to suppliers.
- By checks from suppliers.

Thus ARC plays a large role in the flow of payments through the travel industry. Recall that, as discussed in Chapter 4, ARC is an organization owned by major airlines that regulates the sale of airline tickets by appointing those who may sell them. (To review the requirements for obtaining an appointment, look again at page 84.) ARC also issues standardized numbered forms, called *accountable documents*, that serve as tickets, and it operates a centralized system for processing sales. Not only airlines but also an expanding list of other suppliers (including Amtrak and Greyhound) participate in ARC's system for processing sales, which we examine in the next section.

Payments and Commissions through ARC

The *Area Bank Settlement Plan* is the system set up by ARC through which participating suppliers receive payments for sales by travel agencies. Each travel agency pays the ARC suppliers weekly by electronically filing a mandatory **ARC report**, which is an accounting of sales. (The report is also called an *air report* or *sales report*.)

The ARC report is usually prepared by the travel agency's bookkeeping staff or by a designated employee, usually a Certified ARC Specialist, or CAS. ARC requires that in order to receive an ARC appointment, a business must have a CAS Qualifier on staff. To become a CAS, you must complete an application and pass the CAS test. All CASs must take the test and be recertified every four years.

ARC's *Industry Agents' Handbook* gives a full description of the procedures involved in the Area Bank Settlement Plan. Figure 13.3 (on the next page) outlines how the system works.

First, customers pay the travel agency for the airline ticket or other accountable document with cash, check, or credit card. The travel agency deposits cash and checks received from clients into the travel agency's own bank account.

Within two days after the end of each business week, the agency submits an ARC report via computer to ARC's clearinghouse in Arlington, Virginia, so filing for the previous week must take place every Tuesday. (Currently, Sunday is the last day of the business week.) This process is called *Interactive Agent Reporting (IAR)*. The software for IAR, *Interactive Plus,* can be downloaded at no additional charge. When an agency uses IAR, its daily ticket sales are transmitted from their reservations systems nightly to IAR, which prepares the weekly sales summary daily, allowing the agency to verify transactions and correct any errors. Note that voiding of any air tickets must be done within 24 hours of issue, except for Fridays, Saturdays, and Sundays, which can be voided on Monday.

The ARC report itemizes all of the travel agency's sales to ARC suppliers. It also contains adjustments. For example, the ARC report shows the commissions on credit card sales deducted from the cash amount that the agency owes the airlines, as well as adjustments for tickets refunded directly by an airline. It also includes adjustments for *credit memos* and *debit memos;* these are documents sent by a supplier when a travel agency has reported incorrect amounts for commissions or fares.

The ARC processing center acts as a collection point for ARC reports and disburses money to the appropriate suppliers. It calculates the total amount due the suppliers and presents a demand for that money (called a *draft*) to the travel agency's bank.

The amount withdrawn from the agency's bank account equals cash sales minus commissions from both cash and credit card sales. Thus commissions remain in the travel agency's bank account. The commissions are calculated on the **base fare**—the fare shorn of all taxes.

The ARC bank then disburses the money to the appropriate suppliers. It also forwards credit card billings to the credit card companies, which pay the suppliers.

In short, the travel agency reports its sales each week to ARC, and ARC withdraws money from the travel agency's bank and pays the suppliers. Thus, whether clients pay or not, the agency pays for a ticket within a week of issuing it. To protect against miscalculations by the area bank, the agency tells the bank each week the maximum amount to be withdrawn from its account.

After the area bank has processed all transactions, an *agency sales summary* is accessible on the Internet (over a secure connection), usually within three days after the ARC report was submitted. (For an extra charge, the agency can receive a paper version of the summary in the mail.) Along with other information, the sales summary itemizes all of the travel agency's sales to ARC suppliers with a breakdown of commission, tax, and net remittance for each transaction. The travel agency reconciles its weekly ARC

FIGURE 13.3 ARC Settlement Plan

This diagram shows what happens to payments that come to an agency for travel with ARC suppliers. The agency receives its commission immediately because ARC leaves the amount of the commission in the agency's bank account.

report with ARC's agency sales summary to correct its bookkeeping or to request an adjustment from ARC or an ARC supplier.

Agency Payments by Check

To pay suppliers for services not covered by ARC documents, travel agencies send checks to suppliers. These checks are usually for the *net amount;* in other words, agencies deduct their commissions before sending checks to suppliers. Deposits and taxes complicate the process.

■ If clients pay a deposit, no commission is taken from the deposit. The total commission is deducted from the final payment.

■ No commission is received on taxes if the taxes are calculated separately and added to the package. If taxes are not listed separately but included in the cost of the package, the commission is still taken on the entire package. For example, a tour company will include hotel taxes as part of the stated cost of a package and, in effect, pays a commission on them.

Suppose the cost of a tour package, including taxes, is $549 and the commission rate is 12 percent. Twelve percent of $549 is $65.88, and it is deducted from the final payment. The transactions might go as follows:

1. The client pays a deposit of $100 to the agency to hold the reservation.
2. The agency deposits the check.
3. The agency sends an agency check made out to the tour company or to its escrow account for the full deposit, $100. (An **escrow account** consists of funds or other property that is held by a third party, such as a bank, until specified conditions are met for its release.)
4. The client makes the final payment of $449.
5. The agency deposits the check.
6. The agency calculates the payment due the supplier by deducting the commission of $65.88 from $449 and sends a check for that amount, $383.12, to the tour company (or its escrow account).

Notice that the agency sends the deposit in full to the tour operator and later submits a check to the tour operator for the balance less the commission. A record of monies received and disbursed on behalf of a client should be part of the client's file.

As another example, suppose the price of a cruise air/sea package is $1,499 and the commission rate is 10 percent. There are also port taxes of $109, for a total cost of $1,608. The commission, however, is 10 percent of the quoted cost of $1,499, which comes to $149.90. The sequence of transactions might be as follows:

1. The client pays a deposit of $200 to the agency by check.
2. The agency deposits the check.
3. The agency sends a check for $200 to the cruise line.
4. The client makes the final payment of $1,408 by check.
5. The agency deposits the check.
6. The agency deducts the commission of $149.90 from $1,408 and sends the cruise line the net amount, $1,258.10.
7. The taxes are passed from the cruise line to the governments involved.

For payments overseas, a company may calculate the dollar equivalent of the currency amount owed and send a check drawn on its U.S. bank account, but the amount sent will seldom be exact because exchange rates vary daily. The solution may be to send a check in the local currency. International currency specialists write drafts in local currency drawn on that country's banks. Local banks also provide this service, but they charge more for it. For more information, speak with the international department of your bank.

Checks from Suppliers to Agencies

If clients pay suppliers themselves or if clients pay non-ARC suppliers by credit card, the supplier sends the travel agency a check for the commission. The agency must keep careful track of these commissions due. Chapter 12 included suggestions for how to make effective requests for late commissions.

Most suppliers pay commissions in a timely way, but a few become notorious for slow payment or no payment. In some cases, the failure may reflect a simple oversight. But an overdue payment could mean the supplier is in financial difficulty—a fact that the agency will want to know immediately.

Preferred Supplier Relationships

Regardless of how suppliers pay commissions to agencies, most suppliers offer *overrides*, or bonus commissions, to agencies that meet various sales goals or move clients to the supplier's products. For example, a tour operator might offer

- A 1 percent override after the travel agency has sold 25 tours in the same year.
- A 2 percent override after the agency has sold 50 tours in the same year.
- A 3 percent override after the agency has sold 100 tours in the same year, or perhaps the override is based on dollar volume.

The program might be published for all agencies, or it might be set up by contract between particular agencies and the tour operator. Establishing such an override usually results in the preferred supplier relationship discussed in other chapters.

Preferred supplier relationships bring benefits to both suppliers and agencies. Suppliers gain, in effect, a motivated, knowledgeable workforce selling their products every day. It is a workforce that gets paid only when it is successful. Travel agencies gain the possibility of earning higher commissions. Agencies also gain many less tangible benefits. The preferred supplier relationship can be a huge help in their marketing and selling efforts. Joint advertising campaigns, shared information, and special sales seminars may be part of the preferred supplier relationship, along with perks such as free shore excursions on a cruise.

Ideally, an agency chooses as preferred suppliers only the best suppliers for its clients. By concentrating on preferred suppliers, the agency's employees can more easily develop in-depth knowledge of the products they sell. They may also get to know those suppliers' employees. These personal contacts may be invaluable in helping travel counselors solve problems for their clients. But preferred supplier relationships can create ethical conflicts, which are discussed in Chapter 16.

✔ CHECK-UP

Key elements of the Area Bank Settlement Plan include
- ✔ The ARC report, which is sent by the travel agency each week and accounts for all sales of airline tickets and other accountable documents.
- ✔ The area bank, which receives the ARC report from the travel agency, withdraws money from the travel agency's own bank, and sends payments to the appropriate suppliers. It also puts commissions from credit card payments into the travel agency's account.

When travel counselors obtain commissions by prededucting the commission from a check being sent to a supplier, no commission is taken on
- ✔ Deposits.
- ✔ Taxes that are calculated separately and added to the cost of a package.

The Economics of Travel Agencies

■ HOW DO TRAVEL AGENCIES MANAGE TO BE PROFITABLE?

For many years, the economic health of travel agencies was tied to the commissions earned from airline ticket sales. The elimination of those base commissions and the public's use of the Internet to book travel posed immense challenges. In earlier chapters we examined how new marketing strategies met those challenges; our focus here is on financial operations.

Income and Expenses for Travel Agencies

Travel agencies today derive their income from numerous sources:
- Commissions on sales of transportation, accommodations, cruises, tours, insurance, and other travel components.
- Override commissions.
- Fees and service charges.
- Markups on net charges.
- Miscellaneous amounts from passport photographs, travel guides, luggage, travel accessories, credit for bookings on GDS contracts, and any other services or products the agency decides to provide.

Commissions. Commissions used to account for the largest share of travel agencies' income, but this share has been rapidly falling and is likely to slide further. The commission rates for different travel products vary significantly. For example, in mid-2001 the *average* commissions paid to travel agencies ranged from 3.75 percent for domestic air tickets to 10 percent for Amtrak tickets and 20 to 35 percent for travel insurance. For hotels, commissions were usually 8 to 10 percent; for car rentals, 5 percent on discount rentals and 10 percent otherwise. Today agencies must depend on fees to the client, which do not truly compensate for the lost commissions.

Outside agents who work through a travel agency usually split their commissions with the agency. The split varies. Outside agents may keep as little as 20 percent of the commission if they refer clients to an agency but do not handle details of the trip, or as much as 100 percent. In the latter case, the outside agent pays a fee to the agency to use its services or facilities. This is often referred to as a ***rent-a-desk*** arrangement.

Overrides. Overrides can determine whether an agency survives. If an agency handles a gross volume of $2 million worth of commissionable business and its commissions average 10 percent, it earns a net of $200,000. If an agency's travel counselors concentrate on preferred suppliers, it might earn an average override of 1 percent on that gross volume of $2 million. The agency therefore earns an extra $20,000, increasing its gross earnings 10 percent. If its previous profit was $20,000, the profit now becomes $40,000. In other words, a 1 percent override can result in a 100 percent increase in profits. Well-run agencies can earn an average of 3 percent or more of gross volume on overrides if they sell the right suppliers' products.

Fees, Service Charges, and Markups. Almost all travel agencies now assess fees for most transactions. Service fees account for a growing percentage of a travel agency's revenue, and that percentage is expected to continue to rise. Agencies that charge fees should have clear policies concerning when they are imposed, how much they will be, and when they can be waived. (See Table 13.1.)

Some agencies charge a fee on all transactions; some find that the commissions paid for most tours and cruises negate the need for fees for these arrangements. Certainly any service for which the agency is not receiving a commission warrants a service charge. Those can include items such as helping clients obtain passports and restaurant reservations or buying noncommisionable air tickets, hotel reservations, and some adventure trips.

Travel agencies also gain revenue through markups on net. They can apply markups when they create packages, taking on at least some of the functions of a tour operator.

Miscellaneous Income. Some travel agencies offer services such as passport photos, currency exchanges, and visa services. To differentiate themselves from competitors, some offer home-security services, pet sitting, grocery delivery for the client's return home, or other special services. Some large firms are becoming "one-stop travel stores" that offer luggage, guidebooks, leisure wear, videos, and other travel-related products. Many more agencies are going in the opposite direction, offering just a few unique services related to their specialties.

Expenses. The expenses of a travel agency are at least as varied as the sources of income. Salaries and the taxes and benefits related to salaries, however, are by far the largest expense.

Strategies for Success

How do the expenses and sources of income add up for travel agencies? Since 2000, the number of ARC-approved U.S. travel agencies has declined

TABLE 13.1 Sample Travel Agency Service Fee Schedule

Service	Fee
Cruises, packages, tours	No fee
Standard domestic airline ticketing service	From $29 per ticket
Standard international airline ticketing service	From $39 per ticket
Ticket exchange	From $60 per ticket
Special circumstances (includes coupons, certificates, manually priced energy fares, upgrades, mileage tickets, paper tickets)	From $60 per ticket
European Rail passes	No fee (rush fee $29)
International rail tickets/reservations	$29 each
Hotel or car only (with no air or rail)	From $25
Travel insurance (with no other travel product)	From $20
Accounting record research	From $25

Actual fees are at the discretion of the individual travel agency. All agency fees are nonrefundable. These fees are in addition to any charges imposed by individual airlines/suppliers.

significantly, to about 23,000 in 2004. The average sales at each location have risen, however, and a majority of existing travel agencies are profitable.

Cost-benefit analysis is one tool travel managers use to hold down expenses and ensure profits. A cost for something that sounds like a frill, such as flowers or gifts for clients or counselors, may be worthwhile if it results in loyal clients and low staff turnover. In light of cost-benefit analyses, some agencies stopped selling airline tickets—thus eliminating expenses associated with ARC and reducing computer costs—and then focused on a niche market or on the sale of more-profitable products such as cruises. According to one CLIA study, on average, selling a cruise earns an agency more than twice as much per hour worked as selling a land package. Thus it is not surprising that most agency managers emphasize cruise sales.

One financial strategy for holding down expenses and increasing income is consolidation. With size come economies of scale and influence with suppliers. In recent years many agencies have merged. Large agencies have bought small ones, and equal-size agencies have united to form larger ones. Each of the largest U.S. travel agencies—such as American Express and Carlson Wagonlit Travel—does more than $1 billion in sales a year.

Most U.S. travel agencies, however, are small and independent, with only one location. Most survive in part because they have entered into some kind of partnership—perhaps as a member of a network, co-op, or **consortium**, which is an association of agencies that retain their independent identities but pool their resources for certain purposes.

Some of these consortiums (also called consortia) have quite a large membership across the United States and Canada. Others may be smaller and regional in nature. Travel agency management decides which consortium the agency will join, and the individual counselors in the agency are asked to book through that consortium's preferred suppliers to assure the maximum benefits for the traveler and maximum profit for the agency. The counselors do not hold individual memberships.

In addition to the preferred supplier relationships available through the consortium, the individual agencies are offered a menu of possible services to which they may subscribe depending on the agency's needs and budget. Those range from marketing resources, technology, customizable Web sites, database programs, client newsletters, access to research, and staff training (through seminars, conferences, and online webinars).

Some well-known consortiums include Signature Travel Network, Ensemble Travel Group, The Western Association of Travel Agencies (Westa), and Virtuoso. Some specialize in upscale travel products and their agencies and specialists often garner superior reviews in travel magazines such as *Condé Nast Traveler* or *Travel and Leisure*.

Most agencies—like most U.S. businesses—have also used another strategy in recent years in order to lower expenses and earn a profit: they have tried to reduce the expenses associated with employees. How much employees cost relative to the revenue they produce is a key factor in agency success. In travel agencies, as in other U.S. businesses, recent years have seen cuts in benefits (such as health insurance and vacation time) while salary increases have been slight or nonexistent for the average employee. In addition, travel agencies have reduced labor costs by significantly increasing their use of part-time employees, of employees paid in part or solely through commissions, of home-based agents, and of independent contractors, who bring income to an agency while adding little to the agency's fixed or variable expenses. To learn about the work of independent contractors and home-based agents, see Chapter 14.

Key elements in a travel agency's financial picture are
✔ Commissions, fees, and overrides.
✔ The cost of employees, which is the largest expense of travel agencies.

Important trends in the economics of travel agencies during the last decade include
✔ Consolidation.
✔ Increased membership in joint marketing organizations.
✔ Specialization.
✔ Increased hiring of commissioned salespeople.

Transactions with Clients

■ WHAT DO TRAVEL COUNSELORS NEED TO KNOW ABOUT HANDLING DOCUMENTS AND MONEY?

As conduits between clients and suppliers, travel counselors assume the role of trustees, charged with protecting the financial interests of their clients and their suppliers. In their transactions with clients, they handle both valuable documents and large sums of money.

Accountable Documents

Several of the documents handled daily by travel counselors with ARC-appointed agencies fall into the category known as *accountable documents*—that is, forms issued by ARC that the travel agency must account for. Each accountable document is numbered. If the document is not to be used, the travel counselor must write "VOID" on it. Records of voided documents must be kept for at least 2 years.

Airline tickets are the principal type of accountable document. As discussed in Chapter 4, most airline tickets are electronic tickets. If the trip is canceled, e-tickets must be voided, refunded, or exchanged like any other accountable document.

Two other types of accountable documents are the miscellaneous charges order and a prepaid ticket advice.

■ A *miscellaneous charges order*, or *MCO*, records deposits and full prepayments for transportation, tour packages, supplemental charges, accommodations, or additional collections. A clear description of the type of service for which it is issued must be indicated on the MCO.

■ A *prepaid ticket advice*, or *PTA*, is an authorization for an airline ticket to be issued at a point other than the point of payment. A PTA is most often used when someone in one city wants to pay for the airline ticket of someone in another city and there is no time for the travel agency to issue and send the actual ticket. Electronic ticketing has lessened the use of PTAs.

These documents are like blank checks to those who know how to use them, and they should be handled with as much care as cash. ARC has specific rules about where accountable documents may be kept during and after business hours.

Invoices and Receipts

In addition to accountable documents, travel counselors also handle vouchers, invoices, and receipts. A *voucher* is any document used to confirm arrangements, identify clients, or indicate payments made. An *invoice* indicates the amount due from a client and constitutes an implied contract between the agency and the client for services rendered in exchange for payment. *Receipts* are invoices that indicate an amount paid and the method of payment.

An invoice must be clear and concise and avoid abbreviations unfamiliar to clients. Besides the amount due, a standard invoice may also carry notices and advice to the client that limit the agency's liability. Additional information on an invoice varies with the agency, but often invoices include the serial numbers of tickets or vouchers and some indication of the itinerary.

GDSs can generate invoices or itineraries, or they can put all of this information into a document called a *computerized itinerary/invoice* or *layman-language invoice* (see Figure 13.4 on the next page). The GDS takes the booking information from the client's PNR (passenger name record) and translates it into easy-to-understand language. It also allows the travel counselor to indicate details of the itinerary and payments, and it can include standard notices or advice to the client such as a reminder to reconfirm international flights.

In short, computerized itinerary/invoices can itemize the complete details of a client's trip. The information can then be automatically transferred to the agency's accounting system, allowing agencies to track sales and unpaid commissions easily. Thanks to these documents, vouchers are usually unnecessary.

Handling Payments from Clients

Usually most travel agencies do not release tickets or other documents until they have been paid for. Agencies encourage corporate clients to use a credit card. That way, the travel agency receives its income for the sale while the corporate client does not actually pay until it is billed by the credit card company. But a few corporate clients pay through a central financial office and must be billed.

Travel counselors should scrupulously follow an agency's rules for handling payments. In general, cash should be counted and recounted and a receipt prepared in the client's presence. Personal checks, company checks, traveler's checks, and credit cards require even more care because they can be forged, stolen, or invalid for other reasons. One agency manager describes the consequences.

> Just think, if we accepted one bad check for $500, we would have to sell $5,000 worth of commissionable travel to make the commission back just to break even. That means eleven times the work and we wind up with no income at all. Actually, we lose big time because I am paying everyone's salary and overhead to do the business.

The following are some guidelines for handling credit card payments and checks.

Credit Cards. Most travel agencies prefer receiving payment by credit card, and a large majority of ARC sales are by credit card. Suppliers largely dictate policies for accepting credit cards. For example, most airlines accept the major

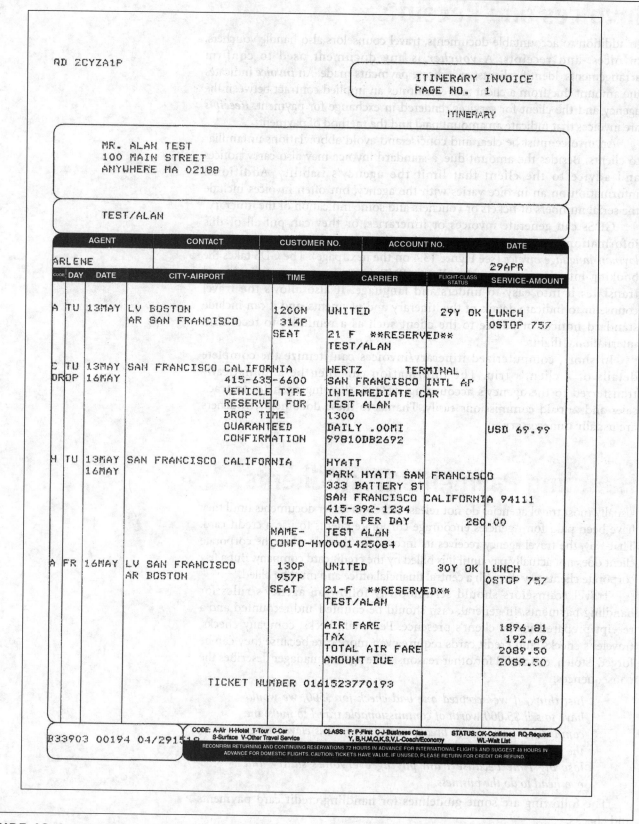

FIGURE 13.4 Computerized Itinerary/Invoice

One copy of the computerized itinerary/invoice is filed at the agency; another is given to the client with the tickets. A more complete itinerary may also be sent to the client.

credit cards such as MasterCard, Visa, and American Express. A few issue their own credit cards (called *airline cards*) for paying for travel-related services. In addition, the *Air Travel Card (ATC)*, the world's first charge card, is currently issued by more than thirty airlines and is accepted by more than two hundred airlines worldwide. Unlike other major charge cards, the ATC can be used only for certain travel-related services. ARC's *Industry Agent's Handbook* lists the forms of payment accepted by specific airlines, and CRSs indicate if a particular credit card payment is not acceptable to the airline being used.

Some travel agencies become *credit card merchants* themselves. In other words, like a store or restaurant, they accept credit cards on their own behalf, not a supplier's, and may set their own policies for accepting credit cards. But they must also pay the credit card company a percentage of each sale.

ARC has set up a system—the *Travel Agency Service Fee (TASF)* program—that allows agencies to accept credit card purchases for non-ARC items such as service charges and to process them through the Area Bank Settlement Plan for a 3.5 percent fee. This program eliminates the need for agencies to have agreements with each credit card company.

Agencies that accept a credit card on behalf of a supplier may be liable for any problems the supplier encounters in collecting payments unless the following steps are taken:

1. Ask the cardholder to give proof of identification by showing a picture ID that also lists a current home address. Only the cardholder whose authorized signature appears on the back of the card may sign for a charge; cardholders cannot authorize a spouse or a child to use their cards.
2. Check the charge card's expiration date.
3. Be sure the cardholder signs the charge authorization form in your presence.
4. Compare this signature with the signature on the credit card.
5. Validate the charge form.
6. Obtain proper authorization from the credit card company (through the computer or over the phone) and show an approval code on the charge form.

Usually travel agencies accept credit card payments over the phone only if the client is known and trusted or if doing so is part of a legal agreement between the client and agency. Take care not to give cash refunds for tickets originally charged to a credit card and to credit refunds only to the credit card that was used for the purchase. Occasionally thieves try to charge tickets to a stolen credit card and then resell the tickets. Suppliers and travel agencies are reluctant to reveal much about these problems for fear of giving ideas to potential thieves, but ARC publishes information to help travel agencies protect themselves from fraud.

Checks and Traveler's Checks. Checks require careful handling. Unless an agency has a different policy,

- Do not accept a personal or company check from anyone, regardless of how much identification the person produces, unless (1) you can hold the tickets or other negotiable documents until the check clears the bank or (2) you know the person and are willing personally to cover payment if the check bounces.
- Do not accept second-party checks (checks with a name and address different from the bearer's).
- Do not accept checks larger than the amount due and then give change.
- Write the client's address and phone number, as well as driver's license number or other proof of identity, on the back of the check.

Some agencies use a check verification service (such as ACHcheck.com or TeleCheck) to verify that the client's account has sufficient funds to cover the check. Another option is an electronic funds transfer, which credits one account (the agency's) and debits another (the client's) automatically by computer.

For traveler's checks, precautions similar to those for personal checks are needed.

- Write the client's address, phone number, and proof of identity on the back.
- Never accept presigned traveler's checks. Have the client sign them again in your presence, and be sure the signature matches that on the proof of identity.
- Accept checks only from reputable, recognized companies.
- Be willing to give some change for traveler's checks; but if the value of the checks far exceeds the amount of the actual sale, advise the client to cash them at the nearest bank.
- Be certain that the checks are in U.S. dollars rather than Canadian or other funds.

These rules should be followed in a matter-of-fact way to preserve the client's goodwill. If the situation is properly handled, few clients will take offense. Those who take offense are usually people you do not want as clients anyway.

Customer Service and the Bottom Line

■ WHAT IS THE RELATIONSHIP BETWEEN CUSTOMER SERVICE AND FINANCIAL SUCCESS?

Money has been the topic of this chapter, but concern for the bottom line must be balanced with attention to customer service. Many services and actions that do not pay off in the short run may do so in the long run if the company's plan is to gain repeat clientele and a reputation for impeccable service.

What does this mean in the case of travel agencies? Travel counselors should analyze the services they render: Will the service bring in extra income now or create a good chance that the client will return next month or next year? Is it in keeping with the image and reputation that the agency seeks?

When faced with specific decisions about service (which clients should receive "Welcome Home" cards, which get flowers or wine in their stateroom, and which get an extra hour of consultation?), travel counselors will find some answers addressed by the agency's policies. But good customer service is an art, not the science of following procedures. Sometimes a counselor does something for a client just because it feels right or spends time sharing ideas because that is why the counselor went into the travel industry. Special occasions when no reward is sought can be the ones that make clients for a lifetime.

Repeat clients are key to financial success. It costs a good deal of money to find new clients. In contrast, superb customer service leads to repeat clients and creates word of mouth that brings in new customers at little or no additional cost.

CHAPTER WRAP-UP

CHAPTER HIGHLIGHTS

To work effectively, travel professionals should understand how their activities influence their companies' financial well-being as well as how to handle the documents and money involved in transactions. This chapter provided the foundation for understanding these issues. Here is a review of the objectives with which we began the chapter.

1. **Describe three types of expenses and two types of financial statements.** Expenses are classified as fixed (which are costs that do not depend on the volume of business), variable (which are costs that are proportional to the volume of business), and semivariable or mixed (which change by less than a proportional amount as the volume of business changes). An income statement summarizes revenues earned and expenses incurred for a particular period. A balance sheet shows the financial position of a business at a particular time, indicating the business's assets, liabilities, and equity.

2. **Outline how suppliers receive their payments and how travel agencies receive their commissions.** Suppliers receive payments directly from clients or their credit card companies, through ARC's Area Bank Settlement Plan, or in the form of checks from travel agencies.

   Travel agencies receive commissions in three ways. First, for the sale of accountable documents for services from ARC vendors such as airlines and Amtrak, commissions are handled through the Area Bank Settlement Plan. Each week the agency sends an ARC report to an area bank, accounting for all sales of accountable documents. The area bank withdraws the money due suppliers from the travel agency's bank account; thus the agency retains the commission once the client's payment is received.

   Second, when clients pay the travel agency for services not covered by ARC suppliers by cash or check, the commission is prededucted from the check that the agency sends to the supplier as final payment. The commission is taken on the total package but not on any separately stated taxes.

   Third, when clients pay suppliers directly and when they pay for non-ARC services by credit card, the suppliers send the commissions to the travel agencies at a later date and need to be carefully monitored.

3. **Identify three benefits of preferred supplier relationships.** Suppliers gain a dedicated, knowledgeable workforce that only gets paid when it is successful. For agencies, preferred supplier relationships make it easier to provide in-depth knowledge to clients, simplify the task of promoting products, provide personal contacts that can help solve problems, and give them the opportunity to earn override commissions, which have a huge financial impact.

4. **List at least five sources of income for travel agencies, key expenses, and**

major strategies used by agencies to hold down expenses and increase income. Commissions on some airline tickets, car rentals, hotels, cruises, tours, rail travel, and travel insurance are major sources of agency income. Other revenue sources include overrides, fees and service charges, markups, and miscellaneous income such as money from the sale of travel guides and other travel-related items. Expenses are varied, including fixed expenses such as rent, variable ones such as postage, and semivariable expenses such as telephone and office supplies. But salaries and the taxes and benefits tied to salaries are the largest expense for travel agencies. Cost-benefit analysis helps businesses make decisions that will maximize income and minimize expenses. Frequently used strategies for ensuring or enhancing profits are consolidation, membership in consortiums, specialization, and reducing the expenses associated with salaries, often through paying employees on a commission basis and through increased use of independent contractors.

5. **Describe precautions that should be taken when accepting credit cards and checks.** A person accepting payment with a credit card should always ask for a picture ID, check the card's expiration date, be sure that the customer signs the charge form and that the signature matches the one on the credit card, get an authorization code, and write the code on the charge form. If a personal check is being accepted, proof of identity should be received and noted on the check. Second-party checks should not be accepted, and change should not be given for checks larger than the amount owed. Tickets and other negotiable documents should be held until the check clears. Whether a credit card or check should be accepted in the first place, however, depends on the agency's policies.

6. **Discuss the relationship between customer service and a travel agency's success.** Giving service costs money, and not every service is worth the expense to a business. But services that do not pay in the short run are sometimes worthwhile in the long run. High-quality service leads to repeat clients—who are key to an agency's financial success—and can create word of mouth that brings in new customers.

KEY TERMS

A list of key terms introduced in this chapter follows. If you do not recall the meaning of these terms, see the Glossary, which begins on page 393.

accountable document
ARC report
Area Bank Settlement Plan
base fare
cash flow
consortium
escrow account

income statement
invoice
miscellaneous charges order (MCO)
prepaid ticket advice (PTA)
receipt
rent-a-desk
voucher

REVIEW QUESTIONS

1. What can an individual travel counselor do to help control company expenses?

2. What can an individual travel counselor do to increase company income?

3. Why do companies need cash readily available?

4. If a company were to hire one new employee, what extra expenses might be incurred?

5. Why are override commissions important to a travel agency?

6. How has technology eased the agency's job of collecting income?

CHAPTER 14

Home-Based Agents

Many home-based agents wonder why they didn't set out on their own sooner. Their earnings exceed what they would have made working for someone else or paying the high overhead costs of maintaining a traditional bricks-and-mortar agency, and they thrive in their new freedom to make business decisions and pursue specialties that match their interests and skills. According to a report from PhoCus Wright, the home-based population soared to 40,000 in 2011 from 31,000 in 2006. Along with those increasing numbers, home-based agents accounted for a substantial portion of agency leisure sales; in 2010, home-based agents racked up nearly $10 billion in gross travel sales or more than one-third of all agency leisure sales.

Still, even travel professionals with years of experience may not be suited to going independent. Some people are surprised by how much they miss the office environment and interaction with coworkers. They also miss the support of departments of experts such as accounting and tech support to call on when things go wrong. Some people discover too late that they do not have the discipline or ambition to work on their own. Some discover that they do not like the risks of owning their own businesses.

Being independent means that you are responsible for all aspects of your business and must weather its ups and downs. What skills do you have that will

Based with permission on Tom and Joanie Ogg, *Home-Based Travel Agents*, published by The Travel Institute © 1999. The Travel Institute gratefully acknowledges the contribution and expertise of Tom Ogg, leading industry authority on home-based travel agencies. This chapter would not have been possible without the help of Tom Ogg, founder of HomeBasedTravelAgent.com, and Joanie Ogg, CTC, the president of Joanie Ogg Marketing Group. Tom and Joanie Ogg together have more than seventy years of travel industry experience.

help you to operate a successful business? How can you strengthen and develop the skills you have and acquire new ones? How do you get started? How do you build a network of support for your business? Should you work with a host agency, or join a consortium, an association of home-based agents and other industry associations? What are the legal considerations for opening your own travel business? This chapter will examine questions such as these.

Of course, this chapter is only an overview of the opportunities, issues, and considerations faced by home-based agents. You can find more detailed information in Tom and Joanie Ogg's *How to Start a Home Based Travel Agency* (published by Tom Ogg & Associates © 2012).

Opportunities for Home-Based Agents

■ WHAT ARE THE OPPORTUNITIES FOR HOME-BASED AGENTS?

The Trend toward Home-Based Work

Many factors have contributed to the growing numbers of travel professionals who work at home. In fact, this change in the travel industry reflects trends in the overall U.S. economy over the past two decades. In many industries several developments have encouraged businesses to use people who work outside traditional offices while also encouraging people to work at home. For example,

■ Advances in technology have made it possible for people to conduct business from almost anywhere while keeping in touch with a central office.
■ Businesses have intensified their cost-cutting efforts as they aim to remain competitive. They may try to save not only on salaries but also on office space, Social Security taxes, pensions, health insurance, workers' compensation, and so on.
■ In many parts of the country, the increased hassles associated with commuting—whether in the form of increased transportation prices or rising commuting times—make home-based work more attractive to employees.
■ The search for a better balance between work and family life makes home-based options alluring to many.

Changes specific to the travel industry have boosted the growth in home-based work among travel professionals. These include the declining importance of air tickets as a source of travel agency income, a shift to pay-for-performance models of compensation, and the emergence of many niches within the travel market, as well as changes in the expectations of travelers and in travel distribution channels.

The changes in travelers' expectations and travel distribution channels are especially significant. Today's travelers have embraced the opportunity to obtain travel services through multiple forms of contact—in person, on the phone, by fax or e-mail, or through a Web site or *social media* channels such as Facebook, Twitter, LinkedIn, or Pinterest. Meanwhile, through the integration of Global Distribution Systems (GDSs) with the Internet and online booking engines (discussed in Chapter 3), travel distribution channels have evolved so that travel professionals can provide a full menu of services even if they are not linked with a traditional agency.

Types of Home-Based Agents

Travel professionals working at home fall into three categories:

- Employees doing some or all of their work at home. Using the phone, e-mail, and the Internet, they can stay in close touch with the home office.
- Part-time or full-time independent contractors.
- Independent entrepreneurs who operate their own agencies.

Home-Based Employees. Many travel agencies, like many other businesses, can now be flexible about when and where many of their employees perform their jobs. Opportunities have increased for agency employees to *telecommute*, conducting business from their homes while staying in touch with the agency's office through the phone and online.

Which agency employees can work from their homes? Job responsibilities at a travel agency may allow not only travel counselors but also those working in Web design, social media marketing, accounting, and sales representative positions to work at least partly from a home office. Work at home is an especially attractive option to *outside sales agents,* people who bring new clients to a travel agency. Outside sales agents may be employed by an agency or work as independent contractors.

Much of what we say in this chapter applies to home-based employees.

Independent Contractors. An *independent contractor* is a self-employed person who is paid by a business to provide certain services. By using independent contractors instead of hiring their own employees, a company saves the cost of paying for benefits, Social Security taxes, office space, office equipment, and other costs, as discussed in Chapter 9. But to avoid violating tax laws, the company must be certain that it truly treats these people as independent contractors, not employees in disguise.

What is the difference between an employee and an independent contractor? Independence is essential. According to the criteria set by the Internal Revenue Service, a business cannot impose control over the independent contractor's time or require certain sales levels. Independent contractors must be free to work where and when and how much they choose. They also must be free to conduct business with whomever they choose; a business cannot require that an independent contractor work exclusively with that company.

The criteria set by the IRS also limit the support that a company can give to an independent contractor. Independent contractors may have a desk at the host agency, but the IRS requires that agencies charge independent contractors a fee for any desk space in the agency's office. Independent contractors must pay for their own supplies, reference materials, and other "tools of the trade" necessary to conduct business, as well as for training. The IRS specifies that independent contractors cannot attend training sessions with a company's employees. Table 14.1 (on page 341) summarizes the major criteria that the IRS uses to determine whether a person is an independent contractor or an employee.

In the travel industry, independent contractors are often travel counselors who choose to become affiliated with one or more *host agencies*. The host agency gives them a means of obtaining domestic airline tickets, override commissions, marketing support, operational support, clout, and credibility.

A formal written contract must be signed between the independent contractor and the host agency. The contract specifies the commission split, which varies but typically is 70 percent to the independent contractor and 30 percent to the host agency for sales made by the contractor. Some agreements allow contractors to retain 100 percent of their commissions while paying the host agency a fee for each transaction. Host agencies may charge a monthly fee to the independent contractor to cover expenses, such as agency-supplied GDS connections, invoices, and other supplies.

Owners of Home-Based Travel Agencies. Home-based agents who do not affiliate with an agency are a growing sector of the travel industry. These business owners make all the decisions for their businesses. They work

CLOSE-UP: ON THE JOB WITH SARA MCLAREN, AT-HOME AGENT

After graduating from a two-year college, Sara McLaren enrolled in a ten-week travel program and became a full-time travel counselor. Eight years later, when she got married, she was one of the most productive people in her office. A year after that, with her first child due and hopes for another, she decided to quit, but after a talk with her manager, she became an "at-home agent" instead.

"My manager, Dolores, introduced me to the possibility that I could work at home. I was skeptical. How would I set up an office at home? And where would I find the time to manage the kids, the house, and the agency work?

"Dolores assured me that I could have GDS access just as if I were in the next cubicle at the office. And she assured me that the agency would work with me. I could take in as much work as I thought I could handle and could stop taking in new clients whenever I wanted. I decided to give it a try and am still doing it three years later.

"Much of my morning is filled with feeding the family and getting the kids involved in something. I try to get to my computer, check my e-mail, and turn the phone on by 10:00 A.M., but sometimes it is a bit later. The pattern for the rest of my day consists of alternate bouts of work and attention to the children as needed. At 2:30 on the dot, we all go out for a walk, whether we feel like it or not and no matter how busy I am. I will often work into the evening.

"Wednesday mornings we have a staff meeting at the agency. It's as important for me to be there for business reasons as it is for me to keep in touch with my colleagues on a personal level. I've hired a neighbor to come in and stay with the kids while I attend the meeting. She also

comes in on the rare times that I go out to lunch with a client or my mother.

"The agency paid for all my computer hookups and expenses, and I furnished our third bedroom as an office. I produce a little over half of the volume of business that I used to do in the office, and I am compensated accordingly. I am trying to better that by increasing my efficiency without lessening the attention I give to my family.

"There are distinct advantages and time-saving opportunities. I put on a pair of jeans and a top, stride barefoot to my computer, and my commute is complete. My coffee cup and snacks in the refrigerator are always an arm's length away. No traffic, no gas stations, and no time wasted. I may be making 40 percent less, but I certainly save money on clothes, dry cleaning, gasoline, and taxes. And if I decide to go to the pool for an hour in the summer, for all my clients know, I am busy on other calls. One downside is that on days when my printer needs a new ink cartridge or for some reason I can't dial in to the Internet, I've got to solve the problem myself.

"Most days you couldn't tell me from any other agent if you were on the other end of the phone. Commercial accounts might call me five times a day, or I might be scrambling to get a room in a sold-out convention area in New Orleans. If I am really going to be inaccessible during the day, the agency picks up my calls. Yes, there have been times when a client has heard baby cries in the background, and I laughingly remarked, 'I'll bet you can tell that I'm working from home.' I figure that when the kids go off to school, I might decide to get to my computer earlier in the morning, but I'll continue my regimen of a long walk in the afternoon or a stop at the pool in the summer."

completely independently and deal directly with suppliers. Operating a travel agency from the home is more complicated than using the home as the base for work as an employee or independent contractor with a host agency.

Relationships with the Industry: ARC, GDSs, and IDs

If you are on your own, how do you maintain relationships with the rest of the industry? How do you shop for travel products and book them for clients?

One key decision is whether you will sell airline tickets. In order to issue airline tickets, agents must obtain an ARC appointment (see Chapter 4) or have an ARC-appointed agency issue their airline tickets for them. Host agencies usually provide home agents with remote access to their GDS and the ability to issue airline tickets with the host agency's ARC number. Home-based agency owners who decide to obtain ARC accreditation in order to issue airline tickets must follow the procedures set forth by ARC in the same way that a retail storefront agency does. As discussed in Chapters 4 and 13, ARC has very specific requirements regarding bonding, financial condition, reporting and bank accounts, security requirements, and personnel training and experience. Accredited agencies are given an ARC number that is used throughout the travel industry to identify them as bona fide sellers of travel in order to receive commissions and travel benefits.

Due to the expenses involved and the limited profitability of issuing airline tickets, fewer agencies are choosing ARC appointments. Most home-based agencies do not concentrate on making domestic airline reservations. For international air reservations, they most often book consolidator tickets that do not require ARC appointments or GDS access.

GDSs provide a quick, easy, efficient way of shopping for airfares and making reservations with many types of travel suppliers. But obtaining GDS access is no longer a stumbling block for independent agents. All major GDS companies have a variety of products that provide access to their systems through the Internet. Many non-ARC independent agents serve their clients well without direct access to a GDS. The majority of non-airline travel suppliers allow travel counselors to make reservations directly with them through a special "agent" section of their Web sites or by calling a toll-free number.

TABLE 14.1 Who Is an Independent Contractor?

Criteria	Employees	Independent Contractors
Behavioral control	Work hours that are set by the company	Determine for themselves which hours to work
	Are hired or fired by the company	Contract to work
	Are trained by the company	Provide their own training
	Are supervised by the company regarding how and where they work	Work independently, where they please
Financial control	Are paid a salary	Are paid commissions
	Are guaranteed their pay	May incur either a profit or a loss
	Are reimbursed for expenses	Pay their own expenses
Relationships between the parties	Work exclusively for one company	May contract with other companies
	Receive employee benefits such as health insurance	May or may not be eligible for employee benefits

Note: The criteria described here are the major ones used by the Internal Revenue Service to determine whether a person is an independent contractor. For additional details, see IRS booklet 1779.

TABLE 14.2

Identification Numbers of Home-Based Agents

1. CLIA membership number
   www.cruising.org.
   Issued by CLIA (Cruise Lines International Association.

2. Pseudo Identification Numbers (establishes an account with the supplier; agent is entitled to commission for sales).
   Issued by individual suppliers and recognized only by that specific supplier.

3. Registered Seller of Travel.
   Issued by your state—if required by law.

4. TRUE (Travel Retailer Universal Enumeration) www.ossn.com.
   Issued by OSSN (Outside Sales Support Network) and the Association of Retail Travel Agents (ARTA), maintained by IATA.

5. VTC (Verified Travel Consultant).
   Issued by ARC (Airlines Reporting Corporation).

If you choose to deal directly with suppliers without using a host agency, you should consider ARC's Verified Travel Consultant (VTC) program. This program allows agents who do not issue air tickets and who meet other criteria to be recognized by, and receive commissions from, certain travel suppliers and organizations. Verified Travel Consultants also receive the VTC Tool Kit, which contains resources and tools.

If you do not have an ARC number or if you are a Verified Travel Consultant, you will want some other identification number that certifies that you are a professional travel seller. Table 14.2 lists numbering systems recognized by major travel suppliers to identify professional travel agents who are entitled to receive commissions for their sales and qualify for travel discounts and benefits. Each has its own requirements for membership.

Networks of Support

Both independent contractors and home-based agency owners face special challenges because they are on their own. Independent contractors no longer have colleagues on hand for on-the-spot advice; nor can they rely on supporting departments for accounting, marketing or computer expertise.

Home-based agencies lose the opportunity for walk-in business. Success will probably require an existing network of potential clients, specialization in a particular type of travel, and links with a traditional travel agency or with an association of agencies. Many independents join a consortium to increase their buying power, to qualify for override commissions, and to take advantage of the additional support that these organizations offer, as discussed in Chapter 13. Many are members of CLIA.

Becoming an active participant in travel industry organizations and taking advantage of opportunities for continuing education will help independents to build a network of support. There are many educational opportunities that we have discussed throughout this textbook; additional educational opportunities are discussed in Chapter 16. In addition, two leading national associations are specifically designed to provide support to home-based agents: the *National Association of Career Travel Agents (NACTA)* and the *Outside Sales Support Network (OSSN)*.

NACTA. Established in 1986, NACTA is a nonprofit national trade association that represents independent contractors, outside sales agents, cruise- and tour-oriented agents, group-oriented travel professionals, and traditional ARC-appointed travel agencies that provide services and support to such professionals. NACTA is a wholly owned affiliate of ASTA, the American Society of Travel Agents. A few of the many benefits that NACTA delivers to its members include a member-only Web site with resources such as recorded webinars, as well as lists of suppliers, hosts, and affiliate members that provide special offers to NACTA members.

OSSN. Founded in 1990, OSSN is a travel industry trade association that represents and supports the home-based travel agency, the independent contractor who sells travel, and the outside travel agent. The many benefits that OSSN provides its members include the Online Member Handbook containing information about how to set up your home-based business, legal issues, marketing, selecting a host agency, and more. Members also gain access to educational meetings, fam trips, lists of host agencies and suppliers that work with independent contractors.

OSSN also offers the TRUE (Travel Retailer Universal Enumeration) code. The recognition of the code by travel suppliers allows travel agents or meeting planners to receive commissions directly from them.

Home-based travel professionals may be
✔ Employees who telecommute.
✔ Independent contractors.
✔ Home-based agency owners.

To be considered independent contractors by the IRS, individuals
✔ Must be free to work where and when and how much they choose.
✔ Must be free to conduct business with whomever they choose.
✔ Must pay for their own supplies, reference materials, and other "tools of the trade" and cannot attend training sessions with a company's employees.

✔ Must pay for the space if they have a desk at a host agency.
✔ Must have a written contract if they work with a host agency.

To increase their chances for success, independent agents should
✔ Become active participants in travel industry organizations.
✔ Take advantage of educational opportunities within the travel industry.
✔ Join an association of home-based agents.

Setting Up Your Business

■ WHAT SHOULD HOME-BASED AGENTS DO IN ORDER TO SET UP A BUSINESS IN A PROFESSIONAL MANNER?

■ WHAT SPECIAL TASKS FACE INDEPENDENT CONTRACTORS AND HOME-BASED AGENCY OWNERS WHEN THEY ESTABLISH A BUSINESS?

Successful businesses are usually those that are well planned. A key question to consider is whether there is a market for what you have to offer. Marketing research, which is discussed in Chapter 9, can help you answer this question. Let's suppose you have determined that you have the skills and personality to work on your own and that there is a market for your services. What's next? You should devote the time and effort to develop a business plan.

The Business Plan

A *business plan* is a summary of what is expected from a business effort, including the level of income, benefits, and investment, along with a statement of mid- and long-term goals. Here are some basic elements of an informal business plan:

■ *Your expectations.* For example, how long do you expect it to take before you will generate income from the business? Do you expect to work part-time or full-time? Do you expect eventually to obtain all of your income from this business?

■ *Your business concept, or the profile of your business.* What is its niche? What is the competition? You may want to specialize in two or three niches to cushion your business for seasonality and unpredicted marketplace changes.

- *A mission statement.* It should clearly communicate your company's purpose.
- *Specific objectives.* Based on your expectations, you can identify specific goals that will direct your efforts and help you set priorities for your activities.
- *Projections for the business.* What income do you project for the first year? For the first three years? What expenses do you project? Do you need outside funding?
- *Your name.* Choose a name that is descriptive of your business's focus. For example, "World Diving Cruises and Tours" is much more descriptive than "Suzy's Travel Shoppe."

If you need outside funding or loans, you should create a formal business plan. There are many books and computer programs that can help you do so.

Legal and Accounting Requirements

Turn to the experts to help you set up your business correctly. In particular, find a good attorney and accountant who specialize in small businesses or travel agencies.

An attorney's advice and assistance should help with the following:

- *Establishing and filing a Fictitious Business Name Statement* (DBA, or Doing Business As) with the appropriate government officials (county and state). Typically, you must file forms with the county recorder's office and place an announcement in a local newspaper for a specified time.
- *Choosing the type of business you will establish: sole proprietorship, partnership, corporation, or limited liability company (LLC).* Evaluate the benefits and drawbacks of each type. Most home-based agencies are established as sole proprietorships.
- *Obtaining the proper business license.* Check with your city hall or county officials to determine if a local license is required to operate a business from your home. Some states require travel sellers to register with the state attorney general's office.
- *Evaluating your business insurance needs.* Your attorney can explain your liabilities and the type of insurance you will need. For example, **errors and omissions and general liability insurance** provides coverage if you are sued by a client for a mistake or negligence. You may purchase insurance through an insurance company of an association of independent agents, such as NACTA or OSSN.
- *Preparing disclosure forms.* A disclosure notice is a written statement that identifies the information you have communicated to clients and is signed by clients. (Figure 10.1 on page 256 shows an example.) A disclosure notice should include receipt of documents, the responsibilities of the seller, cancellation and refund policies, and offers of insurance. Ask your attorney to evaluate the disclosure forms that you plan to use. Disclosure forms are meant to prevent legal problems, but they only help if you keep the client's signed notice on file.
- *Using a limited power of attorney.* Some independent agents use a limited power of attorney as authorization to process phone orders charged to the client's credit card in order to protect themselves from disputed charges. It does provide limited protection and should be reviewed by an attorney.

- *Reviewing your contracts.* Have an attorney look over your contracts with a host agency (if you choose to go that route) as well as any contracts that you have prepared for suppliers.
- *Complying with Seller of Travel Laws.* Check with your attorney to make sure you are in compliance with the Sellers of Travel Law. These consumer protection laws are designed to protect residents of its state, and the laws apply to any Seller of Travel who sells to residents of the regulating state.

An accountant's advice and assistance should help with the following:

- *Assessing the tax implications* of the type of business that you have selected (sole proprietorship, partnership, etc.).
- *Evaluating your business plan.* An accountant can give you advice about the format and content of your business plan.
- *Setting up your books.* Your accountant can help you set up reports needed for funding requests and taxes as well as an accounting system. There are many good accounting programs designed for small businesses that you can customize; see the discussion in Chapter 3.
- *Opening bank accounts.* Most home-based travel agencies set up two checking accounts for their business: a trust account for client funds and a checking account used for operating expenses.
- *Establishing a merchant account.* If you are planning to charge service fees or provide any services or products in addition to those purchased from travel suppliers, you will need to set up a merchant account with the major credit card companies. You may want to use a service (such as Card Service International) that will set up a merchant account with multiple credit card companies and provide the capability to process charges over a secure connection online. This also allows you to accept customer credit card charges via your Web site. If you are working with a host agency, you may opt to use its merchant account. OSSN and NACTA both have merchant account programs.
- *Setting up a federal tax ID number.* An employer identification number (EIN), also known as a federal tax identification number, is a nine-digit number that the IRS assigns to business entities. EINs are used by employers, sole proprietors, corporations, partnerships, nonprofit organizations, trusts and estates, government agencies, certain individuals, and other business entities. Sole proprietors may use their individual Social Security numbers for tax reporting, but suppliers may view an EIN as more professional.

Your Office

Setting up a home office requires time, effort, planning, and money. The investment is worthwhile if the result is a space that gives you a professional atmosphere and convenient access to the required tools of the trade. Here is an outline of the basic elements that you are likely to need for a well-equipped home office.

Stationery and Business Cards.
Use a professional-looking logo on everything—from letterhead and envelopes to brochures and business cards. A graphic designer can create a unique logo that will project a professional image for your business.

Office Space.
In order to take tax deductions for the expenses of a home office, the IRS requires that an area of your home be set aside for "exclusive use" by your business. The dimensions of the office are used to calculate the

percentage of your home that is for business use. You may then be able to deduct that percentage of home expenses (such as mortgage payments and electricity) as a business expense.

Setting aside an area of your home exclusively for your business has psychological as well as financial advantages. It helps you and your family separate personal activities from business tasks and is likely to make it easier to reduce the noise and distractions that inevitably occur in a home. Having an area set aside exclusively for your business is also likely to make it easier to efficiently store and organize everything you need to conduct your business.

Office Furniture. You will need a desk with enough space to conduct business effectively, a comfortable office chair, shelves, and file cabinets.

Office Equipment. Here is some advice about the telephone and computer equipment that you are likely to need.

- Install a phone line under your business name, or consider a Voice-Over-IP service, such as Ring Central or Google Voice. These services allow you to set up multiple extensions, follow you wherever you choose to work and e-mail your voice messages to you. These services can work in conjunction with a land line or independently of one. They also can include toll-free numbers for as little as an additional $5 per month.
- Install voice mail or an answering machine exclusively for your business.
- Answer your phone with a professional greeting, and record a voice-mail or answering machine greeting that identifies your business and your hours of operation.
- Most faxes today can be sent via e-mail or through an online program, such as efax.com, for a small fee, which is often less than the monthly cost of a dedicated fax line.
- If you need to purchase a new computer, consider investing in a notebook (laptop) computer with wireless capabilities. Mobility is especially beneficial to home-based agents who may be meeting clients at locations away from their home offices and may need to keep in touch with customers or perform business tasks while traveling.
- When setting up your account with an Internet service provider, also known as an ISP, (see Chapter 3), consider the high-speed access options available in your area.
- Word processing software is a must-have for letters, flyers, and other marketing and promotional materials. In addition to the desktop options in Microsoft Office, many agents choose *cloud* options, such as Google Docs or Zoho.com. Those are Web sites with software programs that are stored on a remote server. They can be accessed via desktop computer, smartphone, or tablet, such as Apple's iPad or the Kindle Fire. The sites offer much of the same features as traditional software packages for much less, but there are limitations to the features, and a careful evaluation should be conducted to make the right choice for your business needs.

In addition to word procession options, an accounting program is necessary. Choices include desktop software, such as Quicken or Quickbooks by Intuit, and a Web-based option, such as Freshbooks.com or LessAccounting.com. Those are not programs designed for travel agencies, but they use accounting standards adopted by many Certified Public Accountants, which can be useful when preparing taxes.

Web site design software also comes in many varieties. Desktop programs, such as Adobe's Dreamweaver or Microsoft's Expression Web, have an easy-to-use graphical interface, but the learning curve can be steeper than Web-based programs, such as WordPress, and cost can be a consideration. WordPress is free and available as an add-on to most Web site hosting packages.

Depending on the number of office machines you install, you may need to add electrical outlets to your home office. If additional outlets are required, put them on a separate circuit breaker and invest in a good surge protector.

Your Web Site

A Web site can be especially important for home-based travel agencies because they lack a physical storefront. You may want to develop a site on your own, but many companies specialize in creating, hosting, and maintaining Web sites for travel agencies. Here is an overview of the steps to take to establish an online presence for your business.

1. *Determine the purpose and the goals of your online presence.* Do you want your site to act as an electronic brochure and advertisement? Do you want to provide additional services to your clients online, such as destination information, or even the capability to make reservations on your site? Once you have defined your goals, you can design the site to include the features that meet those goals.
2. *Register your company's domain name.* Your URL should be as close to your business name as possible. To find out if your chosen domain name is available, go to www.internic.com. Go to www.icann.org for a list of accredited domain name registrars.
3. *Choose a hosting company.* A reliable hosting company is the foundation of your Web presence and your e-mail. When choosing a hosting company, look for one that offers a service guarantee and the option of an online database. Some offer Web-based design packages, such as WordPress or Joomla, for free. Those programs are database-driven, meaning there are not pages to upload but that the design and the content are separate for ease of changing the design or making text updates via a Web browser. HostGator.com and TravelWebServer.com offer nominal hosting packages that include everything an agent needs to get started.
4. *Develop and design the site.* Using HTML editors, or Web-based services, such as WordPress, novices can create and maintain Web pages without learning HTML coding. However, there are many Web designers and Web-development firms that will design and maintain your site for you, for a fee. CrossoverConsulting.com maintains a list of travel-centric designers and is a good first stop in your selection process.

   If you need to give your customers the ability to make reservations through your Web site, you can obtain tools for online booking through (1) a travel-specific technology company, (2) a GDS, (3) a travel supplier's booking engine, or (4) an agency network or consortium.
5. *Maintain the site and plan for growth.* Web sites must be constantly updated, maintained, and improved. Anticipate and plan for the maintenance and growth of your site in a way that works in harmony with your marketing plan.
6. *Evaluate the effectiveness of your site, and adapt to changing needs.* For each goal that you defined in step 1, you need to develop a method of measuring your success in achieving it. Measure, track, and evaluate the effectiveness of your site on a regular basis. You must be willing to adapt your online presence to the changing needs of your customers.

Surveys and feedback forms on your site are valuable tools to help you make this evaluation. In addition, most Web-hosting companies provide access to reports, called *log analyses,* that contain important information about the visitors to your site. They track information such as the number of hits, page views, and unique visitors to help you evaluate the success of your site.

One free service worth noting is Google Analytics, which offers an independent assessment of Web site traffic and gives comprehensive reports and evaluations of where traffic comes from and how it finds your Web site through keywords.

7. *Use search engine optimization (SEO).* One way to increase the traffic to your Web site is through SEO, which means finding ways to have your Web site appear as high as possible in search results. Different ways to do that include placing key words throughout your site and having fresh content that is updated frequently.

8. *Keep your customers coming back.* Interesting and up-to-date content keeps customers coming to your site. Base the content of your site on your knowledge of your customers. Give them something of value. Make the site as interactive and as customer-friendly as possible. Ask your clients for suggestions about how you can better serve them. Don't be afraid to try something new. Your site can be an effective way of earning your clients' trust and loyalty.

9. *Consider a blog.* A blog is an extremely effective way to connect with your site visitors in a personal way and showcase your unique qualities and experience. It can give your Web site visitors a sense of trust that can be lacking in the faceless world of the Internet. Blogs also give you conversation starts in social media, such as Facebook, Twitter, and Pinterest and can be one part of a full online marketing plan.

Working with a Host Agency

If you are an independent contractor seeking to work with a host agency, you must first complete two tasks: selecting a host agency and signing a contract with that agency.

Selecting the host agency partner that is right for you and a good fit with your business is a key decision. You may choose a local retail agency that has experience working with independent contractors, or you may select an independent contractor network that specializes in working with independents.

Although a neighborhood agency may be convenient, the location of the agency is less important than other features and benefits provided by the host agency. When evaluating a host agency or independent contractor network, consider the following issues:

- *Specialization.* Is the host agency compatible with your business and marketing plan? Does the agency specialize in the products and services that are your business focus? If it does, it will have preferred vendor programs, offering support and overrides that will benefit your business.
- *Training.* What training programs does this agency provide? Does it typically work with experienced agents who require little training? Or does it focus on new entrants to the travel industry and provide extensive training? What level of training do you need?
- *Support.* What level of support does the agency provide? Does it provide

You are a travel counselor who just gave your business card to a friend of a friend. She mentions that she's planning to go to the Caribbean for her honeymoon and expects that she and her fiancé will check the Internet and reserve the trip themselves and save some money. How would you respond?

You almost always want to respond to a person by finding an area of agreement. "Yes, it's amazing what you can do on the Internet," you might say. "We keep a file of some of the best honeymoon hotels in the islands in our agency computer. I'd love to tell you about the ones our clients have raved about, to make sure you don't book at one they were disappointed with. If you two would like to get together with me next week and describe your dream hideaway, I can tell you which ones might fit."

If she seems responsive, follow up with, "What day would be best for you?" If she seems reluctant, you might ask for her phone number or e-mail address. You want to keep as personal a connection as possible, so a meeting or phone number is better than an e-mail address. Your object in the future will be to have another face-to-face meeting to plan her honeymoon—hardly a trip she would want to leave to chance.

quality control of bookings and automated access to a GDS with technical support? If a problem arises with your customer, will the agency provide support and help through relationships it has built with suppliers' representatives?

- *Experience.* How many years has the agency been in business? What experience does it have in working with independents? How many independent contractors does the agency currently work with? How successful are these independents?
- *References.* Ask for a list of references and contact them. Check with the Better Business Bureau to see if it has unresolved complaints filed against the agency. Check industry references and independents already working with the agency.
- *Professionalism.* What memberships in travel industry associations does the agency hold? Does the agency carry errors and omissions insurance? How professional is the owner, manager, and agents who will be working with you?
- *Compatibility.* Can you work well with this group, including the agency owner, manager, inside agents, and other independents? Is your respect for them reciprocated?
- *Benefits.* What travel benefits will the agency extend to you? Will you qualify for discounts on travel and be eligible for fam trips?
- *Finances.* What are the total costs involved, and what do you get for your money? What is the commission split for your sales? What percentage do you get, and what percentage does the agency retain? How are overrides handled? Do you get the same commission split for overrides?

Note that many host agencies do not allow nonagents to work on live GDS systems for at least 12–18 months.

A written agreement that states the terms of your relationship with the host agency or independent contractor network and that clearly identifies you as an independent contractor is required by the IRS. Without this written agreement, the IRS considers you to be an employee of the agency. If you intend to serve as an employee, a written employment agreement between you and the agency should be prepared and signed. An attorney should look over any contract before you sign it. A variety of sample contracts are available through ASTA, NACTA, and OSSN. Table 14.4 on the next page shows important components that should be included in your contract.

Establishing Relationships with Suppliers

If you are setting up a home-based agency, one of your first tasks is to establish and begin building relationships with carefully chosen suppliers. Research and choose suppliers that you know you can trust—ones that can deliver services in the specialties you have chosen. Focus on creating a network within your niches. You must be prepared to prove yourself as a professional who can help your suppliers' bottom line by delivering substantial sales.

Fully develop your network for each of your chosen niches. For example, if you choose cruises as a specialty, become a CLIA member. Once you are a member, you will have access to resources to help you sell more cruises. These include a listing in their Cruise Expert Locator plus free classroom, online, and DVD sales training. Establish relationships with suppliers that specialize in shore excursions so that you can offer your clients a unique and high-quality product with expanded services. Join a cruise consortium to obtain access to overrides, special commissions, and extra services for your clients so that you can maximize your profitability and increase your client loyalty. If you follow a similar process for each of your chosen niches, you will soon develop a complete support network for your business.

TABLE 14.4 Elements Needed in Contracts for Independent Contractors

Parties to the agreement. Clearly identify all parties to the agreement, including Social Security numbers and mailing addresses.

Purpose of the agreement. Define and state the purpose of the agreement. Be as specific as possible.

Term of the agreement. Define a specific length of time (term) in which the agreement will be valid. You may want to include a rollover clause so that the contract can be automatically renewed at the end of the term. For example, "the agreement shall be month to month and will automatically renew at the beginning of each new month." Always include a statement that allows for termination of the contract by either party for any reason. For example, "this agreement may be canceled by either party for any reason, with or without cause, with 60 days' written notice of intent to cancel."

Duties of the parties of the agreement. Describe the specific duties of both parties. Be as thorough and complete as possible. If the agency has verbally stated that training or support will be provided, include the details of what will be provided in the agreement.

Independent contractor statement. The agreement must clearly state the working relationship between you and the agency, identifying you as an independent contractor and not an employee. Include characteristics of the relationship that further define you as an independent contractor, such as nonexclusivity; your paying for "tools of the trade"; your freedom to work where, when, and how much you choose; and the risk of profit and loss.

IRS reporting. The agreement must state that all commissions paid to the independent contractor will be reported on an IRS 1099 form and that the independent contractor is responsible for reporting and paying taxes.

Commission split or other remuneration. The exact details of the commission split, the override split, charges or fees due to the agency, and the timing and method of payments to the independent contractor should be specified. The agreed-upon method of resolving disputes over commissions and payments should also be clearly defined.

Ownership of accounts. A clear, concise statement of who owns the accounts that the independent contractor brings into the agency will eliminate problems when the relationship between the independent contractor and the host agency has

ended. This is a common area of dispute that should be agreed upon at the outset of the relationship.

Payment for services. Details of the collection of funds and the policies for holding client funds need to be clearly defined. How are clients' checks and credit card charges processed and handled? Does the independent contractor collect a client check and then issue a business check to the host agency? What is the procedure for handling bounced checks or denied credit card charges? How and when are commissions paid when the client uses a credit card for payment?

Indemnification. *Indemnification* means protection against or compensation for damage, loss, or injury suffered. Your agreement should contain an indemnification clause that specifies in what circumstances each party will indemnify the other from loss created by errors and omissions. For example, if the host agency issues an airline ticket for the wrong date, the agency should be responsible for the expenses incurred to correct the situation; however, if the independent contractor made the error, he or she should bear the expense. Defining resolutions for these issues in advance goes a long way in ensuring that each party acts in the best interests of the other.

Miscellaneous operating and service fees. Both parties need to agree upon charges that the independent contractor will pay to the agency to perform tasks that service their clients but do not create revenue, such as reissued tickets, voided tickets, coupons, and frequent-flyer tickets. Any additional fees should be clearly identified in the written agreement.

Travel benefits. The complete extent of travel benefits the independent contractor will receive and the procedure for obtaining these benefits should be specified in the written agreement.

Compliance with local, state, and federal laws. The written agreement should include a statement that both parties will comply with all local, state, and federal laws during the term of the contract.

Miscellaneous clauses. Your attorney may suggest specific wording and clauses that should be added to the agreement—for example, which state laws apply if the host agency and independent contractor are located in different states, which party will be responsible for paying attorney fees if there is a dispute, and other specifics that should be explicitly stated and agreed upon by both parties.

Note: This list is not comprehensive. For a more detailed list with explanations, see Tom Ogg & Associates, *How to Start a Home Based Travel Agency*, available from www. homebasedtravelagent.com.

To set up a home business, you should
✔ Develop a business plan.
✔ Obtain expert advice from an attorney and an accountant.
✔ Invest the time and money to create a professional, convenient office space.
✔ Establish a Web site.

✔ Consider whether to work with a host agency if you are an independent contractor.
✔ Establish relationships with suppliers if you are an independent agency owner.
✔ Establish a support network.

Growing Your Business

■ HOW DO HOME-BASED AGENTS EXPAND THEIR BUSINESSES?

Now that you have all the components in place for your business, you need to bring in customers and grow your business. As with all aspects of your business, purposeful and careful planning is required to ensure that your marketing efforts are effective. You will need to define your market, establish a marketing budget, and design a marketing plan to achieve the objectives in your business plan. Business growth requires finding the right marketing mix and differentiating your products and services from the competition.

The Marketing Mix

Chapter 9 explains why developing a marketing plan is critical to the success of any business. A *marketing plan* selects a target market and describes how to handle four basic characteristics of the business called the *marketing mix* or the *four Ps of marketing:* product, promotion, place, and price. Although each home-based agent creates a marketing mix based on his or her business goals and budget, here are some common choices made by home-based agents:

■ *Product.* Most home-based agents specialize in a type of product or activity, a type of client (target market), or a destination.
■ *Promotion.* Many home-based agencies use a combination of methods of promotion. A review of Chapter 9 will remind you of the many forms of promotion that travel sellers can use. Consider your target market when choosing promotion methods, in addition to your budget.
■ *Place.* Although their offices may be in their homes, many home-based agents conduct business over the Internet, make "house calls" at clients' homes or businesses, and conduct travel seminars in meeting rooms of hotels or public libraries.
■ *Price.* Some home-based agents specialize in upscale, luxury travel; others provide products and services in a variety of price ranges. Although most home-based agencies cannot compete by offering the lowest price, they provide value to their clients. Often they can deliver extra services through personal attention to each client and through expert knowledge of their niche.

TABLE 14.3

■ **Tip 1: Look around you.**

Look to your right, look to your left. Your next client is only three feet away from you. Whether you are standing in line at the grocery store or sitting in the bleachers at a little league baseball game, that person next to you is a potential client. Start a conversation; tell people what you do. Pass out your business cards, and give them to your family and friends to pass out for you. That is an inexpensive way to advertise your business.

■ **Tip 2: Promote yourself.**

There are lots and lots of travel agents out there and there is the Internet. How do you compete? Promote your customer service. People want the best value for their money, and they want to feel that someone cares about their vacation. Be accommodating; meet your clients where and when it is convenient for them. Let them know you are there whenever they need you. Deliver their travel documents in clever, creative ways. They will appreciate it and will share your name with others.

■ **Tip 3: Don't be a couch potato.**

Clients will not just show up on your doorstep. You have to go out and find them. Become involved in local organizations, such as the Chamber of Commerce. Volunteer to work on community or church events. Join a networking group in your area. Advertise in church and school bulletins. Wear a shirt or jacket or carry a tote bag with your logo and agency name when you attend functions. Be visible in your community.

Source: Nancy Kist, CTC, president of Career Quest Training Center (www.careerquesttraining.com).

Whatever your marketing mix, develop a brochure that describes and promotes your business. Include a mission statement, a list of the services you offer, the benefits that you provide your clients, and your credentials as an expert. Consider adding testimonials from satisfied customers and the professional organizations that your business belongs to. Also include any guarantees that you offer to ensure that your customers are satisfied. See Table 14.3 for some additional marketing tips.

Differentiating Your Services

Independent agents are actually in a better position than many large companies to deliver personalized, customized service to individuals. As we discussed in Chapter 9, travel sellers across the globe are striving to become more skillful at delivering personalized service through customer relationship marketing and customer relationship management.

Customer relationship marketing enables companies to use information about the individual's preferences and interests to create effective marketing. They build, maintain, and use customer databases that include information such as an individual's travel patterns and preferences, demographic information (age, gender, income level, and so on), hobbies and interests, and more. Based on this information, businesses can customize market offerings, services, programs, and messages. *Customer relationship management (CRM)* is a strategy that weds personal attention and technology in order to provide personalized service and build lasting relationships with clients.

Contact management software has evolved to allow you to keep track of your customers and prospects in ways never before possible. Among effective programs are online services, such as Batchbook.com and SalesForce.com, which allow you to synchronize your e-mail, mobile phone, and other points of contact into one place. They also can run reports, as well as sort, filter, and e-mail directly from the program or connected third-party applications. Using the data that comes in natively, you then can send targeted offers and make calls to people who have expressed an interest in that destination, niche, or supplier. Most are also compatible with online services that perform specific functions, such as Freshbooks.com for invoicing, Mailchimp.com for e-mail blasts, and Shoeboxed.com for expense management. TRAMS ClientBase (a division of Sabre Holdings) and ClientEase by ITAMS Ltd. are popular CRM programs designed for travel professionals.

Managing the relationships that you have built with your customers is essential to the success and growth of your business. If you keep your customers' needs as your focus, you will keep your customers loyal and your business growing.

CHAPTER WRAP-UP

CHAPTER HIGHLIGHTS

Here is a review of the objectives with which we began the chapter.

1. **Distinguish three types of home-based agents.** Employees of agencies may work out of their homes. Home-based agents may also be nonemployees who work as independent contractors. The IRS has several criteria for distinguishing employees and independent contractors. Basically, independent contractors must

in fact be independent—free to establish where, when, how, and with whom they work and limited in the support they can receive from a company. Some independent contractors work with a host agency; they must have a written agreement stating that they are not employees of the agency. There are also a growing number of independent home-based travel agencies.

2. **Discuss the importance of developing a business plan and seeking professional advice when setting up your own business.** A business plan is a summary of expectations from a business effort, including the level of income, benefits, mid- and long-term goals, and investment. Without a business plan, activities are likely to lack direction, decreasing the chances for success. Developing a business plan helps the business owner to keep clear objectives in mind and to set effective priorities. It is extremely important to invest in the services of an attorney who specializes in the travel industry and small businesses in order to obtain advice about legal issues and to check the wording of contracts, insurance policies, and other documents. An accountant who specializes in setting up small businesses or travel agencies can provide valuable information and advice about setting up the books and tax reporting.

3. **Identify the issues that should be considered when selecting a host agency or suppliers.** To determine if a host agency is a good match for your business, you should consider the host agency's specialization and preferred supplier agreements; training offered; the specific types of support that the host agency will provide, such as GDS access and technical support; its experience working with independent agents; references from the industry, clients, and other independents; the professionalism and compatibility of the staff; travel benefits offered; and the financial arrangements, including commission splits, override splits, fees, and collection and refund polices. In establishing a network of suppliers, choose suppliers that you know and trust and focus on suppliers within your areas of specialization.

4. **Describe how home-based agents can differentiate their services and grow their businesses.** Like other travel businesses, home-based agents should develop a marketing plan in order to determine how they will differentiate their business. Many travel businesses today are emphasizing customer relationship marketing and customer relationship management, using technology in order to provide customized, personalized marketing and service and to build lasting relationships with clients. Home-based agents are often in a better position than many large companies to achieve this marriage of technology and personalized service. Managing the relationships that you have built with your customers is essential to the success and growth of your business.

KEY TERMS

A list of key terms introduced in this chapter follows. If you do not recall the meaning of these terms, see the Glossary, which begins on page 393.

business plan
cloud
errors and omissions and
    general liability insurance
independent contractor
National Association of
    Career Travel Agents (NACTA)

Outside Sales Support Network
    (OSSN)
social media
telecommute
Verified Travel Consultant (VTC)

REVIEW QUESTIONS

1. What actions can home-based agents take to project a professional image of their company of one?

2. Outline the steps to take when establishing an online presence.

3. What industry organizations are especially helpful to home-based agents, and what type of services do they provide?

4. Why must sellers of travel acquire an identification number that is recognized by suppliers? Describe the numbering systems available to independent contractors.

CHAPTER 15

Finding Employment

OBJECTIVES

After completing this chapter, you should be able to

1. Design a plan for your search for employment.

2. Describe the items to include in a portfolio and in a résumé.

3. Identify at least six sources of information about possible openings.

4. Discuss at least three keys to a successful interview.

If you have completed a travel program, are pleasant with people, and are willing to work hard, the travel/tourism industry needs you! Nevertheless, finding the position you want may require skill and effort. Both those who are new to the employment market and those who are changing careers and entering the travel/tourism industry for the first time will probably begin with an entry-level position. Our focus in this chapter is on how to obtain one of these entry-level positions; jobs further up the career ladder are discussed in Chapter 16.

OUTLINE

PREPARING FOR THE EMPLOYMENT SEARCH

- What steps should you take to prepare for your employment search?
- What should your portfolio and résumé include?
- How can you find possible openings?

APPLYING FOR A JOB

- What can you do to increase the chances that your application for employment will succeed?

Preparing for the Employment Search

- WHAT STEPS SHOULD YOU TAKE TO PREPARE FOR YOUR EMPLOYMENT SEARCH?

- WHAT SHOULD YOUR PORTFOLIO AND RÉSUMÉ INCLUDE?

- HOW CAN YOU FIND POSSIBLE OPENINGS?

In the years before the popularity of the Internet, the newspapers advertised travel/tourism positions extensively, as did industry magazines and special employment agencies dedicated to this segment of the work force. That is not the case today. Now most entry-level employment opportunities are found by a concerted effort on the part of the seeker. This includes a variety of methods such as networking, researching extensively about potential companies, applying "cold" to companies of interest, or being an intern.

No two people and no two positions are precisely the same; neither are any two searches. Still, following certain steps can increase your chances of success, no matter what position you are looking for. A first step is to prepare yourself for the search by clarifying your goals and possibilities. What types of positions exist, what type of position do you want, and what are your strengths as a potential employee?

Evaluating the Possibilities

In previous chapters we described many different positions in the travel industry; Table 1.1 (page 16) listed more than a hundred. You probably meet the requirements described for many of these positions. One way to sort through the possibilities is to classify them into three types of jobs: (1) nonpersonal phone work, (2) personal intermediary of services, and (3) in-person supplier of services.

Almost all positions that handle reservations fall into the first category, nonpersonal phone work. These jobs are not "impersonal"; you are expected to be friendly and personable. But they are "nonpersonal" because you will probably never talk to the same person twice. You are trained to sell and reserve a particular hotel, airline, car rental, cruise line, or tour. You hang up and seconds later take your next call. Your employer monitors how pleasantly you treat callers, how accurately you give them information, and how often you sell your company's product. When you take off your phone headset and walk out the door each day, you can usually forget about the job until the next day. On the other hand, you do not get the satisfaction of seeing a person's travel through to the end or of developing relationships with clients. Some people find that the work becomes repetitious and the pressure fierce.

The second category—personal intermediary—includes almost all jobs in travel agencies as well as many positions as representatives of suppliers. In these jobs, no two days are alike. You are expected to develop and maintain a personal rapport with clients. You are personally responsible for creating and keeping repeat customers. You gain satisfaction from meeting your clients' needs, but you are likely to feel that the job never ends. Tasks are extremely varied. You must be able to organize your work and assign priorities.

The third category—in-person supplier—refers to the people who deal with travelers while they are traveling. Flight attendants, airport ticket agents, tour guides, cruise activity leaders, and front desk personnel at hotels are examples. You deal with clients face-to-face. You are on your feet, perhaps on the move, throughout the day. Most of these jobs take a lot of energy. They are ideal for people who do not want to stay behind a desk, who want to be out in public, and who enjoy dealing with people in person.

Whatever type of employment suits you, particular companies and specific positions offer varying advantages and disadvantages. One might offer a nice starting salary but little chance of advancement; another might provide challenging responsibilities but a tense work environment. What is most important to you?

- *Think experience.* You might view your first year on the job as a paid internship. You may wish to take whatever position becomes available in order to gain experience.
- *Think career.* If you view this first position as a stepping-stone, the

opportunities for advancement may be the most important characteristic to evaluate.

- *Think salary.* If you expect to remain in the same position for a number of years, consider its earnings potential. Is the pay at the prospective employer equivalent to that at similar companies?
- *Think benefits.* Both tangible and intangible benefits may be much more important than an extra dollar or two an hour. Tangible benefits might include travel, vacation pay, health insurance, profit sharing, and so on. Intangible benefits may be even more important. Does the atmosphere of the company match your style? Will you be comfortable there? What type of training will you be given? It is usually better to take a position with a company that has a specific training program than one that trains haphazardly or expects you to learn on the job. Large companies probably have a formal training program whereas small retail agencies may not. (Be very cautious about agreeing to pay an employer to train you.)
- *Think location.* Travel agencies and hotels are located almost everywhere, and most small towns are within reach of an airport that may need personnel. Also, cars are rented at all airports and in many towns without

CLOSE-UP: ON THE JOB WITH MEGAN MATTHEWS, TRAVEL AGENCY INTERN

Megan Matthews spent a year and a half at a four-year college and then switched to a travel school. Her friendly attitude, excellent grades, and ambition resulted in her immediate hiring after graduation. She chose a medium-size agency that is increasing its emphasis on leisure travel.

"I learned a lot in travel school. After the first week, I realized I had an awful lot more to learn, but now after three months I feel I'm making great progress. Luckily my manager helps me and answers a million questions even when she is busy. When she isn't very busy, she leads me through the steps so I can find the answer myself.

"I'm called an 'intern' right now. Let me explain because there are two kinds of interns. The first is a person who is still in school and is sent for some on-the-job training (usually unpaid) at a travel company. At our agency 'intern' is what they call a new agent for the first six months. After that, we're expected to be 'productive agents,' which at first means making enough sales to at least pay our salary.

"I was kind of surprised that the agency didn't have a Web site. The manager said she had been thinking about it for a while but hadn't gotten around to looking into it—mainly because she couldn't decide what its purpose should be. Even while I was in school, I had wanted to start a site. It was my younger brother who inspired me. He and I always loved hiking, climbing, and other outdoor activities. That got us thinking about putting up a Web site giving information about our area to people around the world. My brother helped set up a Web site for me at my job. The manager even paid him a little something for doing it.

"The agency's job description for new agents includes greeting walk-ins, answering the phones, steering clients to the travel counselors they want to talk to, answering simple questions, sorting all the mail, and doing the filing. For me, the manager has added working on a Web site, using the small one that I have as a model. She mainly wants to see if we can develop in-bound business from overseas to our area but also wants something for current clients to look at.

"When the agents get very busy, I also research prices at hotels or for cruises by making calls or checking the Internet. I've had to run to the office supply store, and I've delivered documents with the owner's car. Actually I enjoyed getting out of the office and doing that.

"I canvass my family and friends on trips that they might take. I don't really do it to get their business, although that's a good possibility, but so I can practice on the computer. I search out the best fares and schedules and then call and give them the information. They've had some questions so I researched further. When I get new clients, I'll be ready for them.

"The agency is going to have me work particularly on Vegas packages and Disney World when I take clients because I've been to both. So I've been studying the brochures and seeing what other counselors book for clients. It's amazing what you learn just by hearing experienced counselors talk to clients.

"Soon I'll be doing trips all over the United States and then North America. And the rest of the world had better look out after that, because here I come."

airports. Small, receptive tour companies may be located in any area that receives tourists. But large reservations offices, often referred to as **call centers**, are located only in certain cities. Unless you are willing to relocate, your choices and your chances for advancement might be somewhat limited by location.

As you research, you'll find that while there is still opportunity for employment in this huge travel/tourism industry, there may not be the openings you'd like as a travel counselor in a retail travel agency. You'll need to look at the industry as a whole and, perhaps, get an introductory position in one of the other sectors such as at a hotel or a tour operator, for example. Then with a year or so of work experience, it's possible to move on from there. Any sector of the broader tourism industry is a good starting point.

Begin planning your job search while you're still taking travel classes; don't wait until that magical moment when you receive your graduation certificate. And be sure to appraise yourself realistically. You may find you'll have to forgo certain employment possibilities if your life does not permit you to relocate to another city, work irregular hours, get by the first year on minimum wage, or perhaps drive to and from the airport in the middle of the night.

Assessing Yourself

If you do not recognize all of your positive qualities, you obviously cannot present them to a potential employer. Here is one way to conduct a self-assessment that will allow you to present yourself in the most favorable way.

First, take seven blank sheets of paper and list all of your qualifications and qualities, including

- Skills (for example, being able to book PNRs [passenger name records] in a GDS, build Web sites, or figure out complex airfares).
- Destination knowledge (maybe you know a lot about the major Caribbean islands and their highlights).
- Talents (ballroom dancing, a memory for names and faces, leadership ability—everything counts).
- Interests (outdoor sports, the arts).
- Personal preferences (working together with a team, having a lot of variety in your work).
- Accomplishments (received perfect attendance award, recognized for charitable work).
- Personal travel, if any (including domestic and international).

List as many of your qualities and qualifications as you can, and then set the lists aside. If additional entries come to you, jot them down. After a few days, reexamine your lists. Can you add to them? Check the curriculum of your travel program. Have you listed all of the areas you mastered and skills you developed during the program? Talk to your friends and relatives to determine whether you have overlooked any qualities and qualifications. Now read over your lists. As you go about your job search, remember all that you have to offer.

Most likely, you will also think about negative qualities as you do this exercise. Perhaps you have few contacts, you lack self-confidence, or you tend to ignore other people's opinions. Think about how you can either overcome these drawbacks or transform them into positive characteristics. Write down a plan for doing so and follow it. Do not dwell on your shortcomings; everybody has some. Some may be fairly easy to overcome (such as lack of contacts); others may take longer. In the meantime, think about your positive qualities.

Developing a Portfolio

To be ready for any situation in your job search, prepare a complete portfolio. Every component of the portfolio should be available in both print and electronic form. It should include

- The original of your *résumé*, which is a summary of your qualifications and work experience.
- The original of a list of references.
- Diplomas from all schools attended.
- The final transcript from the last school you attended—if you had good grades.
- Any special certificates or awards.
- Samples of your work, such as itineraries or tests.
- Two or three extra copies of your résumé and list of references.

Everyone needs a good résumé. Although résumés do not by themselves win jobs, a poor one will usually eliminate you from consideration. The goal of the résumé is to gain an interview and then to serve as a convenient summary.

Figures 15.1 and 15.2 show sample résumés. Notice that their formats are slightly different: each résumé is structured to highlight different points. Similarly, you should adjust your résumé so that the emphasis suits the positions you are applying for. If you are applying for diverse positions or in different types of companies, you should prepare more than one résumé. Store them on your computer, and customize for each company you apply to.

Guidelines for Résumés. Usually a résumé should be no longer than a page. It might follow a conventional structure such as the following:

- *Career objective.* Keep your statement of the objective somewhat general so that you do not limit your possibilities.
- *Work experience.* For each job you have held, gather the following information: beginning and ending dates of employment, company name, complete address and phone number, job title, and short description of your duties. List the positions in reverse chronological order, putting your latest job first. Remember, customer service is paramount for most travel jobs. If you have experience dealing with the public, emphasize it. To some employers, experience waiting on customers at Burger King might be the most meaningful item on a résumé. Do *not* list every short-term job you have held since childhood.
- *Education and specialized training.* List the names and complete addresses of schools, dates attended, degree or diploma received or credits earned, and honors and awards. Also list specialized training such as computer classes, destination seminars, and language courses. If you are finishing travel school and have little work experience, you might list your educational background before your work experience.
- *Skills and accomplishments.* List your skills. Use descriptive, active words, and list accomplishments that apply those skills. Emphasize the most valuable areas of your experience, and be specific. For example, "Managed seven-person team at Burger King for eight months. Absenteeism was 30 percent lower than the average team. Was offered position of day manager." Quantify accomplishments whenever possible. Also include any volunteer work.
- *Personal travel.* Extensive travel to other countries should be noted, especially for jobs with travel agencies.

Usually, a line stating that references are available is no longer included on résumés, nor are the actual references listed on the résumé itself. Employers assume that you will produce a separate list of references when requested. Prepare a list of work, educational, and personal references on a separate page. Make sure that each person listed has agreed to be a reference and knows that he or she may be called.

To make an effective presentation in the résumé, use short paragraphs. Avoid exaggerated claims, unnecessary information, repetition, jargon, slang, and abbreviations.

The appearance of the résumé matters, too. Use wide margins. Avoid gimmicks such as unusual paper or fancy lettering, but highlight the most important points by using bullets, underlining, or bold print. Finally, have someone else proofread your final copy, and be sure to use spell-check.

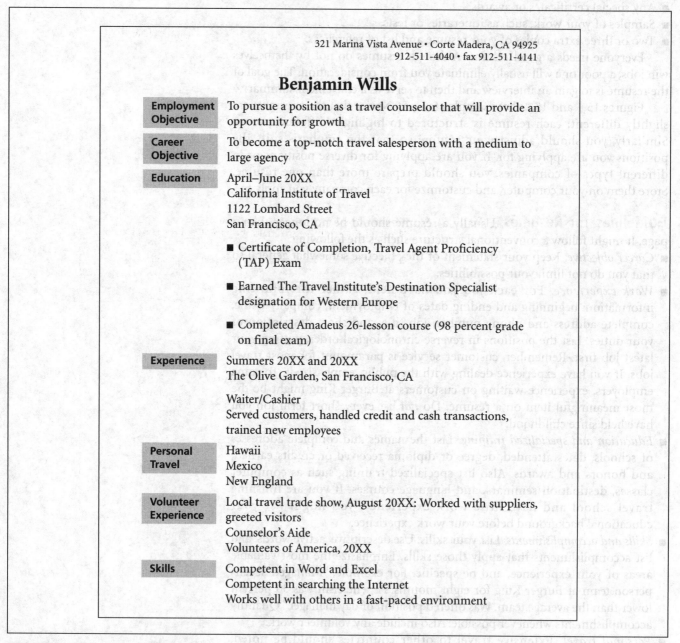

321 Marina Vista Avenue • Corte Madera, CA 94925
912-511-4040 • fax 912-511-4141

Benjamin Wills

Employment Objective	To pursue a position as a travel counselor that will provide an opportunity for growth
Career Objective	To become a top-notch travel salesperson with a medium to large agency
Education	April–June 20XX California Institute of Travel 1122 Lombard Street San Francisco, CA ■ Certificate of Completion, Travel Agent Proficiency (TAP) Exam ■ Earned The Travel Institute's Destination Specialist designation for Western Europe ■ Completed Amadeus 26-lesson course (98 percent grade on final exam)
Experience	Summers 20XX and 20XX The Olive Garden, San Francisco, CA Waiter/Cashier Served customers, handled credit and cash transactions, trained new employees
Personal Travel	Hawaii Mexico New England
Volunteer Experience	Local travel trade show, August 20XX: Worked with suppliers, greeted visitors Counselor's Aide Volunteers of America, 20XX
Skills	Competent in Word and Excel Competent in searching the Internet Works well with others in a fast-paced environment

FIGURE 15.1 A Sample Résumé

This sample résumé is for a candidate with no previous experience in the travel industry; therefore, he elected to describe his travel education first. Another option if you have no experience is to emphasize your skills.

Preparing an E-Résumé. Many employers require an e-application or an e-résumé. An e-résumé follows the same structure as a traditional résumé; Figure 15.3 shows an example.

Most employers that request an electronic résumé will list the format that is compatible with their systems. If the site states that electronic résumés must be in ASCII text, then you must use plain-text format (see Chapter 12). This format does not allow special fonts, italics, bold, or underlining. Keep text lines 65–70 characters long; it is acceptable if the e-résumé exceeds a page.

Amy Perkins

111 High Street	Lexington, MA 02173	508-332-5955

Employment Objective:	To obtain a sales position with a supplier to the retail travel industry
Experience Summary:	Extensive experience in the retail travel industry Experience selling leisure, corporate, and group travel Consistent record of top sales performance

Employment History:

April 20XX–Present	All Seasons Travel, Lexington, MA

Cruise Department Manager
- Responsible for managing sales, marketing, and training operations
- Negotiated for overrides to ensure profitability
- Established training seminars and incentive programs for the sales staff
- Developed and executed marketing seminars, mailings, and advertising
- Improved employee retention rate by 30 percent
- Achieved an average increase of 5 percent per year in sales by the Cruise Department

Director, Group and Incentive Travel
- Responsible for identifying and closing the sales of group travel
- Developed unique group travel events
- Organized incentive programs for corporate accounts
- Built marketing programs to attract groups

Assistant Manager
Responsible for daily operations, including sales and personnel management

January 20XX–April 20XX	Sun and Fun Tours, Boston, MA

Travel Consultant
Responsible for sales of leisure travel

Education History:

20XX–20XX	Massasoit Community College, Brockton, MA 02402 Travel and Tourism Certificate
20XX	Certified Travel Counselor (CTC)

FIGURE 15.2 A Sample Résumé

This sample résumé is for a candidate who has worked for two travel companies. Notice that she featured her experience and accomplishments in these jobs and relegated her schooling to the end of the résumé.

Large employers might have a *résumé builder* on their Web site, in which each user fills in the blanks, or they might ask that you e-mail the résumé. If you are sending a résumé via e-mail, the cover letter should be in the body of the e-mail, not in an attachment. You should even include your résumé in the body of the e-mail unless you have received permission to send the

FIGURE 15.3 Submitting E-Résumés

Carlson Wagonlit Companies gives job seekers three ways to submit their cover letter and résumé: (1) by manual entry, (2) by uploading the résumé and cover letter as an MS Word document, or (3) by pasting the items into separate fields.

résumé as an attachment and have verified that the recipient can open it. Many companies have strict policies against opening attachments from unknown senders.

Finding Current Openings

Most job openings never appear in want ads. Most are offered by employers to people they know, people who are recommended to them, or people who contact them directly. If any of your friends or relatives know someone in the travel industry, they may be able to help you. Try **networking**—using personal contacts to make business contacts and to advance in the business world.

If you are professional in your approach to school or your current job, then your instructors, employers, fellow students, or coworkers will be able to help you make contacts. Your classmates are your first network. As each classmate finds a job, that person becomes a contact for the others and can provide information about what is happening in his or her company. Also, your travel instructors have a multitude of contacts in the industry.

The placement department of your educational institution may help you find a job, but do not depend on it alone. The department may be helping a hundred other students. Once the placement department gives you information, follow up on it and let the placement people know the result.

Also consider any guest speakers in your classes. Did any of them impress you? Did they tell the class to contact them? If they passed out business cards, they are inviting you to keep in touch. Call and reintroduce yourself.

Use information interviews to develop your network. An *information interview* is one in which you are seeking knowledge about an industry or company. It should not be a disguised attempt to get a job. Many of these interviews do bring job offers or information about job openings, but never bring up the subject first. Many people will be gracious in giving you their time.

The telephone directory may list travel companies you never knew existed. You might call and ask for a contact from whom you can obtain an application or to whom you can send a résumé. Send a cover letter (discussed in the next section) and résumé. Ten days after sending your résumé, call and ask if it was received.

The larger the company, the more likely a phone call is the way to get started in the right direction, but many travel agencies and tour operators are small entities. Often a personal visit is your best chance to make an impression. Many jobs are obtained by people who just show up at an office with their résumé and ask to fill out an application. Timing and luck are important. Treat the visit just as you would an interview; it may turn out to be one. Dress professionally. Do not take it personally if people do not have time to talk with you. Ask for the name of the person to contact by phone or mail.

Also, call employment agencies and ask if they handle travel positions. Describe clearly the type of positions you are looking for, and do not be steered into others. Employment agencies that specialize in the travel/tourism industry usually concentrate on finding experienced "gems" or in filling higher management positions, but these people may have some of the best contacts in the industry. Private employment agencies earn money only when an applicant is hired. Make sure that the company, not you, pays the fee. "Temp" agencies that may send you to work in a company temporarily are, at times, a good way to get your foot in the door.

ON THE SPOT

You see the following job ad on your local newspaper's Web site under "classifieds": "Corporate or leisure travel agent wanted, no exp nec. E-mail résumé to xyztravel@abcweb.com." How would you go about answering this ad?

Travel agencies have perfectly good reasons for advertising without revealing their name or phone number, though few ask for people without experience. Although it is perfectly possible that this is a legitimate job ad, the best advice is either to skip it or to check with your newspaper to see if the source of the ad is a bona fide agency. Another option is to e-mail something about yourself, describing your sterling qualifications but not revealing your identity or any personal details. Then explain why you do not wish to send personal information until you know the receiver.

Check online. A large percentage of all employers now use the Internet for job posting and recruiting. Many companies have employment information on their Web sites. Often the sites list available positions, describe how to apply, and say where to send a résumé or application. Also check popular job-listing sites (such as Monster.com, Yahoo! Jobs, and craigslist) as well as online employment services that specialize in travel and the Job Search area on the Web site of the *International Council on Hotel, Restaurant, and Institutional Education (CHRIE)*. Most positions listed by online services require experience, but by reviewing them, you can learn what employers are looking for and can pick up the general tenor of the business and the jargon that is used.

Many online services will help you create an e-résumé that includes searchable keywords and will send your résumé to potential employers—for a fee. At ASTA's Job Board, job seekers register online and an advanced matching engine automatically notifies them every time a new job is posted that fits their skills and experience. Also, applicants can give permission for employers to search their résumés.

Other sources of information about job openings include libraries and state employment services. The listings at state employment services cover only a fraction of job openings, but job counselors may give you fresh ideas. In some places these services offer classes on interviewing and résumé preparation, job-search libraries, or computerized job listings.

✔ CHECK-UP

Three types of positions in the travel industry are
✔ Nonpersonal phone work.
✔ Personal intermediary.
✔ In-person supplier.

Qualities and qualifications to consider in a self-assessment include
✔ Skills.
✔ Knowledge.
✔ Talents.
✔ Interests.
✔ Personal preferences.
✔ Accomplishments.

Applying for a Position

■ WHAT CAN YOU DO TO INCREASE THE CHANCES THAT YOUR APPLICATION FOR EMPLOYMENT WILL SUCCEED?

If you are reading this book, we assume that you like travel and that you like working with people; these are two essentials for getting a job in the travel/tourism industry. As we discussed in Chapter 1, for an entry-level position you also need an ability to speak and write clearly, to handle basic math, and to learn. Beyond these fundamental ingredients, what makes a successful candidate for a travel job?

Employers look for (1) intangible qualities such as personality, attitude, and friendliness; (2) experience; and (3) travel education. Although most employers prefer someone with experience, they know that people with education and intangible qualities will turn into top-notch performers quickly. People who have all three characteristics have the best chances. Throughout the job application process, highlight your strengths in these three areas, beginning with your cover letter.

The Cover Letter

If you hear about a job opening that interests you, respond with your résumé and a *cover letter*, which is a letter of introduction that accompanies a résumé and is designed to obtain an interview or an application form. And because many openings are not posted, approach companies "cold" anyway with a cover letter. A good cover letter creates a positive impression and makes a prospective employer want to talk to you. It not only describes your talents but also says how they will benefit the company. The more you can customize your letter to a specific company and to a specific person, the better the chance that your letter will stand out.

To create a successful cover letter, follow the guidelines for business letters described in Chapter 12. Keep the sentences, paragraphs, and letter short. Proofread carefully. The following structure is usually effective:

- In the first paragraph, state the position you are seeking; Figure 15.4 shows an example. If you know anything about the company, use that knowledge to describe why you would like to work there.
- In the second paragraph, refer to your enclosed résumé. Do not repeat the information in the résumé.
- In the third paragraph, point out some personal qualities and accomplishments. Be positive but not cocky.
- If the position was advertised and the ad asked for a salary history, use the fourth paragraph to meet this request. Give a salary range that you believe overlaps the company's range. Keep your comments about salary general. Note that an acceptable salary is negotiable, and do not state exactly what you currently earn.
- In your final paragraph, ask for a personal interview and give your telephone number during business hours. Close with a positive statement that encourages a response. If you want the company to send an application, enclose a stamped, self-addressed envelope.

Send a résumé to a company even though you do not know whether it has any job openings. In this case, the résumé should be accompanied by a type of cover letter called an *application letter* or *unsolicited cover letter*. First take the time to learn something about the company. Carefully assess companies before applying to them. If certain companies appeal to you, (whether or not they have advertised for employees), learn everything you can about them in advance. If it's a tour company, read their latest brochures backwards and forwards. If it's a hotel, perhaps visit one of their properties and read about them in a hotel management magazine. If it's a cruise line, familiarize yourself with their various itineraries, ships, and special features. And, for a retail travel agency, check their Web site, if they have one.

In the first paragraph of your letter, introduce yourself and state why you are writing. Show that you know what the company does, its interests, and its problems. Try to identify something about yourself that would interest the employer. A surprising number of employers will not agree to meet people who call because they are looking for employment but will make time to talk with someone who seems unique or who has taken the trouble to learn about the company. In today's market, employers are often interested in someone who has a unique talent, such as Web site maintenance, an ability to cold call potential commercial accounts, or another language.

Your Street Address
Your City, State, Zip code
December 18, 20XX

Personnel
United Airlines
P.O. Box UAL 123
Chicago, IL 60666

Ladies and Gentlemen:

The position sought → This letter is in response to your recent advertisement in the *Chicago Tribune* for reservationists. Having recently graduated at the top of my travel class, I think I'd be an ideal choice for the top airline in the United States.

Reference to résumé → As you can see from my enclosed résumé, I achieved almost perfect grades in Apollo as well as other courses. I was able to go much further in the computer program than was required and believe I would do extremely well in your training program and eventually become an outstanding salesperson for United.

Personal qualities → What may be a little harder to see on paper is that I am an energetic, congenial, and happy person who enjoys dealing with people. I do have references from former positions dealing with the public that will bear this out, and I would enjoy sharing them with you. I am willing to work at the airport or at your downtown reservation center.

Request for interview → I am eager to discuss the possibility of working for United Airlines and look forward to the opportunity of a personal interview. You may reach me at the above address, by telephone at (708) 343-0105 most days after 2 p.m., or by e-mail at anncarbone@myemail.com. I look forward to hearing from you.

Sincerely,

Ann Carbone

Ann Carbone

Enclosure

FIGURE 15.4 A Sample Cover Letter

This job candidate has a lot of good things to say, but notice that she gets to the point of the letter and also sells herself in the first two sentences, in case the personnel manager does not have time to read a four-paragraph cover letter.

Application Forms

If you have reached the point where you are filling out an application form, things are going well. Keep the following in mind:

- Don't leave anything blank.
- Follow all directions.
- Use black ink and your neatest printing. If you have the option, type the information.
- Read each question carefully, and think before you answer.
- Be sure the information matches your résumé. Do not leave any gaps in your employment history.
- Make sure your spelling and grammar are correct.
- If you are asked to state your "reason for leaving" previous positions, never state a negative reason. Instead of "quit" or "personality conflict," write "left for better job environment" or "received better career opportunity."

Take care that the information you submit is correct. Most employers conduct background checks. If your application and résumé don't match the information from the background check, employers may think you are dishonest. It is a good idea to run a background check on yourself before starting your job hunt to reduce the chances that you or the potential employer will be surprised by information found in the process.

The Interview

On average, it costs thousands of dollars in time and training to bring a new person into the staff of a travel company. An interview represents your best opportunity to show that you are worth that investment. You should be selling your abilities to the employer, showing that you are the ideal solution to the employer's problem (needing a good employee). Put your best foot forward, showing your strong points honestly. Dishonesty or even insincerity is likely to backfire.

Preparing for an Interview. Sometimes an employer calls to arrange the interview; sometimes an employer writes and asks the job applicant to call to arrange it. This initial phone contact might be used to screen applicants. In fact, whenever you talk with a representative of the company, be prepared for a mini-interview. Have your résumé handy and be prepared to answer questions. Be as professional as possible. Eliminate all background noise, and give the person on the phone your undivided attention. Use your best phone manners and English, have a pen and paper ready, and do not hesitate to ask questions or directions.

Before the interview, be sure you find out its exact time, the name and title of the interviewer, and the name and address of the company. Prepare thoroughly. In particular,

- If you are unsure of the company's location, go there the day before if possible.
- If you live far away from the company, be prepared to say how you would get to the job. Do not allow a potential problem to eliminate you from consideration.
- Learn everything you can about the company (their brochures, destinations, properties, ships, price point, and itineraries, for example). Check their Web sites, and you also might read about them in trade publications.
- Be prepared to take tests.

- Prepare any questions you may wish to ask.
- Be prepared to answer all questions.

"Tell me about yourself." "What is it about this position that interests you?" "What do you expect from the company you work for?" "Why should I hire you rather than someone else?" These are all *open-ended questions* frequently asked by interviewers; Table 15.1 lists others. Be ready to take advantage of the opportunity that open-ended questions present. Before the interview, plan key points that you want to get across about yourself. If you are applying to a European air consolidator, for example, be ready to emphasize your knowledge of major European airports. Prepare examples to prove your points.

You might prepare further by becoming a "beginning expert" in some niche in the market. Keep up-to-date by reading the trade publications of whatever field you are most interested in. Or come to the interview with a list of possible prospects, including any organizations you belong to that might have potential clients. Employers love to hear how you are going to help sell their products and services.

Like an athlete getting ready for a game, you should prepare for an interview and then relax. Look at the interview as a conversation and an opportunity. The least that can happen is that you make a contact and find out more about your future.

Avoiding Elimination. When there are many candidates for a position, the interviewer's first task is not to choose the best person but to narrow the field. The best person may be eliminated because of a crucial early mistake. The following guidelines will help you avoid that fate:

- Be on time. In fact, be ten minutes early.
- Call if you are going to be late or if you cannot report for the interview. You should have a very good explanation, but be prepared for the fact that this

TABLE 15.1 Frequently Asked Interview Questions

Topic	Example
Previous work experience	Why did you leave your previous job?
	What did you dislike about your boss?
	How did you deal with the pressure?
	What did you like about your job? Dislike?
Education and interest	What did you like most in your travel program?
	What course gave you the most difficulty?
	Will you be taking other courses?
	What do you do in your free time?
	Do you have a hobby?
	How do you think your education prepared you for this job?
	What leadership roles have you held?
	Where have you travelled?
Work style and preferences	How do you feel about overtime?
	Do you like working alone?
	How well do you work with a team?
	What kind of supervisor do you prefer?
Personality	What five words best describe you?
	What are your strong points? Weak points?
	What do you see yourself doing five years from now?

may eliminate you anyway. Car trouble or problems with a baby sitter are unacceptable excuses.

- Dress appropriately. Regardless of the style of dress in the office, dress professionally and conservatively for the interview.
- Go to the interview by yourself.
- Smile, be friendly, and be polite. Assume that you are being observed from the time you enter the parking lot until the time you leave. Many interviewers will ask receptionists or others their impression of a candidate.
- Fill out forms neatly and completely.
- Greet the interviewer, introduce yourself, and offer a firm handshake. Do not sit down until you are offered a seat or until the interviewer sits down.
- Have good posture and positive body language.
- Be enthusiastic and ask pertinent questions.
- Speak clearly and correctly.
- Stress your sales ability, even if in a different field.
- Don't immediately ask what benefits exist.
- If applying to a retail travel agency, perhaps mention the possibility of your bringing a personal following of clients to the agency.
- Don't schedule yourself too closely. If the interviewer would like you to stay a bit and meet some of the key people, you don't want to refuse because you have another appointment or a baby-sitter waiting.
- Bring your portfolio with you and present it.
- Ask for the interviewer's business card at the end of the interview. Thank the interviewer and even the receptionist.

Remember that the company is not looking to spend thousands of dollars on someone who will soon quit. Emphasize your commitment to a travel/tourism career. Whatever you do, be confident.

Selling Yourself. If you are applying for a position that involves meeting and serving the public, the impression you make on the interviewer amounts to a test of how well you would perform on the job. A successful interview should be a pleasant experience for both you and the interviewer.

Whatever the position you are applying for, the interview resembles a sales situation. Much as a salesperson needs to develop rapport with clients and understand their needs, you should put yourself in the interviewer's shoes and ask yourself what is important to the company. Focus on issues that are relevant to the company and to the job opening. Show that you understand today's business environment and the challenges it poses to the company. Be positive about the working environment.

Also, be prepared to turn any of your liabilities into positive characteristics or at least to neutralize them. Do not bring them up unless the interviewer does or unless they are obvious. Younger people emphasize their energy; older people emphasize their experience.

Illegal Pre-employment Questions. It is illegal for an employer to ask certain questions of a job applicant. Unless employers can demonstrate that applicants' ability to perform a job depends on the answer, employers are not legally allowed to ask about gender, race, religion, marital status, number of children, disability, or current economic status. They may ask if you have been convicted of a crime or if there are felony charges pending against you—but not about an arrest record. Legally, you may be asked if you are a citizen of the United States—but not whether you (or your parents or spouse) are a naturalized or native-born citizen. And you may not be asked what country you are a citizen of. The employer is allowed to ask about your age only to determine whether you are old enough to work legally.

Of course, pointing out that a question is illegal is not likely to help your chances of being hired. (Reporting an employer to the authorities won't put you on the top of the candidate list either, but it may help future job seekers.) You might try to address the concern of the question without answering it directly. For instance, if an interviewer asks the illegal question, "Do you have plans to raise a family?" the interviewer's concern is whether you will stay with the company. A response that affirms your commitment to the position would probably satisfy the interviewer.

Asking Questions. An interviewer expects an intelligent applicant to ask questions. For example, unless the topics have already been covered, it would be appropriate for you to ask

- What are the daily responsibilities of the particular position?
- What is the most important responsibility?
- Is training provided?
- To whom would I report?
- With whom would I be working?
- Are there advancement opportunities?
- What other skills are required?
- When can I expect to hear from you regarding the position?

Questions regarding salary, benefits, travel opportunities, and so on should wait until the second interview or the job offer.

Once you have experience and confidence, you will see interviewing as a two-way street. In the best of situations, you will be evaluating the company as much as it is assessing you.

Following Up. As soon as the interview is over, take time to send a brief thank-you letter to the person who interviewed you. Be prepared for a second interview with a different person. If you have not received feedback from a first interview after approximately ten days, you may write a letter or call to ask about the status of the position.

Group Interviews

Many airlines and other large companies like to give group interviews. You should prepare for a group interview as you would for a personal interview. Keep in mind that the interviewer may be watching how you react throughout the session. The interviewer wants to see if you are friendly and interact well with others.

The interview may offer several opportunities for you to ensure that you will be remembered. Plan a statement introducing yourself that indicates why you would be an effective employee and that shows you know something about the company. There is a good chance that the interviewer will ask for volunteers to answer the first questions. Those who are ready will be remembered for their initiative. Sometimes the interviewer asks applicants to sell something to the group; how you handle yourself is usually more important than what you say. Even asking for the interviewer's card at the end of the session or having an excellent question may earn you a place in the interviewer's memory.

Remember that the interviewer is not only looking for outstanding candidates but also eliminating people from consideration. First impressions count, and negative ones will disqualify a candidate. Do not do anything to eliminate yourself. Your goal is to get to the second interview, which will be a personal one in which your chances for success are good.

CHAPTER HIGHLIGHTS

Résumés, cover letters, and interviews all represent opportunities for you to introduce yourself to prospective employers. How to take these and other steps in a way that will lead to an entry-level job was the focus of this chapter. Here is a review of the objectives with which we began the chapter.

1. **Design a plan for your employment search.** Begin with an evaluation of the type of position you are looking for and of your own strengths. Preparation of a portfolio and a hunt for job openings are logical next steps, followed by preparation of a cover letter or application letter. Eventually, these steps should lead to an interview.

2. **Describe the items to include in a job-seeking portfolio and in a résumé.** A résumé, a list of references, school diplomas, transcripts, certificates or awards, and samples of work make up a portfolio. Each component should be prepared in both print and electronic form; many employers require that applications and résumés be submitted electronically. Traditional and e-résumés follow the same structure. Career objective, work experience, education, and skills and accomplishments are the key features of a good résumé. The best order depends on the specific position, the type of company, and the applicant.

3. **Identify at least six sources of information about job openings.** Networking is one of the most productive sources. Newspaper ads, a school's placement office, information interviews, employment agencies, state employment services, and online services such as the one sponsored by ASTA also provide information about openings. In addition, positions may be discovered by checking telephone directories for the names of companies and then phoning or visiting them.

4. **Discuss at least three keys to a successful job interview.** Preparation is one key. It should include learning about the company, going over sample questions, and planning key points to convey. Courteous, professional behavior (such as being on time and dressing appropriately) is another key to success; it is needed in order to avoid early elimination from consideration. During the interview, it is important to be confident, to focus on issues that matter to the interviewer, to emphasize one's strengths, and to ask intelligent questions. And every interview should be acknowledged with a thank-you letter.

KEY TERMS

A list of key terms introduced in this chapter follows. If you do not recall the meaning of these terms, see the Glossary, which begins on page 393.

application letter
call center
cover letter
International Council on Hotel, Restaurant,
    and Institutional Education (CHRIE)

networking
résumé

REVIEW QUESTIONS

1. Name three characteristics you would consider in evaluating a potential employer.

2. Describe how you are going to overcome or transform one of your weaknesses as a potential employee.

3. What are four parts of an effective cover letter?

4. List four behaviors at an interview that might eliminate an applicant from serious consideration.

5. Outline steps you would take to use the Internet in your employment search.

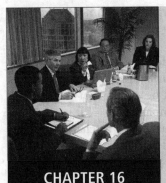

CHAPTER 16

Building a Career

OBJECTIVES

After completing this chapter, you should be able to

1. Suggest at least four ways to ensure success in a new job and four steps to take to prepare for advancement.

2. Outline a path for advancing in a travel/tourism career.

3. Identify at least four ethical responsibilities of travel professionals.

4. Describe how to develop your skills and knowledge as a travel professional.

Your first day on the job will be the first day of the rest of your career. Where will you go from there? This chapter suggests some destinations and directions. After discussing how to meet the challenges of a new job, we examine how to build a successful career in the travel/tourism industry. We conclude with a closer look at two keys to success and professionalism: ethical behavior and continuing education.

OUTLINE

SUCCEEDING ON THE JOB

- How can people in the travel/tourism industry increase their chances of success in a new job, and how can they prepare for a better position?

CAREER PATHS IN THE TRAVEL INDUSTRY

- What steps make up the career ladders for travel professionals?

ETHICS IN THE TRAVEL INDUSTRY

- What ethical dilemmas are most likely to face travel professionals, and what principles should guide their reactions?

CONTINUING EDUCATION FOR TRAVEL PROFESSIONALS

- Where can travel professionals obtain the continuing education and training to build their careers?

Succeeding on the Job

- HOW CAN PEOPLE IN THE TRAVEL/TOURISM INDUSTRY INCREASE THEIR CHANCES OF SUCCESS IN A NEW JOB, AND HOW CAN THEY PREPARE FOR A BETTER POSITION?

The New Position

The first step toward success in a new job is to have appropriate expectations and attitudes, enthusiasm, a willingness to learn, and patience with yourself as you encounter new situations. With these, you can begin to establish yourself and earn credibility and respect. Following are tips for starting a position.

- Make all your first impressions good ones. Always be on time. Notice how those around you dress. At first you might dress slightly more formally than you think is expected.
- Don't pretend to know something when you don't. Ask questions. Realize what you don't know; then learn it. Admit mistakes and look at them as opportunities for learning. Let your mistakes be errors that result from taking initiative, not from being immature or impatient.
- Look for a *mentor*, a person who serves as an unofficial teacher, counselor, role model, and advocate. Your mentor should be someone who can give you advice, whose knowledge and character you respect, and who will appreciate your eagerness to learn.
- Be a team player. Help out colleagues whenever possible.
- Demonstrate initiative. Successful people do things on their own and watch for opportunities to do more. Be involved. Don't wait for things to happen.
- Have a positive attitude. Be optimistic and cheerful. When something goes wrong, take it as a challenge to find a solution. Love your work and work hard at it.

Table 16.1 presents some examples of failures and successes in carrying out these tips.

Striking a balance between prudence and initiative can be especially difficult when you begin a job. Remember that every company has its own *corporate culture*—its own set of values, beliefs, priorities, and practices. In one company, for example, people may saunter in anytime between 9:00 and 9:15 A.M. and no one cares; in another, if you are consistently five minutes late, you may be fired. The policies and procedures described in the company manual may differ from the reality in many ways, large and small. You may be told, "Well, when Sally isn't here, we check with Joe even though we're supposed to check with Dottie because Dottie is always tied up on the phone with clients."

Most likely, you will need to learn the elements of the corporate culture piece by piece over the first few months. Be prudent at the beginning, and operate according to the manual or the practices of your coworkers. Eventually you may decide that it is worthwhile to challenge existing procedures. But don't try to change things overnight. Remember that (1) your coworkers have been doing the job for a lot longer than you have, (2) it is human nature to resent criticism from a new person, and (3) there is bound to be a lot going on in the company that you do not know about yet.

TABLE 16.1 The Professional versus the Order-Taker

Unsuccessful New Employees Say	Successful New Employees Say
Their lines are always busy; this is a waste of time. I'll never get through.	Does this phone have automatic redial and speed dial? We've got to get through.
They'll never answer. What a waste of time.	I think I'll open all the mail while I'm on hold.
How should I know that's the way I was supposed to do it?	Sorry. I never really learned how to do an exchange notice before. Do you have time to show me?
I've finished my job.	I finished filing all those brochures faster than I thought. Can I make some calls and help you research those rates?
Sorry, that fare is all sold out.	Sorry, the fare on that train is sold out, but I can get you the best current fare, which is $95, or get you the lower fare on the next day's train.
So, do you want to make this booking now? Client: "Thank you." Counselor: "No problem, no problem."	Which can I reserve for you, the 10th or the 12th? Client: "Thank you." Counselor: "It was a pleasure to serve you. See you again."

Your Next Position

Many people are happy in an entry-level position for many years and become very valuable to their companies. Others are eager to move into positions with more status, responsibility, and earnings. You will have to gauge the possibilities for advancement with your first employer. Changing jobs, sometimes a number of times, is an accepted part of the travel industry and sometimes necessary to move up in the industry.

If you are interested in moving up the career ladder, your first step is to establish yourself as being excellent at whatever you are doing. Find positive ways to stand out. For example, volunteer to take on extra work or to help organize a company function. When the opportunity arises to talk with a supervisor, don't be shy about describing your accomplishments.

Maintain and extend your networks. Your coworkers and managers are potential members of that network. Make a special effort to be friendly to those whose personalities do not mesh with yours, and avoid office gossip.

Also, join and take an active part in local industry associations. In previous chapters we described many of these nationwide organizations, such as ASTA (American Society of Travel Agents) and MPI (Meeting Professionals International). They offer opportunities not only for networking but also for learning. Other smaller groups often can be found on a local level, providing an opportunity for travel professionals to share experiences and hear speakers on a variety of industry-relevant topics.

Remember to keep your portfolio and résumé up-to-date. Add anything you accomplish to your portfolio. Mention seminars, trade shows, courses, and any other experiences that have added to your expertise. Did a client write a letter of praise and thanks? Cherish and protect it.

Above all, be professional. A *professional* has learned a body of knowledge, mastered skills needed for a certain occupation, and demonstrates a commitment to the standards of that occupation and the interests of his or her clients. People have no trouble knowing when someone is or is not being professional. Professionals treat others with respect, follow through on commitments, and take responsibility for their work. Professionalism requires both ethical behavior and continuing education, and we take a closer look at both of these topics at the end of the chapter.

Skills to Develop

Continuing development of your skills and knowledge is essential to professionalism and to career advancement. Take advantage of on-the-job training and personal travel. Learn another language, take a geography class, do Greek dances, take classes toward a business degree, or go to a one-day seminar on African pottery. Just keep learning and gaining new experiences. You can continue your education on your own; take advantage of educational opportunities offered by organizations in the travel industry, take courses at a college or university, or attend seminars or webinars from industry suppliers.

Which skills are most likely to help you as you advance in the travel industry? Chapter 1 described general skills required for entry-level positions (in interpersonal relationships, language, math, technology, and the ability to learn). To perform professionally in the travel industry, you will need not only to build on those skills but also to develop others, such as those listed below:

- *Business communication.* Every travel professional should refine and develop communication skills constantly. They cannot be stressed too much.

- *Organization.* Travel professionals manage massive amounts of information. The ability to determine which information is relevant and to obtain up-to-date information when it is needed is crucial.
- *Time management.* Many jobs in the travel industry require the ability to perform multiple tasks simultaneously while meeting deadlines. Travel professionals need skill at assigning priorities to tasks to manage their time well.
- *Negotiation.* Travel professionals negotiate daily. To be successful, you need to communicate effectively and to offer creative ideas for solving problems.
- *Understanding consumers and trends.* In order to deliver excellent customer service, travel professionals must develop skill at understanding their clients' needs and motivations and at noticing shifts in patterns of consumer spending and travel.
- *Planning and crisis management.* To advance in the travel industry, you should be able to manage crises effectively. Planning how to deal with problems is one of the best ways to ensure that you will be able to handle a crisis. Good planning also allows a business to remain competitive.
- *Embracing cultural diversity.* Increased knowledge about different cultures will help the travel professional overcome problems that cultural differences can bring, especially as the workplace and business interactions become more culturally diverse.
- *Staying current.* The travel industry is renowned for constant change. Failure to prepare for and adapt to change leaves your success up to chance. If you try to avoid managing change, change will manage you. If you expect and accept change, then change will become not an obstacle but an opportunity. That includes staying up-to-date on new travel products, policies, and any world events that may affect travel.

✔ CHECK-UP

A corporate culture
- ✔ Includes values, beliefs, priorities, and practices.
- ✔ May be inconsistent with the policies and procedures described in a company manual.
- ✔ Is not a formal structure and is learned piece by piece.

Professionalism requires
- ✔ Mastery of the body of knowledge and skills required by the specific occupation.

- ✔ Commitment to the standards of the profession.
- ✔ Commitment to the best interests of clients.

Implicit in professionalism is a willingness to
- ✔ Abide by ethical standards of conduct.
- ✔ Engage in continuing education and development of skills.

Career Paths in the Travel Industry

■ WHAT STEPS MAKE UP THE CAREER LADDERS FOR TRAVEL PROFESSIONALS?

You have succeeded in your first job. You have an excellent reputation, an extensive network, and an up-to-date résumé. You have developed your skills and attended numerous seminars. Now you want a new job with more status, pay, and responsibility. What is your next step?

No one structure describes all companies in the travel industry, and there is no one set of steps that constitutes the career ladder for all companies. The Close-Up: Careers in Chapters 1 through 9 described many positions, including the principal entry-level jobs. Here we outline some of the key opportunities for advancement in the industry.

Travel Agencies and Home-Based Offices

The smaller the travel agency, the more likely it is to be family-owned and to have people entrenched in positions. Medium-sized to large agencies or agency chains usually provide more opportunities for promotions. To keep up-to-date, travel counselors should read trade journals such as *Travel Weekly*, *Travel Agent*, and *TravelAge West*.

Travel counselors in small to medium-sized travel offices might advance by steps to lead agent, assistant manager, or manager—if these positions become available. They are more likely to advance by becoming better travel counselors—able to handle more clients, to do so more efficiently, and to contribute to a higher profit margin for the agency, which may, in turn, qualify them for higher earnings as salary increases often are tied to increased sales and agency profit.

For counselors with several years of experience, other options for advancement are

■ To work for a mega-agency. A mega-agency is likely to have many specialized jobs and levels of management.
■ To work as an outside sales agent.
■ To work as an independent contractor.
■ To start their own travel agency.

Striking out on your own has obvious attractions as well as risks. Chapter 14 discusses the benefits, challenges, and steps involved in starting your own agency or setting up as an independent contractor.

For any of the career paths we have described, your best chance for success as a travel counselor is to specialize. Just as travel agencies need to carve out market niches, individual counselors should select an area of specialization. Figure 16.1 on the next page outlines steps to take in establishing a specialization.

Earlier chapters described types of specialization. They include

■ *Particular kinds of travel based on an activity or interest,* such as adventure trips, ecotours, and different kinds of sports tours. If you earn a reputation as the one counselor in your community who knows about the specialty, your success is likely to be guaranteed for a number of years.
■ *Specific demographic or affinity groups,* such as particular ethnic groups, specific age groups, honeymooners, doctors, or firemen. To develop this kind of specialization, you also form bonds with the group. One travel counselor who became a specialist in travel for gays and lesbians reported that her first step was to join the International Gay Travel Association (IGTA). She wrote to all the suppliers on its membership list, studied their brochures, and started running weekly ads in a local gay and lesbian newspaper publication.
■ *Specific geographic areas.* Pick the place about which you are or would like to become most knowledgeable. Make yourself known as the specialist in that area for your agency, your city, or even nationwide.

FIGURE 16.1

Developing a Specialization

Everyone has interests that can be developed into sales specialties that will enhance a career. These five steps have proved to be a successful path for counselors to follow.

Step 1: Look at Your Interests, and Select A Potential Specialty.
What do you do with your spare time, or what did you enjoy doing as a child? What vacations have you enjoyed? What trips do you most enjoy working on? Do you have a special skill?

Step 2: Check Out the Niche.
Survey existing clients. Are they part of the potential market? Is there enough interest to justify the specialization? How much will it cost to penetrate the market? What volume of sales could be expected? Is the market adequately served now? If not, why not? How will your service differ from already available services?

Step 3: Educate Yourself.
Read as much as you can. Take fam trips related to the specialty. Contact related tourist boards and magazines. Consider courses offered by The Travel Institute, ASTA, CLIA, and other professional organizations. Learn about relevant suppliers.

Step 4: Develop A Marketing Plan.
Identify your potential clients and the marketing mix you will use to reach them. Don't overlook less expensive types of promotion. Check your database for people who have expressed interest in the specialty. Send newsletters and press releases. Consider ways to use your Web site and the Internet. Arrange speaking engagements or theme nights. Attend events and exhibitions. Get involved with organizations related to the specialization.

Step 5: Stay Fresh.
Monitor the market through trade publications. Take trips. Keep in touch with tourist boards and suppliers. Ask your clients for feedback.

Sources: Based on *Travel Agent*, August 5, 1996, p. 40; *Building Business*, July 1, 1996; The Travel Institute's *Special Interest Travel* (1996).

■ *Cruise travel.* Some agencies work only on cruises; many others sell a range of types of travel but have cruise departments. If your specialty is cruises, do not look just for cruise-only agencies as possible employers; most successful agencies want to emphasize cruise sales.

These specializations are not mutually exclusive. For example, if you decide to specialize in an ethnic group, you would establish a network within that ethnic community, attend community events, learn about its culture and develop expertise in destinations popular with that group. If you specialize in a geographic area, the specialty might take longer to develop than others because you might have to build your market one client at a time, but you can combine this specialty with others. A specialist in Italy, for instance, might also become expert in trips devoted to art, wine, or cooking; a specialist in Latin America might develop expertise in ecotourism or Mayan culture. Cruising is a field with almost endless opportunities for specialization— adventure, family reunions, the Greek islands, and more.

During the coming decade, leisure travel is expected to grow more than business travel. But if you want to advance and increase your salary quickly at the outset of your career, consider concentrating on business travel. Large commercial agencies often call themselves *travel management companies* and include many specialized jobs, such as corporate account manager and customer service agent (see the Close-Up on page 19). Sales representatives keep business coming in; negotiators make sure suppliers are giving the agency the best possible rates and overrides. In addition, Web specialists handle bookings via the Internet or keep the agency's Web site updated; systems administrators respond to users' calls to the help desk; database administrators provide technical support and maintenance for computer networks. In addition, companies often have separate departments for group sales, incentive travel, and convention and meeting coordinators. To keep up-to-date with these areas, read *Meetings and Conventions Magazine*.

Online Agencies, GDSs, and E-Careers

Online companies such as Travelocity, Expedia, and Orbitz need people proficient in computers and people familiar with air reservations and other sectors of the travel industry. A combination of computer and travel knowledge can put you on the fast track.

Many small online companies have locations all over the nation. Most online travel companies, including airline reservation centers, hire fulfillment companies to provide customer service, ticketing, and reservation services through call centers in the United States and other countries such as India.

A growing number of careers in the travel industry—beyond just online agencies—focus on electronic communication. Every sector of the travel and tourism industry has an electronic component. Many companies are looking for people within the travel industry who have computer and Internet skills rather than hiring technical experts who are unfamiliar with the industry. Thus, there are many opportunities for travel professionals who would like to specialize in e-marketing, Web design and maintenance, database management, distribution systems, Web-based applications, and customer relationship management (CRM).

GDSs (global distribution systems) have been the traditional employers of travel professionals specializing in computers although it remains to be seen if the GDS system will be as strong as it has been. Travel computer specialists may begin their careers by working at a GDS help desk and move into sales and then management. However, because computer specialization now extends to all sectors of the travel and tourism industry, you may begin your career with computers in any sector of the travel industry.

Tourism and Destination Management

Careers in the tourism industry range from dealing with activities (festivals, gambling, skiing, music) to promoting single attractions to marketing entire nations as destinations. Opportunities exist in destination management companies (DMCs), government tourist offices (GTOs), and convention and visitors' bureaus (CVBs). (See the Close-Up on careers in destination management and promotion, page 27.) Career paths may begin with behind-the-scenes support jobs and move to highly visible positions planning events.

Airlines

If your career lies with the airline industry, *Aviation Weekly* and publications of the Future Airline Professionals Association can help you keep in touch with developments in the field. In recent years the business has been volatile. Many employees have moved from one carrier to another because they wanted to look for advancement or because their employer ceased operations or cut its workforce.

Those who work in the reservations office of an airline might seek advancement by applying for openings in specialty areas such as the agent desk, tour desk, rate desk, group desk, or computer help desk. Supervising and training positions are logical promotions. Another path is to move into sales, advertising, or marketing. For example, you might aim to become a district or regional sales manager, often referred to as a ***business development manager***.

If you work at the airport as a ticket agent, gate agent, or customer service specialist, you might aim for supervisory roles such as schedule coordinator, shift manager, or airport station manager (who manages the day-to-day operations of an airline at a particular airport).

Flight attendants can advance to become senior flight attendants, supervisors, or training instructors. If flight attendants decide to end their flying days, they have a good chance of securing a position in other areas of the airline. They often make excellent travel counselors or tour leaders.

Accommodations

Because of its large size, the hotel industry is likely to have more job openings and more opportunities for advancement than other segments of the travel/tourism industry. Those who want to take advantage of these opportunities need to gain expertise in areas such as room inventory management, housekeeping, facility maintenance, and food and beverage sales. These can be studied in hospitality courses and hotel training programs. AH&LA (American Hotel and Lodging Association) can help you stay in touch with changes in the industry.

Many top-grade hotel chains are dedicated to promoting from within and have programs to help their personnel advance. Supervisory and assistant managerial positions may be the obvious steps after an entry-level job. The resident manager at some properties not only supervises all hotel operations, departments, and personnel but also is the principal contact with guests to resolve special issues and build goodwill. Usually the resident manager completed study at a hotel school or a hotel management program and rose from a front-desk position to assistant manager or executive housekeeper.

At many resorts, you can combine hotel skills with an interest in a specialty. For example, gambling resorts, spas, and western ranch resorts need people who know the special features of their operations.

Ground Transportation

Because ground transportation is often sold as part of a travel package, many jobs in this travel sector involve vendor relations and marketing relationships with other segments of the travel industry. Generally, positions related to yield management and computer-based distribution and marketing are growth areas. Fleet acquisition and logistics offer fascinating career paths. For example, the fleet manager for motorcoach companies monitors and allocates equipment used for charters, tours, and regularly scheduled service and figures out how to get equipment where it is needed in the most efficient way.

In car rental companies, rental agents who excel may move up in the management structure at a particular location—perhaps from shift manager to station manager to city manager. But advancement might require relocating to another city. Becoming a district manager and then being promoted to regional manager are logical steps. Other opportunities are available only at the company's main office, where operations, sales and marketing, and management and administration functions are performed. *Auto Rental News* is the publication to keep you current in the industry.

For careers in passenger rail travel, future opportunities depend not only on market forces but also on changes in government funding. Advancement within Amtrak may be slow, but longevity and dedication may pay off. Amtrak prefers to promote people from within its system and people who believe strongly in rail travel. Those in reservations might look for advancement in supervisory roles, training, and sales, much as with the airlines. Management positions are possible for those who further their education. Attendants might look to advance to onboard chief (the supervisor of the train's onboard crews). After one year of service, attendants can transfer to a different union within Amtrak if they want to advance in other parts of the company. Representing international rail or small local excursion rail companies may be another avenue.

Cruises

Because of the impressive growth of cruising, chances for advancement are excellent for those who are ready to seize opportunities. Land-based personnel might move into specialized areas such as capacity control, group sales and reservations, air/sea operations, and air/sea ticketing. Most positions are in U.S. port cities, and most of these are in Florida. Watch for openings in supervisory or managerial positions, marketing, and sales. Account executives or sales representatives who are stationed in different parts of the country can make excellent salaries. Most of them have a large sales territory and usually work out of their home. A lateral or upward move might take you into cruise-only travel agencies. Expertise and sales ability could lead to an excellent position in one of these companies.

For ship-based personnel, possible career moves into specialized areas are much like those for hotel personnel, because a cruise ship is a floating resort. Travel management, hotel, financial, or ship experience might lead to the position of purser or even hotel manager (called *chief purser* on some lines). These positions are responsible for the passengers in almost all respects: overseeing cabins, handling the guests' finances and securing their valuables, handling the ship's other income and expenditures, making sure the ship complies with local documents and regulations, and much more. Those involved in entertainment and activities might aspire to be assistant cruise director or cruise director. Shipboard experience as part of the cruise staff is the best preparation for these jobs.

Tours

Wholesalers tend to be larger companies than tour operators, which are often small operations in the United States. Even some large tour operators are family-owned and -operated, which means the number of upper-level positions is limited. The best opportunities lie with the largest domestic tour companies. High growth has increased openings, particularly in product innovation and quality control. Every company is seeking to promote itself on the Internet, providing opportunities for those knowledgeable in e-commerce.

To advance in a career in tours, you might take one of three general paths.

- If you start as a tour guide or tour escort, your advancement may come by working more often, with larger groups, or on more prestigious tours. Successful escorts work well with diverse people and get to know the inner workings of the product. Thus, many can rise to high levels in the company when they decide to "come in from the cold" and work in the company's home office.

- If your entry-level position is in the office, your career path might involve moving into groups, sales and marketing, or operations (that is, keeping track of clients and vendors and communicating with them).

- If you are committed to working on tours and have something special to offer, you might start your own operation or begin a new program for an existing tour operator. New destinations, activities, and ideas are needed constantly. Ski instructors, river-raft enthusiasts, art teachers, ranch hands, chefs, animal lovers—all might involve themselves in starting or helping to build tour programs.

✔ CHECK-UP

Travel counselors increase their chances of advancement by selecting an area of specialization, which might involve
- ✔ Particular kinds of travel.
- ✔ Specific demographic or affinity groups.
- ✔ Specific geographic areas.
- ✔ Cruises.

Career paths in the travel industry
- ✔ Vary from one sector of the industry to another.
- ✔ May require a willingness to change locations or change companies or both.

Ethics in the Travel Industry

■ WHAT ETHICAL DILEMMAS ARE MOST LIKELY TO FACE TRAVEL PROFESSIONALS, AND WHAT PRINCIPLES SHOULD GUIDE THEIR REACTIONS?

Professionalism implies a commitment to ethical behavior, which means following certain principles of proper conduct. In fact, ethical behavior is often in the long-term best interests of a company and an individual. If you earn a reputation for unethical behavior, you forgo the trust of clients and ultimately are likely to lose business as well. But these considerations about whether a behavior will pay off have nothing to do with ethics.

There are ethical standards and ethical dilemmas in every facet of business life, from hiring and firing to relations with colleagues and customers. A company may establish policies that encourage or discourage ethical behavior, but ultimately each individual is responsible for acting ethically.

Sometimes the ethical choice is difficult to determine. No law prohibits many unethical behaviors. It is not against the law, for example, to tell outsiders about a client's travel plans or to neglect to cancel space that you know will not be used, but usually these acts are unethical.

One aid in determining the ethical course of action comes from codes of ethics published by professional associations. ASTA's code, for example, states that "all ASTA members pledge themselves to conduct their business activities in a manner that promotes the ideal of integrity in travel and agree to act in accordance with" the principles of the code; Table 16.2 reprints those principles.

Often, however, no rule clearly defines what should be done in a particular situation. For a great many situations, you can determine what is ethical only by consulting your own conscience and by asking, Is this action fair? Is it just? Will it harm anyone? In this section we look at some of the situations that most frequently raise ethical questions for travel professionals, and particularly travel counselors.

Confidentiality

Duties to preserve confidentiality protect and restrict travel agencies, travel counselors, clients, and suppliers. A salesperson should not disclose information gained from a client to anyone except others in the industry who need that information in order to provide services. (By requesting services, the client has given implied approval for these disclosures.) Clients' travel plans should not be discussed outside the office, and information about their plans should not be given over the telephone to anyone except those clients.

Similar restrictions apply to information given to an employer. Travel professionals should never discuss with the public the cost of travel benefits received from suppliers, and supplier representatives should treat information about travel counselors as confidential.

Travel Benefits

Anyone actively engaged in the travel industry and meeting certain minimum requirements is eligible for benefits and discounts offered by hotels and resorts, sightseeing attractions, airlines, cruise lines, and other travel companies. People who misrepresent themselves as travel industry employees in order to obtain these benefits are guilty of unethical conduct. It is also unethical to encourage or help others to misrepresent themselves.

This type of misrepresentation became a business of its own in the 1990s, when companies popularly known as *card mills* began selling travel agency credentials. Card mills advertise for outside sales agents as if they were bona fide travel agencies, but they provide minimal support and training. They pay members a fee for each new person recruited. Training often focuses on how to recruit new members, not on travel products and how to sell them. Some people pay the initial fee and join simply to use the identification cards in order to take advantage of discounts on travel that are intended for bona fide travel professionals.

These card mills may harm the traveling public, the suppliers cheated out of discounts, and professional travel counselors whose reputation they cheapen. ASTA, IATA, and the Association of Retail Travel Agents (ARTA) have been working to stop this abuse of travel agent credentials.

TABLE 16.2 ASTA Code of Ethics—Guiding Principles for Members

Responsibilities of travel agent, premium, international travel agency company, and international travel agent associate members

1. **Accuracy.** ASTA members will be factual and accurate when providing information about their services and the services of any firm they represent. They will not use deceptive practices.

2. **Disclosure.** ASTA members will provide in writing, upon written request, complete details about the cost, restrictions, and other terms and conditions of any travel service sold, including cancellation and service fee policies, before accepting payment. Full details of the time, place, duration, and nature of any sales or promotional presentation the consumer will be required to attend in connection with his or her travel arrangements shall be disclosed in writing before any payment is accepted.

3. **Responsiveness.** ASTA members will promptly respond to their clients' complaints.

4. **Refunds.** ASTA members will remit any undisputed funds under their control within the specified time limits. Reasons for delay in providing funds will be given to the claimant promptly.

5. **Cooperation.** ASTA members will cooperate with any inquiry conducted by ASTA to resolve any dispute involving consumers.

6. **Confidentiality.** ASTA members will treat every client transaction confidentially and not disclose any information without the permission of the client, unless required by law.

7. **Affiliation.** ASTA members will not falsely present a person's affiliation with their firm.

8. **Conflict of Interest.** ASTA members will not allow any preferred relationship with a supplier to interfere with the interests of their clients.

9. **Compliance.** ASTA members shall not have been convicted of a violation of any federal, state and local laws and regulations affecting consumers. Pleas of nolo contendere, consent judgments, judicial or administrative decrees, or orders, and assurances of voluntary compliance and similar agreements with federal or state authorities shall be deemed convictions for purposes of these provisions.

Responsibilities of all members

1. **Notice.** ASTA members operating tours will promptly advise the agent or client who reserved the space of any change in itinerary, services, features, or price.

2. **Delivery.** ASTA members operating tours will provide all components as stated in their brochure or written confirmation, or provide alternate services of equal or greater value, or provide appropriate compensation.

3. **Credentials.** An ASTA member shall not, in exchange for money or otherwise, provide travel agent credentials to any person for whom there is no reasonable expectation that the person will engage in a bona fide effort to sell or manage the sale of travel services to the general public on behalf of the member through the period of validity of such credentials. This principle applies to ASTA members and all affiliated or commonly controlled enterprises.

Conclusion

Failure to adheere to this Code may subject a member to disciplinary actions, as set forth in ASTA's Bylaws.

Source: Adapted with permission from ASTA.

Misrepresentation and Disclosure

Deceptive advertising is unethical. The facts in an advertisement should be clear and complete. It is unethical to advertise services that are not available or that are so limited that very few can obtain them (in other words, bait-and-switch schemes). When services are limited, the advertiser should clearly spell out the limitations.

Similarly, it is unethical for salespeople to misrepresent a product. For new salespeople, it is easy to misrepresent a product unintentionally, through inexperience or overeagerness. Salespeople should avoid overgeneralizations such as: "Oh, it's just great on that island; everyone loves it."

Failure to disclose facts necessary for the client to make an informed decision is also unethical. The fact that a client does not know enough to ask the right questions does not alter the salesperson's responsibility to disclose vital facts. Travel counselors are ethically obliged to warn clients about facts such as code-shared flights and drawbacks of a destination. In fact, the U.S. Department of Transportation now requires that travel agencies give travelers information in writing about a code-shared flight or a flight listed as "direct" that actually requires a change of planes.

Ticketing

Travel counselors are contracted to sell suppliers' services according to the suppliers' rules and regulations, and counselors must make a good-faith effort to follow and enforce those rules. Certainly they should not tell clients how to circumvent the regulations. But when clients find their own way around the rules, the ethics of the situation sometimes become murky.

In particular, the rules regarding discount airfares have created difficult situations. Many travelers learn how to manipulate these rules with no help from travel professionals. Back-to-back ticketing and hidden-city ticketing are two examples.

In *back-to-back ticketing*, the client buys two discount tickets and rearranges the departures and returns. The practice occurs when the cost of two discount round-trip tickets is less than the cost of one round-trip ticket at full fare, but the discount tickets have restrictions that the client cannot meet. For example, a client might want to make a round-trip flight to New York but be unable to meet the restriction on the discount fare that calls for staying over on a Saturday night. So the client buys two discount round-trip tickets for different dates and then uses just one leg of each ticket in order to complete his trip.

In *hidden-city ticketing*, a client who wants to go to City Y buys a ticket for a flight from City X to City Z with a connection at City Y because the fare for a ticket from City X to City Z is less than the fare from City X to City Y. The client actually gets off the plane when it lands at City Y. For example, to go to Atlanta from Chicago, a client might buy a ticket for a Chicago-to-Orlando flight with a connection in Atlanta—and get off at Atlanta—because the airline has a special discount fare for the Chicago-to-Orlando flight.

The airlines argue that these practices violate ticketing agreements. Many travel counselors complain that it is not their job to police clients' requests. But if travel agencies practice back-to-back or hidden-city ticketing, they risk incurring fines from the airlines and even the loss of their ARC appointments.

Reservations

Ethical considerations also limit reservation practices. It is unethical

- To try to book travelers who have already made reservations or paid for travel with another agency.
- To book reservations that you do not intend to use and then cancel them at the last moment to open up space for standby passengers or those hoping for an upgrade.

You should cancel, in a timely manner, all space that clearly will not be used, and you should book only one reservation that a client can use at a time. Booking two reservations for an individual at the same time is called *doublebooking* and is unethical. But if clients ask you to doublebook far in advance and for only a very short time so that they can confer with others, the ethics of the situation are less clear. Many agents feel ethically correct in doing so even though they are technically violating a supplier's regulations.

Selecting Suppliers

Some agencies could not survive without the override commissions given by preferred suppliers. As an employee, the travel counselor has a duty to concentrate on these preferred suppliers. Ideally, only companies that are leaders in their fields, providing value and service, have been selected as preferred suppliers. Thus, in principle at least, by selecting preferred suppliers the travel counselor is meeting the needs of both the agency and the client.

In practice, preferred supplier relationships obviously raise the possibility that the interests of the agency and the client will conflict. Disclosure helps: the agency should make a list of preferred suppliers available to clients. In any event, the travel counselor has an obligation to help the client choose the service or supplier best suited to that client. If the preferred supplier does not meet that test, the travel counselor should recommend a supplier that does, even though the result is a lower commission.

Gifts, prizes, awards, and contests offered by suppliers to travel agencies or directly to travel counselors may also tempt counselors to put their own interests ahead of the client's. Given the fact that employees in many businesses and governments are not allowed to accept any gift worth more than $25, the policy of offering gifts worth $100 or more is questionable. Agencies should set clear policies regarding their employees' participation in reward programs. The counselor, in any event, has an ethical obligation to serve the client's interests.

Fiduciary Responsibilities

If you are a travel counselor, once a client gives you money, you are considered the guardian of those funds. You have an obligation to try to deal only with reputable suppliers, and you have a specific duty to disperse the funds as the client intended. This means doing so in a way that meets deadlines and other requirements of the supplier. By the same token, the supplier has an ethical duty to guard funds entrusted to it toward a particular end. It is unethical to risk a client's funds on other purposes when there is a chance those funds may be lost before the client's trip.

In some states, these responsibilities are regulated by requirements that travel agencies or suppliers place client funds in escrow accounts under

ON THE SPOT

Mr. Dehere, a frequent business traveler, has a meeting that ends two hours before his departing flight. He is not certain he will make it to the airport for this flight, but he says he really needs to get on that flight if possible. If he doesn't make it, he will be even more desperate to get on the next flight. So he asks you to make a reservation for him on both flights. What should you do?

This is clearly a case of doublebooking. Savvy clients know that they can pick up the phone, call the airline, and doublebook themselves. Mr. Dehere might want to engage in this unethical practice on his own, but you should not violate the airline's rules by doublebooking (nor should you encourage him to do so). Urge him to reserve the later flight. He can then try to make the earlier flight and see if a seat is available.

ON THE SPOT

RentUsNow is offering travel counselors a free car rental for a week if they make ten bookings with it this month. Your agency approved the contest, and you would certainly like that prize for your upcoming vacation. It's the end of the day on the last day of the month, and you have sold nine rentals for RentUsNow so far. Now a client calls and wants a rental. You determine that for this location, renting from Top Rentals, which is just as reliable as RentUsNow, would save the client $15. Which supplier do you select?

Your client's best interests must come first. But before giving up on RentUsNow and the prize, you might try calling the company and asking it to match the other supplier's price, or you might offer your client a $15 rebate check (which you would pay for personally), explaining your reason for wanting to book with RentUsNow. If neither strategy succeeds, booking with RentUsNow would be unethical.

certain situations. (Recall that an *escrow account* consists of funds or other property that is held by a third party, such as a bank, until specified conditions are met for its release.) In a sense, an operator should consider all client funds "in escrow" until the trip has been completed.

Government Regulation of Travel Sellers

The higher the ethical standards of those in a profession, the less need there is for laws and regulations by government. But even if travel professionals adhere to the highest standards, frauds and other unethical behaviors may be carried out by people outside the travel industry. Many travel organizations such as ASTA try to prevent or uncover these problems, but they persist.

When an industry's attempts to police itself fail, government may provide a last line of defense. For example, ASTA asked the Federal Trade Commission (FTC) and the National Association of Attorneys General to investigate the problem of card mills, and its request brought some results. And in 1999 Operation Trip Trap was established to stop unethical companies from tricking consumers (mainly teens and seniors) into thinking they had won trips that they had not won.

In addition, a number of states either have laws licensing or regulating travel sellers or are considering them. Their chief aim is to protect consumers from scams and from losing their money if a travel seller goes out of business. These laws often require that travel sellers register with the state in some way and either post a bond or contribute to a consumer restitution fund.

✔ CHECK-UP

Ethical choices are
✔ Based on principles of right conduct.
✔ Not determined by the balance of costs and benefits or by how a choice affects your interests.

For travel counselors, practices that raise ethical problems include
✔ Deceptive advertising and other misleading sales techniques.

✔ Clients' requests for back-to-back ticketing, hidden-city ticketing, and doublebooking.
✔ Preferred supplier policies or offers by suppliers that encourage the selection of suppliers other than those that would be best for the client.

Continuing Education for Travel Professionals

■ WHERE CAN TRAVEL PROFESSIONALS OBTAIN THE CONTINUING EDUCATION AND TRAINING TO BUILD THEIR CAREERS?

Effective travel professionals are always learning. Four types of continuing education might enhance your career:
■ *College or university education.* In the travel industry, top positions in

particular may require completion of courses that teach advanced business, marketing, or management skills.

- *Industry education,* which includes seminars, trips, and specialized courses. We examine some of these opportunities later in this section.
- *Computer education.* Representatives from computer companies often visit offices to give brief seminars and practice sessions. Also, the airlines' computer centers in various cities offer advanced computer training programs that last from one to five days.
- *General education,* which includes keeping current with events on the international scene and in the business world. Your personal travel is one invaluable resource. The travel, business, and international news sections of your local newspaper and of national papers such as *The New York Times* (in libraries and online) will often include valuable reports. Subscribe to at least one of the trade publications listed in earlier chapters. Consumer publications such as *Condé Nast Traveler*, *National Geographic Traveler*, *Travel and Leisure*, and *Budget Travel*, as well as public television, travel videos, guidebooks, and travel literature can round out your education.

Keep in mind that you can pursue each of these types of education using the Internet. If you take a class via the Internet, in most cases you will be able to study when and where you want. But the advantages of this freedom prove to be disadvantages to many. Being able to study "whenever" can become "never." Choose a specific place and time for study, or look for Internet courses that present online seminars at scheduled times or that set a strict schedule of assignments that must be e-mailed.

Educational Resources of the Travel Industry

Suppliers are a tremendous source of educational opportunities. At their seminars you can learn about the company and the industry, make contacts with others, and enjoy yourself—at little or no cost.

Discounted trips, familiarization trips, and ship inspections offer unique and enjoyable opportunities for learning. On *discounted trips,* you join with others to sample a company's service or tours; these trips may require little of you other than sampling the services as any traveler might. A true *familiarization* (or *fam*) *trip* is a working trip: you travel with a group of other travel professionals on a specially arranged itinerary and are expected to participate in all scheduled functions and to learn as much as you can. In some cases, an accompanying spouse or another person may come along; in other cases, that is not allowed. The airlines, hotels, tour operators, or other suppliers involved count on your participation to warrant their sponsorship of the trip. Active attendance at events is your most important "payment" for the trip. Suppliers should make clear the level of participation expected, ensure that participation is worthwhile, avoid overburdening participants, and monitor who participates.

The tourist boards of many countries offer special training programs. The Magic of Mexico programs are some of the best known. Other popular specialist programs are offered by Puerto Rico, Aruba, Peru, and the U.S. Virgin Islands. More are added every year.

Other educational opportunities come from professional organizations. For example, ASTA holds seminars in cities and online on a variety of subjects—such as selling to the youth market, group pricing, and net versus commissionable pricing. ASTA also offers home study courses, with certificates for completion, on mature adult travel, family travel, special-interest travel, and travel marketing.

Numerous organizations provide advanced training programs, and some certify travel professionals who complete the requirements of a program. For example, ARC (Airline Reporting Corporation) offers a number of self-paced tutorials and virtual classes.

CLIA (Cruise Lines International Association) offers one of the best-known training programs. Its certificate program has two levels: *Accredited Cruise Counselor (ACC)* and *Master Cruise Counselor (MCC)*. The program includes classroom training, sales and marketing seminars, cruise conferences, exams, ship inspections, and cruises. Employees from many parts of the industry benefit from CLIA's one-day seminars and courses offered in cities throughout the country and aboard ships.

CLOSE-UP: ON THE JOB WITH TALULA GUNTNER, TRAVEL AND TOURISM EDUCATOR

Talula Guntner, CTC, is a professor of travel and tourism at Northern Virginia Community College in Annandale, Virginia. She has also been the director of a proprietary travel school. She holds a B.A. in elementary and library education from Columbia College, an M.A. in education and human development with a specialization in travel and tourism, and an Ed.S., the latter two from George Washington University. The following are excerpts from an interview by Kate Rice for *Travel Professional* magazine.

Kate Rice: "Travel became your passion early on. Why?"
Talula Guntner: "I guess it was just seeing there is so much more of the world than what I knew about firsthand. A guy I dated in college would ask me how I knew there really was an Arizona if I had never been there. He would talk about how he wanted to touch the pyramids to see if they were real. Now I have actually been inside a pyramid and know they really do exist, not just in pictures.

"I've been to the jungles of Ecuador, visited Mount Bromo in Indonesia at sunrise, ridden a donkey to the top of Santorini, gone horseback riding in the water in Jamaica, gone tubing through a cave in Belize, and stood on a glacier in Alaska.

"In 1969, when I was an elementary school librarian, I went on one of the tours to Europe—'If This Is Tuesday, This Must Be Belgium,' a thirty-day tour of Europe for $850. That's what really sold me on travel. I quit teaching and did outside sales. Of course I had no training. I didn't know what I was doing, so I had to go back to teaching.

"Then I moved to Washington, and a woman who just did groups hired me. I had no training, but I kept myself a lifelong learner. I was always going to seminars and conferences. I got my CTC and then found out that, at that time, your CTC counted toward a third of your master's degree at George Washington University. So I went back and got my master's in education and human development. If I got it now it would be a master's of tourism administration. All this time I was working in the industry.

"When I got into the business there weren't even training schools, not even six-week schools. Now you can get a doctorate in business at George Washington University with an emphasis in travel. And there's such opportunity out there.

"We need to encourage people to join our industry; we need to add good people to it. I speak to schools all the time—elementary schools, high schools. When I speak to students I tell them to look at travel. It's important to do work you enjoy; you don't need to wait to retire to enjoy life.

"We have a lot of what I call the chronologically gifted, people who are retiring [from another industry] or people who realize they just don't want to be tied to a computer all day and that they want to deal with people more.

"Now in travel there are so many different things to do. You can have two or three careers in travel—a car rep becomes a cruise line rep; the cruise rep becomes a travel agent. We have certificates in travel and tourism, groups, meeting planning, tour guiding, cruises, selling events, and exhibition management—that's a very strong program.

"Travel has enriched my life. I have made lifelong friends in the industry and through travel. I have been privileged to share some of what I have learned with my students. It is rewarding helping people enter such an exciting field. If I had my life to live all over, there is very little I would change besides marrying my husband earlier, taking more trips, and saving more money so I could travel more!"

Source: Adapted with permission from "Training for a Wealth of Work Options," Travel Professional, August/September 2004, pp. 48–49, 52.

Among the many other examples of certificate and training programs are the following:

- Advanced training for the hospitality industry is available from CHRIE (International Council on Hotel, Restaurant, and Institutional Education), an organization devoted to education and training for the hospitality and tourism industry, and from AH&LA, which conducts an educational institute that offers training in all facets of the hotel industry.
- Organizations such as the National Business Travel Association (NBTA) and the Association of Corporate Travel Executives (ACTE) can help you keep up-to-date with developments in business travel. For special training related to meetings and incentive travel, the Convention Industry Council (CIC) offers the *Certified Meeting Professional (CMP)* certificate, and the Society of Incentive Travel Executives (SITE) certifies members who complete its requirements as *Certified Incentive Travel Executives (CITE)*.
- The NTA (National Tour Association) awards a *Certified Tour Professional (CTP)* certificate, and the Association of Destination Management Executives (ADME) offers a *Destination Management Certified Professional (DMCP)* designation for successful completion of their programs.

Programs from The Travel Institute

Certifications, specializations, and other training resources are also available from The Travel Institute, an international nonprofit organization that aims to increase professionalism within the travel industry and to create standards of excellence for all travel professionals. Since 1964, it has been the premier educational resource for members of the travel industry at all stages of their careers.

This textbook prepares you for the first of a series of professional credentials offered by The Travel Institute: the *Travel Agent Proficiency (TAP) Test*. It measures entry-level knowledge for all aspects of the travel industry. By taking and passing the TAP Test, you will earn the nationally recognized TAP credential and shorten the waiting period to receive the IATAN Travel Agent ID card after meeting IATAN's requirements. Passing the TAP Test also reduces (by 6 months) the work experience required to complete the first part of The Travel Institute's two-level certification program, which consists of the Certified Travel Associate and Certified Travel Counselor designations.

The *Certified Travel Associate (CTA)* program focuses on core competencies and skills needed for work in the travel industry. The curriculum includes communication, geography, sales and service, and niche markets. To receive the CTA designation, you must complete the CTA curriculum, pass the CTA test, and have 18 months of cumulative experience in the travel industry. Continuing education each year is required to maintain the CTA designation.

The *Certified Travel Counselor (CTC)* designation requires at least 5 years of full-time experience in the travel industry and reflects study in topics related to advanced accomplishments in the travel industry. The curriculum covers business development, contemporary issues, and professional development. CTC candidates are required to complete 10 courses in which they learn how to negotiate effectively, make dynamic presentations, analyze business opportunities, implement technological solutions, plan for the future, and more. Continuing education and membership each year are required to maintain the designation.

The *Certified Travel Industry Executive (CTIE)* program teaches business-to business travel professionals how to analyze new business opportunities, develop marketing strategies, negotiate, manage more effectively, and master technical skills. Like the CTC, the CTIE program requires at least 5 years of full-time experience in the travel industry. Continuing education and maintaining membership each year is also required to keep up the designation.

The Travel Institute's other educational programs include Destination Specialist and Lifestyle Specialist courses. Together, these courses offer in-depth knowledge about several regions of the world as well as popular niche markets.

Current Destination Specialist courses include Alaska, Caribbean, France, Hawaii, India, Mexico, North America, Northern and Central Europe, Southern Europe, and Spain. Lifestyle Specialist courses include Sustainable Travel and Villa Vacations.

The Travel Institute's TRIPKit contains a comprehensive collection of essential tools for entry-level professionals. It includes this textbook as well as *Exploring the World*, a Travel Agent Proficiency (TAP) Test Voucher, and a six-month membership with The Travel Institute.

The Travel Institute also offers more than 600 online courses on technology, business, finance, and social media through its Communiversity. Premium members of The Travel Institute can access all these courses for no charge. Both Basic and Premium Membership offer many benefits. including free webinars, white papers, and podcasts.

All of The Travel Institute's educational programs can be completed either through self-study, group study, or online. Regardless of which program you choose, The Travel Institute's programs provide essential knowledge as you begin your travel career.

Prospects

For travel professionals ready to learn and to adapt, this is a time of opportunity. Experts offer varying predictions about what will happen to specific segments of the travel industry in the near future. In the long run each segment is likely to grow, although the jobs of travel professionals will change.

Travel itself will also change. Globalization is shrinking the world and making it more homogeneous. The Nepalese wear their jeans while sipping Cokes and watching MTV. Chinese basketball stars arrive in the United States while American players go to Europe. And wherever people are, they can get a Big Mac. Yet the variety of distinct human cultures persists as individuals struggle to keep their unique identities intact, whether they be Somalian or Norwegian.

A hundred years ago only a tiny percentage of people could get to even the most accessible places around the globe, and many places were inaccessible. A hundred years from now, will there still be reasons to leave home? Will the twenty-first century end up being one in which people can go everywhere but where there is nowhere worth going to? We think not. Instead, it will offer travel opportunities undreamed of a century ago. Physical presence in a different place will still trump any form of "virtual" or "cyber" presence.

Like other citizens, travel professionals have a role to play in determining tomorrow's travel paths. They can influence how the peoples and environments of destinations near and far are treated. In fact, some argue that travel professionals have a special ethical obligation to help protect the cultures and environments of the destinations they profit from, and many companies offer "green" programs. Meanwhile, this is a time during which you can go almost anywhere on earth, yet a time in which there are still adventuresome and culturally distinct destinations to visit.

CHAPTER HIGHLIGHTS

This chapter discussed the keys to making the most of the opportunities in the travel industry. Here is a review of the objectives with which we began the chapter.

1. **Suggest at least four ways to ensure success in a new job and four steps to take to prepare for advancement.** New employees especially should aim to make a good first impression, to be a team player, to take initiative, to have a positive attitude, and of course to work hard. The path to success is easier for those who find a mentor and learn to understand the corporate culture. Steps to take to prepare for future advancement include establishing a reputation for excellence, extending and maintaining networks, keeping a job portfolio up-to-date, continuing to learn, and being professional. It is important for travel professionals to develop skills at business communication, organization, time management, negotiating, understanding consumer trends and motivation, crisis management, cultural diversity, and managing change. Successful travel professionals look at change as an opportunity to position themselves and their companies for success.

2. **Outline a path for advancing in a travel career.** Specific steps depend on the career and the company. Large companies often offer more opportunities for advancement than do smaller ones. Sometimes advancing in a career will require relocation, specialization, or additional formal education, whether through college courses or through programs offered within the travel/tourism industry.

3. **Identify at least four ethical responsibilities of travel professionals.** Travel professionals have a responsibility to preserve the confidentiality of information provided by clients. They also have an obligation to present clear and complete information about their products or services, avoiding deceptive advertising and disclosing all facts necessary for clients to make informed decisions. In addition, they are obliged to serve the client's interests in selecting suppliers and to act as guardians of any funds entrusted to them (sometimes by maintaining escrow accounts). Travel counselors also have a responsibility to follow suppliers' rules and regulations when they sell suppliers' services. Thus clients' requests for back-to-back ticketing, hidden-city ticketing, and doublebooking all raise ethical questions for the travel counselor.

4. **Describe how to develop your skills and knowledge as a travel professional.** General education on your own—through on-the-job training and experience, personal travel, and reading—is one important path to professional development. College and university courses provide another route and may be necessary for some positions. In addition, suppliers and professional organizations in the travel industry offer innumerable seminars, trips, and formal courses. Among the programs are courses leading to certification as a Certified ARC Specialist (CAS), Accredited Cruise Counselor (ACC), Master Cruise Counselor (MCC), Certified Meeting Professional (CMP), Certified Incentive Travel Executive (CITE), Certified Tour Professional (CTP), Destination Management Certified Professional (DMCP), Certified Travel Associate (CTA), Certified Travel Counselor (CTC), Certified Travel Industry Executive (CTIE), and Destination Specialist.

KEY TERMS

A list of key terms introduced in this chapter follows. If you do not recall the meaning of these terms, see the Glossary, which begins on page 393.

back-to-back ticketing

business development manager

card mills

corporate culture

doublebooking

hidden-city ticketing

mentor

professional

REVIEW QUESTIONS

1. What is a mentor?

2. What is meant by a company's corporate culture?

3. What are some of the factors that shape the opportunities for advancement in a company?

4. What are four skills that every travel professional should develop, and why are they important for career growth?

5. Describe three situations that would create an ethical conflict for a travel counselor.

6. List three ways that the Internet can help you continue your travel education.

Glossary

24-hour clock A timekeeping method that eliminates the A.M./P.M. distinction and uses a different numeral for each hour of the day.

■ **A** ■

AAA See *American Automobile Association.*

ACC Accredited Cruise Counselor, training and designation program offered by Cruise Lines International Association.

accountable document A standardized, numbered form issued by *ARC* that the travel agency must account for.

Acela Express *Amtrak's* high-speed train serving the Northeast corridor of the United States.

ADA See *Americans with Disabilities Act.*

additional liability insurance (ALI) Extra coverage for injury, death, or other liability to a third party, beyond both what state law mandates that car rental companies include in the cost of the rental and what the renter's own insurance might cover.

adjoining rooms Rooms next to each other that have separate entrances but no means of going directly from one room to the other.

adventure cruise A *special-interest cruise* designed to appeal to an audience of similar tastes and interests, often on ships accommodating between 90 and 250 people.

adventure tour A *special-interest*

tour that focuses on outdoor physical activity. See *hard adventure* and *soft adventure.*

affinity group A club, team, or other membership organization made up of people who share a particular interest or characteristic (such as age or ethnic background).

aft Toward the rear of a ship.

AH&LA See *American Hotel and Lodging Association.*

Airline Deregulation Act The U.S. law that ended the government's economic control of the airlines; enacted in 1978.

Airlines Reporting Corporation (ARC) The organization owned by major U.S. airlines that regulates the sale and distribution of airline tickets. It accredits agencies that sell airline tickets; supplies documents used in selling airline tickets, rail transportation, and related services; and provides a centralized system for processing these sales.

airport hotel A lodging built to be convenient for travelers departing on early-morning flights or for people not needing to go downtown to conduct their business.

air/sea A package that includes the cost of the cruise and flight arrangements to the port of embarkation.

Air Transport Association (ATA) The trade association formed by major U.S. airlines that represents them before governmental bodies and promotes the safety

and efficiency of the air transport system.

ALI See *additional liability insurance.*

all-inclusive A *resort* that offers a complete package of vacation activities for one price, typically including meals, accommodations, entertainment, and use of sports and recreational facilities.

all-suite A hotel that offers rooms with separate sleeping and living areas.

altitude The elevation above sea level.

Amadeus One of the four major *global distribution systems.*

American Automobile Association (AAA) A motor club that offers members a variety of travel and motoring services.

American Hotel and Lodging Association (AH&LA) The trade association that represents the lodging industry in the United States.

American plan (AP) An arrangement in which the room rate usually includes three meals; also called *full board.*

American Society of Travel Agents (ASTA) The trade association that lobbies governments, presents educational programs, and speaks to the public on behalf of its members, who include travel agents as well as others in the travel industry.

Americans with Disabilities Act (ADA) An act passed in 1990 stipulating that people with

disabilities have the right to access the same travel services as those without disabilities.

Amtrak The corporation that operates intercity passenger rail service in the United States.

AP See *American plan.*

APEX fare The most frequently used discount fare for international air travel.

application letter An unsolicited *cover letter,* accompanied by a *résumé,* sent to a company when the sender doesn't know if the company has any job openings.

Apollo A computer reservation system owned by United Airlines.

ARC See *Airlines Reporting Corporation.*

ARC report A weekly accounting of a travel agency's sales of airline tickets and other *accountable documents;* also called a "sales report" or "air report."

Area Bank Settlement Plan The system by which airlines that are members of *ARC, Amtrak,* and certain other *suppliers* receive payments for tickets sold by travel agencies.

arrival tax A tax imposed on passengers entering a country.

ASTA See *American Society of Travel Agents.*

ATA See *Air Transport Association.*

atlas A compilation of maps.

■ **B** ■

back-to-back ticketing The practice of buying two discount tickets and rearranging the departures and returns in order to avoid restrictions on the discount ticket.

baggage and personal possessions insurance Coverage in case baggage or personal possessions are lost, stolen, or damaged while traveling.

bait-and-switch The deceptive practice of advertising something that is not available.

bareboat charter A chartered *yacht* without a professional crew.

base fare Airfare exclusive of taxes, fees, commissions, or other surcharges.

B&B See *bed-and-breakfast.*

bed-and-breakfast (B&B) A small establishment emphasizing personal attention and offering individually decorated rooms with special character.

benefit A positive result that a *feature* brings to a particular client.

Bermuda plan (BP) An arrangement in which the room rate includes a fully cooked breakfast.

berth A bed on a cruise ship.

block A group of cabins on a cruise line all at the same price.

boarding pass A document that allows a passenger on a flight.

boatel A motel, which can be a boat, on a river or waterway for guests who arrive by boat.

body language Nonverbal signals such as facial expressions, posture, and gestures.

bow The front of a ship.

BP See *Bermuda plan.*

brand An identity associated with a company name.

bricks-and-clicks agency A travel agency with a *marketing plan* that calls for using both a Web site and a physical location as points of sale.

BritRail pass A *rail pass* that allows travel throughout England, Scotland, and Wales.

browser Software that provides access to material on the Internet (for example, Explorer, Navigator, and Firefox).

buffer zone The 225-mile zone extending from the U.S. border into Canada and Mexico within which the *U.S. ticket tax* is assessed.

bulkhead A movable partition that divides an airplane into compartments.

bullet train Japan's high-speed passenger train.

bumped Denied a seat on a flight even though one has a confirmed seat because the airline oversold the flight.

business class A class of service ranging between first class and coach in amenities; also known as *executive class.*

business development manager An airline sales position that is equal to being a district or regional sales manager.

business plan A summary of what is expected from a business effort, including the level of income, benefits, and investment, along with a statement of mid- and long-term goals.

business travel Travel undertaken for the purpose of conducting business, including meetings, conventions, and *incentive travel;* also known as *corporate travel.*

■ C ■

cabin A bedroom on a cruise ship.

call center Large reservation offices maintained by airlines, hotels, and other travel/tourism companies.

cancellation penalty A charge incurred for canceling travel arrangements after a specified time.

Canrailpass A pass offered by *VIA Rail* that provides 12 days of unlimited travel anywhere in Canada during a 30-day period.

card mill A company that sells travel agent credentials to outside sales agents but provides minimal support and training.

cash flow The pattern of expenditures and income that determines the availability of cash.

casino A center for gambling, often operated in conjunction with hotels or resorts.

CDW See *collision damage waiver.*

CEIR See *Center for Exhibition Industry Research.*

Center for Exhibition Industry Research (CEIR) An organization that advocates for and represents the exhibition industry.

chain A group of affiliated properties that bear the same name, follow the same operating procedures and standards, and share a reservation system.

charter A specially scheduled flight reserved by a private group or *tour operator.*

château, castle, and villa An upscale inn in a unique property, such as a medieval castle or an entire villa, often with amenities that include an on-site chef and private swimming pool.

CHRIE See *International Council on Hotel, Restaurant, and Institutional Education.*

Chunnel The tunnel beneath the English Channel that links England and France.

CIC See *Convention Industry Council.*

circle trip A journey that returns to the city where it began but that follows a different route on the return trip. It is like a *round-trip* but involves two or more *stopovers.*

CITE Certified Incentive Travel Executive designation program offered by the Convention Industry Council.

civil aviation All cargo or passenger air travel done for hire, including *scheduled service* and *charters.*

classes of service Compartments that distinguish levels of service; for example, *first class, business class,* or *coach.*

CLIA See *Cruise Lines International Association.*

climate The weather that characteristically prevails in a region.

close To obtain the client's firm commitment to buy.

close-ended question A question inviting precise answers or simple facts.

cloud Web sites with software programs that are stored on a remote server.

CMP Certified Meeting Professional designation offered by the Convention Industry Council.

coach A class of service in the least expensive and most frequented compartment on an aircraft or Amtrak; called *economy class* on many international airlines.

code-sharing agreements Agreements that allow an airline to use the same two-letter code as a larger, better-known airline.

collision damage waiver (CDW) Insurance that waives the car

rental company's right to charge the renter for damages if the rental car is involved in an accident. See *loss damage waiver (LDW).*

command interface A system of communication between a computer and its user in which the user types strings of keystrokes in order to control the computer.

commercial agency A travel agency specializing in *business travel.*

commercial hotel A hotel that is centrally located in a city and caters mostly to business travelers but is suitable for leisure travelers as well.

commission A percentage of the sale or a fee paid to a salesperson for selling a product.

commodity Something that varies little and has the same value everywhere.

commuter airline A small carrier that services one region (such as the Midwest or New England).

computer reservation system (CRS) An electronic system that links distributors and suppliers to a centralized database and is set up for making reservations; a *global distribution system (GDS).*

concierge A lodging staff member whose function is to provide information and other services to guests.

conference system A system by which a group of *suppliers* controls the sale of their product, appointing agents to sell it and establishing a standard contract.

configuration The layout of seats in an aircraft.

confirmed A reserved travel arrangement.

connecting flight A flight that has a stop that requires the passenger to change planes.

connecting rooms Rooms that are linked by a common door inside the rooms.

connection A stop that occurs when the passenger deplanes with the sole purpose of boarding another plane.

consolidator A distribution company that negotiates with airlines to buy seats on flights at bargain rates and then resells the flight tickets.

consortium An association of travel agencies that retain their independent identities but pool their resources for certain purposes, such as advertising and training.

construction principles Rules and guidelines for formulating the airfare for itineraries other than simple round-trips; usually used for international air travel.

consulate A regional office of an embassy.

continent One of the earth's seven large landmasses: Africa, Antarctica, Asia, Australia, Europe, North America, and South America.

Continental plan (CP) An arrangement in which the room rate includes a light or continental breakfast.

convention hotel A hotel that focuses on hosting meetings and conventions.

Convention Industry Council (CIC) A group of organizations representing the convention, meeting, trade show, and exposition industries.

convention rate A discount rate for accommodations offered to participants at meetings and conventions.

cooperative advertising An arrangement in which an advertisement by a supplier or distributor includes information about a travel agency as a contact for reservations in return for the travel agency's contribution to the cost of the advertising.

corporate culture A company's set of values, beliefs, priorities, and practices.

corporate rate A special rate sometimes offered to all business travelers, sometimes just to listed corporations, and sometimes to anyone who asks.

corporate travel Travel undertaken for the purpose of conducting business; also known as *business travel*.

couchette Sleeping accommodations on a train consisting of a compartment with six bunk beds; found on European trains.

Council on Hotel, Restaurant, and Institutional Education See *International Council on Hotel, Restaurant, and Institutional Education*.

country of registry The country from which a cruise ship is legally recorded as doing business and by whose laws and financial regulations the ship is governed.

cover letter A letter of introduction that accompanies a *résumé* and is designed to obtain an interview or an application form.

CP See *Continental plan*.

CRM See *customer relationship management*.

cross-selling Selling products or services beyond those originally requested by a client.

CRS See *computer reservation system*.

Cruise Lines International Association (CLIA) An association that promotes cruising to both the selling agents and the buying public through public relations and advertising as well as by training travel counselors.

cruise ship An all-inclusive floating *resort* that moves from port to port.

CTA Certified Travel Associate, educational and designation program offered by The Travel Institute.

CTC Certified Travel Counselor, educational and designation program offered by The Travel Institute.

CTIE Certified Travel Industry Executive, educational and designation program offered by The Travel Institute.

CTP Certified Tour Professional, educational and designation program offered by the National Tour Association.

customer relationship management (CRM) A strategy that combines technology and personalized service to meet the specific needs of customers, provide excellent service, build lasting relationships with clients, and increase customer loyalty.

customer relationship marketing The use of information from databases to direct marketing efforts so that promotions and services match clients' preferences and interests.

■ **D** ■

database An organized collection of data.

deck plan A diagram of the layout of a ship.

demi-pension A meal plan at a European lodging in which breakfast and one other main meal, usually dinner, are included in the room rate; called *Modified American plan (MAP)* in the United States.

demographic segmentation The process of categorizing people according to characteristics such as age, sex, or marital status.

denied boarding compensation Compensation owed to a passenger who is *bumped* if the airline cannot get the passenger to his or her destination within an hour of the originally scheduled time.

departure tax A tax imposed on passengers leaving a country.

dependables In Plog's analysis, people who value familiarity and comfort and focus on everyday problems tend to visit popular places when they travel and to return to the same places each year.

destination A location that a traveler chooses to visit.

destination geography The study of those characteristics of locations that influence travel.

destination management and promotion The overall marketing of an area, whether a city, region, or other location; usually done by a government entity.

Destination Specialist Site-specific educational program and designation offered by The Travel Institute.

dine-around plan A meal plan in which a credit toward dinner at other hotels or separate restaurants is included in the room rate.

direct flight A flight that has one or more stops at which the passenger does not have to change planes; also known as a *through flight*.

direct link A seamless flow of information between a distant computer and a *computer reservation system*.

direct mail A form of advertising that consists of letters, newsletters, or other printed material mailed to potential customers.

discount fare See *promotional fare*.

distributor A company that acts as an intermediary between *suppliers* and travelers, helping travelers obtain the goods and services owned by suppliers.

DMC A destination management company that specializes in inbound travel.

domestic air travel Flights between and within the continental United States and parts of Alaska, Hawaii, Puerto Rico, the Virgin Islands, and Canada.

doublebooking The practice of booking two reservations for a client at the same time.

double open-jaw trip An arrangement similar to a round trip that allows the passenger to depart from and return to different airports in a city or a neighboring city.

dual distribution A practice whereby travel *suppliers* sell to the public both directly and indirectly, through travel agencies and other intermediaries.

dude ranch A resort, usually in a western U.S. state, where guests can participate in horseback riding, hayrides, and square dancing.

duty A charge or tax.

duty-free port A port in which no duties or taxes are levied on goods.

■ **E** ■

economy class See *coach*.

ecotour A *special-interest tour* designed to appeal to those interested in the environment.

electronic reading device Lightweight, portable electronic tablets with a large storage capacity for downloading and reading books and periodicals.

electronic ticket Flight information stored in a computer but not printed on a conventional ticket; also called an "e-ticket."

ELI See *extended liability insurance*.

e-mail Communication sent from one computer to another.

embarkation point The port from which a cruise begins.

embassy The office of the ambassador who represents a nation in another country.

EP See *European plan*.

equator The imaginary line that circles the globe halfway between the North and South Poles.

errors and omissions and general liability insurance A type of insurance that protects a business from a claim of alleged negligent acts, errors, or omissions in the performance of its services; also called "professional liability insurance."

escorted tour A *tour* in which participants travel together as a group and are always accompanied by a professional escort.

escrow account Funds or other property that is held by a third party, such as a bank, until specified conditions are met for its release.

ethnic agencies Travel agencies or tour companies specializing in travel for people of a particular ethnic background or language.

Eurailpass A *rail pass* that allows unlimited first-class travel through specific European countries for a specified time.

European plan (EP) An arrangement in which the room rate includes no meals.

Eurostar The train that operates through the Chunnel, the tunnel beneath the English Channel that links England and France.

excess baggage charge The fee that airlines (or other modes of transportation) charge for exceeding a stated limit on the weight or number of pieces of baggage that may be transported.

exchange rate The rate at which the currency of one nation can be exchanged for the currency of another.

executive class See *business class*.

expedition A trip taken on a small cruise ship by a group with a specific objective, such as a particular *soft adventure* or cultural or educational experience; generally features a nontraditional itinerary and expert lecturers.

extended liability insurance (ELI) Additional insurance for injury, death, or other liability to a third party, beyond both what state law mandates that car rental companies include in the cost of the rental and what the car renter's own insurance might cover.

extended-stay hotel A type of *all-suite* geared to those staying at a destination for a few weeks or more.

■ **F** ■

FAA See *Federal Aviation Administration*.

familiarization (fam) trip A trip offered to travel professionals at a reduced rate so that they can inspect hotels and restaurants and sample an area's attractions and services.

fax Written documents electronically transmitted over telephone lines.

feature An inherent characteristic of a product or service.

Federal Aviation Administration (FAA) The agency of the federal Department of Transportation that has primary responsibility for airline safety regulations and that licenses pilots, certifies aircraft as safe, and enforces rules regarding passenger safety.

feedback question A question that confirms details that have emerged in the conversation.

ferry A ship that carries passengers, vehicles, livestock, and supplies across a body of water on a regular schedule.

first class (1) A class of service on an airline or train that provides more comfortable travel than other classes of service, usually by providing better service, more complimentary amenities, and more spacious seating; (2) a very good to excellent hotel, but not as luxurious as a deluxe hotel.

FIT A custom-designed *tour*.

flag of convenience A term used to refer to a ship that a company registers in a country other than its own to avoid regulations or taxes.

flight insurance Coverage for accidents that occur in connection with air travel.

fly/cruise An arrangement whereby a cruise line offers air transportation.

fly/drive An *independent tour* that includes air transportation as well as car rental and permits participants to stay at a number of hotels.

forced single An additional amount that a single traveler may have to pay when a tour operator cannot find a roommate.

fore Toward the front of a ship.

four Ps The four characteristics of a business—product, promotion, place, and price—that constitute the marketing mix.

franchise company A company that provides the use of a name, a central reservation system, advertising, and training.

freighter A ship whose principal purpose is to carry cargo.

frequent-flyer plan A bonus program for people who fly frequently on a particular carrier.

frequent-guest program A program that rewards repeat guests with bonuses such as a free room night.

full board See *American plan*.

■ **G** ■

Galileo One of the four major *global distribution systems*.

gateway A city that serves as the arrival or departure point for international travel.

GDS See *global distribution system*.

geography The science that studies the earth and its features and life, as well as how these interact.

global distribution system (GDS) An electronic system that links distributors and suppliers to a centralized database and is set up for making reservations; once known as a *computer reservation system*.

GMT See *Greenwich mean time*.

graphical interface A system of communication between a computer and its user in which the user can control the computer by clicking on pictures or symbols that are displayed on the computer's screen.

green sheet The Summary of Sanitation Inspections of International Cruise Ships. It can be viewed on the Web site of the Centers for Disease Control and Prevention (CDC).

Greenwich mean time (GMT) The time at Greenwich, England, from which world time zones are calculated; also known as *universal time coordinated (UTC)*.

gross registered tonnage (GRT) The amount of enclosed revenue-producing space on a cruise ship.

group rate A rate that reflects a discount offered to a group that uses a certain number of rooms on the same night.

GRT See *gross registered tonnage*.

guaranteed for late arrival Situation in which a client can hold a reservation past the standard arrival time by paying a deposit for the room.

guaranteed rate Situation in which a client is guaranteed a cabin in a given price range by the cruise line, which arbitrarily assigns the client a cabin.

guaranteed share rate Situation in which a cruise line or *tour operator* guarantees a per-person double-occupancy rate if a single client is willing to share a cabin or room with another person of the same sex; if another person is not available, the client still receives the share rate.

gulf A body of salt water bordered by a curved shoreline, such as the Gulf of Mexico.

■ **H** ■

hard adventure A type of *adventure tour* that features strenuous outdoor activity (for example, mountaineering or white-water rafting), remote locations, or risk.

hidden-city ticketing The practice in which clients buy a ticket for a flight between two cities with a stop at the desired destination, where they actually get off, because that ticket is cheaper than a ticket for a flight between the originating city and the desired destination.

higher intermediate point (HIP) The term used in the *mileage system* for international airfares that designates a point on an itinerary that has a higher fare than the *through fare* between the origin and destination cities.

high season The season when rates and traffic peak.

HIP See *higher intermediate point*.

hold time The deadline for holding a room without payment.

honeymoon specialist A counselor with expert knowledge of resorts and cruises appropriate for couples and requirements for marriages abroad.

hospitality industry The industry that supplies hotel accommodations and food and beverage services.

host A representative of a tour or ground operator who helps tour participants to plan and arrange activities.

hosted tour A *tour* in which individuals travel independently but have access to a *host* to assist them at each destination on the tour.

hostel Dorm-like accommodations, usually open to all ages, and less expensive than some other types of lodging.

hotel consolidator An intermediary company that purchases blocks of hotel rooms at favorable prices and resells the rooms.

hotel manager The person on a cruise ship who ensures that all passenger services run smoothly.

hotel representative firm A firm that accepts reservations and provides marketing and sales on behalf of individually owned properties; also known as a *rep firm*.

hotspot A location that offers access to a *WiFi* network.

hub-and-spoke system A system by which an airline uses certain cities as connecting centers, or hubs, for as many flights to and from outlying cities as possible.

■ I ■

IATA See *International Air Transport Association.*

IATAN See *International Airlines Travel Agent Network.*

IDP See *International Driver's Permit.*

inbound travel Companies that specialize in travelers arriving from other parts of the country or from abroad.

incentive house A travel agency that specializes in arranging *incentive travel.*

incentive travel Travel offered as a prize or reward for employees, usually for productivity or sales performance.

income statement A financial statement summarizing revenues and expenses for a particular period.

independent contractor A self-employed person who is paid by a business to provide certain services. The IRS has specific criteria to distinguish independent contractors from employees.

independent tour A *tour* in which participants travel independently; often called a *package.*

inn A lodging that offers local character, personal service, and a dining room; is somewhat larger than a *bed-and-breakfast* and functions more like a hotel.

interline agreement An agreement among airlines.

International Air Transport Association (IATA) An association of international airlines, whose goal is to create stability in international aviation.

International Airlines Travel Agent Network (IATAN) The organization that appoints U.S. travel agencies to sell tickets for international airlines serving the United States.

International Council on Hotel, Restaurant, and Institutional Education (CHRIE) An organization dedicated to continuing education in the *hospitality industry.*

international date line The imaginary line roughly corresponding to 180° *longitude* that, by international agreement, separates one calendar day from another.

International Driver's Permit (IDP) A translation of a driver's license into an internationally recognized format.

Internet The global network of computer networks that enables anyone who accesses it to communicate with any other computer connected to it.

Internet service provider (ISP) A company that connects users to the *Internet.*

invoice A document that indicates the amount a client owes.

island A body of land completely surrounded by water.

ISP See *Internet service provider.*

isthmus A narrow body of land connecting two larger bodies of land.

■ J ■

joint fare The fare for a trip through a connecting city when the flights involve different airlines that have agreed on one published fare.

■ K ■

knot The measure of speed at sea; equivalent to about 1.15 land miles per hour.

■ L ■

land rate The tour rate that does not include airfare to the destination.

latitude The distance measured in degrees north or south of the *equator.*

LDW See *loss damage waiver.*

leeward The side sheltered from the wind.

legacy airlines Major airlines that were among the first in the industry.

leisure travel Travel done for pleasure in the broadest sense of the term (travel to visit family and friends is generally, but not always, included in this category).

LGBT travel specialist An agent familiar with destinations friendly to the lesbian, gay, bisexual, and transgender traveler.

Lifestyle Specialist Specialty-specific educational program and designation offered by The Travel Institute.

lodge Historic, rustic accommodations, often found in U.S. national parks.

lodging Another term for the hotel industry.

longitude The distance measured in degrees east or west of the *prime meridian.*

loss damage waiver (LDW) Insurance that waives the car rental company's right to recover damages resulting from theft or vandalism as well as from collisions involving the rental car. See *collision damage waiver (CDW).*

low season The season when rates and traffic are at their lowest; sometimes called the *value season.*

■ M ■

management contract An arrangement by which a hotel company manages but does not own a hotel.

MAP See *Modified American plan.*

marketing A series of decisions and actions taken by a seller to create a match between consumers' preferences and a product or service.

marketing plan A set of decisions that identifies a *target market* and determines what to sell, how to promote it, where to sell it, and at what price to sell it.

market research The gathering and analyzing of information about consumers and products.

market segment The process of identifying clusters of individuals who have similar needs and can form a *target market.*

maximum permitted miles (MPM) The number of miles assigned by *IATA* to every pair of cities around the world for which international fares are published. Passengers are assessed a surcharge if they exceed this mileage by making additional stops.

MCC Master Cruise Counselor, training and designation program offered by Cruise Lines International Association.

MCO See *miscellaneous charges order.*

Mediterranean climate A *climate* with warm, dry summers and mild, wet winters.

meeting A gathering arranged by a business or other group and involves an overnight stay.

meeting planner A specialist who plans *meetings* for sponsors.

Meeting Professionals International (MPI) An association of meeting professionals that promotes the meeting industry.

meeting travel Travel to organized gatherings such as conferences and conventions.

megaship A large cruise ship that measures at least 70,000 *GRT* and holds more than 1,600 passengers.

membership organization A not-for-profit association in which individual members own and operate hotels that share a global reservation system as well as other common services.

mentor A person who serves as an unofficial teacher, counselor, role model, and advocate.

metric system The system of units of measurement based on decimals (10s); used by most countries.

mileage system The method of determining airfares that ties the fare to the number of miles flown. Most simple domestic *round-trips* are *not* based on the mileage system.

minshuku A traditional-style private guesthouse in Japan; similar to a European *pension.*

miscellaneous charges order (MCO) An *accountable document* issued by travel agencies when standard ticket stock cannot be used.

Modified American plan (MAP) An arrangement in which the room rate includes breakfast and one other main meal, usually dinner; called *demi-pension* in Europe.

monsoon A wind system that changes direction seasonally; also may refer to the heavy rains that accompany the wind.

motel A lodging with only one or two stories, ample parking, and very limited food service.

motor inn More hotel-like than the traditional *motel* yet catering to the auto traveler; often found in or near large cities.

motorcoach A bus.

MPI See *Meeting Professionals International*.

MPM See *maximum permitted miles*.

■ N ■

NACTA See *National Association of Career Travel Agents*.

National Association of Career Travel Agents (NACTA) A trade organization that specializes in representing *independent contractors* in the travel industry, outside sales agents, and host agencies.

National Tour Association (NTA) The association of *tour operators, suppliers,* and destination marketing organizations that are insured and comply with the NTA Code of Ethics.

national tourist office (NTO) A government-sponsored office that works within the country to make it attractive to tourists and works outside the country to present it in the best light.

National Transportation Safety Board (NTSB) The government agency that tracks aviation fatalities, publishes annual safety statistics, investigates accidents, and recommends safety enhancements.

negotiated corporate rate A rate that has been negotiated with a company or its affiliate or association.

net rate A rate that does not include a *commission*.

networking Using personal contacts to make business contacts and to advance in the business world

neutral unit of construction (NUC) A special counting unit established by *IATA* to calculate airfares that involve countries with different currencies.

niche A specialty market.

niche cruise A cruise designed around a theme to appeal to the interests of a special group.

nonstop flight A flight with no intermediate stops.

no-show A person who does not show up for his or her scheduled flight but does not cancel or change the reservation.

NTA See *National Tour Association*.

NTO See *national tourist office*.

NTSB See *National Transportation Safety Board*.

NUC See *neutral unit of construction*.

■ O ■

occupancy rate The percentage of rooms occupied.

ocean A major division of the earth's huge body of salt water; the four major oceans are the Arctic, the Atlantic, the Indian, and the Pacific.

one-way trip A trip from an originating city to a destination city with no return to the origin.

online travel agency Usually refers to a travel agency that does business almost exclusively online but can refer to any travel agency that uses the Internet for a portion of its business.

open-ended question A question that invites answers that include whatever facts, opinions, or feelings the respondent thinks are relevant.

open-jaw trip A trip in which the passenger either returns to a city different from the point of origin or departs for the return trip from a city other than the original destination.

open-skies policy The policy that eliminates governmental regulations in order to allow international air carriers to fly where they choose, charge what they want, and make deals among themselves.

option date The date by which a deposit or full payment must be made when there is a time period between booking and payment.

OSSN See *Outside Sales Support Network*.

outside sales agent A person who brings in new customers, beyond the travel agency's existing clientele. This person may be an employee or an *independent contractor*.

Outside Sales Support Network (OSSN) An organization that specializes in representing and supporting *independent contractors* in the travel industry, *outside sales agents,* and host agencies.

overbook To sell more tickets than there are seats.

override An extra payment made by a *supplier* as a bonus for a large volume of sales. See *preferred supplier relationship*.

oversold A situation in which the number of confirmed passengers who show up for a flight exceeds the number of seats.

■ P ■

package Two or more travel components bundled together and offered at one price; often used to refer to an *independent tour*.

PAI See *personal accident insurance*.

paper ticket The conventional airline ticket, which consists of a booklet of coupons, including one kept by the passenger.

parador A traditional-style, government-operated hotel of Spain, usually in a historic building with atmosphere. (Puerto Rico also applies the term to some of its local inns.)

passenger facility charge (PFC) A surcharge imposed to pay for airport improvements.

passenger load factor The percentage of available seats on a flight that are actually sold; it can be stated for any length of time.

passenger name record (PNR) A record of a passenger's reservation information in a computer.

passport A document issued by a government to a citizen in order to establish an individual's identity and nationality and to request protection for the citizen while he or she is abroad.

peninsula A body of land with water on three sides.

pension A small family-run European lodging that may be run much like a hotel or a *bed-and-breakfast*.

personal accident insurance (PAI) Car rental insurance that covers bodily injury to the renter.

personal selling Selling conducted through person-to-person contact.

PFC See *passenger facility charge*.

Pied Piper A well-known and popular leader for a special-interest tour.

pitch (1) The amount of space between one seat on a plane and the seat directly in front of or behind it; (2) the up-and-down motion of a ship.

PNR See *passenger name record*.

point-to-point tickets The fare from one *stopover* point to another.

port charges On a cruise, charges to cover fees levied by governments or port facilities for the use of the port.

port of call A stop on a cruise ship's itinerary.

pousada A government-operated, traditional-style hotel of Portugal, usually in a historic building with atmosphere.

preferred supplier relationship An arrangement in which a travel agency is committed to maximizing its use of a particular *supplier;* in turn, the agency can receive *overrides*.

prepaid ticket advice (PTA) An authorization for an airline ticket to be issued at a point other than the point of payment.

price segmentation The process of dividing a population into segments based on the amount they are able and willing to pay for a product.

prime meridian The imaginary line running through Greenwich, England, that connects the North and South Poles.

professional A person who has learned a body of knowledge, mastered skills needed for a certain occupation, and demonstrated a commitment to the ethical standards of that occupation and the interests of clients.

promotion An effort to communicate information about a product or service to the market.

promotional fare A lower fare offered by an airline to generate more business; also called a *discount fare*.

properties A term for the various types of accommodations in the hotel industry.

psychographic segmentation The process of categorizing potential consumers based on their attitudes, interests, and beliefs.

PTA See *prepaid ticket advice.*

public relations Any activity conducted to establish recognition and respect for a company or product.

purser The person on a cruise ship who handles financial matters and operates the information desk.

■ Q ■

qualifying The process of identifying potential clients by determining how ready and able they are to make a purchase.

■ R ■

rack rate The regular posted or off-the-street price of a room.

Rail Europe A company owned by Swiss and French railroads that acts as a booking agent for rail travel in Europe.

rail pass A pass that allows train travel for a specified time and region with unlimited stops and unlimited mileage.

rate desk A part of an airline or travel agency staffed by specialists in international airfares.

receipt An *invoice* that indicates an amount paid and the method of payment.

record locator number Numbers or letters assigned to each air reservation, called the "reservation number" by the general public. Various forms of the term can be used for other travel components.

rent-a-desk A situation where an outside counselor works through a travel agency and shares commission based on the service provided by the agency.

rep firm See *hotel representative firm.*

repositioning cruise A cruise that moves a ship from one cruising area to another between seasons.

resort A hotel that provides a vacation in itself, offering various activities, facilities, and services.

résumé A summary of qualifications and work experience.

Retreat-style accommodation Often a full complex used by companies or organizations for meetings and educational activites.

river A moving body of fresh water that flows from a basin to a termination point.

ROH See *run-of-the-house.*

roll The side-to-side motion of a ship.

rondavel Circular lodgings in southern Africa with varying levels of amenities.

round-trip A journey that returns to the same city where it began.

routing system The method of setting international airfares in which the fare depends on the specific route flown; used for most international *discount fares.*

run-of-the-house (ROH) A flat discount rate at which a hotel offers any of its available rooms, whatever their location, to members of a group.

ryokan A traditional-style inn in Japan; usually superior to *first class.*

■ S ■

Sabre One of the major *global distribution systems.*

SATH See *Society for Accessible Travel and Hospitality.*

scheduled service Regularly scheduled flights, in contrast to *charter* or on-demand flights.

schooner A large sailing ship that uses both sails and motors.

sea A body of salt water surrounded or defined by land, such as the Mediterranean and Caribbean Seas.

search engine Web-based software that indexes and searches the Internet, finding and displaying Web-based sources for information requested by users.

seat width The total side-to-side space available at seat cushion or chest level.

security fee A fee established in 2001 to pay for increased security measures.

segmental analysis An evaluation of the profitability of different products and services.

segment tax A tax on each takeoff and landing at U.S. airports.

self-catering rental apartment Furnished flats or apartment available in some major cities and beach communities.

selling An aspect of *marketing* that ensures that a product or service is purchased.

selling up Upgrading a client to a more expensive or inclusive version of a product or service.

shell An incomplete brochure

provided by *suppliers* that has one or two photographs and some generic text; travel agencies or *tour operators* then add the details about their product.

shoulder season The period between *high* and *low seasons.*

single supplement An additional charge, over the per-person double-occupancy rate, for single occupancy of accommodations.

SITE See *Society of Incentive and Travel Executives.*

Skype A software application available through a computer that lets you talk with others by voice, video, or instant messaging.

social media Electronic communication through which people interact, such as Facebook, Twitter, and LinkedIn.

Society for Accessible Travel and Hospitality (SATH) A nonprofit organization devoted both to promoting awareness, respect, and accessibility for mature travelers and those with disabilities and to promoting their employment in the industry.

Society of Incentive and Travel Executives (SITE) A worldwide organization of professionals dedicated to the development of *incentive travel.*

soft adventure A type of *adventure tour* that involves mild activity but little physical challenge or danger; for example, a walking tour through vineyards or rafting on a mild river.

sound A long, wide body of water connecting two larger bodies of water.

spa A type of *resort* that emphasizes health, diet, and fitness.

space ratio The measure of spaciousness on a cruise ship; computed by dividing the ship's *GRT* by the number of passengers.

special-interest tour A *tour* designed to appeal to the interests of a very specific *market segment.*

special-interest travel Travel devoted to a particular interest or activity.

specialty train A train taken by passengers mainly for the experience, not the transportation.

spread A range of cabins at various prices on a ship.

stabilizer A mechanical device

that can be activated from the side of a ship to minimize its *roll* and create a smoother cruise.

standard ticket A form of airline ticket accepted as valid by all airlines that are members of the *ATA.*

standby A person trying to obtain space on a flight listed as full.

step-on guide A person who joins a *tour* briefly to conduct sightseeing.

stern The back of a ship.

stop Occurs whenever a plane lands.

stopover A planned break in a journey; occurs whenever the traveler stays at a domestic location for more than 4 hours (or 24 hours for international flights), unless the *stop* is necessitated by the airline's schedule.

strait A narrow channel of water connecting two larger bodies of water.

supplier A company that owns and provides the goods and services (including transportation, food, shelter, entertainment, and attractions) sold to travelers.

supporting businesses and organizations Entities that either provide travel-related services such as maps and travel insurance or aid or regulate the travel industry.

■ T ■

TAP Test An entry-level competency test developed by The Travel Institute and the American Society of Travel Agents.

target market A *market segment* that a seller aims to reach.

telecommute To work from a remote location and communicate with the business office via computer and other communication devices.

template The electronic version of a *shell,* an incomplete brochure provided by *suppliers.*

tender A small boat for carrying passengers from ship to shore and back when the larger ship cannot dock because a harbor is too shallow or too crowded.

tented camp Accommodations for travelers on safari in Africa, ranging from simple to more luxurious.

TGV A high-speed train in

France that travels close to 200 miles per hour.

The Travel Institute The international nonprofit organization that educates and certifies travel professionals at all stages of their careers.

third/fourth person rate The price for additional persons, after the first two, who share either a cabin on a cruise or a room on a *tour*.

through fare The fare through a connecting city when the connection involves flights by the same airline.

through flight See *direct flight*.

TIA See *Travel Industry Association of America.*

tour A package of travel features sold as a single unit.

tour escort The person responsible for the smooth running of a *tour* and the welfare and satisfaction of the clients; also called a "tour manager" or a "tour director."

tour guide A specialist who dispenses in-depth knowledge about his or her particular topic on an *escorted tour*.

tour operator A company that assembles the components of *tours* and may own facilities or vehicles or employ personnel used on tours; may also sell tours directly to the public.

tour wholesaler A company that packages the components of *tours* for later sale by retail outlets.

tourist card An entry document used by some countries in lieu of a *passport*.

tourist court Individually owned cabin accommodations built in the 1920s.

transfer Transportation between hotels and airports, docks, or railroad stations.

Transportation Security Administration (TSA) The agency of the federal government responsible for developing

policies to ensure the safety of U.S. transportation, including airport security and the prevention of hijacking.

travel accident and health insurance Coverage that protects the insured in case of accidents and sickness while away from home.

travel agency A business that sells travel products and services directly to the public.

travel counselor An individual who advises travelers and who sells travel arrangements to the public for *suppliers*; also known as a "travel agent."

travelers with disabilities Those travelers who have impaired mobility and require special arrangements.

Travel Industry Association of America (TIA) The nonprofit organization that represents the U.S. travel industry and works to promote increased travel to and within the United States.

tree lodge Accommodations on stilts for travelers on safari in Africa, ranging from simple to luxurious.

trip cancellation or interruption insurance Coverage that reimburses clients for nonrefundable prepayments if they must cancel or discontinue a trip for a reason covered by the policy.

TSA See *Transportation Security Administration.*

■ **U** ■

uniform resource locator (URL) The address of a Web site.

United States Tour Operators Association (USTOA) The professional association for *tour operators* that conduct business in the United States; members pledge adherence to a code of ethics and participate in a consumer protection plan.

universal time coordinated (UTC) See *Greenwich mean time (GMT).*

URL See *uniform resource locator.*

usage segmentation The process of categorizing potential consumers according to the purpose for which they would use a product.

USA Rail pass A *rail pass* on *Amtrak* that can only be purchased outside the United States.

U.S. ticket tax A tax charged on airline tickets purchased in the United States for travel among the fifty states or in the *buffer zone* in Canada and Mexico.

USTOA See *United States Tour Operators Association.*

UTC See *universal time coordinated.*

■ **V** ■

value-added tax (VAT) A tax levied on a product at each stage of manufacture or distribution and included in the price charged.

value season The time of year at a destination when prices are lower; sometimes called *low season* or "off-season."

VAT See *value-added tax.*

venturers The term used by Plog to describe travelers who tend to be confident and curious, to have varied interests, and to enjoy discovering new vacation spots.

Verified Travel Consultant A designation issued by the Airlines Reporting Corporation that provides an identification number to a counselor.

VFR travel Travel to visit friends or relatives.

VIA Rail Canada's passenger train network.

videoconferencing A meeting where cameras allow participants in various parts of the country to see and talk with each other.

visa An endorsement, stamp, or separate paper placed in a *passport* by officials of an international government specifying the conditions under which the traveler may enter the country.

voice mail An automated phone-answering system that handles incoming calls.

voucher A document used to confirm arrangements, identify clients, or indicate payments made; issued by a *tour operator*, cruise line, or travel agency.

VTC See *Verified Travel Consultant.*

■ **W** ■

waitlisted Placed on a list of people seeking a service that is sold out.

walking the guest Practice whereby a hotel substitutes nearby accommodations of equal or better quality when it has no rooms available for a confirmed guest.

webcasting A meeting held over the Internet where computer cameras allow viewers in various parts of the country to see, hear, and talk with a remote presenter.

WiFi A wireless network that broadcasts over a particular part of the electromagnetic spectrum; short for "wireless fidelity."

windjammer A large sailing ship with multiple sails.

windward The side exposed to the wind.

Worldspan One of the four major *global distribution systems*.

World Wide Web The system that organizes information on the *Internet* into interconnected pages that can be easily presented and retrieved.

■ **Y** ■

yacht A boat used for private excursions.

yield The average amount of revenue earned per passenger mile.

yield management system A fare structure designed to maximize revenue.

Index